JOURNEYING BOY

John Evans completed his doctoral studies on Benjamin Britten at the University of Wales in 1984. After five years as Research Scholar at the Britten-Pears Library and Archive he joined BBC Radio 3, becoming the network's Head of Music in 1993. His publications include *Benjamin Britten: Pictures from a Life 1913-1976* and *A Britten Source Book.* He is currently President and Executive Director of the Oregon Bach Festival in the United States.

Journeying Boy

THE DIARIES OF THE YOUNG BENJAMIN BRITTEN 1928–1938

Selected and edited by
John Evans

faber and faber

First published in 2009
by Faber and Faber Ltd
Bloomsbury House
74–77 Great Russell Street
London WC1B 3DA
This paperback edition first published in 2010

Typeset by RefineCatch Limited, Bungay, Suffolk
Printed in England by CPI Mackays, Chatham

Published with financial support from the Britten-Pears Foundation bpf

A CIP record for this book
is available from the British Library

ISBN 978-0-571-23884-2

2 4 6 8 10 9 7 5 3 1

For my parents, Leslie and Avis,
and my siblings,
Joan, Ann, Sue and Chris,
with love

Contents

Illustrations

ILLUSTRATIONS IN TEXT

PLATES

Plates 1–4, 10–25, 28–9, 31–4 are reproduced by permission of the Trustees of the Britten–Pears Foundation. Plates 1, 12, 16–18, 20, 22–4, and 31 were taken from Benjamin's personal albums, and photographed using the Zeiss camera he purchased on 5 May 1934 for £4.10, from the proceeds of his father's will. I would like to thank Dr Nicholas Clark, Librarian of the Britten-Pears Foundation, for his invaluable assistance in sourcing these images and providing them for reproduction.

Plates 5–9 are reproduced by permission of Gresham's School, Holt, and I would like to thank Liz Larby, of the Gresham's School Archives, for her assistance in providing plates 5 and 6 for reproduction, and for authorising the rights on the remaining Gresham's plates.

Plates 29, 33 and 35 are reproduced by permission of Bridget Kitley, née Slater, to whom I am most grateful; her mother's wonderful photographs of her father, Montagu, and of Wulff Scherchen and Benjamin Britten, are amongst the very best available from this period.

John Evans

A sketch by Marjorie Fass of the young Benjamin Britten completing a composition exercise for Frank Bridge. Signed *MF 1928.*

Once upon a time there was a prep-school boy. He was called Britten mi., his initials were E.B., his age was nine, and his locker number was seventeen. He was quite an ordinary little boy; he took his snake-belt to bed with him; he loved cricket, only quite liked football (although he kicked a pretty 'corner'); he adored mathematics, got on all right with history, was scared by Latin Unseen; he behaved fairly well, only ragged the recognised amount, so that his contacts with the cane or the slipper were happily rare (although one nocturnal expedition to stalk ghosts left its marks behind); he worked his way up the school slowly and steadily, until at the age of thirteen he reached that pinnacle of importance and grandeur never to be quite equalled in later days: the head of the Sixth, head-prefect, and Victor Ludorum.

But . . . there was one curious thing about this boy: he wrote music. His friends bore with it, his enemies kicked a bit but not for long (he was quite tough), the staff couldn't object if his work and games didn't suffer. He wrote lots of it, reams and reams of it. I don't really know when he had time to do it. In those days, long ago, prep-school boys didn't have much free time; the day started with early work at 7.30, and ended (if you were lucky not to do extra prep.) with prayers at 8.00 – and the hours in between were fully organised. Still there were odd moments in bed, there were half holidays and Sundays too, and somehow these reams and reams got written. And they are still lying in an old cupboard to this day – string quartets (six of them), twelve piano sonatas; dozens of songs; sonatas for violin, sonatas for viola and 'cello too; suites, waltzes, rondos, fantasies, variations; a tone-poem 'Chaos and Cosmos'; a tremendous symphony, for gigantic orchestra including eight horns and oboe d'amore (started on January 17 and finished February 28); an oratorio called 'Samuel': all the opus numbers from 1 to 100 were filled (and catalogued) by the time Britten mi. was fourteen.

Benjamin Britten, from his introduction to *A Simple Symphony* (1934)

Preface

What past can be yours, O journeying boy
Towards a world unknown,
Who calmly, as if incurious quite
On all at stake, can undertake
This plunge alone?
Thomas Hardy, 'Midnight on the Great Western'

For Christmas 1927 Edward Benjamin Britten was given a *School Boys' Pocket Diary and Notebook* for 1928, printed and published by Charles Letts & Co., Diarists and Manufacturers of London. Facing the title-page the inscription reads 'Ben from Aunt Nellie': the diary was a Christmas gift from Mrs Frederick [Ellen] Harmer, the elder sister of Britten's father, Robert. Beneath the inscription Britten signs his name with a flourish (a signature that remained largely unchanged over the years) and lists his home address, '21 Kirkley Cliff Road, Lowestoft', and the two schools he attended during that calendar year, 'South Lodge School Lowestoft', which he later deleted (presumably at the end of term) adding '& Farfield [House] Gresham's School, Holt.' From the diary's *Personal Memoranda* we learn that he was five feet, six and a half inches tall, that his collar size was fourteen-and-a-half and his boot size eight. Britten had just turned fourteen, and for the next ten and a half years he kept a daily journal, the entries growing in length, complexity and private reflection; intimate thoughts were committed to a succession of pocket and desk diaries, a period of self-reflection that ended abruptly and finally on Thursday 16 June 1938. Though a diary exists for 1939, it is by then little more than an appointment book with but a handful of entries, and so it is not included within this volume. After 1938 Britten was never again to keep a private diary; the only first-hand account of his life thereafter is to be found in his letters, whose editing has been a labour of love for his former publisher and authorised biographer, Donald Mitchell. So the present volume of diaries provides a unique opportunity to get inside the mind of a very complex and sometimes troubled creative artist during his early, formative years. And while Britten himself was very suspicious of the practice of interpreting the work of a creative figure as a reflection of his or her inner soul, these diaries speak volumes about the man and artist he was to become.

As the prodigiously gifted son of a doting mother and the very highly regarded young protégé of one of the most enlightened British composers of the day, Britten's childhood was in many respects charmed. Yet it was not without its challenges. The diary entries from his days at boarding school are particularly anguished, and it is painfully clear that he left behind his home and his childhood only very reluctantly. With the help of these diaries and in the company of the young Benjamin Britten, we trace the progress of this journeying boy through his time at the Royal College of Music, and on to his early apprenticeship in London, working on contract for the GPO Film Unit, the Group Theatre and the British Broadcasting Corporation. The relationship he established in 1928 with his teacher and mentor Frank Bridge was extraordinarily positive and influential, and sustained him throughout this period – the Bridges and their circle are a constant presence. But Britten's remarkable progress during these years was also tinged with pain and loss: international success in Florence, Barcelona and Salzburg counterpointed at home by the death of both parents within three years; a steady flow of commissions, publishing contracts and performances through the 1930s, but with the growing threat of Fascism, the Spanish Civil War and the rise of the Nazi party as a gruesome backdrop to life; the liberating influence of W. H. Auden and his intellectual circle alongside Britten's own inner turmoil, as he slowly came to terms with his homosexuality while rejoicing in the company of children – it must have seemed an irreconcilable problem. So the story he tells through his journals is compelling, very personal but also very much of its time.

Milton would have us believe that 'The childhood shows the man, as morning shows the day',* and these early diaries of the young Benjamin Britten provide ample evidence for the claim. In them we discover a boy, at the tender age of fourteen, reluctantly yielding to the inevitable progress of puberty, adolescence and early manhood, journeying in body and spirit, and leaving his personal account of that journey suspended in mid-thought, on the eve of the Second World War. At the age of twenty-five, Britten was at last coming to terms with his homosexuality, was yielding for the first time to an emotional connection with a younger man, and had just embarked on a friendship with the tenor, Peter Pears, a soulmate who was soon to become his life partner and principal interpreter. Britten was also on the brink of a major international career, and not just as a composer – he was also a pianist,

* Milton *Paradise Regained* (1671), Book IV, 1.220

conductor, arts administrator and co-founder of the English Opera Group and the Aldeburgh Festival, two of the most influential arts institutions in post-war Europe. Britten's international standing was not equalled by any other British composer in the second half of the twentieth century, and scarcely by any of his contemporaries abroad: his career as a composer for lyric theatre alone was comparable to that of Puccini and Richard Strauss. These diaries provide a fascinating insight as to how that came about: how a boy from a modest family, the son of a dentist, brought up in a remote East Anglian fishing town, for whom life was often a struggle, achieved so much in one short lifetime.

Editorial notes and acknowledgements

To reproduce every word of Britten's diaries in their entirety, together with the annotations necessary for their comprehensive understanding, would have led to a substantial multi-volume publication – so first, a word about the careful process of selection that has taken place. One has to remember that Britten began keeping these journals as a schoolboy, whose life was governed largely by family circumstances and the school rules at South Lodge and Gresham's. Sundays revolved around church and his leisure time was largely devoted to composing and music-making, but also tennis and badminton parties and the occasional cricket match. When the harsh East Anglian climate and the cold North Sea permitted, there were bathing parties and tea at the family hut on Lowestoft beach. Accounts of these activities are very matter-of-fact in content, but the roll call of his many church-going, musical, sporting or bathing companions is always extraordinarily detailed. So the exclusion of many such entries, as part of a broader process of selection, became both obvious and necessary.

Thereafter, the key aim in the selection process was to sustain the narrative flow of Britten's journey from boyhood to early manhood, and to chart the fast-changing and expanding musical tastes that began to define him as a musician and artist. To that end, the diary entries that have survived this selection process are reproduced in their entirety, not least because they illustrate the extraordinary juxtaposition of private thoughts, industrious routine, and increasingly public activity. Inevitably, as the years go by and these entries grow in length and deepen in self-reflection, fewer are omitted and the text becomes more complete. It should also be stressed that no entries have been omitted for reasons of confidentiality or sensitivity, nor have any entries undergone internal editing for any reason.

By their very nature, private diaries involve a good deal of compression and personal shorthand. Unlike letters, which are intended to communicate ideas and feelings to another person, diaries contain an individual's most private thoughts and intimate confessions, with no particular intention by the author that anyone else should be privy to them. In the first year of his diary-keeping Britten used a pocket diary that allocated four entries to the page, so space was at a premium. From 1929 the diaries were largely in a page-a-day format. But whatever the space available to him, Britten always seemed to have more to commit to his journal than space would allow: in his attempts to get his thoughts down on paper, his writing is occasionally illegible (or imprecise at best) and his punctuation often erratic or idiosyncratic, the end of a line often sufficing to mark a sentence as finished, more often than not without a full stop.

Britten also bordered on dyslexia when it came to spelling, a condition he retained throughout his life, and he would always keep a dictionary to hand when writing letters. He also developed, and again retained, the habit of joining certain sequences of words such as 'abit' and 'alot', while also adopting the practice of the day in hyphenating words such as 'to-day' or 'to-morrow' that we now expect to read as joined. All of these idiosyncrasies have been retained and never silently edited or corrected in the text; and the many deletions in the diaries (some more emphatic than others) have also been preserved and replicated as accurately as possible, as they demonstrate the efforts he made to express himself more clearly, and the struggle he had to overcome his dyslexia-like battle with spelling. Words and names that are routinely misspelt, but never corrected, are also left as they appear on the page, as they are (almost without exception) easily interpreted phonetically. Britten's original punctuation is retained also, which can again be idiosyncratic, particularly when it comes to the use of full stops – often omitted altogether or used when one would expect a comma. Britten often ran out of space too (hardly surprising when one considers his extraordinary industriousness) and entries will run on to almost any adjacent space available – under previous entries, over the page, and often above the date for the day itself. However it is rare that this has any bearing on what is actually being communicated, so this has not been preserved in the layout of the entries, unless complete statements of note were made in their entirety above the date, in which case this is where you will find them in the text.

In the later diaries, when the political turmoil in Europe was troubling him greatly, Britten would leave a number of line spaces in the middle of entries, so as to divorce the more profound issues from the more domestic and routine. This has not been replicated here, as it would have taken up far too much space in the entries from 1935 onwards; but if a new paragraph accompanies serious comment on the political scene, one can assume that Britten had allowed enough space to convey the change of focus.

A great many hyphens, abbreviations and other oddities result from the fact that Britten has come to the end of a line and these are often determined by little more than the shape of the page. To edit these silently (or insert '*sic*', or the correction, or a footnote on every occasion) would have either peppered the text with amendments or doubled the number of annotations, which would soon have become tedious for the reader. So I have decided to aim for complete authenticity in the presentation of the diaries (in so far as one can achieve it without reference to their author) and trust that the reader will go with the flow, as it were. For today's text-messaging generation, this should prove no distraction.

In the course of ten and a half years of diary-keeping, Britten identifies by name more than a thousand individuals – from family and school friends to teachers and tennis partners; and amongst this great roll call are the many fellow musicians who were to become increasingly significant in his life. Some of these were mere acquaintances, while others were personal friends or collaborators; many more were fellow composers or performers, often featured in concerts and operas that he attended, or on wireless broadcasts or gramophone recordings that he heard, courtesy of the new technologies of the day. To have identified all of these on the page, as they first occur in each entry, would have seriously impeded the diaries' narrative flow; and annotating them within the text would have significantly increased the number of footnotes. Moreover, if the *dramatis personae* were to be identified only on their first appearance, the reader would probably have to spend rather a lot of time referring back through the general index, in order to locate the first appearance of the person in question and find the relevant annotation. Instead, I have provided a list of personalia towards the back of the book that identifies every significant figure, musical ensemble or institution, and provides such fundamental information as I believe necessary for a rounded understanding of the diary entry itself. This has the added benefit of providing one easily accessed source of biographical information on the many individuals who recur regularly in the diaries, and also those who arise only occasionally here but played a much more significant role in later periods of Britten's life.

Annotations to the entries themselves fall into two basic categories. The first is a minor clarification, when a shorthand reference or abbreviation on Britten's part (such as the initials of a person's name or a particularly distorted misspelling) might impair the reader's ability to refer to the Personalia. On these occasions the necessary clarification appears in square brackets within the diary entry itself. On rare occasions Britten himself uses square brackets, as is the case on 22 January 1936 and, coincidentally, again on the same date in 1937, and we have preserved the use of his square brackets here, as the context makes clear that they are Britten's clarifications on the text, not mine. More substantial and detailed footnotes appear at the end of each section. The footnotes themselves are as concise as possible. Their main purpose is to provide salient information, and sufficient reference-points for the reader to explore chosen avenues further, should he or she so wish. It is not my aim to provide the subtext of a secondary narrative – that, I hope, will be adequately provided by the brief introductory essays that articulate the sequence of the diaries, each introducing a significant new phase in Britten's life. These are primarily designed to place Britten's personal narrative in a broader context, providing information in advance that will help the reader to get more out of the diary entries themselves.

While I believe that this volume will be both accessible and fascinating to a wide range of readers, if it is also to be useful to musicians, scholars and those with a professional interest in the arts, then it needs to identify as precisely as possible all Britten's reading matter, including the scores he was acquiring and studying. Equally important is the need to identify the music he was rehearsing, performing and listening to at the time of each entry – in this respect, then, the annotations are very detailed whenever possible, though very occasionally Britten's references to music are too imprecise to allow a definite identification. The process of identifying the music he was actually *writing* has been more consistently successful, as every reference has been cross-checked with the manuscript database of the Britten–Pears Library and Archive at Aldeburgh, and double-checked with Britten's original manuscripts. To be able to read Britten's comments about the progress of a composition, identify in each case which score he was referring to, then finally handle the manuscript pencil sketch or ink fair copy itself in order to cross-check the reference, was a very special privilege for me, and one of the most rewarding experiences in what has been a very happy editorial process.

Every publication and author acknowledged in the Bibliography has contributed to my ability to interpret and annotate these diaries effectively, but two essential sources and a few individuals deserve particular mention here. Dr Donald Mitchell and Dr Philip Reed have done much pioneering work on this period of Britten's life, in a variety of publications (all listed in the Bibliography), but I am particularly indebted to them for their tireless research and scholarly editing of Britten's selected correspondence, *Letters from a Life* (Faber and Faber, 1991), the first volume of which proved a vital source for my own researches as it covers the precise period of the diaries. Beth Britten's very personal, touching, and affectionate profile of her younger brother, *My Brother Benjamin* (The Kensal Press, 1986) provided a unique perspective on the family's history, its daily routine and interpersonal dynamics; how I wish Beth had still been alive to consult when I began work on the diaries in 2006.

My colleagues at the Britten–Pears Library in Aldeburgh are much to be congratulated for the wonderful work they do in the preservation of a truly exceptional collection and archive, and for their dedication to making the collection accessible to new generations of scholars, academics and music-lovers. Their personal support of me through this enterprise was first-rate and I am very grateful to the Library Director, Dr Chris Grogan, and his colleagues Nicholas Clark, Anne Surfling and Pamela Wheeler. But very particular thanks must go to Anne and Pam, who have worked tirelessly to ensure that the original typed transcripts of the diaries – made over a long period of time, by different transcribers on different machines, and transcribed (more often than not) for content rather than precision – are now as accurate as is humanly possible. I am eternally grateful to them for this, and for many helpful suggestions they have made along the way about my draft text. Thanks also go to my commissioning editor at Faber and Faber, Belinda Matthews, for her enthusiastic support of this project, and her sound advice along the way. I am also grateful to Colin Matthews and John Bridcut, both of whom read my final manuscript, and generously shared their well-informed perspectives on the text.

At Faber, Elizabeth Tyerman, Anne Owen and Michael Downes were tireless in applying their professional skills to the project, and have given freely of their time and good counsel; and book designers, Eleanor Crow and Ron Costley, have made a most handsome job of the book's design, in the very best traditions of the Faber catalogue. I would also like to thank Eugenie Woodhouse for her proofreading, Kate Ward for her work on the plate section design, and Patricia Hymans for compiling the index.

Finally, I must express my gratitude to the trustees of the Britten–Pears Foundation and the directors of The Britten Estate Ltd for entrusting me with this wonderful project and for making the diaries and all associated source and research materials available for this publication.

It is said that Persian carpet makers deliberately weave a mistake into their patterns, because perfection offends the gods. I can claim no such excuse for any of my shortcomings, but I do hope that any errors or omissions that I have failed to tease out from the fabric of this book will not impede the reader's understanding, appreciation and, above all, *enjoyment* of Edward Benjamin Britten's very remarkable early journals.

John Evans
Aldeburgh, London, Eugene
November 2009

Prelude

A time there was as one may guess
And as, indeed, earth's testimonies tell
Before the birth of consciousness
When all went well
Thomas Hardy, 'Before Life and After'

Edith Rhoda Hockey, Benjamin's mother, was one of seven children – the oldest daughter of William Henry Hockey, a Queen's Messenger in the Home Office at Whitehall, and Rhoda Elizabeth Niblow, the daughter of a box-maker in Shoreditch. Edith and her three sisters were educated at Miss Hinton's School for Girls in Maidenhead, where they were contemporaries of the Britten girls, daughters of a Maidenhead family and sisters of the man who was later to become Edith's husband, Robert Victor Britten, the son of a draper turned dairy manager. When Robert moved to London to study dentistry at Charing Cross Hospital, he began to call on Edith's younger sister Sarah, whom he had presumably met through his sister Florence, an exact contemporary of Sarah at Miss Hinton's. The courtship was short-lived, however, as Robert soon transferred his affections to the oldest daughter, Edith, then in her late twenties and four years his senior. He would confess many years later to his eldest child, Barbara, that he had felt sorry for Edith and wanted to extricate her from an invidious situation – her mother had a drinking problem and as the eldest girl, Edith had assumed much of the responsibility for running the family home. The Hockeys lived in a staff flat at the Home Office, from where Edith and Robert were married, on 5 September 1901; the service was held just down the road at St John's Smith Square.

However prosaic the impulse for this union might have been, theirs was to be an enduring and, by all accounts, happy marriage. They first settled in Ipswich, where Mrs Britten's eldest brother, William, was organist of St Mary-le-Tower. Here Mr Britten began his career as assistant at Penraven's dental practice on Fonnereau Road, and they had their first child, (Edith) Barbara, on 11 June 1902. In 1905 they moved to Lowestoft, where Mr Britten set up his own practice, initially at 46 Marine Parade, where a son, Robert (Bobby) Harry Marsh, was born on 28 January 1907. The following year the family moved up the hill to 21 Kirkley Cliff Road, a larger house to the south of the town centre with wonderful views of the North Sea and town harbour, where they were to remain for almost thirty years. It was here that their third child, Charlotte Elizabeth (Beth) was born on 10 June 1909.

Edward Benjamin Britten was born at Kirkley Cliff Road on 22 November 1913 – by happy coincidence, this was St Cecilia's Day, on which the patron saint of music and musicians is celebrated. The boy's arrival was probably not planned by his parents; indeed his sister, Beth, has suggested that his parents chose his name in the hope that he would, indeed, be the 'Benjamin' of the family, the last of the line. But he did not lack for love and attention, perhaps *because* he was an unexpected gift; he was certainly treated as such and doted on. Barbara, Robert and Beth were eleven, six and four when Benjamin came on the scene; his father was in his mid-thirties, his mother in her early forties, both rather on the old side as parents for that time. As an infant Benjamin contracted pneumonia and very nearly died; according to Beth he was saved by the fact that his mother continued to breastfeed him, and when he was too weak to draw milk from her, she expressed her milk and fed him with the aid of a fountain-pen dropper. He survived, but this brush with death left him with a weak heart and prone to infections over the years, which would ultimately lead to the heart condition that required surgery in 1973, leading to his early death in 1976.

But we are getting ahead of ourselves, because this frailty as a child had a much more immediate effect on Benjamin's life. There seems to have been a sense within the family that he was special, and that his life had been saved for a purpose; and when, at the tender age of five, he began commandeering the piano stool and attempting to write music of his own, his mother saw it as her mission thereafter to ensure that his full potential would be realised. There seems to have been very little doubt in her mind that her youngest son was destined for greatness, and she soon became convinced that Benjamin would become one of the great 'B's in music, alongside Bach, Beethoven and Brahms. Britten's father had a much more pragmatic and practical approach to his son's upbringing, so Mrs Britten, out of respect for her husband, was apparently as discreet as possible about the nurturing and management of Benjamin's musical development. Even his siblings considered him to be special, certainly his sisters, who doted on him; the relationship with his older brother was more complex and even at times competitive, despite the six-year age difference.

Mr Britten's attitude, despite Benjamin's physical frailties, was that he should have as normal a childhood as possible, and be provided with a rounded education that would fully equip him for life. Mrs Britten was happy to go along with this strategy, but only up to a point. The fact that Benjamin boarded at Gresham's School, Holt, in order to pass his School Certificate, *before* going to music college, must have been a great concession on her part, because she was never really in any doubt about his true potential. For her, it was a waiting game, and in the meantime she would carefully put in place all that was required in the way of musical training, and find opportunities for Benjamin to perform in public. She was a capable amateur musician herself: she had sung in the National Choral Society in London and was Secretary, a regular chorister, and sometimes soloist with the Lowestoft Musical Society. She supervised Benjamin's earliest piano lessons, used her many local contacts to further his musical education, and hosted regular musical soirées at Kirkley Cliff Road where she, with Benjamin at the piano, would often be centre-stage.

For the young Benjamin, composing music, poring over scores, playing piano duets with friends or accompanying his mother in her favourite songs became as natural to him as breathing. His diaries attest to the fact that music was never far from his thoughts, even when other, perhaps more pressing, matters (such as school work) should probably have demanded more of his attention. But music was not his only passion. Despite his bouts of ill health he was a very keen, accomplished and competitive sportsman, skilled at tennis, badminton, cricket and swimming. In his last year at South Lodge Preparatory School he was Captain of Cricket and *Victor Ludorum*. At Gresham's he spent almost as much time at the nets, or playing on the cricket field or the tennis courts, as he did in the music room, listening to gramophone records, playing the viola in trios or piano duets with his fellow students. And this is where we pick up the story of Benjamin's life through his diaries, in 1928, as he moves from South Lodge Preparatory School in Lowestoft to board at Gresham's School in Holt: the start of an often painful transition, from the security of home life to a more independent existence, from childhood to adolescence.

Lowestoft – Gresham's

. . . everything seemed so simple when he was a boy . . . simple and delightful for the most part. But as he grew up, he began to be increasingly disillusioned – in man – I suppose.

Sir Peter Pears, interviewed in *A Time There Was . . .* (*The South Bank Show*)

Britten's life has been so well documented, and his career so celebrated, that sometimes a true perspective on his early years is hard to achieve, clouded as it is by the public nature of almost everything he did after the now legendary premiere of *Peter Grimes* at Sadler's Wells on 7 June 1945. It is very easy to forget that he was born shortly before the Great War and grew up in a very provincial fishing town on Suffolk's east coast – a community populated by retired colonels, the widows and orphans of the war, and spinsters for whom marriage was now unlikely, as too many eligible young men did not return to their families and loved ones in 1918. At times, reading Britten's own account of life in Lowestoft, one is reminded not so much of the characteristically East Anglian 'Borough' community of *Peter Grimes*, but rather the more quaint provincial society of the 'Loxford' of *Albert Herring* – full of charitable good causes and committee meetings, church fêtes and musical gatherings, with the ever-present town worthies in attendance: the vicar, church organist and schoolmistress. Indeed, Mrs Britten herself was at the heart of community life in Lowestoft, as a regular worshipper at St John's Church, where all four of her children were baptised and confirmed. She seems, however, to have been less successful in persuading her husband of the virtues of regular prayer or church-going; his Sunday routine involved visiting patients in the morning, returning via a friend, Decar Blowers, landlord of a farmhouse pub in Sotterly; after the traditional family Sunday lunch and tea, Mr Britten's early evening port-of-call was Lowestoft's Royal Yacht Club. It would be safe to say that Mr and Mrs Britten made rather different interpretations of the day of rest.

Meanwhile Mrs Britten continued her charitable work as Secretary of the Lowestoft Musical Society, supporting the 'Care of Girls' charity, and running a soup kitchen for the Scottish Girls who worked at the fish-markets, whose job it was to gut and pack the herring catch from the Scottish boats during the season. Beth, meanwhile, ran the local lacrosse team and the Brownie troupe. The children were encouraged to take their social responsibilities and civic duties seriously, and despite a degree of snobbishness on Mrs Britten's part the family was brought up to respect individuals from all walks of society. They were devoted, for instance, to Mr Britten's secretary, Miss Hayes, and to the domestic staff, Rose, May and Phyllis; but highest in their affections were the two sisters from Farnham who managed Mrs Britten's home from the polar extremes of the house. Annie Walker, the children's nanny, joined the household in 1907, six months after Bobby was born, and remained with the family until 1932. Her empire was the nursery on the top floor. After Benjamin came along it was thought that Mrs Britten needed more help with running 21 Kirkley Cliff Road, so in May 1914 Annie's sister, Alice, joined the household as cook and remained for almost twenty years, leaving only in January 1933 to marry a man to whom she had been betrothed for almost her entire time in Lowestoft.

In this extremely well-run establishment, education and general improvement were also taken very seriously. All four children began their education at Southolme, Miss Astle's pre-preparatory school in Lowestoft, where her younger sister, Miss Ethel Astle, was the music teacher. Both Britten girls went to the Woodard School of St Mary and Anne, Abbots Bromley, in Staffordshire. Barbara became a health visitor in London (first in Peckham, then Hampstead) and during the Second World War became Assistant Superintendent of the Child Welfare Department of the Middlesex Hospital in London. Beth studied at the Paris Academy of Dressmaking in London's Old Bond Street; during the 1930s, in partnership with a student friend, Lilian Wolff, she founded Elspeth Beide, a dress-making establishment at 559 Finchley Road in Hampstead, before marrying Christopher (Kit) Welford and starting a family of her own. After Southolme, Bobby went to preparatory school at Forncett in Norfolk during the First World War, then boarded at Oakham School, Rutland (1921–6) before going up to Cambridge. After graduating he became a schoolmaster at the Elms School in Colwall (near Malvern), and then headmaster of Clive House in Prestatyn, north Wales – the school for which Britten was later to write his *Friday Afternoons* children's songs.

After Southolme, Benjamin went to South Lodge Preparatory School, just down the hill on Kirkley Cliff, where he was academically successful and, above all, happy. From the age of five he had been receiving piano lessons from his mother and started scribbling music of his own. Two years later he began music theory and piano lessons with Ethel Astle, and in 1923 Benjamin started viola lessons with one of the leading string teachers in East Anglia at the time, Mrs Audrey Alston in Norwich. By the time he heard

Frank Bridge conduct his orchestral suite *The Sea*, at the 1924 Norfolk and Norwich Triennial Festival, Benjamin was pouring out his own musical thoughts on manuscript paper at an astonishing rate, but was still receiving no formal teaching in composition. Thanks to Audrey Alston all that changed. On 27 October 1927, at the next Norwich Festival, Alston introduced him to Bridge after a performance of *Enter Spring*, and on inspecting some of Benjamin's compositions the following day, Bridge agreed to take the boy on as a private pupil the following year. Again through Alston, Britten also started piano lessons with Harold Samuel in London, later in 1928. So by the time Benjamin began keeping his daily journal in January of that year, he was about to enjoy some of the best private teaching available in the country. The lessons with Bridge, in particular, were long and arduous, and Bridge seems to have made no concessions to, and very little allowance for, the boy's youth. He instilled in him a creative discipline, and a level of professional application, that was to stay with Benjamin for life.

Meanwhile, the Britten household regime was becoming increasingly complicated. Now exposed to this extraordinary level of professional tuition, and all the opportunities it afforded, Benjamin was eager, not to say impatient, to study full-time at a conservatoire. But his father, strongly supported (according to Beth) by Barbara and Bobby, insisted that he continue his formal education to secure his School Certificate. Concerned about the boy's future, Mr Britten thought him too young and immature to live alone in London (even if chaperoned); and despite Benjamin's obvious gifts, Mr Britten was yet to be convinced that the boy could make a good living as a musician. Beth Britten, in her lovingly personal profile of her brother, described her father as a cautious man, apparently always worrying about money. She even suggests that her mother's constant entertaining of local friends and neighbours was encouraged by Mr Britten's nervousness of losing valued patients. Surprisingly, the Britten home had neither a gramophone nor a wireless at this time; and though Beth attributes this to a concern on her parents' part for the possible impact on the very healthy music-making within the family (Bobby was also a good pianist and violinist), it might also reflect Mr Britten's anxiety about the family finances. As Beth recalled:

> My father used to say things to us such as 'Make money, honestly if you can', or 'Don't marry money, but go where money is.' My mother would be horrified and say 'Robert, don't say things like that to the children,

> you know you don't mean it.' He certainly was the most honest man, but overcome with the need to make ends meet.*

But if there was one thing Mr Britten was not prepared to scrimp on, it was his children's education and welfare. By the time we enter Benjamin's personal account of his life in January 1928, the decision had already been made that he was to board at Gresham's School in Holt, Norfolk, and though the outcome was largely satisfactory (Benjamin certainly emerged stronger and better equipped for London as a result), the move also led to a great deal of turmoil and unhappiness, which manifested itself in constant and sometimes prolonged periods of sickness and depression that seriously impacted on the boy's academic work. As soon as he arrived at Gresham's on 20 September 1928, for the start of the Michaelmas term, he began a count-down in his diary to the end of term, labelling each successive week: 'END OF WEEK . . .' By the start of the 1929 Midsummer Term, from 19 May, this had become a daily obsession and remained so till he left school in August 1930, each entry headed with a boxed count-down to the end of term: [1–84] – [2–83] – [3–82] and so on.

Nonetheless, whatever Benjamin's mental or physical state, he never stopped composing, even when in the school sanatorium. The diaries also speak of his obvious frustration with the quality of music teaching at Gresham's, where he seemed merely to tolerate Miss Chapman (his viola teacher) and Hoult Taylor (the junior music master), while barely tolerating and at times actively despising Walter Greatorex, the Director of Music. Perhaps he never recovered from Greatorex's suspicious and less than welcoming greeting on his first arrival at the school: 'So you are the little boy who likes Stravinsky!' But it is important to recognise the sheer amount of musical activity at the school at this time, and to acknowledge that Gresham's was considered an impressively progressive and enlightened school (a reputation it still enjoys today), with an enviable commitment to the arts. Indeed it had already produced many highly distinguished alumni, including Lord Reith (founding Director General of the BBC), the poets W. H. Auden and Louis MacNeice, the painter Robert Medley and the composer Lennox Berkeley; coincidentally, all four of these great men would play their part in Benjamin's journey through the 1930s.

His experience of Gresham's, however, was hugely influenced by desperate homesickness and an overwhelming sense of deprivation at the loss of his

* Beth Britten, *My Brother Benjamin* (Bourne End: The Kensal Press, 1986), p. 52.

mother's loving support. But by the end of the Gresham's years the clouds began to lift, and much to his own surprise, Benjamin received his School Certificate. At the end-of-term speech day, the headmaster J. R. Eccles proudly celebrated 'the largest [honours list] I have ever had the pleasure of recording', including three Cambridge College Fellowships, three Commonwealth Fund Fellowships, eight first-class degrees, four scholarships won by OG's at Oxbridge colleges and six by those straight from school. 'Crowning these triumphs', however, in Eccles' estimation, was Benjamin's Open Scholarship to the Royal College of Music: his name was inscribed on the Honours Board in Big School for 1929–30, alongside the names of future diplomats, academics, senior civil servants and scientists.

Diaries: 1928–1930

Gresham's School, Holt

Benjamin's pencil sketches for *May in the Greenwood* and *A Hymn to the Virgin*, written 'in secret on lines drawn on my writing pad', while in the school sanatorium at Gresham's. © The Britten Estate Limited. See diary entries for 8–9 July 1930.

1928

TERM BEGINS. – HOLT

Thursday 20 September
~~We go~~ Mummy, Daddy, and Bobby, take me to Holt, to school, worse luck! Met Purdy and we wander about for about 1 hour, until the crowd arrive.

Friday 21 September
We do ~~are~~ our Studies (I am in a study 3 boys, who might be worse, but might be better. They are full of swearing and vulgarity), in the morning, and have chapel at 10.30. Work in the afternoon. Bed at 9.30. I do not like the outlook of 13 weeks of this!

In my study I have a ghastly time in the evening, Corner and 3 other boys Meiklejohn Savory Briant, are positively vulgar. It makes me feel sick to think of it.

Sunday 23 September
Chapel 10.30, and 6.30 (a memorial service to some dead master.). Go to tea with Mrs Gaunt, and have a ripping time. Walk with Purdy in afternoon.

Saturday 29 September
Usual work, walk, and practise. In evening Mr. Greatorex, + Miss Chapman. give a recital.[1] Mr G. is simply terrible, played no 2. notes together, and everything [BB writes a squiggle here] To think that he ~~was~~ is professor of music here! Miss C. was quite good if only she could tune her strings![2]

Saturday 6 October
Recital in the evening. Bach's Air on G string,[3] Gavotte in E and Handel sonata in E[4] (Miss Chapman) very good. Mr. Greatorex, Mr. Taylor (piano) and Miss Chapman, Mr. Taylor was given a great Reception, tho' he didn't deserve it.[5] It looked as if he was a bad sight reader, and as if he had never seen the music before; the way he stopped when he came to a hard passage and looked at it.

Wednesday 10 October
Orchestral Practice at 5.45. (Haydn, 1st move. of Oxford Symphony), Schubert Moment Musical, Marche Militaire, March Heroique, Mozart

Menuett from G min Symphony).[6] Gramophone Records and Practice Piano in Mr. Greatorex's room

4th WEEK OF TERM ENDS

Choir practice 12.25, Viola lesson 11.40.

Thursday 18 October

Have a nice letter from Mr. Bridge. I am ~~feal~~ feeling very queer all day, as if something terrible is going to happen. My old feeling of terror comes much. Apart from that, ordinary work.

5th WEEK OF TERM ENDS

Thursday 25 October

I am reading a book on Beethoven by P.K. Bekker.[7] I don't know if I like it very much; it is far to fanciful and always fixes programmes to every work. I wish people would let us enjoy works without distracting our attentions with programmes.[8] Walk in the afternoon. Choir practise.

Tuesday 13 November

Brahms has gone up one place in my list of Composers. Beethoven is still first, and I think always will be, Bach or Brahms comes next, I don't know which![9] Ordinary work, and walk in aft.

Monday 19 November

182~~7~~8 Schubert died

Ordinary work. It is getting cold ~~to ge~~ and dark every morning to get up!! Ordinary work. Schubert Centenary, but, of course being at school I can do nothing in memory of this immortal man.[10]

1929

TERM BEGINS – HOLT

[Farfield, Holt, Norfolk.]

Thursday 17 January

In the morning I pack for going back to school where I go in the afternoon in the car with Beth and Mum & Pop. Have a nasty skid this side (Lowestoft) of Norwich.

I do detest leaving home, there is that utter loneliness at school, which I loathe

Friday 18 January

In the morning we unpack our tuck-boxes and put our studies in order. I am in the same study as last term, Marshall II, Savory, Meiklejohn. Chapel at 10.30. Work in afternoon, the work in the new form, IVc. is going to be very hard.

Because of 5 schols. ~~next~~ this term ends on the 4th instead of the 10th, ~~hurrah!~~ only 11 more weeks!

END OF FIRST WEEK

Thursday 24 January

Ordinary work up to ~~till~~ break, and then I go to bed with my usual bilious complaint plus a nasty feverish cold.

Feel too ill to do any reading at all, that being my only recreation in the sick-room. (I have had to lapse into red-ink because my ordinary fountain pen has run out, and in my present state with Matron so busy I cannot have it filled).

Friday 25 January

I am still laid up in bed. The house is pestered by this 'disease' of a feverish cold. One by one they are going down, and to the San [Sanatorium]. By a lucky stroke when I fell ill, there was a bed in a sickroom empty so here I am!! Do a little reading (Pathfinder – Cooper).[1]

Sunday 27 January No.II.

Still in bed, so no Chapel for me. I am slightly better. More boys from Farfield fall to the "disease".

Finish 'Pathfinder', Happy find! A good book at last, 'The Caravaners' by the author of Elizabeth & her German Garden.[2] So I'm deep~~ly~~ in that.

Monday 28 January

Same as yesterday, progressing slowly. 8 people of Farfield, with disease, 2 in the two sickrooms at Farfield and 6 at the san.

Finish 'Caravaners' quite good, but I did not like it as much as I had hoped to, however!

The people at home are wonderful with writing, letters pour in. I really am lucky!

Wednesday 30 January

15 boys (not counting 3 not back) out of Farfield ill! Slightly better, progress maintained! (This is like the bulletins outside the Palace!)[3] I am still lying down, as I feel rather bad when sitting up.

I finish the book, Bat-wing, rather as I expected.

END OF SECOND WEEK.

Thursday 31 January

N.S.Q.C. concert at Lowestoft; afternoon and evening. Mummy is most hard-working about it, has been for about the last 3 weeks.

Programme:

1. String Quartet in G maj., Mozart (which, I don't know, movements are – Allegro, Andante – Romanza, Minuetto etc, Rondo – allegro.)
2. 2 Spanish Dances (Bolero & Seguidillas) for Piano Trio (with Mr. Winter) – Fernandez Arbòs.
3. Mendelssohn, String Q. in E^b maj. op.12.

Harrington Kidd | Jocelyn Bates
Audrey Alston | Charles Finch
Marjorie Winter (Pft.).

Saturday 2 February

In response to an appeal home, they rippingly send me a parcel of Books – St Ives, Little Duke, & the Toilers of the Sea (Hugo).[4] The first I read & finish to-day. I am still lying down, tho' much better. But I am haunted by a horrible sickness feeling of which I can't get rid.

The N.S.Q.C concert was not at all successful, financially only £4 gain on 2 concerts! What is to be done with Lowestoft music?!!

Wednesday 6 February

Get up and go down stairs, and have meals with the rest of the house, tho' still sleeping in the sickroom.

Finish the Quartett (Rhapsody)[5] for Mr. Bridge, though I shall go on altering it for a long time, I expect!

Begin reading "Loorna Doone"[6]

End of 3rd Week

Thursday 7 February

To-night I get up and go back into the dormetry.

I go about downstairs all day, but mostly I sit in my study writing music.

I go through and alter: Song of Enchantment[7] & the Rhapsody.

Write a short Minuet in an old style, ~~for~~ a very easy quartet for home & school use, (sketched for a long time, before).[8]

Friday 8 February
Just the same as yesterday, only I get up for breakfast. I scarcely slept a wink last night.

I work hard at my music. Copy the parts of the minuet & some of a new Novelette[9] written to-day. I am still stuck over my Rhapsody. I can't start properly or end properly, at that. Mummy sends 3/- for some oranges. I've got to have 2 a day.

Tuesday 12 February
Still no school for me. Yesterday and to-day have been ~~some~~ two of the coldest days I have ever known. To-day I go out for 2 short walks before & after lunch. I write a short Romance to complete the "Miniature Suite".[10] Now Novelette – Minuet – Romanze – Gavotte. I have copied out all the parts except those of the Rom.

<u>End of 4th Week</u>

Thursday 14 February
Still absent from school work. Everso much more snow, it is quite deep, allowing as well as skating, tobogganing, in the afternoon. But of course I'm not allowed to go out!

In the afternoon after a lie down I listen to the wireless, a concert, orchestra & Paul Wittenstein [Wittgenstein] (I think that's his name, the left-handed pianist). Quite good, tho' I didn't like the programme very much.

Monday 18 February
In morning the snow begins to melt, but it freezes towards nightfall. I go out for two short walks. No School. I am still unsatisfied with my Rhapsody. I don't know what to do with it. I have another attempt to rewrite it again to-day, <u>unsuccessfully</u>! I write a short Etude for viola solo, and continue to patch up "Lilian".[11]

Do quite a lot of reading "Vanity Fair".[12]

Wednesday 20 February
The same events as yesterday practically. I go out twice, in morning & aft. Do a little writing & much reading.

Begin a Piano quintet which I leave off in disgust.[13]

Also I begin a piece for Piano quartet which looks as if its going to be variations on an unoriginal theme (only I wrote it)[14]

END OF FIFTH WEEK.

Thursday 21 February
Still no school; it's getting very, very boring, and as there is not much outward appearence of any illness, it looks rather queer (one might almost say suspicious) that I'm out of school so long. If they only knew how bored I am! ~~and~~ I do very little writing, only a short song, "the Witches' Song"[15] in afternoon. I even give up the unoriginal theme etc. in disgust! Nothing from Mummy about next Sat.

– LOWESTOFT.

Saturday 23 February
Mummy, Pop, Beth and the car arrive ~~home~~ at about 2.15. After collecting a little luggage and start home! On the way home we stop at the Warners and have tea (just the Lowestoft side of Norwich). Arrive home at about 7.0. It is ripping to be home!

Monday 25 February
In the morning I go and see Dr Evans, who says I had better stay at home for a while until I am completely well. He also forbids me going out while the wind is so beastly. I begin to sort out all my M.S.S.[16] I have got a lot! Miss Ethel (Astle) comes in to coffee.

Wednesday 6 March
I get up and stay in the room, half dressed. I do a lot of altering, Rhapsody & Miniature suite.[17] Also I do alot of reading. Yesterday I read and finished Master of Ballantrae.[18] I loved it, very much. I am not sleeping atall well now-adays.

– HOLT AGAIN.

Tuesday 12 March
Dr Evens says I can go back! So of[f] I have to go in car with Pop, Mummy, Beth, Bobby, feeling absolutely rotten. We arrive at about 5.45. and they go back home. I don't do prep, but go to bed early, feeling worse than ill. I don't sleep much to night.

Wednesday 13 March
I spend probably one of the most miserable days in all my life. Lying in bed in the dormetry, feeling absolutely rotten. Yearning for home and everybody there. Am sick once in morning. Why did they send me back, to go to bed

directly? I think Miss Margerye Goldson ~~comes~~ goes to stay, at home. Mummy rings up in evening to see how I am.

END OF EIGTH WEEK

Thursday 14 March
I am if anything worse to-day, & certainly not more cheerful. I am moved into the small sickroom in the morning. Mummy rings up again in the evening, it is a disappointment for her!

Lowestoft Musical S. concert at Marina Theatre,[19] Bach's Peasant Cantata [BWV212] & A. Rowley's "By the Deep in G"

Friday 15 March
Mummy rings up in morning to say she is coming, and will stay night at the "Feathers".[20] She arrives just before tea. I am still in bed. It is marvellous being with her.

She goes out about 6 o'c. to see Dr Hendrie, then she comes back to me and stays until 8.30.

Bliss!! Mummy brought me some lovely grapes

Saturday 16 March
I am still in bed, all day. Mummy comes at 10.15 and stays the whole morning, bringing a plant and some sponge-cakes. She has dinner with Mrs. Thompson. Daddy comes to fetch her, and he goes after tea, in car. Barbara comes to stay at home.

There is a chance of me going home next Saturday. Pop wanted to-day, but Mummy wouldn't allow it until I am better.

End OF NINTH WEEK

Thursday 21 March
I get up about 9'o having had breakfast in bed, in the sickroom. I hear from Mummy who says that I shall probably go home next Tuesday. Not Saturday because Beth has a Lax Match away at Aldeburgh and wants the car. I finish off the copy of the Rhapsody[21] and begin transcribing a viola Ètude for violin.[22] I ~~sh~~ have to sleep in the dormetry to-night.

Friday 22 March
Last-night it was frightfully hot, I scarcely slept at all. and I fear to-night's going to be the same. I get up for breakfast, and go to bed about 7.15. I finish the Étude copy a violoncello part (of the miniature suite), and write a short Madrigal. "Song from nice valour", J. Fletcher.[23] I go out for a tiny walk

in afternoon, tho' feeling pretty rotten. I am getting better, tho'. Marshall II goes to San. with Scarl. Fever.

– LOWESTOFT

Tuesday 26 March

Mummy and Pop arrive in car about 4.o'clock. In morning I go and say good-bye to J.R. Eccles. We leave Holt about 5 o'clock & get home before 7 o'c. Bobby & Beth are at home. It is marvellous to be at home, such bliss! We had a marvellous run home, 50 miles in under 2 hours.

Garland goes to the San. with Chicken Pox. There is a case of mumps at Woodlands.

Wednesday 27 March

Go out along the beach with Beth in morning. And with Mummy in afternoon; & in the evening when nearly dark by myself. Play alot of Viola, especially Beethoven Vlc. sonatas arranged, by myself. Duets with Mummy after tea, Beethoven's 7th Symphony. Great fun.

What Bliss is home!

Thursday 28 March

Barbara comes home from London, at 6.10 (really about 6.25!). Go shopping with Mummy & Beth in morning, in the car. Go for a walk with Beth in the afternoon.

Play Cesar Franck Sonata with Bobby (violin) in evening, quite fun. The gorgeous weather continues since March 8th, it really is more like August, than March.

Sunday 31 March

I am at last out of quarentine, and so I am allowed to go to Church. Communion at 8.0, everso many people there, about 200 I should think, and Morning Prayer at 11.0. Sawdon & Foster (from South Lodge) come to tea; I asked Francis (Barton) but, worst luck he couldn't come. Walk with Mummy, ~~before supper~~ after tea, and after that some Vla. & pft duets with her (Beethoven Vl.c. sonatas).

TERM BEGINS – HOLT

1 (pas~~t~~sed) – 84 (to come)

Wednesday 8 May

Return to School in the afternoon, worst luck! Beth comes with Mummy & Pop to bring me over. We start at 2.0. approx. and have tea at Sheringham.

They eventually go about 6.0. Oh! It is a ghastly feeling to be away from ones own darlings for so long. Do ~~most of~~ the packing in the morning.

2–83

Thursday 9 May

Remake our studies in the morning and unpack. Chapel at 10.30. Play tennis with Williamson, Hinde II, & Roberts, ~~who~~ (the last 2 are pretty hopeless) at 4.15–5.15.

Have a slight practise at piano, and a little gramophone (1st mov.s. of Brahm's 4th symph. & Piano quintet, & last of Mozart Jupiter).[24] Feel pretty miserable, especially as there is no news from home.

END OF FIRST WEEK

8–77

Wednesday 15 May

I have a beastly cold which gets steadily worse all day. Ordinary work in morning, except that I'm feeling rotten. Orchestra practice 12.25–1.5. Go to Miss Gillett after dinner & she gives me some quinine,[25] and a gargle. I go into school in afternoon, & practise after tea, and do prep, but I feel worse & go to bed early in the sickroom. It is a blessed nuisance as I have so much work to do.

14–71

Tuesday 21 May

Continue with School. I seem to be doing very badly this term. I expect it is because I missed so much last term. I am still off games. This term we have 3 half-hols. a week; ~~Mond~~ Tues. Thurs. Sat. On the other 3 days we have an extra period. I do alot of practising both after breakfast, dinner & tea. Miss Chapman gets me Kreuz's Viola Studies book 4. They're very good I think. I don't have a bad music lesson. (viola of course). Have a letter from Mummy.

20–65

Monday 27 May

Ordinary work. Cricket at 12.0. Practise viola after tea. I am doing badly at work this term, I expect it's to do with ~~the~~ missing so much last term. In German I feel it especially. I don't think I've learnt a word this term. I came straight up from the C block german to the B block (in my double move) and consequently I'm ~~write~~ right behind. Most of the boys are going in for the School cert this term, and I've only done 1 term's work! The Master (Addleshaw) won't stop to explain, and I can't understand.

<u>END OF 3rd WEEK</u>

22–63

Wednesday 29 May

A pretty unsuccessful day for me. For one thing the prep I did for J.R.E. (Mostly Unitary method still) he greeted me with the fact that it was very bad, in that I had put in "ditto" signs (i.e. "); I expect that I'll have a rotten time in Physics tomorrow, as he is always disgustingly rude when he is furious, as he seems to be now. I can't see how I was to know, as it is my first writing prep for him.[26] Orchestra practise, 12.25. Viola lesson, 9.30, Cricket net after tea with non-recruits.

23–62

Thursday 30 May

The storm came at the Physics period, it was bad but not as much as I had expected, and what was more it was not ~~me~~ I alone. J.R.E seems pretty fed [up] with me altogether now! Play cricket this afternoon in 3rd game, which is a pretty rotten one. Have a topping game of tennis after tea, with Miles, Roberts, Williamson. Have so much prep. to do that I again have to stay up to extra. I have ~~had~~ nothing from Mummy ~~now~~ (the last time she wrote was 24th), I wonder what's up.

27–58

Monday 3 June

I am school bell-fag, this week; the school-pre. of the week chooses a ~~person~~ boy to ring all the school-bells. Marshall I. has chosen me. It's rather a fag, but it's not bad fun. It rains, so there's not ~~much~~ any cricket. We have the quarters order,[27] I go down one, & up two. I really must do better next quarter, tho' I have been working hard, I know. Have a letter from Pop. Write a song for voice & strings, "The Birds", by H. Belloc.[28]

<u>END OF SIXTH WEEK</u>

43–42

Wednesday 19 June

Ordinary work all day. I struggle over it somehow, how I don't know, except that God was helping me. Have a lovely long letter from Laulie, most cheering. Practise Violin & Viola after tea as there is no Corps. I seem to be going down & down in form, this quarter. How I shall pass the school cert. next summer I don't know. Still, nothing from home.

58–27 Play hymn at prayers

Thursday 4 July
A simply pelting morning & part of afternoon. There should have been a match v. J. Zingari but it was naturally put off. I spend most of afternoon in music rooms, gramophoning & practising viola & piano. ~~After~~ (there is a new record of Wagners Overture to the Mast.)[29] After tea I play duets with Berthoud (Mozart Vl. concerto in D maj) & Trios with Floud Schumann Quintet (Floud Pft, ~~Vl~~ Berthoud Vl. 1 & 2, me the rest)

60–25

Saturday 6 July
In the morning it rains hard, but it clears up enough for us to play a nice but cold game of cricket. Spend all ~~afternoon~~ evening in the music rooms practising viola, piano, playing trios (Schumann Quintet) with Mr. Taylor (pft) 2nd music master. After that I play pft. duets with him, Mozart's Symphony ~~no~~ (Jupiter). Play hymn at Prayers.

61–24

Sunday 7 July
Service at 10.30–11.0, ~~for~~ Thanksgiving for the King's recovery.[30] Very nice service tho' too short. Play Schumann's Quintet as last night only with Floud as Vln. 2. Play 1st & 2nd movs. of G min. symph duet with Taylor. There is a study tea for pres. in the house. 4.30–5.30. I & 3 others (Crawford, Johnson Hinde II) fag. Play in string quartet (see Jan. 20th), quite good [with Miss Chapman, Berthoud and Diver]. Play 2 Haydn Quartets. (Serenade & B♭, same as last time), great Fun. Write home.

71–14 END OF 10th WEEK

Wednesday 17 July
The day before J.R.E Practical physics. Oh! for the time when I could say that it ~~was~~ is over. I spend most of a broiling hot day in revising for that & chemy practical. The day ends with some atrocious bullying in our Study, Marshall & Savory v. Williams (the small new boy), who ends in tears.

Unfortunately I was out of the room. And this a school of the honour system![31] Nothing from home, I wonder what's up.

RETURN TO HOLT.

1–90 TERM BEGINS

Thursday 19 September
Pack in morning with Mummy. Hair cut at 11.30. Bathe with Mummy & Beth, at 1.0.–1.30. approx. Set off in car with Pop. Mummy, & Beth, for Holt, via. North Walsham, at 3.0. Arrive, having had tea about 10. miles from Holt, at 6.0. They leave at 7.0. See about studies etc. after. Oh, God! Home!! And Parents!!! Why ever was school invented; at least school away from one's beloveds.

33–58

Monday 21 October
Feel absolutely rotten & sick in the morning & go & tell Miss Gillett so. I see Dr. Hendrie & he keeps me out of school all day. Stay in my study all the time, feeling worse than ill. I can't think why I'm not to go to bed, because I have to keep absolutely still on the "lounge", which is very uncomfortable. Begin a piece for Viola & strings.[32]

34–57

Tuesday 22 October
Same as yesterday, feeling little better. I am fed completely on milk. Stay in study as yesterday. Reading much; yest. I read a play of G.B. Shaw. "Overruled". ToDay Tolstoi's Forged Coupon, & start the "Unbearable Bassington" of "Saki".[33] Quite good I think. Continue writing the Viola thing and studying music, Orchestration (Forsyth, lent to me by Mr. Taylor), & a little Counterpoint.

38–53

Saturday 26 October
Eat a piece of bread & butter at breakfast which sends me down with the sickness again! It is a blithering nuisance. However, I manage to finish the Introduction & Allegro for Viola solo & String Orchestra.

Finish the "Unbearable Bassington". It really was very good. Begin another by 'Saki'; Reginald, & R. in Russia.[34] Which I like quite, but not to same extent. Match v. Norwich R.F.C. – School win. Recital at which Mrs. Wilkinson sings. Attend neither.

40–51

Monday 28 October

A terribly rainy day & very cold. Am still out of school. I wonder what they thought at home of my letter to-day! There was (1) News of my illness (2) Want of 3 new shirts (3). Birthday list (a massive list of min. scores). (4). Mummy wants to come to recital which she thinks is on Dec. 2nd instead of Nov. 2nd. Quite a bombshell! I write "Wild Time" for Sop. & strings.[35] I've got quite a craze for string orch. now. Spend most of afternoon with Miss Gillett in her room & turning out clothes. Have a little more food. Hair cut.

41–50

Tuesday 29 October

Still out of school but better. I have some fish for dinner – the first substantial thing since Sunday week! – in the dining hall. Other meals (except breakfast (bread & milk) in dining hall) in study & supper in dorm. per usual. Letter from Mummy. Short walk in morning. Then rain for rest of day. Few sets of ping-pong in afternoon with Miles. Bath in evening. Write fresh copies of "Song of the Women", & begin f.c. [fair copy] of "Int. & All°"

42–49

Wednesday 30 October

Still out of school, but I am determined to go back to-morrow. If I don't go then, I shan't play in the recital on Saturday & Mummy won't come over. I go out twice, in morning & afternoon. There is a match v. an Emmanuel College team which wins 11–6. I don't watch it however.

Copy & rewrite sheets of "Int & Allegro". There is a foully strong wind. It is fairly shaking the house now – I am sitting up in bed at 8.0 waiting for my supper (bread & Milk!).

45–46

Saturday 2 November

From the heights of happiness (4.15 meeting Mummy, Pop, Beth & "Seizer"[36] in the car) to the very depths of misery (lying in bed after they have gone at 8.0.) Ord. work in morning no P.T. Pingpong walk, practise in afternoon. Tea with Mummy & Pop Mr & Mrs. Thompson. Recital with Gog & Miss Chapman, Mozart Trio & Brahms.[37] Play horrible badly in former, &

less badly in latter. Play house-prayers, & go to bed, not to the Debate. In depths of misery.

49–42

Wednesday 6 November

I begin a perfectly awful day, with Gog telling me that my piano style (incidentally learned from Miss Astle & approved of by H. Samuel) was no good, & thereupon showing me the (his!!) style. After a pouring morning, & a meagre lunch, we watch a match v. ~~Old~~ Cambridge O.G's, & have a near scrape from J.R.E. (he ticks the 2 boys with whom I was watching off for not watching etc.); return to Music rooms, & have a play & gramophone with Floud & thereupon Gog finds us together & is livid.[38] Horrible orch. practise. Get into row with Docker for not staring Mr. Thompson in the face all the time in a house jaw![39] Music lesson 12.0 only cheerful thing in a silly day!!!

60–31

Sunday 17 November No 9

Ordinary Sunday with – well – quite a nice sermon by Rev? Thomas?? I spend most of the day anyhow the most enjoyable part of the day talking with Floud ma. and occasionally his satelite Floud mi. He really is a remarkable boy. One of the Very few (about 4) boys who think, in the school. He doesn't think any worth of games; disagrees [runs on into entry for 18 November]

61–30

Monday 18 November

with practically all the habits of the "normal public school boy", e.g. corps., prefects (he should be heard on that!). Very clever, knows much of art, music, & literature etc. Specially modern. A joy to talk with!!

Yesterday I began sketching a trio for Vln, Vla, Pft.[40] Do a little more to day. Quite pleased. Ordinary work, walk, pingpong. Letter from Mummy. Play house prayers. Go to bed, instead of extra prep.

62–29

Tuesday 19 November

It is a pretty bad thing to think how this school is degrading its name. It is laid on modern lines. In 1905 perhaps it was Modern, but really ~~it~~ what was Modern in 1905 is not in 1930. Originality (oh! that blessed thing) is completely discouraged. If you are original, well you are considered a lunatic, & consequently become unpopular. Unpopularity is then a thing to be aimed for in Gresham's School Holt then. Ord. day.

63–28

Wednesday 20 November
I go to bed once again. I had a beastly sore throat all yesterday, & as it didn't go I had to tell Nurse, who is deputizing for Miss Gillette who is ill, and I am put to bed. Do much thinking, a scrap of writing (see Monday). I am thinking much about modernism in art. Debating whether Impressionism, Expressionism, Classicism etc. are right. I have half-decided on Schönberg.[41] I adore Picasso's pictures.

86–5

Friday 13 December
Utter misery somehow, to day. Everything seems to go wrong from the beginning of the day. I have a letter from Pop. saying that they are coming over tomorrow & not on Thursday (not to fetch me then, but to be here for concert), inspite of my continued entreaties. That means they will want to take the majority of my things home tomorrow, & on top of the play, practising for concert, work which I can't get done, I have to pack.

87–4

Saturday 14 December
Day begins as light as a bad thunderstorm & ends as dark as a sunbeam. I have a chance to pack in afternoon, whilst waiting for Mummy & Pop + the car, which eventually don't arrive until 5.0. approx. They come to concert at 8.15 which doesn't go too badly considering, orch. was awful, & choir not so bad. Mummy & Pop are sleeping at the Feathers. (Work goes very badly in morning)

88–3 SUNDAY no 3 [of Advent]

Sunday 15 December
Go out to breakfast with Mummy & Pop in morning, at 8.30. They go + my luggage just before chapel. Berthoud has come down; play Beethoven vln & pft sonatas with him aft. Morning chapel & aft. tea. Spend aft. with Floud in music rooms, gram.& playing pft. & discussing possibilities of getting rid of the Bullying etc of Farfield. Come to no conclusion Sermon by J.R.E in morning. Typical J.R.E., but nicer than usual.

89–2

Monday 16 December
Last day of House play, and consequently everything is more in a mess than usual. Bed. at 11.0. I am now sleeping in the Junior dorm, having been moved to the senior dorm. to make room, for the women (boys, of course), in the play. Sat. night seems to have softened many people towards me!!![42]

90–1

Tuesday 17 December
The main trouble to day is the remaking of the study list. Purdy evidently wishes to go out, (no wonder!) & Tyler is going, our wishes this time. It is hard to find place for former, & few people wish to come in because of Blanco W. I have one Very tempting offer (Balls, Williams, Bellerby) but on acct. of our effort to stop Bullying (see Sunday) it is wiser I feel for us to remain together.

91–0

Wednesday 18 December
Have to say good-bye to Floud, most unfortunately. I have had a marvellous time with him & I am terribly sorry he has gone. I have learnt piles from him. While playing house games in the evening, in being "tossed", I get dropped on my head luckily my fall was broken, so nothing serious happened.[43] But it ~~was~~ is very uncomfortable. Yearning for tomorrow.

MEMORANDA

[Supplementary entries to 1929 diaries]

Tuesday–Thursday, April 19–21st
[BB must mean May here, as he was on holidays from school at this period in April 1929 and the only month during which these dates fall on a Tuesday and Thursday in term time is in the month of May.]

In these three days, rather a nasty business has arisen, that I didn't have room to note in the diary of the 3 days. E.A. Robertson's, our late housemaster, friends & relations want to give Farfield a memorial, ~~for~~ of him, and suggestions were asked to be given into Lavender, the captain of the house. On Tuesday a not too nice, by any means, suggestion was put into the study (Lavender's). Of course the Pres. wanted to know who this was who give it in, and nobody owned up. A day passed still nobody owned up and so

Lavender had to punish the whole house, so the whole house went for a run (the people off runs (including me) walked the distance and wrote an essay on "Honour System"). I don't think now the person will own up, only I think he might have done before.

Saturday Nov. 9th

When Playing the Gramophone after Choir & Orch. practice with Whittow, the spring unaccountably gave way, & the wretched instrument refuses to work. We told Gog on Sunday (10th) but as it wasn't our fault he doesn't seem to mind much, as there is a chance of us having a new one. The old one was a terrible old thing. (Monday.) The gramophone is now as good as it was on Sat. Some poor wretched person has mended it.

Tuesday Dec. 17

Docker has taken it into his head to alter studies again (Reasons as yet ungiven). So study remains as before except for a newboy instead of Tyler.

1930

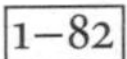
1–82

TERM – BEGINS – HOLT

Thursday 16 January

Go back to school with Pop & Beth in the car, having packed in the morning & said good-bye to Mummy at home, because of the Musical Soc. concert to-night. How I loathe this abominable hole. I am still in the Biddy-hole, with the most impossible crowd. I simply cannot see how I can bare up through it, & suicide is so cowardly. Running away's as bad; so I suppose I've got to stick it. But 83 days!

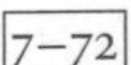
7–72

Wednesday 22 January

Balls has brought back some good records with him, and they are the only source of my joy. (Schuberts unf. Symp (very cut), Casse Noisette, & both Peer Gynt Suites).[1] No letter from Mummy. She hasn't written since Friday, & then only a note. I play Hockey for first time, & consequently I'm very tired now (in evening). Orchestra practise 5.45. (Beethoven ov. Prom.) (Bach Peasant Cant.)[2] ~~Oh!~~ The music's lovely, but Oh! the playing!!

8–71 END OF 1st WEEK

Thursday 23 January
I really am getting alarmed at the lack of a letter from Mummy. Especially, as I dreamed about death 2ce last night, & both times tho' not she, it was connected with her. I don't like to write in case our letters cross, but I shall certainly write soon, in a long day of work (stay up, to extra prep), the only cheering thing is the hearing of Part of Brahms 2bl concerto on gramophone,[3] & pt. of it on a new one in the music rooms (it is not in use yet, & it was only being tried).

10–69

Saturday 25 January
Ord. work in morning, game in aft. & then go to tea with Miss Chapman. After that directly [BB arrows 'directly' to the start of the sentence here, meaning it to read 'Directly after that'] both of us return to music rooms & for ¾'s of an hr. practise the Vln & Vla parts (together) of the Bagatelle;[4] then go to a most ghastly recital, all Chopin (which surely needs a great personallity to be bearable), by Mr Taylor. Truely he was very courageous, but that's all. It included the Ballade in A♭, which was the funniest thing I've heard for a long time (as was the C♯ Scherzo).[5] Laulie sends me a "Music & Youth."[6]

11–68

Sunday 26 January No.2
Chapel at 8.15, 10.30 & 6.30. Quite nice services, with a typ. J.R.E sermon at 6.30. Quite harmless but striking out no new path & lacking any orig. or helpful thought. Write letters in morning, & then listen to grm. in aft. (pt. of time Brahms D'bl concerto on new grm.) It is a marvellous thing, I adore the first mov. & 2nd also but not so much the 3rd as yet. Try over with Greatorex & Miss Chapman my Bagatelle & scrap of Mendlesohn D min.[7] It goes quite well. better than I expected.

14–65

Wednesday 29 January
Watch a match in the afternoon, against the masters. The school wins after quite a good match, 4–1. Orchestra practise in evening, quite interesting but oh! the orchestra is bad. It consists of 6 first. vlns, 8 seconds 2. vlas., 6 Vlcs.,

1 pft, 1 trombone, 2 flutes, 1 Clarinette, but there is about ½ a person in the orchestra who can play. Why a school of this musical reputation cant get up an orchestra of decent standard, I don't know; lack of energy?!!

27–52

Tuesday 11 February
I really think that last night was the most miserable night, of my existance. 1. I couldn't get to sleep (not. unusual). 2. I had litterally about 6 terrible dreams, seperated by about ½ hr of sleeplessness. In 1. Mummy was killed by a chimney stack falling through the roof. 2. Pop was killed when driving a bus (!) over Kessingland dam. 3. Beth (or Barbara) was burned in the house catching fire. I cannot remember the others. Musical Times is sent from home. Ord. day, with ping-pong in aft. with Ouseley. Play that most glorious of hymns the "Churches one foundation" (Wesly) for prayers.

28–51

Wednesday 12 February
I really wish I didn't dream every night; and every dream is about home, which is lovely while it lasts, only at the revaille it is literally foul. Last night I dreamed of going home, as last Easter term. I ~~am~~ play a very energetic game of hockey (League, as last Wednesday); we win in spite of the abominable lack of self-control of Matthews – 4.0. Orchestra practise in evening.

30–49

Friday 14 February
We have a mild game of hockey in the afternoon; probably the funniest game I've ever seen; every one plays worse than they ever have done before I should think. I am getting absolutely "fed to the teeth" with Blanco White. He is as selfish a boy as ever lived; takes no interest whatever in any ~~subject~~ thing besides himself, & cannot even make himself agreeable. Gratitude for all I've done for him! It is because of him that I can't get a decent study, no one'll come near him & I don't wonder!!!

31–48

Saturday 15 February
Have the most miserable game of hockey imaginable. We play in spite of the driving snow; because we lose (1-0, shot in about first ¼ hr) Matthews loses

his temper the whole time, & tho' probably we don't play well (he played worse than any), when we are doing our best, it isn't pleasant to be sworn at the whole time. Go to a frightful (& ∴ typical) Gog "Bach" recital, oh! for Samuel! In evening there is the most glorious lecture I've ever been to by Mr. John Rothenstein on Modern Art. He compared M. Art to M. Music, & talked for quite a time on Cézanne, Van Gogh & Géricault–

32–47

Sunday 16 February No 5

Typical, unsatisfactory school Sunday. Services at 10.30 (frightful congregational practice & 10.) & 6.30 with a good sermon by Rev. A.L. Watt on the "Inequality of the World". I completely lose my temper with Gog (luckily he wasn't present). He has now written the most abominable Benidicite which is performed in Chapel; unfortunately for everyone concerned I lost my temper on a piece of M.S. paper, & the most frightful bit of unplayable rubbish for pft. was the result.[8] Ord. practise in evening; a bit better than usual in spite of ourselves!

33–46

Monday 17 February

I do frightfully badly in Geography in the morning; but luckily I wasn't bottom. I get 4½ out of 30!! Have a good practise in 12–1. on viola, which is progressing quite well, I think. I wish the piano were more but I do have such a ridiculous time for practising (perhaps 5 min a day?). A lovely letter from Pop in the evening, most comforting.

34–45

Tuesday 18 February

Another simply frightful day of work. I simply cannot do a thing right this week, or rather quarter. I am droping marks, ridiculosely, all over the place, & yet God knows (I speak absolutely reverently) that I am doing my utmost best. I work the whole of the afternoon, except a break of about 5 mins for practise with Piano, & 5 mins for a game of ping-pong. Oh God, how will this end?

35–44

Wednesday 19 February

I am simply astounded at my ridiculousness. I cannot get over it. Today I do as badly as possible in all possible subjects. I feel absolutely frightfully bad in the morning, but I can't go to bed (1) because of the work I've got to do

(2). because of the recital on the 1st, & various other things. Orchestra practise, & ~~much~~ match in the League business in aft. We lose 2–1.

36–43

END OF 5th WEEK

Thursday 20 February

I am afraid I succumb in the morning. I go to the Gillett (Matron i.e.) & tell her how bad my throat is; I can hardly speak. I see the Doctor [Hendrie] who orders me out of school, & indoors all day. He the~~r~~/n~~fore~~ tells me that he likes the "Song" (see Jan. 4th) that I wrote for him, & is going to sing it at the ~~same~~ recital (March 1st) ~~at~~ in which my Bagatelle is being played. Of course it is nice to have my things done, but I wish they could have been other than these two, for I don't like them. Do alot of writing (Little Idyll)[9] & bit of Quartett (see Jan 3rd)

37–42

Friday 21 February

Spend to-day out of school again. My throat is better, but still rather painful. I write & write – it is glorious to get some time to think, & to put ones thoughts down! I finish my quartet piece; but I have everso much altering yet to do. I listen to the most frightful bit of music, about 4.45 to 5.15. A string ensemble with Pft (&harmonium?) (?). A violinist scrambles thro' 2 last movs. of Mendlesohn Concerto. Leaves the rest of the people behind, except poor pianist!!

38–41

Saturday 22 February

Yet another day out of school. My throat is better in the morning, but comes on with increased painfulness towards evening. At various times, I get news of Quarter's orders of various subject (this quarter ends on Monday); & as I feared I have done rather badly in practicly every subject! I write little today (1). ~~as~~ I have much altering & rewriting to do (2) After dinner until bed (as always at 7.30) there is nothing but gramophones to be heard. I am very interested in "Bridge of San Luis Rey"[10] of which I read much today.

39–40

Sunday 23 February No. 6

I spend this day out of school per usual. I am frightfully bored really, because there is so little to-do. Music is the only thing – what I should do without it, God only knows; but even that you cannot do always in a place full of rowdy, inquisitive ("what's that you've got there?") boys. I finish S.L. Rey in morning & begin Keble Howard's Fast Lady. V. funny but tosh![11] I write letters (Home & Harold Samuel)

40–39 HALF-TERM

Monday 24 February

At last we are at the top of the hill. I always imagine the term as a gigantic hill beg ∩ ½ ∩ end., & me as an awful [?] car trying to climb it. I have a happy surprise in ¼'s order & ½ term's too. I am 5th in 1st & 4th in 2nd; in spite of my conduct & stupidity last week! I write a little song (pft. sketch) in about ½ hr. in morning (S. Sassoon's Every~~body~~one sang.),[12] & then copy it out orchestrated in between lumps of P.G.W.'s Inimitable Jeeves.[13] V. Funny, but absolutely awful [?] rubbish!

41–38

Tuesday 25 February

Still out of school. I rewrite "Tit for Tat"[14] in the morning, & then begin a slow movement for S. Quartet on same subject as the Quartet piece finished on Friday. I finish the Wodehouse, & begin G.K. Chesterton's Innocence of Father Brown.[15] I am only reading light stuff, now as I have writing to do, & I find that if I ~~read~~ have to think about my books I can do less in writing. Go out for a short walk in morning. Play ping-pong with Andrews in afternoon.

42–37

Wednesday 26 February

I finish the slow movement & finish also a fast movement of the Quartet pieces. I don't know yet if I like it, as there is still everso much to do to it. I am still out of school, but I hope to return to-morrow to my labours. I can do no writing from Dinner until prep. ~~& consequently~~ because of the incessant din of gramophones & so I do some copying of Hist. notes that I have missed, & also finish Father Brown. It is a very "innocent" book, but quite amusing.

44–35

Friday 28 February

I am longing forward infinitely to to-morrow, especially as Mummy & Pop & Beth are coming, or rather because of their coming; but I want to hear Dr. Hendrie ~~hear~~ sing my song, altho' I don't like it too much. Ordinary day's work. I go to a lecture in evening on "Separating Substances from one another", By Dr ?, very int. for that kind of thing. I practises & work in afternoon. I have alot of pft. work to do.

45–34

Saturday 1 March

And Now It is all over! I am sitting up in bed alone. All (or most of) the others have gone to a Debate, but I haven't because I'm so tired. Mummy, Pop, & Beth & the car arrived at 2.15, & they are staying the night at the Feathers. I go out for a drive with Beth & Mummy, to Cromer & then come home for tea at the F. Then we go to the Recital. It goes very badly! My thing is ~~not~~ quite well appreciated but not understood Dr Hendrie is ill & doesn't sing my song! I go back to dinner at Feathers & return in time for prayers 8.30

46–33

Sunday 2 March No.7

I go out to Breakfast, with Pop & the rest at Feathers; then Pop & Beth go~~es~~ off in car back to Lowestoft, & Mummy stays. After chapel I go for a long walk with Mummy round the Town, & go back to lunch at F. About 4. we go to Music rooms & I play to M. a little. Tea at F. & then go & see Dacams for about 5 mins. Mummy comes to Chapel & hears sermon by Eccles, which was less typical & ∴ much better, than usual. I say good~~bye~~night to Mummy after that, & return to do my divinity prep.

55–24

Tuesday 11 March

Have a very hectic day, with rather a comforting end. In morning, when deep in prep. (no P.T. on account of snow), I have a letter from Mummy, saying write to H.S. [Harold Samuel] & demand lesson on Friday as she has to see Auntie Queenie (why?). I see Thomson & Eccles, who say yes, & in aft. I send a prepaid telegram to H.S., who answeres in evening, saying yes. on Friday aft. at 3. I have now all arranging to do; but what prospects! Tell Hines what I think of him, much to his discomfort!!

57–22 End of 8th WEEK.

Thursday 13 March

I spend most of to-day getting my leaves signed & making arrangements for tomorrow. I jolly well hope that I do meet Mummy to-morrow; but I have heard nothing from her. In the finals of the Senior house matches Farfield beats Woodlands 2–1; which accounts for the ~~riotous~~ gay behaviour in Evening. I don't go into prep but pack & go through my M.SS. for Bridge. Orchestra practise.

58–21

Friday 14 March [Holt/London]
Have two of the most hectic days in my life. To begin with, the Taxi ordered to take me and my heavy bag & music case to station doesn't turn up & I run ½ mile in 6 mins & leap into train, more dead than alive, without ticket or breath as it is moving. Meet Mummy at Kings X, & have meal, & go for talk with H.S. at 3.0, about my future. Have tea there & go immediately to Bridge at 5.45 & have 1 hrs lesson & leap back to Belvedere Hotel in time to have a short dinner with Barbara & Mummy, before going (incidently 5 min late) to topping concert at Queen's H. with Mummy. Backhaus was simply ideal; I enjoyed the Bax, but didn't understand it. Orchestra marvellous.[16]

59–20

Saturday 15 March [London/Holt]
Mummy goes off in morning to see about Auntie Queenie (who has a fit of melancholia), & I go out with Ruth complete with car, brother-in-law, & niece & nephew (aged 6, & 10). Go about London incidently to Augeners where I buy Delius' two orch. pieces (~~coo~~ cuckoo etc.).[17] Dinner at a Slaters with Mummy, Barb. & Friend. Only just catch train at King's X at 3.0. Mummy goes off to Lowestoft by later train. I arrive at 7.15 absolutely dead, & go to bed immediately.

Monday 7 April [Lowestoft]
Bobby arrives in aft. & Margorie after tea. Go to Playhouse with Beth, for rather a poor (silent) film, "The 4 feathers", little similarity to the book.[18] I go to a marvellous Schönberg concert on the Billison's wireless. Including "Chamber-Symp.", Suite op. 25 (pft.). & Pierrot Luniere [*Lunaire*].[19] I liked the last the most, & I thought it most beautiful. It was of course perfectly done.

Tuesday 8 April
I do 4 hrs pft. practise to-day, as yesterday. Play 2¼ hrs of glorious tennis in aft. with Beth, Pamela Handley, Ann Arnold. The others go to Yarmouth. Oh, I ~~nev~~ didn't realise how true, or not true enough, love-stories were. It is

positively unhealthy with Bobby & Marjorie. The latter as far as I can see, is an empty jar, & spends all her time "darling"ing him as much as he, her. Schönberg got a terrible report in the D. Mail!!

Monday 14 April

Go in morning, after trying over the Vla piece (See Sat.) with Bazil & also one of his, to get my Schönberg (6 Short pieces) ordered on Friday (also Smetana's Overt. Verk. Brant)[20] I am getting very fond of Schönberg, especially with study. Play tennis in aft. with Beth & 2 Crowdies (Mollie & Stevan) & Marjorie & Bobby (pt time)

Thursday 17 April

Practise & Bazil in morning, & then go up to Morlings to see if some catalogues have come Barbara comes home by 1.45(?) train. Laurence Talbot comes to tea. I finish the copy of my quartet,[21] only, now I shall go on altering minute details until the year dot. I suppose. Anyway I like it quite now; at any rate the last movement pleases me.

Wednesday 30 April

Practise with Charles & Bazil in morning, & then a short walk with latter. Have a "modern music" evening. 20 people including ourselves. All by contemporary composers (excluding 1 of Scriabin & a nocturne of Chopin (by request!) played by myself). Trio plays my bagatelle; pt. songs (2 of Holst); Mrs. Taylor & Mr. Coleman play J. Ireland Vl. Son (no. 1.) complete. 6 pft. pieces (Schönberg).

43–42 HALF-TERM. End of 6th Week.

Wednesday 18 June [Holt/London]

Mummy rings up about 9 o'clock to tell me to meet her at Norwich (Mr. Thompson takes me to Sheringham) which I do at 1.49. We go up to London by 2.7; my final of comp. Schol. is tomorrow, & Mummy only had the postcard this morning. See Barbara in evening & after her dinner go out to a Lyons for some ices etc. Spend night at Belvedere.

44–41

Thursday 19 June [London]

I go to College at 10.0. & have a writing exam (Pt. Song, Scherzo, modulations to write) from 10–3.0 with break for lunch at Barkers with Mummy 1–2. & oral from 3 – 5.30 (I was in room with R.V. Williams, John Ireland, &

Waddington (?) for about ½ hr.). After that I have surprise of winning comp. Inspite of ~~the~~ 2 brilliant others in final (5 altogether in it), including Alec Templeton, a blind boy. In evening Dinner with Barb. & Mummy at Hotel, & then with Mummy go to a marvellous performance of Hiawatha at Albert Hall.[22] Perfectly glorious singing staging, & ballet.

45–40

Friday 20 June [London/Holt]
Shop with Mummy all the morning in Hugh Rees[23] (to get my prize books) & in Harrods, where we have lunch. I go off by 3.0. train at Kings X to Holt once again, arriving at station early so as to enable (? I've not heard to contrary yet) Mummy to catch 3.10 at L'p'l. Street. Everyone full of congratulations; apparently Eccles told them about it at prayers this morning. I have 3 telegrams (Miss Ethel, Bobby, Family)

46–39

Saturday 21 June [Holt]
Quite a successful day considering it is the first away from my darling. Eccles makes quite a fuss of me at school prayers, & I receive alot of congrats.[24] 2 telegrams (Marjorie Goldson; South Lodge) Play tennis 2.30–3.30. Peacock, Seymour, Pearson – 4.30. ~~Willcock~~ Goolden Hinde I & Miles – 5.15. Willcock & Goolden & Hinde II. Great fun but broiling. 6–8. Full rehearsal of play with orchestra.

49–36

Tuesday 24 June
My prize books come in morning (I get 2 vols of Drinkwater's plays; Oxford book of English verse. Strauss Don Quixote & 5 orch. Songs. Schönberg Pierrot L. & Rimsky Kos. Coq d'or Suite. total £2–10).[25] Play cricket in inter house afternoon. No net after tea because of match. German extra 7.0. Oh, I love my books!

58–27

Thursday 3 July
I feel rotten in morning, but I keep in school, & play in a house game in afternoon, making 41. not out. Lie down before tea & go to Miss Gillett & to bed at prep.time I see doctor as I have a temperature. I am in the larger sick-room, as it is cooler.

59–26

Friday 4 July
In bed all day, with temp. still. Read quite alot. Green Mantle & Hunting Tower, of John Buchan.[26] I am not allowed to work worst luck. Choir Holiday – I wish I could go. It is marvellous weather for it.

63–22

Tuesday 8 July
Still in bed (My temp. refuses to be steady) Write a canon (in secret on lines drawn on my writing pad) May in the green wood – simply something to do.[27] Do much reading espec. Chaucer (for exam) & Musical Times which Mummy sends me today.

64–21 End of 9th Week

Wednesday 9 July
Still in bed, I have got absolute "wind-up" about the School Cert.; what little hope I might have had I've lost now, as I was depending upon this time for revision. Write (in similar fashion) "Hym to the Virgin",[28] & a set of variations (¾ of it) for organ,[29] which are rather rubbish – I rather like the Hymn tho'. Don't read much – Letter from Pop.

65–20

Thursday 10 July
I finish the Variations in morning (now called Passacaglia) In afternoon read E.P. Oppenheim's Mystery Road[30] – absolute piffle! In evening I set (¾s finished only) W.S. Blunt's Song,[31] Write a long letter to Mumm. & Pop, having a letter from the former. I am up & about the room all day. Lady Buxton gets in in bye election in N. Norfolk.[32] Great distress

Thursday 31 July
I see boys off by 8.20. I am terribly sorry to say goodbye to many of them, especially David. Mr. Taylor gives me Forsyth's Orchestration & Kitson's Counterpoint; both of which I am very pleased with.[33] Mummy & Pop arrive in car at 10.30 to take me home. We have ~~dinner~~ lunch at West Runton, & arrive home 5.30. It is marvellous to be home, but I didn't think I should be so sorry to leave

Thursday 4 September [Lowestoft]

I hear from Bazil that I have passed my School cert. He saw it in the E.D.P.[34] besides seeing that he'd passed the higher. I'm relieved, but I did not expect it in the least. Go up to Morlings & practise with him 12–1. I begin arranging Brahm's 4th Symphony, for 2 pfts. Hard work, but experience. I do it all afternoon & after tea.

Friday 5 September

I hear on a P.C. from GRT. [Thompson] that I have passed School Cert. with 5 credits.[35] It is simply extraordinary the luck I am having now. Margaret Stewart comes over for the day; we were supposed to have had a tennis party, ~~but~~ in afternoon but instead (owing to weather) we go to pictures (Playhouse). Rottenest feeblest show imaginable (except Micky Mouse). Do more transcription.

Notes: 1928–1930

NOTES: 1928

1. Greatorex played a Scarlatti Pastorale, a Bach Choral Prelude, an F Major Sonata by Mozart, a Chopin Mazurka and the Brahms Intermezzo in A major, Op. 118 No. 2; Miss Chapman played a G minor Sonata by Tartini.
2. Amusingly Miss Chapman's first school-report comment on Britten's viola playing suggested that he needed to improve his intonation!
3. An arrangement of the Air from the Orchestral Suite No. 3 in D (BWV1068).
4. Sonata in E for violin and continuo (HWV373).
5. The very warm reception Hoult Taylor received on this occasion was probably because it was his first appearance in the School's recital series, as he had only recently joined the school staff, a fact that Britten might not have been aware of. He played two pieces of Schumann, the Romance in F sharp, Op. 28 No. 2 and the Novelette No. 7 in E, Op. 21, and the first movement of Grieg's E minor Piano Sonata, Op. 7.
6. For a Christmas concert at the school on 15 December.
7. Bozman's translation of Paul Bekker's musical study and biography of Beethoven, published in Britain by Dent in 1925.
8. Britten remained suspicious of commentators reading too much into music, not least his own works – even (or perhaps particularly) those stage works that might invite an autobiographical interpretation.
9. It is interesting to note that as time went by Britten's admiration for Beethoven and Brahms waned; in the case of Brahms this happened remarkably quickly, largely because of the particular quality of his orchestration, which Britten grew to detest. His admiration for the music of Bach, however, was constant, and he became a noted interpreter of the *Brandenburg* Concertos, the *St John Passion* and the *Christmas Oratorio*.
10. Britten had already developed a deep affection for Schubert's chamber music by this time, but as the years went by he was hailed as one of the finest Lieder accompanists of his generation, particularly noted for his performances of Schubert's songs through a now legendary recital partnership with the tenor Peter Pears.

NOTES: 1929

1. *The Pathfinder* (1841) by the American novelist James Fenimore Cooper (1789–1851), famous for his tale of frontier adventure, *The Last of the Mohicans* (1826).

2. Elizabeth von Arnim (1866–1941).
3. King George V's health had been a cause of concern, and it was customary to leave updates on his progress on the gates at Buckingham Palace. The detective novel Britten was reading while in the sickroom was *Bat-wing* (1920) by the Fu-Manchu author, Sax Rohmer (1883–1959).
4. The first of these books may have been *Anna St Ives* (1792) by Thomas Holcroft (1754–1809), the first revolutionary novel to be published in England; the other two books in the family parcel were *The Little Duke or Richard the Fearless* (1854) by Charlotte Mary Yonge (1823–1901) and *The Toilers of the Sea* (1866), a seafaring melodrama by Victor Hugo (1802–85).
5. The *Rhapsody* for string quartet, begun on 28 January; see 21 March.
6. The famous seventeenth-century historical romance by R. D. Blackmore (1825–1900), published in 1869.
7. *A Song of Enchantment* (Walter de la Mare) for soprano and piano (1 January–7 February 1929), later published as the first song of *Tit for Tat* (1968).
8. For his *Miniature Suite*.
9. Also for his *Miniature Suite*.
10. The completion of his first draft of the *Miniature Suite* for string quartet (26 January/7–12 February); see 6 March.
11. Unidentified, and not to be confused with a later piece for solo viola, written on 1 August 1930, and published posthumously as *Elegy* for solo viola by Faber Music in 1985; *Lilian* (Alfred Lord Tennyson) for voice and piano (15–19 February 1929).
12. *Vanity Fair: A Novel without a Hero* (1847–8) by William Makepeace Thackeray (1811–63).
13. Pencil sketch, abandoned and never developed.
14. Similarly abandoned.
15. *The Witches' Song* (Ben Jonson) for voice and piano (21 February 1929).
16. Britten begins compiling a detailed manuscript catalogue of all his compositions written between January 1925 to December 1927, now preserved in the Britten–Pears Library.
17. *Miniature Suite* for string quartet (26 January–8 March 1929).
18. *The Master of Ballantrae: A Winter's Tale* (1889) by Robert Louis Stevenson (1850–94).
19. A theatre still active today on Lowestoft's marina sea-front.
20. The Feathers Hotel, 6 Market Place, Holt, Norfolk, where the Britten family usually stayed when visiting Benjamin at Gresham's.
21. *Rhapsody* for string quartet (28 January–21 March 1929).
22. The *Etude* for solo viola (18 February 1929).
23. *Song from 'Nice Valour': 'Hence all you vain delights'* (John Fletcher) for *a cappella* voices (22–3 March 1929); Britten also set a companion piece, *Song from 'Valentinian': Care-charming sleep* (John Fletcher) for *a cappella* voices (24–5 March 1929).

24. Brahms Symphony No. 4 in E minor, Op. 98 and Piano Quintet in F minor, Op. 34; Mozart Symphony No. 41 in C, 'Jupiter', K551.
25. Quinine is a natural white crystalline alkanoid with fever-reducing and pain-killing properties, in common use in the UK until the 1940s, when more sophisticated medication came into use.
26. As Britten learnt to his cost, Eccles was notoriously punctilious in these matters.
27. The School published the boys' relative academic standing on a quarterly basis.
28. Abandoned sketch, which later became a setting for voice and piano.
29. Wagner's Overture to *Die Meistersinger von Nürnberg*. As Britten grew older and began to doubt the reliability of his sense of perfect pitch, he used to check it by thinking of this overture as it always pinpointed the key of C major clearly in his inner ear.
30. Frequent bouts of ill health had dogged King George V for several years, but his illness reached grave proportions late in 1928, when a pleural abscess weakened his heart. An operation saved his life but his recovery was very slow. Not until February 1929 was he able to journey to a house near Craigwell, on the outskirts of Bognor in Sussex, for several weeks of convalescence. In the spring of 1929 he returned to London and in July he was able to attend a National Service of Thanksgiving for his recovery.
31. Gresham's prided itself on its Honour System, which placed the onus on the boys themselves to behave honourably, own up to their mistakes and, if necessary, either persuade others to own up or report the misdeeds of those who didn't subscribe as faithfully to the code as they should. It was introduced from the outset by the school's founder, Howson, and sustained throughout his headship by Eccles.
32. Britten begins the *Introduction and Allegro* for viola and orchestra afresh.
33. *Overruled* (1912) by George Bernard Shaw; *The Forged Coupon* (1905) by Leo Nikoleyevich Tolstoy; *The Unbearable Bassington* (1912) by Saki [H. H. Munro] (1870–1916).
34. *Reginald in Russia* (1910), short story by Saki.
35. *Wild Time* (Walter de la Mare) for soprano and strings (27–8 October 1929).
36. A pun on Britten's part, as their dog Caesar, was a Springer Spaniel (a gun-dog) hence "Seizer".
37. They performed arrangements for violin, viola and piano of the Mozart Trio in E, K498 (originally for clarinet, viola and piano) and the Brahms Trio in E flat, Op. 40 (originally for violin, horn and piano); and P. C. Floud played Palmgren's *Night in May*, 'The Little Shepherd' from Debussy's *Children's Corner* suite and Ravel's *Le jardin féerique*. The review of the concert in the school magazine, *The Gresham*, described E. B. Britten as 'a very reliable musician in ensemble work, always the most difficult of tasks'.
38. As Britten and his musical schoolfriends spent so much time together in the music room, it is perhaps surprising that Greatorex reacted so strongly to find Britten and Floud alone on this occasion; though he might have suspected that their friendship was a little too close. There seems to have been a belief, as a

result of the 'honour system', that affectionate or 'inappropriate' relationships between the boys did not in fact happen.

39. Public-school slang for 'a good talking to', in response to bad behaviour or poor academic results.
40. The first of *Two Pieces for Trio* (17 November 1929–5 January 1930).
41. Britten became a great admirer of Schoenberg around this time and was later overwhelmed by the music of Alban Berg, with whom he wanted to study after leaving the RCM.
42. Britten's performance of Chopin's Nocturne in F sharp, Op. 15 No. 2, the B minor Waltz, Op. 69 No.2, and two of Roger Quilter's Studies, Op. 4, would seem to have made its mark and perhaps gone some way to making his fellow students more understanding of his special gifts.
43. This would seem to have been more boisterous fun than bullying.

NOTES: 1930

1. Schubert Symphony No. 8 in B minor, 'Unfinished', D759; Tchaikovsky ballet suite, *The Nutcracker*, Op. 71a; Grieg *Peer Gynt*, Two Concert Suites, Opp. 46 and 55.
2. Bach Cantata *Mer hahn en neue Oberkeet*, BWV212.
3. Brahms Concerto in A minor for violin, cello and orchestra, Op. 102.
4. The new title for the *Rhapsody Piano Trio*.
5. Chopin Ballade No. 3 in A flat, Op. 47 and Scherzo No. 3 in C sharp minor, Op. 39.
6. Popular music magazine of the day.
7. Mendelssohn Piano Trio No. 1 in D minor, Op. 49.
8. *A Poem of Hate* for piano, inscribed 'Written at W.G.' – a violent flourish of forty-three bars marked 'Presto fuoco'.
9. *A Little Idyll* for piano (20 February; rewritten 8 March 1930). The earlier works to which Britten refers (with back references to earlier entries from his diaries) are his setting for voice and piano of Charles Sackville's 'Oh, why did e'er my thoughts aspire', and the *Quartettino* for string quartet (3 January–9 April 1930).
10. *The Bridge of San Luis Rey* (1927), the Pulitzer Prize-winning novel by Thornton Wilder (1897–1975).
11. *The Fast Lady* by Keble Howard, pseudonym for John Keble Bell (1875–1928): a story of a trip on the Broads in the eponymous boat, *The Fast Lady*.
12. *Everyone Sang* (Siegfried Sassoon) for tenor and small orchestra.
13. *The Inimitable Jeeves* (1924) by [Sir] P(elham) G(renville) Wodehouse (1881–1975).
14. *Tit for Tat* (Walter de la Mare), originally set on 31 December 1928; revised and published in 1968 as the final song of the de la Mare collection *Tit for Tat*.
15. *The Innocence of Father Brown* (1911) by G(ilbert) K(eith) Chesterton (1874–1936).

16. Arnold Bax's Symphony No. 3 (1929).
17. Delius *Two Pieces for Small Orchestra: On Hearing the First Cuckoo in Spring* (1912) and *Summer Night on the River* (1911).
18. *The Four Feathers* (1929), a silent-film adaptation of the British adventure novel (1902) by A. E. W. Mason (1865–1948), directed by Meiran C. Cooper and starring Richard Arlen and Fay Wray; playing at Lowestoft's local cinema.
19. Schoenberg Chamber Symphony No. 1, Op. 9 (1906); Suite for Piano, Op. 25 (1921/23); *Pierrot Lunaire*, Op. 21 (1912).
20. Schoenberg *Six Little Pieces* for piano, Op. 19 (1911); Smetana Overture to *Die verkaufte Braut* (*The Bartered Bride*). The viola and piano piece to which Britten refers had been written over the previous weekend.
21. *Quartettino* for string quartet (2 January–17 April 1930), published posthumously by Faber Music in 1984.
22. *Hiawatha's Wedding Feast* (1898), cantata by Samuel Coleridge-Taylor, staged at the Royal Albert Hall, Kensington Gore, London SW7.
23. Hugh Rees Ltd, specialist bookshop on Regent Street, London W1.
24. Gresham's liked nothing better than the academic success of its boys and a great deal of fuss was made of Britten, whose name was added to the Honours Board in Big School.
25. Two pounds ten shillings went a long way in 1930!
26. *Greenmantle* (1916) and *Huntingtower* (1922) by the author of *The Thirty-Nine Steps*, John Buchan (1875–1940).
27. *May in the Greenwood* (anon.) for two high voices and piano.
28. *A Hymn to the Virgin* for *a cappella* voices and solo quartet; revised in 1934 and published by Boosey & Hawkes.
29. *Passacaglia* for organ.
30. *The Mystery Road* (1921) by E. Phillips Oppenheim (1866–1946).
31. *O fly not, Pleasure* (Wilfred Scawen Blunt) for soprano, contralto and piano (10–11 July). An ink fair copy of this song (dated 20 July 1930 and inscribed 'to S. M. Courtauld) is now the property of Gresham's School, Holt; see 3 January 1931.
32. Lady [Lucy] Noel-Buxton (1888–1960), a Labour candidate, and one of only thirty women MPs elected to the British Parliament in the 1930s.
33. *Orchestration* (1914) by Cecil Forsyth (1870–1941) and *The Art of Counterpoint* (1902) by C. H. Kitson (1874–1944), two seminal books for music students.
34. *Eastern Daily Press*, published in the North Suffolk and Norfolk area, which listed the School Certificate results for Suffolk and Norfolk pupils.
35. *The Gresham* (Vol. III, October 1930) lists E. B. Britten as one of the boys who obtained five or more School Certificate credits; he also came second in 'Throwing the Cricket Ball'!

London
– Royal College of Music–
Lowestoft

> *. . . if a man has been his mother's undisputed darling he retains throughout his life the triumphant feeling, the confidence in success, which not seldom brings actual success along with it.*
> Sigmund Freud, 'A Childhood Recollection' from *Dichtung und Wahrheit*

Benjamin's time at Gresham's had clearly been traumatic, but also character-building. Whether or not his father's strategy of preparing him for the outside world was successful (and it probably was, to a degree) it was unquestionably a painful rite of passage and distressing for much of the time. It is unlikely, from everything we know about his relationship with his parents and siblings, that the desolate state he got himself into during term-time was fully communicated to his family. And yet the Gresham's years ended on a high, with Benjamin getting five credits in his School Certificate and securing an open scholarship to the Royal College of Music in London. The RCM Scholarship attracted great praise from the school, not least from Eccles himself, and Benjamin ended this otherwise unhappy chapter of his life feeling that he had at least justified himself in the eyes both of the sometimes sceptical school authorities and of his fellow pupils, some of whom had, no doubt, been unsympathetic to his often fragile health and perhaps even suspicious of his unusual talents. So the summer of 1930 was a much more positive period of renewal, with the great adventure of advanced musical training in London to look forward to, and the possibility of a career in his chosen vocation firmly on the horizon.

Benjamin was doubtless nervous of yet another extended period of separation from his mother and the security of home life in Lowestoft, but Frank and Ethel Bridge lived in Kensington, within walking distance of the College, and on Bridge's recommendation he was to study composition there with John Ireland and piano with the composer/pianist Arthur Benjamin. Lodgings were arranged in Princes Square in Bayswater and Benjamin soon settled into a routine, not so very far removed from that which he had enjoyed in Lowestoft. Surrounded in his lodgings by doting (often spinster) older women, and with the opportunity to indulge entirely in his musical passions (and with the Bridges, close at hand, as surrogate parents), this was an environment that was much more conducive to his creative temperament than boarding at Gresham's. The amateur music-making of Kirkley Cliff Road, St John's Church and Morlings was replaced by more professional music-making at the RCM, notably with the piano trio he soon formed with the violinist Remo Lauricella and cellist Bernard Richards. Meanwhile the Bridge household and their wider musical circle (which included the virtuoso Catalan violinist, Antonio Brosa) provided further opportunities, and the Bridges themselves were fine string players – Ethel a violinist and Frank, like Benjamin, a viola player. Benjamin also joined a chamber choir with his sister Barbara (who was now living and working in Chelsea), and within a year Beth too moved to London, and lodged with him at Burleigh House on the Cromwell Road. On Sundays they replicated the familiar Lowestoft routine of church-going and high tea with fellow lodgers; tennis was a constant and favourite pastime and old Lowestoft and Gresham's friends (some with homes in London) were still firmly on the scene.

But there were musical and creative frustrations nonetheless, and from time to time Benjamin's health suffered as a result of the daily tensions of trying to make his way in the world. Indeed the College was not always the most welcoming of institutions. Famously, one of the professors involved in his scholarship audition was heard to comment: 'What on earth is an English public school boy doing, writing music like this?' The profound conservatism of this institution was no doubt a disappointment to him, and despite a very promising start in his relationship with John Ireland, problems soon arose as Ireland became unreliable and unpredictable. But the personal confidence and dedication that Benjamin had inherited from his mother, and the supreme professionalism he had learnt from Bridge, stood him in good stead, and enabled him to seek opportunities outside the College – notably through the Macnaghten–Lemare concerts of new music and, even while still a student, from within the BBC. He was also beginning to get noticed by some of the major publishing houses in London, and his exposure to the London concert scene, particularly the very enterprising programming promoted by the BBC in London during the 1930s, developed his musical tastes, professional standards and confidence in the validity of his own opinions.

The influence of Frank Bridge is still very much in evidence of course – perhaps most notably in the sometimes harsh opinions teacher and pupil shared about Henry Wood and Adrian Boult. Indeed, as the reader will discover, Benjamin could be quite vitriolic about Boult, but this may have been, in part, as a result of his loyalty to Bridge, whom he clearly felt had been passed over at the BBC, when Boult was appointed its Musical Director and Chief Conductor of the BBC Symphony Orchestra in 1930. As the diary entries themselves reflect, Bridge was rarely engaged to conduct anything other than more popular or light-music programmes for the BBC, which in retrospect is particularly surprising, given his progressive tastes in music, and his awareness and appreciation of the more contemporary musical trends on the Continent. These tastes rubbed off on young Benjamin, and soon we see his love of Brahms giving way to a passion for Wagner, Schoenberg and Berg, while it's doubtful that he ever needed to be persuaded to dislike Vaughan Williams, Bliss and (sometimes) Walton, of whose technique he is often critical. Where Bridge and Britten did eventually agree to disagree (evidence, in time, of Benjamin's growing maturity and independence) was over the music of Mahler, of whom Bridge was sceptical; Britten, by contrast, was an early admirer and advocate, and retained a lifelong affection for Mahler's music.

Meanwhile, Benjamin continued to be just as prolific in his own writing. The *Rhapsody* quartet, *Quartettino*, D major String Quartet, *Sinfonietta* for ten instruments, *Phantasy* oboe quartet, and the choral variations, *A Boy Was Born*, all date from his time at the RCM. His musical allegiances moved away from Brahms (immediately) and Beethoven (more gradually), towards Mahler, the composers of the Second Viennese School, and the contemporary masterpieces of Stravinsky. Wagner was a new discovery that became a passion, sustained throughout the 1930s.

On a personal level, new friendships were made throughout this period, with fellow students (including the Welsh composer Grace Williams, and his chamber-music partners, Lauricella and Richards), and with colleagues and friends of the Bridges, including Brosa and the artist Marjory Fass. But there is no doubting that here was a very young sixteen-year-old, even by the measure of the day. Relationships with both sexes were entirely platonic and there is a sense of his resisting the adolescent process in all but that which guided his chosen career. It is remarkable, however, how mature his musical skills and individual creative personality became during these three short years. This may well explain, in part at least, why John Ireland became less and less effective as a teacher and mentor, as Benjamin became more and more judgemental about everything he encountered, both inside the College and out in the profession. Increasingly his attention turned towards mainland Europe.

Diaries: 1930–1933

Royal College of Music, London

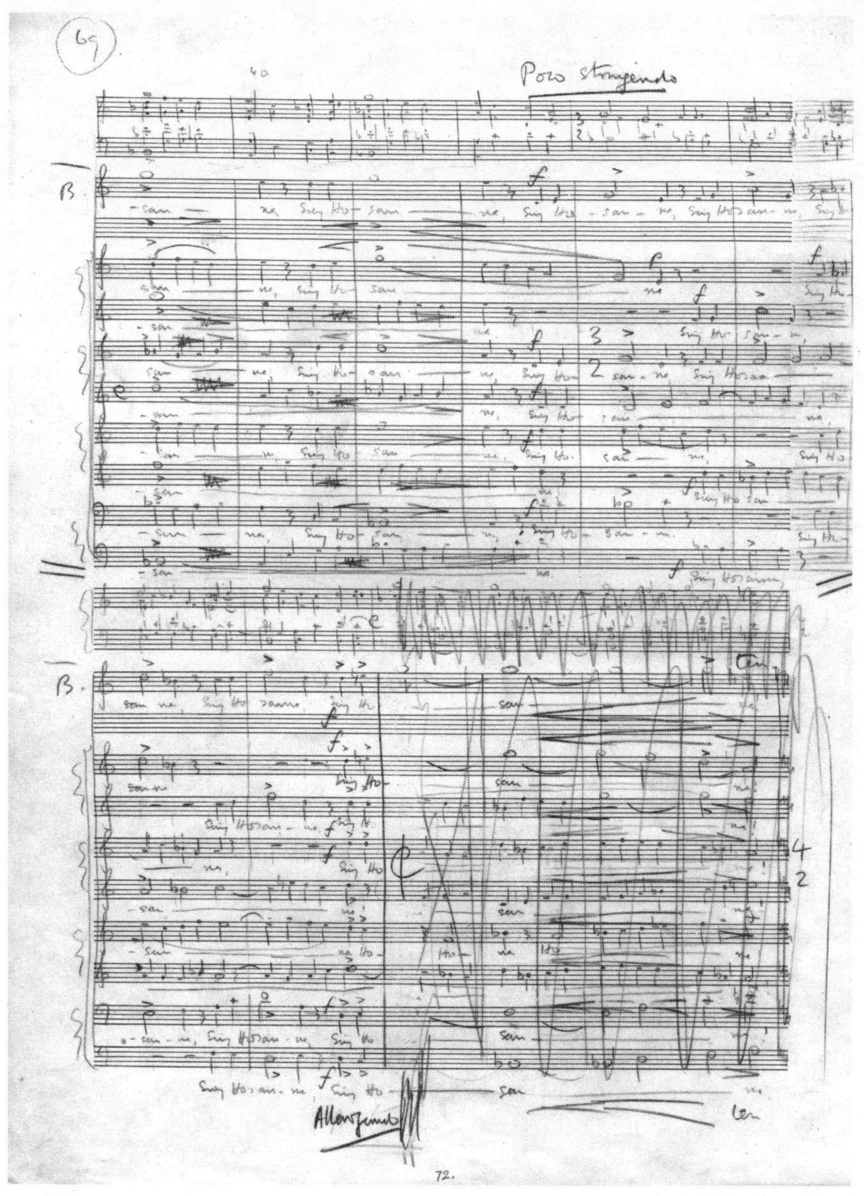

Autograph composition draft (pencil) for the closing section of the finale to the choral variations, *A Boy Was Born*, Op. 3, demonstrating the struggle Britten had in perfecting the finale to his personal satisfaction. See diary entries for 7, 20 February, 22, 24–5, 27 March, 3, 18, 25 April and 8–9, 11 May 1933.

1930

– LONDON

Saturday 20 September

Pack all morning, & then Beth takes Mum. & me in car to station to catch 1.15. Arrive 25 mins late and get to Miss Thurlow Priors[1] at about 5.0. It is rather a nice place, but rather full of old ladies. A respectable boarding house. Go to coffee at Barbara's flat.[2] Miss Hurst & she were coming to dinner but Barb. is in bed with chill.

Monday 22 September

Go directly after breakfast with Mummy to College. Make stupid mistake in ridiculously easy entrance exam. All matters are simplified extraordinarily by us Meeting Mr. Voke, who shows us all over the place. Lunch with him at Pontings[3] 12.30. Sir H. Allen's address. 1.'o'clock. Tea at Prince's Square. Walk after to find practice rooms (New School of music). Barbara to dinner. Find out that a Miss Prior[4] (who lives here) is a member of the National Chorus[5] & knew Mummy at Lowestoft.

Tuesday 23 September

Get my time table from the College in morning. I am with J. Ireland & A. Benjamin. Shop with Mummy in morning, and go to college at 12.0. I have no lessons to-day. See Mummy off at the bus for the 3.10 home. Oh, God, I wish she were here. Practice Pft after that, & after tea go for a drive with Miss May Prior, & a German man. Go to Queen's Hall Prom.[6] with Howard Ferguson Mozart concerto (K. Long) delicious & Mahler 4th. Much too long, but beautiful in pts.[7]

Get W. Walton's Sinfonia Concertante (pft score) for pt. of Maths Prize.

Wednesday 24 September

Practise in morning 9.45–10.45. Lesson (pft) with Mr. Benjamin 12.0–12.20. Very nice, tho' he says I must have 4 hrs a day practice (15s) & an extra Pft Lesson a week (3 guineas), if I am to take Pft seriously. Have music class with Dr. Buck in aft. It is so petty (Mus. dictation) that I ask to be moved up, & am eventually in a set 2 higher. Practice 4.0–5.0. Drive with Miss Prior & a Miss Henderson after tea. Barbara rings up 8.30 a.m & p.m.

Thursday 25 September

Am at College from 10–1. Waiting for J. Ireland for 1½ (10–11.30), & he eventually doesn't turn up. Very difficult aural training with Mr. Allchin, 12–1. Practise Pft 2–4. Tea at 51, & then go by bus to meet Floud near Queen's Hall (at a Lyons) at 7.0. Have a small meal at an A.B.C. & then go to very good Prom. "Enter Spring" (Bridge) marvellous – that man's a genius. "Sinf. Concert." W. Walton – quite good, but immature. Bax, Symph. 3.[8] Lovely in pts; Very good. English Singers, excellent. Speak to Mrs. Alston afterwards

Friday 26 September

Practise 9.30–10.30, then go to Coll. & have ½ hr (waiting ½ hr outside his door) lesson with Ireland. Very nice, but he is even more critical than Bridge – no that's not possible – anyhow he's very good. Practise in afternoon 2.0–3.30. Mummy & Pop arrive from Norwood (where they are at Dental Meetings) at ab't 4.0. Go out to tea with them, inspite of pelting rain to Whiteley's.[9] Barb. comes to supper. They all go at 9.30. worst luck. Vol. 1. Tchecov's [Chekhov's] plays, & op. 115 overture (Beethoven)[10] – prizes.

Wednesday 1 October

Practise pft in morning, 10–12.0. I have an interview with Sir Hugh Allen at abt. ~~4~~ 3.45 in afternoon. I should have been there at 3.0, but I am kept waiting. He is very nice. I miss ½ Dr Buck's class because of this (3.30–4.15). Have a short but nice lesson with Mr. Benjamin 4.30. He wants me badly to go into a hostle, where I can practise in the house, but I want to stay here. Dinner in, play cards in evening, with Hendersons.

Thursday 2 October

I go to College for lesson with Ireland, but he doesn't turn up (rehearsal); & I walk back to Prince's Sq. for a time, & go back at 12.0 for Mr. Allchin's class. Practise 2.0–4.0 in afternoon. Go (having had early dinner) to Queen's Hall & prom. – Purcell trumpet Voluntary, Goossen's Oboe Concerto (beautiful, monotonous, impossibly gorgeously, immortally played by Léon [Goossens]). Two V. William's songs; J. Ireland Pft Concerto (very beautiful, interesting & excellently played). Elgar 2nd Symphony, (dreadful (nobilmente sempre) – I come out after 3rd movement – so bored. He [Elgar] conducts – ovation beforehand (!!!!!!!!!!)[11]

Thursday 9 October

Have 1 hrs. lesson with John Ireland (after waiting ¾ hr): very nice tho' very subduing! He's going to take me thro' a course of Palestrina; tho' to reassure me he tells me that every musician, worth his salt has done this. Practise

1 hr (right hand alone) 2.30–3.30; write a little more of concerto. I go to dinner (there & back, tube,) with Howard Ferguson; jolly nice time. He plays me his Symphony,[12] which I like immensely. Also go through Ravel trio,[13] & some of my things. Return 9.15–10.0.

Thursday 16 October

I go to College in morning & have a topping lesson with John Ireland for nearly 2 hrs. 10.15 or less – 12.0. He is terribly critical and enough to take the heart out of any one! Go to see the Director in afternoon. My appointment was at 2.30, but I don't see him until 3.20. So, as really the talk tho' very nice, wasn't very helpful, the aft. was practicaly wasted. Go to Selfridges[14] to tea with Barb. at 5.15. & then to sing (bass) in English Madrigal Singers (Foster).[15] Marvellous. She sings 2nd soprano. Return home. 7.45.

Tuesday 21 October

Usual practice with a bit short in afternoon, as I leave at 3.45 to return to write the Mass in the style of Palestrina for Ireland.[16] I spend most of after tea & after dinner doing it (in Henderson's room): this strict counterpoint does take ages to write! Barbara rings up.

Friday 24 October

I practise as usual, 10–12 2.–4. I begin writing a piano piece – Hush; I know I'm not supposed to be writing but I had to put this down – after afternoon practise. After tea, I go to call on Ruth Turner who is out; & then to see Mrs Bridge. Frank B. seems to be having a magnificent reception in America (with the Brosa String Quartet & Harriet Cohen). I am so glad, & bucked. The Hendersons go out after dinner. I am in drawing room & play (ugh!) to Miss Prior etc.

Sunday 26 October

Go to St. Pauls (?) Paddington[17] to service with Tumtpy Henderson & May Prior. Hear Bishop of Westminster, v. good. Go to Marvellous L.S.O. concert at Albert Hall 3.0–4.50. Mengelberg. Der. Freischütz ov. 3rd Symphony Brahms. Saint-Saëns ~~3rd~~ 2nd pft. concerto (Anie Dorfman. v. good). Bolero Ravel. The Brahms. was thrilling & so was the Bolero, in which I was nearly hysterical! Orchestra good but not flawless. Mengelberg, superb, magnificent, great.

Wednesday 29 October

Ordinary practise in morning, with Mass afterwards. Practise 2–3, then College. V. nice lesson with Benjamin. Go to Shaftsbury Avenue to

H. Reeves;[18] get Tchaikovsky concerto (B^b) cheap ed. & Ravel. Bolero soiled (4/6) Go to B.B.C. Symphony concert with Mrs. Bridge in evening. The orchestra is most magnificent material; but I dislike Boult; he doesn't play a stringed instrument & you can tell it by listening to the strings. Beethoven 8th disappointing. Rubenstein played the Tch. [Tchaikovsky B^b] concerto magnificently, but rather as if he didn't like it.

Thursday 30 October

Go to College at 10.0 for lesson with Ireland (He arrives 10.30!). V. fierce! I had done rather a bad bit of pt. writing in the mass – those consecutive 5^{ths} always escape my notice![19] Practise in afternoon. Go for an ice to Selfridges with Barb. after tea at 5.0. She doesn't go to choral because of theatre, & I don't go because of going to Howard Ferguson, where I arrive at ¼ to 7. Dinner & 2 pft duets after. Mozart E^b concerto, Brahms Quintet, Fêtes (Debussy), La Valse (Ravel).[20] Back by 10.15

Monday 10 November

Usual Palestrina work & practise in morning. Practise pft. from 2.15–3.15 in afternoon but then come back & lie down as I felt very tired & sick. Get up for tea & go out afterwards to see Mrs. Bridge only she wasn't back from Mrs. Alston's yet. I make up my mind to go to the Carlyle Singers in the evening, & only at dinner decide to go to bed, as I do, immediately. Barbara comes to see me. I'm not at all bad.

Tuesday 11 November

I am in bed all day, although I am everso much better, really practically well. I read a lot of the "Three Musketeers"[21] write three letters (to Mummy, & the editors of the books out of which I took the poems for the Carols to be performed, re Copyright). The Hendersons are with me alot. Miss Gwynne (who stays here) brought me some grapes. Do alot of counterpoint. Letter from Barbara.

Wednesday 12 November

I get up for Breakfast. Go to see Mrs. Bridge 9.30. Usual practices, & College in afternoon. Mr. Bridge takes me to B.BC. Queens Hall Concert. 6 Brand. Concertos & 2 Arias, Keith Falker. Soloists H. Samuel (marvellous), A. Catteral (v. good technique), etc. (Brain, marvellous & L. Goossens). I am rather tired of sequences at the end, tho' it was v. enjoyable. Don't v. much like Wood's Bach. Disappointed with no. 2. 6 (with a mass of violas) very fine, & 5. 3 was thrilling.

Saturday 22 November [Lowestoft]
I have some lovely presents; inc. Waterman pen (Pop & Mum), & Poetry Books (W de la Mare Barb: Davies Beth) & Brahms Song of Fates & of Destiny[22] Miss Hayes & Maids; 6/- Miss Norman. Walk with Mummy & then Beth morning; with Beth aftern. Marjory Phillips, Dr White, come to dinner, & Mr. Sewell (new ass.) & his fiancée Mrs. Rogers, afterwards. Great fun with Pit & Cheating.[23] ~~My~~The copies of my 2 songs come. I also learn that I am accompanying the Choral Society in Bridge's Prayer[24] at the concert.

Wednesday 26 November [London]
I go to see Mrs Bridge after breakfast, about tonight's concert, which she's not going to. I practise 10.30–12.45. Go to College, & have v. nice lesson with Benjamin. I play March & Pastoral for 2 pfts out of his new suite[25] (M.S.S still) with him; they're jolly fine & great fun. Go down to H. Reeves & get Brahms 2nd pft concerto, & 2nd Quintet, Schubert 7th Symph. & Beethoven Flute serenade all for 8/6!!![26] Tumpty Henderson's Birthday. I don't go to the Concert, because of letter writing.

Filthy Fog. until evening. John Ireland away, so don't go to College until 12.0.
Thursday 27 November
Practice Pft afternoon, no Madrigals write letters bet. tea & early din. Go to Philharmonic concert. Ov. Schwanda[27] amusing. Rubenstein in Brahms concerto no. 2. He is really superb. His playing & the heavenly music makes me feel absolutely hopeless. After that the Schubert 7th symphony,[28] disappointing although it's vandal to say so; this symph annoys me with its ceaseless repetitions. Beautiful in parts but 1000 times too long. Orchestra not too good, but L Goossens adorable; the man's a marvel. Back at 10.55. Hendersons out to theatre.

Wednesday 3 December
I write & practise (10.40–12.40) in morning. Go to College in afternoon and have a v. depressing time. Benjamin although quite pleased, says that I am not built for a solo pianist – how I am going to make my pennies Heaven only knows.[29] Then I discover that the Easter term begins on Jan 8th (instead of as I expected Jan 22nd). Go to Kensington Town Hall to Festival at 7.0. The Carlyle singers are 1st in their lot (we didn't sing too badly, I think, because the other choirs weren't at all bad). After until 10.15 combined rehearsal under R.V. Williams.

Thursday 4 December
I go to College at 10.0 & have v. nice lesson with Ireland – he is quite pleased with my Credo. I practise 2.15–3.30 & then go to College to get ticket written

for concert tomorrow – as Ireland said I must go, although all the tickets were gone! I go to the combined concert of the Kensington Festival.[30] Quite well attended, & not at all bad of it's sort. R.V.W conducts. The best of the evening was Mothers singing of Bonny Lighter boy[31] – marvellous rhythm, words & everything. R.V.W. Xmas Fantasia thrilling to sing & I should think to listen to. V. Beautiful.[32] Back 11.0

Friday 5 December

I write until 10.45 & then go & practise till 12.45. I practise 2.30–4.30 in afternoon. Write a little after tea. I go after dinner to a concert at the R.C.M. (1st Orchestra). Cockaigne (Elgar) J. Ireland pft. concerto (which I like better each time – Helen Perkin played it beautifully) [Beethoven] 5th Symphony (ensemble bad) & suite – Boutique Fantastique (I cannot think why Vienna went mad over Rossini). Back at 10.15

Monday 15 December [Lowestoft]

I arrange the Sea Foam from the Sea Suite [Bridge] for 2 pfts, beginning in the morning & working in afternoon & evening. I finish it, but there is plenty to alter. I am afraid it's very hard – at anyrate the 1st pft. Walk – Xmas Shopping with Beth (return with Mummy) in late morning. Walk with Mummy in afternoon. Mrs. Owles comes to tea.

Tuesday 16 December

I work, continuing the alteration & arrangement of the Bridge (I begin the 1st movement) in morning – 12.0, (walk with Beth) & afternoon. Ann Arnold comes to tea & to go with Beth to Brownies at 6.0. Walk with Mummy (& Caesar) after tea. Go to a Rehearsal of the Musical Society. I thought that the Madrigals were bad – but! They do my 2 songs – disappointingly, & the Prayer, badly. (men especially so)

Wednesday 17 December

Work in morning (Mass – copying out) & evening (Bridge transcription). Walk, with Mummy before lunch. Pictures (Grand) 3.0–5.0 with Beth – Disraeli[33] – Most interesting & awfully good. Go to B.B.C. Symph. Concert at St Luke's Hospital – Dr. Colvin's Wireless. Why they gave this Mass in D to Scherchen – Heaven only knows.[34] Of course there were beautiful bits – Sanctus & Benedictus & Kyrie – but the end of the Credo was incredibly scrambled. Chorus good[35] – seemed to me that all their work was wasted. Soloists – tenor [Parry Jones] – not too bad: – Soprano [May Busby] – dreadful. Orchestra respectable – what I could hear of it – it didn't come through too well – I thought

Tuesday 23 December

I work a very little in morning, & practise the viola a little. Walk with Caesar at 9.0, & 12.0 (up the town to buy the remnant of my Xmas presents). I write all the afternoon – Vigil[36] by W. de la M.: I don't yet know if I like it. Choral practise – after some holly decorations in the house – at St. John's School rooms. I play the piano through out. 2nd choral song will never be a success I fear. Chorus not at all too good!

Sunday 28 December

Walk in morning, 10–11.30 with Pop, Beth & Caesar. Mr. Voke & Mrs. come in to tea at 4.0. Mummy, & Mr. Voke & I go in to Coleman's at 4.15 to try over the solo quartet parts[37] etc. for the Musical Society concert. Mum. Mrs. Coleman (sop). Mary Cannel (cont). Mr. Catchpole (Ten). Mr. V. (bass). They sing quite well. Come back for tea. After which Mr V. sings my Vigil most beautifully. I like it now. Work all before Supper, read Lyndesey aft. & evening; I like it immensely in parts.

[Britten's diary for 1930 ends with a detailed record of his personal and professional accounts.]

1931

Saturday 3 January [Lowestoft]

Practise at 11.45 at the Colemans with Charles & Bazil. Musical Evening at 8.0. Chief Attraction – Mr Voke's singing. He sings esp. well, Boris' Monologue (twice).[1] About 30 altogether came. We try my W.S. Blunt Song for Sops. & Altos[2] – utter failure. People terrified by accidentals and manuscript (copied by Aunt Q [Queenie] – & self). Play Bach 2ble concerto. Mozart Sonata in D [BB notates sonata rhythm here] Merry Andrew, etc.[3]

Monday 5 January

Do a good deal of Counterp't in the morning, & walk with Beth afterwards. I go down to the church in the ~~morning~~ afternoon, practically all the time, to go through the "Prayer".[4] & to arrange the chairs etc. Walk with Pop after tea. The concert goes quite well; my things are quite well done (the 2nd better than rehearsal)[5] the Prayer also not too badly done – it's an absolute marvel. Rest of programme – carols & very good organ solos by Mr. Coleman.

Tuesday 6 January

The reporter of the E. Anglian Daily Times rings up to know about my songs! Scream!! Walk around the golf course with Aunt. Q. while Beth has a golf lesson 12–1. Work at Agnus Dei II (Canon)[6] & cp't all the afternoon. Play 2 pft duets with Bazil at Morlings 5–6. It's ghastly to think of to-morrow – of course London's marvellous but home's so good.

Friday 9 January [London]

Practise in morning & afternoon (11.30–12.30 & 2.15–4.15) – Beethoven Sonata in G. (op.49?) L'st Movement & Schumman "Pappillons".[7] Write up to 11.30. Go to Dinner with Barbara, arriving at her flat at 6.0. Listen to the Wireless – especially to a concert of contemporary music – Schönberg – Heaven only knows!! I enjoyed his Bach "St Anne"; & quite liked his "Peace on earth" for Chorus – but his "Erwartung" – ! I could not make head or tail of it – even less than the "Peace on earth".[8] Back at 10.50

Monday 12 January

Usual writing & practise during the day. Writing 9.30–11.30; I finish the Agnus Dei II moderately successfully, only looking over I find hundreds of slips in partwriting (consecutive 5ths esp.). Do some quite good work at pft. Go down to Augeners to see about the frame for my Brahms picture, after tea; only it costs 15/- & I therefore don't get it.

Write a small carol (Women's voices & alto) "Sweet was the Song",[9] after Supper. Hendersons go to Theatre.

Wednesday 14 January

Usual practise ~~until~~ & writing (9.15–11.0) in morning. Go to College in afternoon, & have 20 mins. pft. lesson (not 40. mins in spite of Mum's plea with the Director). I also get leave to drop Music classes, (Dr. Buck) as they're so easy. Go to H. Reeves after lesson, & get some music 2nd hand. Listen to BBC concert on Miss Prior's (quite good) wireless in evening. [Handel] E min Concerto Grosso, Concerto 1 (Liszt – Solomon) Iberia (Debussy) – the tragedy was, that in the middle of the Schubert C maj (End of Slow mov.) The only performance I've ever really enjoyed, the battery ran out. Still, the 1st 2 movs. were very good.

Friday 16 January

I am writing songs now for Ireland – not necessarily in Palestrinian style. I spend alot of my time this morning searching (for words), as yet unsuccessfully, although I have got some likely ones. Copy the Agnus Dei II out also, which finishes my Mass.[10] Practise 11.30–12.45 2.15–3.30, & then go to

College in an unsuccessful attempt to see the Bursar [Edwin Polkinhorne] about my extra pft. lesson, which the Director said he'd see about, and about which, so far, nothing's been done. Work in evening. Henderson's out ~~for~~ to theatre. Beastly wind.

Tuesday 20 January

I spend 2 hrs reading poetry solidly, & then write – in desperation a very short song – "Sport" of W.H. Davies.[11] I don't like it; even less than usual. Practise 11.30–12.30; 2.~~30~~15–4.15 ~~6~~5.0–6.0 (the extra hour to make up for some of the time I've missed. I listen to Delius (1st Cuckoo & Summer Night)[12] on Miss Prior's wireless at 8.0 against a background of Jack Payne[13] – even then they were miraculous. He is a wizard.

Wednesday 21 January

I have an appointment with the Director at College at 11.0. I go there & find he's out. Before that, I copy out ~~of~~ "Sport". Return and have an hour's practice. Lesson with Benjamin at 2.40 I go through 2nd & 3rd movs. of his new Vln. Concerto,[14] which I like very much. It is ext. fine & original. I have an appointment (made this morning) with the Director at 3.30. Wait from 3.0–~~4~~3.40 unsuccessfully, & return to "52".[15]

Thursday 22 January

I go to John Ireland's studio for my lesson at 10.0. Have a very instructive one, if not very encouraging! Certainly I seem to be doing nothing right or worth doing nowadays. Come back walking via the College to make an umpteenth attempt to get my Aural training lesson fitted in. Ordinary practise in afternoon. Meet Barbara at 5.0. at Selfridges, only she is too tired and busy to come to Madrigals in which we do some new things – they are great fun.

Friday 23 January

I write until 11.0. when I go to college, for my apptmt at 11.30 with the Director, for whom I wait until 12.40. (doing nothing in the meantime save seeing about my aural training class unsuccessfully). He suggests me giving up 20 mins. of my ~~class~~ lesson with Ireland for extra pft. lesson (!!!) I practise all afternoon. Go to see & have a 2nd tea with Mr. & Mrs Bridge (to ~~see about~~ take back Sea Suite). I finish a Madrigal[16] in evening – don't like it. Hendersons are out.

Saturday 24 January

I go down to Harold Reeves about 11.30, to get a Mozart Symphony (E^{b})[17] that I hope to hear tomorrow. I also get Mahler's Wayfaring Songs.[18]

The Hendersons go out to tea. I attempt to do some selecting of poetry (for songs & madrigals) but drop off to sleep, in afternoon! (the wind was terrific last night, & I didn't get much sleep.) Alter my madrigal after tea. Play cards with Tumpty Henderson after tea.

Sunday 25 January
Church at 8.0 (Malcolm Sargent takes collection) at St. Matthews, & 11.0 with Tumpty Henderson at ~~Alls~~ Holy Trinity, Paddington. The Hendersons take Miss Gwynne & me to L.S.O. Albert Hall concert & Mengelberg. Mendelssohn Midsummer's night's dream. Mozart Prague Symph. [K504] Liszt 2nd pft concerto (Vronsky), Wagner Prelude & Finale (Tristan). Quite good. very enjoyable. Go to Supper at Bridges & then to B.B.C Studio (at Waterloo)[19] for Symphony concert which He conducts. Marvellous show. Glinka (Russlan. ov.). Mozart K.543. Miriam Licette in Willow & Ave Maria (Otello – Verdi),[20] Bridge Poem 2[21] – Magnificent – Tchaik. ov. Rom. & Juliet. Speak to Brosa & Mrs., sit with them & Mrs. Bridge. Back by Taxi at 11.30. It was terribly interesting to see everything. Orchestra very good – especially Lauri K.[Kennedy] & cellos. & Horns.

Wednesday 28 January
I finish copy of To the Willow-tree, & write a short, unsatisfactory song "Autumn".[22] This I copy out in spare moments, after lunch & tea. Go to College at 2.40 for Pft. lesson. Benjamin seems more pleased, although I play even more abominably than usual. Listen all the evening to St[r]avinsky concert.[23] Remarkable, puzzling. I quite enjoyed the pft. concerto. Sacre, – bewildering & terrifying. I didn't really enjoy it, but I think it's incredibly marvellous & arresting.

Saturday 31 January [Lowestoft]
Write in the morning & then walk with Beth along cliffs; write most of afternoon & then walk with Mummy. Haircut at Priggs[24] at 5.30 & then walk with Pop down to Club.[25] I am writing a choral piece for 8-voices on a bit of Psalm.[26] It's jolly hard to write, & I am certain to find hundreds of consecutives when revising.

Wednesday 4 February [London]
Usual writing & practise in morning. Pft lesson at 2.40. There is a large gathering of Norland (?) Nurses[27] for tea at Miss Prior's.

I go to Queen's Hall (Area) for B.B.C. Concert. Weber. ov. Oberon: Mendel. Vln concerto (Szigeti): Brigg Fair: Bax – November Woods. Schumann 4th (D min.). I am v. disappointed with orchestra; marvellous material but ensemble, bad. Lauri Kennedy & Cellos good. A. Boult – beastly played about with Schumann – Szigeti magnificent. Didn't like Bax – bored with it – not much November about it. Delius delicious.

Friday 6 February

I practise as usual & write. Go to H. Reeves after tea to get Berlioz Sym. Fantas. [*Symphonie fantastique*] Go to Magnificent Harty Concert with Hallé Orch. Handel Water Music – Brahm's 1st pft. Concerto (Backhaus) literally thrilling. – What a marvel that first movement is. Berlioz Symphony Fant, which the orchestra played marvellously, it isnt much good as music, but a topping entertainment. Orchestral ensemble topping. Drummer superb. Backhaus was a bit unsympathetic in places, but he brought out the strength of the first movement marvellously. ~~With~~ Incredible technique. Audience v. enthusiastic. Back at 11.5. Sat with interesting man (rather blind). Amateur, & v. keen!

Saturday 7 February

I go for walk with Tumpty Henderson to Hyde Park Corner via Whiteleys (on return), getting back about 12.15. I work all afternoon & after tea at choral piece – merely choosing words for 2nd half. I eventually select some (rather unsatisfactory). Read through whole of Psalms, & Daily Light.[28] Play cards in evening with Tumpty, Mrs Walker & Skelton – Snap, Rummy.

Monday 9 February

Practise & write as usual. [Albert] Sammons is practising & writing in the room next to mine in the afternoon. I go to Queen's Hall to get tickets, & Augeners to get my Brahms picture framed after tea. Practise viola after supper, & then as I settle down to write, I notice in Radio Times[29] that Brahms quartet 3 is going to be broadcast by Hungarian S.Q.[30] So I borrow Miss Prior's Wireless, & have marvellous ½ hr listening to the purest music in the purest of possible forms. What a marvellous craze for the viola Brahms had! What a humorous theme the last movement has!

Wednesday 11 February

Lesson with Benjamin at 2.40. Meet an Italian (?) Violin Scholar at College and arrange to practise duets with him. See Mabel Ritchie, also, & she gives me her address. I listen to B.B.C concert on Miss Prior's wireless. First half (Schuman, Manfred ov. – marvellous work – Beethoven 4th concerto (Beautifully played by Backhaus)) ~~did~~ does not come through v. well. 2nd Half – Planets.[31] These works arn't very much to my taste, but they are v. fine & clever. Jupiter has some good tunes; Mars v. striking. Altogether, too much, harp, celesta, Bells etc. Beginning of Saturn & end of Neptune v. beautiful. Uranus great fun. I suppose they were well played.

Thursday 12 February
Go to John Ireland's Studio at 10.0. He is quite pleased with my work (more or less i.e.) except for numerous consecutive fifths. Walk back. Practise in afternoon, & then meet Barbara at Selfridges & have something in the Soda Fountain business with her & Miss Gibson. Go to Madrigals afterwards. Listen to a bit of Appalachia[32] after dinner. Luxurious monotony; rather disconnected, I thought. Hallé chorus & orchestra.

Friday 13 February
I begin writing a new choral carol (4 voices).[33] I'm afraid it'll be considered v. discordant but I like it. Practise in afternoon with Remo Lacricella [Lauricella], a brilliant violinist (scholar at College of 4 years' standing) We play concerto (Violin & pf of Mozart A maj).[34] Meet Barbara, have tea at Lyons at 4.45. Meet Pop from Ireland at 5.45 at Euston. Taxi to Lip'l St to leave his luggage & tube back, leaving Barbara at Oxford Circus. Pop stays at 51 for night. Walk with him round Piccadilly & Charing Cross after dinner.

Monday 16 February
I finish my carol in the morning, and also do acres of revision. Practise at usual times. Go to see Mr. Bridge after tea. He offers (and then refuses to let ~~be~~ me do it, because of eyes) to let me correct the copied out part of his Concerto Elegioso ('Cello).[35] I should have loved to have done it. Spend about 1 hr & ¼ hr there. Mrs. Alston & Miss Fass (?) were there. They are all going to hear Kreisler to night. Lucky bounders! Practise Vla after dinner.

Wednesday 18 February
Finish copying out Carol & do a considerable amount of 4 part florid Cp't, 9.15–11.0 & after dinner. Practise & piano lesson as usual. I listen to half of a B.B.C. concert in evening. Egmont overture (marvellous work) & Brahms 1st Pft Concerto with Dohnanyi. Horrible scramble it sounded; anyway the strength of the first movement was there; but oh! the third movement! The wireless gradually faded in the first movement & so I missed the recap. & 1st half of movement 2. When I got a new accumulator, I listen to 1 min of Elgar Symphony 2, but can stand no more.

Thursday 19 February
I go to Ireland's studio for my composition Lesson. It is, I suppose, a very good one, but certainly not a cheering one! I am now "getting it" for variety

of styles in my carol – it is quite right, but that doesn't make it any the more pleasant! Meet Barbara at Selfridges as usual at 5.0. & then to Madrigals

Tuesday 24 February

Continue with my choral movement a good deal in morning, after lunch & tea. Practise with the Italian boy in afternoon – he's jolly good. Go to Wigmore Hall in evening with Barbara (see yesterday)[36] to hear Pirani Trio. A very good concert. Beethoven B^{b} Trio – marvellous work, beautifully played. Casella – Siciliana & Burlesca – very beautiful & amusing. Tchaikovsky A minor Too long, & much too orchestral although beautiful in it's sentimental way. All v. excellently played.

Thursday 26 February

Composition lesson at 10.0. Ireland is quite pleased with my latest carol. Go to Augeners & Chesters[37] for Brahms op 21. variations & Prokofiev op. 12 prelude for pft. study.[38] Practice in afternoon. No madrigals. Walk with Hendersons after tea. Go to Chamber Concert at R.C.M. 8.15. In a long programme Helen Perkin (Ireland's star & best comp. pupil) plays her own Ballade for pft. V. competant with only about 1 bit of original work. Too long, I thought, for material. Beethoven A min (op 132) quartet, tolerably played. Divine Work! as also is Brahms G maj vln sonata.

Wednesday 4 March

Walk after breakfast for about ¼ hr. as is now the rule. Usual writing (continued unsuccessful attempts ~~for~~ at new carol) & practising.

Lesson with Benjamin at 2.40, & then go to University Library to get some books with Lacricela. Get Stravinsky ~~Vln Concerto~~ Sacre; Brahms Vln Concerto; Franck Symphony (Min scores) & Beethoven: Impressions of contemporaries.[39] Walk with Tumpty after tea. Work (again unsuccessfully) after dinner. Little Viola practise.

Friday 6 March

Go to R.C.M. Patron's Fund at 10.0. Here [Hear] rehearsal & performance by L.S.O, Adagio & Scherzo (Edric Cundell conducting himself) – terribly Elgarian & Wagnerian. César Franck Symph. Var.[40] (under M. Sargent) well played by P. Cory (R.A.M). & ~~some~~ very good Dance Suite of D. Moule Evans. Quite original Go with Bridges to B.B.C. Studio no. 10 (Waterloo) for Contemporary concert at 9.0. Van Dieran quartet no 5. – rather puerile, I thought for him – not too well played by international Quart. Peter Warlock's Curlew – rather fine, but overdrawn. & Hindemith's v. fine Concert music for Pft (Emma Lübbecke-Job), Brass & Harps.[41] Magnificently played under

Frank Bridge. I really thought, that although there was a certain feeling of experiment running through it, it contained some fine stuff!

Sunday 8 March

Go to church at 11.0 with Miss Prior at St. Mark's.[42] Have v. fine sermon by Bish. of London,[43] & v. fine Anthem "Many Waters" of Ireland[44] v. well sung. Walk with Miss Prior after dinner. Write letters for rest of afternoon & evening until supper at the Bridges at 7.30. Go to BB.C. Studio for concert which Mr. B. conducts. with Mrs. B. & Miss Fass (?). Revel in Haydn (Symp. 104), & Bridge 2 Tagore Songs – marvellous creations, not superbly sung by Astra Desmond. P. Herrman plays Schumann Vlc Concerto poorly, R-Korsakov Cap. Espagnol, Marvellously played by the orchestra as was every item,[45] the B.B.C. Orch is awfully fine, but discipline (owing to No. of conductors) faulty. Wind-excellent; L. Kennedy & F. Thurston (clar.) simply superb. Bridge conducted marvellously. Back by taxi at 11.10.

Wednesday 11 March

Finish my carol in morning.[46] Practise. Lesson with Benjamin 2.40. Go to University Library get Chopin – Godovsky Studies vol. 1.[47] Brahms ~~g~~F 5^{tet} & Bruchner no8 Symph. Go to very fine B.B.C. concert conducted by O. Fried. ~~Col~~ Coriolan ov. (v. finely played). Brahms 2nd Concerto (Gieseking) – simply magnificent. He was as brilliant as Rubenstein, but put the music to the fore simply magnificently – I've never heard a Concerto played so well. Berlioz Fantastic Symphony – more polished than the Hallé, & consequently March to Scaffold lost a bit. But the orchestra was simply superb, all the evening. Kennedy's solo in the Brahms too gorgeous.[48]

Friday 13 March

Begin completely re-writing "Christ's Nativity".[49] Practise 11.45–12.45. Go to College in a fruitless effort to find out about R.C.M. Union.[50] I practise 3.30–4.30. Go to quite a good concert (British Women's Symphony Orch)[51] at Queen's Hall with Barbara (tickets given by Miss Atkinson). They play Sibelius' beautiful En Saga, quite well, & also (with Emilo Columbo [Emilio Colombo]) Max Bruch's G min. Vln concerto. C. plays some pifling little solos (including Debussy's charming fille aux chevaux de lin)[52] competantly To finish with Bantock's Hebridian symphony[53] – mediocre stuff!

Saturday 14 March

I go to the Leicester galleries[54] (starting before 10) to see Epstein's new sculptures & Southal's paintings. The latter are quite beautiful. Some of the former are entrancingly delightfull (esp. Joan Greenwood).[55] Re.

Genesis, I do not know, altho' I spent ages looking at it, I do not understand it. It's very marvellous & amazing. Do some music shopping on way home H. Reeves Dvorak Cello Concerto (B min) & M.S. (Augeners). Go to concert – Maud Randall in afternoon – with Miss Bicknell – the lady-cook here – who was at school at St. Anne's. & afterwards tea at Maison Lyons with her. There was nothing striking abt. the concert – only competant playing. – Schuman Symph ~~Var~~ Etudes. Group of modern pieces & Chopin B min. sonata.

Tuesday 17 March

Go to John Ireland's via the college at 10.30. Have v. good lesson. I think he quite likes "Preparations". Practise 12.15–12.45. & all aft. Lauricella doesn't turn up as arranged – Go to recital with Tumpty by Sheridan Russel (Vcl), assisted by var. others. All English programme – some old music, well played by Russell, & v. interesting suite of L. Berkeley for Vlc & Oboe (H. Gaskell). Rather dull Idyllic Fantasy of C. Scott for Voice (Dorothy Moulton), vlc & ob. New Sonatina (pleasant & competant) for Vlc & Pft of Ben Burrows; nothing striking or original at all.[56]

Wednesday 18 March

Lesson at 2.40. Mummy arrives at 4.0 by bus from Lowestoft. Barbara comes to dinner Go with Mummy to B.B.C – Beethoven concert, conducted by Oskar Fried. Fidelio, 4th & 9th Symphonys. The first two were played beautifully. But Fried seemed to frighten the orchestra in the 9th. He altered scoring right and left. 1st movement, impressive, 2nd mov. too fast, the 3rd two slow. Last movement was notable for fine singing of Nat. Chorus & soloists. All considering it was rather a disappointing performance – of the conductor's. He was raging all the way through the 9th – there is no reason why he should blame the whole orch & choir for the slips of the 4th Horn (C^{b} scale (3rd mov.) & Timpani (2nd mov.)

Thursday 19 March

Quite good lesson with Ireland in Chelsea at 10.0. Practise afternoon, tea with Barbara & Mummy at Selfridges at 4.45. Go with Mummy (with tickets from Mrs. Brosa via. Mrs Bridge) to topping recital by Antonio Brosa. He is simply superb. Incredible technique, with beautiful interpretation. His Bach Chaconne was great. Prokofiev op. 16 Vln. Concerto[57] didn't contain much music, but was rather like a compendium of School for Virtuosity vln exercises. He played it toppingly. A great violinist.

Sunday 22 March

Get up early & go to St. Matthews with Mummy at 8.0. Spend all morning (11.0–1.0) & afternoon (2.30–4.45) with lunch back here – at Bach Choir, St. Matthew Passion, cond. A. Boult, with D. Silk, M. Balfour, S. Wilson, H. Eisdle, K. Falkner & A Cranmer. A very good performance on the whole, & very moving. Keith Falkner & St. Wilson were great & Dorothy Silk also. Choir quite good – oh, it's a great work! Tea with Barbara; back here for supper. Write to Pop afterwards. Early bed, by 10.0

Wednesday 25 March

Mummy returns home by bus from Charing X at 10.5. Stay in bed for breakfast, owing to v. bad night with pains. Have caster oil & suffer for it for the rest of the day. Don't go out but get up at 12.0 (consquently missing Pft. lesson). Do some copying out. Listen to B.B.C. concert on Miss Prior's Wireless (I had my ticket but sold it). Rossini Semeramide ov. & Dvorak's sentimental vlc (B min) concerto sentimentally played by Suggia, & Morning Heroes.[58] I cannot say much about the last, because it came over v. badly, the choral writing sounding confused, & I had no score. There seem to be some fine bits in the work (2nd movement) & some terribly ordinary bits.

Friday 27 March

I don't go out in the morning, because of beastly weather cold & fog, & so I do my writing & practising in the drawing [room] (in spite of beastly pft). Go to Queen's Hall to hear R.A.M. Students (under Henry Wood) do Franck's Beatitudes, in afternoon at 2.30. Sit pt. time with May (Comp. student at R.C.M.) who gave me the ticket. It is a poor work in comp. with Symph. Var, Symphony & Les Djinns etc. partly because of the inane words. Competant performance. Work in evening. – Variations.[59]

Monday 30 March

Write some more var. in morning & stick my "Thy King's Birthday" together.[60] Usual practise, go to R.C.M at 3.30 to see Miss Darnell, Lady Superintendnt about oculist. Go to see "Tell England" in evening (with some Complimentary tickets of Louis Ledérer) at Palace Theatre with Tumpty.[61] It is a simply amazing film, not much like the book. Terribly realistic and too harrowing really to be enjoyable. Exhilarating in a way, to see all those lives given up, – but for nothing. Parts very well played.

Tuesday 31 March

Practise & write as usual. Play with Lauricella in afternoon. Go to lunch with Laulie in morning at Mackies[62] – she is staying up here for a day or two. Go to Waterloo Studio (B.B.C). to hear Contemporary concert, with Bridges. He conducts B.B.C. orch "Enter Spring" & "Willow aslant a Brook" (Bridge)[63] rather badly played, but magnificent, inspired works. Brosa St. Quart. plays with orch concerto by Conrad Beck. Interesting, but that's all, incredibly played. And to end up with an absurd Concerto Grosso by Igor Markievitch.[64] Intoleraby difficult, & consequently only mod. played by the orch. This must have been written with the composer's tongue in his cheek.

Wednesday 1 April
I finish my variations with a fugue in morning. Some of them I quite like; some of them – muck. Practise as usual. Lesson in afternoon, with Benjamin. Both of us too tired with term to do any work! So he looks at my "Thy Kings Birthday," which he likes, & thinks quite original! Laulie comes to dinner in evening. I pack all after tea, & after Laulie goes at 8.45. Early bed.

Saturday 11 April
Copy out Viola part of Rondo[65] in morning & practise pft. See Bazil who is still laid up at 12.0. Play tennis 3–4, 5–6 on Clyffe courts, with Beth, Mr. Sewell & Mrs. Rogers. Tea at Hatfield House (where they live). Go to Cinema (Palace) with Pop (who comes out v. soon), Mum. Barb. & Beth. 2 Putrid Films & "Paramount on Parade";[66] v. interesting in a way. M. Chevalier's wonderful, considering what ~~little~~ a voice and looks he has.

Monday 13 April
Charles Coleman comes in morning to practise Trio (Vln & Vla only). Walk up to Morlings, to pay a bill, order some music, at 12.15 with him. Walk with Caesar up to golf course to meet Beth in afternoon. Putt with her on putting green after tea. Long walk with Pop after dinner along cliffs. I arrange Klärchens 1st song from Egmont[67] for pft. duet, having translated it into English, for Mum.

Wednesday 15 April
Finish one of the Fugues, more or less satisfactoryly. Practise Rondo with Charles & Mr. Coleman (Bazil is waiting to find out whether he is infectious for measels (Hilary Reeve is the probable culprit).), at 11.0 at their house. Walk up to Morlings afterwards. Write a little in afternoon. Walk with Caesar after tea. Go with Pop, Mum, & Beth to Lowestft Amateur & Dramatic Show "Vagabond King".[68] Quite well done (Funny men & female sec. of Chorus esp. good), & quite amusing – tho' of course nothing in it. 7.30–11.0

Saturday 18 April

Practise Rondo in morning. at Colemans. Should have played tennis with Mr. Sewell & Mrs. Rogers, 3–4, –5.6, but it rains all aft. Tea with them at Hatfield.) Musical Evening (all Beethoven) at 8.0. 2 Owles, Dr. Mead, 3 Colemans, 2 Phillips 2 Boyds, Mrs & John Nicholson, Mrs. Taylor, Miss Goldsmith. Sing a good many Rounds & Canons. Mrs. Taylor played 5th Sonata (F maj) with Mr. Coleman (rather Wonky intonation). I play op 10. no 3 (D maj) sonata. Mummy sings Klächen's 1st song from Egmont. (with Pft. duet acc. Mr. Coleman & Me). I also play Brahms (Hungarian Song) ~~variatns~~ variations[69] as a last resource as I have no more Beethoven at the moment. Every one seems to enjoy themselves, especially singing the Rounds.

Wednesday 22 April

Walk with Mum before Lunch Go to John Nicholson's to tea at 2.45. & to hear Gramophone records on his new Radio-Gram Hear. Brahms. Pft. Concerto Mov. 1. (Rubenstein) Tchaik. Pft. Con. (Solomon). Hear my prayer (E. Lough – beautifully sung) & Schubert B^{b} Trio (v. well played by D'Aranyi, Salmond, & Hess).[70] Play Pingpong also after tea. I am reading Drinkwater's Abraham Lincoln; marvellous play.[71]

Thursday 23 April

Walk up town in morning (via Station, sending off a parcel to Beth at Norwich (for a dance tonight), by train). to Morlings getting – on appro: – 2 records of Temple Choir[72] (Hear my prayer; & I waited for the Lord etc.)[73] from which to choose one – Heaven only knows which. They are both v. beautiful; personaly I think the 4^{tet} singing in "O come everyone that thirsteth" to be superb. Walk after lunch with Caesar. Play tennis with Mr. Sewell on Clyffe courts from 5.50–7.5. V. good & equal games,

Saturday 25 April

Very windy & rainy all day, so only go out after breakfast with Caesar, & after tea with Pop, Beth & Caesar up north end via Morlings to pay for "Hear my prayer", which we have chosen after much discussion and now with many misgivings. 2 Astles, 2 Phillipps, Ethel Boyd, & Mrs. Owles come in to sing Beethoven rounds after supper. We have a very hilarious time, if we don't give very perfect performances of these lovely little creations! I play 2 movs. of Beethoven op. 10 no 3. & a Prokoview prelude.[74] Bobby & Marjorie go to a dance.

Sunday 26 April

Walk with Pop & Caesar all morning. Beth & Mummy go to St. John's at 11.0. Read, & finish R.E. Lee (Drinkwater)[75] in afternoon. I think I prefer it to Lincoln, but they are both marvellous plays. Play a little Viola & pft. with Mum, before supper. Census is taken before we go to bed – What a business.[76]

Wednesday 29 April

~~Shake~~ Shave in morning; I shave once every 2 days now, with a cut-throat, which Pop has taught me to use. Practise all morning until 12.15, when I walk with Mummy. Play Tennis in afternoon (3–4.15) with Beth, Mrs. Black & a Nephew (?), Not by any means excellent Tennis, but great fun! Miss Bradley & Dr Mawson (of St. Luke's)[77] come to tea. Cut Front Lawn before tennis & after tea. Beth goes to cinema with Blacks in evening. Walk with Pop to Club after dinner.

Saturday 2 May

Do a bit more packing in morning. Go out with Ma. at 12.0 to Boughtons to have my photo retaken[78] as the others were worse than they need have been. Play tennis 3–4, 5–6 with Mrs. Black & Trixie Greville, who come back here to tea in the interval. V. feeble tennis. It's beastly ending hols with tennis like that. Cut Back & front lawns, before lunch & dinner resp. Play bit of Rockaway, & Rummy in evening. Pop & Mummy take their tea in car to South Cove. Lovely day

Tuesday 5 May [London]

I finish my rewritten Variations in morning & after lunch. Practise 11.30–12.45, & 2.15–4.15 with Lauricella, with whom I play Greig G min. Sonata & Mov 1 of Dvorak's Vln Concerto (A min) which he plays magnificently. Go to H Reeves after tea & get Saint Saen's 4th Pft. Concerto, ~~soiled~~ soiled (where, I know not!) for 3/- instead of 4/-. Play cards (Rummy) with Mr Gates & Mr Summers 2 of the new people here. Barbara rings up.

Wednesday 6 May

Have my hair cut before 9.30 at Whiteleys. Revise my Variations until 11.0. Practise 11.0–12.0 Go to College to ~~do~~ make various business arrangements, & have lesson with Benjamin 12.40–1.0. Practise all aft. 2.15–4.15. Practise Viola after tea. V. hot day, for this time of year. Dinner early at 6.45. & go to Queen's Hall to B.B.C. Concert.

[Written on two sides of a small card and inserted by Britten into the diary at this point.]

B.B.C. Orch. conducted by Adrian Boult. Euryanthe ov. (Weber), beastly bit of music, mauled about by Boult (2nd Subject more than 2ce as slow as 1st sub.). Bad slips on part of orch. V. Williams Tallis Fantasia. V. beautiful (wonderfully scored), but over long. well played. Cortot in Saint-Saëns 4th Con, very wonderful playing in spite of many wrong notes, which one didn't mind. Encored, playing (marvellously heavenlily) a Chopin Walse ($C^{\#}$ min). Mahler's Lieder eines Fahrenden Gesellen (Maria Olszewska, wonderful singing). Lovely little pieces, exquisitely scored – a lesson to all the Elgars & Strausses in the world. Enigma Variations, a terrible contrast to these little wonders. I listened with an open mind, but cannot say that I was less annoyed by them, than usual. Of course there must be alot in them, but that type of sonorous orchestration (especially in Var. V, IX, XII, (which seem exactly alike to me)) cloys very soon. Of course there are lovely moments (Dorabella is good, but is spoilt by trite ending~~)(~~Var. XIII is very effective~~)~~. on the whole I thing Ysobel's the best) but Oh! no XIV !! The orchestra played their exacting, but effective parts very well, & Adrian Boult was a sympathetic conductor, I suppose. I suppose it's my fault, and there is something lacking in me, that I am absolutely incapable of enjoying Elgar, for more than 2 minutes.

Thursday 7 May

Go to College, after beginning an unsatisfactory piece for violin & pft,[79] for aural training with Mr. Allchin at 11.0–12.0. Back for lunch. Practise 2.15–4.10. Meet Barbara at Selfridges at 5.0 after having gone to the Aeolian Hall [Bond Street] for some Music. The Madrigal choir is bigger than before, & is I think v. good. Back to dinner at the flat with Barbara. Have wireless; Harold Williams (?) singing Somerville's 'pleasant' Maud suite.[80] And a few Chopin preludes, exquisitely played by Cortot.

Friday 8 May

Begin last movement of a St. Quartet[81] in morning, before going to 1st Comp. lesson with Ireland. He is quite pleased with My fugues,[82] more especially with the last. I practise all afternoon. See Mr & Mrs Bridge after tea. Have long talk with them, & do a bit of correcting of proofs of his marvellous opera "Christmas Rose".[83]

Walk with Mr Summers & Gates (two new men here) after dinner.

Monday 11 May

Write a bit more of 1st mov. of St. Quartet in morning, most of it completely out of place & unsuccessful. Practise 11.45–12.45 & 2.15–4.15. Meet Barbara at Boots (Buck. Pal. Rd.) at 5.0 to take back ~~Drink~~ Galsworthy's Plays.[84] She comes on here to dinner & then we go to Playhouse (Char. X) to get some tickets for Sat. night. She goes to Chelsea, & I return here.

Wednesday 13 May

Write some more Quartet, before practising 11.0–12.0 & after supper. Go to quite a good pft. lesson (on the Brahm's Var. (Hungarian Song) with Benjamin, 12.40–1.0. He has now given me Ravel's Sonatine & Beethoven op 2 no 1. Son. (E^b). Practise 2.15–4.15. Walk after tea, & in the Gardens (of Prince's Sq.) after dinner with Tumpty Henderson.

Thursday 14 May

Finish the first movement of my Quartet before going to an Aural Training class at 11.0–12.0. See Lauricella & walk back with him afterwards. Practise all afternoon, & meet Barbara at Selfridges at 5.0. Madrigals afterwards at 6.0. Great fun. Read a Tchekov Play in evening, the Bear.[85] A great work! I think alot about a slow movement to my quartet.

Friday 15 May

Begin Slow Move of Quartet before going to Coll. at 11.45 to find my Comp. lesson has been moved to Thursdays, only the Coll. has not informed me of this, so that I miss a lesson this week. This Establishment! Practise 2.15–4.0. Go st. to Barbara's flat where Beth is, having travelled up from Lowestoft by Bus arr. 3.30. Walk with her before dinner (all 3 of us there). Go to 'Stand up and Sing'[86] (3/6 seats at Hippodrome) – Jack Buchanan Elsie Randolph, Anton Dolin, 7 Hindustans (marvellous gymnastic feats) in a perfectly topping, side-splitting, rolicking good show. Back at 12.0.

Wednesday 20 May

Write until 11.0, practise till 12. & then go to College to find that Benjamin will teach me tomorrow instead. Practise in afternoon. Go to Augener's for M.S. paper, & to Hills for gut for my broken viola, after tea. Go to a recital of D.F. Tovey & Adila Fachiri (tickets from Hills via Miss Atkinson). Beethoven Kreutzer & op 96, & Brahms D min Sonatas. No. 1 played with fire, & spirit, but rather inaccurate. No 2. with right lucid touch, for this delicious idyll.[87] Players well matched in last; fine interpretation, if rather rough. Mr. Summers goes with me.

Thursday 21 May

Go for a lesson at J. Ireland's Studio, at 10.0 until 12.0. Have very good & instructive lesson. Come back via. R.C.M. Practise 2.15–3.15 & then go for tea at Benjamin's house in Kilburn.[88] Look thru the libretto of a future operetta of his,[89] & have very good pft. lesson. Return immediately for Madrigal practise, when we do some good work. Practise Vla after dinner (at 8.0), after mending my viola.

Wednesday 27 May

Pop, Mum, & Beth go to Gloucester by car from Lowestoft, to stay. Go to Covent Garden after breakfast in an unsuccessful attempt to get campstools to put in a queue. Have my hair cut a Whiteleys, before practising (11.0–12.0) & v. good pft. lesson 12.40. Practise in aft. & then meet Barbara & Miss Hurst, have dinner at Eustace Miles,[90] & then go & sit in queue for Cov. Garden op. Lohengrin at 7.30.[91] Op. very well done; orch moderate. Elsa v. good actress only distressing wobble (E. Teschemacher). Loh. (Willi Wörle) excellent; best of all Olkzewska as Ortrud. What a voice! The opera is (except for one or two banal bits) exceedingly beautiful – no wonder it's so popular.

Thursday 28 May

At 10.30 have nearly 2 hrs of most damning (tho' v. good) critisism from Ireland at Chelsea.

Practise in afternoon. Meet Barbara at Selfridges at ~~5.0~~ 4.50, & then Madrigal very hard together. Go back to her flat for dinner (Miss Hurst's out). Hear Brahm's Horn trio on wireless from Paris. I am afraid that I prefer our Philistine viola version,[92] to this overswamped by horn business. Horn – Horn – nothing else. Back by ¼ to 10.

Friday 29 May

I finish the 1st mov. of my Quartet again, in morning, & begin a new 2nd mov. in evening.[93] Practise as usual, 11.45–12.45, 2.15–4.15. Walk with Summers after tea. Go to Madrigals at about 8.15 with Barbara, at Morley College, until about 9.50. We are rehearsing Madrigals & ~~Folkes~~ Folksongs for Tuesday's E.F.D.S.[94] Concert, back at 10.50.

Sunday 31 May

Go to Church with Summers to St. Marks, N. Audley St, at 11.0. V. nice service, altho' it is too high for my liking. Miss Prior brings us back in her Austin 7. Go to Madrigal Practice at Cecil Sharpe House,[95] meeting Barbara at Hyde park Corner, having walked across park, & progressing by bus. Tea with her at a A.B.C. in Oxford ~~Circus~~ st, & walking by myself back here. Practise Viola a bit after dinner.

Tuesday 2 June

Finish (after one or two attempts) the Slow movement, of My quart. I am quite pleased with it. Practise as usual, in aft. with Lauricella. Go to sing (in evening dress) at the Cecil Sharp house, at a Folk song, & Folk-dance concert at 8.30. Patuffy Kennedy Fraser also sings, quite charmingly, some Hebridean Songs with harp. We sing a group of Madrigals, & a group of Folk song arrangements. Interspersed with these are many & monotonous (I am heretic enough to say!) folk dances, tho' some were beautiful Barbara, of course, sings, & Miss Hurst also goes. Back at 11.15.

Wednesday 3 June

Do a deal of revision (ie. altering) of my Quartet before practising 11.0–12.0. V. good lesson with Benjamin, 12.40. He was quite pleased with my Ravel Sonatine (mov. 1.)[96] Practise afternoon. Walk with Tumpty after tea, down to Wigmore St., & with Skelton & Davies after dinner in park.

Thursday 4 June

Lesson with Ireland 10.0–11.30; quite helpful. He likes my second slow. mov. better than the 1st one. Practise as usual. 2.15–4.15. Walk with Nora Henderson after tea. Barbara comes for dinner, & a bath afterwards. She is v. amusing, & we have a great time.

Friday 5 June

Write a bit in morning, & then go to Patron's Fund rehearsal in morning.[97] Only new work is Howard Ferguson's Short Symphony in D minor.[98] V. fine work not too well played by N[ational]. Symph. Orch under Sargent. Schuman's ineffective Vlc conc. (Audrey Piggott), Chausson's Chanson Perpétuelle (well sung by Veronica Mansfield) & Strauss's v. long & meandering Burlesque for Pft & orch. Practise in aft. Go to R.C.M Chamber concert with Tumpty in evening, at 8.15. V. dull show. Sibeliu's, Voces intimae, Quart. well played, but blurred out of all recognition by the hall. Ravel's delicious Int. & Allegro, (Harp etc.). quite well played, made the concert worth going to.

Monday 8 June

I write "Aspatia's Song"[99] in morning, quite successful, & also begin a de la Mare, unsuccessful.[100] Practise as usual. Begin "Hymn to Pan" before meeting Uncle Sheldon at Queen's Road and bringing him back here to dinner with Barbara. He takes us to the Royal Tournament at Olympia – marvellous show. I enjoyed every moment of it. The P.T. Squads were superb, & the musical drives. It quite makes me long to be a soldier!

Wednesday 10 June

I do, in morning & evening, a good deal of arranging of Bridge's Melodie (orr. Vlc & pft) for Vla. & Pft.[101] I begin an unsuccessful song, before that.[102] Pft. Lesson. as usual; Benjamin shows me the beginning of his opera (The Devil take her(?)), of which I have already seen the libretto. Practise in afternoon. Go to Westminster Central Hall to take some music (Nat. Chorus) back to May Prior. Walk all way home thro' the parks. Walk with Summers in evening.

Friday 12 June

Write much more of Vln Part in morning. usual practise. Walks after tea with Tumpty, Gates, & Summers in the park. After dinner go to marvellous B.B.C. concert (at 9.45) at Studio, with Bridges. Wagner Faust ov. & Strauss Don Juon. Marvellous works, thrilling & moving. Glazunov's dry & academic 6th Symphony. I have never heard the orch. play better; they were enthusiastic about his conducting, & I don't wonder! He introduced me to Harry Barlow, the world's greatest Tuba player, who showed me alot about the instrument, & also told us a little about his life's study of the instrument, which is treated so badly in the orch. – the yard-dog of the orch – as he puts it.

Monday 15 June

Write a more-~~of~~or less satisfactory song "Love is a Sickness"[103] in morning, & do a bit more copying of part. Practise as usual. Have Hair cut after lunch, at Whiteleys. Go to Morley College for Madrigals (etc.) practise for Hyde park show. Terrible shout. Go via the Lyceum, where I get tickets for Sadko[104] on Thursday. Ring up Barbara. Walk with Gates after tea in gardens. He! is simply topping.

Wednesday 17 June

Begin Viola part. Usual Practice. Walk with Gates after tea. Frank Bridge rings up at dinner to know whether I can go to Russ. Ballet[105] (at Lyceum) instead of Mrs Bridge who's not well with toothache. So I go with him & Miss Fass. See De Falla's El Amor Brujo – Wonderful. Glinka Ratmir's Dream, mod. & most glorious of all Petrushka; this is an inspiration from beginning to end. Wonderful dancing esp. Voizikowsky as P. Finish with a rolicking Danses Polovtsiennes (~~Bir~~ Borodin – P. Igor).[106] I have never even imagined there could be such dancing.

Thursday 18 June

Go to Ireland for good comp. lesson at 10.0. Come back via R.C.M with Lauricella. Play tennis 4–5 with Gates; play v. badly. Go to opera (Lyceum) with Miss Hurst & Barbara (B. & I take Miss H.) to see Sadko.[107] v. well done – voices all good, save for excessive wobble. Music v. pretty, tuneful, but v. thin. Opera a mass of spectacular scenes; not really an opera. Scenery v. good. Chorus good; orchestra mod. not as good as last night (under E. Goossens both nights – v. fine). Orchestration wonderful of course. Back about 12.0.

Saturday 20 June [London/Friston]

I have early breakfast & go to Victoria & catch 9.20 to Eastbourne, where Mrs. Bridge meets me in Miss Fass's car (a friend of theirs who lives v. near & is with them most of the day) & motors me to their lovely cottage in Friston.[108] I play tennis all afternoon & after tea with Mr. Bridge who is really very good, & amazingly steady. Great fun. Miss Fass is here for tea & dinner, & Mr. B. & I go to her house & listen, after supper, to a bit of Carmen, on her wireless from Rome. The country around here is too superb for words. No one about at all – lovely!

Sunday 21 June [Friston]

After breakfast at 9.30, I go for a long walk over the Downs with Mrs. Bridge. After that Mr. Bridge looks at my choral work (Thy K's B. [*Thy King's Birthday*]) – he is mod. pleased with my progress. Lunch with Miss Fass. Play tennis abit in afternoon with Mr. Bridge, & again after tea – he really is remarkably good. Tea at Miss Fass' & dinner (the 3 of us) back here. Listen to a Stratton Quartet[109] concert on wireless at Miss Fass's. She lends me some madrigals.

Monday 29 June [London]

I write in morning & evening a piece for Vln & Pft (going down hill on a Bicyle – after H.C. Beeching). Practise as usual. Play tennis (abominably badly) with Gates on Commodore Hotel court 5–6. Hear that H.W. Austin is beaten in Wimbeldon by Shields (U.S.A). Ò râge, ô desespoir!

Tuesday 30 June

Gates goes away at mid-day, for good I'm sick to say. I write a Vln & Pft piece, "Moon," in morning[110] – more satisfactory than the Bicycle one. Copy parts out, & Lauricella plays them in aft. He's going to practise them, but plays them already well. Meet Beth at 5.59 at Lv'pl St. She comes here to dinner. Walk in park with her, & then go with her to Barbaras, where she stays the night, befor departing for Switzerland (Basle with Yvonne Clar), in morning at 9.0 Back at 11 0.

Wednesday 8 July

I copy out in morning Vln. pt. of Bridge Vlc Mélodie, for Lauricella to play in aft. Act. he doesn't do it, as he only comes for a short time without Vln. Practise in morning as usual, & also begin a mediocre setting of Psalm 130.[111] Play tennis with Mrs. Johnson in Cadogan Gardens 4.30–6.30 Have some quite good games, alto' I'm not yet by anymeans on form. Go onto dinner with Barbara and Miss Hurst. Back at 10.0.

Thursday 9 July

I write a good deal more Psalm in morning. Go to Patron's Fund rehearsal at 11.40. Hear a long meandering Petrouchka-like Ballet of Betty Luytens [Lutyens] (Infanta's Birthday)[112] which suffered being away from Stage, & "Riding together", M. Blower. mod. good. Irene Morden sings, "Thou Monstrous Fiend" [from *Fidelio*], tolerably, orch. v. bad. Practise as usual. Walk with Tumpty after tea. Write letters after Supper.

Monday 13 July

Write more Psalm, practise 11–12, lesson (to make up for last Wed.) with Benjamin 12.40. Practise in afternoon Walk after tea with Miss Alford, a great collector of Folk songs & dances, writer of books & novelist who is staying here. She is amazingly interesting & knows tons about ballet, & proposes that I should write music to one of her ballet "books".

Tuesday 14 July

I copy out my 3 fugues in morning, & pratice. Practice with Lauricella in aft. Go to Covent Garden with Miss Alford to see Ida Rubenstein's ballet. Psyche & Cupid – (Bach-Honegger) David (Sauguet) – Ravel's Mère L'oye (orch. only – v. bad) & Bolero.[113] Don't think much of Rub. but scenery & corps de ballet – Wonderful. Bach v. beautiful (quite brilliantly arranged by Honegger) tho' long. David, dramatic~~que~~ but music poor. Bolero taken very slowly; interesting but not exhilerating.

Wednesday 15 July

I go for a lesson to Chelsea with Ireland at 10.30 He is quite pleased with my Psalm so far. Go to College for lesson with Benjamin at 12.40. He is quite pleased with my Ravel Sonatine, which I play at my second study Pft Annual Exam. in aft. at about 3.30. Exam Mr. Morrison (Angus?). I play rather badly.

Monday 20 July

I revise my Psalm, & several old works for exam. Begin a poor piece, supposed to celebrate our beating U.S.A in the Davis cup.[114] Practise as usual.

Pick up a second hand copy of 4 quite good songs (including "Madrigal" – charming) of Herbert Howells,[115] at Whiteleys – ½ price.

Wednesday 22 July
I go to comp. exam. at Coll. at 12.0. Absolute Farce. Examiners – V. Williams, Waddington, Edgar Bainton. (not, unfortunately, Ireland). I have ½ hrs exam on all the work done this ~~term~~ year! Of course they look at the wrong things & make me play the wrong things out of the hundreds of things I take them! I don't practise in afternoon, but lie on my bed, as my feet are v. red & swollen. Write to Gates after dinner.

Thursday 23 July
I practise Vla. & pack a bit in morning; I can't go to practise yet as my foot is still rather bad. I go to Victoria to take back Adrian Glynde after tea, only have to bus all the way. Listen to Contemporary Music concert, broadcast in evening. v. Schönbergian Suite op. 18 of Knipper; uninteresting. Some vague weird Jap. songs of Maklakievicz. An extraordinary unacc. Choral "Ame du peine" of Hare; best of all 3 choruses of Wellesz. Quite well sung by Wireless Singers. Ended by a Sinfonietta, of Halffter, amusing tho' over-long.[116]

Friday 24 July
I hear from Lauricella that I have ~~one~~ won the Farrar Comp. prize,[117] & go to College soon after breakfast to confirm this. I pack all the rest of the day, with breaks for meals, 1 hrs. Practise, 11.45–12.45, 1 hrs. v. enjoyable & quite good tennis with Mrs Johnson[118] at Hotel Commodore, 4–5. Barbara comes after dinner to help me in my packing. Go to say good-bye to Mr. Bridge abt. 10. & don't get home till abt. 12.30. V. interesting talk, he's been to International festival at Oxford.[119]

Thursday 30 July [Lowestoft]
Usual playing, but walk with Beth, going to Molls & buying a new tennis racquet with prize money – Austin – 75/- (paying 70/-) a superb one.[120] I play tennis 5–7 on court opposite (too wet for grass) with sometime Beth & sometime Mr Sewell, but even this racquet cannot raise my play ~~about~~ above the most execrable standard. Walk with Pop before bed.

Friday 31 July
Walk with Beth in morning; after playing Viola with Aunt [Janie]. Go to Meads to tennis at 3.0, playing on Mrs. Woodger's court. Just Kathleen Mead, Beth, Tommy Pedder, & I. We have some quite good tennis on the

whole. Get back rather late, at 7.30. Miss Alford sends me a libretto for a ballet – it looks amusing but will be dashed difficult to cope with.[121]

Sunday 2 August
Walk with Pop in morning after which I play Beethoven's Diabelli Var. all through – what an incredibly marvellous work! Willcock, who has been on the broads, comes to see me in the afternoon & we walk together. Walk with Pop, Beth & Rosemarry [Pollard] after tea & with Pop before bed. Begin reading Long Road of John Oxenham.[122] So far jolly good.

Monday 3 August
We all, except Pop (who stays to play golf) go out for lunch & tea to a lovely spot near Covehithe,[123] near the sea. Picnicing is very nice. Back at 6.o. Go to Sparrows Nest in evening (including Pop this time) to hear Paul Robeson & an Vaudville company. He has a remarkable organ, but didn't seem able to use it. I am not an enthusiast of the Negro Spirituals. The rest of show tame, except a man called Halls v. funny & clever, & a Clown & acrobat.[124]

Wednesday 5 August
Bathe with Beth & Rosemary before lunch – Mummy has a care of girls Committee meeting, & with Mummy, Beth, Rosemary, Mr & Clive Chartres before tea. Mr & Mrs. Jean, & Clive come to tea on Beach. Bobby arrives by 6.53 from West Hartlepool. His marriage to Marjorie (Alas) is arranged now.[125] Go to Palace to see Talkie film Charlie's Aunt,[126] with Beth & Rosemary in evening. Screemingly funny.

Monday 10 August
Practise Viola & Piano in morning, & walk with Mummy in morning. Go up to Morlings with Bobby in aft. to get "A-Roving" (Plymouth-Town),[127] on which Miss Alford's Ballet (which I am going to set to Music) is based. Mr. Horne (& his wife) come in after Supper. He used to dig with Pop in Ipswich when they were young.

Thursday 13 August
Write a bit more ballet in morning, & walk with Beth. Go to Marina Theatre to see Charlie Chaplin in "City Lights",[128] with Mum, Beth & Bobby. A wonderful piece of acting. There should have been a party on the beach, but this the weather puts out of the question. It clears up however for some tennis, 5.30–7.30 with Mr. Kelway, Mr. Sewell & John Nicholson; on court opposite.

Monday 17 August

Practise Pft in morning. I am stuck over the Bad Girls'dance [for *Plymouth Town*]. Walk with Bobby before lunch. The Nicholsons come to tennis – Elizabeth & John, on court opposite. No tennis is possible before tea, because of rain; but after tea we have over 2 hrs. of windy tennis. tho' fun. Play with Beth – 6–4, 5–7, 7–5. & with Elizabeth; 6–2, 6–3, 6–2. Finish [André] Maurois Wonderful "Ariel" in evening. What a wonderful man Shelley was!

Saturday 22 August

Walk with Bobby up to Morlings, after breakfast to get Ravel's Intro-duction & All° (played by Cockerill, Virtuosos, Murchie & Draper) & Bridge Novellette no 3 (Virtuosos) on 2 Records.[129] Absolutely thrilling!

Go to Chartres with Beth in car at 3.30 for tennis; have only rather feeble tennis on a very wet court.

Sunday 23 August

Bobby, Beth, Alice (to see her mother), & I go over in car to see Nanny at ~~Fanham~~ Farnham in morning.[130] Go also over to Capel (where) & see Mrs. Chambers (with whom we used to stay as children.)[131] Back for lunch. Barbara goes back to London by 5.10. Walk with Pop, & then Beth after tea (Pop & Ma. go to Southwold – Pop for a case).

Wednesday 26 August

Dorothy Graham-Brown (who used to live here) & Charles & Herbert (who went to S. Lodge) come to see us, D. for lunch, & tea; & 2 boys for tea. Bathe in morning with them all & Beth, & David Boyd. Have John & David Boyd & 2 Graham B's on beach in aft. & for tea; Beth plays tennis with D.G.B. & 2. Boyds (Miss) in aft. & has tea down at hut. Nanny comes over for day & has tea with us. Pop goes out for dinner to Club. (Yacht). The 2 Boyd boys are abt. the nicest boys I know.

Saturday 29 August

Bobby goes off to W. Hartlepool[132] by 9.48. Go to Stat. with him, with Mummy, & Beth (driving). Walk with Caesar before lunch. Beth & Mum. go to Norwich at 1.0, & then come back to Warners at Bramerton, where Mr. Sewell takes me for tennis at 3.0. Have some good singles, & a double with Beth & Mrs. Warner. Go to dinner with Sewells in their new house up North End. Go rather late (8.30!) because Pop is ill with Broncitus, having had a bad cold all the week, & refusing to go to bed.

Thursday 3 September [West Hartlepool]
Walk with Bobby & Dick Shorter (Best man) in morning, round the docks; have elevens in Bins (all of us, Family, Rishworths (with whom Bobby stays). Wedding at St. Pauls at 2.0; I ush with 2 Goldsons & a cousin (Oliver).

Lord Thurlow marries them, Uncle Sheldon & a Curate assisting. Reception at Goldson's afterwards (Westside). Follow Bobby to Sunderland in cars (several) where he goes on in train to Lakes, & we bring our car back here. We all have dinner at Goldsons in evening (16 of us) & go to see Picture – "Plunder" afterwards.[133] Back at 12.15 at Hotel.

Much rain on first half of journey.

Friday 4 September
We intend to start home at 9.0, but the car won't start & Beth doesn't arrive at the Hotel until 10.10. Have breakdown before near Wetherby. We take Dick Shorter (best Man) back to his home at Leadenham. Roads very flooded, North of Newark generally. Have lunch at Bell hotel, Barmbymore ~~3.0~~ 3.15–4.15. Stop at Dick's home at 6.0–6.15. Have more car trouble before East Dereham, where it is seen to at 10.30. Back at ¼ to 1 in morning.

Saturday 5 September [Lowestoft]
Get up late. Walk with Beth before lunch. Get some flowers for Mum & Pop, as it's their wedding day. Go with Beth to Hippodrome, to see Tom Walls & Yvonne Arnauld in "Canaries sometimes sing".[134] Screaminly funny. Walk with Beth after tea (getting caught in rain). Barbara & Miss Hurst cross to go to Switzerland this afternoon, I believe.

Sunday 6 September
Pop is still in bed, but his temp. is normal for first time since Sat. week. Beth & I take Caesar for walk & then go to St. John's at 11.0. My nose bleeds hard for most of the service. Go to tea with Mr & Mrs. Laurence Sewell in their house at North End with Beth. Walk with her afterwards.

a Car runs away down hill in morning, & hits a woman & child, by our gate

Wednesday 9 September
I get W. Walton's Viola Concerto from O.U.P.[135] It's a fine work but difficult. Walk with Beth before lunch. Go with Beth & 4 Chartres (– Gordon) to "Hell's Angels" at Marina in aft.[136] Marvellous photography spoilt by Slop. Stuff. Listen on a hired wireless to Brahms prom. Rhapsody – wonderful work, spoilt completely by atmospherics, as was rest of concert. D'ble Concerto, Arthur Catteral, good, L. Kennedy wonderful – tone comparable to Casals. Magnificent 4th Symph to wind up with.[137]

Thursday 10 September

Go in car up town in morning with Mum. & Beth, & walk back with Caesar. Play tennis, 3.30–4.30, 5.30–7.30 on cort opp. with Beth, K. Mead, Mr. Amery, Mrs Sewell, Teddy Rogers & after tea Mr. Sewell. Listen to Prom. after dinner; British Composers' night. Walton's wonderful Vla Concerto (beautifully played by Tertis) stood out as a work of genius. Lamberts' Rio Grande very interesting & beautiful, as was Holst's Ballet from Perfect Fool, & Warlock's Capriol Suite. Boughton's 2 songs (beautifully sung by Trefor Jones) amusing, quite delightful. Smyth's songs Chrysella, & the Dance – the reverse – despicable![138]

Friday 11 September

Finish an arrangement of Haydn's D maj. 'cello concerto[139] in morning for viola, & practise it. Walk with Beth also, & in afternoon Play tennis with her 5.30–6.30 on court opposite. Listen to a section of Beethoven Prom; Marvellous Leonora no 2. (In many ways I prefer this to no. 3; there is no anticlimax); Concerto no. 2. beautifully, & joyously played by Cyril Smith. "Thou Monstrous Fiend" (Fidelio)[140] sung by Stiles Allen; – a wonderful organ, naught else. At this moment we were cut off for a wretched babble from Snowdon.

Monday 21 September [London]

Beth takes me to station in car to catch the 8.30 to Liverpool St. Go at once at 11.30 in taxi to my new rooms at 173 Cromwell Rd; then to R.C.M to Sir Hugh Allen's address at 1.0; back to Burleigh House for lunch at 2.0; meet Barbara & Miss Hurst from Switzerland at Victoria at 3.30 (+ 30 mins late). Tea with Barbara at her flat. Then meet Mummy & Pop from Cornwall (Fowey) at 6.55 (+ 20 mins late) at Paddington. They stay here the night. Walk with Pop before Bed.

Walk & shop (Harrods)[141] with Mum & Pop in morning.

Tuesday 22 September

Go to Liverpool St. to see them & Barbara off to Lowestoft by 3.10. Tea here. Walk after. Go to Prom. after early dinner (6.30). Volga Boatman's Song (blatently arranged). Song of Flea (Moussorgsky) – Harold Williams excellently sung. – very amusing. Rachmaninov's terrible – vulgar, old-fashioned 2nd Pft. Concerto (Solomon). Mossolov's Factory – amusing – nothing more. Tchaikovsky's 4th Symphony – which makes one long for Chamber music & Mozart, & makes one deplore the discovery of "Fate".[142] Rather ragged orchestral playing. I prom, only till ½ time.

Cannot practise in morning, as Lounge is full of people.

Wednesday 23 September

Lesson with Benjamin 12.30–1.0. Arrange about practice at New S. of Music [the RCM's new practice studios] in aft. & go on to Augeners to buy some music. Go to Prom. (Brahms) in evening with Peter Floud & his sister. 3 Magnificent works – orch. moderate – Haydn Var. – Concerto no 1. (Myra Hess – v. creditable & moving performance) & the glorious 3rd Symphony. After interval Myra Hess plays the Symphonic Var. of Franck. Delightful work (~~quite~~ his masterpiece), equally delightfully played.[143] Considering the diff. between this & the Brahms. M. Hess did splendidly.

Thursday 24 September

Go up to Harrods in morning to see abt a Pft for Pop to give to Bobby. Practise in Lounge 11–1.0. Practise in N. School of M. 2.40–3.40. Go to Madrigals at 6.0; General meeting as well as singing. Get back for dinner at 8.0, & listen afterwards, on wireless in Lounge to Prom[144] – Ireland's Pft Concerto & Holst's Planets. I still think the first very loosely put together, & second too sugary (celeste); both have v. fine & beautiful moments; but I feel no music of that generation can be compared to works like Walton's Viola Concerto

Friday 25 September

Practise here, 11.0–1.0, & in N.S. of M. 3.0–4.0. Go to College [illegible] after lunch to see Lauricella. Go to Prom.[145] in evening with Floud's sister (he cannot come). Beethoven 3. Leonoras – (I think I prefer 2. it is so dramatic), An de Ferne Geliebte, beautifully sung by Steuart Wilson as we[re] 3 Kodaly Songs in second ½ of programme. 5th Symphony (of which I am not v. fond – rather weary). Respighi's Fountains of Rome – brilliant but not very deep. Orchestral playing – still moderate, with most astonishing slips!

Tuesday 29 September

More scoring in morning & evening. Practise as usual only 2.30–4.0 with Lauricella in N.S.M. We do the Beethoven Vln concerto, which he plays really very well. Listen, in evening on a rather poor wireless, to Mozart's Jupiter Symphony,[146] Even then it was magnificent, especially the exhilerating & gorgeous last movement. What a marvellous man Mozart is! (It was from the Prom.).

V. good lesson with Benjamin 12.20–1.0. Practise in afternoon at N.S. of M. & go afterwards to Augeners to get Music.

Wednesday 30 September

Go to Prom (Bach) with Mollie Floud at 8.0. V. long programme to stand for. Sarabane, Andante, & Bourée (Strings), v. good & well played. Murchie in B minor Flute Suite (delightful playing). 2 Conces. (C. & C min). 2 pianos (Ethel Bartlett & Rae Robertson)[147] – wonderfully played. Thalben Ball in B min Prelude & Fugue; only bit of organ music I've ever really enjoyed. Also arias by Stuart Robertson (excellent) & Gladys Ripley (not so good). Also Suite no 6 Bach – Wood – Even Wood's garish orchestration could not spoil some of this music.[148] Back at 11.25.

Wednesday 7 October

Lesson with Benjamin 12.20. Start a new Psalm (150) before that. Practise N.S.M. 2.30–3.30, hair cut at Whiteleys. After dinner I go to Arthur Benjamin's House in Carlton Hill. To hear William Primrose play his Vln Concerto (new) & Sonatina (Vln & Pft)[149] – both v. fine works. The rest of the London St. Quart ~~were~~ are there (Primrose is the violist);[150] & seem to be very nice. The 2nd Violin (John Petri ?) brings me to Edgware Rd. underground in his car. Arrive home abt. 12.45 a.m.

Thursday 8 October

John Ireland cannot have me at 10.0, which I find when I arrive at his studio at this hour, but I have a lesson at 8.45 in evening, ~~lasting~~ being back at 11.30. Mostly talk, – his opinions of various contemporary composers![151] Practise 12.0–1.0, 2.30–3.30 at N.S.M. Go to Queen's Hall for tickets after this & Meet Barbara for tea at Selfridges at 4.50. She goes to Madrigals but I don't because of a filthy cold.

Friday 9 October

Write, until 11.0 (a new Piano version of 3 Orch. Songs, begun yesterday).[152] Pack, & then practise till 1.0. Catch 3.10 from Liverpool St home. Travel all ~~the~~ way with Elizabeth Nicholson. Fairly quick journey. Pop & Beth meet me in car. – Mummy being in middle of tea party. Our new Erard (or rather 2nd hand) has arrived, & the Kemmler gone to Bobby. The Erard is superior in touch (& in case) but inferior in tone. It is a full grand (6′ 8″)

Monday 12 October [Lowestoft]

Walks ~~with M~~ in morning with Caesar, & with Mummy. In Interval continue Psalm 150. Play tennis in aft. 3.0–4.30, with Beth, Mrs. Hodges & Dr More (?) from St. Luke's.[153] Quite good tennis, & great fun. In evening, in auspices of Lowestoft Mus. Soc, Fred. Woodhouse, with Mable Ritchie[154] (staying here for night) & Geoffrey Dunn give an evening of "Intimate opera," in St. Margaret's Institute,[155] at 8.15. Programme, – Coffee Cantata (Bach), [BB leaves gap here] (Arne), & Bastien & Bastienne, (Mozart).[156] All very delightful & amusing The three come back to supper afterwards. Mum. Beth & I go, – Pop, going to a Masonic.

Tuesday 13 October [Lowestoft/London]
Mabel Ritchie sings my 3 songs before going off by train at 9.48. Walk with Mummy, Beth, & Caesar, & pack in morning. Catch 2.31 to London. Mum & Pop bring me to station in car. Pretty good journey, on time. Meet Barbara, by accident, in Metropolitan,[157] at Nottinghill Gate. Attempt to write in evening, but am driven to desperation by a loud wireless on landing outside.

Wednesday 14 October [London]
Write & Practise Pft before going to R.C.M. for lesson with Benjamin at 12.20. Practise before, & write after, tea, both here. Go to Queen's Hall, with Mrs. Bridge, who gives me ticket, to B.B.C. Symp. Conc. Orch, material wonderful, Adrian Boult – muck! Brandenburg Conc. no. 3. – heavily played – tone wonderful. Ensemble of Beethoven Symph. 4, bad; otherwise moderate – not sparkling enough. Best of all, Backhaus in Schumann Concerto. Really inspired. Florence Austral sings Closing scene from Gotterdämerung wonderfully. Back by 11.0

Wednesday 21 October
Score, practise, & then good pft lesson at 12.40 at Col. Practise & hair cut in aft (Whiteley's). Go to. B.B.C Concert (1st half – Area,[158] 2nd half – Stalls with Bridges). Strauss – conducting Mozart E^{b} Symphony, his own three Hölderlin Prayers (beautifully sung by Margarete Teschemacher), & Domestic Symphony.[159] Dull & annoying Mozart – can it be he who wrote Don Juan? Hölderlin songs; boring & monotonous Straussian sounds. Domestic: amusing, & annoying by ~~tern~~ turns; but with some lovely bits. Orch. as good as could be with such a conductor (or rather beater). Come home by bus, via. Bridges by 11.5.

Sunday 25 October
Church at St. Judes with Diana May & her Grandmother at 11.0. Go to Albert Hall Concert 3.0 L.S.O. Beecham. Smetana's sparkling Bart. Bride ov. Mozart 34. C maj, delightful, Symphony, Edna Iles in Beethoven's Fine 3rd Concerto – Delius Marvellously beaut. but Wagnerian Walk to Paradise

Garden (Vill. Rom. & Juliet) – & Bizet's Charming 1st L'Arlesienne Suite. Orch. probably very good (also Edna Iles) but Echo was more than usually vile where I was sitting (Stalls – ticket given by Lauricella). Thomas Beecham. v. good tho' too spectacular – we want a screen! Tea with Mr & Mrs Turner (Ruth), just back from Lowestoft, supper with Barbara. Write home there afterwards. Back by 9.50.

Wednesday 28 October

No lesson in morning so score & practise instead. Play tennis in afternoon 3–4 with Miss Gillespie on Lincoln's Inn Fields. She is very good, & we have marvellous fun. Back for tea. Listen to B.B.C Symp. concert on wireless in evening. Henry Wood. Beethoven – Coriolan; "Der [Die] Frist ist um" (Flying Dutchman)[160] – well sung by Herb. Janssen (wobbly intonation occasionally tho'). Sibelius 1st Symphony – amazingly fine – rather Brahm's like. He does some very commonplace things tho'. Har. Bauer in G maj Beethoven Concerto. 1st & 2nd mov.s magnificent. 3rd too fast, & rather ragged. To end – Liszt's brilliant & amazing Mephisto Walser.

Friday 30 October

Lesson with Ireland at Coll. at 11.10. V. good; on orch. of ballet. Practise (NSM) with Lauricella in aft. We speak (abt. L.'s violin) to Albert Sammons afterwards. Then I go to O.U.P. (Aeolian Hall – Bond St.) to get some music – C. Franck Symph. Variations (which I am to do for Benjamin) & Gordon Jacob – Orchestral Technique.[161] Little more copying in evening.

Saturday 31 October

Work at Bridge nearly all morning. Play tennis at 3.0 at Cartwright Gardens with Mrs Johnson, Miss Gillespie & a friend (girl). Great fun. Play as long as light lasts (4.30) Go to see Ireland as soon as back (6.0). He wants me to copy out into score, ~~of~~ some pts. of a new Haydn Pft Concerto which has been discovered at Brit. Mus. [British Museum][162] Can't very well refuse, & so I start work on <u>that</u>, in evening. It's interesting, work; but too much, that, the Bridge, & my own stuff. Ireland is going to reorchestrate it.

Pft lesson 12.40 – I play (2nd pft) Franck Symp. Var. with Benjamin (1st pft. V. good.

Wednesday 4 November

Play tennis with Miss Gillespie, 3–4 Lincoln's Inn's Fields – great fun. Bath before early dinner (6.50) & go to B.B.C. concert – ½ time Area & ½ time Circle with F.B. Adrian Boult (<u>terrible execrable</u> conductor) leads the show.

Elgar Intro. & All° nice spots but terrible – "Toselli's Serenata"! H. Samuel in Brahms 2nd Conc. – v. disappointing reading tho' excellent technically – too pompous & slow. Schuman 1st delightful symphony – indifferently played. Go home with F.B. & Brosas (Mr. & Mrs.), for lemonade, back here 11.15.

Friday 6 November

Bit of scoring before going to RCM. to see Herbert Howells – show him Psalm 130 – he is very encouraging & nice. Meet a pupil of his – Lord (Howard de ?) Waldon. Go to Orchestral (in part~~)~~ vocal) rehearsal of Benjamin's opera – Devil Take her, in opera theatre. It's very amusing, & in places quite beautiful. Go for a walk after tea with Diana. Play Bridge with her & her grandmother, & Mrs. Fairley after ~~supper~~ dinner.

Lord Mayor's show.

Monday 9 November

Score more in morning, & bit in evening. Practise as usual in morning, & bit early afternoon; here. Go to R.C.M. at 3.0 to hear rehearsal of Bridge's opera "Christmas rose".[163] He conducts – I sit with Mrs. B. It sounds very attractive, & in parts v. beautiful. Back for tea at 4.30. Play a bit of viola & Vln. with Diana after tea; & some card games after dinner (including 3 handed Bridge with Mrs. Jonas). Ireland rings up at 10.15.

<u>Opening of Parliament</u>

Tuesday 10 November

Finish Haydn in morning, & take it to Ireland at lesson at R.C.M. at 11.10. Also have talk with Gordon Jacob on scoring. See Mr & Mrs Bridge before practising (with Lauricella 2.30–4.0 at N.SM) & after at 4.15 for tea and go to oculist (Bazil Reeves – Wimpole St.) with him at 5.0. I am to wear glasses for close-work. Get back here – via Bridges – at 7.30. Play (3 handed & then an invented 2 handed) Bridge with Diana & Mrs Jonas. Mrs Fairley goes away to-day.

Friday 13 November

Do alot more scoring before lesson at R.CM. with Ireland at 11.10 – which causes my eyes to go v. blurry & a beastly headache all day. Lie down until 3.0 in aft. & go to Whiteleys for hair cut. Aft. supper go in to a Miss Farquhar's niece's flat (Miss F. is living here) to meet alot of nieces & nephews & people – including Mr. Mrs & Miss Montague Nathan (he is secretary of Camargo Society). They are awfully nice. Get back abt. 11.45.

Saturday 14 November

Walk (to various Libraries – Boots & Public) in morning, 10.0. with Diana. Practise Pft & vla a bit after that. Go to take pts of my quartet to

Mr. Howard-Jones (to whom Mr. Ireland has shown my score) – as there is a faint chance of some quartet playing it over.[164] Diana & her Grandm. have a Mr. Jonas (cousin) to dinner, & I sit with them & afterwards. Walk with him (& D.) ~~go home~~ a little way to his home at 9.30.

Sunday 15 November
Church at St. Judes[165] at 11.0. After that walk to Marble Arch & back with Diana – to get some exercise! Go to tea with the Montague Nathans at 4.0 – many people there including Miss Farquhar. He looks at My ballet & says I am to send it to the committee of the Camargo Society (of which he is secretary) for consideration.[166] Write letters after supper,

Wednesday 18 November
Lesson with Benjamin at 12.20. Practise with Lauricella at N.S.M. all afternoon. Go (Frank Bridge takes me) to Q.H. to B.B.C. Symp. Concert at 8.15. Locatelli's Concerto di Camera in E^b. Gieseking in Bach. D min (not at all a good performance – dull & heavy) Schönberg 5 orch. pieces [Op. 16] (some quite fine – better than I expected – Colours – no. 3 [*Farben*] – marvellous) & a Dull & unscholastic (especially in treatment of grace notes in 2nd mov.) perf. of Beethoven's marvellous 7th symph. Orch. as before – material marvellous – but badly trained in ensemble & everything by that worst of all conductors (?) Adrian Boult

Thursday 19 November
Write & Practise here in morning. Go & see Bridges in afternoon, & then on to tea with Barbara at Selfridges (she also buys my birthday present there) & Madrigals. Write letters in evening, & also listen to Philharmonic Bach concert (Herbert Menges). Really quite good – excellent, superb, soloists, Concertos, F min (H. Samuel) & A min (Isolde Menges) – Both with supreme Slow mov. Marvellous Performance of 5th Brandenburg (above two with Gerald Jackson) & creditable, very, performance of 3rd Brandenburg – marvellous work.

Sunday 22 November [Lowestoft]
Birthday. Presents – Fur gloves (Mum & Pop) & choice of records – Stavinsky & Delius (ditto). Books – (Beth, Barbara Bobby, Lazy) – M.S. Paper (Maids & Nanny) – Money (Miss Turner 6/6). Church with Mum. at 11.0 – St. Johns. Finish scoring of "Plymouth Town" in aft. Miss Turner comes to tea – & Mum. & I walk home with her after. Walk with Pop after dinner; also play gramophone records – the Stravinsky, L'Oiseau de Feu Delius "Brigg Fair".[167]

Wednesday 25 November [London]
No lesson with Benjamin. Go to O.U.P to get Walton's Belshazzar's Feast – & to Langham St. (Cranz) to get Delius Serenade.[168] Practise with Lauricella in aft. Have tea with F.B. afterwards – he gives me the score of his 6^tet^.[169] Go to B.B.C. Symph. Concert at 8.15. Sit first 1/2 in area – Haydn Symphony 88 (G) & Mozart Symph. Concertante (Sammons & Tertis (2nd rather disappointing)) – both played with over 60 strings!! Rather ragged & uninspired playing under Boult. 2nd Half in stalls with Bridges (speak to V. Williams, Howells & Bliss) Holsts's – Hammersmith[170] – interesting. but not H. at his best. Walton's Belshazzar's Feast (National Chorus – mod. good) – very moving & brilliant (especially 1st half) – but over long – & to continuously loud – I felt, Back via Bridges at 12.0

Friday 27 November
Am up by 7.30 – breakfast at 8.0 & practise (to avoid people) 8.30–9.45. Write until abt. 12.30 & practise till 1.0. Go to dress Rehearsal of Benjamin's "Devil Take her" at College. (Trefor Jones & Sarah Fischer in chief parts – Beecham conducting) It is a very brilliant affair & comes off marvellously. Very effective on stage & humourous. Performance really very good. A very capable, amusing, if not great, work. Walk (to Boots) with Diana after tea. Write letters, & listen to ~~gramophone~~ wireless after ~~su~~ dinner. An amusing Cyril Scott operetta – Singing Sickness.[171]

Sunday 29 November
Leave Here at 11.30 to go to Harold Samuel at Hampstead for lunch & tea. Have marvellous time – he plays Partita in E min [Bach] to me (magnificent) & also I play (ugh!) some Schubert duets with him. Isolde Menges & Ivor James come into tea with him & to rehearse afterwards – but I go immediately after tea. It's frightfully foggy. Barbara comes to supper. After she goes I begin some variations (Sop. Cont. Vln. Vla. Pft) & a French Carol.[172]

Tuesday 1 December
Can only get 1 hrs. practice in morning & ¼ hr in aft. rest of time writing – go to R.C.M. at 4.0 for Pianoforte Technique exam (act. 4.45) – exam. Mr. Whitehead – scales & arpeggios – pretty mouldy. Go with Mr. & Mrs. Bridge to first performance of R.C.M. opera – Holst – Savitri[173] (rather dull, but beautiful in a way) & Benjamin's op. "Devil Take Her". Brilliantly done. Marvellous little work – every note comes off – charming & witty to a degree. The College students in it were not put in the shade by Trefor Jones (Poet) or Sarah Fischer (Wife) – excellent as they were – which is saying alot. Enthusiastic reception.

Wednesday 2 December

Practise for abt. ¾ hr. in morning, – score, – then lesson, v. good with Benjamin. Practise with Lauricella all aft. & walk with Diana after tea. Write letters & bath after dinner. More rows about my practising – people threaten to leave if it doesn't stop! It is all so stupid, because it could be perfectly simple if people could say straight out to me – "not to-day thank you", instead of going & moaning round Miss Wrist. As it is they tell me they don't mind it. The av. person seems to be a dishonest fool.

Friday 4 December

No lesson with Ireland again which I find out after tramping to the R.C.M. Finish Bridge copying[174] after lunch, & take it to him after practising 2.45–4.30 at N.S.M. Have tea with Mrs Bridge. Then he looks at the end of my score of Plymouth Town – which has to be sent in soon to the Camargo Ballet. He also gives me the vocal score of the "Christmas Rose" – marvellous thing. Read after dinner.

Saturday 5 December

Play tennis 12.0–1.0 at Cartwright gardens with Miss Gillespie – rather badly, but great fun. Rains in aft. which prevents me going with Diana for a walk. After tea begin copying out a Soprano part of my Carol Variations, which I finish after dinner. Listen to Wireless also after dinner – some very good Vaudeville & a bit of Tantivy Towers.[175]

Monday 7 December

Go for lesson with Benjamin at 12.40. ~~Pr~~ Score & copy out some more carol parts beforehand. Go at 2.0 to the dress rehearsal of Christmas Rose. It is a darling little work – but it is being done execrably (chorus & orchestra especially – Miriam however being very good). If well done it would come off admirably on the stage. Mrs Bridge & Miss Fass are also there, & I go home to tea with them & Mr. Bridge. Do some more copying after dinner. Mr. Ireland rings up about lesson (about time too – 3 weeks!)

Not v. satisfactory lesson with Ireland at 11.10.

Tuesday 8 December

Practise all afternoon at N.S.M. More copying out of carol after tea. After dinner I go with Barbara to R.C.M. to operas (sitting with Mrs. Bridge & Miss Fass) – Christmas Rose & Blue Peter (Armstrong Gibbs).[176] The performance vocally quite good (Miriam excellent)[177] orchestrally bad. C. Rose may not be an excellent opera from the stage point of view, ~~wh~~ but when there is little action the music is always sublime – & that is O.K. for me! the Blue Peter was an amusing little thing – merely Musical Comedy – clever in its way – but as different as anything from the adorable C. Rose.

Wednesday 9 December
Score a bit & then lesson with Benjamin at 12.20. Practise with Lauricella all afternoon. Go to B.B.C. concert (area ticket) at 8.15. Henry Wood. Haydn symphony (at usual break-neck speed & with usual battalion of strings) – Bach concerto E maj (Thibaud) – disgraceful performance – bad technically (rhythm out of control & intonation bad) & interpretively (impossible portamento). Thibaud was better in Chausson's long & sentimental Poem with orchestra. Delius' Song of High Hills – amazingly beautiful – incredibly long & monotonous even for Delius – but what marvellous sounds, he creates! Chorus (National) helped admirably in these.

Score in morning & pack in afternoon.
Thursday 10 December
Go at 6.15 to dinner with Bridges & then to Northampton Polytechnic institute (Clarkenwell)[178] for concert for poor people by Audrey Chapman Orchestra cond. by F.B. Amateur strings (marvellous) & prof. wind (quite good). They play Brahms Tragic ov. Schubert B min. Symp.[179] Dvorak Serenade for Strings (rubbish) & Tchaikovsky's adorable Romeo & Juliet.[180] Harold William's sings Non piu Andrai (Figaro)[181] not too ~~welll~~ well, but Song of the Flea (Moussorgsky)[182] marvellously so that it ~~had~~ has to be repeated. The orch ~~was~~ is magnificent althro', & F.B. of course superb. The performance of the Tchaikovsky drives me potty. Supper at Bridges & back by 12.0

Friday 11 December
Score more in morning, & Lesson with Ireland nominally beginning at 11.10 actually past ~~12~~ 11.45 as he was rehearsing a trio of his. Pack all afternoon, & Barbara comes after tea at 5.45 to finish it all for me. Go to RCM. in evening for 3rd performance of Bridge's Christmas Rose & Armstrong Gibbs' Blue Peter (awful tripe). I like the Xmas R. more than ever – altho' the second ~~Mir Miriam wasn't~~ Miriam was not as good as the first (Eugenie Walmsley). Go back to Bridges afterwards with Miss Fass, & Mr (just back from America) & Mrs Brosa. Back at 12.15.

Thursday 17 December [Lowestoft]
Walks with Caesar in morning, & then practise with Bazil (vla & pft) 12.15 – lunch (1.15). Viola concerto – bits of – (Walton). Delius – Hassan Serenade; Bridge – Melody (both orig. Vlc). Beth & I write invitations for a prospective

dance here, in afternoon. Also I copy out Vla. part of Carol Variations. Walk with Pop before dinner & before bed. Play bridge (Mum. Beth & Pop), in evening. I play with Beth.

Friday 18 December

Practise with Bazil & Charles (Vln Vla Pft) at Colemans at 11.0. Play ~~my~~ the acc. parts to my Carol-var & my two pieces (1930)[183] – both pretty measly. Play Badminton with Mrs. Boswell's club in afternoon 3–6 in Drill Hall; Besides Beth, Marj. Phillips; Doris Tamplin; & Elizabeth Jacquiers. Have some awfully good games – M. Phillips & D. Tamplin being marvellous. Walk with Pop after dinner.

Wednesday 23 December

Score in morning & then shop with Mum & Beth & car. All of us (including Mum. & Pop who go on to Southwold but are back to C's for tea) go in afternoon to Sotterly in car to Chartres; for holly picking. Get quite alot Tea at Chartres: back by six. More scoring before dinner.

After dinner Beth & I sing carols up this Road (from Wellington Esplanade). with Guild of Fellowship.[184] 8.30–11.0 (with food at Reeves). Get quite alot of money – quite fun – tho' I'm hoarse now.

Church 8.0 (St John's) (with Mum, Barb. Beth)

Friday 25 December

& 11.0 with Mum. Marvellous presents. inc. Petroushka & Minnie Maylow[185] (John Masefield) – Mum & Pop: Pencil. Beth – Mozart Vl. Vla. Symph – Laulie: Ride of Valkyrie[186] – Maids. Barbara gives me Monthly Musical Record[187] every month. Beth & I prepare for evening in afternoon. Mr & Mrs Sewell (Laurence & Fernande) & Teddy Rogers come to Xmas dinner. We have quite fun afterwards. Bed 12.30.

Saturday 26 December

Score more after breakfast at ~~8~~ 9.30 & before dinner. I finish the scoring of 150th Ps. & am quite pleased – now for no. 130. Walk with Pop. at 11.0 until lunch. Beth & I should have played Hockey in afternoon (arr. by Bill Arnold) but we have to stain the dining-room floor for Tuesday's dance & there is no other time. This we do & move various bits of furniture in aft. & after tea a bit. Mum & Barbara sing abit after dinner. Usual walk – bed.

Sunday 27 December

Walk with Pop & Beth & Caesar in country (ie. Golf links) in morning. Mum. Barb. go to St. Johns at 11.0.

Write letters most of afternoon & after tea. Read some of A.A. Milne's marvellous "If I May"[188] – the man's a genius.

Walk – Bed.

Tuesday 29 December

Walk with Beth up town in morning to Morlings to choose records (to hire) to play on hired Radio gram. for to-night. Various odd jobs – final movings for dance in aft. & after tea. Dance 8–1.0 In dining room. abt. 33 people come. I think it goes pretty well. After they have gone we put back majority of furniture getting to bed at 2.30 abt.

Wednesday 30 December

Morlings don't fetch back Radio Gramophone so spend much of the day listening to all our records & to wireless. In evening have stage-version of Eric – or little by little[189] – absolutely fatuous, but screamingly (unintentionally) funny.

Walk with Barbara in morning. Begin reorchestrating Psalm ~~130~~ 130 in aft.

Walk – Bed.

1932

Friday 1 January

More Scoring of Psalm 130 in morning. Beth & I go to Badminton Holiday club in aft. (about 12 there). Quite fun, but not excellent badminton. Pop, Mum, Beth & I go to St. Lukes dance for Nurses in evening at 8.0.

I come away and go to Phillips at 9.35 to listen on wireless to concert F. Bridge is conducting – marvellous – Rimsky-Korsakov. Scheherazade – brilliant. Sachs' Monologues & extracts from Act III Meistersinger.[1] What a conductor that man is – what tone he gets from his strings. After that the dance seemed deadly dull. But don't leave till 12.30

Wednesday 6 January

Practise a bit (Pft) & with Mum (singing) in morning & also score abit before Mr. & Charles Coleman (Pft & Vln) come in to rehearse for Saturday – Last 2 movements of Mozart concerto (E^{b}) (Vln Vla Pft).[2] Walk with Beth & Caesar in afternoon before: Mrses Phillips, Nicholson, Back, Coleman, Misses Astle & Goldsmith come to rehearse (2 part & 3 part-songs), for Sat. We do a Shipbuilders' Song of Holst (v. fine), an ordinary little Shepherd's Song of

W. Davis[3] & my variations on a French Carol, which really go v. well considering lack of balence, difficulty of reading French, & strangeness with any idiom except that of "I passed by your window" & Tosti's "good-bye". Beth & I should have gone to the Rouches to Whist, but car won't start & generally misbehaves. Play card games etc after dinner.

Thursday 7 January
Practise with Charles Coleman, chez lui, 10.0–10.45 for Sat. Hair cut at Priggs at 11.15. Go up to Morlings with Aunt Q before lunch to get 2 records of Petrouchka, marvellous music – playing quite good. L.S.O. Coates. Go to tea with John Nicholson at 3.0 for his gramophone & records. Hear Beethoven B^{b} (op 90 odd) Trio[4] (Cortot, Thibaud, Casals) Superb music & playing. Also Mendelssohn Concerto (Kreisler) – of course efficiently played. Back at 7.10. Bridge in evening. Walk with Pop – bed

Saturday 9 January
Beth & Mum do most of my packing (I help) before 11.30. Practise with Charles Coleman at his house for evening. 11.30. Walk with Mummy up town at 12.30–1.30. Practice with Mr. Coleman as well as Charles at their house 2.15–3.15. Walk with Caesar before tea. Go & see Miss Ethel after & practise pft abit. Musical Evening. at. 8.0. Besides ourselves 3 Colemans, Mrs. & John Nicholson Mr & Mrs Back (who both sing) Mr & Mrs. Owles. Mrs & Miss Phillips. 2 Miss Boyds. 2 Miss Astles (Miss Ethel plays). Miss Banks. Miss Goldsmith. Sing alot of Part Songs including My variations[5] – quite good! I play Ravel "Jeux d'eau" & Debussy "Reflets" & Franck Symp. Variations. Mum sings Ireland "12 Oxen" & Armstrong Gibbs "to one who passed Whistling". Quite a success. They go about 11.45.

Monday 11 January [London]
Pop Mum, & Beth take me down to station to catch 8.30 back to town. Arrive after good journey at 11.30, taxi to Burleigh House (which is very full) & then go straight to R.C.M for Director's address at 1.0. See Lauricella after. Go to New School of Music to arrange about practising, but I probably am going to have pft. in my room here (now I am top floor). Unpack abit after tea; I cannot much as I probably shall have to change rooms when one large enough becomes vacant. Go to Barbara after dinner, at 8.0 Listen to wireless abit; talk – write home; back at 9.45.

Tuesday 12 January
I am to stay in this room & so I unpack all morning, and arrange about Piano & what not.

Go to R.C.M. in afternoon at 2.15 & play with Lauricella until about 5.0 (Brahms Concerto move. & bits of Bridge Trio which we are going to play). Go to see Mr. & Mrs. Bridge after dinner – talk alot he lends me his Piano Trio Fantasy & gives me 2 pft pieces "Hidden Fires" & "Graziella".[6] Magnificent. Get back before 11.0.

Wednesday 13 January
My piano is brought in the morning. It fits in the room quite well. Score abit before going to R.C.M. for Lesson with Benjamin (pft.). Have a talk with him & Howells (& play Psalm 150). In afternoon go to Augeners to get Brahms Pft. Sonata 1. & Rachmanff Preludes (op. 32)[7] – 10/5!!! Walk all the way back by 3.30. Practise abit before & after tea & Score abit before dinner. Afterwards play card games with Mrs Jonas & Diana May (her grand-daughter). Early bed.

Sunday 17 January
Dr (Miss) Gillespie wakes me in time to go to 8.0 service at St. Judes. I go there again with Mrs. Jonas at 11.0. Quite a nice service. Mum, Pop, bring Beth in the car to start work to-morrow. The Former are sleeping at 183 Cromwell Rd. as there is no room here, but all food's here. Beth is going to live here. She hasn't her permanent room yet, but will have it tomorrow. Walk with Pop & Beth, to Beth's dressmaking acadamy after tea. Barbara comes to supper; & goes about 9.0 (¼ to-). Go to bed, all of us, early.

Tuesday 19 January
Mum & Pop leave by car at 10.30. I go with them as far as Baker St. to help them on their way. It's beastely that they've got to go. Return & finish scoring of Psalm 130. In afternoon I go to R.C.M. & play with Lauricella until 4.0 & then play trio (Bridge – Phantasy C min.) with addition of a 'Cellist – [Bernard] Richards, who is nice & very good. Great fun. We mean to do this regularly. Barbara comes in in the evening, to have a talk with us. Sit in Beth's room (no. 26) all evening.

Wednesday 20 January
Practise all morning before going to R.C.M. for very good lesson with Benjamin at 12.30. In afternoon practice abit & also begin a Phantasy 5^{tet} (first page only – rather unsatisfactory).[8] After tea I go to O.U.P. Bond St. to get some music (Bach Italian Conc. & a book on Strauss)[9] – Meet Beth & walk home. Listen to "Rope" on Wireless after dinner. Play by Patrick Hamilton[10] – very clever & thoughtful, & excellently done & acting marvellous.

Friday 22 January

Have about ¼ hrs. lesson with Ireland at (nominally) 10.35–~~12~~11.50. He spends the rest of the time telephoning, finishing someone else's lesson & talking about his concerto.[11] Practise Pft. all afternoon & after ~~even~~ tea.

In evening Beth & I go to Bridges to listen to a Busoni concert on wireless. very wretched Music (Violin Concerto & Turandot Sweet).[12] Back by 10.15.

Sunday 24 January

We [he and Beth] both sleep rather late & breakfast at 9.45. Both go to Church at St. Judes. Fernande Sewell calls to see us at abt. 12.0 but we are out unfortunately. Write letters in afternoon. Go for a walk before supper. Listen to pt. of B.B.C. symph. concert at 9.5 – Ansermet ~~and the~~ very good. Egmont ov. quite well played. 2 songs from Egmont (Irene Morden) quite well sung. Bach 2nd Brandenburg with E^b Cl. instead of Trumpet (most of time). One gained in confidence but missed the power & character of the trumpet – but the E^b Cl. sounds very like a small trumpet, & there was better balance. Honnegger's Symphony (1930)[13] to end with. Some amazingly beautiful ideas: but it seemed to me too complex. I liked the slow mov. best for one long broad string (afterwards brass) theme. Last mov. began well but meandered: beautiful ending – Delius!!

Tuesday 26 January

I write some more Phantasy in morning – more successful. Practise Pft. a bit also. Go to R.C.M. at 2.15 to Practise with Lauricella; at 4.0–5.0 do a bit of Trio with Richards. Go straight to Hampstead to dinner with Howard Ferguson at 6.30. Go to concert with Him & Gerald Finzi at Conway Hall The Erhart Chamber orchestra. Rather a bad show – orch. not very good R.V. Williams Charterhouse Suite. 3 Canzone Ricercate (R.O. Morris, which we went to here). V. contrapuntal & academic. A terribly long & meandering "Ode to Nightingale" for Strings, Pft & Tenor by Dorothy Erhart. & 2 ~~Grang~~ Grainger pieces.[14] Back by 10.45

Wednesday 27 January

Lesson with Benjamin 11.40. Practise before that. Write more Phantasy in aft. Go to dinner with Bridge's at 6.20. & to concert afterwards with them (Mr. Bridge coming at half time). Ansermet (Queen's Hall) conducting B.B.C. Eroica, badly played under not inspired conducting. Stravinsky Capriccio for Pft (Strav. himself) & Orch. Amusing but not much more. Marvellous Symphony of Psalms (Strav.) tho'. Bits of it laboured I thought but the end was truly inspired. Chorus, not too bad (National) & orch. better in 2nd half of programme. The performance left much to be desired tho' Ansermet was good. Back at 11.15.

Sunday 31 January

Go to the Zoo with Beth & Diana, leaving at 10.30 & getting back at 1.45. V. interesting & a lovely day. Go with Lauricella to a L.S.O. concert at Albert Hall – Beecham. Hänsel & Gretel ov. – charming. Haydn's delightful 3rd Symp.[15] v. well played. Delius' Pft. Conc. (Katherine Goodson). Don't like the work – Liszt & Tchaikovsky, not much Delius. ~~Barbara comes to~~ Beethoven Symp. 2 very well played. V. spirited under Beecham only first mov. too fast. Barbara comes to supper. Listen to Tchaikovsky's marvellous Romeo & J.[16] on wireless at 9.15.

Tuesday 2 February

I write more of the slow mov. of my Phantasy & also practise piano in morning. After walking a good way with Beth towards her acadamy.

Go to practise with Lauricella at R.C.M. in aft. & have great difficulty in finding a room. We have some quite good practise at the Bridge trio – it's less Greek than before now. Practise pft. a bit before supper, & do more vocal scoring in evening. I have just finished reading David Copperfield[17] again. It is an absolutely first rate book – inspired from beginning to end.

Sunday 7 February

Rather late breakfast. Go to Church at St. Judes' with Beth at 11.0. In afternoon Mr. & Mrs Bridge take me to Albert Hall to Berlin Phil. Orch. (Fürtwängler). Hackneyed Programme. Haydn London Symp. [No. 104 in D]; Wagner, Siegfried Id. & Flying Dutchman ov.; Tschaikovsky's Pathetic Symp. F's readings were exaggereated & sentimentalised (esp. so in last item – no wonder a member of the audience was sick!! The orch. ~~was~~ is a magnificent body, tho' slightly off colour to-day (~~N.B.~~ e.g. wind intonation, 1st Clar & 1st Horn). Strings are marvellous. Timpanist great. Marvellous ensemble & discipline

Go to tea with Barbara (also Beth) at her flat.

Back, walking, by supper.

Wednesday 10 February

Go to College after finishing Vocal score & practising at 11.40 for lesson (v. good.) with Benjamin & to give Vocal Score of both Psalms to R.V. Williams (teaching there. Go up to Augeners in aft. to get some music. Listen to Irelands Pft. conc. from ~~Boun~~ Bournemouth before tea. Practise Pft. after tea. Go to B.B.C. concert Queen's Hall (area). Beethoven's miserable King Stephan ov. miserably ~~play~~ played under Boult. Brahms Vln conc. (Busch – marvellous technically but as hard as nails with little feeling for music). Ireland's magnificent Mai-Dun – quite well played for the B.B.C. orch. Bax's new Winter Legend's (Harriet Cohen) longwinded rambling boring stuff – so feeble and dull after the Ireland.[18] Orchestra bad all evening; Boult worse. Come back via Bridges at 11.15.

Thursday 11 February

Walk with Beth as usual a bit in morning. Finish Phantasy, & practise the rest of day. Go to Bridges for supper at 6.30 & then. F.B, E.B, Miss Fass, & I go to Audrey Chapman Orch. at Northampton institute, Clarkenwell. F.B. conducts the most marvellous musical thrill of my life yet. Beethoven, ov. ~~L~~ Corolian, 9th Symphony (1st 3 movs) Elgar Serenade Strings (rather dull), Mozart Symp. Conc. Vln Vla (Isolde Menges & Bernard Shore – only moderate) & Beethoven Egmont ov. The strings (all amateurs!) were the best I have ever heard. The 2nd class Professional wind were quite good (3rd & 4th Horns especially in slow mov. of 9th). The Beethoven overtures were electric; but as for the 9th Symph. – !!

Back, via Bridges for supper, at 11.45. Beth waits up & we have some tea.

Wednesday 17 February

Practise all morning. R.C.M. rings up to say no lesson with Benjamin. Beth is still in bed, but abit better. Write a part song (canon) "Rainbow" in aft.[19] Walk with Diana after tea. Go (Area) to B.B.C. concert at 8.15, Queen's Hall. Henry Wood. Mozart Flute (typical up-to-date Mozart – presto & fff). Strauss's Master-piece of Characterisation Don Quixote.[20] Cassordo [Cassadò] solo 'cello. Quite good but not perfect. This work is too diff. for performance under modern conditions. 20 rehearsals are needed. Hindemith's Konzertmusic (Brass & Strings).[21] Some magnificent stuff & lovely scoring, quite well played. In 1st ½, Maggie Teyte sang Ravel's Schererazarde marvellously – gems of songs as they are. to end Concerto in G. min (Wood-Handel(!)) – Marcel Dupré. I suppose his playing was good.

Saturday 20 February

Beth's in bed all day but a bit better. Go & shop for a bit in morning. Finish "Ship of Rio" (Pt. song) after that. Alan Bush rings up about a Musical magazine "Pro Musica" & some things of mine.[22] English Madrigal Choir (Arnold Foster) gives a concert at Vict. & Albert. Mus. at 3.0.–4.15. All ~~Mag~~ Madrigals with some Pipe & Tabor Solos by Joan Sharpe. Not very good – we have done better than this. Have tea with Barb. (also singing in chorus) & Miss Hurst nearby, after & then I go to Liverpool St to meet Mum by 5.59. She stays here (come to see Beth). Barbara comes to dinner.

Monday 22 February

Beth's better & gets up in the room most of the day – tho' not properly dressed. Go with Mum to a Mrs. Barrett's to see a Pft (grand) that a Mrs. Audrey Melville is going to lend me here. Practise abit in morning. Go with Mum to Liverpool St. to see her on the 3.10 home. Come home via Queen's Hall for some tickets. Barbara comes in after tea, which I have with Beth. Sit with her after ~~tea~~ dinner. Do a bit of revising of pt. songs & Phantasy.

Thursday 25 February

I finish copying Phantasy in afternoon working most of aft. & morning when I'm not practising. Go out for a walk 12–1 with Beth. Go to Madrigals (meeting Barb. for tea at Selfridges) alone – Barb has cold. Go out afterwards to Phil. concert (Queen's Hall) – Malcolme Sargent – Idomeneo ov. & Surprise Symphony – tepid performances – rather bad in detail.[23] Ravel's New pft. concerto which I cannot take seriously. Brilliantly played by Marguérite Long & inefficiently conducted by Ravel.[24] The slow movement is piffle! Léon plays Eugene Goosen's attractive~~ly~~ Oboe Conc.[25] superbly as can only he. De Falla's El Amor Brujo, which wears very well, to end an interesting concert. Sargent not too bad in modern works seemed out of place in the classical.

Saturday 27 February

I walk across the park to Whiteley's to have my hair cut after breakfast. Afterwards do some more work – rewrite end of Ps. 150. Also go & return some records to Gertrude (Barbara's maid at Sloane Sq.) Howard Ferguson comes to tea at 3.30. Have talk & playing, & tea in drawingroom. V. nice. he goes at 5.45. In evening listen to wireless; Spencer Dyke quart[26] playing (roughly, lack of polish). Smetena's Aus mein Lieben – a fine tho' scrappy & long work. & Bridge's delicious Idylls. Also Leslie England plays (v. well) Brahms marvellous Handele var.[27]

Monday 29 February

I finish my copy of the 3 pt. songs in morning, before going to lunch with Hubert Foss at the Oxford University Press (Amen House) at 1.0 He looks at a good many of my things & keeps the part songs. I come back via the R.C.M. giving in my Phantasy for the Cobbett competition.[28] Go to the Bridges for tea & a talk, & to Barbara after supper until 10.15.

Tuesday 1 March

Lesson with Ireland at 10.35: have nothing to show him, except orchestrastion of Psalms, as I have been ~~doing~~ copying over the week-end. Go to R.C.M. via Augeners (to get Debussy quart.) at 3.0 to practise trio until 4.30. Do some quite good work at Bridge – lovely work.[29] I go to a concert at the Y.W.C.A. (Grt. Russel St.) with Mrs. Bridge (actually go with Mr. & Mrs. Brosa in taxi as well) Brosa Quartet~~te~~ – Haydn Emperor, Beethoven $C^{\#}$ (Miracle) & Debussy G. min.[30] They played superbly (except for a slip on part of new 'cellist – Meurice – in Beethoven). Brosa is, of course superb. Go back to a Mrs Pember(?) in Sussex Gardens, after for supper. A whole crowd goes including Bridges (+ Mr) Brosas & a very nice Miss Bowes-Lyons. Back before 2.0.

Friday 4 March

Mrs. Melville's pft. is brought here & my other taken away ~~by~~ between 10.15–11.15. Spend along time sorting out room – there really is quite alot of room in my room now surprisingly enough. Practise Pft in afternoon – also write home. Walk to R.C.M. ~~in~~ after tea with Diana to see if anything from V. Williams. Listen to Bartok concert broadcast 9.0–10.30. Suite no 1. contained some charming moments, but meandered 'a la Liszt &' Strauss much. Rhapsody (with composer at piano) more striking & the "Amazing Manderin" most original of all.[31] I cannot say I love this music, but it is amazingly clever & descriptive.

Sunday 6 March

Church at St. Judes with Mrs. Jonas & D. at 11.0. Do some writing in aft. var. on a theme of Bridge.[32] Barbara comes to tea – in Drawing room. Go to supper with Bridges & then (+ Brosas) to B.B.C Studio for orch. concert (F.B. conducting) Brahm's 3rd Symp. Orchestra rather poor. Isolde Menges in Amin. Bach. conc. – very good, but not my Bach – finally F.B. magnificent & lovely Enter Spring which the orch. played quite well. Beth comes back, by 6.25–9.15. Barbara's here to meet her, but gone when I get back at 11.15.

Monday 7 March

Work at Var. in morning. Practise Pft. in aft.

Walk with Beth a bit of her way to the Acadamy in morning & with Dian after tea. Listen to Leners (on wireless) playing Schubert D min. quart.[33] which irritated every feeling of taste I've got. Sentementalised, exaggerated, violated in every way – playing suited for a provincial Lyons. Debussy G min – followed was also bad – with shocking intonation. So much for them!

Wednesday 9 March

Practise Pft. before going to R.C.M. for a v. good lesson on Bach. Chromatic Fant. & Fugue with Benjamin at 11.40. In aft. I write one or two feeble variations, & begin a Violin & Viola concerto.[34] Also write after tea & a bit after dinner Then, I also write home & listen to a bit of a B.B.C. concert. Lamond playing Tsch. B^{b} min. conc. what appeared to be rather clumsily, also Berlioz's Carnival Romaine.

Sunday 13 March [Friston]

Long talk with Mr. Bridge in his studio in morning. Also walk with Mr. & Mrs. B. – Mr Graves (oculist) & secretary before lunch. Go to Miss Fass' in afternoon over the downs & tea at her house. Also play darts after tea. She comes to supper. We all listen to B.B.C. concert – Malcolme Sargent conducting ordinary performances of De Falla's 3-cornered hat – L'apres-Midi [Debussy] – Rachmaninoff 2nd concerto (Solomon – v. good) & Stravinsky L'oiseau de Feu After lunch Mr. Bridge plays alot of his things – including bits of his apparently beautiful Piano Sonata.[35]

Wednesday 16 March [London]

Practise Pft. before going to R.CM. at 11.40 to find Benjamin away examining. Go to Bridges for lunch to listen to broadcast performance of his Phantasy Quart. (Pft – F$^{\#}$)[36] Go to Queen's hall after to get rid of a ticket for Weigarner B.B.C. concert tonight. Go to Howard-Jones' after dinner. He has got the Stratton Quartet to try over my St. quart[37] and one by a Mr. [David] Cox. Considering it was sight-reading it was very good. I am v. pleased with it – it sounds more or less as I intended it. Back by 11.45.

Thursday 17 March

I do some altering & a good deal of addition to my 1st mov. of concerto in morning. Practise Pft in aft. Go to Bridge's to supper at 6.30 (Miss Fass is there as well.). All 4 of us go to Audrey Chapman Orch. concert at Clarkenwell which F.B. conducts. Lauricella & Richards also go; Mr & Mrs Brosa as well. Magnificent playing for an amateur orchestra from strings. Wind not so good – only 2nd rate professionals. Oberon ov. Brahm's Vln Concerto – Eda Kersey, a v. sensitive performance – showing wonderful promise. Meistersingers Apprentice's dance. Scheherezade (R. Korsakov) is amazingly well played considering that the wind had only 1 rehearsal. What wonders F.B. can do! Come back by 11.45 – via supper at Bridges + Brosas

Wednesday 30 March

Practise Pft. before going to R.C.M. at 11.40 for lesson with Benjamin. See V. Williams, who tells me that he cannot get my Psalms done where he was trying.

In aft. rewrite a bit of quartet & also listen to wireless (Bournemouth) Beethoven Concerto (Syble Eaton – disgraceful). & Bràhms-Ha~~d~~ydn Variations. Go for long walk after tea. Barbara comes in after supper.

Saturday 2 April [Lowestoft]

Leave at 9.0 to go to Liverpool St to catch 10.3 home arr. 1.37 after v. long journey – Met by Mum, Beth, Caesar & Car. Go to South Lodge Gymnasium Display after lunch (Mum, Beth & Self).

There are some very good boys there. Walk with Pop before dinner & before bed.

Tuesday 5 April

Go down to Church with Mum at 10.30; she to ~~decorate~~ do flowers with a cousin of Amories & me to meet a Douglas Fox (one armed organist – friend of Bridges) (with Mr. Coleman) for whom I turn over at Helen Amory's wedding at 12.45 at St. Johns. Mum & Beth also go & to the reception at Royal Hotel after – which I cut. Walk with Caesar in aft. Mum Pop Beth & I go to Marina in evening to see amateurs do "Rose Marie".[38] Quite good acting but some atrocious singing.

Thursday 7 April

Hair cut at Priggs at 11.0. Walk with Basil Reeve & Caesar before an early ~~bed~~ lunch at 12.45. Mum & I both go to Norwich. Mum with Mrs. Dance (in her car) & Mrs. Owles & I with John Nicholson in his car. We go to N.S.Q.C. concert. 2.45. Beethoven no. 1. in F; Dittersdorf E^{b}; Elgar.[39] Playing rather ragged & lifeless. Mrs. Alston is by far the best in a rather bad team. Elgar I didn't like – the Dittersdorf was amusing. Back by 6.15. Take Caesar for a walk before dinner. Walk with Pop before bed; & bath.

Monday 11 April [Worcester]

Rain most of day. Uncle S. [Sheldon Painter] is in bed until tea with bad cold, & without a voice. Read (or rather finish) the Hill – by H.A. Vachell – v. good,[40] if too full of Harrow & Sentimentality. Walk (by self) to station before lunch, & along river before tea. Most of the odd moments of the week-end have been spent in helping to do an enormous Jig-saw puzzle. Bed at 10.0.

Wednesday 20 April [Lowestoft]

Practise with Bazil & Charles in morning, after finishing Slow mov. Go with Bazil up to Morlings for 2. piano duets all aft. 3–5. Do Cesar Franck Symp. Var.; Brahms D min. conc. (1st mov.). Schumann Var. (2 Pft.). Beethoven 2nd Conc (1st & 3rd mov.). My arrangements of Bridge Sea suite (mov. 1 & 3) & Brahms 4th Sym. mov. 1.[41] Back to Reeves for tea. Play in garden aft. V. rainy day in spots. Pop goes to Marina. Mum to Flick with Miss Haes evening.

Saturday 23 April

Get by post, the min. score of L'apprenti Sorcier from Harold Reeves. Walk with Beth & Caesar before lunch. Mum & Pop go to Ispwich by car to see Aunt. Janie in aft. Beth & I go too, & take Alice to see her mother at Farnham.[42] Beth & I have tea at Restaurant. I borrow vocal scores of Elektra & Otello[43] (which used to belong to Uncle Willie). Arrive home abt. 8.30. Walk with Pop – bed.

Wednesday 4 May [London]

Finish the last mov. of my concerto before going to R.C.M. for Pft. lesson with Benjamin, but I expect I shall scrap it all. I find out that I have won the Cobbett prize – £13–13s to the better! Go to O.U.P. to get some music in aft. & come home & practise. Walk with Diana after tea. Listen to B.B.C. concert on wireless after ~~tea~~ dinner. Rather a shaky performance by Nat Chorus of Jesu, Joy & Treasure Motet. They certainly made a loud if not a joyful noise in the 9th Symphon (Beethoven). Boult conducts an uninspired performance (turn back) [because entry is concluded on previous page, under 3 May] Some instrument parts played v. well; but on whole v. ragged considering amt. of rehearsal. Boult is beginning to fool abt. with things – he has dropped his so-called "letting the music speak for itself".[44]

Sunday 8 May

I catch 12.10 from Marylebone to Gerrards X, where Sir Leonard Hill meets me & takes me to Chalfont St. Peter where his family lives – + Lady Hill & Nannett Hill. Have lunch & tea – with games of Badminton in garden in between & return by 5–5.8–620 with Nannett. Listen to B.BC. concert after supper Fogg – Bassoon concerto. Tho' well played by Archie Campden – I hate a whole work for Bassoon – anyhow there wasn't much music in it.[45] Dvorak's 5th Symphony[46] – which I really enjoyed in spite of it's being so hackneyed & some v. ragged playing. But Dvorak does things so well.

Tuesday 10 May

Lesson with Ireland, instead of last Friday, at 10.35. In the aft. Lauricella & Richards come to my room to practise Bridge Trio at 2.30 (I go to fetch them) – 4.0. Finish cutting back lawn & play tennis against wall with Mrs Fairly after tea. Go to dinner at 7.30 with Bridges, back from Friston for 2 days. He looks at some of my things (Phantasy & 3 Canons[47]) & lends me Meistersingers. Back before 12

Wednesday 11 May

Practise Pft. before going to R.C.M. for lesson with Benjamin at 11.40. Bit of Pft practise & Viola practise in aft. Rain most of day until aft. Roll lawn after tea. Go to Cinema (Kensington) with Diana after dinner – & see some utter tosh – Strictly Dishonorable.[48] Listen to Prelude to Tristan from Covent Garden, before dinner, under Beecham – Disgraceful![49]

Monday 23 May

Copy out Cello part of Scherzo[50] in morning, also bit of pft. practise. Go to R.C.M. in aft. to see people & on to Oxford Circus etc. to get music. Pft. practice after tea After dinner go with Hall to marvellous but terrible film, Kamaradschaft.[51] Enough to make one dream for ages.

Mum has big League of Pity[52] show at Sparrows' Nest

Thursday 26 May

~~Cop~~ Rewrite Part song no. 2 in morning before Lauricella & Richards come at 12.30 to practise for an hour. Pft practice in aft. Meet Beth at 5.0 & go up to Reeves where I pick up a second hand min. score of Tristan – marvellous work![53] Beth & I go to Kamaradschaft again in evening; even more impressing than before – if possible.

Friday 27 May

Lesson with Ireland in morning at 10.37 & investigate about coming Mendelssohn schol. Pft practice in aft. & copyout part song no. 3.[54] Walk with Beth to Ireland's after tea about Mendelssohn S. Play Mah Jongh with Mays (Mr. & Diana) after dinner.

Sunday 29 May

Beth gets up after breakfast & I go for a walk with her in the park, after doing some writing. Write home in aft. & read (David Copperfield for the umpteenth time). Go ~~to~~ with Barbara to Madrigal practise at 4.15. Have tea at Barbara's flat with Beth as well, & go on to Wesleyan Church Chelsea (where practise was) at 7.30 to give concert. (Same programme as last Sunday). When back here listen to Brosa's on wireless playing Schubert A min quart. beautifully. Battery runs down before I hear Borodin no II.[55]

Tuesday 31 May

Send off my entries for Mendelssohn Schol in morning (2 Psalms – score: Phantasy 5^{tet} – Cobbett: & 3 Sop. Songs – Vocal Score).[56] Practise Pft after that. Lauricella & Richards come in aft. We practise my Phantasy Scherzo all time. Listen to Act, I of Mastersingers on wireless after dinner.[57] What struck me most is what little attention anyone paid to the written music. Beckmesser v. good – Habich; & Schorr as Sachs & Lehman as Eva – what little I heard of them.

Wednesday 1 June

Practise Pft before lesson with Benj. at 11.40. He gives me Walton Symph. Conc. & Schuman Phantasy to work at. Begin a partsong (I loved a lass) in aft.[58] After tea I go to Augeners & Chesters to get music (De Falla – El Amor Brujo) – walk back thro' park – marvellous day. More pt. song after dinner. Also listen to Wireless – Saint-Saëns Carnval des Animaux – and a wonderful, impressive but terribly eerie & scary play "The Turn~~ing~~ of the Screw" by Henry James.[59]

Thursday 2 June

Finish 'I loved a lass' in morning – quite pleased with it. Trio practise here at 12.20–1.30 with Lauricella & Richards – work at my Scherzo all time. Pft in aft. Walk with Diana in aft. (Her parents have gone to Lowestoft). Listen to Act I of Tannhauser in evening – tolerable, but bad singing of Tannhauser & Das Hirt (why not a boy for this?)[60]

Friday 3 June

Go to R.C.M. at 10.0 & Lauricella & Richards & I play my trio to Ireland who is pleased with it. Have lesson with him 11.0–12.0. In aft pft. & walk after tea with Beth. In evening listen to wireless – a very amuzing Musical Comedy skit – the Pride of the Regiment by Walter Leigh.[61]

Sunday 5 June

Church with Beth at St. Judes at 11.0. & walk after with Diana & her. Write letters in aft. Barbara, Diana & Beth & I all have tea in Beth's room. Walk with Beth after supper, & listen to Kutcher St. Quartet playing, raggedly, Haydn G min (74. no 3) & Brahms A min.[62] Sarah Fischer also sings.

Monday 6 June

Pft. lesson, after pft. practise, at R.C.M. with Benjamin at 11.40 to make up for one missed last term – on Walton Symp. Conc & Schuman Phantasy.[63] Write another part song (The Sad-day)[64] in afternoon. Walk with Diana after tea. A friend of hers comes to dinner (& Mrs Cooper) & we four play Mah-Jong after ~~sup~~wards

Thursday 9 June

Rotten day for writing. Only write a putrid song after tea.[65] Trio practice 11.30–1.30. (Lauricella alone for 1 hr). Good work at Bridge Scherzo. I practise Pft abit in aft.

Barbara, Beth, & I go to His Majesty's to see "Dubarry" at 8.15.[66] V. spectacular Musical Comedy. V. entertaining but not exactly intelleigent. Anny Ahlers is most attractive & Heddle Nash sings well Back by 11.30

Saturday 11 June [Friston]

Play abit of tennis with Mr. Bridge before lunch, after a long talk with him. We four (Mr & Mrs B. & Miss Fass) go to Eastbourne in aft. to see pt of U.S.A. v. gt. Britain Tennis. U.S.A win 4–1 (matches). We see S.B. Wood bt. H.W. Austin. 6–3, 3–6, 6–4, 6–4 (?). Incredible play – unbelievable. Austin gave the impression of being the greater master though out of practise. After, Mauglin [Gregory S. Mangin] (U.S.A). bt Oliff [John Olliff] in 3 sets. Rain prevents us having tennis after tea. Listen to wireless after Hazard (Com. Stoker of Dardanelles fame)[67] & Tannhäuser from Rome.

Monday 13 June

Pft practise at Miss Fass' for a bit before going to Willmington[68] in her car, from there. Mr. & Mrs B. & I walk back here (all but a bit at this end) abt. 4 miles, while Miss Fass paints.

Tennis here in aft. & also after tea. Wireless ~~and also~~ after supper at Miss Fass'. Here [hear] Sir Francis Floud's talk in "Rungs of Ladder".[69]

Wednesday 15 June [London]

Pft practise before going to R.C.M. for lesson, v. good, with Benjamin at 11.40.

In aft. I start, unsatisfactorily, a new Ballet[70] (by Miss Alford) but can't make much head way with it. Walk with Beth after tea.

Friday 17 June

Go to R.C.M. to find Ireland not there at 10.0. Return, after listening to a bit of a Patron's Fund Rehearsal, to pft practise. Bit more of that in aft. & also read much poetry (on roof – on acct. of marvelous weather) on off chance of finding something to set to music. Beth & I go up to Oxford St. for her to shop aft. tea. Getting some stalls thro' Lauricella, Beth & I go to "Hiawatha"[71] at Albert Hall. Taxis both way, as we change. An amazing show. V. impressive.

Monday 20 June
I begin a movement which might be a bit of a Chamber symphony in morning.[72] Practise Pft in aft. Go up to Hawkes[73] after tea & get Kodaly's Psalmus Hungaricus – marvelous work.[74] Beth goes to Hampstead to play tennis with Kathleen Mead after tea. I listen to a Vaudeville on wireless and write letters after dinner. Too full of Psalmus to write music!

Wednesday 22 June
Practise Pft. before going to R.C.M. for Pft. lesson at 11.40. Hear from R.V. Williams that he can't get my Psalms done anywhere.[75] Write more Symph. in afternoon. Walk with Beth after tea. Go to R.C.M. with her at 8.15 for part of Chamber concert. Stravinskys 3 pieces for Str. Quartet[76] (marvelous works) are creditably (not more) played by a quartet including Richards. Then a dismal, disgraceful in technique & musicianship, performance of "La Folia" by R.C. Onley.[77] A dull Cantata ("Non sa che sia dolore" – but it might have been in Sanscrit) by Bach followed.[78] After that we fled.

Friday 24 June
Bobby & Marjorie have a son born yesterday.[79] Great rejoicings. Go to. R.C.M. for good lesson with Ireland in morning. Practise Pft all aft. & walk with Beth. After supper we meet Kathleen Carter and go to Gaumont Palace ~~Theatre~~ Cinema, Hammersmith. Amazing no. of shows for money. 2 films – including news – & three stage shows – all pretty putrid tho' – including De Groot

Saturday 25 June
Practise Pft. & walk with Beth in morning. In aft. we queue at Drury Lane for Cavalcade[80] at 2.30. (Gallery 2/-). Magnificently produced – & with some fine & moving ideas. Not an especially great play tho'. Walk back to Hyde park – via Embankment & ~~grat~~ St. Jame's Park. Barbara comes to dinner.

Tuesday 28 June
Barbara makes arr. for Pop to go & see a specialist – because of his trouble[81] – a Mr. Cassidy – v. good. She comes round early in the morning. We all go with Pop – Beth & I shopping whilst he is seen. the Dr. does know what's wrong – v. cheerful! They go home after lunch – Beth going with him to help with the driving. I practise with Lauricella & Richards in aft. Barbara rings up after ~~supper~~ dinner. Austin beats Sheilds (U.S.A.) at Wimbledon – great rejoicings. V. hot day.

Thursday 30 June
Write more of slow mov. in morning, afternoon & after dinner – practically finishing it. Lauricella & Richards come 12.30–2.0. Good work at Bridge.[82] Meiklejohn of Gresham's comes to see me after tea – very pleased to see him.

Austin beats Satoh at Wimbledon, thus being in final – greater rejoicings! Rain at last, tho' still hot.

Friday 1 July
Finish Slow mov. of concerto [for violin, viola and orchestra] before going for lesson with Ireland at RCM at 10.35. Afternoon listen to a Patron's Fund Rehearsal. Grace Williams' 2 Psalms[83] – in competant music – Delius. Go to Bond St. for Beth & return via. Whiteleys for hair.cut in aft. Practise Pft also a bit. Nannette Hill (daughter of Sir Leonard) comes to dinner, & we both go (tickets given by Lady Hill) to the Ballet (Carmargo etc.) at Savoy Theatre. Not particularly impressed by Fête Galante of ~~Glik~~ Glinka. Tchaikovsky's Lac des Cygnes was effective & Anton Dolin danced v. well in this & Lord of Burleigh (Mendelssohn – arr. E. Evans)[84] which was very amusing.

Monday 4 July [Lowestoft]
Pop still the same with aches and pains. Write more of last mov. of symph. in morning; & Beth & Diana & I bathe from hut at 12.0. Walk with Beth & Caesar up town in aft. After tea Beth gives me some lessons in driving the car the other side of ~~Cal~~ Carlton After that we bathe (Diana as well) at 6.0. Cold but fun. Bridge abit after dinner

Thursday 7 July [London]
Write more of last mov. in morning & aft. Lauricella & Richards come to practise 11.15–1.30. Do good work. Beth & I go to Booseys after tea to see abt. a presentation Baton from Lowestoft Musical Soc. to Mr. Coleman.[85] Write home & listen to wireless after supper. Prokofiev's attractive overture on Yiddish Themes, a Bax carol, Elizabeth Maconchy's ordinary Pft concerto (Kathleen Long) some amazing Begger Songs of Hermann Reutter. Pft solos of Bartok & Walton's Delightful & attractive Façade.[86] Performances on the whole inadequate under Stanford Robinsons – except for the Wireless Singers who sang brilliantly

Saturday 9 July
Writing all aft. & after tea I finish my Symphonietta for 10 intruments. Beth & I go to Clapham Common to play tennis (practice) 11.0–12.30. V. Hot. We go in the Gallery of the New Theatre[87] to see Twelfth Night in evening. 8.30

Marvellous show – very funny, & superbly acted – Jean Forbes-Robertson (Viola) & Phyllis Neilson-Tery (Olivia) & ~~Malvolio~~ Arthur Wontner (Malvolio) being especially good.

Monday 11 July

Begin to score my Symphonietta in morning. V. Hot day with Thunderstorms. Practise Pft in aft. Go to R.A.M. [Royal Academy of Music] Marylebone Rd. ~~for~~ at 5.0 to hear result of Mendelssohn Scholarship with 2 Others (inc. Grace Williams & a Mr. Baxter). Complete~~ly~~ fiasco. Owing to a muddle at beginning between Dr. Sargent & Walter O'Donnell the proceedings have to start from beggining again, so we wont hear until September. Marvellously efficient!! Beth & I go to dinner with Hanworth at Temple[88] at 7.0. Great time Dr. (Mrs). Hanworth & Mr. Hanworth & Dr's sister Dr. Wallace there. Back by 11.~~25~~30

Tuesday 12 July

Still very hot – R.C.M. for lesson with Ireland. He's very pleased with my Sinfonietta. Write home before lunch. Trio practise here in aft. Do more scoring of my Sinf. after dinner.

Wednesday 13 July

Pft. lesson; after pft. practise in morning at ~~1140~~ 11.40 at R.C.M. with Benjamin. In it I also play B. & Herbert Howells my sinfonietta, of which they approve. Spend rest of day copying out Sinf., except after dinner when I go & see the Bridges, back in town for a few days. Beth ~~gos~~ goes to Barbara.

Saturday 16 July

Ring up Anne Macnaughten abt. the concerts of British Work[89] at which they're probably going to do my Sinfonietta. I finish Copying this in morning, aft. & after tea. Beth & I meet Barbara at Selfridges for some iced elevenses. I buy a vol. of Grave's marvellous poetry. Barbara comes in evening. Beth is out to dinner, with Elinor Bond.

Sunday 17 July

Beth & I go to church at St. Judes at 8.0. I rewrite a Song. Elizabeth Ann[90] in morning. Barbara, Beth, & I, catch 12.10 to Gerrade's Cross where Sir Leonard Hill meets us & takes us in car to his house at Chalfont St Giles, where we spend day. Play Badminton with Nan & Sir Leonard in aft & After tea. Catch 5.58 back arr. here abt. 7.15. Write home & begin to copy out Pt Song "I loved a lass", after supper.

Monday 18 July

Walk abit of the way with Beth to her academy in morning. I finish "I lov'd a lass", & write a new part song to go with it "The Lift Boy" – R. Graves.[91] Anne Macnaghten comes to see me before lunch – she is going to do either my Quartet (1931) or the phantasy quintet.[92] Practise Pft in afternoon. Walk after tea. Copy out Elizabeth Ann after ~~supper~~ dinner.

Tuesday 19 July

I rewrite bit of my intro. & allo. for Trio (alias Phant. Scherzo) in morning, & copy out "Lift-boy". Richards & Lauricella come in aft. Don't do much work. Bridge trio no. 1., & Mozart Pft. quart.[93] Walk ~~with~~ in Park after tea. Kathleen Carter comes to dinner, & Barbara comes after – Card games etc.

Wednesday 20 July

Go to College at 11.0. for comp. Exam. Examiners. R.V. Williams, S.P. Waddington & Ed. Bainton. Richards, Lauricella & I play my Intro. & All^{o}. to them, & they see my Ballet, Sinfonietta, 2 latest pt. songs, etc. Seemed quite pleased Go to H.M.V., Regent St. to get gram. records in aft. intending to get Till Eulenspiegle. I get Stravinsky's great Psalm Symphony.[94] Come back via. Hair cut at Whiteley's Rewrite bit of old Quart[95] after dinner.

Thursday 21 July

Practise Pft. before the Trio comes at 11.30 to practise until 1.30. We do Bridge Quintet[96] & Mozart Pft. Quart (G min.). I pack all afternoon. After tea I go for Second Study Pft. exam (examiners – Benjamin – Bainton & another – horrors!) at 4.30. Come back via Anne Macnaghten's, where I leave my old Quartet. I find that I have won the Sullivan prize[97] (£10) cheers! Pack after dinner & write letters.

Friday 22 July

Go to R.CM. at 10.30, after finishing packing etc. to hear ~~result of~~ competition Cobbett prize – performance of my 5^{tet} – bad – but I expected worse. Ivor James & Waddington there – including Cobbett himself. The Trio (Lauricella & Richards) & Beth & I set off for Friston at 1.0 from 173. C.R. [Cromwell Road] in Richards car (Beth helping him with the driving) arr. after good journey at 5.0. We 3 stay at Miss Fass' & Beth with B's. Tennis after tea, & games after supper

Saturday 23 July [Friston]

Practise Trio from 9.30–11.30. & tennis at B's after that. We all picnic at Willmington at David (giant) for lunch. Come back & Mr. B. Miss Fass & Beth, Bernard & I bathe in sea. Tennis after tea (with Mr. B, Beth, Miss Fass

& Bernard). After supper at Miss Fass' we play (with F.B as a superb Vla & Mrs B. as Vl. 2) Mozart Pft. quartet in G min & Bridge Pft. Quintet – marvellous fun.

Sunday 24 July

Pelting with rain & wind all day. We practise my Phant. Quintet (me playing Vla. 2!!) in morning. Lunch at B's play about in garden in rain in aft. with Bernard. Mr. Graves & Miss Spiling come over after tea. After supper & tea more playing – my ~~Phant~~ Intro, & Allo. for Trio, Bridge Phant quartet (Pft) & his marvellous trio in which he coaches us.

Late bed.

Friday 29 July [Lowestoft]

Finer day – less rain. Practise Pft in morning & walk with Beth up town. My Sinfonietta arrives, beautifully bound. Finish copying out Flute pt. in evening & write letters. Bobby & Marjorie & son John arrive 5.54 from Prestatyn. Met by Beth & Mum in car. The son is a trouble in evening. Walk with Pop before dinner & with him & Bobby before bed.

Saturday 30 July

I have vocal score of Stravinsky's great Psalm Symph sent from Chesters. More copying of Horn part of Sinf. in morning. Walk with Beth, before Bathe with her & Mum at 12.30. In aft. Beth & I go to tennis party at Mrs. Dance's. Not v. excellent tennis. Among those present ~~was~~ is Mrs. Owles. John cries alot in evening. Walk with Pop before bed.

Sunday 7 August

I go to help Ethel Boyd at St. Johns at 10.0 with the Children's Holiday Fund, as last Sunday. Not nearly as good tho', as the service was taken in a sentemental ~~egga~~ exaggerated, Sankey & Moodeyish manner by the Church Army. Church after at 11.0 with Mum. Bazil Reeve comes in afterwards to hear Strav.'s Psalm Symph. Read more 'Grub St.'; & bit more copying in aft. Walk with Pop, Bobby, & Beth after tea, to club. Grub St. in evening & walk with Pop.[98]

Tuesday 9 August

Finish 2nd Fiddle part in morning (only 2 more, thank heaven!), & practise Pft. Bathe with Bazil Reeve, & Mum & Beth before lunch. Also Bathe with Chartres (Mr., Clive & Jean) when they (+ Mrs.) come over to tea down at hut. Pop takes Mum, Beth & me to Sparrow's nest to see "Mr. Cinders" – musical comedy.[99] Very amusing & principal parts, very good.

Laurence is ill, & Pop has his work to do.

Thursday 11 August

V. hot day. Have 4 strenuous sets of tennis with John Nicholson in morning on his court. Go st. down to huts after, to bathe with Beth & Kathleen Mead – v. warm, at 12.30. Beth & I go to tennis, in car, at Chartres (Sotterley) at 3.30. Have quite good tennis. Back by 7.25. After dinner I run into Boyd's to hear F.B's 'Blow out you Bugles'[100] (sung by Frank Titterton, very well), from Promenade Concert – conducted by him. Seemed very fine. More copying afterwards, & walk with Pop Get Walton's Portsmouth Point, ov., on gram record.[101] Disappointed. Ineffective & apparently bad & careless workmanship.

Monday 15 August

Beth & I take the two Davids (see yesterday) [Boyd and Gill] to a picnic given by the Boswells (taking one's own nourishment) at Winterton. Arrive at about 12.15. Bathe before lunch, & before tea. Great fun, v. rough. Rounders in aft. Back by 7.0. Great fun. David (alias "Terry") Gill is a nice boy.

Read some Ingoldsby Legends[102] in evening. Early bed. Long letter from F.B.

Tuesday 16 August

Practise Pft. & Viola in morning & bathe with Mum & Beth before lunch. In aft. Beth & I go to Normanston Park[103] to help the Boyds entertain the slum children from town (see previous Sundays). Play cricket with them, & arrange races for them. Quite fun. They are nice children. Back by 7.0. Write letters after dinner.

Friday 19 August

Walk before breakfast as usual with Caesar – this time with Ethel, David & John Boyd as well. Go up town in morning to Boots, Morlings, & Public Library,[104] where I pick up 2 books of Lyrics (Elizabethan & 17th cent.)[105] for 2/6 instead of 10/6 each! Bathe with Beth & Cyril Reeve. V. rough but fun. V. hot day as yesterday. I go to tea with Reeves to meet a Christopher Gledhill from Oriel (Bazil's college). Go to "Mata Hari" at Palace[106] with Beth to see Greta Garbo. She is most attractive, I suppose, but what slop!

Yacht-club regatta week.

Monday 22 August

Pft. practise before going to Bungay in car with Beth at ~~11.30~~ 12.0 We play in Tennis Tournament.[107] Our Handicap Singles take place to-day; both of us lose. Beth (playing v. well) to Elizabeth Nicholson 7/5 - 6/2. & I (playing atrociously) to a Mr. Watts 6/4 - 6/4. Quite fun tho'. Back by 5.0. Go up to Morlings after tea. Walk with Pop before bed.

Tuesday 23 August

As Pop is going to Southwold (because Laurence is ill with quinsy)[108] we can't have the car; & the Nicholsons take us over to Bungay. We don't play our mixed Double until abt. 12.30 & then we very stupidly loose 6/2, 1/6, 6/1. to Lt. Col. & Miss Eardly-Todd. After watching some more matchs David Boswell brings us back by 5.45. Walk with Barbara before dinner. Dr & Mrs. McNab come to coffee. We putt opposite.

Thursday 1 September

My records of "Sacre du P." arrived yesterday.[109] They are magnificently played in spots, but the speed seems unreasonable in places, eg. The Dance of the Earth, where the 8 Horns are left high & dry struggling. To-day Mum, Barb. Beth (driving), & I go to the Priests[110] at Harleston, at 12.30 We have lunch up the river & tea in the house – owing to rain. Back by 7.0 Bath before dinner. Right thro' the "Sacre" after.

Friday 2 September

Go up to Morlings & Library after pft. practise in morning. At former I pay for the World's Wonder (Sacre – 24/-) & at the latter, I get some Ravel pft. music. In afternoon John & David Boyd come to tea on beach. Mum Barb. Beth & I bathe.

Friday 9 September

Masterson is making me some Tails (bought with my Sullivan Prize) & I have them fitted in the morning. Begin abit of a new Phantasy[111] (doubtful) & Bathe with Mum & Beth before lunch. In afternoon we have a tennis party – up at the tennis.club at 3.0–6.30 Barbara Spashett, Mrs. Speak & T.J.E. Sewell come. Have tea up there.

Marvellous day after pelting rain until 10.30 a.m.

Saturday 10 September

Mum goes to Ipswich to see Aunt Janie's new house,[112] by bus starting 9.45 arr. back 6.30 Go up town before lunch to libraries. From the public I get Cecil Gray's Contemporary Music.[113] Very fine, but I don't altogether agree with everything he says. Read this & walk with Caesar ~~up~~ in afternoon. Pop goes to the Hospital to be X-rayed after tea at 5.0.[114] Beth & I go with him in car.

Monday 12 September
Rewrite bits of my 5^{tet} Phant. in morning & walk with Mum before an early lunch at 1.0. Beth & I go out to a joint picnic with Boyds – Ethel & Mrs (Junior) & David & John. In the 2 cars. We go to a place near the river at Beccles. Blackberries – & general fool about. Aunt. Queenie arrs. by 6.10. We have a Radio- Gramophone on approval – Pop is going to buy one. But it is anything but satisfactory.

Monday 19 September [Lowestoft/London]
Catch. 8.30 to town. Beth takes me to Station in car & Mum to see me off. Arr. 11.30. Go to R.C.M. for Allen's termly address. at 1.0. See Lauricella. Unpack all afternoon. After tea I go shopping with Mrs. Millar. Listen to a Wagner Prom after dinner on a very bad wireless. Mastersinger ov. Bachannale, Siegfried Idyll. Hagen's Songs[115] (Norman Allin). Funeral March & finale from Götterdämmerung (Florence Austral) – orchestral playing rough, but some good wind playing.

Tuesday 20 September [London]
I write more of my Oboe Phantasy[116] in morning & practise. Bernard Richards & Lauricella come in afternoon & we read through Ravel's Trio.[117] Walk with Lauri after tea. After dinner I listen to Prom on wireless – British Programme. Delius' marvellously beautiful, tho' meandering & too long, Song of the High Hills, completely dwarfs the rest of the aenemic programme – Cyril Scott's dismal Noel, Elgar's typical Sea pictures & Ethel Smyth's "Aubrey Brain". Vl & Hrn. Concerto.[118]

Thursday 22 September
Practise Pft before going to R.C.M. for a rehearsal of my Sinfonietta at 11.0 in Mr. Buesst's class. I have never heard such an appalling row! However when we have a flute & a 'cello & when the players have looked at their parts, I think it will be all right. Another fruitless attempt to ~~finish~~ continue the Phantasy in the afternoon. Walk after tea, round about the place. Beth & I go to Barbara after ~~sup~~ dinner.

Friday 23 September
Lesson with Ireland at 10.35. Practise Pft. in afternoon. Ring up Hubert Foss about the Agreement re. my pt. songs.[119] Walk with Beth after tea. Listen to Beethoven Prom on the atrocious wireless here. Beethoven's 1st & 8th Symphonies played without care or thought. Ria Ginster sings the 2 "Egmont" songs, & Myra Hess plays the 4th Conc. Write letters also.

Saturday 24 September

Bit of pft. practise in morning & walk – shopping – with Beth. After lunch we go on a river-trip, with Mrs. Millar, down to Greenwich from Westminster. Very int. all thru' docks. Start at 2.30, back by 4.45 with 45 mins walk at Greenwich. Walk back from West. via the Tate Gallery. See a marvellous picture of a "Dead boy", by Alfred Stevens (?).[120] Go to Barbara after dinner, hear bit of Prom. concert.

Thursday 29 September

I go to R.C.M. at 11.0 for the most execrable rehearsal of my Sinfonietta without proper D.blbass & flute this time. In afternoon I practise with Lauri & Bernard at Ravel at R.C.M. 3–4.10. ~~Go~~ Meet Barbara at Selfridges & then go to Madrigals with her. Whole lot of new stuff. Back for dinner at 8.0. Beth has Elinor Bond to dinner.

Friday 30 September

Write more Phant. before going to R.C.M. for good lesson with Ireland at 10.35. & in afternoon, & abit before bed. After tea I go to Augeners & return via the Bridges, when I post some music to the copyists for F.B. (they are at Friston). Listen to a typical Beethoven Prom. on putrid wireless hear. Leonora 3. Tremati Trio[121] (not first rate B. but jolly in spots) & 9th Symphony Whole programme done with Woods usual exaggeration & lack of detail. The chorus was heroic if naught else.

Saturday 1 October

I spend morning scraping ~~off~~ old green paint off my book-shelf & start painting it black. In afternoon Beth & Barbara go to the Zoo with some small child. I spend aft. in Tate gallery until abt. 5.15. See some great pictures. Listen to Last "Prom" on wireless after dinner. Gigantic enthusiasme for Wood. Chief features of a rowdy programme – Dennis Noble's wonderful singing of Largo al factotum (Rossini) & the Ravel Bolero.

Friday 7 October

Go to Anne MacNaghten's to fetch my 5^{tet} on the way to R.C.M. before lesson from Ireland. at 10.35. Write more Oboe Phantasy in afternoon. Walk with Beth after tea. Write letters & listen to amusing play on wireless "House Party" by Frances Poulenc (Les Biches) & Denis Freeman.[122]

A new suit arrives for me from Mastersons – Blue.

Tuesday 11 October

Practise Pft & Rewrite bits of Phant. in morning before going to hear a Rehearsal of Anne MacN's quartet at 12.0 at her house. Practise Pft in afternoon. Go to St John's Institute at 5.0. for a Concert of the Music Club: – Mangeot's International St. Quart. (pretty poor) play some Locke & Purcell & then with B.B.C. wind a long meandering Pastoral Phantasy by Helen Perkin who plays Ireland's fine Sonatina rather poorly, & with Mangeot Delius' 3rd Sonata.[123] Also a work by ~~Warlock~~ Van Dieran in memory of Warlock with John Goss etc.[124] Go straight to Sadler's Wells, where I have a bit of a meal (meeting Kenworthy – late of Holt) & meet Bridges (up in town for a few days) and go to Ballet at 8.0. V. good Ballet with Anton Dolin & Markova etc. [Britten leaves a long gap here] by Gretry,[125] rather uninteresting. Manhattan Serenade, [126] solo by Dolin – marvellous. Poor music by Geoffrey Toye in a very amusing "Douanes" with Dolin & Ninette de Valois.[127] Sylphides[128] to end with. Back with Bridges to supper.

Wednesday 12 October

Practise Pft. before going to R.C.M for lesson with Benjamin at 11.40. Hubert Foss (of O.U.P.) comes to lunch at 1.0. Play him my Oboe Phant. after & show him my Antithetical Songs.[129] Begin to copy out my Intro. & Allo. for trio[130] in afternoon & after dinner. Walk with Beth before dinner.

Thursday 13 October

More copying before going to R.C.M. in morning for the most atrocious of all rehearsals of my Sinfonietta. Only 8 inst. out of the 10 (& of these 3 new!). What an institution. Rehearse there in aft. with Bernard & Remo. Meet Barb. & Beth at Selfridges – tea – Madrigals with Barb at 6.0 – Dinner with Bridges with moaning about R.C.M. Back by 10.30.

Friday 14 October

Lesson with Ireland at 10.35 – v. good & after, we go & see Mr. Waddington & new arrangements are made that my Sinf. should sound less like ~~an anaem~~ aenemic cats. Copy out in afternoon until 3.15 when I go to ~~Sel~~ Whiteley's to have my hair cut. After tea write home. Go to Bridges at 7.0 & with Miss Fass we go to B.B.C. Studio at Waterloo Bridge, where at 8.0 F.B. conducts a concert. Frank Titterton with a magnificent voice sings two F.B. Songs – Adoration & Love went a-r. – heavenly things, & the Prize song.[131] Leonora 3 (taken slower than usual – with gain in effect) Borodin Symph. no. 2 (not particularly impressing as a work but the playing was, in spots delightful) & an exuberant perf of Rimsky's Wedding March from Coq D'ore Back to 4. B.G's[132] for supper until 11.45.

Sunday 16 October

~~Ca~~ Walk with Beth before catching 1.0 train to ~~Rickmean~~ Rickmansworth with Alan Frank (colleague of H.F. [Hubert Foss]). I have lunch with Mr. & Mrs. Foss.

Play something of mine to them in aft. Catch 5.21 back after tea. After supper write letters, & listen to Spencer Dyke Quart. playing Beethoven F min quart. (sure a wonder of the world) & Bridge 3 Idylls (marvels in another way).[133] Even ~~their~~ the Quartet's murderous playing couldn't murder them.

Monday 17 October

More copying out in morning & after lunch, & ~~after~~ before bed. Practise Pft. in afternoon. Go to R.C.M. in morning to see Léon Goossens about my Oboe Quart. I also go to his Studio at 5.45 to play it again to him & also a dancer Miss Burrows. He seems to like it. Go to Carlyle Singers after ~~tea~~ dinner at Lansdown Rd. They do my 3 pt-songs,[134] which seem to be effective enough. & v. easy.

Tuesday 18 October

Finish copy of Intro. & Allº. in morning. Bernard & Lauricella come in aft. Try the str. bits of my Oboe Phantasy. Go to dinner with Iris Lemare at 7.0. & afterwards to the first of the MagNaghten-Lemare concerts. R.O. Morris Canzon no. 6. (Dull & academical I thought). Dorithy Gow's Phant. some amusing music, but bad str. writing. Stuart Wilson sings 8 Oliver Gotch songs – works of a clever Amateur. Maconchy Vln Sonata (Helen Perkin & Anne MacN) interesting tho' lacking in individuality & Haydn's 1st quart. played v. roughley.[135] After the concert I go back to supper at Iris Lemare's Ireland was there as well as André Mangeot, Herbert Lambert & all the performers & Gerald Finzi. etc. etc. Back by 12.15.

Friday 21 October

Practise Pft before & after going to R.C.M. for lesson with Ireland at 10.35 & to hear Iris Lemare conduct abit of Patron's Fund (H.K. Andrew's Oboe concerto – Evelyn Rothwell playing well), rather a dull work – conventional.[136] Begin copy of Oboe Phant. in afternoon. Meet Beth at 5.15 at Austin Reed's (to buy evening waistcoat) via Queen's Hall & Augeners. Victor & Gordon Clark come to dinner here at 7.0 & we all go round to Barbara's for games etc. after. Back by 11.45.

Saturday 22 October

Practise Pft. & copy abit in morning. Beth packs. I go to Gloucester Rd. St. with her. She catches 3.10 home. More copying of Phant. in afternoon & after tea. Meet Barb at 8.15 at Broadcasting House for concert (tickets from

R.C.M.) in concert Hall at 8.30. English Ensemble – Kathleen Long (poor in spots). Marjorie Hayward (good) Rebecca Clark (musicianly but not inspired). May Mukle (poor tone). Mozart G min Quart. Fauré C. min. (marvellous work) Brahms. A maj.[137] Good 1st 2 mov. but too terribly long & boring for words. But 2nd mov. was wonderful.

Tuesday 25 October

Copying all morning, I finish score of Phant.[138] A long job. Now for parts! Bernard & Lauri come in afternoon. Ber. stays until 6.0 to do the Bridge Vlc. Sonata lovely work.[139] Go to Bridges to dinner at 7.15 & listen to a performance of Act II of Tristan on wireless. Beecham spoils it by hurrying & there is only a very poor orchestra. Florence Austral & Walter Widdop (Isolde & T.) very good. The rest rather poor. Even they couldn't spoil this wonder of the world. Back by 11.30.

Wednesday 26 October

~~Begin oboe part of Phant in morning before lesson~~ Practise Pft before Benjamin at 11.40. Copy out ob. part of Phant. in aft. Go for walk after tea. [Frederick] May comes to see me before tea. After dinner B.B.C. Symphony Concert with Bridges. Bantock's ghastly Sappho ov. Bridge's heavenly Enter Spring. Tchaikovsky's Violin Concerto – atrocious work (Mischa Elman – superb ~~musician~~ fiddler but impossible musician), & Franck's symphony, lovely in spots.[140] Boult's speeds were wrong almost without exception. There is magnificent material in the orchestra but it's tired out. Back to Bridges until 12.30 & back for a bit of copying.

Thursday 27 October

Finish Oboe part before going to College for rehearsal of my Sinfonietta; a great improvement – although no doublebass!! Trio in afternoon, Bernard to stay to do Bridge sonata after. Go to dinner with Nan Hill at her club (New Victorian) & to the Ballet Club[141] after. See L'aprés-midi – quite good, only with piano tho'. Lord Berner's – Le foyer de danse,[142] very amusing. Markova was very fine.

Filthy night

Friday 28 October

No lesson with Ireland owing to intense amount of copying to be done. Finish viola part in morning. May[143] comes in afternoon to say he hasn't had time to do 'cello. I begin that after tea & then go to dinner with Howard Ferguson at 7.0. Play 2 pft duets with him after. Back by ten. Then finish 'cello part by abt. 12.45.

Saturday 29 October

~~Copy a bit~~ Alter bits of May's 1st Fiddle part, before packing & catching 12.45 to Croydon, via Daily Telegraph, where I leave my entries for the comp.[144] Meet Bernard Richards at Croydon & he drives me down in his car to Friston where we spend the weekend arrive in gale & rain at 6.45. Miss Fass comes to dinner, games. etc. afterwards.

Sunday 30 October

Sleeping with Bernard, we both stay in bed until 11.0 with breakfast. Play bits of [Bridge's] Vlc Sonata to F.B. & then walk abit with Him. Mr F. Spiers (+ family) come over in aft. to have music at B's. Play Bridge Quintet, & they 4 play Beethoven C min St. Quart. Tea & Dinner at Miss Fass'. More Chamber music including Bridge Vlc Sonata & Schubert B^b Trio. (Mr. B. Vla).[145]

Monday 31 October

Bed with breakfast until 10.0. We all go into Seaford in car to see (& get wet) the rough sea. The wind is terrific all the week-end. In aft. Mr Spiers comes over again, & we play the last Trio, & the Phantasy Pft Quart[146] (with F.B. as Viola.) After tea we pack, Bernard fetches the car from East Dean and at 7.0 we leave for London. Arr. at Croydon at 9.10 & catch train arr. here abt. 10.0. Beth arrives from home also tonight.

Wednesday 2 November

Every single spare moment of day is spent in a ~~feav~~ feverish attempt to get a score of my Sinf done by Sat. Lesson with Benjamin at 11.0. Go to B.B.c concert at 8.15 (Area). Inc. H. Samuel playing well (but not perfectly) Bach's D min concerto. Not as good as I have heard him. Ireland's beautiful Forgotten Rite. & a by no means perfect performance of Belshazzar's Feast by B.B.C. Chorus. Denis Noble is v. fine singer. It is amazingly clever & effective music. with some great moments, I feel. Back at Bridges until 11.30 & then an hour's copying.

Friday 4 November

Copying before & after lesson with Ireland at 10.35 & after lunch & tea, I get my copy of Sinf. finished, thank God! The committee of the Mendelssohn Scholarship meet at R.C.M. Ivor Walsworth is the Scholar this time. (See July 11th.) He wasn't even in the original trio. ~~App~~ Apparently as he was at the <u>R.A.M.</u> An R.C.M. person got it last time, so it must needs be an R.A.M. this time. So much for an Anonymous exam! However they give me a grant of £50 ~~if~~ so as not to discourange me in composing!!!!!! Beth & I go to dinner at the Bridges & all of us to the Corona ~~the~~ Cinema after. See Thark[147] (R. Lynn T. Walls etc. & Claude Hulbert). v. funny.

Sunday 6 November [Lowestoft]
Mum goes to St. Johns at 110 & I go for walk with Pop round golf links. Listen to wireless all afternoon (Mum & Pop are having a Marconiphone on approval.). Mengelberg from Hilversum. An excellent performance of Mozart G min[148] Thibaud plays Lalo's Symph Espagnol very well, but sentimentally. Walk with Pop & Mum after tea, & with Pop before bed. Wireless & gramophone as well.

Wednesday 9 November [London]
Go to Ireland at 9.45 to run through Heldenleben on his gramophone. Lesson with Benjamin at R.C.M. at 11.40. Alter some parts in afternoon. Go to B.B.C. Concert (area) at 8.15. Henry Wood. Myra Hess ~~played~~ plays the Beethoven G maj. after rather a ragged Brandenberg no. 6. She plays it technically v. well, but ridiculous cadenzas, & she & Wood have no idea of the 2nd movement – it's Andante not adagiossississimo. A fine performance of Strauss' Heldenleben to finish with. It contains some marvellous things, & some great scoring, but the common-place harmony of alot of it kills me. The programme is vile I think.[149]

Thursday 10 November
Rehearsal of ~~Symp~~ Sinf. at R.C.M. at 11.0. Back to old style of rehearsal, only 8 people & 2 new!! However – See Grace Williams after. In afternoon, bit of pft. practise & Michael Halliday (late of South Lodge & now in Mercantile Marine) comes to tea & walk with him after across park, when I go to Madrigals & after to Bridges (up for day & night) for dinner, & he goes to Theatre. He stays the night here, however.

Friday 11 November
Michael goes at 7.30. Lesson with Ireland at 10.35. at R.C.M. Bit of service in concert hall at 11.0. Beth & I go down to Albert Dock (Plaistow) in afternoon to see Michael & over his ship S.S. Cornwall. V. interesting. Walk abit of way back via Whitehall. Back for dinner about 7.30.

Saturday 12 November
Go to Whiteley's in morning to have hair cut, & then on to St. Martin's Lane to Chatto & Windus to get a copy of Ancient English Carols.[150] I am setting some in a work for Chorus soon, I expect.[151] Read & practise Pft in aft. Beth goes to a theatre with some old St. Anne's girls. Go to see Grace Williams after tea. Read in smoke-room after dinner.

Walk back with G. Finzi & G. Holst. [after the Ballet Club concert]

Tuesday 15 November

Practise Pft all morning & a bit in afternoon. Also do some searching for Carols before Bernard comes at 3.45 for tea & a rehearsal of the F.B. Vlc sonata. Michael Halliday comes to say good-bye before off to Italy after tea. Walk with him. After dinner I go to Lemare-MacN. concert no.2. at Ballet club. Desparately dull. Quartets by Locke, Gordon Jacob (not even competant, I ~~don't~~ feel) & Phant. of Helen Perkin (the best of the programme, in spots amusing but never really felt. Among these Muriel Herbert (acc. by Alannah Delias for whom I turn over) sings some of her impossible songs, & ~~some~~ one each of Betty Lutyens & E. Maconchy.[152]

Wednesday 16 November

Lesson with Mr. Benbow in morning (deputising for Benjamin – examining) at 11.40. Practise before that & in afternoon. Also write letters & read carols. Walk after tea. Go to B.B.C. concert (in area) at Queen's Hall at 8.15. Ansermet conducts a poor perf. of Der Freischutz, & a not too thrilling one of Debussy's incomparable Nocturnes. Eliz. Schuman sings 3 delightful Mahler songs[153] & Et Incarnatus (C min. Mass) of Mozart marvellously. A competant performance of the ~~still~~ astounding Sacre to finish with. Back with Grace Willliams to Bridges.

Tuesday 22 November

Practise Pft. & more sketching of Xmas work in morning.[154] Bernard comes in aft. &, work at F.B. Sonata. Beth arrives back by bus at 4.0. Tea with her & B. in her room with my birthday cake. Walk with her afterwards. Barb. comes to dinner; cards after & with Miss Wheatley. Write to Mum & Pop after that.

For my birthday I have: Gold Watch from Mum & Pop: Come Hither (W. de la Mare)[155] from Beth & Barb. Letter & sweets from Bobby: 6/- from Aunt. Nellie: 6/- & sweets from Miss Turner. M.S. paper from the maids.

Wednesday 23 November

Pft practise in morning. Go to R.C.M. for unfruitful attempt to see Allen. Read in aft. & sketch things. Write letters & walk with Beth after tea. Go to B.B.C. Concert with Mrs. Bridge. Henry Wood makes a great mistake playing a garish arr. of Beranice ov. (Handel) before a perf of Mozart Haffner Symph. with reduced orch; which sounded ridiculously thin. Casals plays Haydn's conc. marvellously technically but does one or two things I don't like. But the treat of the evening was 2 mov. from Bach C min Suite as encore. Superb! Ends with Dvorak 5th Symp. This wonderful work was rather spoil by a rough perf.[156] Back via B's at 12.30.

F.B. gives me a copy of his Pft. Sonata.

Thursday 24 November

Usual style of R.C.M. rehearsal at 11.0 – with 3 new people – only with 10 altogether – rather a wonder! After lunch I see Allen about Schols. etc. Rehearsal with Ber. (Sonata) & then + Lauricella (Trio – F.B.). Walk to Selfridges, & then to Madrigals with Barb. New Bass in Madrigals – Paul Wright – very nice. I have imported him from Carlyle. Beth & I go back to dinner with the Bridges. Listen to a faked perf. of Petroushka by Beecham – within an inch of a collapse all the time.[157] Back by 11.30.

Friday 25 November

I write the theme of my Choral variations in morning. Write letters in aft & walk Mrs. Millar comes to tea in Beth's room. Go to Grace Williams at 5.0 to Meet Dr. Wellesx from Vienna. Walk with Beth after. After dinner go to Broadcasting House for a Van Dieran concert at 8.0 with Bridges (ticket from Gerald Finzi). Quite the most dull, dismal & boring music ever written. Megan Foster's singing was the only bright spot.

A marvellous day but with a good wind. Rain after dark.

Sunday 27 November [Friston]

Breakfast in bed; after which Miss Fass takes us in the car first to Birling Gap & then to Willmington to see The Giant (otherwise "David") of which she has done a splendid painting for me. After lunch I write letters & then Mr & Mrs. B. drive me into Seaford to fetch John Boyd (David can't come) from school (Seaford Col.) & bring him back to Miss Fass' for tea. Take him back by 6.30. Miss Fass comes here to dinner. Listen to Casals conducting – very dully & ignorantly – Brandenberg no. 3. Haydn London Symp [No. 104 in D] & Brahms 4th.

Tuesday 29 November [London]

Go for lesson with Ireland at R.C.M. at 10.35. Bernard comes & we play Vlc. Sonatas all afternoon. Beth & I meet Victor Clark at 6.30 at Savoy Theatre – have a meal – & (having queued for Pit) see Mikado.[158] A first rate show. The performance was excellent, tho' not perfectly perfect. Lytton was outstandingly funny. What ~~a~~ heavenly shows these operas are!

Thursday 1 December

As Mr. Buesst is away, a Maj. Hobey deputises for him, & he lets me direct a rehearsal of wind only at 11.0 (for my Sinff.). Do alot of work. See Ireland after that. Write abit more of variation – unsatisfactory in afternoon, before going to R.C.M. at 4.30 on purpose to accompany Lauricella – who very annoyingly departs home before I arrive without letting me know – in consequence I waste an hour before going to Madrigals at 6.0 Barbara doesn't go, as Helen Hurst has Mumps. I go to dinner with the Bridges after, at 8.0. Back by 11.30

Saturday 3 December

Practise Pft before going to Anne MacNaghten's at 12.0 for a rehearsal of my quintet.[159] After a bit of telling they get the spirit of it quite well. It ought to be quite good in time. Lunch with Anne at an A.B.C. Barbara comes to tea in Beth's room. Walk back with her after tea & then walk back here. Beth goes out to Kathleen Mead for ~~after~~ dinner & a play. I attempt to listen to Act II of Mikado after dinner, but the wireless expires.

Sunday 4 December

Church at St. Michael's Chester Square with Beth. V. good sermon by W. Elliot. Write letters & read in aft. Walk after tea with Beth. Go to ~~Ba~~ Camargo Ballet after supper with Bridge's and Miss Fass. Pretty dismal show except for Wendy Toye's magnificent dancing in F.B's "Willow".[160] There were things I didn't like about her choreography tho'. Other ballets were Sylphides – Infanta's Birthday – amusing stage show but putrid music by Betty Lutyan's & Constant Lambert's "Adam & Eve" in the same style[161]

Tuesday 6 December

I write more choral work before lesson with Ireland at R.C.M. After that go to Bridges where I have lunch. Rehearse the F.B. Cello Sonata all the aft. with Bernard. Early dinner with Beth at 6.15 & then go to ~~queue for~~ the Gallery of Queen's (with some tea at Lyon's before) to see Edith Evans in Beverly Nicholl's very moving "Evensong".[162] A most tragic play.

Wednesday 7 December

I finish the 1st variation before going to lesson with Benj. at 11.0. After lunch I go to Bridges to acc. Lauri. playing Tschaikov. concerto to F.B., who gives him a lesson on it. Come back to tea, to which Howard Ferguson comes; talk & play. Listen to Elgar concert after dinner.[163] The Intro. & Allo. makes some nice sounds, but the form seems so unsatisfactory & bits of Toselli's Serenata & the fugetta annoy me. So does most of the Enigma Var & all of the Second Symph.

Thursday 8 December

Write letters & post Mum's birthday present before going to R.C.M. Buesst doesn't turn up & four of the players do, so we have a scratch perf. of bits of the Schubert octet.[164] Play for Lauri. abit after. Rewrite bits of my var. in afternoon before going to Anne MacNaghten to tea to meet Mr & Mrs Frank Howes. Go to Carlyle Singers "dress" rehearsal at the Ballet Club theatre. Miss Taylor brings me back in her car by 11.30.

Friday 9 December

Don't have much of a comp. lesson with Ireland in morning, owing to him rehearsing a Vla. Sonata. After abit of rehears. with Lauri at R.C.M. at 2.0 I go to Anne MacN's for a rehearsal of my 5^{tet} – not so good. Kathleen Mead comes to dinner. I go to Courtauld Sargent-concert[165] with Howard Ferguson at 8.15. Kodaly's rather dull "Theatre Overture." Suggia plays ~~Hay~~ Haydn's conc. v. well. An amusing Concertanti by him (Vln. Vlc. Ob. Fag.). Bax's fourth Symphony.[166] V. disappointing after 3rd. But one can't judge by one hearing, I suppose Back, after going to a restaurant with Howard by 11.30

Sunday 11 December

Beth's not frightfully well. Walk with her abit in park – with foul weather as yesterday – in morning. Rest of morning & afternoon – besides writing letters – I begin a transcription of F.B's lovely Willow for Viola & Pft.[167] Grace Williams & Barbara come to tea. Walk with Beth before supper. Listen to wireless after – inc. Elgar's Falstaff [168] which contains some v. fine stuff – also some. . . . . .!!!

Monday 12 December

More transcribing before meeting Mum at Liverpool St. at 11.25 – she's not frightfully well. After lunch the Bridges come here for a bit & I do a bit more transcribing. Walk with Beth & Mum. before changing. Barb. comes to dinner. No. III of Lemare MacN. Concerts at Ballet Club. Choral & String programme Arnold Foster – 3 Manx Songs. Lillian Harriss – Phantasy Trio. Jane Joseph – a little Child – Female voices & St. quint. My 2-pt. Songs (3 – Oxford Press – W. de la Mare) – sung v. well. I accompany. They go down well. Helen Perkin plays a Suite of Christian Darnton (I turn over). Betty Lutyens – 5 Os.[bert] Sitwell Poems for Chorus & Vlc. 'CB. Hrn. Trpt. & Pft. My String quintet Phant. v. badly played by Anne Mac N's quart + Vla. Worse, by far than rehearsals. 3 Three Madrigals. The Choir was poor. I sang bass & Barbara Soprano, Iris Lemare conducted quite well. I go to Lady MacN's [Macnaghten] for a party after wards – but not for long. I collect ~~Barb~~ Beth & Mum from B's after & we are back soon after 12.

Friday 16 December [Lowestoft]
Do alot of work at F.B. Pft Sonata[169] in morning before walk with Caesar (& Mum for abit) before lunch. Walk with C. also ~~before~~ after lunch & before dinner. Mum has a singing aft – they do my songs[170] & some Beethoven canons. Only Mrs Owles, Mrs. Back & Miss Newsum come tho'. Play some viola with Mum before a walk with her & Caesar in evening.

Tuesday 20 December
Practise Pft & walk with Caesar along beach in morning Morling comes in morning & aft to fix up our new Wireless (Echo-superhet. built into H.M.V. Gram pick-up.) – absolutely superb. Aunt. Flo. arrives by car at 4.15. Walk with Pop & Beth after tea. After dinner listen to F.B. conducting a B.B.C. Concert. Oberon-ov. Paradise Garden – Delius – Miriam Licette singing a rediscovered (let sleeping dogs lie) aria.

Abit of Hansel & Gretel & abit of the Coc d'or Suite. Orchestra not superb – but F.B. on form – & you know what that means!

Wednesday 21 December
Practise, pack parcels & other Christmas duties & 2 walks with Caesar in morning. I walk with Caesar in aft. before Listening to Lauricella playing Tschaikov. conc. from Bournemouth. He is not a fiddler yet, but may be a fine one. Walk with Beth – shopping after tea. More wireless after dinner a Nativity play from St. Hilary Cornwall[171] & A. Benjamin playing, beautifully, Prokofiev's 1st conc.[172]

Thursday 22 December
See Bazil after breakfast & ~~get~~ arrange Carols for Sat. Hair cut & walk with Pop before lunch. Practise Vl. & Vla. with Charles Coleman in aft. probably for Saturday. Shop abit after tea, & walk with Pop.

Write letters after dinner & also listen to beginning of Hely-Hutchinson's Carol Symphony – utter bilge.[173]

Saturday 24 December
Post parcels & shop in morning before Aunt. Flo takes Beth & me to Sotterly to get some holly. Barbara arrives in aft. by 3.24 – & goes straight to bed with a feverish cold. Have a rehearsal at 5.30 for to-night. Shop with Beth after. Listen to Yeoman of the Guard[174] after dinner, do up parcels & decorate. Go carol-singing, starting here at 12.0. Marj. & Connie Phillips, 2 Boyds, 2 Reeves, Laurence Sewell & Charles Coleman & Miss Goldsmith & Beth & I. Sing about 8 carols in all. Go to 12 places singing about 3 at Each. In parts (so-called!) of course. All old carols, including my arr. of "Unto us a boy".

At 2.0 a.m. They come into Kitchen for refreshments. Beth & I wash up & we go to bed by 3.30.

Sunday 25 December
Church at 8.0 at St. Johns with Mum, Beth, & Aunt Flo. Walk with Pop in morning. Read in aft. Walk with Pop & Beth before supper. Xmas dinner mid-day. Presents include marvellous Swan "Eternal Pen" from parents.[175] F.B. sends me score of Francesca da Rimini.[176]

Boxing day no.2.
Tuesday 27 December
Pop takes Beth, Aunt Flo & me over to Farnham in new car to see Nanny. Start at 10.15, back by 12.30. Beth & I go to Mead's badminton – 12 there, inc. John Nicholson. Play games in evening, & also Listen to Brosa's playing, excellently (what a joy to hear something in tune!) Malipiero's Cantari chè madrigalesca.[177] which I think may be v. fine.

1933

Monday 2 January [Lowestoft]
Begin Var. II of Christmas work[1] in morning & after tea. Result of thinking & searching for poems all these hols. Long walk with Caesar before lunch & in aft. – shopping. Listen to Wagner 'Prom'. on wireless in evening. H.J. Wood's usual eccentricies & meaningless vandalism – but he must be getting tired – poor old man! Usual pop. Wagner.

Thursday 5 January
Practise pft & walk with Caesar in morning, & after lunch. John Nicholson comes to tea to have gramophone records. Try to listen to Delius Prom after dinner – but the wireless is hopelessly out of order. There is some doubt as to whether I shall continue with Ireland at R.C.M. Pop wrote to him, & he replies very agitatedly + a telegram (& he also rings up F.B.)[2]

Friday 6 January
In morning Morling's man puts radio-gramophone right – it is a wonder now. Practise with Bazil – 2 Pfts At Morlings. Bach D min Concerto & Schumann 1st mov.[3] Badminton in aft. Beth – having been in bed yesterday – tho' up, cannot go. 8 there. Quite fun – tho' not super badminton. Read more of Jame's glorious & eerie "Turn of the Screw."

Alice leaves us – having been here for just on 20 years (next May).[4] New cook arrives.

Saturday 7 January

Walk with Caesar, practise Pft, & walk – shopping with Mum in morning. Read more of the "Turn of the Screw" & walk with Caesar before going out to tea with Mr & Miss Bank's (he is organist of St Margerat's Church) at 4.30. Walk back. Listen to bits of Messiah sung by Sheffield Union from Prom – v. strong voices – tho' not especially well trained. Finish the 'Screw'. An incredible masterpiece.

Tuesday 17 January [London]

Bit of pft. practice & rewriting in morning. Walk across park to Selfridges in aft. for hair cut. Lauricella comes at 5.0 & play abit with him. Meet Mrs. Scoular (late Mrs. Buck of Gisleham), Marion Buck & David Scoular (step son – now at Farfield, Holt) at Globe theatre at 8.5. They take me to see Lilac Time.[5] (very amusing in ~~parts~~ parts, scenery v. pretty. Music arranged excruciatingly). Go back to their hotel (~~Reb~~ Redbourne). until abt. 12.0.

Thursday 19 January

After alot of deliberation I begin another variation in morning (in drawing room downstairs – saving gas. – all by myself – luckily), which progresses quite well. No. IV. More of it in afternoon before going to R.C.M. at 4.0. to run through the Tschaikov. Concerto with Lauricella. Meet Barbara at 5.0 at Selfridges & Madrigal after. See Paul Wright. Dinner at Bridges afterwards. Back by 10.30. Miss Fass there.

Friday 20 January

Lesson with Ireland at 10.35. Write letters, in aft, & practise Pft abit. Go to tea with Anne MacNaghten at 5.0; they rehearse the string parts of my Sinf. after. Dinner at Bridges, before we 3 go to B.B.C. house to Contemporary concert. B.B.C. orch. conductor Adrian Boult. 3 Escales of Ibert. 2^{bl}. Pft. conc. of Arthur Bliss & G min Symph. of Roussel.[6] Frightfully noisy things one after the other – thats all I know!

Saturday 21 January

Having packed, go to R.C.M. for rehearsal of Sinfonietta by Iris Lemare at 10.0. Not at all good, although everyone was put out by the absence of Doublebass, Bassoon, & the normal Clarinet. The Bridges pick me up from there in their car at 12.30 & take me down to Friston for the week-end. Arrive 3.45. Go into Eastbourne after tea. Listen to wireless after dinner.

Thursday 26 January

Writing all morning, also in aft. I rewrite & finish Var. IV. Go to R.C.M. at 3.0. to rehearse F.B. Vlc. Sonata with Bernard. Go to London Academy at 4.0 for a rehearsal of Sinf. with Iris Lemare. J. Ireland comes. Not good – only 7 there! On to Madrigals at 6.0. ~~Was going~~ Am going to dinner with the Wrights, only cancelled at last moment. Write letters & altering Var IV after dinner.

Friday 27 January

V. good lesson with Ireland in morning. Write letters & rewrite end of Var. IV in aft. Also bit of pft. practise before Stephen Crowdy comes to tea in my room at 5.30. Bit of walk with him before dinner, to which he stays & we go together to Kensington cinema (via 'Doggens'). See Grand Hotel[7] – amazing cast in a way; but not particularly convincing acting. Heavenly Micky Mouse[8]

Sunday 29 January

Church at St. Michaels at 11.0. Elliot has ~~'flu~~ sore-throat & cannot preach. Walk back via parks. Read & write letters in afternoon. Go to tea with Barbara at 4.30. She is v. tired & stays in bed all day. After supper go with Bridges to B.B.C. Studio no. 10 concert at 9.5. V. good playing, tho' not perfect owing to under-rehearsal. Haydn Clock. Symp. Delius Cuckoo (a miracle) & Tschaikovsky's wonderful Francesca de Rimini which F.B. made sound terrifying. Before Fran. Arthur Benjamin conducts his Vln concerto (Brosa – magnificent).[9] Not pleasing as a whole; there are some good things, but many week ones. Back to Bridges with Brosas.

Tuesday 31 January

Finish Var. in morning, & practise Pft. Laurr comes for a practise in aft. Long walk, all after tea. Mrs. Bridge comes to dinner. Go to last of series of Lemare-MacNaghten concerts at 8.30 at Ballet Club. Andrews. Oboe. Conc. (Sylvia Spencer) My Sinfonietta; Jacob. Wind 5^{tet}, Finzi Introit (Anne M.), Grace Williams – Tr. & orch. (Walton).[10] Considering amt. of rehearsal & nature of same, my work went quite well – but oh! Bit of party at B Club. after & to the Bridges after with Bazil Reeve, who came up.

Wednesday 1 February

Lesson with Benj at 11.40 on F.B. Sonata. Practise Pft. ring up people, see Miss Taylor about Carlyle Singers in afternoon. After supper go to Queen's Hall (ticket from Vaughan Williams). to B.B.C. concert. Adrian Boult gives a possitively aenemic performance of Unfinished. Harriet Cohen plays V.

Williams new Pft. Concerto. I am afraid that I don't like his music, however much I try. Bax's Garden of Fand, & Delius' Sea Drift (Roy Henderson & Philharmonic Choir). latter v. beautiful.[11] Back to Bridges for a bit with Brosas.

Thursday 2 February

Copy out the Vlc. part of a bit of a Beethoven Sonata to try with Ber. when he comes at 11.0–1.30 to practise. Work at F.B. Sonata. Practise Pft before that. Read abit of ~~poet~~ carols in aft. before going to Mangeot's for a rehearsal of my 5tet [12] at his house (Creswell Place), at 3.30. Meet Barb. at Selfridges at 5.10 & Madrigal with her afterwards. Back by 8.0. Read abit after.

Sunday 5 February

Go to Broadcasting House at 11.30 for a rehearsal of my Sinfonietta with Clark. He only has time to do ¾ hrs at it, which, of course, isn't nearly enough. So we agree to withdraw it from this afternoon's (4.15) programme; and it is announced then to be done in the near future. Spend most of the afternoon telephoning. Grace Williams comes to tea, after which I go and see Anne MacNaghten who is in bed with 'flu. Paul Wright comes to supper with a riotous evening after, on Pft. Write letters after he goes at 9.45.

Tuesday 7 February

I write abit more (v. unsatisfactory) of Finale in morning. Practise Pft in aft. abit. Walk in park after tea. Go to dinner with Howard Ferguson at 7.0 at Hampstead. Play two piano duets after, with him – Bax Sonata. Also play over his Vln Sonata.[13] It contains some good things, esp. in 1st 2 mov. 3rd I'm not sure about – hand of Brahms is heavy over it. He lends me some Schönberg. Back by 11.0.

Wednesday 8 February

Good lesson with Benj. at 11.40. Go to see Bridges after tea. After supper I go with them (Tickets from B.B.C. – front row dress circle – dinner jacket – top hat!) to Queen's Hall, B.B.C. Concert. Euryanthe ov. – disgraceful perf. under A. Boult. – wrong in tempi & mood from start to finish (although, notes pretty well played), as was the Eroica at the end – of which I can only stand 3 movs. Elina Gerhart sings 4 Strauss Songs, v. well, although her voice is ob. past it. Intonation v. bad in Wiegenlied. Schönberg conducts his op. 31. variations.[14] What I could make of it, owing to a skin-of-its-teeth performance, was rather dull, but some good things in it. ~~Beth~~ Meet Sch. in interval. Beth comes ~~by~~ back by 11.0.

Sunday 12 February [Lowestoft]
Marvellous day. Pop takes Barb, Mum & me to Burgh Castle (Nr Yarmouth) in morning in 'Snipe'. Read & walk with Caesar in aft. Mum goes to station with Barb. who catches the 5.25 back to town. Walk with Pop after tea. Listen to Maestersinger Ov. after supper – Adrian Boult. This perf, like the Eroica, an absolute disgrace. Of course the notes were correctly played, & more or less together but – tempo, phrasing dynamics, shape, etc. etc!!!!

Monday 13 February
Long walk with Caesar in morning; & before lunch with C. (& part way Mum) & before tea with C., & before dinner with C. & before bed with C. & Pop. Begin an easy mov. for St. Quart.[15] between walks with C. in morn. & aft. Miss Ethel Astle comes in, after tea. Play Ping-Pong with Lawrence Sewell after. Listen to the Kolisch Quart. playing astoundingly, Berg's astounding Lyric Suite.[16] The imagination & intense emotion of this work certainly amaze me if it not altogether pleases me.

Thursday 16 February [London]
Rehearse Sinfonietta with Buesst at 11.0. & Rehearse with Bernard (F.B. Son) after until 2.0. (at R.C.M.). Mr. Brosa comes here at 3.30 to rehearse with me – what fiddling! Has tea & leaves at 6.30. I go to Audry Chapman Orch at Clarkenwell with Bridges after an early dinner. F.B. conducts as usual, & the strings of the orch. are for amateurs marvellous – quite the best of all in town. Mozart – Figaro ov. & Jupiter. Brahms-Haydn Variations, Schumann Pft. conc. (Irene Scharrer intensions v. fine but execution not so good). Beth & Mum go to "Richard of Bordeaux".[17]

Friday 17 February
Instead of lesson with Ireland go to Broadcasting house for rehearsal all morning. Practise Pft all afternoon. Mum. goes to dinner with Barbara. Beth & I pick her up after & go to B.B.C. at 9.0, where Mangeot etc. broadcasts my Fantasy 5^{tet}, quite creditably. It isn't a good work, but the rest of the programme – Darnton's Trio, & Erik Chisholme's 2^{bl} Trio[18] – 45 mins!!! Bridges & Brosas there.

After Hockey Match, Beth & I go on to Bromley for tea with Aunt Louise & Uncle Willie.

Saturday 18 February
Mum & Beth shop in morning. I practise pft. Write a letter & odd job. Mum goes off from Liverpool St. by 3.10. Beth & I go to Beckenham to see 'Varsity Hockey Match. Camb. 2–0. John Hardie (D.F. Walker too.) of S. Lodge,

Docker, Wynne Willson & Marshall of Holt playing. See various old Greshamians & J.J.E. [T. J. E.] Sewell, who brings a contingent from Lowestoft. Barbara goes to E. Mad. Soc. concert at League of Arts, which I cut. Beth goes to Theatre in evening. I read – Forsyte Saga.[19]

Monday 20 February

Go back to my variations in morning for abit; but I cannot get on with the wretched Finale at all. Go to R.C.M. to try, unsuccessfully, to get something out of the Library. Go via. Park – v. snowy. More variation – effort & practise Pft abit in aft. before going out to tea with Christian Darnton; see much of his stuff. Listen to Brosas after dinner. Beethoven 1st Rasoumov.[20] Not my Beethoven but some of it ~~was~~ is very beautiful Quartet playing. It's a treat to hear someone playing in tune. Then the Cantari alle Madrgalesca of Malerpierro,[21] which I like. They play it magnificently, as far as I can tell.

Tuesday 21 February

Read gallons of poetry in morning, for Choral work, but unsuccessfully. Lauricella comes in aft. to play, & I go over some of his work (a quartet) with him after tea. Walk with him after that. Beth goes to a lecture after dinner, while I copy out 1st Fiddle part of 'Alla Marcia' Quartet, & finish 'A Man of Property'.[22]

Wednesday 22 February

Practise F.B. Pft. Sonata before going to R.C.M. at 11.40 to have a lesson with Benjamin on it. After ~~dinner~~ lunch, I go to Hampstead with Beth to see her new premises[23] & for a walk on the heath with her. Back to her room for tea; after which I practise viola. After dinner I copy out Vl. 2. & Vlc. parts of March, & listen to 2nd half of B.B.C. concert. Lamond playing Liszt Concerto clumsily & dully, & Ravels glittering 'Daphnis & Cloe'.[24]

Thursday 23 February

R.C.M. at 9.30, to rehearse with Bernard, & at 11.0. to rehearse strings of Sinfonietta. & after to rehearse again with B. in morning some coats are stolen from cloak-room, among which is my new one – & my fur gloves – curses & swears! Practise Pft before going to R.C.M. again to rehearse F.B. Trio with B. & Lauricelle. Meet. Barb. & Beth at Selfridge at 5.15, & Madrigal after. Write letter after dinner & listen to a quite creditable perf. of Sinf. Fantastique[25] under Beecham.

Sunday 26 February [Friston]

Breakfast in bed, & up by 11.0. Talk with Frank B; we all lunch at B's, with ping-pong before and after. Tea too. Supper at Miss Fass's, where we sing the birthday round, written by Miss Fass, & music (so-called) by me (in afternoon).[26] Chamber music (as well as listening to a bit of wireless) after – inc. my Quartet – alla marcia. 2 movs. of F.B.'s Pft. Quintet, & his new Vln. Sonata played by him and Toni Brosa.[27]

Monday 27 February [Friston/London]
Breakfast in bed, with a walk with F.B. & Bernard after. Play Haydn Woods Vln conc.[28] with T. Brosa after at Miss Fass's (he's to play it on wireless on Wed.) & some pieces. Lunch at F.B's; Brosas come back to town by train, I go with Bernard (via Newhaven) & Bridges together in car & they pick me up at Croyden (Bern's home) & land me here at 7.0. Bath – dinner – wireless – bed.

Tuesday 28 February [London]
Begin a ~~walze~~ valse movement for St. quart. in morning.[29] Rest all afternoon owing to foul headache. After tea Beth & I go to R.C.M. Second Orchestral Concert to hear Bernard play Dvorak 'Cello conc. (2nd & 3rd movements), with great promise, & in places real achievement. But the orchestra & the student conductors – ! Write letter & more valse after dinner. Beth goes to a lecture.

Wednesday 1 March
Practise Pft before going to Benj. for a lesson at 11.40. Go with Beth to get new coat (exactly like the last) from Barkers[30] in aft. Get £2 from College for it. Practise Pft after tea. Go out to dinner with Bridges & then with Mrs. B. go to ~~Adolphe Buschf~~ Adolf Busch, & Rudolf Serkin conc. at Wigmore hall – all 3 Brahms. Pft & Vln Son.[31] B. is technically perfect – except for a curious inability to play a phrase legato, & Serkin is wonderful. But there was a lack of subtlely about Busch, & the interpretation left much to be desired, I felt – annoyingly so. The ensemble was perfect (except for 1 disagrement in phrasing of a mov. – op. 108 – mov. 3 – (little beauty)

Friday 3 March
Finish Valse in morning before lesson with Ireland at 10.35 at R.C.M., and in afternoon. Tea with Grace Williams. After dinner read more Forsyte Saga, which is making a terrific impression on me. Also listen to a clever tale by "A.J. Allen",[32] & two brilliant folk-song arrangements of Percy Grainger – 17 come Sunday & Father & Son, knocking all the V. Williams and R.O. Morris arrangements into a cocked-hat.[33]

Wednesday 8 March
Pft practice & Pft lesson on Kreutzer in morning.[34] More practise & alterations in scoring of bits of Sinf. in aft, Meet Beth & Lilian Wolff at 4.50 at

Marble Arch. She goes away for a week – until Friday with Wolff's, & week-end home. Walk home via parks & Bridges. Tickets from B.B.C. I take Mrs Bridge to ~~Smpyh~~ Symphony Concert at Q.H. at 8.15. H. Wood conducting. Egmont ov. (à la Valse), Haydn Symp. Horn Call & D. with some first-rate horn playing. Busch plays E maj. Bach Vln concerto badly for a first- rate fiddler. 3 Excerpts from Berg's Wozzeck – thoroughly sincere & moving music. Tod & Verklärung seemed dull & banal after this.[35] Orchestral playing throughout evening technically good but dull & uninspired as usual. Back via Bridges

Thursday 9 March

Usual ~~Sym~~ Sinf. rehearsal at 11.0 v. bad; 2 players missing! F.B. Sonata with Ber. after. Kreutzer with Lauri. at 3.30 & Trio (F.B.) after. Meet Barb. & Madrigal as usual.Write letters & listen to wireless after late dinner. Fall of House of Usher[36] – unbearably creepy & terribly well done. 10.30. Sermon by Elliott – very fine – typical.

Friday 10 March [London/Friston]

Bit of alteration of Valse & Romance before lesson with Ireland at R.C.M. at 10.35. Back via Bridges for lunch. Beth comes in after it before off to Lowestoft. Pack & go to Bridges at 2.30, where Mrs. B drives us, Mr. B, a ½ sister, at whose house near Brighton we have tea & me to Friston. Come via Brighton & Newhaven, & Seaford. Marvellous day, scenary heavenly. Arr. about 7.0. After dinner listen to House of Usher again.

Sunday 12 March [Friston]

Perfectly heavenly. There literally hasn't been a cloud in the sky since Friday morning; bit of a wind earlier on, but it dies down later. Walk before break-fast on downs. Write letters & a bit of an "Alla burlesqua" after.[37] Lunch at Miss Fass'. Then Mrs. B. takes me to Seaford to fetch out John & David Boyd. Go to White Horse for a bit, & then back here for ~~tennis~~ tea & ping-pong. Take them back by 6.15. Listen to Stravinsky's Vln. Conc. after dinner, to which Miss Fass comes, & a disgraceful perf of Pastoral Symph (under Boult).

Monday 13 March [London]

Start back at 7.15 arr. (after heavenly drive with Mr & Mrs B.) at 10.15. Lauri comes in afternoon to practise Kreutzer. Walk after with him for abit. I get tickets from B.B.C. for Broadcasting House Chamber concert at 8.0, to which I take Grace Williams. Stravinsky & Dushkin. Pergolesi transcripts. Duo Concertante (2[ce] performed) & some incredible arrangements from the Ballets – all for Vln & Pft.[38] Dushkin is a fine fiddler, but I am not so impressed with Stravinsky as pianist.

Tuesday 14 March

Pft. practice all morning. Rehearse Trio at R.C.M. all aft. 2.0–4.0. After tea with Miss Wrist write letters. After dinner I go with F. May (his tickets) to Oriane Madrigal Society concert at Aeolian Hall. under C.K. Scott. This choir sings quite well – but no remarkable tone, ensemble, or intonation. Although pitch was maintained well, as in Harrison's interminable & dull-as-ditchwater "Blessed Damozel" for female voices.[39]

Thursday 16 March

Go to R.C.M. at 11.0 for final rehearsal of Sinf. It goes v. well. Pft practice at abit before going to R.C.M for Trio rehearsal 4–5.30. After dinner R.C.M. Chamber Concert at 8.15. Mum & Beth go. Bridges & Brosas also there. Beethoven C$^{\#}$ min quart competantly but dully played; an atrocious perf. of Delius Vl. Sonata no. 1. F. May plays. bit of Phantasy of Schuman, & I conduct a show of my Sinfonietta which goes quite well.[40]

Friday 17 March

Lesson with Ireland at 10.35. Mum sees Allen at 10.45 & gets details of Octavia Schol. out of him.[41] After lesson, I listen to bit of Patron's Fund – Kathleen Long play Duncan Rubbra's Pft. Concerto,[42] mild, unoriginal, ill constructed inefficient music. After lunch I go to R.C.M. to hear 1st orch. (under G. Toye) run throu F. May's Scherzo.[43] Beth & I go to ~~Station~~ Liverpool St. Station to see Mum off with Barb. by 4.45. Walk back as far as Piccadilly. Beth has Kathleen Carter to ~~dinner~~ dinner.

Sunday 19 March

Hear the most incredibly brilliant & moving sermon on War by Elliot when Beth & I go to St. Michael's at 11.0. Do abit of writing in aft. Grace Williams & Elinor Bond come to tea; walk with Grace after, along Embankment. After supper write letters & Grace comes in to hear wireless; Henry Wood conducting slack & incompetant perfs of Haydn Drum Symp. Hindemith's Vla Concerto (with H.), which has some awfully fine & exhilarating things in it; & L'oiseau de feu, 1st Suite.[44]

Wednesday 22 March

Another day of useless struggle with Finale. Lesson with Benj. at 11.40 & walk after with Beth. Go to dinner with Bridges at 7.0 & go to B.B.C. concert with Grace (Beth & Joan Wynne-Reeves also go) afterwards. Wood conducting Hindemith's Unaufhörliche.[45] Perf. mediocre competant but not inspired choral singing not even that [BB arrows back to 'competant' here] & some soloists. Adeleid Armhold was frightfully good tho'. The work is frightfully long & disconnected, naturly being wedded to such ludicrous words. It contains some fine things (esp. in second half), but it is too monotonous seeming to me a work of devices (clever enough) rather than inspiration.

Friday 24 March
Write a good deal more of Finale in morning before lunching with H. Foss at a Resteurant near Amen House.[46] Play him what is done of my var. & I think he'll publish them, with luck. Back by tea time, walk with Beth to see Bridges after, she is making a dress for Mrs B. After dinner Beth & I go to B.B.C. to see & hear Hindemith's Lesson.[47] V. amusing & witty, and with apparently a very deep philosopy underneath it, which I was quite oblivious of. Harry Tate & Co. were clowns & Tudor Davies, Arthur Cranmer, B.B.C. orch. wireless singers, Military Band, & Adrian Boult (in full form!).

Saturday 25 March
Write abit more of Finale in morning. After lunch Beth & I go to Kew Gardens as it is such a God's own day. Back at 6.0. Grace takes Beth & me to the Shilling Theatre, Putney, after dinner to see the Irish players in the Plough & the Star.[48] Very good acting in a fine tho' over long play. Arthur Sinclair, & Mary O'Neil were esp. good. Rather poor melodrama in spots, but very harrowing on whole.

Monday 27 March
In morning do alot of rewriting of Finale. Practise pft abit in after noon before walking pt. of way to Lilywhites to meet Beth + to take Tennis racquet for repairs. Also see George Hockey (cousin) there. After dinner listen to Amar Quart. playing Brahms C min[49] & Mozart F. (K.590). Efficient playing – that's all. Not superlative ensemble, tone balance, or to my mind interpretation. The Brahms was very stuffy. The Mozart was delicious after it – some of it they played well.

Fritz Rasp as the 'man with bowler hat' Emil was Rolf Wenkhaus.
Both 1st rate.

Tuesday 28 March
Bit of rewriting before lesson at R.C.M. with Ireland at 10.35 (instead of Friday as he's been examining). Rehearse Trio in afternoon & then with Lauri. alone. Walk across park with him & back (as it is such a glorious

day – still perfect weather) before dinner. After Beth & I take Grace to Cinema House to see 'Emil und die Detektive',[50] which is the most perfect & satisfying film I have ever seen or ever hope to see. Acting as natural & fine as possible – magnificent & subtle photography – plot very amusing & imaginative – a collosal achievement

Friday 31 March
Lesson with Ireland at R.C.M. at 10.35. Afterwards go & see Bridges before they leave for Friston at 1.15. Go up to Westend to get pt. songs for home etc. & to get Emil & die Detektive which is going to be very interesting – when I can understand it! (Kästner wrote it).[51] Back by 4.45. See Grace after tea. Begin to pack after that. George Hockey & Barbara come in to coffee after dinner. The marvellous ~~day~~ weather has begun to break up with a vengeance.

Saturday 1 April [London/Lowestoft]
Pack all morning. As Mrs. Melville is having her grand pft. (she lent it me) back on Monday, I am able to give up my room these hols – so that means clearing everything out of my room, which is an enomous business. Catch 3.10 home with Beth. Pop meets us at 6.0 in Humber. Mum is laid up with a sprained ankle. After dinner, gramophone & listen to Edward Clark conducting a performance of Petrouchka. to say nothing of interpretation (which was ludicrous) it was disgracefully incompetant – the orchestr 'swam' completely about 6 times & it is a wonder of wonders how they ever got to the end together. The inst. playing was bad throughout

Sunday 2 April [Lowestoft]
Walk with Pop & Beth in morning. In aft. listen to Pt. 2 of Matthew Pass. Bach Choir cond. A. Boult. Choir lazy & inefficient; Boult typically annoying & dull. Walk with Caesar before tea & with Beth after. After supper listen to Bazil Cameron cond. Sibelius Impressive (tho' there are some things that irritate me) 3rd Symp. & Till [Strauss *Till Eulenspiegel*]. Dull & laclustre.

Monday 3 April
Hundreds of schemes are in the air at the moment, but none of them are connected with the Variations, unfortunately. One of them is a Suite on 'Emil';[52] & another is a Suite for Fl. Ob. Pft, commissioned by Sylvia Spencer. I arr. the 'Alla Valse' for that combination in the morning,[53] after doing odd jobs about the house. Finish it after lunch. Walk with Caesar in aft. up town, shopping. Hair cut at Priggs & walk with Beth before dinner. Listen to wireless 'What's In T'ilt', & write letters after.

Wednesday 5 April

Begin transcribing 'Alla Romanze' for Fl. Ob. & Pft. in morning, before long walk with Bazil Reeve. In aft. I go & play cricket with South Lodge boys, up on their field.[54] Great fun; have a glorious knock, making 33 & eventually retiring with bust bat! Not stylish cricket tho'. Back for tea by 5.10 Walk with Beth after; & after dinner play a bit of Bridge with Mum, Pop & her.

Monday 10 April

Lilian catches ~~q~~ 10.7, back home, (Beth drives her down to station; I go too). & Beth the 5.45 back to town (I walk down with her). Play tennis at at Everett's Park, Oulton with John Nicholson, 11.15–12.45. He takes me. Walks at various odd times with Caesar. Listen to Fürtwängler & Berlin Phil. from Berlin in Eroica.[55] Not what I want exactly in one or two places; but very lively & what orchestral playing! Strings superb.

Friday 14 April

Work in morning, & walk before lunch with Beth. Section of 3 Hour's [Good Friday] service with her, 2.15–3.0. After that go to Normanston park to watch bit of Hockey Match. Ipswich v. London Hosp. George Hockey came over with a Geof. Mason playing for Former, & we watch with him, & bring him back here to tea. Long Walk with Caesar before dinner. Listen to Brahm's Requiem after from Mühlacker.[56] V. stogy perf. which didn't come over well.

Tuesday 18 April

Seem to get moving at last with Finale of Variations.[57] Work all morning at it, except for the arrival of Nan Hill to see us. Walk up town with Michael in aft. Go with him to have a look over South Lodge (he's there with me) after tea. Play abit of Bridge after dinner & listen to Chamber Concert after that (Cobbett prize works). Phant. of Hurlstone capable but undistinguished, I felt.[58] Brosas played it well. Ireland's 1st Vln Sonata (himself & that superb Brosa). Fine material but over long. V. Williams 5^{tet} has some good things in it, but technically inefficient & imitative, & didn't seem to hang together.[59] The playing didn't do much to redeem it either.

Sunday 23 April

Not up especially early. Walk with Pop & Beth in morning. Copy out more Variations – very slow job, before lunch & tea, to which last the 3 Colemans come. More copying after tea. Listen to Webern conducting Mahlers' lovely 4th Symphony from London Regional.[60] This work seems a mix up of everything that one has ever heard, but it is defintely Mahler. Like a lovely spring day. The orch. seemed to have caught the spirit but not over many notes of it!

Tuesday 25 April

Catch 10.7 to Darsham where Peter Welford meets me & takes me to Peasenhall Hall, where I spend day with him. Mr & Mrs Welford there. As it rains all day except for a bit after lunch, when we play deck-tennis, we have to be in doors; play much ping-pong. Peter takes me to Darsham to catch 6.7, arr 7.8. home Write abit of alteration in Var. after dinner, & listen to wireless. 1st (& I hope, last) broadcast perf of Bliss' Clar. Quintet.[61] I only listened to 1 ½ movs. V. unoriginal piffle. & it wasn't even amusing, but intensely dull

Wednesday 26 April

I copy out & rewrite most of morning & afternoon with occasional walks with Caesar. Mum & Beth go to Norwich in afternoon to shop. Walk with Pop after tea. Beth & I go to Marine at 7.30 to see the Amateurs do 'Chu Chin Chow'.[62] Quite a good show for amateurs, & the costumes & scenary were very lavish. Total lack of voices & of much art of acting spoils it. Gladys Mumford is an exception, however.

Saturday 6 May [London]

Alot more copying of Var. – i.e. that portion of which is finished more or less satisf. – in morning & afternoon & after tea. Shop abit in morning & go to Ambassador's Theatre for tickets. Gwen Rice comes to dinner with Beth. I go to Amb. Th. at 8.45 – ticket paid for by Miss Fass – to see Uday Shan-Kar & his Hindu dancers (inc. Simkie & Robindra – quite young) & musicians (inc Vishnu Dass – marvellous drummer & Timir Bewan).[63] I haven't seen anything for ages which has thrilled me more. Marvellously intellectual & perfectly wrought dancing. Finest I have yet seen Music, full of variety, rhythmically & tonally. one perfect creation of Shan-kar – an ecstatic dance. Tandava Nrittya was a longer ballet with a very exciting fight.[64]

Monday 8 May

More copying in morning, more or less rewriting as I go along. 9000th attempt also at finale.[65] Go to Whiteley's for hair cut in aft, walking there & back. Practice Pft after tea on Miss Gapper's piano. Listen to Schnabel playing Brahms B^{b},[66] in London Musical festival after dinner. Wireless v. bad unable to judge much. Technique seemed excellent & the idea of the work as a whole But many details annoyed & irritated me.

Tuesday 9 May

Alot more copying in morning, after lunch, & after dinner, but it's a dashed slow business. Go to Cramer's in morning to hire piano. R.C.M. Jubilee. Concert at 3.0 attended by T.M. the K. & Q.[67] Unfortunately as they're in the balcony I can't see them. Programme of music by late students & conducted by same. Elizabeth Aveling, faints after singing atrociously, in Music – Charles Wood. Dan Godrey conducts V. Willliams appaling Wasps, Ireland conducts 2 moves. of his pft. concerto (H. Perkin) v. dully, Holst Plantet-Jupiter (L. Ronald) 3. Songs of Fleet – Stanford (Hugh Allen). Bliss conducts his 2 pft conc. Jerusalem, God save the King. Back to tea with Bridges (Mrs. was there). Frank wasn't even asked to conduct!!! Some College

Thursday 11 May

Go to F.B. in morning re proofs, return & do odd alterations of my 'Boy'. Practise pft in afternoon. Tea in Beth's room at 3.30. lesson with Benj. at 4.10 – see Constant Lambert & play him the variations. Go on to Covent Garden & meet Beth & Grace before 6.0. ~~see ma~~ Tristan begins at 7.0. Good seats (3rd row of Gallery – 3rd for preference). Frida Leider suddenly [in]disposed, Henny Trundt is rushed from Cologne in the aft. V. good; rather ungainly but sings & acts well. A mild Isolde, who is most impressive at the end. Melchior is simply superb. What a voice! The subtlety of his movements is incredible. Olczewska & Janssen (Bran. & Kurn. [Brangena and Kurnewal]) ~~wh~~ were worthy of themselves – colossal & moving achievements. Beecham & orchestra, only blots on the marvellous show. Cor Anglais v. good. But what music! Dwarfs every other art creation save perhaps 9th. [Symphony – Beethoven]. The glorious shape of the whole, the perfect orchestration: sublime idea of it & the gigantic realisation of ~~it~~ the idea. He is the master of us all. Since heard that Beecham was vilely rude to Leider who refused to sing in morning. I am not surprised.

Saturday 13 May

Bit more copying in morning & also some pft. practise. Still too full of Tristan to do much. Attempt to rig up a 'Come-back'[68] [BB sketches diagram here] in aft. in garden. Elinor Bond & Barbara come to tea. See Grace after; lend her Tristan to get rid of the wretched thing. Listen to the winning ~~comp.~~ 3 of Telegraph comp on wireless. Armstrong Gibbs 4tet. competant I suppose, dull as ditchwater & v. unoriginal. E. Maconchy Ob. 5tet. Not so competant, but one or two fresh Ideas. Edric Cundell (1st prize), technically efficient I suppose. Superficially brilliant & disonent fast movs. Ordinary & rather cheap slow ones.[69]

Monday 15 May

Tons of copying all day except pft practise abit before & after tea. Walk with Beth after that. Dinner at Bridges at 7.15. T. Brosa & an American composer there. Go on to London Musical Festival concert (B.B.C. orch) after with Grace. (Good seats from B.B.C.). Conductor Serge Koussevitzky. Not so startling as I imagined. He seemed too finicky & not at ease. He wasn't very enlightning in Sibelius 7th Smph, abt. which I can't make up my mind. It contains some fine things & some utter tosh. A hectic perf of Tsch. 5th finished. An uneven work. Concert began with Prokofiev's Classical Symph. Brilliant, witty scoring. Rather dull second movement.

Wednesday 17 May

Practise Pft in morning & copy in aft. Go to see Bridges with Beth (she's doing a dress for Mrs. B.) after tea. Anne MacNaghten comes to dinner & we go to B.B.C. Lond. Musical Festival after. Q. Hall. Koussevitzky again. Walton Portsmouth Pt. V. well played, as was Bax's v. long & meandering 2nd Symphony. Wagner excepts. 2nd half. – Venusberg Music, Siegfried Idyll & Meistersinger Ov. Details v. good, but tempi v. erractic. S. Idyll. Irritatingly slow & laborious.

Thursday 18 May

Copying in morning & pft practice abit. lunch at 12.30. Rehearsal of My Phant. 4^{tet} at R.C.M. at 1.0. Natalie Caine is playing Oboe, Lauri (Vln), Riddle (Vla) Bernard (Vlc).[70] Goes v. well. Pft. lesson with Benj. 4.10. Meet Barb. & Beth at Selfridges. at 5.15. Don't go to Madrigals. Bit of cold being an excuse. Miss Wrist has bought us a 'Kum-bak' in garden; use it much before & after dinner.

Friday 26 May

Bit of copying before lesson with Ireland at 10.35. We play my Oboe. Quart. to him. More copying & pft. practise in aft. & after tea. See Grace too. Beth & I go to B.B.C. at 9.0 for a perf. of Kodaly's Spinning Wheel.[71] Mostly folk-song. There is some very attractive stuff – beautifully done. Choral writing excellent. Some of it was rather dull, banished from the stage. Performance, conducted by K. was rather perfunctory tho' chorus, Roy Henderson, & Enid Cruickshank. v. good

I hear that Stokowski conducted Meistersinger Ov. at the end as a surprise item!!!

Monday 29 May

Copying in morning, Pft in aft. 'Kumback' after tea. Go to another Jubilee Concert of R.C.M. with Beth. Adrian Boult conducting orchestra of old students. V. Dull programme. Schubert, Rosamunde scrapily & dully played – in the true Boult fashion. Somerville's ghastly Normandy var. 3 Butterworth songs (Keith Falkner) P. Hadly 'The Trees so high'. R.O. Morris Sinfonia (help!) Coleridge Taylor bit out of Hiawather. – then we fled!

Thursday 1 June

Revise & begin to bind "Boy" in morning before long rehearsal at R.C.M. 12.0–2.0. It goes better; in fact parts very well. Practise Pft before pft. lesson at 4.10. Alter bits of Phant. after that, & after dinner continue binding. With Grace I go to very amusing (supposed to be Tyrolean) party at Spencers. (Mrs. & Sylvia – at home). Ivor James, Sybil Thorndyke, Anne MacNaghten, Anthony Spurgeon, Penelope S., ~~among~~ Frank Howes, among those there

Friday 2 June

Finishing binding "Boy" in morning before lesson with Ireland at 11.10. Have rehearsal of Phant. in it, at 12.0 to which Foss comes. unfortunately it goes very badly, so he doesn't get too good an impression. However he comes back to lunch at 173, & hear's "Boy" & seems very pleased with that. At 4.0 the Quartet (N. Caine, R. Lauricella, F. Riddle, & Ber. (B. Richards)) go to R. Acadamy to play my Phant. to the Mendelssohn Schol. Committee. Unfortunately it goes v. badly once again. Of course they are only students, but Lauri made in both performances some unforgivable howlers, – Lack of experience of course. After dinner & packing Grace comes in to listen to Elizabeth Bergner in "Wild Duck"[72] – incomparable artist.

Monday 5 June [Lowestoft]

Begin altering 'Lift Boy' into full Chorus & pft in morning.[73] Bathe & Bask in sun, (it's a perfectly celestial day – v. hot & lovely sun & a good breeze) with Barb., Mum & Beth before lunch. Beth drives Mum & me over to Farnham where we see Nanny & Alice, & picnic for tea with them. Listen to Otello from Covent Garden, or rather Act II of same What a work! Melchior was v. fine as Otello.

Friday 16 June [London]

As I've done so little work, I don't go to Ireland at R.C.M. until 11.0. Go to B.B.C. at 3.30 to see Hely-Hutchinson, Cyril Dalmaine (Chorus master) & Foster Clark. They seem to like my 'Boy'. After dinner I go with Grace (her tickets) to R.C.M. to see Vaughan William's Hugh the Drover.[74] It needs a larger stage, of course – even so the First Act was very exciting & the rest was a dreadful anticlimax. V.W. has shown in places apt use of chorus, in others dreadful disregard of natural movements. The music was full of folk-song.

(if you like that sort of thing) – it was best so – when not (as between Scenes in Act II), it was dreadful. Mona Benson (excellent) & Trefor Jones & Mable Ritchie (good towards end) Leyland White – v. good.

Monday 19 June
Mum & Pop go back in morning, taking Beth to 559 [Finchley Road] on way. Start about 10.0.[75] I go to Mangeot's at 11.0 to hear them run through ~~at~~ my Oboe Quartet which they're to broadcast some time; also play pft. for them in a run through of Hely Hutchinson's "Idyll & Diversions" – muck![76] Copy out – or rather begin to – parts of "Boy" in aft & after dinner. It's an awful business.

Tuesday 20 June
Alot more copying in morning. Bit of pft practice. Rehearse trio at R.C.M. 2.0–2.40. Catch 3.15 with Mr. Mangeot from Waterloo to Effingham Junction out to Cobham where we play tennis with his two sons – who are excellent. esp. Faulk (?). He brings me back in his car & drops me at 31 Mayfield Avenue where I have dinner with Fred. May & have gramophone records after with him. Pajola's Daughter – Tapiola – & 5th Symphony – all Sibelius. I enjoyed Tapiola v. much & bits of the 5th – but it is hard to see what he's driving at. Food for thought, tho'.[77]

Wednesday 21 June
Hear from Foss. that Scherchen is going to do my Sinfonietta in Strasbourg this August.[78] Consequently spend all day revising parts & score & metronome marks etc. Pft. practice abit before dinner, also abit of 'Kum bak'. Write letters after dinner.

Friday 23 June [London/Friston]
At 11.30 I go to York Hotel, Berners St, to see Hugh Ross about having my 'Boy' produced in New York.[79] Pack in afternoon, rather unsuccessfully, leaving behind both pyjamas & sweater!, & meet Miss Fass & Mrs Bridge at Chelsea Polytechnic at 4.0. Miss Fass drives ~~me~~ us down to Friston, arr 7.0. Bit of tennis before dinner with F.B. The Brosas are down too, staying with Miss Fass. They all come in after dinner.

Monday 26 June [Friston/London]
The Brosas go back to town by train at 11.30. The Bridges have to come up to town for a bit on business & return to Friston to-night, so they bring me back, starting at 11.30 eating on way, arr. 3.15. Unpack & practise pft before tea. Go & see Kennedy Scott at 5.0 about my "Boy". He frankly doesn't like it, – thinks it ineffective, too difficult, & not 'cantabile'nough. We'll see

about that. At anyrate he's not going to do it with the Philharmonic Choir. Write letters after dinner.

Tuesday 27 June [London]
Copy rest of 'I lov'd a lass' in morning (for English Singers), & also begin 'Lift Boy' after dinner. Begin negotiations with B.B.C. about 'Boy', in morning. Rehearsal of F.B. trio in aft. at R.C.M 2.15–4.0. Hair cut at Whiteleys after – walk there & back thro' park. V. Hot day.

Thursday 29 June
Alter more Phant in morning & also practise Pft before rehearsing Trio at R.C.M 12–1.30. Pft practice & then lesson at 4.10. Grace comes to dinner. Then at 9.15. Beth goes with her, & I go with Bridges to Gala perf of Carmargo Ballet (in honour of Delegates of Congress) at Covent Garden. V. good seats. Coppelia Act I dull (spoilt by bad rhythm of Lambert conducting). Lopakova excellent in rest tho'. Anton Dolin in v. marvellous España; & Lac des Cygnes with Dolin & Markova.

Saturday 1 July
Alot more copying in morning. Beth & I go to Wimbledon in aft. for tennis championships. V. Hot. Only see edges of various matches (F. Krahwinkle v. Mrs. King) Helen Jacobs v. Miss Burke, Austin v. Spence etc) until we were presented with a very good centre court ticket from a stanger where we see Cochet v. Jones, & Hughes & Mrs Moody (marvellous) v. W.E.M. Collins & Miss Webb.[80] Owing to crowds take 80 mins getting back, arr. 8.10.

Monday 3 July
More copying in morning, also odd jobs (iron trousers etc); lunch at Piganis with Cyril Dalmaine to see about 'Boy'. Practise pft after shopping abit (get L'isle joyeus for AR.CM)[81] & after tea. More copying ~~after~~ before dinner & after a bit of 'Kum-bak' after dinner.

Monday 10 July [Lowestoft/London]
Mum comes down with me to station when I ~~to~~ catch 8.30 back to town. Taxi at once to B.B.C. where I hear end of rehearsal of wireless singers (8 + 2 for boys pt.) doing my Boy.[82] That from 12–12.45; & again aft. lunch back here 2.30–3.30, then a run through for the B.B.C. music staff to hear. I am relieved to say that it all comes off splendidly. They sang it excellently considering they were sight-reading it from M.S. parts (copied at 5.30 in morning!). I am very pleased & bucked. Beth (who comes by 9.58–1.13) & I go to Barb. after supper. Write letters also.

Tuesday 11 July

Practise Pft all morning after a walk with Beth on ~~the~~ her way to Hampstead. Also abit of pft in aft. after an unsuccessful attempt to alter Ob. Quart. Beth & I go to Jubilee Recital at R.C.M. v. dull. Irene Kohler plays alot with excellent technique. Ber. & a May Barrett give a competant perf. of Ireland's cello. Sonata.[83] The rest negligible

Thursday 13 July

Have hectic rush to get alterations of Phant. copied into parts before going to R.C.M. at 12.0 for rehearsal with Natalie Caine (ob.) Lauricella, Riddle & Bernard. Some of the alterations are O.K. Some arn't. Play abit with Lauri after. Practise pft after a late lunch & after tea. Long walk in Battersea park with Beth after dinner.

Monday 17 July

Finish off parts before going at 11.20 to R.C.M. for Benjamin. Play Choral Variations to Howells. Also meet a Mr. Boys, Critic studying at College[84] – Have a rehearsal of Phant. at 2.0. previous to a perf. of it at my -comp. exam at 3.0. Examiners – Waddington, Rootham & R.O. Morris, who find it a bit excru~~t~~ciating. Hear abit of my Var. Walk with Boys after & play him Var. Kum-bak after tea; nothing after dinner.

Wednesday 19 July

Beth leaves here to sleep at 559 Finchley Road. She leaves with all her goods & shattels soon after breakfast. I copy parts & rewrite bits of Phant. in morning. After lunch take these parts to Mangeot, & run thro' a Goossens Lyric Poem with him.[85] Practise Pft after that & after tea. Shop, & then go up to Beth's for dinner. Help her pack & get straight. Get back by 11.0.

Pft. Exam at 10.0 (Ernest Walker, Barton & Fryer. Exam).

Friday 21 July

Go to B.B.C. with Mangeot after to play over Lyric Poem of Goossens with him for Benefit of Edward Clark. He takes me back to lunch with Anne MacNaghten. Meet Boys at R.C.M. in aft. Shop after tea & pack. After dinner Beth & I (getting 2 10/6 tickets – Because of Farrar prize just won) go to Alhambra for Ballet.[86] See Petrouchka, that marvel, with Woisekovsky, Riabouchinska, & Lichene. The perf. was worthy of the Ballet. Jeux D'Enfants (Bizet), & Cottillon (Chabrier tho' good, were rather an ~~at~~ anti-climax after the other.[87] Mangeot takes both Beth & me back to our respective dwellings in his car after.

Tuesday 25 July [Friston/London]
Ber & I leave at 8.0 for town arr. (he has to go to town so brings me) at 10.45. I go to O.U.P. to see Foss at 12.0 abt. publishing "Boy". Back to lunch with Mangeot & rehearsal of Phant at 2.0. only Leon Goossens dosn't turn up. So Silvia Spencer runs it through for us. Hair cut after that. Dinner at Bridges' (where I'm staying the night). F.B. conducts a Symphony Conct at Waterloo Studio (no. 10) of B.B.C. at 9.35. Dvovak (in Der Natur). Debussy (L'Après Midi). His own very brilliant Dance poem (v. orig since written (& hissed) in 1913) & Schumann (4th Symph.).[88] Everything is thoroughly thought out & done in the right & only way. Orch. always plays much better under F.B. than any one. The Brosas come back for a supper after.

Abit cooler, thank Heaven.
Friday 28 July [Lowestoft]
Write many & long letters in morning. Bathe before lunch. Go to tennis at Boswells in aft (Barb. Spashett & Dr. Palmer there). Rains a bit. I use my new racquet (not in rain of course) bought this morning (Austin 60/-). We win 2 first matches in challenge round of Davis Cup v. France. Walk with hound before dinner & bed. Listen to Mangeot playing 'Lyric Poem' (E. Goossens) in evening. It is a thousand pities that this man, interested in music & a musician, is simply incapable of playing the fiddle.

Saturday 5 August [London]
Rehearse at 10.0 with Goosens, Mangeot etc. Lunch at Miss Wheatley's (from Burleigh House) Estab. Back to B's for a read & rest; go to Amrid Johnston's for tea & talk abt. "Boy" cover.[89] Go to dinner with Brosas. V. amusing & good time. Back by 11.30.

It's really too hot to go out in morning. Mum & Pop arr. at Burleigh house for lunch, which I have there with them.
Sunday 6 August
Laze in afternoon there – listen to Brosa recitaling 5.30–6.0. Go to B.B.C. for reheasal (& control balance) at 7.45. In the Chamber Concert (Mozart G maj. & Faure – International Str. Q.). at 9.5.[90] Goossens & Mangeot, Bray, & Shineborne broadcast my Phant. Ob. Quart. Mum Pop, Mr. & Mrs. Brosa come to listen. Goossens does his part splendidly. The rest – altho' they are intelligent players, arn't really first class instrumentalists.

Thursday 10 August [Lowestoft]
Get up after breakfast, & spend day about house & garden. Read (Begining 'Scenes of Clerical Life')[91] Gramophone (Sacre, & Tristan), Pft. (Beethoven

& Bach mostly – especially that marvellous op. 103(?) – D maj. Sonata of the former).[92] Mum & family have tea party on beach in aft. I stay here with Pop who goes to bed for evening.

Saturday 12 August

Practise Pft; write abit more of ~~alla~~ arr. of "Boy" in morning; & walk with hound before lunch. In aft. Bobby, Mum, & Marj. & I go over to Priest's for tennis. Not excellent tennis, but fun. After dinner listen to opening night of Proms – in which Toni Brosa plays Symp. Esp.[93] marvellously – except for a lapsis memoriae in the last mov. After that Bobby & I go on Speed Boat fr. S. Pier. Marvellous thrill.

Monday 14 August

Begin for umpteenth time Rag for St. Quart. in morning.[94] David (Jerry) Gill comes to try over bit of 'Boy' for me at 11.30; & all Reeves come & bathe after (Bazil, Cyril, David – & Jerry). In aft. Jerry & David come to Bathe & tea at hut, with me alone. Bobby & Marjorie are out for day, & Barb. & Mum look after John. After dinner Barb, Bobby, Marj. & Me all go on Electric boats in Kens. Gardens

Saturday 2 September

Practise pft. abit before going over with Laurence & Teddy to Bungay at 11.0. L. plays his handicap singles final v. Gibson abt. 12.0, & wins in three sets. After lunch, Mum & Fernande come driven by Beth. L & I play in the men's Handicap doubles final v. Gibson & Jewson losing a v. good match, 9/7, ~~6/4~~ 4/6, 6/2. Tea there, brought by Mum; back by 6.30. We all four go to Sparrow's nest to see 'Fresh Fields' by Ivor Novello.[95] Well acted, & v. amusing in spots. Tho' on whole a weak attempt of satire on social custom.

Monday 4 September

Write, abit (only a fraction) more of 'rag' in morning & aft. Walk with Beth up town before bathe with her & Mum & then lunch. Play tennis with Fernande ~~Rogers~~ Sewell, & Teddy Rogers & Beth before dinner. Listen to Florence Austral & Walter Widdop hacking their way thro' the Love Duet [*Tristan und Isolde*] – a badly chosen & ill balanced bit too.

Wednesday 6 September

Pft. Practise & sketching in morning. Also bathe before lunch with Beth & David Boswell v. rough & high tide. My gramophone records (1 already here, 3 new ones) of Missa Solemnis come. V. disappointed with perf. (soloists excru~~t~~ciating – chorus pretty bad – orch. v. good cond. Bruno Kittel, rather incompetant).[96] Read, laze, cut grass in aft. All Boyds come to tea. Putt with John & David after; then Bathe with Beth, John & Ethel Boyd at 6.30.

Friday 8 September
Letters, pft practise, revision, walk up town shopping with Hound in morning. Also much playing of records of Mass in D.[97] I like them better. with abit of careful toning down, the soloists can be made to sound more normal. But what music! The end of the Gloria (fugue esp.) drives me potty. We have the 2 Welfords & Peggy Haes to bathe & tea at hut in aft. Putt & go on electric boats in Kensington gardens. Listen to Beethoven's raelly delightful Triple Concerto from prom.[98]

Monday 11 September
My proofs of a 'Boy was born' come in morning; Spend much time beginning to correct. Also copy more. Walk with hound & pt. way Mum before lunch. Correct in garden in aft. After tea go to Teddy Rogers & play singles. Mum helps abit to correct after dinner.

Wednesday 13 September
Finish Copying Rag in morning, & more correcting. Kit Welford calls for me at 12.0. & takes me back to Peasenhall for lunch, tennis, & tea. Stephen Crowdie's there. Catch 6.0. train back from Saxmundham. More correcting after dinner – it's perfectly frightful the number of mistakes there are. I've just bought Pop the records of Ravel's Bolero – his latest craze.

Thursday 14 September
Alot of correcting in morning then walk with Mum & hound, & pt. way Bazil Reeve up town before lunch. In aft. instead of tennis party – abandoned thro' rain, Anne Rix takes the party (me included) to Grand to see 'the Sign of the Cross'.[99] Charles ~~Laugth~~ Laughton is excellent as Nero; & there is some marvellous photography & production. Tho extremely melodramatic, it is frightfully harrowing, & I can't get out of my head what those ceatures suffered. More correcting in evening.

Friday 15 September
2 Welfords, Stephen Crowdie, Bazil Reeve come to lunch, & bathe on beach. Walk shopping before they arrive at 11.15. They go, after going on electric boats abt. 3.15. After tea I walk with Caesar as far as Kessingland Dam to meet Pop, & drive back. Listen, at 10.30, to Clark conducting a perf of my Sinfonietta from B.B.C. V. rushed in places & obviously thoroughly under-rehearsed. Some of the soloists were good.

Monday 18 September
Begin packing in morning. Bathe before lunch (in spite of rather rainy weather) with Mum & Bazil Reeve. Finish packing, walk with hound in aft. Pop takes me to station with Mum intending to catch 5.45 – but finding that I have to change at Beccles, he takes me on to there to catch 6.9. It's frightful having to say good-bye to him & Mum. Arr. after long & dirty journey, at 9.29 & at 173, Cromwell Rd; before ten. Ring up Beth & Barbara.

Tuesday 19 September [London]
Go to R.C.M. in morning to see Authorities about me returning thither this term – there seems to have been some doubt about it. Also see Herbert Howells about my 'Boy'. proofs. On to Anne MacN's about my Quartet pieces[100] after. Lunch with Mangeot, & try various things over with him. Unpack in aft. After tea play tennis with Mangeot, Son (Faulk) & friend at Melbury Club. V. good tennis, & grt.fun. Go to see Beth after supper rather late back.

Friday 22 September
Go to R.C.M. to arrange about lessons, & see Ireland first thing in morning. For rest of morning go to Bridges & practise on their piano – they're away at Friston. Lesson with Benjamin at 2.0. Go after that to meet Francis Barton (see S. Lodge days) at Liverpool St. at 4.0. Walk & have tea with him. See him off to Haileybury at 6.0. It's good to see him again. Listen after dinner to bit of Prom. on very bad wireless here. H. Samuel plays Beethoven 2nd Concerto simply beautifully.[101]

Monday 25 September
Go to College to fetch proofs of 'Boy' from Herbert Howells – which he's been correcting, in morning. Final revision of proofs for rest of morning & afternoon. See Ireland after tea at his studio. Write letters after dinner, & then see Grace Williams.

Tuesday 26 September
See Hugh Allen about future job at 10.30. Go on to Oxford Press after to see about details re proofs. Practise Pft all aft (I've got one in my rooms, now that I've decided to stay here this term). Beth comes after dinner for bath. Many letters.

Friday 29 September
Alot of pft practice, & alittle writing during day. Play at 4.0, at R.C.M. with Kathleen Long F.B's Phantasm, which she is playing on B.B.C. soon. She

plays it excellently. See Grace after that. Listen to [Beethoven] Choral Fantasia & 9th from Prom, after dinner. Even Wood's eccentricacies, and the rather roughness of performance couldn't hide the unapproachable genius & inspiration of the whole of the latter.

Saturday 30 September

Odd jobs in morning; bit of writing & pft practise. Tuner comes for pft. Tennis with Mangeots at Effingham. Mrs. Currie takes me in her car. Mangeot brings me back for a hurried dinner, after which I meet Barbara at Q. Hall for Prom (tickets from B.B.C.). Thoroughly light & vulgar 1st half, which I thoroughly enjoy – selec. from Mignon, Carmen, Rigol. Pagliacci, Walton's Façade, & above all Strauss's wonderful, moving Don Quixote, excellently played by L. Kenneddy, but v. scrappily by orch. 2nd half we only stuck a garish arr. of Handel Org. Conc. played (when one could hear him) by Stanley Marchant.

Sunday 1 October

Walk with Grace in morning, in parks. After lunch I go down to Croyden to the Richards for tea & supper (combined). Alot of people there (+ instruments) – enough to play 3rd Brandenburg, & Dvorak Pft. 5tet [102] etc. etc. Also much ping-pong with Bernard. Back by 11.30.

Monday 2 October

Spend all morning & aft. (except for abit of practising before tea) at March. Get on quite abit with it. Go to a concert by Schusster (of Berlin Phil), 'cello. at 8.30 at ~~Wigmore~~ Grotrian Hall. V. dull programme – ~~rather~~ inadequately played. Good technique, with wobbly intonation & an almost complete lack of rhythm. I go with Grace, tickets from Miss Bond via Barbara

Tuesday 3 October

Work at march in morning – rewriting & continuing. Bit of pft practise. Rehearse F.B. 'cello sonata with Ber. all aft. in my room. After tea Grace & I go bargain hunting in the Charing X Rd. She finds several scores she wants, but I find nothing. Listen to Delius' new Idyll[103] in evening – judging from perf on a disgraceful wireless, this just says what D. has said so often before, & perhaps it doesn't say it as well.

Thursday 5 October

Go to Queen's Hall with Mr. Bridge at 10.0 to Prom. rehearsal. He conducts his 'Dance Poem'. Back to Lunch with him & Mrs. Work abit in aft. Ber. comes after tea. Go with him to Prom at 8.0 (tickets from B.B.C.). Bartered Bride. ov. 6

attractive, yet flimsy Catalan Folk Songs (Sophie Wyss). Elgar's Impossible Vln. concerto (not perfectly played by Sammons). Schubert Unfinished. All played by orch without any enthusiasm, altho' they worked up abit of that for F.B's Dance Poem, which he conducts splendidly.[104] It's a haunting work.

Friday 6 October [London/Lowestoft]
As I'm leaving town I have to make many arrangements re proofs etc. See Bridges at abt. 11.0 re various matters. Go on to R.C.M. for short lesson from Ireland at 12.25. Catch 3.10 from Liverpool St. Travel some of way with David Green, & Laurence Talbot. Mum meets me. Pop is not too bad, but he really might be a good deal better.

Wednesday 11 October [Lowestoft]
Much pft practise in morning. After that finish my 'Physical Training', with much effort.[105] Walks, in aft & after tea. Pop's cough is dreadful; why in the world can't something be done for it? I'm reading H.G. Wells the Bulpington of Blub,[106] which seems very interesting.

Thursday 12 October
Finish picking apples in back garden after breakfast. Pack etc. Take Mum out in car for a drive before lunch. Practise Pft abit in aft. Also walk with Caesar. Mum walks down to station with me to catch 5.45 back to town. Arr. 9.24, at 173 at 10.5. It's impossibly ghastly leaving home with Pop like this.

Tuesday 17 October [London]
Finish part before going to R.C.M. at 11.40 to Ber's lesson with Mr. Whitehouse. Do 'Eccles, & Bridge Sonatas. Ber comes all afternoon to rehears, & I go to play with him in R.C.M. Concert Hall at 5.0. See Bridges on way back. Begin & finish Viola part before & after going to rehearsal of Carlyle Singers of my 2 pt. songs – Love'd a Lass & Lift Boy.

Thursday 19 October
So-called lesson with Ireland at 9.45. Copy much after that & in aft. Go to R.C.M. to do some arranging, via Bridges. Back here for tea to which Howard Ferguson comes, in my room. See his Octet.[107] Go to concert at R.A.M. with F.B. after dinner. Works of Comp. masters there – not a single bit of music among the 9 items (didn't hear all of the Bush Quart[108] – tho' end was well done of it's kind). An excellent quart. did some work – led by David Martin.

Saturday 21 October
Quartet rehearsal postponed. Walk to see Ireland & deliver a book token in morning. Odd job. Meet Meiklejohn (from Holt) & lunch with him in

Soho. He is up with a friend from Oxford & we three go to Sadler's Wells at 2.30 to see R-Korsakov's diverting & ext. clever 'Tsar Saltan'.[109] A good all round cast; ensemble in orch a good deal lacking – owing to cond. – Laurence Collingwood. Stephan Crowdie comes to dinner. We go out to a Fair at Hammersmith after that. Back & talk.

Monday 23 October

More copying of parts all morning before early lunch; rehearsal at R.C.M. 1–2.30. Irene & Bernard Richards (Vl.1.,Vlc), Nora Wilson (Vla) while I deputise for F.Riddle on Vl.2. They do movs. 1,2, 5 of my 'Go play Boy, play',[110] which comes off well, I think. Rehearse with Lauricella all aft, & practise pft after tea. Go to see Bridges after dinner; John Alston's there.

Wednesday 25 October

More attempts & failures to write, & copy more parts, in morning.[111] In aft. I go to Steinway studios to play orch. part of F.B's 'Phantasm' with Kathleen Long. Mr. & Mrs. B. are there too, & we all tea at M.M. Club after.[112] Meet Beth at 6.15, shop, eat & then go to Old Vic, with Mrs. & Elizabeth Boyd & Miss Wheately, to see Cherry Orchard[113] with Charles Laughton, Flora Robson, Léon Quatermain etc. in a superb cast. But what a play! Dwarfs every other. The acting, production & play were a revalation.

Thursday 26 October

Pts, arranging at R.C.M. & elsewhere in morning. Rehearse (with new Viola – Beryl Blunt) at R.C.M., ~~at~~ 1–2, my 'Go play, Boy play' (or what's done of it) with Quartet. Lunch after, here. Amrid Johnston comes in aft. about cover of 'A Boy was born'. Lauricella comes to be accompanied after tea. Beth comes to dinner & we both go to an 'At home' of Lady MacCormick's at Doughty House Richmond where the Wyn Reeves play some quartets – Schubert & Brahms in A min, & F.B's Cherry Ripe & Sally.[114]

Thursday 2 November

Pft. in morning. Write a song, for R.H.M.B. & Clive House, very light & bad – 'I mun be married a Sunday', in aft.[115] After tea go to Ireland's Studio where the Quartet (Richards Etc.) play the existing 3 movs. of 'Go play, boy'. Go to dinner with Bridges – Mrs. Brosa is there too. After dinner, they take her back in their car – I go too & then they drop me here.

Friday 3 November

Practise pft. before pft. lesson with Benj. at 11.10. Rehearsal with Quart. at 1–2. Lunch. Irene Richards, Margot Stebbings, Beryl Blunt, & Ber play the

3 existing mov. of my 'Alla Quartetto Serioso' to the Mendelssohn Committee at 4.0 at R.C.M. (They have granted me a 2nd £80 & want to hear the result (?!!)). Grace comes after ~~tea~~ dinner to listen to 1st ~~pf~~ perf. of Bliss new Vla. Sonata.[116] On a very bad wireless, this work seemed very dull tho' beautifully played by Tertis & Solomon. Letters also.

Saturday 4 November
Practise pft. before going to Bumpus's to shop in morning. The Queen (~~ing~~ 'incognito') comes in when I'm there.[117] Go for a long walk over Wandsworth Common with Grace all aft. On way back, by bus, I give my seat to a woman, & being discovered standing by conductor am ordered off bus – Which means much waste of time, altho' next conductor (on learning facts) gives ~~me~~ us the remainder [page torn here] ride free. Tea with Grace.

Final revision of proofs of 'Boy' in morning; also abit of pft. practise.
Wednesday 8 November
Go to lunch in South Ken. with Stephan Crowdy 12.45–1.30. Then to O.U.P. Back via Poetry Bookshop.[118] Lauri comes for a rehearsal after tea. Go to B.B.C. Symphony concert, cond. so called, by A. Boult. Rimsky Korsakov's Easter ov. sounded dead. Bartok (a v. fine pianist) played his 2nd Conc. I don't want it. To finish with Bliss's truly dated Morning Heroes. Massacre of fine words. Scherzo was best – but, what a concert! The Bridges bring Grace (who went with me) & me back in their car.

Thursday 9 November
Grace comes to see me abt. some matters after breakfast. Practise pft. rest of morning. Ber. & Irene Richards come here 1.45–4.45 for long rehearsal at Beethoven & abit at Ravel Trios. I go to Ireland's Studio at 5.0, for lesson. But the dear man doesn't turn up. So far in 8 weeks of term I have had 4 (so-called) lessons from him. Write letters etc. after dinner.

Saturday 11 November
After 2 mins silence[119] I walk across park to Whiteleys to have my hair cut. Long walk in park & tea afterwards with Grace Williams. Meet Lucy & Stephen Crowdie at 6.30 at Piccadilly. Beth was to have come too, but she has gone home for week-end. We eat at Brasserie Universale & then go to see Matheson Lang in the 'Wandering Jew'.[120] The Acting is very fine in this impressive but rather overdrawn play. Some of the crowd scenes & noises weren't exactly thrilling, but the end was very fine.

Tuesday 14 November
Rewrite bits of & patch up score of Phantasy before going to lunch ~~at~~ with Foss (Holbon Restaurant). Go to Trio rehearsal at 3.30 at Mrs. Brosa's studio, until 6.30. Go to Badminton club for ½ hr, & then rush back to Carlyle Singers rehearsal (at 179 Crom. Rd) of my 2 part songs at 9.30.

Wednesday 15 November
Write all morning, a piffling little song – 'Jazz Man';[121] also search for words for more. Walk after lunch. Pft. practice; then play with Lauricella 3.30–6.0. Go to B.B.C. Symphony Conc. with Beth at 8.15. Cond. Weingartner. H. Samuel plays Beethoven 2nd Conc. delightfully – tho' abit inaccurate in spots. W. ~~do~~ is disappointing; the Brahms (Variations)[122] was rough, & rather dull (tho' who could make that antidiluvian scoring sound interesting); & the Symphony Fantastique of Berlioz didn't sound as electrifying as it should – in spite of all the din & speed.

Thursday 16 November
Practise pft before the Richards come at 11.0 for Trio Rehearsal until 1.0. Rewrite bits of Quartet parts (Ob) & send them off to Mangeot together with parts of the existing 'Boy' Quartet to Anne who wants to do them so much that I have weakly given way.[123] Barb. at Selfridges at 5.0. & John Nicholson at Piccadilly at 6.15. Go to a News Theatre & Dinner after. Walk most of way home. Letters – bed.

Friday 17 November
Open banking account at Lloyds early in morning. Practise pft before lesson with Benj. at 11.10. See Bridges (Mrs. is off to Hanover) for lunch; lesson with Ireland at 2.30. Meet Francis Barton at Whitehall at 4.0 & wait for him until 5.30 while his is medically examined for Navy. Tea with him at my digs & see him off at 7.20 from Charing X. Letters & have a tea party (!) with Miss Wheatly & Sylvia Buckland before bed. Also pack.

Sunday 19 November [Lowestoft]
Walk with Pop (rather slowly tho') down to club in morning. Read in aft – H.G. Wells' Joan & Peter,[124] very interesting & amusing – & then walk with Caesar. Letter & pft. & gramophoning (Beethoven's acme of beauty – the Mass in D) before supper. Reading & more letters after. Mum & Pop have given me for my birthday (held to-day instead of Wed.) a marvellous pair of fur gloves.

Wednesday 22 November [London]
Practise pft & arrange matters most of day. Lauricella comes to play at 4.30–6.30. Dinner with Mrs. & Miss Hurst & Barbara at the flat. Beth comes

after. As it's my birthday – more presents: Money – Aunts Julianne & Nellie & Miss Turner. Umbrella – Barbara & Beth. Book – Bobby. Sweets – Miss Hurst. Alice tho' the looking glass – Mrs. Hurst. & of course the fur gloves.

Monday 27 November

Write another School Song (Abram Brown) in morning also practise pft. Trio in aft. Meet Beth & have photos taken (gratis of course) at Swaines Bond St. after tea.[125] At 31 Tite St.[126] I go to a concert of modern chamber music (arr by D. Ponsonby) – Mangeot etc. & Goossens. They do – not well – my Oboe quartet. I turn over for Yvonne Arnaud playing Ravel Trio & Poulenc for Ob. & Fg. (G. & Newton).[127] Excellent performances. Meet Many people – on to Waterhouses for supper after.

Wednesday 29 November

Pft more or less all day. Lauri. comes 4.30–5.30 for rehearsal of Tschaikov. concerto. Go to Trinity Hall at 6.0 with him to hear first London perf. of Foss' Vln Sonata – afraid it's bad.[128] Perf. by him & Barbara Pulowmacher (bad). After dinner Miss Wheatley & I go to Rialto, to see French Film 'Poil de Carrotte' with Robert Lynen (Poil) & [Harry] Baeur (Pére).[129] Simply superb show. Photography & Acting, producing & plot all first rate. The father is grand & as for Poil – he is a magnificent emotional artist. I was thoroughly harrowed, intensely amused, & thrilled beyond measure, the whole time

Friday 1 December

Practise pft before going to R.C.M. for a pft. lesson with Angus Morrison (deputising for Benj). Pft in aft. Go to lesson with Ireland after tea 5.0–6.30. Go to Chamber concert at 8.30 with Grace at B.B.C. – Kolisch Quartet. playing Mozart D min. & Beethoven A min. Krenek – var. from op 5. & five pieces of Webern.[130] All from Memory – astounding. Amazing technique & the perf of modern works all to be desired. The classics ought to have been perfect too – but spoilt by erractic speeds (esp. finale of B.) & general lack of understanding. The Krenek, as music, was dull. The Webern interesting & very beautiful in parts.

Saturday 2 December

Hair cut & shop (for 'Poil de Carrotte') in morning. Tea & Talk with J. Ireland in aft. After an early dinner go to Studio no. 10 at Waterloo with F.B. where he conducts a concert with B.B.C. orch. at 8.15. Strauss' superb Don Juan is very well played. Astra Desmond sings Saint Saens' 'Fiancée du Timbalier' – very moving. 2 Bits from Hänsel & Gretel; F.B.'s two lovely

Tagore songs, & Chasseur Maudit of Franck to end with. Back to 4 Bedford Gardens with F.B. for supper.

Thursday 7 December

Pft practise & then Trio. 11.0–1.0. Go to R.A.M. to a New Music Society concert. Where the Grinke Trio (G. (Vl), Florence Hooton (Vlc) & Dorothy Manley (Pft)) play F.B.'s last Trio magnificently.[131] It is a thrilling work, & I enjoyed & wondered at it enormously. The rest of the programme (except for an interesting Sonatina of Casella) was negligible.[132] Tea after at M.M. club with F.B., Miss Fass, & Mrs Brosa. Meet Beth & see Poil de Carrotte for second time. Just as impressed, harrowed, & thrilled. I understood it more easily; probably thr' knowing the book. What an artist that, Mde Lepic is; & that kid, & his father.

Monday 11 December

Practise pft before going to Anne's for rehearsal of St. Qu. at 11.30–12.30. Back via R.C.M. See Grace in aft (abt. Rudiments) & then on to tea with Ireland to play him pft pieces for A.R.C.M. Paul Wright comes to dinner, & go to Ballet Club with him by 8.30. 2nd of MacN. Lemare concerts – Choir (select (!!)), & quart. Do. Elizabeth Machonchy's Motets, & Syke's Motet. My 2 part songs (which I accompany) go quite well – esp. Lift Boy.[133] But really there isn't a singer in the lot of them. Anne did her best with my 'Go Play, Boy, Play' – but again, I want 1st class instrumentalists besides enthusiasm. Beth & Miss Wheatly go from here. Go on to MacNaghtens for supper after.

Tuesday 12 December

A.R.C.M. paper work & harmony (!) takes ½ hr at 10.0.[134] Practise at R.C.M. after that. Henry Boys (of R.C.M. – critic) comes to lunch. Pft in aft. Go to dinner with Beth before badminton.

Wednesday 13 December

Practise pft abit, & arr. matters with O.U.P. & Daily Telegraph etc. in morning. Go to A.R.C.M. Aural Exam at 2.40 & Practical Solo Pft. at 3.0. (Examiners. M. Barton; Kendall Taylor; Edwin Benbow) I hear after the [Beethoven] Mass that I've got through. See Mrs Bridge after exam; & then tea with Grace after that See Lauricella abit before dinner. Go to Queen's Hall for B.B.C. Concert. Beethoven's supreme Mass in D. I feel at the moment that it is impossible to conceive music greater than this. Boult even couldn't ruin it. Chorus not bad. Orch ditto though intonation poor, & Catteral [solo violin] was too hard in the Benedictus. The soloists – Adleheid Armhold (disappointing in a way, but very lovely in spots), Mary.Balfour (not too good); ~~Trefor~~ Parry Jones (better); Keith Falker (too insignificant) – weren't a good quartet. But even all this couldn't spoil this God of a work

Thursday 14 December
Rehearse at Northampton Institute with A.M.O. (late A.C.O.) orch.[135] under F.B. at 10.0 onwards, with F.B. I am playing cymbals! Back for lunch. Change into tails; go to Brosas' studio where I rehearse trio with Ber & sister at 3.30 to 6.0. Dinner with Mrs Brosa; Then Beth & I & she go on to concert. Play cymb. in 'In the South' of Elgar – a very beautiful work in parts. The rest of programme. Ravel 'Pavane'; Beethoven Vln Conct. (played by Orrea Pernel – quite good): Franck Symphony Back to supper with Bridges – after which F.B. drives us all home in turn – me last.

Friday 15 December
Pack in morning & aft, with much telephoning etc. Go to Bridges for tea & then on in there car to No. 10 Studio (Waterloo) of B.B.C. where F.B. conducts a run through of his Phantasm. I turn over for Kathleen Long, who plays it excellently. Beth comes to dinner; & Barbara after. They help me with packing. It's a fearful job, as I have to clear everything out of my room.

Saturday 16 December [London/Lowestoft]
Finish packing in morning. Go to see Grace, & Anne. Catch 3.10 home. Travel as far as Beccles with Moeran, & 'Harry', his folk-singer.[136] Mum meets me. Pop seems about the same – perhaps abit weaker.

Monday 18 December [Lowestoft]
Practise pft in morning. Walk with Mum before lunch, & with Caesar before tea. Letters & revise one or two M.S.'s between tea & dinner. Letters after dinner. Pop stays in bed all day until 8.0 He took some morphia last night & consequently (tho' one hopes <u>not</u> consequently) feels much better.

Tuesday 19 December
Make an attempt to write a feeble kids' song in morning.[137] Shop before lunch – also abit in afternoon. Gramophone before dinner. Listen to abit of Radio adaption of 'Christmas Carol' after dinner.[138] Pop seems much worse to-day. Effects of morphia going off I'm afraid.

Thursday 21 December
Hunt through tons of old M.S. for material for School String suite in morning; afternoon.[139] Walk up town (shopping) before lunch. Pop isn't really so well, I'm afraid. Miss Ethel Astle comes in, in evening.

Friday 22 December

More M.S. hunting in morning. Shopping with Mum before lunch, & all aft (with Caesar) alone. Tie up parcels & write letters after tea. Listen to 'Cris du Monde' of Honegger after dinner.[140] Difficult to judge, as it came over badly; some of it was very impressive (esp. the end) & extraordinarily beautiful.

Saturday 23 December

Hair cut after breakfast. Have a drive alone in Humber, before going down to meet Beth and Barbara off 1.26 from town (actually it arr. at 2.0). Shop in aft, & late tea. Begin pizz. scherzo for Str (arr. of piece written when abt. ~~10~~ 11 or 12)[141] Listen to Wireless (Walton's Façade) after dinner.

F.B. sends me a colossal box of chocolates & Mrs B. a tool combination – v. good. Laulie an eversharp.[142]

Monday 25 December

St. John's early (8.0) with Barb. & Beth. Presents ~~after~~ at breakfast – to which Pop comes down. He & Mum give me new overcoat – books (Carroll) from Barb, & Beth, & also one from Aunt Flo. 5/- Aunt Julianne. Musical handkerchiefs from Bobby, Writing paper from Miss Hayes. Walk with Beth & Barb. along cliffs before lunch. Listen to very good broadcast in aft – Absent friends scenes from all over British Isles, & then from all over the Brit. Empire.[143] Bit of Scherzo after tea.[144] Pop struggles down to dinner (Xmas one), but is feeling rotten. Listen to v. fine broadcast of Act II of Mikado (glorious thing).[145]

Sunday 31 December

Go for a drive in car (last day of Humber)[146] with Barb. & Beth, & then for short one with Mum. Read in aft. – finish Barries' little wonder – 'The Little White Bird'.[147] Walk with Barb. before tea. See her off at Station with Bobby, back to town at 5.28. Walk with Bobby before bed. Pop's pretty bad in evening – sick with cough. [BB leaves a two-line gap at this point, separating the remainder of this entry with a wavy line.]

I'm not sorry this year is over, tho' in many ways it's been a good year. Beth has started building up what looks as if it's going to be a fine business. Bobby's school is progressing, slowly though surely.[148] I have had a good deal of publicity – Broadcasts & D. Telegraph especially. But the slur on the whole has been Pop's dreadful illness. I know that every one of us would give all ~~they~~ we have to see him well & fit again. Mum's nursing & ~~spirit~~ pluck has been the only bright spot in the whole dreadful time. – So, farewell 1933. Let us see whether 1934 can give us back what seems to us the impossible – Pop's health.

Notes: 1930–1933

NOTES: 1930

1. The boarding house in Bayswater, 52 Princes Square, London W2, where Britten lodged for his first year at the Royal College of Music. The RCM was just across Kensington Gardens, on Prince Consort Road, SW7.
2. 81 Holbein House, Holbein Place, London SW1.
3. One of three department stores then on Kensington High Street, London SW1.
4. Sister of Miss Thurlow Prior and fellow lodger at Princes Square, who worked at Central Hall, Westminster, and was an old friend of Mrs Britten from the National Choral Society.
5. Formed by the BBC in 1928 for the first performance of Granville Bantock's oratorio, *The Pilgrim's Progress*; renamed the BBC Chorus in 1932, the BBC Choral Society in 1935, and the BBC Symphony Chorus in 1977.
6. London's Queen's Hall, at Langham Place, W1 (adjacent to All Souls, Langham Place and BBC Broadcasting House) was the premier concert hall in London before the Second World War. It opened in 1893, and from 1895 it was the home of the Promenade Concerts, founded by Robert Newman and Henry Wood. It was destroyed by an incendiary bomb in 1941.
7. Three decades later Britten was to conduct this symphony (with Joan Carlyle and the London Symphony Orchestra) at the 1961 Aldeburgh Festival, a broadcast recording of which was later released commercially by the BBC on their *Britten the Performer* archive series in 1999.
8. Bridge *Enter Spring*, Rhapsody for orchestra (1926–7); Walton *Sinfonia Concertante* for piano and orchestra (1927); Bax Symphony No. 3 (1929).
9. The department store in Bayswater, now a shopping mall.
10. Beethoven Overture, *Namensfeier* (Namesday).
11. Britten did come round to Elgar later in life, conducting at the Aldeburgh Festival and recording for Decca both the *Introduction and Allegro* for strings and *The Dream of Gerontius*.
12. A student work that does not figure in Ferguson's published output.
13. Ravel Piano Trio in A minor (1914).
14. The department store at 400 Oxford Street, London W1.
15. Founded in 1929 by Arnold Foster (1896–1963), its conductor until the ensemble's demise in 1940. Britten (singing bass) and Barbara (soprano) were members (1930–3); Barbara was also Secretary of the Choir.
16. Britten worked for the best part of three months, under Ireland's guidance, on his 'Palestrinian Mass', preserved in the Britten Archive in an ink fair copy dated 'Oct. 4th 1930–Jan. 16th 1931'.

17. Probably St James's, Sussex Gardens. As there hasn't been a Bishop of Westminster since the 16th century, Britten is probably referring to William Foxley Norris, KCVO (1859–1937), then Dean of Westminster Abbey (1925–1937).
18. A specialist music shop at 210 Shaftesbury Avenue, London WC2.
19. It is interesting to note that Britten had not received any strict harmony and counterpoint lessons with Bridge, but it was Bridge who recommended that Britten study with Ireland at the RCM, so perhaps he was aware that a different, more theoretical approach (for a while, at least) would be of some benefit to his young protégé. Consecutive parallel fifths between voice parts are considered inadmissible in terms of the strict harmonic principles of Palestrinian counterpoint. See 12 January 1931.
20. Mozart – either K271 or K482; Brahms Piano Quintet in F minor, Op. 34; Debussy *Fêtes* from *Trois Nocturnes* (1899); Ravel *La Valse*.
21. *The Three Musketeers* (1844), novel by Alexandre Dumas, père (1802–70).
22. Brahms *Schicksalslied*, Op. 54, for chorus and orchestra (1868–71).
23. 'Pit' is the classic game of commodities trading.
24. *A Prayer* (Thomas à Kempis), Bridge's only work for chorus and orchestra (1916), an invocation to peace that must have appealed to Britten's pacifist sensibilities.
25. This must have been an early sketch in piano reduction (or possibly a potential arrangement) of the first two movements of Benjamin's *Light Music Suite* (1928–33) for orchestra.
26. Brahms Piano Concerto No. 2 in B flat major, Op. 83, String Quintet No. 2 in G, Op. 111; Schubert Symphony No. 9 in C, D944; Beethoven Serenade in D for flute, violin and viola, Op. 25.
27. Polka and Fugue from Weinberger's fantasy opera, *Schwanda the Bagpiper*.
28. Britten refers here to the 'Great' C major Symphony of Schubert, D944, finished in 1826 and now numbered as the Ninth, but commonly referred to at this time as the Seventh, before the modern renumbering of the symphonies took into account the incomplete E major Symphony, D729, (sketched in 1821 and chronologically the seventh of the series), and the B minor 'Unfinished' Symphony, D759, dating from 1822.
29. This isn't entirely borne out by Arthur Benjamin's comments in Britten's end-of-term report, which were much more positive about Britten's prospects of a career as a pianist.
30. An amateur vocal and choral festival, supported by Vaughan Williams.
31. *The Bonny Lighter Boy*, an English folk-song most probably sourced by Mrs Britten from the collection of *One Hundred English Folksongs*, edited by Cecil Sharp and first published in 1916.
32. The impression that Britten dismissed all of Vaughan Williams' music is not borne out by his response to the *Fantasia on Christmas Carols* (1912, for baritone, chorus and orchestra) or indeed an earlier positive reference in the diaries to the *Tallis Fantasia* (1910). His criticism was largely directed at Vaughan Williams' symphonic writing and orchestration.

33. *Disraeli* (1929), an historical film (though fictionalised) about the great diplomat, starring George Arliss in an Oscar-winning performance, directed by Alfred E. Green.
34. Hermann Scherchen's reputation was founded on his performances of new music rather than the central classical repertory.
35. This was the broadcast debut of the National Chorus.
36. *Vigil* (Walter de la Mare) for bass (or contralto) and piano (23 December 1930/17 January 1931); revised in 1968 as the fourth of the de la Mare sequence, *Tit for Tat.*
37. The third of the *Three Character Pieces* for piano: 'Michael' [Tyler].

NOTES: 1931

1. The famous monologue from Act II of Mussorgksy's opera, *Boris Godunov.*
2. *O fly not, Pleasure*; see 10 July 1930.
3. Mozart K311 and John Ireland's piece for solo piano, *Merry Andrew* (1918).
4. Bridge's setting of Thomas à Kempis; Britten's annotated score is in the Britten Archive.
5. Britten's *A Hymn to the Virgin* (9 July 1930) and *I saw three ships* (12–13 September 1930).
6. For the Palestrina Mass exercise he was completing for John Ireland.
7. Beethoven Op. 49 No. 2; Schumann Op. 2.
8. Schoenberg's arrangement for orchestra (1928) of Bach's Prelude and Fugue in E flat (BWV552); *Friede auf Erden*, Op. 13 (1907) for chorus; and the monodrama *Erwartung*, Op. 17 (1909); a BBC Symphony Orchestra concert conducted by the composer, with Margot Hinnenberg-Lefebre as soloist.
9. *Sweet was the Song* (William Ballet's Lute Book) for alto and female voices, the start of an ambitious project for a 'Christmas Suite' for voices, referred to variously in these diaries as his choral symphony (23 February) and suite (20 March) and finally *Thy King's Birthday* (13 January–26 March 1931); published posthumously as *Christ's Nativity* by Faber Music in 1994.
10. *Mass for Four Voices* [Agnus Dei II for five voices] (4 October 1930–16 January 1931).
11. *Sport* (William Henry Davies), a setting of an anti-hunting poem, for bass and piano.
12. Delius *Two Pieces for Small Orchestra: On Hearing the First Cuckoo in Spring* (1912) and *Summer Night on the River* (1911).
13. Clearly Britten's fellow lodgers had a preference for dance-band music.
14. Arthur Benjamin Violin Concerto (1932).
15. His lodgings in Princes Square, Bayswater, London W2.
16. *Love Me Not for Comely Grace* (Anon.) for *a cappella* voices (SSAT).
17. Mozart Symphony No. 39 in E flat, K543.
18. Mahler *Lieder eines fahrenden Gesellen* (*Songs of a Wayfarer*) for low voice and orchestra (1884/1896).

19. A converted warehouse on the south bank of the Thames near Waterloo Bridge.
20. Desdemona's 'Willow Song' and *Ave Maria* from the final scene of Verdi's opera *Otello* (1887).
21. The second of Bridge's two *Poems* for orchestra (1915), after Richard Jefferies' *The Story of My Heart*.
22. *To the Willow-Tree* (Robert Herrick) for *a cappella* voices (SATB).
23. Ernest Ansermet conducted the BBC Symphony Orchestra in Stravinsky's *Mavra* (1922), the Concerto for Piano and Orchestra (1923–4), with the composer as soloist, *Apollon musagète* (1927–8), the UK premiere of *Four Studies* for orchestra (1928), and *Le sacre du printemps* (1911–13).
24. Bertie Horace Prigg, barber, 261/263 London Road South, Lowestoft.
25. Mr Britten was a member of the Royal Norfolk and Suffolk Yacht Club, Royal Plain, Lowestoft.
26. *O Lord, forsake me not* (from Psalms 28, 38, 39 & 116), motet for double chorus.
27. Founded by Norland College in 1892, nurses trained in childcare, to work with children in private homes and institutions.
28. *Daily Light on the Daily Path: A Devotional Textbook for Every Day of the Year in the Very Words of the Scripture* (*c.*1875) compiled by Jonathan Bagster and members of his family.
29. The *Radio Times* is the broadcast listing magazine of the British Broadcasting Corporation.
30. Brahms String Quartet No. 3 in B flat, Op. 67.
31. Holst's orchestral suite was broadcast from a concert given at London's Queen's Hall, by the BBC Symphony Orchestra and Wireless Chorus, conducted by Adrian Boult.
32. Delius *Appalachia: Variations on an Old Slave Song with Final Chorus*, for chorus and orchestra.
33. First draft of his setting of C. W. Stubbs' *Carol of King Cnut* for *Thy King's Birthday*.
34. Mozart Violin Concerto No. 5 in A, 'Turkish', K219.
35. Bridge *Oration: Concerto Elegiaco*, for cello and orchestra (1929–30).
36. Beethoven Piano Trio No. 4 in B flat, Op. 11; Casella *Siciliana* and *Burlesca*, Op. 23, for piano trio (1914–17); Tchaikovsky Piano Trio in A minor, Op. 50. Britten's fellow lodger, Miss Atkinson, had provided the tickets for this concert in London's premier recital room on Wigmore Street, W1, a hall that was to be of great importance to Britten throughout his career.
37. The music publishers J. & W. Chester and Augeners in Great Marlborough Street, W1.
38. Brahms *Variations on a Hungarian Song*, Op. 21 No. 2; Prokofiev 'Prelude' from *Ten Pieces*, Op. 12 (1906–13); see 25 April.
39. *Beethoven: Impressions by His Contemporaries* (1926), by O. G. Sonneck (1873–1928).

40. Franck *Symphonic Variations* (M46), for piano and orchestra.
41. Hindemith *Konzertmusik* for piano, brass and two harps, Op. 49, (1930).
42. St Mark's Church, North Audley Street, London W1.
43. Arthur Foley Winnington-Ingram (1858–1946), Bishop of London (1901–39).
44. Ireland *Greater Love Hath No Man*, motet for treble, baritone, chorus and organ (1912; also known as *Many Waters Cannot Quench Love*).
45. Haydn Symphony No. 104 in D, 'London', Hob:I/104; 'Day after Day' and 'Speak to Me My Love' from Bridge *Three Tagore Songs* (1922–5); Schumann Concerto in A minor for Cello and Orchestra, Op. 129; Rimsky-Korsakov *Capriccio Espagnol*, Op. 34.
46. *Preparations* (Christ Church manuscript) for double *a cappella* chorus.
47. Chopin *Etudes*, in virtuoso transcriptions by Leopold Godowsky (1870–1938).
48. Brahms' Piano Concerto No. 2 has an exquisite cello solo in the slow movement, played on this occasion by the BBC Symphony Orchestra's principal cello, Lauri Kennedy, an artist much admired by the young Britten.
49. See 30 March.
50. The society of past and present students of the RCM, founded in 1905.
51. Founded in 1922; this concert was conducted by Malcolm Sargent.
52. 'La fille aux cheveux de lin' (The girl with the flaxen hair) from Book 1 of Debussy's *Préludes* for piano (1910).
53. Granville Bantock *Hebridean Symphony* (1915).
54. Noted gallery of contemporary painting and sculpture in Leicester Square.
55. This is a famous portrait bust of the actress and theatre director Joan Greenwood (1921–87) as a child.
56. A recital at the Grotrian Hall, Wigmore Street, London W1; Harold Craxton's editions of early English music; Lennox Berkeley *Petite Suite* (1927); Cyril Scott *Idyllic Fantasy* (1921); Benjamin Burrows *Sonatina* (1930).
57. Brosa's Wigmore Hall recital, with the pianist George Reeves, also included Veracini's Sonata in A minor.
58. Bliss *Morning Heroes* (1930), symphony for orator, chorus and orchestra, dedicated 'To the memory of Francis Kennard Bliss [the composer's brother] and all other Comrades killed in battle', setting texts by Homer, Walt Whitman, Wilfred Owen, Li Tai Po and Robert Nichols. Though Britten was clearly unimpressed by this work, it may well have influenced his own *War Requiem*, in spirit, if not in substance – both works are linked to the First World War and both set the poetry of Wilfred Owen.
59. *Twelve Variations on a Theme* for solo piano.
60. *Thy King's Birthday*, 'Christmas Suite' for soprano, contralto and *a cappella* chorus (13 January–26 March 1931) published posthumously as *Christ's Nativity* by Faber Music in 1994.
61. *Tell England* (1931), British film about a group of school friends who perish in Gallipoli during the First World War, based on the novel by Ernest Raymond, with a screenplay by Anthony Asquith, directed by Asquith and Gerald Barkas.

62. Britten was meeting his godmother, Miss Mabel Austin (known affectionately to the family as Laulie) at Mackies cafe, 11–12 Marble Arch, London W2.
63. Bridge *Enter Spring*, Rhapsody for orchestra (1926–7), and *There is a Willow Grows Aslant a Brook*, 'Impression' for small orchestra (1927).
64. Beck Symphony No. 4: *Concerto for Orchestra* (1929); Markevitch *Concerto Grosso* (1930).
65. Britten had made an arrangement for violin, viola and piano of Beethoven's *Rondo a capriccio* for piano ('Rage over a Lost Penny'), Op. 129, for the 'Beethoven Evening' on 18 April.
66. *Paramount on Parade* (1930), considered to be the best all-star musical of the time; it featured and promoted the talents of virtually everyone on the Paramount Pictures payroll, under the supervision of British musical-comedy favourite Elsie Janis and eleven top directors.
67. 'Die Trommel gerühret', Klärchen's Song from Beethoven incidental music to Goethe's play, *Egmont*.
68. *The Vagabond King* (1925), highly successful Broadway operetta by Rudolf Friml, William H. Post and Brian Hooker adapted from an earlier stage version of the novel *If I Were King* by Justin Huntly McCarthy (1830–1912).
69. Beethoven Sonata in F, 'Spring Sonata', Op. 24, for violin and piano; Sonata in D, Op. 10 No. 3 for solo piano; 'Die Trommel gerühret', performed on this occasion in an arrangement made by Britten on 13 April for voice and piano (four hands); and Brahms' *Thirteen Variations on a Hungarian Song*, Op. 21.
70. Schubert Piano Trio in B flat, D898.
71. *Abraham Lincoln* (1918), play by John Drinkwater (1882–1937).
72. Choir of the Temple Church, just off Fleet Street, London EC4.
73. 'O For the Wings of a Dove' is the famous passage from Mendelssohn's sacred anthem for soprano, chorus and organ or orchestra, *Hear My Prayer* (1844); 'I waited for the Lord', popular duet of the day, is taken from the fifth movement of Mendelssohn's Symphony No. 2 in B flat '*Lobgesang*' (Hymn of Praise), Op. 52.
74. The Prelude (No. 7) from Prokofiev's *Ten Pieces for Piano*, Op. 12; see 26 February 1931.
75. *Robert E. Lee* (1923), play by John Drinkwater.
76. The UK has conducted a census of its population every ten years since 1801, though no census was conducted in 1941 because of the Second World War. The first four censuses (1801–31) were mainly statistical (that is, they were mainly headcounts and contained virtually no personal information); the returns for the 1931 census, undertaken on this day, were destroyed by fire during the Second World War.
77. Formerly the Empire Hotel, St Luke's Hospital on Kirkley Cliff Road was established in 1921 as an isolation hospital for the care of tuberculosis cases under the Metropolitan Asylums Board.
78. See Plate 11, and *Pictures from a Life*, Plate 40.
79. Possibly the first sketches for the *Two Pieces* for violin and piano, for Remo Lauricella; see 29 and 30 June.

80. *Maud* (1898), song cycle (Tennyson, Rossetti and Kingsley) by Sir Arthur Somerville (1863–1937).
81. String Quartet in D major (8 May–2 June 1931), revised in 1974, towards the end of Britten's life, and published by Faber Music the following year.
82. *Three Fugues* for piano (14–21 April 1931), written as an exercise for John Ireland.
83. Bridge *The Christmas Rose* (1919–29), opera in three scenes, with a libretto based on a play for children by Margaret Kemp-Welch and Constance Cotterell.
84. Boots (the Nottingham firm of pharmacists still trading today) ran a subscription lending-library service in their shops throughout the UK from 1899 to 1966. The tickets Britten purchased later that evening (for Saturday 16 May) were for the original West End production of *The Church Mouse* (1931), an English adaptation by Benn W. Levy (1900–73) of the Hungarian play by Ladislas Fodor (1898–1978) staged at the Playhouse Theatre (formerly The Royal Avenue Theatre) on Northumberland Avenue, London WC1.
85. *The Bear* (1888), one-act play by Anton Chekhov (1860–1904). Sir William Walton made an operatic setting of this play for the English Opera Group (at the suggestion of Peter Pears), which was premiered at the 1967 Aldeburgh Festival.
86. The original West End production of *Stand Up and Sing*, a musical play by Douglas Furber (1885–1961), with music by Philip Charig (1902–60) and Vivian Ellis (1904–96).
87. Britten still greatly admired the chamber music of Brahms at this time – though not so much in later life.
88. 66 Carlton Hill, St John's Wood, London NW8.
89. The libretto by Alan Collard and John Gordon for Arthur Benjamin's one-act opera, *The Devil Take Her* (1931).
90. Health-food restaurant at 40–2 Chandos Street, London W1.
91. Conducted by Robert Heger; see Personalia.
92. Brahms Trio in E flat, Op. 40 for horn, violin and piano; Britten had made his own arrangement of this trio, for viola, violin and piano, for a school concert with two of his tutors while at Gresham's; see 2 November 1929.
93. String Quartet in D major.
94. The English Folk Song and Dance Society.
95. The home of the English Folk Song and Dance Society, 2 Regent's Park Road, London NW1, named after its founder Cecil Sharp (1859–1924).
96. Ravel *Sonatine* (1903–5) for solo piano.
97. Founded by Ernest Palmer in 1903 to provide open rehearsals and promote new music.
98. Later withdrawn.
99. *Aspatia's Song* (Samuel Daniel), the first setting completed for the *Three Small Songs* for soprano and small orchestra (8–19 June 1931).
100. Unidentified.

101. Bridge *Mélodie* (1911) for cello and piano.
102. Unidentified.
103. *Love is a Sickness* (Samuel Daniel), another setting (placed first in the set) for the *Three Small Songs* for soprano and small orchestra (8–19 June 1931).
104. *Sadko* (1892–8), opera-legend in seven tableaux by Rimsky-Korsakov.
105. Members of the Ballets Russes who had continued to perform together after Diaghilev's death in 1929. This group joined with other former Ballets Russes dancers in 1932 to establish a new company– the Ballets Russes de Monte Carlo – which subsequently gave a very successful season of performances at the Lyceum Theatre in London's Covent Garden.
106. Manuel de Falla's one-act ballet, *El Amor Brujo* (1914–15); an adaptation of music from Glinka's opera *Ruslan and Lyudmilla*; Fokine's original Ballets Russes choreography of Stravinsky's 'burlesque' in four scenes, *Petruchka* (1911); and the 'Polovtsian Dances' from Borodin's opera, *Prince Igor*.
107. The UK stage premiere of *Sadko*.
108. Friston Field, the country retreat near Eastbourne built by Frank and Ethel Bridge in 1923; see *Pictures from a Life*, Plates 47–8.
109. The Stratton Quartet was to give the premiere of Britten's *Three Divertimenti* at the Wigmore Hall in London, on 25 February 1936.
110. *Moon* (after Shelley) for violin and piano.
111. *Out of the Depths have I cried to Thee, O Lord*; see also 19 January 1932.
112. An early run-through of Lutyens' ballet *The Birthday of the Infanta* (1932).
113. The programme included Bach/Honegger *Les noces d'Amour et de Psyche* (1928), *David* (1930) by Henri Sauguet, and Ravel's *Ma Mère l'oye* (1912) and *Bolero* (1928).
114. The annual international tennis competition for men.
115. Howells *A Madrigal*, Op. 22 No. 2 (Austin Dobson) for voice and piano (1916).
116. Lev Konstantinovich Knipper Suite, Op. 18; Jan Maklakiewicz *Four Japanese Songs* (1929) for soprano and orchestra; Egon Wellesz *Mitte des Lebens*, Op. 45, for soprano, chorus and orchestra (1931); Ernesto Halffter Sinfonietta in D (1925).
117. Ernest Bristow Farrar (1885–1918) was a composer and organist, a student of the RCM and a friend of Frank Bridge, killed in action at the end of the First World War. The prize was founded in his memory and Britten was to be awarded it again in 1933, his last year at the College.
118. A parlour-maid at Britten's lodgings.
119. The ninth annual Festival of the International Society for Contemporary Music, held that year in London and Oxford.
120. Britten bought a much-favoured racquet of the time, named after the famous English tennis champion 'Bunny' Austin, at Moll's Sports House, 173 London Road South, Lowestoft.
121. Violet Alford provided Britten with the scenario for his ballet score *Plymouth Town*.

122. *The Long Road* (1907) by the English novelist John Oxenham (1855–1941).
123. A village between Lowestoft and Southwold.
124. Alec Halls, Clown Argo and the acrobatic duo, Christopher and Columbus.
125. Robert Britten and Marjorie Goldson were to marry on 3 September 1931.
126. *Charlie's Aunt* (1930), film adaptation of Brandon Thomas's hilarious play, directed by Al Christie, with Charles Ruggles in the title role; playing at the Palace Cinema, London Road South, Lowestoft.
127. 'A-Roving: In Plymouth Town There Lived a Maid', traditional capstan or heaving shanty, quoted in Violet Alford's ballet scenario and used as the basis of Britten's ballet score.
128. *City Lights* (1931), romantic comedy directed by and starring Charlie Chaplin (1889–1977) as the lovable tramp, struggling to help a blind flower girl with whom he has fallen in love.
129. These recordings of the third of Bridge's three *Novelletten* (1904), played by the Virtuoso String Quartet, and Ravel's *Introduction and Allegro* (1907), played by the Virtuosos, John Cockerill (harp), Robert Murchie (flute) and Charles Draper (clarinet), were released by HMV in May 1929. Britten's set is preserved in the Britten–Pears Library and Archive at Aldeburgh.
130. Annie Scarce, *née* Walker.
131. On their farm in Capel St Andrew, Suffolk.
132. The wedding of Britten's brother Robert with Marjorie Goldson was to take place in his fiancée's home town of West Hartlepool.
133. *Plunder* (1931), British farce directed by Tom Walls (1883–1949).
134. *Canaries Sometimes Sing* (1930), another British farce, starring and directed by Tom Walls.
135. Walton Viola Concerto (1929), bought in readiness for the broadcast on 10 September.
136. *Hell's Angels* (1930), American war film directed by Howard Hughes (1904–76).
137. In view of Britten's later dislike of Brahms and Henry Wood, a somewhat surprising entry; see also 23 September.
138. A BBC Orchestra concert in which William Walton, Constant Lambert and Dame Ethel Smyth conducted their own works.
139. Haydn Concerto in D for cello and orchestra (Hob.VIIb:2); only the viola part of Britten's arrangement of the first movement (Allegro moderato) survives.
140. 'Abscheulicher, wo lebst du hin', Leonora's great Act I recitative and aria.
141. The department store on the Brompton Road, Knightsbridge, London SW1.
142. A reference to the 'motto' theme of the opening bars of the symphony's first movement, identified as the 'Fate' motive.
143. Brahms *Variations on a Theme by Haydn* (*St Anthony Chorale*), Op. 56a; Piano Concerto No. 1 in D minor, Op. 15; and Symphony No. 3 in F, Op. 90; Franck *Symphonic Variations* for piano and orchestra.
144. A BBC Symphony Orchestra concert conducted by Henry Wood and Gustav Holst.

145. Beethoven Leonora Overtures Nos. 2 and 3, Op. 72; *An die ferne Geliebte*, Op. 98, for voice and piano (sung by Alois Jeitteles); and Symphony No. 5 in C minor, Op. 67; Kodaly *Three Songs*; Respighi *Fountains of Rome* (1915–16).
146. Mozart Symphony No. 41 in C, 'Jupiter', K551. Britten conducted an Aldeburgh Festival performance of this symphony, with the English Chamber Orchestra, at Blythburgh Church on 14 June 1966.
147. The piano duo for whom Britten was later to write a number of two-piano pieces; see Personalia.
148. One of Henry Wood's own suites, compiled from various Bach sources and orchestrated in grandiose fashion.
149. Benjamin Violin Concerto (1932); see 29 January 1933. The *Sonatina* was never published.
150. Britten was later to write his *Lachrymae*, Op. 48, for William Primrose in 1950.
151. It would be interesting to speculate to what extent Britten and Ireland agreed about their contemporaries.
152. *Three Small Songs* (Samuel Daniel) for soprano and small orchestra.
153. The St Luke's doctor to whom Britten refers could have been Dr Mawson or Dr Moor.
154. A favourite guest artist on the Lowestoft musical scene who, many years later, was to become a member of Britten's English Opera Group, creating the roles of Lucia in *The Rape of Lucretia* (1946) and Miss Wordsworth in *Albert Herring* (1947).
155. St Margaret's Institute, a Parish Mission on Alexandria Road, Lowestoft.
156. Bach Cantata *Schweight stille, plaudert nicht* (BWV211); Mozart *Bastien und Bastienne*, K50, one-act *Singspiel* to a libretto by Friedrich Wilhelm Weiskern.
157. The Metropolitan and District Station, now Notting Hill Gate Underground Station.
158. The seatless Promenaders' section of the Queen's Hall, London.
159. Mozart Symphony No. 39 in E flat, K543; the UK premiere of Richard Strauss's *Drei Hymnen von Friedrich Hölderlin*, Op. 71; and his *Sinfonia domestica*, Op. 53 and tone poem, *Don Juan*, Op. 20.
160. The Dutchman's Act I aria from Wagner's opera, *Der fliegende Holländer*.
161. *Orchestral Technique* (1930) by Gordon Jacob (1895–1984).
162. It has not been possible to identify this Haydn manuscript, despite searches via both the British Museum and the British Library.
163. Bridge *The Christmas Rose* (1919/1930), opera for children in three scenes.
164. The Stratton Quartet played through Britten's String Quartet in D (1931) on 16 March 1932.
165. St Jude's Church, Collingham Road, London SW5.
166. Britten's *Plymouth Town* (1931) was not taken up by the Camargo Society, much to the regret of Montagu Nathan, who years later wrote about the missed opportunity in the *Radio Times*. Britten put the score to one side and it was eventually published posthumously by Faber Music and The Britten Estate Ltd in 2005, almost thirty years after the composer's death.

167. Columbia recordings conducted by Stravinsky (*Firebird*) and Beecham (*Brigg Fair*).
168. Walton *Belshazzar's Feast* (1931), cantata for baritone, chorus and orchestra; Delius 'Serenade' from *Hassan* (1920–1), his incidental music for the five-act play by James Elroy Flecker (1884–1915).
169. Bridge String Sextet (1906–12).
170. The premiere of Holst's orchestral arrangement (1931) of his earlier work for military band, *Hammersmith: Prelude and Scherzo*, Op. 52 (1930).
171. Scott was a very prolific composer, writing well over four hundred works, many of them withdrawn or now missing.
172. *Variations on a French Carol* (Carol of the Deanery of Sainte Menehould), for women's voices, violin, viola and piano (29 November–1 December).
173. Holst *Savitri*, Op. 25, one-act chamber opera (1908–9); a College production conducted by Sir Thomas Beecham.
174. Britten acted as copyist on Bridge's *Phantasm* (1930–1) for piano and orchestra.
175. *Tantivy Towers*, Op. 73 (1931), popular light opera by Thomas Frederick Dunhill (1877–1946) to a libretto by A.P. Herbert (1890–1971).
176. Armstrong Gibbs *The Blue Peter*, comic opera in one act, with a libretto by A. P. Herbert. A large collection of the original manuscripts of Armstrong Gibbs is now in the Archive of the Britten–Pears Library at Aldeburgh.
177. The role of Miriam was sung by the soprano Eugenie Walmsley.
178. A Technical College in St John's Street, London, EC1, now part of the City University.
179. The 'Unfinished', D759.
180. Britten retained a great affection for Tchaikovsky's concert overture, making his own arrangement for organ in April 1934, and much later in life conducting it at the 1968 Aldeburgh Festival with the English Chamber Orchestra, a recording released in the BBC's *Britten the Performer* archive series in 1999.
181. Figaro's famous Act I aria from Mozart's *Le nozze di Figaro*.
182. Mussorgsky *Mephistopheles's Song of the Flea* (Goethe).
183. *A Hymn to the Virgin* and *I Saw Three Ships*.
184. A club at St John's Church that met for devotional and social activities.
185. *Minnie Maylow's Story, and Other Tales and Scenes* (1931) by the English Poet Laureate, John Masefield (1878–1967).
186. Britten's inscribed scores of Stravinsky's *Petruchka*, Mozart's *Sinfonia concertante* in E flat, K364, and the Prelude to Act III of Wagner's music drama, *Die Walküre*, all survive in the Archives of the Britten–Pears Library at Aldeburgh.
187. A monthly periodical published by Augener from 1871 to 1960.
188. *If I May* (1920), novel by A. A. Milne (1882–1956).
189. *Eric, or Little by Little* (1858), a cautionary tale set in a Victorian boarding school, by Frederic W. Farrar (1831–1903).

NOTES: 1932

1. 'Was duftet' and 'Wahn! Wahn!' sung by the baritone Arthur Fear, and the *Prelude, Dance of the Apprentices, Procession of the Masters* and *Homage to Sachs* from Wagner's comic opera *Die Meistersinger von Nürnberg*. Bridge was conducting the BBC Studio Orchestra.
2. Mozart *Sinfonia Concertante* in E flat for violin, viola and orchestra, K364.
3. Holst 'Song of the Ship-builders', the first of the *Four Part-Songs* (1910); Walford Davies 'The Shepherd', the last of the *Four Songs of Innocence*, Op. 4 (1900).
4. Beethoven Piano Trio in B flat, 'Archduke', Op. 97.
5. The premiere of Britten's *Variations on a French Carol*.
6. Bridge *Phantasy* in C minor for piano trio (1927–9); *Hidden Fires* and *Graziella* (1926) for solo piano, the original copies of which are in the collection of the Britten–Pears Library.
7. Again, both of these scores are in the collection at the Britten–Pears Library.
8. *Phantasy* in F minor for string quintet (2 violins, 2 violas, cello).
9. *Richard Strauss* (1908) by Ernest Newman (1868–1959).
10. *Rope's End* (1929), a rather gruesome thriller by Patrick Hamilton (1904–62).
11. Ireland Piano Concerto (1930).
12. A BBC Contemporary Music Concert devoted to the music of Ferruccio Busoni, given by the BBC Orchestra (Section D) under Adrian Boult: *Comedy Overture*, Op. 38; Violin Concerto in D, Op. 35a, played by Joseph Szigeti; and *Turandot – Orchestral Suite from the Music to Gozzi's Drama*, Op. 41.
13. Honegger Symphony No. 1 (1930), commissioned by Serge Koussevitzky for the Boston Symphony Orchestra, for whom Britten was later to write his *Spring Symphony*, Op. 44 (1949). Koussevitzky also commissioned Britten's first opera, *Peter Grimes*, Op. 33 (1945).
14. Though Britten mentions the Percy Grainger only in passing, he was to develop a great love for Grainger's music, performing it at the Aldeburgh Festival and making a very significant recording of a collection of his music for Decca.
15. Haydn Symphony No. 3 in G (Hob:1/3).
16. Tchaikovsky's fantasy overture *Romeo and Juliet* was performed by the BBC Orchestra (Section B) conducted by Nikolai Malko.
17. *David Copperfield* (1850) by Charles Dickens (1812–70); see 29 May.
18. Ireland *Mai-Dun*, symphonic rhapsody for orchestra (1920–1); Bax *Winter Legends*, Sinfonia concertante for piano and orchestra (1930).
19. A setting of Walter de la Mare, published along with further settings of de la Mare's *The Ride-by-Nights* and *The Ship of Rio*; see 23 September.
20. Strauss *Don Quixote*, fantastic variations on a theme of knightly character, for cello and orchestra, Op. 35 (1896–7).
21. Hindemith *Konzertmusik* for brass and strings, Op. 50 (1930), here given its first performance in the UK.

22. Britten was eventually to write his *Russian Funeral* (march for brass and percussion) for Alan Bush in 1936.
23. Haydn Symphony No. 94 in G (Hob:1/94); *Idomeneo* would be the only Mozart opera Britten was to conduct during his career – a series of outstanding performances with the English Opera Group (directed by Colin Graham and with Peter Pears in the title role) at the 1969 and 1970 Aldeburgh Festivals and at the 1970 BBC Promenade Concerts at the Royal Albert Hall.
24. The UK premiere of Ravel's Piano Concerto in G (1929–32), performed by the dedicatee, Marguerite Long, with the composer conducting.
25. Eugene Goossens Oboe Concerto, Op. 45 (1927), written for his brother Léon.
26. See Personalia.
27. Brahms *Variations and Fugue on a Theme of Handel*, Op. 24.
28. Britten submitted his *Phantasy* String Quintet for the Cobbett Prize at the RCM; see entry for W. W. Cobbett in Personalia.
29. Bridge Piano Trio (1929).
30. Haydn String Quartet in C, Op. 76 No. 3; Beethoven String Quartet No. 14 in C sharp minor, Op. 131; Debussy String Quartet in G minor (1893).
31. Bartok Suite No. 1 for orchestra, Op. 3 (1905); *Rhapsody*, Op. 1, for piano and orchestra (?1904); and *The Miraculous Mandarin*, Op. 19 (1918–19), concert suite from the pantomime in one act.
32. This incomplete set of variations for solo piano is based on the same theme, from the second of Bridge's *Three Idylls* for string quartet (1906), on which Britten later based his *Variations on a Theme of Frank Bridge* for strings.
33. Schubert String Quartet No. 14 in D minor, 'Death and the Maiden', D810.
34. Concerto in B minor for violin, viola and orchestra (9 March–1 July 1932), which was left incomplete in draft score, eventually edited and scored by Colin Matthews for a performance at the 1997 Aldeburgh Festival, and subsequently published by OUP in 2002. See 1 July 1932.
35. Bridge's Piano Sonata (1922–5) was dedicated to the memory of Ernest Farrar; see note 117 to the diary entry for 24 July 1931.
36. Bridge *Phantasy* in F sharp minor (1910) for piano quartet.
37. String Quartet in D major.
38. *Rose Marie* (1924), American operetta by Rudolf Friml and Herbert Stothart with book and lyrics by Otto Harbach and Oscar Hammerstein II.
39. Beethoven String Quartet in F, Op. 18 No. 1; Dittersdorf String Quartet No. 5 in E flat; Elgar String Quartet in E minor, Op. 83.
40. *The Hill* (1905) by Horace Annesley Vachell (1861–1955), a controversial novel for its day, set at Harrow, exploring the more intimate side of schoolboy relationships.
41. For Britten's arrangements of Bridge's orchestral suite *The Sea* (1910–11), see the diary entries for 15 December 1930, 17 and 20 May 1934, and 9 July 1934; his two-piano arrangement of the first movement of Brahms' First Symphony has not survived.
42. Village near Saxmundham in Suffolk where the Walker sisters retired.

43. Strauss's one-act opera *Elektra* (1906–8), libretto by Hugo von Hofmannsthal; Verdi *Otello* (1884–7), libretto by Arrigo Boito after William Shakespeare. While Britten remained ambivalent about the merits of *Elektra*, he greatly admired *Otello*, which had a profound influence on his opera, *Billy Budd* (1951).
44. A live relay from the Queen's Hall given by Isobel Baillie (soprano), Muriel Brunskill (contralto), Walter Widdop (tenor) and Horace Stevens (bass), the National Chorus and the BBC Symphony Orchestra, conducted by Adrian Boult. The Bach item sung by the National Chorus was the motet *Jesu meine Freude* (BWV227).
45. Eric Fogg Bassoon Concerto in D (1930); the concert, given by the BBC Orchestra (Section B) conducted by Sir Henry Wood, also included Handel's Concerto Grosso Op. 6 No. 4.
46. Britten is here referring to the Symphony No. 9 in E minor, 'From The New World', Op. 95. At this time the first four Dvorak symphonies were largely unknown and the accepted numbering began with the Symphony No. 5 in F, Op. 76. The now-familiar numbering of the Dvorak symphonies became current only as recently as 1959–63, with the publishing and dissemination of the first four symphonies in the new Dvorak Complete Edition.
47. *Phantasy* String Quintet in F minor and the *Three Two-Part Songs*.
48. *Strictly Dishonorable* (1931), American film directed by John M. Stahl, based on the stage-play by Brock Pemberton (1885–1950).
49. Though the BBC relayed Act I of this performance live from Covent Garden – with Frida Leider (Isolde), Maria Olczewska (Brangäne), Herbert Hanssen (Kurnewal) and Lauritz Melchior (Tristan) – Britten seems to have abandoned his listening thanks to Beecham's conducting of the Prelude.
50. Britten's *Phantasy-Scherzo* for piano trio.
51. *Kameradschaft* [Comradeship] (1931), a profound and moving German film directed by G.W. Pabst (1885–1967) about a rescue mission of entombed French miners by German workers on the Franco-German border.
52. Another of Mrs Britten's good causes, a charitable organisation that flourished in the UK between the wars, in which children from good homes were enrolled by their parents to raise money for the poor.
53. As these diaries attest, Britten became a fervent admirer of Wagner during the 1930s.
54. Transcription of the first of the *Three Small Songs* for soprano and small orchestra.
55. Schubert String Quartet No. 13 in A minor, 'Rosamunde', D804; Borodin String Quartet No. 2.
56. Britten's settings of Psalms 130 and 150, the *Phantasy* String Quintet in F minor, and *Three Small Songs* for soprano and small orchestra. For a detailed account and analysis of Britten's relationship with the Mendelssohn Scholarship Foundation see *Letters from a Life*, Vol. I, pp. 252–4.

57. Another Beecham performance from Covent Garden, with Friedrich Schorr as Hans Sachs, Fritz Wolff as Walter and Lotte Lehmann as Eva.
58. *I lov'd a lass* (George Wither), the first of the *Two Part-Songs*; see 18 July 1932.
59. A dramatised adaptation of Henry James's novel, written and produced for the BBC by E. J. King Bull. Britten was to make his own operatic setting of the *The Turn of the Screw* (to a libretto by Myfanwy Piper), which was commissioned by the Venice Biennale and premiered by the English Opera Group at the Festival of Contemporary Music at La Fenice in 1954.
60. Tannhäuser was sung by Kurt Taucher, Wolfram by Herbert Janssen and Venus by Josephine Wray; the shepherd boy (at the start of scene 3) was sung by the soprano Norah Gruhn, as has always been the custom in this opera. It is entirely characteristic of Britten that he would have preferred the raw vibrant tone of an unbroken boy's voice for this short unaccompanied solo.
61. *The Pride of the Regiment, or Cashiered for his Country* (1932), musical comedy by V. C. Clinton-Baddeley (1900–70) with music by Walter Leigh (1905–42).
62. Haydn String Quartet No. 59 in G minor, 'The Rider', Op. 74 No.3 (Hob.III:74); Brahms String Quartet No. 2 in A minor, Op. 51 No. 2.
63. Walton *Sinfonia concertante* (1927) for orchestra with obbligato piano; Schumann *Fantasy* in C, Op. 17.
64. *The Sad Day* (Thomas Flatman) for two voices and piano.
65. Possibly a first attempt at setting John Drinkwater's *This is the Tale of Elizabeth Ann*; see 17 July.
66. *The Dubarry*, a comic opera by the Austrian composer Carl Millocker (1842–99), was playing at His Majesty's Theatre in the Haymarket in a new revised version, with new English lyrics by Paul Knepler and J. Williminski.
67. Harry Stoker [Lieutenant Commander Henry Hugh Gordon Dacre Stoker, DSO (1885–1966)] had been a hero of the Battle of Gallipoli, during which he captained the first submarine to breach the Dardanelles. In his post-war career he became a noted actor and Irish croquet champion.
68. Wilmington (close to the Bridge's country retreat at Friston) is famous for the 226-foot figure carved into the chalk soil of the South Downs, known as 'The Long Man of Wilmington', but referred to locally as 'David'.
69. A BBC Radio talk in the series *Rungs on the Ladder* (on the subject of social mobility and the English system of education) given by the father of Britten's Gresham's friend, Peter Floud, whose sister Mollie was also a concert-going friend of Britten's. Sir Francis was Permanent Secretary at the Ministry of Labour from 1930 to 1934.
70. Britten began sketching two scenes from another ballet scenario by Violet Alford (this time a pastoral tale set in a Basque village) but abandoned the project very quickly. The scenario of these first two scenes is reproduced in *Letters from a Life*, Vol. I, p. 257.
71. Coleridge-Taylor's cantata performed as a pageant at the Royal Albert Hall.
72. First sketches for the Sinfonietta, Op. 1; see 9 and 16 July.

73. The music publishers and retailer, Boosey and Hawkes, 295 Regent Street, London W1, who were to become Britten's publishers from 1934 to 1963.
74. Kodaly *Psalmus Hungaricus*, Op. 13, oratorio for tenor, chorus, children's choir and orchestra (1923).
75. Vaughan Williams was trying to arrange performances of Britten's recent settings of Psalms 130 and 150 and had written to Sir Ivor Atkins (1869–1953), organist of Worcester Cathedral and Director of the Three Choirs Festival, to no avail.
76. Stravinsky *Three Pieces* for string quartet (1914, rev. 1918).
77. Fritz Kreisler's arrangement for violin and piano of a set of variations by Corelli.
78. *He Knows Not the Meaning of Sorrow* (BWV209), now considered of doubtful authenticity.
79. The birth of Robert and Marjorie's first son, John.
80. Noel Coward's *Cavalcade* was playing at Covent Garden's Drury Lane Theatre.
81. It was some time before Mr Britten's condition was diagnosed, but the sad progress of his final illness is movingly documented by Britten over the next two years.
82. A rehearsal of Bridge's *Phantasie* Piano Trio in C minor (1907); see 19 July.
83. Grace Williams *Two Psalms* for contralto, harp and strings (1932).
84. Tennyson-inspired ballet with music by Felix Mendelssohn; scenario and arrangement by Edwin Evans, orchestrated by Gordon Jacob.
85. On 12 July the Lowestoft Musical Society presented C. R. J. Coleman with a silver-mounted ebony baton in recognition of his thirty years as a leading musician in the town.
86. Prokofiev *Overture on Hebrew Themes* for chamber ensemble (1919); Bax *Of a Rose I Sing a Song*, carol for choir, harp, cello and double bass (1920); Maconchy *Concertino* for piano and small orchestra (1928); Hermann Reutter *Four Beggar Songs*; Bartok *Romanian Dance* No. 1 (1915), *Burlesque* No. 1 (1908), *Allegro barbaro* (1911); Walton *Façade*, first suite for orchestra (1926).
87. Now known as the Albery Theatre, St Martin's Lane, London WC2.
88. The Temple Bar restaurant, 227–8 The Strand, London WC2.
89. Part of the Macnaghten–Lemare Concert series at the Ballet Club Theatre in Notting Hill Gate, London W11.
90. *This Is the Tale of Elizabeth Ann* (John Drinkwater), unpublished setting for voice and piano.
91. *Two Part-Songs: I lov'd a lass* (George Wither) and *Lift Boy* (Robert Graves) for two-part boys' or female voices and piano (1–2 June 1932; 18 July 1932); revised 5–28 June for mixed chorus and piano.
92. See 12 December 1932.
93. Bridge *Phantasie* Piano Trio in C minor (1907); Mozart Piano Quartet in G minor, K478.
94. Stravinsky *Symphony of Psalms* (1930), the composer's first recording, for Columbia Records, with the Alexander Vlassoff Choir and the Walter Straram Orchestra; Britten's copy is preserved in the Britten Archive.

95. Probably the String Quartet in D major (1931); see 18 July 1932.
96. Bridge Piano Quintet in D minor (1904–5; rev. 1912).
97. The RCM composition prize in memory of Sir Arthur Sullivan (1842–1900)
98. Britten refers here to Ira D. Sankey (1840–1908), the American gospel singer and composer, associated with evangelist Dwight L. Moody (1837–99). He was reading *New Grub Street* (1891), a novel set in the literary and journalistic circles of late-1800s London, by George Gissing (1857–1903).
99. *Mr Cinders* (1929), musical comedy by Clifford Grey and Greatrex Newman with music by Vivian Ellis and Richard Myers.
100. Bridge *Blow Out You Bugles* (Rupert Brooke) for tenor and orchestra (or piano) with optional trumpet (1918).
101. Recorded for Decca by the New English Symphony Orchestra conducted by Anthony Bernard. Britten's copy is preserved in the Britten–Pears Library.
102. Two collections of myths, legends, ghost stories and poetry (1840/1843), written by 'Thomas Ingoldsby of Tappington Manor', the pen-name of Richard Harris Barham (1788–1845).
103. Normanston Park, Peto Way, on the outskirts of Lowestoft.
104. The Carnegie Public Library and Museum, Clapham Road, Lowestoft.
105. *Elizabethan Lyrics* (1925) and *Seventeenth Century Lyrics* (1928), chosen, edited and arranged by Norman Ault; purchased by Britten with the proceeds of the Sullivan Prize. The latter inscribed volume is preserved in the Britten–Pears Library.
106. *Mata Hari* (1931), the famous MGM film directed by George Fitzmaurice (1885–1940) with Greta Garbo in one of her signature roles as the First World War spy.
107. The 22nd Waveney Valley Championship was held in Bungay, a small market town sixteen miles west of Lowestoft.
108. A complication of tonsillitis when a peritonsillar abscess develops between the back of the tonsil and the wall of the throat; much more difficult to treat effectively before the availability of antibiotics.
109. Stravinsky's 1931 recording for Columbia of *Le sacre du printemps* (1913) with L'Orchestre Symphonique de Paris.
110. Friends of the Britten family who lived twenty-two miles west of Lowestoft, in Harleston, and coincidentally had a London home very near Frank and Ethel Bridge in Kensington.
111. Probably the earliest draft of the *Phantasy* for oboe and string trio, Op. 2.
112. Mrs Britten's sister-in-law had moved from 88 Berners Street, Ipswich, to 14 Fonnereau Road, the Hockey family home until the death of their daughter, Elsie, in February 1984.
113. *A Survey of Contemporary Music* (1924) by the Scottish composer and critic, Cecil Gray (1895–1951).
114. Mr Britten's illness still remained undiagnosed, despite extensive tests and X-rays.

115. 'Hagen's Watch', 'Hier sitz ich zür wacht' (Act I) and 'Hagen's Call', 'Hoi-ho' (Act II) from *Götterdämmerung*, a performance by the BBC Symphony Orchestra conducted by Sir Henry Wood.
116. *Phantasy*, Op. 2, for oboe and string trio (20 September–20 October 1932).
117. Ravel Piano Trio (1914).
118. Delius *A Song of the High Hills* (1911) for chorus and orchestra; Scott *Christmas Overture* (1913) for orchestra with optional chorus; Elgar *Sea Pictures*, Op. 37, five songs for contralto and orchestra; Smyth Concerto for Violin, Horn and Orchestra (1927), receiving its premiere in this Promenade concert by the dedicatees, Jean Pougnet (violin) and Aubrey Brain (horn) with the BBC Symphony Orchestra under Henry Wood.
119. Britten *Three Two-Part Songs* (Walter de la Mare): *The Ride-by-Nights, The Rainbow, The Ship of Rio* (15–29 February 1932: rev. 25–7 May 1932).
120. *Dead Boy*, pencil drawing by Alfred Stevens (1818–75). See *Letters from a Life*, Vol. I, p. 277.
121. Beethoven *Tremate, empi, tremati* (Bettoni), Op. 116, for soprano, tenor, bass and orchestra.
122. A radio-drama adaptation by BBC producer C. Denis Freeman based on Poulenc's ballet *Les biches* (1923), inspired by the paintings of Watteau that depicted Louis XIV and various women in his *Parc aux Biches* – the word *biche* usually translated as hind, or a female deer. Poulenc described his work as a 'contemporary drawing room party suffused with an atmosphere of wantonness', hence the English title *The House Party*.
123. Perkin *Pastoral Phantasy* for piano; Ireland *Sonatina* (1926–7) for piano; Delius Violin Sonata No. 3 (1930).
124. Bernard van Dieren *Hommages: In Memoriam Philip Heseltine* (1931) for voice and seven instruments.
125. *Grétry Pas de Deux*, Constant Lambert's arrangement of excerpts from *Zémire et Azar* (1771), and *Léphaleet Procris* (1773) and *L'embarras des riches* (1782) by André Ernest Modeste Grétry (1741–1813).
126. *Manhattan Serenade*, solo for Dolin choreographed to one of the hits of the Swing Era, composed in 1928 by Louis Alter (1902–80).
127. *Douanes* [Customs] (1932), comic ballet by Ninette de Valois about the daily life of a French customs office.
128. *Les Sylphides* (1907), short non-narrative ballet by Fokine with music by Chopin orchestrated by Glazunov.
129. Britten's original title for his *Two Part-Songs: I Lov'd a Lass* and *Lift Boy*.
130. Britten *Introduction and Allegro* for piano trio (20 May 1932).
131. Bridge *Adoration* (Keats) and *Love Went A-riding* (Coleridge); Walther's 'Prize Song' from Act III of Wagner's *Die Meistersinger von Nürnberg*. Britten and Pears often included *Love Went A-riding* in their recital programmes.
132. 4 Bedford Gardens, Kensington, London W8, the Bridges' London home.
133. Beethoven String Quartet No. 11 in F minor, Op. 95; Bridge *Three Idylls* for string quartet (1906).

134. *Three Two-Part Songs* (de la Mare): *The Ride-by-nights, The Rainbow, The Ship of Rio* (15–29 February 1932; rev. 25–27 May 1932).
135. Haydn String Quartet in B flat (Hob.III:1).
136. H. K. Andrews Oboe Concerto in C (1932); see 31 January 1933.
137. Mozart Piano Quartet in G minor, K478; Fauré Piano Quartet No. 1 in C minor, Op. 15; Brahms Piano Quartet No. 2 in A, Op. 26; a recital given in the Concert Hall of BBC Broadcasting House, Portland Place, London W1.
138. Britten *Phantasy* for oboe and string trio, Op. 2 (9 September–25 October 1932).
139. Britten retained a great affection for Bridge's Cello Sonata (1913–17), performing it many times in later life with the Russian virtuoso, Mstislav Rostropovich, with whom he recorded it for Decca in July 1968.
140. Bantock *Sappho* Prelude; Bridge *Enter Spring*, Rhapsody for orchestra (1926–7); Tchaikovsky Violin Concerto in D, Op. 35; Franck Symphony in D minor.
141. New Victorian Club, 30a Sackville Street, Piccadilly, London, W1 (founded in 1893 as a club for professional gentlewomen, and re-launched as the 'New' Victorian in 1897), and Mercury Theatre, Notting Hill Gate, London W11.
142. Berners *Le Foyer de Danse* (1932), derived from *The Triumph of Neptune* (1926), was choreographed by Frederick Ashton.
143. Frederick May (1911–85), Irish composer and a contemporary of Britten's at the RCM, undertaking copying work on his behalf.
144. Britten submitted his *Phantasy* Op. 2 for the *Daily Telegraph* chamber music competition that year, which was won by Elizabeth Maconchy for her Quintet for oboe and strings (1932).
145. Bridge Cello Sonata (1917) and Piano Quintet in D minor (1904–12); Beethoven String Quartet in C minor, Op. 18 No. 4; Schubert Piano Trio in B flat, D898.
146. Bridge Piano Trio No. 2 (1929) and *Phantasy* Piano Quartet in F sharp minor (1910).
147. *Thark* (1932), the film adaptation of the farce by Ben Travers (1886–1980) directed by Tom Walls (1883–1949) was playing at the Coronet Cinema, Notting Hill Gate, London W11.
148. Mozart Symphony No. 40 in G minor, K550; a favourite of Britten's, who recorded it with the English Chamber Orchestra for Decca in 1968.
149. Britten reacting badly to the autobiographical nature of Strauss's tone poem, *Ein Heldenleben* [A Hero's Life], Op. 40.
150. *Ancient English Christmas Carols 1400–1700* (1928), collected and arranged by Edith Rickert (1871–1938), a volume preserved in the Britten–Pears Library.
151. Britten was researching texts for his choral variations, *A Boy Was Born*, Op. 3.
152. Britten is consistent in his criticism of much of the work aired at these Macnaghten–Lemare concerts of new music (particularly their technical deficiencies) and is often also critical of the quality of the performances.

153. *Rheinlegenchen, Ich atmet' einen Linden Duft* and *Wer hat dies Liedlein erdacht?*
154. *A Boy Was Born*, Op. 3.
155. *Come Hither*, an anthology by Walter de la Mare of 'rhymes and poems for the young of all ages' (1923, revised edition 1928). This copy is preserved in the Britten–Pears Library.
156. Interesting and characteristic that Britten should respond most favourably to Casals' encore – the Allemande from Bach's C minor cello suite.
157. A performance given by the London Philharmonic Orchestra and broadcast live from the Queen's Hall – a Royal Philharmonic Society concert that also included Strauss's *Macbeth* and Boccherini's Third Symphony.
158. *Mikado* (1885), operetta in two acts by W. S. Gilbert (1836–1911) and Arthur Sullivan (1842–1900), playing at the Savoy Theatre in The Strand, home of the D'Oyly Carte Opera Company.
159. *Phantasy* String Quintet in F minor.
160. Bridge *There is a Willow Grows Aslant a Brook*, 'Impression' for small orchestra (1927).
161. *Adam and Eve, suite dansée* (1925), choreographed and danced by Antony Tudor (1909–87) and Prudence Hyman (1914–95).
162. *Evensong* (1932), romantic tragedy by Beverley Nichols (1898–1983) and Edward Knoblock (1874–1945), based on Nichols' own novel about the personal sacrifices of an operatic diva facing the decline of her career.
163. Adrian Boult and Elgar (who conducted his Second Symphony) with the BBC Symphony Orchestra.
164. Schubert Octet in F, D803.
165. A popular subscription series at London's Queen's Hall, founded in 1929 by benefactor Mrs Samuel [Elizabeth Theresa Frances] Courtauld (who had underwritten Beecham's Covent Garden seasons in the 1920s) and the conductor Malcolm Sargent, with the express purpose of presenting programmes that featured contemporary works alongside the mainstream repertoire of the day.
166. Kodály *Theatre Overture* (1927); Haydn *Sinfonia concertante* in B flat (Hob.1:105); Bax Symphony No. 4 (1931).
167. Britten's arrangement for viola and piano of *There Is a Willow Grows Aslant a Brook* was published by Thames Publishing *c.*1990.
168. Elgar *Falstaff*, Op. 68, symphonic study for orchestra (1913).
169. Bridge Piano Sonata (1922–5).
170. Probably the *Three Two-part Songs*.
171. *Bethlehem* (Bernard Walke), Nativity Play in three scenes, relayed by the BBC from St Hilary's Church, Marazion, Cornwall.
172. Prokofiev Piano Concerto No. 1 in D flat, Op. 10.
173. Hely-Hutchinson *A Carol Symphony* (1927) for orchestra.
174. Operetta (1888) by Gilbert and Sullivan, broadcast from the Savoy Theatre.

175. The classic fountain pen of the day, manufactured by Mabie, Todd & Co., and trademarked as 'Swan, the Pen of the British Empire'.
176. Britten conducted this work at the 1971 Aldeburgh Festival, on 13 June.
177. Malipiero String Quartet No. 3: *Cantàri alla madrigalesca* (1931).

NOTES: 1933

1. *A Boy Was Born*, Op. 3.
2. Ireland's unpredictable nature, his drinking, and the fact that he began using his gifted young pupil to undertake all sorts of unpaid work as copyist and proof-reader, were taking their toll.
3. Schumann Piano Concerto in A minor, Op. 54.
4. Alice (sister of the children's nanny, Annie) joined the Britten household as cook in May 1914. Beth Britten tells us that Alice's fiancé, a Mr Pratt of Stratford St. Andrew, was unable to marry before this date, because his aunt was keeping house for him, he did not want to turn her away, and the cottage was too small for three people to live comfortably. One assumes that Mr Pratt's aunt had eventually died, and Miss Walker and Mr Pratt could finally marry after a twenty-year engagement.
5. *Lilac Time* (1916), Viennese operetta telling a fictionalised account of the love-life of Franz Schubert, featuring his music in arrangements by Heinrich Berté. The English-language production playing at the Globe Theatre had an adapted libretto by Adrian Ross (1859–1933) with new arrangements of Schubert by G. H. Clutsam (1866–1951).
6. Ibert *Escales* (1921–2); Bliss Concerto in B flat for two pianos and orchestra (1925–9); Roussel Symphony No. 3 in G minor, Op. 42.
7. *Grand Hotel*, epic romantic drama (1932), awarded that year's Oscar for Best Picture, starring Greta Garbo, John Barrymore, Joan Crawford, Wallace Beery and Lionel Barrymore, directed by Edmund Goulding (1891–1959) with a screenplay by William A. Drake, based on his own play adaptation of Vicki Baum's novel *Menschen im Hotel* (1929).
8. Britten retained a boyish love of Mickey Mouse movies all his life.
9. Arthur Benjamin Violin Concerto (1932).
10. H. K. Andrews Concerto in C for oboe and chamber orchestra (1932); Britten Sinfonietta for ten instruments (1932), later published as his Op. 1; Gordon Jacob *Serenade* for five wind instruments (1932) unpublished; Gerald Finzi *Introit* for small orchestra and solo violin (1932) later published as the *Introit* in F, Op. 6; Grace Williams *Movement for Trumpet and Chamber Orchestra* (1932), unpublished – not to be confused with the later Trumpet Concerto of 1963.
11. Vaughan Williams Piano Concerto in C (1926–33; rev. 1946); Bax *The Garden of Fand* (1913–16), tone poem for orchestra; Delius *Sea Drift* (Whitman), cantata for baritone, chorus and orchestra (1903–4).
12. *Phantasy* in F minor (1932) for string quintet.

13. Ferguson Violin Sonata No. 1, Op. 2 (1932).
14. Schoenberg *Variations for Orchestra*, Op. 31 (1926–8).
15. *Alla Marcia* for string quartet (material from which was later expanded and used for 'Parade' in the Rimbaud song-cycle, *Les Illuminations*, Op. 18) posthumously published with *Three Divertimenti* (1936) by Faber Music in 1983.
16. Berg *Lyric Suite* (1925–6).
17. *Richard of Bordeaux* (1932), play by Gordon Daviot [pseudonym for Elizabeth Macintosh] (1896–1952), which was playing at the New Theatre, London, in a production starring and directed by John Gielgud.
18. Christian Darnton *String Trio* (1933); Erik Chisholm *Double Trio* for violin, cello, double-bass, clarinet, bassoon and trumpet – a BBC Concert of Contemporary Music in the Concert Hall of Broadcasting House.
19. *The Forsyte Saga*, a sequence of three novels and two interludes (1906–21) by John Galsworthy (1867–1933).
20. Beethoven String Quartet No. 7 in F, 'Razumovsky', Op. 59, No. 1.
21. Malipiero String Quartet No. 3: *Cantàri alla madrigalesca* (1931).
22. *The Man of Property* (1906), Vol. I of *The Forsyte Saga*.
23. Elspeth Beide, the dress-making establishment that Beth Britten ran at 559 Finchley Road with her college friend and business partner, Lilian Wolff.
24. Ravel *Daphnis et Chloé*, Suite No. 2 (1913).
25. Berlioz *Symphonie fantastique*, Op. 14.
26. See *Pictures from a Life*, Plate 52.
27. Britten *Alla Marcia* (1933); Bridge Piano Quintet in D minor (1906–12) and Violin Sonata (1932).
28. Haydn Wood Violin Concerto in B minor (1932).
29. The first sketches for a five-movement suite for string quartet, *Alla Quartetto Serioso: 'Go play, boy, play'* (the quotation is taken from Act I scene 2 of Shakespeare's *The Winter's Tale*). This project preoccupied Britten, on and off, throughout 1933 and occasionally in the following two years, eventually undergoing a thorough revision in 1936 as *Three Divertimenti* for string quartet, premiered at the Wigmore Hall by the Stratton Quartet on 25 February 1936 and published posthumously by Faber Music in 1983.
30. Barkers Department Store, Kensington High Street, London W8.
31. Brahms Violin Sonatas No. 1 in G, Op. 78; No. 2 in A, Op. 100; No. 3 in D minor, Op. 108.
32. A. J. Alan [Leslie Harrison Lambert] made his name as a radio broadcaster in the 1920s, always insisting on wearing evening dress for performances of his ghost-story writings. His broadcasts were frequently transcribed, and formed the basis of his two collections: *Good Evening, Everyone* (1928) and *A. J. Alan's Second Book* (1933).
33. Britten retained a life-long admiration for Grainger, performing his music at the Aldeburgh Festival and making a classic recording for Decca in the 1960s. He seems to have made a slip of the pen here though, as the arrangement to which he refers is actually *Father and Daughter*, the first of his Faroe Islands

Dance-Folksong settings, scored for five solo male voices, double mixed chorus, strings, brass, mandolin and guitar band.

34. Beethoven Violin Sonata No. 9 in A, 'Kreutzer', Op. 47.
35. Beethoven *Egmont* Overture, Op. 84; Haydn Symphony No. 73 in D, 'La chasse', (Hob.1 : 73); Bach Violin Concerto in E (BWV1042); Hermann Scherchen's concert suite of *Three Fragments* (1924) from Berg's opera *Wozzeck* (1914–22) with May Blyth (soprano); Strauss *Tod und Verklärung*, Op. 24, tone poem for orchestra.
36. *The Fall of the House of Usher* (1839–40), short story by Edgar Allan Poe (1809–49).
37. Another string quartet movement for '*Go play, boy, play*'.
38. Stravinsky *Suite Italienne* (1933) from *Pulcinella* (1920), *Duo concertante* (1932), *Prélude et Ronde des princesses* (1929), *Berceuse* Nos. 1 (1929) and 2 (1933), *Scherzo* (1933) from *L'Oiseau de feu* (1910); *Danse Russe* (1932) from *Petruchka* (1911); *Chants du Rossignol et Marche chinoise* (1932) from *Le rossignol* (1914); and *Divertimento* (1932) from *Le baiser de la fée* (1928).
39. Julius Harrison *The Blessed Damozel* (Dante Gabriel Rossetti) for *a cappella* female voices.
40. It is still remarkable to note that, apart from the earlier premiere of Britten's *Phantasy* string quintet (on 22 July 1932), this was the only performance at the RCM of any Britten work during his time as a student at the College.
41. The prestigious RCM Octavia Travelling Scholarship, awarded in 1930 to Britten's college friend, Grace Williams, to enable her to complete her training in Vienna with Egon Wellesz. It may well have been at this meeting that Britten's mother discussed Britten's desire to study with Alban Berg in Vienna and was warned by Sir Hugh Allen that Berg would be a bad influence on Britten.
42. Edmund [Duncan] Rubbra Piano Concerto, Op. 30, which was later withdrawn by the composer.
43. Frederick May *Scherzo* for orchestra (1933).
44. Stravinsky Concert Suite No. 1 (1911) from his ballet, *L'oiseau de feu* (1910).
45. Hindemith *Das Unaufhörliche* (1931), oratorio for soloists, chorus, children's choir and orchestra, with a text by Gottfried Benn (1886–1956).
46. Amen House, the London offices of Oxford University Press in EC4.
47. Hindemith *Lehrstück* (1929), theatrical cantata for soloists, clowns, chorus, military band and orchestra, with a text by Bertolt Brecht (1898–1956).
48. *The Plough and the Stars* (1926), anti-war play by Seán O'Casey (1880–1964).
49. Brahms String Quartet in C minor, Op. 51, No. 1.
50. *Emil und die Detektive* (1931), a film adaptation of the famous children's novel (1928) by Erich Kästner (1899–1974) supervised by the author himself.
51. Britten had been sufficiently struck by the film to search out Kästner's 1928 novel in the original German, and was struggling to remember his schoolboy German.
52. Britten was rethinking his scheme for *Alla Quartetto Serioso: 'Go play, boy, play'* as a suite fashioned from Kästner's film and the novel that inspired it.

The two '*Go play, boy, play*' arrangements are preserved in the Britten–Pears Library collection.

53. Britten arranged two of his '*Go play, boy, play*' movements for this combination before abandoning the scheme, but in 1935 he was to write his *Two Insect Pieces* (for oboe and piano) for Sylvia Spenser.
54. See *Pictures from a Life*, Plate 56.
55. Beethoven Symphony No. 3 in E flat, 'Eroica', Op. 55.
56. A broadcast via the new international radio broadcasting transmission facility near Mühlacker, West Germany, first put into service in 1930.
57. Brittten was struggling valiantly with the highly complex finale of *A Boy Was Born*, Op. 3.
58. William Yeates Hurlstone was one of six composers awarded the inaugural Cobbett Prize for chamber music in 1905 for his *Phantasy* String Quartet (1905).
59. Ireland Violin Sonata No. 1 in D minor (1909); Vaughan Williams *Phantasy* Quintet for strings (1912).
60. This was undoubtedly the Mahler symphony with which Britten had the most personal connection, hence his desire to perform it during the 1961 Aldeburgh Festival.
61. Bliss Clarinet Quintet (1932).
62. *Chu Chin Chow* (1916), musical comedy by Oscar Ashe (1872–1936) with music by Frederic Norton (1869–1946), based on the tale of Ali Baba and the Forty Thieves.
63. This was the famous touring troupe of Uday Shankar (1900–77) world-renowned Bengali classical dancer and choreographer from India, brother of Ravi Shankar, the virtuoso sitar player and composer.
64. *Tandava Nritya* – according to religious scholars, this dance of Lord Shiva (called 'Anandatandava,' meaning, 'the Dance of Bliss') symbolises the cosmic cycles of creation and destruction, as well as the daily rhythm of birth and death. The dance is a pictorial allegory of the five principal manifestations of eternal energy – creation, destruction, preservation, salvation and illusion.
65. Britten is still struggling with the finale to *A Boy Was Born*, one of many examples of the supreme effort that he put into writing often highly complex music that nonetheless sounds effortless, instinctive and inevitable.
66. Brahms Piano Concerto No. 2 in B flat, Op. 83.
67. Their Majesties King George V and Queen Mary.
68. Bat-and-ball game testing individual dexterity.
69. Armstrong Gibbs String Quartet in A, Op. 73; Maconchy Oboe Quintet (1933); Cundell String Quartet in C, Op. 27. All three works were recorded by the Griller Quartet in April and May 1933, and are now available on a Dutton remastered CD transfer.
70. A rehearsal for a Mendelssohn Scholarship performance of Britten's *Phantasy*, Op. 2, to be given by Natalie Caine (oboe), Remo Lauricella (violin), Frederick Riddle (viola) and Bernard Richards (cello) at the Royal Academy of Music; see 2 June.

71. Kodaly *The Spinning Room* (1932), one-act opera based on Hungarian folk-songs.
72. *The Wild Duck* (1884), play by Henrik Ibsen (1828–1906), considered by many to be the finest and certainly one of the most complex works by the great Norwegian dramatist.
73. Britten begins the process of revising *Lift Boy* (1932: the second of his *Two Antithetical Part-Songs* for two-part boys' or female voices) into the version eventually published by Boosey and Hawkes in 1934, for mixed chorus and piano. A similar revised version was completed of the first of the *Antithetical Part-Songs, I Lov'd a Lass*, later that same week.
74. Vaughan Williams *Hugh the Drover, or, Love in the Stocks* (1911–14), ballad folk-opera in two acts with a libretto by Harold Child.
75. When Beth Britten moved into her living quarters at her new business premises at 559 Finchley Road in Hampstead, Britten moved into her larger room, adjacent to his at Burleigh House.
76. Hely-Hutchinson *Idyll and Diversions* for piano quintet (unpublished).
77. Britten often tested his position with regard to his 'pet hates', such as Brahms and Elgar.
78. Scherchen was a great advocate of modern music.
79. Although there is no record of Hugh Ross conducting *A Boy Was Born* with his New York Schola Cantorum as an immediate result of this meeting, in 1941 he was to be the Music Director for the New York premiere of the Britten-Auden choral operetta, *Paul Bunyan* at Columbia University.
80. Britten's passion for tennis (and indeed his competitive streak as a player) remained undiminished throughout his life.
81. Debussy *L'isle joyeuse* for solo piano (1904).
82. It has long been thought that Peter Pears was a member of the BBC Wireless Singers at this time and sang in the premiere of *A Boy Was Born*. However this has since been proven not to be the case, as Pears' first contract with the BBC ran from July 1934 to November 1936.
83. Ireland Sonata in G minor for cello and piano (1923).
84. An important first encounter with Henry Boys, a musical soulmate and a rare early instance of Britten enjoying a productive musical friendship with a music critic, a profession of which he was to grow more and more suspicious as time went on. Later in life he was to enjoy a similar relationship with Hans Keller and Donald Mitchell, who (like Boys) were both music critics *and* scholars, and won Britten's trust, professional respect and affection.
85. Eugene Goossens *Lyric Poem*, Op. 35, for violin and piano, written for André Mangeot in 1920.
86. The Alhambra Theatre (inspired by the Moorish splendour of the Alhambra palace in Granada) specialised in ballet and music-hall entertainment, and used to dominate the east side of London's Leicester Square. It was destroyed by fire and demolished in 1936; the Odeon Cinema, Leicester Square, was built on the site the following year.

87. This season at the Alhambra was the London debut of Colonel W. de Basil's new Ballets Russes de Monte Carlo, the principal company (founded by Russian impresario Vasily Grigorievich Voskresensky) to succeed Sergei Diaghilev's Ballets Russes after his death in 1929. While they continued to revive the great Fokine ballets of the original company, they also brought in new choreographic talent, including Leonide Massine and George Balanchine.
88. Dvorak Overture *Amid Nature*, Op. 63; Debussy *Prélude à l'après-midi d'un faune*; Bridge *Dance Poem* (1913); Schumann Symphony No. 4 in D minor, Op. 120.
89. Amrid Johnstone designed the original cover for the first edition of Britten's choral variations, *A Boy Was Born*, Op. 3, published by OUP in 1934.
90. Brosa performed Chabrier's arrangement of the Vitali *Chaconne* and the *Tarantelle* by d'Eilanger; the chamber concert comprised Mozart String Quartet No. 14 in G, K387; Fauré String Quartet in E minor, Op. 121; and the premiere of Britten's *Phantasy*, Op. 2, played by members of the International String Quartet (André Mangeot (violin), Eric Bray (viola), Jack Shinebourne (cello)) with Léon Goossens (oboe). The concert also included two groups of songs: Wolf 'Heimweh', 'Bescheidne Liebe', 'In dem Schatten meiner Locken' and Schumann 'Der arme Peter', 'Die Meerfee', 'Widmung', performed by Lily Zaehner.
91. *Scenes of Clerical Life* (1858), three short stories by George Eliot [Mary Anne Evans] (1819–80).
92. Beethoven Piano Sonata No. 7 in D, Op. 10 No. 3.
93. Lalo *Symphonie espagnole* in D minor, Op. 21, for violin and orchestra.
94. Britten was revising the *Alla burlesca ('ragging')*, the last movement of '*Go play, boy, play*', which was performed (together with an *All'introduzione* and *Alla valse*) at the RCM on 3 November (for his application for a Mendelssohn Scholarship), and again on 4 December at All Hallows, Barking, by the Macnaghten String Quartet. The *Alla burlesca* was inscribed 'To Francis' [Barton].
95. *Fresh Fields* (1933), the premiere production from London's Criterion Theatre of the satirical play by Ivor Novello (1893–1951).
96. Bruno Kittel conducting the Berlin Philharmonic Chorus and Orchestra (solo violin Wilfried Hanke), with Lotte Leonard (soprano), Eleanor Schlosshauer-Reynolds (contralto), Eugen Transky (tenor) and Hermann Schey (bass).
97. Beethoven *Missa Solemnis*, Op. 123.
98. Beethoven Triple Concerto in C, for piano, violin, cello and orchestra, Op. 56.
99. *The Sign of the Cross* (1932), epic historical drama starring Charles Laughton and Claudette Colbert as Nero and Poppaea, directed by Cecil B. De Mille (1881–1959).
100. *Alla Quartetto Serioso: 'Go play, boy, play'.*
101. Beethoven Piano Concerto No. 2 in B flat, Op. 19.
102. Bach Brandenburg Concerto No. 3 in G (BWV1048); Dvorak Piano Quintet in A, Op. 81.

103. Delius *Idyll* (1933) for soprano, baritone and orchestra.
104. Bridge *Dance Poem* (1913) for orchestra, conducted by Bridge in a Promenade Concert shared with Henry Wood.
105. Britten was still struggling with *'Go play, boy, play'*. *Physical Training* was the subtitle he applied to this revised march movement.
106. *The Bulpington of Blub: Adventures, Poses, Stresses, Conflicts, and Disaster in a Contemporary Brain* (1933), novel by H. G. Wells (1866–1946).
107. Ferguson *Octet*, Op. 4, for clarinet, bassoon, horn, string quartet and double bass (1933), one of his earliest works to gain wide recognition.
108. Alan Bush String Quartet (1929).
109. Rimsky-Korsakov's *The Tale of Tsar Saltan* (1900), opera in four acts (six tableaux) and a prologue, based on the Pushkin poem, with a libretto by Vladimir Ivanovich Belsky. The cast for this British premiere of the opera, given by the Vic-Wells Opera Company, included Joan Cross, Edith Coates and Roderick Jones, artists who were later to create the roles of Ellen Orford, Auntie and Balstrode in the 1945 Sadler's Wells premiere of Britten's first operatic masterpiece, *Peter Grimes*.
110. A rehearsal of the *Alla'introduzione, Alla valse* and *Alla burlesca* for the Mendelssohn Scholarship presentation of Britten's work on 3 November.
111. Work resumed on the *Theme (What to do?) and Variations*, presumably on the second variation ('On the see-saw'), which Britten began sketching on 20 October.
112. Bridge *Phantasm*, Rhapsody for piano and orchestra, (1931). The Mainly Musicians Club (known throughout the profession and by its members as the M. M. Club) was founded in 1933 by the cellist May Mukle. Its basement premises in Argyle Street, adjacent to Oxford Circus tube station, remained open throughout the Second World War, during which time it also functioned as a bomb shelter. It finally closed its doors in 1948.
113. *The Cherry Orchard* (1904), the final play by Anton Chekhov (1860–1904), produced by Tyrone Guthrie. More than a decade later, as Director of the Vic-Wells Company, Guthrie championed Britten's first opera, *Peter Grimes*, which launched the Sadler's Wells Opera's post-war return to its London home in 1945. Guthrie went on to direct a new production of *Grimes* at Covent Garden in 1947 and the English Opera Group premiere of Britten's new realisation of John Gay's *The Beggar's Opera* in 1948.
114. Schubert String Quartet No. 13 in A minor, 'Rosamunde', D804; Brahms String Quartet No. 2 in A minor, Op. 51 No. 2; Bridge *Two Old English Songs: Sally in Our Alley* and *Cherry Ripe* for string quartet (1916), also arranged by Bridge for string orchestra and piano duet. Many years later Britten was to make his own arrangement of *Sally in Our Alley* for an Aldeburgh Festival recital with Peter Pears in June 1959, and it was published later that year in the fifth volume of his *Folk Song Arrangements*.
115. The first of Britten's settings for a collection that was originally entitled *Twelve Songs for Schools*, and eventually published in 1936 by Boosey &

Hawkes as *Friday Afternoons*, Op. 7, twelve children's songs with piano. They were written for his brother Robert and inscribed: 'To R. H. M. Britten and the boys of Clive House School, Prestatyn, 1934'.

116. Bliss Sonata for viola and piano (1933), written for Lionel Tertis.
117. HM Queen Mary, Consort of King George V. Members of the British Royal Family would sometimes visit leading London stores, such as Fortnum and Mason, incognito, and though they would often be recognised by their loyal subjects, etiquette demanded that they be given privacy and not acknowledged or approached. All transactions were conducted by the personal servants, who always accompanied them on these occasions.
118. The Poetry Bookshop, 35 Devonshire Street, Theobald's Road, Bloomsbury, London WC1; founded in 1913 by the British poet Harold Monro (1879–1932).
119. Observed annually in the United Kingdom at 11 a.m. on Armistice Day, the anniversary of the official end of the First World War – 11 November 1918 – the eleventh hour of the eleventh day of the eleventh month.
120. *The Wandering Jew* (1923), play with Matheson Lang in his most famous stage role as the figure from medieval Christian folklore who, according to legend, taunted Christ on the way to the Crucifixion and was then cursed to walk the earth until Christ's Second Coming.
121. A setting of Eleanor Farjeon for *Friday Afternoons*.
122. Brahms *Variations on a Theme of Haydn*, Op. 56a.
123. '*Go play, boy, play*', for a performance by the Macnaghten String Quartet on 4 December.
124. *Joan and Peter: The Story of an Education* (1918) by H. G. Wells (1866–1946).
125. See Plate 14.
126. 31 Tite Street in Chelsea, London SW3, had been the studio of the celebrated American portrait painter John Singer Sargent (1856–1925).
127. Poulenc Trio for piano, oboe and bassoon (1926), played by Yvonne Arnaud, Léon Goossens and Richard Newton.
128. Hubert Foss Violin Sonata (1933).
129. *Poil de Carotte* (1933), directed by Julien Duvivier and based on the 1894 novel by Jules Renard (1864–1910); a touching story of a young boy driven to consider suicide as an escape from his uncaring mother, only to find strength and love from his father – a story certain to move Britten, who in later life was often to play surrogate father to boys from troubled homes.
130. Mozart String Quartet No. 15 in D minor, K421; Beethoven String Quartet No. 15 in A minor, Op. 132; Krenek 'Variations' from String Quartet No. 5 in E flat, Op. 65 (1930); Webern *Five Movements* for string quartet, Op. 5 (1909).
131. Bridge Piano Trio No. 2 (1929).
132. Alfredo Casella *Sonatina in Tre Tempi*, Op. 28 (1916).
133. *Two Part-Songs* (Wither and Graves) for mixed chorus and piano.
134. Britten was sitting his final exams for his Associate of the Royal College of Music (solo performance) diploma.

135. The amateur orchestra founded by Audrey Melville, *née* Chapman.
136. Harry Cox (1885–1971), English farm labourer and folk singer from North Norfolk.
137. 'Ee-Oh!' for *Friday Afternoons*.
138. *A Christmas Carol* (1843), a BBC radio adaptation of the Christmas ghost story by Charles Dickens.
139. Work begins on Britten's *Simple Symphony*, Op. 4, which he bases on his juvenile songs and piano pieces.
140. Honegger *Cris du monde* (1931), secular oratorio: a timely warning about a world in crisis, with a text by René Bizet.
141. First sketches for the 'Playful Pizzicato' of the *Simple Symphony*.
142. A cut-throat razor.
143. A radio programme linking up friends and family separated throughout the British Empire over the Christmas period.
144. Work progressing on *A Simple Symphony*.
145. A BBC broadcast of the D'Oyly Carte production of the Gilbert and Sullivan operetta from the Savoy Theatre, London.
146. The family car, a 1929 model Humber 23–8 Snipe, purchased second-hand in December 1932.
147. *The Little White Bird* (1902) by the author of *Peter Pan*, J. M. Barrie (1860–1937).
148. Clive House Preparatory School in Prestatyn, North Wales.

Apprenticeship and early successes

Wherever you go you are and probably always will be surrounded by people who adore you, nurse you, and praise everything you do . . . by playing the loveable talented little boy.
W. H. Auden writing to Benjamin Britten, New York, 31 January 1942

There is a famous story that has been told and retold about Britten many times, but is nonetheless worth retelling here, as it illustrates the extent of his single-mindedness about his career. He was asked at a tennis party in Lowestoft, while still a fairly young boy, what he planned to do with his life and what career he wanted to pursue. Britten's answer was, by all accounts, spontaneous, direct and final: 'I'm going to be a composer.' 'Yes, but what else?' came the reply. 'Nothing else,' was his defiant retort – 'a composer!'

This was not altogether how it turned out, of course, because Britten would establish his own opera company in 1947, his own festival in 1948 and remain an active and highly accomplished pianist and conductor throughout his life. But he was undoubtedly one of the most successful professional composers of his generation, creating a career that was the envy of many and equalled by few. He made a very good living as a composer, and this success underpinned (and indeed underwrote) his other musical activities. And it is interesting to see how quickly his career took off, once he left the RCM in December 1933. It might have felt slow to him (as the diaries of the ensuing months suggest), but consider the following as a scenario for a young composer of twenty, straight out of college.

Within two months of Britten leaving the RCM his choral variations, *A Boy Was Born*, were premiered by the BBC Wireless Chorus in a BBC Concert of Contemporary Music under Leslie Woodgate, broadcast live on 23 February. Britten was by then trying his hand at conducting, and on 6 March he directed the premiere of his *Simple Symphony* with the Norwich String Orchestra at Stuart Hall in Norwich. The following month his *Phantasy* oboe quartet was selected for performance at the International Society of Contemporary Music festival in Florence, where it was performed by Léon Goossens and members of the Griller Quartet on 5 April. His progress was halted by the death of his father – long anticipated but no less traumatic for that – just a day before the ISCM concert, while Britten was travelling in Florence with his school friend, John Pounder. Britten took time to come to terms with his loss and devote himself to his family, particularly his grieving mother. He spent much of 1934 either in Lowestoft or travelling with his mother, first to stay with his brother at his school in Prestatyn, and, later in the year, taking her on an extended tour of Europe through much of October and November, visiting Switzerland, Austria and France. Today we would call it 'quality time', and he would later reflect on the importance of this trip for both of them, because his mother was herself to die unexpectedly in January 1937, leaving him bereft.

His account of this European tour is wonderful to read on many levels, not least for its further evidence of his voracious appetite (and highly developed critical judgement) for great musical experiences. It points also to his not insignificant entrepreneurial skills: while in Vienna he made contact with two leading music publishers, Erwin Stein and Hans Heinsheimer, both working at Universal Edition at the time. Both men were Jewish and in the wake of the *Anschluss* they found professional refuge with Boosey & Hawkes – Stein in London and Heinsheimer in New York, where each ended up representing Britten after the war. Stein became something of a musical father to Britten after Frank Bridge's death in 1941. He had been a pupil of Schoenberg and counted amongst his fellow students no less a figure than Alban Berg, one of Britten's greatest musical heroes. The fact that Britten could count upon Stein as his main editorial contact at Boosey & Hawkes after the war was of profound importance, and the foundation of this important post-war relationship lay in the time he spent in 1934 with Stein in Vienna.

Despite the turmoil of his father's death and this extended period abroad, Britten still managed to complete four small-scale works and begin a fifth in the autumn of 1934. The *Te Deum* in C and *Jubilate Deo* in E flat (both for chorus and organ), the unison song, *May* (*Now is the month of Maying*) and the *Holiday Tales* for piano (later re-titled *Holiday Diary*) were all completed between July and October, and at the end of the year he began his Suite, Op. 6, for violin and piano. This was as nothing, however, compared with the feverish activity of the following year. Admittedly, the number of original scores he completed in 1935 was, by his own standards, rather modest: just the Suite, Op. 6 and *Friday Afternoons*, Op. 7, plus a short Blake setting and two movements for an incomplete suite for oboe and piano for Sylvia Spencer. But he had meanwhile been contracted, thanks to a recommendation from the BBC, by the GPO Film Unit, where he met and worked with the poet W. H. Auden. Auden introduced him to the directors of The Group Theatre (Rupert Doone and Robert Medley), which led to further collaborations with many of the most progressive theatre ensembles in London. Britten became in effect a leading composer-in-residence for both the GPO Film Unit and The Group Theatre, writing for many of their most significant productions. In 1935 he hit the ground running, and in this year alone he wrote music for *The King's Stamp, Coal Face, The Tocher, C.T.O. (The Story of the Central Telegraph Office), Telegram Abstract, How the Dial Works, Conquering Space, Sorting Office, The Savings Bank, The New Operator*, and *Negroes* for the GPO Film Unit; *Men behind the Meters, Dinner Hour* and *How Gas is Made* for the British Commercial Gas Association; *Timon of Athens* for The Group Theatre and *Easter 1916* for The Left Theatre, often playing in or directing the stage performances and/or recording sessions for these scores.

Britten's relationship with these remarkable institutions had a profound intellectual and political influence on him. Through them he encountered not just Auden, but men such as Christopher Isherwood, Louis MacNeice, Montagu Slater, Rupert Doone, Robert Medley, William Coldstream, John Grierson, Alberto Cavalcanti, Stuart Legg, Harry Watt and Basil Wright – some of the most original creative artists working in theatre and film between the wars. It was a rich and instructive apprenticeship for him, because he had to learn how to write fast, to order, for prescribed and generally very limited forces, and was often required to experiment with musicians and instruments to achieve musico-dramatic effects and contrive a sense of actuality, particularly in the films. Meanwhile he continued to study with his mentor, Frank Bridge, who constantly challenged him. They seem to have ended up agreeing about all the music that mattered to them most, except Mahler – Britten's passion, but not Bridge's.

This was indeed an intense apprenticeship, but only a composer of Britten's fluency and extraordinary technique could have taken full advantage of the opportunities it afforded. He had been writing music almost every day from the age of nine; from the age of fourteen he had studied intensely with the most demanding of teachers; and thanks to the brilliance of his technique and the steady employment he enjoyed immediately after college, he never looked back. As he had said to his Lowestoft neighbour at that tennis party back in his youth, he was going to be a composer. This was his career and he was determined to make a success of it.

Diaries: 1934–1935

Apprenticeship and early successes

Britten's ink fair copy of the *Sentimental Saraband*, the third movement of *Simple Symphony*, Op. 4. The work is based on his juvenilia – piano pieces and songs written between the ages of nine and eleven; the footnote refers to the source of the main theme of this movement, the Suite No. 3 for piano (1925). © The Britten Estate Limited. See diary for 6 March 1934.

1934

Wednesday 3 January [Lowestoft]
Rewrite bits of Scherzo in morning.[1] Long walk up town with dog. Read & laze in front of fire – first part of aft. Then walk up town shopping with hound. Ping-pong after tea with Laurence Sewell. My new Gram record of Tristan Prelude under Furtwängler comes[2] – it is superb. Pop comes into drawing-room, for lunch, & then for abit after supper as usual. But his cough & sickness is pretty bad. Write letters after dinner.

Thursday 4 January
I can't find any suitable material to continue my kid's finale. See T.J.E. Sewell (head of S. Lodge) in morning. Walk with Bazil Reeve before lunch. Read in aft. (Barrie – Tommy & Grizel).[3] Walk after tea (to which Rev. W.E. Reeve comes), & Bazil comes after that to hear gramophone & some of my new things. Pop's cough is frantic after dinner; he's also suffering a good deal all the time. His birthday to-day.

Friday 5 January
Pop's morphia day, so he's feeling well, tho' wuzzy. Walk up town with dog in morning. Go to Badminton at Drill Hall in aft. 8 there – quite fun. Bath before dinner. Letters & listen to T. Brosa playing A. Benjamin's Vln concerto (much as I want to – I ~~don't~~ cannot like the work – badly put together – tho' T.B. played it beautifully). Miss Ethel Astle comes to see Pop.[4]

Sunday 7 January
Very long walk with hound along cliffs in morning. Do much work at it. Read more 'Nijinsky' in aft.[5] & walk with Caesar. Listen to abit of Prokofiev 3rd conc. & practically all of Verdi's Otello (this from Vienna) on wireless after tea & dinner.[6] Marvellous opera – pretty well done. Fading was rather bad in spots.

Wednesday 10 January [London]
Rehearsal of 'Phantasm' at Queens Hall at 10.0. Go up with Mr. & Mrs F.B. Meet Beth for lunch at Lewis at 1.0. Go up to Oxford Press abt. 3.0. Hear from Foss that my Oboe Quart. has been accepted by international jury for

Contemporary Music Festival.[7] Go and see (for 2nd time) 'Emil & the Detectives' at Cinema House, Ox. Circus.[8] It is a simply delightful film, as great a comedy as 'Poil de Carotte' was ~~in the~~ a tragedy. Early dinner at 6.30 at F.B's & go up with them in car to Q.H. for 5th of Brit. Music Concerts. Landon Ronald doing officiation tho' F.B. conducts his own Phantasm which K. Long plays brilliantly (I turn for her)[9] Audience seems to like it v. much. Rest of programme dull & droning – don't hear all of it (Elgar 1st Symph. – 2 pieces of Howells, Wallace Villon etc.). After show go back to Dennis Grayson's at Knightsbridge. He has home-made some gramophone records of to-night's show of Phantasm – & they really are very good. The Brosas come back for supper at B's. F.B. takes them back to St. John's Wood (go with him) at 2.30. In bed by 3.0.

Friday 12 January [Lowestoft]
See Aunt Flo. off by 10.7 to London. Write letters etc in morning. Badminton in aft. Only 7 there – quite fun. After Dinner ~~walk down~~ meet Barbara from London by 8.4. Listen to last Brit. Music Concts inc. J. Irelands new Legend for Pft (Helen Perkin – inadequate) & Orch.[10] Seemed unsatisfactory & meandering – & rather reminiscent – tho' some nice things in it. Moeran's 2nd conventional folksongy Rhapsody[11] & Belshazzer's feast of Walton. V. exhilerating in parts – but he looses too many opportunities & workmanship is often too bad. I'm afraid there isn't quite enough left when the glitter & icing is taken away.

Thursday 18 January
Write most of 'Finale' for school suite in morning & aft. Walk with hound before lunch, & after tea with Stephen Abell – also play ping-pong with him. Listen to F.B. conducting B.B.C. orch. in a programme of light music – delightfully done. William Tell, ov.; Chant sans paroles; Funeral March of a Marionette was just superb; Sylvia Ballet; Barcorolle etc. from Tales of Hoffman; and Marche – Père la Victoire to finish.[12] The whole programme was just write. (Toni Brosa, & H. Samuel are giving at a Phil. chamber concert to night the 1st perf of his new Vln Sonata).[13]

Friday 19 January
News of my Ob. Quart. being in Internat. Festival becomes public. Finish (or attempt to) Finale of my Kid's Suite in morning. Badminton in aft. Great fun, & some quite good badminton. (6 there). Beth comes back here by 6.10. Listen to Hindemith's last String trio[14] after dinner – (played by Hindemith etc.) – I can't make very much of it but judging by first

hearing, the fast movements have a pleasing vitality which is missing in the slower ones.

Monday 22 January
Go down to station to see Beth off by 8.30 to town. Work at pft in morning – Strav. pft. arr. of Petrouchka. Walk before lunch. Go to Badminton at Drill Hall in aft. John Pounder goes too, & takes me in his car. Listen to Berlin Phil. orch. from Queen's Hall after dinner. Bach D maj. Suite; ~~Sy~~ Schumann's 4th, & Beethoven's 7th Symphonys. Superb orchestra – enormously energetic; & extraordinarily well disciplined. I didn't like everything that Furtwängler did. But most of the Schuman was magnificent.

Tuesday 23 January
Rewrite bits of what is already done of kid's Suite. Walk with dog before lunch & again in aft. I'm now looking for stuff to make a 1st mov. Practise Petrouchka before dinner. After, listen to some early Beethoven Chamber-music from Munich. The Trio for 2 Ob. & Cor Anglais; & Serande in D for Vl. Vla & Vlc.[15] Both of these are extremely attractive – & ingenuously scored if not hair-raising musicly. I must hear them again. Performances quite good.

Thursday 25 January
Practise pft, & sort out music for modern music lecture – in morning. Walk with dog, & pt. way Mum, before lunch. I am endeavouring to force myself to write an overture for 'Telegraph Competition'.[16] Walk with dog before & after tea. Leslie Woodgate (from B.B.C.) rings up about 'Boy was born' abt. 4.0. Listen to Wireless play after dinner 'Trent's last case'.[17] Seemed to be rather far-fetched – but well done on the whole.

Friday 26 January
Printed copies of 'A Boy was Born' arrive in morning – they look pretty good. Send some off to people in morning. Walk with Mum before lunch. Badminton in aft. Am going to a lecture with Laurence, & so have an early dinner – but it is postponed. Miss Ethel comes in to see Pop, after dinner. He seems still better. Listen to a bit of a Contemporary concert from B.B.C. Suite 'The Nose' by Shoshtakovitch.[18] Very amusing & exhilerating – but I shouldn't be surprised if it were found to be uneventful & even conventional with all the glitter taken off – this, especially the Entre Acts.

Sunday 28 January
Walk in morning – right to N. Pier with hound. Short one before tea. Read before that. Letters & gramophone after. Finish Bloody Mary's after

supper.[19] It is unpleasant, but pretty well done. Abit too medodramatic in places to ring true, but really very interesting.

Pop has a bad down day. Lungs & chest are still better, but the stomach's an awful bother – he's sick several times.

Wednesday 31 January [London]
Go to see Dorothy Wadham in morning (abt. performance of my Ob. quartet in florence). Shop abit after that – in Charing X Road. Return to find Bridges back from country. Go to see Leslie Woodgate at B.B.C. at 5.0. Arrangements about 'Boy was Born'.[20] Go with F.B. to B.B.C. Symphony concert at 8.15. Bruno Walter conducting – v. disappointing. Mozart G min. & Brahms E min. Unintelligent on whole – & orchestra rather poor. Prokofiev plays (apparently brilliantly) his new 5th Concerto. I don't want it.

Thursday 1 February
Practise pft. here in morning – also much arranging by Telephone. Have a good lesson (on kids' pieces) in aft. from F.B. After tea, Mr & Mrs Bridge & I go to see film at a 7d Cinema near here – Hell's Divers.[21] V. amazing photography of flying – best I've ever seen. I go to dinner with Mr & Mrs Brosa up at St. John's Wood. Mrs. B. isn't frightfully well, so I dine out with Mr. B. at a restaurant near.

Friday 2 February [London/Lowestoft]
Go to R.C.M. in morning to see Kathleen Long (for F.B.) & John Ireland. After that go up to Beth's for Elevenses. After lunch (before which F.B. goes to a B.B.C. rehearsal for Sunda[y]). F.B. gives me an excellent lesson on my quartet pieces (Go play boy, play). Go to Liverpool [Street], & Meet Barbara & catch 4.54 home. Do alot of ~~walk~~ work in train – arr. my Quartet Alla Valse for pft.[22] Arr. on time at 8.4; Mum waits for dinner for us. Go up to Miss Ethel's before bed, to see abt. pianos.

Saturday 3 February [Lowestoft]
Go to Miss Astle's to practise abit on her pft. in morning. Spend rest of morning here – practising & making notes for afternoon, when I give a lecture-recital on 'Modern Music – its meaning' to the Teachers' Association of the Royal Schools of Music at the Astles – 3.0–4.15 with Tea after. Play alot of pieces & do agood deal of talking. Horribly nervous & talk much rot. John Pounder (Mum & Barbara also) comes; play ping-pong with him at his home after.

Sunday 4 February

Long walk with Barbara in morning along cliffs. Read in aft – beginning Milne's Red House Mystery[23] Walk with dog before listening to the Rothschild Quart. from Vienna[24] playing F.B.'s 3 Idylls – not to well – at 4.10. Go down to station & see Barbara off to town by 5.28. Listen to F.B. conducting B.B.C. orch at 9.5. Orchestra not on form. Bach's 3rd Brandenburg wasn't very satisfactory – uncontroled. Haydn's Clock Symphony was better. Kathleen Long plays 'Phantasm' again; not such a good show as the Queen's Hall, but the great work redeemed it. A riotous performance of Capriccio Espagnol ends the programme. Rhythm excellent.

Tuesday 6 February

Spent all writing-time to-day (most. of morning, aft. & after tea) rewriting bits of Kids' Suite. Walks before lunch & after tea. Listen to wireless after dinner – Bernard Shaw speaking very finely & beautifully in the 'Whither Britain' series;[25] also Toni Brosa & Max Piram in a recital. A really disgraceful perf. of Beethoven F maj. Sonata. T.B. plays some solos after – very beautifully; he is a superb fiddler which makes it more annoying that he is such an indifferent musician.[26] Piram is, of course, a wash-out. Pop's not so well to-day.

Thursday 8 February

Pop is worse, towards night, than I've ever seen him, I'm afraid. Work at Bourée in morning & abit after lunch. Go to tea with Mr & Miss Banks at Corton Road at 4.30 (having cleverly forgotten to reply to their invitation). Listen to a very clever & effective broadcast of the immortal 'Emil' at 8.0.[27] Hugh Green was very good as Emil, & the other kids were very natural. The nightmare was pretty good.

Sunday 11 February

Usual Sunday. Walk in morning with Beth. Read in aft. & short walk before tea with hound. Letters after tea & 5.30–7.30 Listen to a fine broadcast perf. of Shakespeare's incredible Anthony & Cleopatra. Edith Evans was superb (as C.) & so was Robert Farquason & Godfrey Tearle (A). They rather overshadowed the rest, but it was 1st-rate.

Pop's about the same – but rather feeling the after-effects of the morphia.

Wednesday 14 February [Lowestoft/London]

Hair cut, pack & walk (shopping) in morning; Moeran rings up & the Norwich Festival Secretary comes over to see me at 1.30 about writing a work for them for 1936.[28] Catch 2.32 off to town. I am staying with the

Bridges for to-night. After dinner Mrs. B. & I go off to Queen's Hall for B.B.C. concert. Boult conducts a dull & ignorant perf. of Oberon overture & then Schnabel is rather disappointing in Brahms D min concerto – tho' the slow mov. was mostly beautiful. Job of Vaughan Williams seemed interminable.[29] There are some nice things in it if you arn't tired of folk song modalism – but most of it is heavy, dull, imitative & amateurish.

Thursday 15 February [London]

Go to rehearsal of my 'Boy etc' at B.B.C. at 11.0–1.0 under Woodgate It really goes promisingly well. Everyone is very decent about it. In aft. F.B. looks very searchingly at my Kid's pieces in aft – to their great advantage. Go to Audry Melville Orch. concert at 8.0 at Clarkenwell – Miss Fass, Beth as well as Bridges. This is certainly the place to go for sane & inspiring performances. Wagner F. Dutchman ov.; Borodines Steppes; S. Saens exciting Fiancée du timbalier (badly sung by Gabrielle Joachim) & a very beautiful perf. (for an amateur orch.; 2nd rate wind, & a first rate conductor) of Tschaikov. 4th.[30] V. bad fog in evening; Beth & I (I am staying night at Beths) take just under 2 hrs getting back arr. 2.0. V. terrifying in spots.

Friday 16 February

After breakfast go to R.C.M to see Arthur Benjamin & people Lunch at Bridges. In aft. go & see film 'Liebelei' at Acadamy.[31] Personally, in spite of everyone's ravings, I am rather disappointed, tho' some of the acting & all the photography is fine. Abit over-sentimental for me personally. At 5.0 go to St. Marks. N. Audly St. for a rehearsal of the Boys for my choral work.[32] They sing like angels – for this stage of ~~the~~ rehearsal. Go, via Bridges, to Barbaras with Beth, to dinner. I am staying the night with Barbara.

Monday 19 February [Lowestoft]

Pop is terribly weak & dazed all day – exactly as if he has had a overdose of morphia. We are extra specially worried about him, until Dr. Evans comes after dinner to see him, & to tell us that he has been taking overdoses of his cough mixture which has morphia in it.

Spend most of day copying parts of kids' suite – morning aft. & after dinner until 11.30. Go to short badminton after tea – 4.30 to 6.0 with Laurence.

Elgar dies.

Friday 23 February [London]

F.B. comes with me to rehearsal at 11.0. Better than yesterday but not good. Back to late lunch here, to which Julian Herbage comes. In aft. go back to see Mr. Goodwin (Radio Times) at B.B.C. back to tea here, then go up to rehearse Boys again at St. Marks. Bath & dinner at 7.30, then Mr. & Mrs. B. take me up to Broadcasting house for contemporary concert. My 'Boy was Born' goes infinitely better than rehearsals, some of it really going well. It goes down pretty well.[33] Cyril Scott plays 2nd pft sonata; 4 Choral songs of Rubbra (1st 2 very similar) & A Motet of Woodgate (conductor) for a rousing (not much more!) finish. Whole lot of us (Mr & Mrs B, Mr & Mrs Brosa, D Wadham, John Alston, Harold Samuel & friend) meet at M.M. Club for supper. Bad fog; We (Mr Mrs B. & I) drive H. Samuel back to Hampstead. arr. here at 1.40.

Tuesday 27 February [Lowestoft]
Have an awful struggle to get parts finished for to-night. Just manage to, working all morning & aft. – with a ~~short~~ short walk before lunch.

After tea Charles Coleman calls for me in his car, at 5.45. & takes me over to St. Giles Hall Norwich for rehearsal of Mrs. Sutton's (late Alston) String orch. in which he's playing 2nd Vln. V. bad orch. Moeran is conducting 2 concerti, & I my kid's Suite which they play pretty badly. Start home at 10.0 Stop for meal, and arr at 12.0. Very snowy, but lovely night.

Pop's chest is so bad in morning that Dr. Evans is sent for and orders him Morphia.

Tuesday 6 March
Charles & Mrs. C. call for me at 9.30 to go to Norwich in their car. arr. 10.30 at Stuart Hall for rehearsal. Meet Peter Bevan at 11.11 from London – he is a friend of Ber's & is helping us in the 'cello department. Lunch with him and Mrs. Chamberlain. At 2.45 show starts at Stuart Hall. Mangeot (cond. Moeran) plays 2 concerti (Vivaldi & Haydn) with orch. – v. badly. I conduct my 'Simple Symphony' which doesn't go too badly – except for a swim in the Saraband. A Scratch Quartet scrambles through 2 movs. of Mozart G maj. Tea after & then to Mrs Sutton's gift shop – where I have rather a set-to with A. Mangeot about his not playing for me at Florence.[34] See Peter B. & him off to town by 6.45 – & get back here by 8.0. Listen to an interesting story on wireless – delightfully told by 'A.J. Alan.'[35]

Wednesday 7 March
A positive night-mare of a day. Spend most of morning, aft & after tea sitting with Pop, whose chest is unbearably painful. Walk up town before lunch. In afternoon a chest specialist, Mr. Batti-shaw (?) comes down from town to see Pop, & is at any rate hopeful. But the chest is no better after his departure. More morphia at night.

Tuesday 13 March

Pop's about the same – but he still has to take his morphia, as well as the opium pills. Usual morning, polishing up things, pft practice & walk. Read abit in aft; more thinking of writing; & a short walk. Go to Badminton at Mrs Palmer's club for an hour with Laurence from 5.15–6.15. Begin a sketch for 'Poil de Carotte' before dinner,[36] late – because of Dr Evans coming in. He comes in every day now. Long talk with Pop in evening on Finance.

Wednesday 14 March

Pop is better all day until the evening when he has a bad spasm of pain. Do some work at 'Poil', write letters & walk with Caesar at various hours of the day. Listen to broadcast of concert ~~version~~ performance of Wozzeck (1st in England) from Q.H. – by B.B.C. orch & Adrian Boult with Bitterauf as Wozzeck (superb) & May Blyth as Marie (seemed excellent) & a large & efficient cast.[37] It wasn't very satisfactory as a broadcast – voices too loud, & blurring. Only the third Act (& bits of second) were intelligible. The music of this is extraordinarly striking without the action, while that of the first isn't – except for the exciting march & beautiful little lullaby. The hand of Tristan is over alot of the intense emotion, but Berg emerges a definite personality.

Thursday 15 March

Pop gets up & sits in his room in the evening. Otherwise he is abt the same as yesterday. Very unsatisfactory day – I cannot get on with the rewriting of the Alla Marcia from Quartet Suite.[38] Spend most of morning & aft. doing it. Fernande comes to tea for abit, to help me abit with Italian[39] & arranging. Go to Badminton with her & Laurence from 5–6.

Walk with dog before dinner. Listen to Pierre Monteux conducting L.P.O. Thibaud scrambles brilliantly through Symphonie Espagnol; & the orch. likewise thro' Debussy's Nuage & Fêtes[40] – but Monteux is a great man.

Friday 16 March

Pop moves into Spare room as sweep comes. About same – but no morphia.

Letters – bit of altering & walk – household shopping in morning. Long telephone talk with Moeran about various musical matters at lunch. John Nicholson comes to Badminton with me at Drill Hall I go there with Marjorie Phillips. 11 there – quite fun. Doris Tamplin takes me to Station where I meet Barbara off 6.4. Read & gramophone (Mass in D) in evening.

Sunday 18 March

Pop is very comfortable until abt. 6.0, when the effects of the morphia die off. He has 2 gr. morphia again abt. 9.0. Long walk with John Pounder &

Barbara – pt. way – in morning. Read, & short walk with Barbara before tea. Walk down to station with her to see her off by 5.28. Walk abit back with Dunkerley of S. Lodge. Letters between then & supper. Listen to Tertis and B.B.C. orch after. A new & dismal Idyll (?) by Holst.[41]

Monday 19 March [Lowestoft/London]
Rewrite parts of Simple Symphony. Shop with Mum & pack in morning. Catch 2.32 to town after lunch, arr. 6.0. Go st. to Bridges where I'm staying. After dinner go with Mr & Mrs. B. to B.B.C. where he conducts an orch. concert. The orch is very tired and doesn't play too well. Smetana, B.B. ov.; F.B's lovely 'Lament'. Percy Hemming sings some songs (4 of F.B.), but is very out of voice. Long extract from Meistersinger, & Berlioz-Weber Introduction to Valse (splendid rhythm) & Hungarian March (not so good)

Tuesday 20 March [London]
Go to see Foss abt. various matters at O.U.P. in morning at 11.0. Then to hire-depart. of O.U.P. about other matters. Shop abit, & then meet Dorothy Wadham for lunch at M.M. Club. After, go to Grillers for rehearsal of my Ob. Quart which they are playing at Florence. Back by 6.0. Go to dinner with Barbara – but back by 9.30.

Wednesday 21 March [London/Lowestoft]
Go to Italian State Railways in morning to see abt. fares & routes to Florence. Then on to my bank (Lloyds) in Earls Court Road to arrange abt money matters abroad. Collect my luggage from the Bridges & meet Beth at 1.0 at D.H. Evans[42] & have lunch with her. Go to Liverpool St. via Italian Railways (more details), O.U.P. at Soho Square (picking up scores), & catch 3.15 home. V. good train, in at 6.4; Bath Dinner – bit of Wireless – letters – bed. Thank Heaven!

Pop is about the same – pleurasy no worse – but bed sores – aches & pains, pretty bad

Thursday 22 March [Lowestoft]
Pop is much worse than he's ever been – in dreadful discomfort & pain. Mum is up practically all night (after 1. A.m.), & I, two hours of it, with him. Dr. Evans injects (hypodermically (?)) morphia between 7–8 in the morning & he cannot be left all day. Mum sleeps in aft, & I look after him from 2–4.30. I rewrite & alter bits of my 2nd score of my Sinfonietta to take abroad, if I go. Short walks before lunch & after tea with J. Pounder.

Begin Zweig's 'De Vriendt goes Home', which ~~begins~~ promises very well.[43]

Tuesday 27 March [Lowestoft/London]
Pop brightens abit to say 'good-bye' to me – but doesn't seem too well. I leave by 8.30 to London. John Pounder is coming on this journey with me. Mr. P. takes us down to station. Travel with many S. Lodge Boys & Mr. Boase. John & I go to Wilton Hotel on arrival. Lunch with Barbara at Marble Arch – get tickets from It. State Railways after, & then I go up to rehearse with Griller's at 2.45. Go to tea with Mrs. Bridge at 4.30, & back to Piccadilly with John at 6.0. Meet Beth & eat with her at 6.45 then go to 'Reunion in Vienna' with Lunt & Lynn Fontainne. Excellent acting, but rather disappointing as a play.[44] Not particularly attractive.

Wednesday 28 March
After breakfast at 8.30, leave hotel to catch 10.5 at Victoria to Newhaven. Meet an English man and his Swiss wife & son with whom we travel to Paris. Pretty rough crossing – many people succomb. Arr Paris at 5.55, & cross in omnibus provided in ticket. Meet a Miss Cherry (School-mistress) going to Pisa and eat at the buffet of Gare de Lyons. Catch 8.50 train for Turin. Only 4 in carriage (1 besides ourselves), but cannot sleep, although quite comfortable.

Thursday 29 March [Florence]
Arrive at Modane at abt. 7.30. Country is very lovely – snowy & mountanous. No trouble with customs. Arr. at Turin at 12.30 (It. Summer time) & change to very crowded train (don't get seats before Genoa). Get very tired of travelling. Eat on train – food from home, Hotel Wilton, and Modane. Change at Pisa at 5.30, & arr. at Florence abt. 7.45 – pretty exhausted. Go st. in taxi to Teatro Communale, to see Sec. of Fest. – with whom we had an appt. – about rooms. Have much difficulty in making anyone understand, and eventually go to a Hotel Helvetia with one A. Cooke, whom we met on journey – bath – short walk – bed (lovely!).

Friday 30 March
Over sleep, and don't have breakfast until 11.0. Go to see some people (Pearce & his sister) we met on the journey at Pensione Balestri where we decide to stay – ~~moving~~ having our luggage moved. Lunch there with them. See abt. matters at Teatro Comunale in aft. with Cooke, Prof. Dent (Presd. of Fest.), Vladimir Vögel, & (John). After tea in Plaza Vitorio Imanueli, we 4 (– Vogel) (+ 2 Pearces who tram there) walk to Grassina to see Good Friday procession. Enormous crowds see this interesting show – which must have been very impressive as a simple Village show – but not exactly artistic

as it is – electrified & elaborated. We all walk back (abt. 4 miles); eat here, but sleep out at a Pensione near as the Balestri is full.)

Saturday 31 March
After breakfast (at P. Balestri) at 9.30, John & I get some money from a Bank, & then go to the Duomo to see the Annual Fest. Scoppio del Carno (Dove ignites car of Fireworks).[45] Very interesting. After lunch here we spend about 2½ hrs at the Uffizi Galleries, & see some marvellous pictures – notably impressed by some da Sarta, & Fra Filippino, and some Botticelli. Long walk all over Florence, shopping, after tea, & after supper. We + 2 Pearces go to Savoia ~~film~~ cinema to see Film '1860' – abt Garibaldi, but find it extremely hard to follow.[46] Eat on way back – in Piazza V.E.

Sunday 1 April
Go to St. Maria Novella at 11.0 for service – which is not particularly exciting – go to the Duomo for abit after – this is 2 Pearces, J. & A. Cooke & myself. Cooke comes here to lunch & the P.'s go out. Walk all over Florence with J. in aft. At 5.0, he Phyllis Pearce & I go to concert at T. Comunale of Stagione Orch under V. Gui. V. good & sensitive orchestra Cattozzo's ~~Intro~~ L'orazione starts – loud & dull music. 2 Extracts from Parsival (not too well conducted), Franck's Redensione & Beethoven's Pastoral Symphony, which Gui couldn't let run it's natural course – although the last 3 movements weren't at all bad Go to Station after to meet Grillers from London. After dinner 2 Pearces and we go to see Maurice Chevalier & Horton in 'Learn to Love' at the Edison[47] – bit more intelligible than last evening

Monday 2 April
Go with John to inaugural reception of Int. Festival at 11.0 Meet alot of interesting people. Walk after. Correct some quartet parts[48] in aft. before going to concert of Italian music in connection with the Festival at Teatro Communale at 5.0, with J. and Phyllis P. Very dull programme – 2 Sicillian songs of Muré, & beginning of Intro. Aria & Toccata of Casella being the only things of interest.[49] The rest of an interminable programme was merely by Italian Parrys & Stanfords. Walk with Pearces after dinner.

Tuesday 3 April
Letters in morning, & walks to Brit. Institute and Piazza del Independenza to find Grillers. Rehearse with them at B. Inst. in aft. Go to 1st Concert of Int. Festival – Chamber, at Teatrino Communale, at 5.0, with Phyllis & John. Composers were – Martelli, Holzmann, Osterc, Reisager [?], Berg (3 movs. of Lyric Suite) & Francaix (Sonata for Vl. Vla Vlc). Kolisch Quart did most

of playing. The last two were only notable works – B. magnificent & F. very charming & witty. We go to a Segovia Recital at Pitti palace at 9.0; but get bored & leave after ⅓ of it of course he is a superb player, but I don't like the Guitar as a solo inst.[50]

Wednesday 4 April

John & I go to Uffizi in morning, & with Pearces in aft. we go round the town & to St. Miniato outside Florence. At 9.0 p.m. 1st Int. Soc Orchestral concert under Scherchen at Teatro Comunale – Honneger Symph mov. no. 3 (v. fine) – Ravel Lefthand pft. Concerto (not Ravel at his best, but very charming in spots – Witgensten plays it) – Bartoks amusing 1st Rhapsody (Szigeti) – Markievitch Salmo (which causes a bit of a scene, but is not really so important – interesting & original in spots) & Schrechter's Turkamenia [*Turkmenia* – suite for orchestra] – highly coloured but rather cheap underneath. Meet Cooke his friend Baba, & a Marievitch friend of his, aft.

Thursday 5 April

Rehearse with Goossens & Grillers in the morning at Teatro Comunale. In aft. go to Vecchio Palace with J. & Pearce, & to Pitti Galleries with J. & Miss P. after to tea in the Boboli Gardens – a I.S.C.M. Show. After dinner – 2nd Int. Chamber concert at Teatrino Com. Goossens & the Grillers really play my Phant. very beautifully & it's quite well received. Other works – Trio by Neugeboren (apparntly v. conventional – I didn't hear it) – Strurzenegger a Cantata for Various instruments rather colourless – an ~~inster~~ interesting quartet by Spinner – and a fiendish Vln Sonata by Jezek – with quite the worst fiddling I've ever heard – by S. Novak. After that we leave – at 11.30. 2 other items.[51]

Pop dies – see Monday.

Friday 6 April

Go on excursion to Siena ~~with~~ in connection with Festival – with John & Phyllis. Leave Flor. at 8.45 and go by omnibuses – 5 of them. It pours with rain all day, so Siena is rather lost on us. Lunch given by the Mayor etc. – visits to Cathedral. Young Wulff Scherchen (son of Hermann) attaches himself to me, & I spend all the time with him.

Get back by 7.15 – very wet & cold – bath – dinner – sit about until about 9.0 when we suddenly decide to go to see 'Fra Diavolo' at a very low cinema.[52]

Saturday 7 April

Go with John & Cooke in morning to see about stamping & dating of tickets. Meet Wulff & have a short walk with him before lunch. At lunch get a telegram from home – come to-day, Pop not so well. Pack up at once – John marvellously sympathetically insists on coming too – see about things, leave score for Scherchen, & the Pearces come down to station to see us off by 4.53. Change at Pisa at 6.14 – very full train as far as Genoa, but we get seats there – quite good ones.

Sunday 8 April

Have a dreadful breakfast on the train this side of Turin. Arr. at Paris (G. de Lyons) at 2.10. Have to stay there 6 hours – with no money (banks being shut), & pretty tired. Have a good meal at 7.0. – Go to Louvre before this, – and wander about the place. Catch 8.55 from Gare St. Lazare arr at Dieppe at abt. 11.30. Quite smooth crossing – rainy. Sleep for abt. 2 hours.

Monday 9 April [Lowestoft]

Arr: Newhaven at abt. 3.30 (English time) & at Victoria at abt. 6.0. Taxi across to Liverpool St. – hang about for an hour & then we catch 8.15 home – breakfasting on the way.

When I arrive, I learn that Pop died on Friday – a stroke, hastened by general weakness.[53] A great man – with one of the finest brains I have ever come across, & what a father! Bobby, Barbara and Beth are all here. Bobby & Beth came on Saturday, while Barb. ~~was~~ has been here since Easter. Don't do much – except some walks with Bob. Fernande takes Mum, Barb & Beth to Norwich in aft. to get some clothes. We all go to Astles after dinner. Considering what Mum has been through – she is bearing up incredibly.

Tuesday 10 April

Don't do much all day – get up rather late – see Mr. Coleman with Bobby abt. music for tomorrow (decide on last no. of Matt. Pass. and Var. III of my 'boy')[54] – letters & read in aft – walk with Beth after tea. Aunt Florence & Dr. Freda Harmer (cousin) arr. by car before tea; & Uncle Sheldon from London by 8.4. Long walk after dinner with Robert.

Mum is being marvellously brave.

Very rainy day, but the aft. is fine with a little sun.

Wednesday 11 April

Things have to be arranged in the morning – go out with Beth with Freda in her car – many lovely wreaths arrive, – 62 in all. The funeral is at 2.30. It is a very simple & lovely service – Mr Reeve & Uncle Sheldon take it (Lord is my Shepherd – Irish tune for 'The King of Love'). Mum is a perfect marvel, even when we go up to Kirkley Cemetary after, she has control of herself. Laurence, Fernande, & Mr. Reeve come back to tea. Uncle Sheldon goes off by 6.43 – Freda takes him down in her car – I go with them.

Friday 13 April
See Mr Coleman in morning abt. matters – see abt clothes etc. & walk with Bazil. Mum, Barb, Beth shop in car lent by Woodgers.

Letters in aft. & after tea. Mum has been writing everso many so we have been helping her, but she still has over 100 to do. Walk with Beth before dinner. We all go along to Miss Astles' after dinner.

Saturday 14 April
Odd jobs in morning – see Bazil & walk with him. Laurence takes Barbara to station to catch 2.30 to town (Beth & I go too). Mum is busy sorting out Pop's affaires – we help too – everything is in very good order. Mr. Nicholson is the solicitor – & he seems a help.

Go to see Pounders before dinner. Fernande comes in after dinner to cheer us up, as we're feeling rather down.

Sunday 15 April
Mum Beth & I go to Church at St. Johns at 11.0. Mum bears up wonderfully. Go for long walk with John Boyd (staying here) in aft. along Beach. Letters by the dozen after tea. Beth & I go up to Cemetary with Mum before supper. After, Miss Ethel comes in. Much packing.

Monday 16 April
Mum, Beth & I catch 10.7 to Ipswich – taxi to station. Arr. at Aunt Janie's at 12.30. Lunch with her in garden; with Elsie (cousin). in aft. Mum goes to see Uncle Willie (her brother) at a home near (thro' drink).[55] Catch 4.24 to town (3 of us) and go st. to Barbara's flat for dinner with her & Helen Hurst. Go to 36 FitzJohn's Avenue (where Silvia Buckland is living) for 2 nights – Beth comes here too.

Friday 20 April [Prestatyn]
Bobby has two kids to coach in morning. I practise abit. Then walk with him down town. After lunch a spot of ping-pong & then more creasoting the fence. After dinner he & Marjorie go out to Morgans, & Mum & I stay in to listen to a wireless which we've hired. F.B. conducts a light operatic concert – Bizet: 'Le Patrie' ov; [blank] sings a Verdi & Puccini Arias. He makes the Peer Gynt Suite no. 1. sound positively thrilling esp. Asis Tod.[56] What the world has lost in his not conducting enough, cannot be estimated

Sunday 22 April

Robert, Marjorie & I go to Church at Melidon in morning at 11.0. Mum comes to meet us on the hillside. Listen to wireless, read, & write alot of letters in aft. Long walk with Robert between tea & supper. Listen to an Ansermet Concert from B.B.C. at 9.5. H. Perkin plays Ireland's 'Legend' with orch. – an attractive idea, but he hasn't the creative power or technique to do it – tho' there is fine atmosphere in parts of it. Also Debussy – Jeux (Nigensky) – not super Debussy, but very interesting & attractive, with wonderful scoring & colouring.[57]

Friday 27 April

Miss Austen (Laulie) – my late god-mother comes over from Liverpool for day. Mum & I meet her at 11.0. Coffee. After lunch walk with Robert & odd jobs – likewise after tea. Early dinner & R & I go to see Laulie off by 8.15 bus. Listen to Stravinsky contemp. concert under Ansermet from B.B.C. at 9.0.[58] Mavra, comic opera, very interesting & quite amusing, tho' not very satisfactory for broadcasting – neither was Les Noces, which followed, tho' one couldn't help being thrilled by much of it especially the exciting rhythms, and colours; splendid architecture & the beautiful end. A great work.

Sunday 29 April

Mum & Robert go to church at 11.0 at Melidon. I stay & write – re-do an old Choral song (Of one that is so fair & bryte).[59] Walk to meet them. Heavenly day – glorious sun. In aft. help Robert abit with School time-table, & listen (pt. time in garden) to Vienna Phil. Orch. from Albert Hall (under Bruno Walter – who annoys me so much) – light, mostly Strauss & Suppé Waltzs – very beautifully played. Mum & Robert go in to Rhyl for C. Science service at 6.0 & are late back I write letters, read & listen to wireless – a doleful performance of Ravel Quartet by the Kutchers.

Monday 30 April

Robert goes to see a parent at Flynnongroye [Ffynnongroyw]; Mum & Barge[!] go to Rhyl shopping in morning. I stay & work – only very unsatisfactorily – make an ~~arr.~~ re arr of I saw 3 Ships – too elaborate.[60] Play tennis (vilely) with Barge in aft, at 3.30 after shopping down village with Robert. Help him in various matters after tea. Ryle their junior master arrives before supper. After – I listen to broadcast from Covent Garden of Act. I of Beethoven's World-wonder 'Fidelio' – the more I hear of this music, the smaller I feel. Very good cast – Lotte Lehman superb as Leonore (Abscheulicher was thrilling)[61] & a very delightful Marcelline (Berger).

Rocco (Kipnis) very good also. Beecham good but not first-class, & orchestra only so-so. Even then, it was a thrill, and the glorious sound of the 'Canon' was unbelievable.[62] What music.

Wednesday 2 May

Odd jobs in morning – write (alter bit of 3 ships & then decide it's a wash-out) – read – shop for Robert long walk with Mum up hill – Help to coach boys at cricket in aft, after another shopping walk in aft. After tea practise pft. Garden abit after supper – superb weather still, & then listen to Act III of Walküre from Covent Garden.[63] Incomparable Leider as Brünhilde; & Bochelmann as a very good Wotan, also Lehmann as a beautiful Sieglinde. But what music to sing!

Friday 4 May

Sketch a school song in morning & revise another.[64] Walk, shopping with Mum before lunch. Help Robert with a singing class, and at coaching the boys cricket in aft. – this also after tea. Walk to post with him after supper, also listen to a scrap of a mediocre perf. of Beethoven Vln Concerto by Flesch and a dead as ditchwater perf of Brahms' 3rd Symp under Boult – oh; the slow movement – like all the badly played harmoniums![65] This is the first concert of the London (B.B.C.) Musical Festival.

Monday 7 May

Mum is sent for by Aunt Queenie (her sister) who is in the middle of an attack of 'melancholia'. So regardless of the fact that she needs a long rest & holiday, ~~she~~ Mum has to pack up in order to go & nurse her. What the rest of the family thinks of it I don't know. Help her in bits in morning – bit of sketching & copying, – walk shopping before lunch. Read etc. & practise in aft. Walk with Robert after tea. Listen to Die [*Das*] Unaufhörliche of Hindemith in evening. There are some lovely things in it & most of the 2nd half is thrilling.

Tuesday 8 May

Go with Mum to Chester by 8.58, to see her on to 10.18 to Chalford (via Hereford & Gloucester). Shop, have 11'ses with Geoff Wood & see the Cathedral & return by 12.30. Help Robert with boys at Field. Letters & walk with him after tea. Listen to wireless (the hired portable taken away, & a hired electric one in its place – not so good) – Palladium Command perf. & Act II of Fidelio from Covent Garden. Cast as before – Voelker as Flor. & [Alfred Jerger] as Don Fernando. They follow the usual custom of playing Leonore 3 between scenes & irritatingly cut the exciting 1st Chorus of last scene.

Personally, much as I love the ov. I don't want it there. They can change scenes pretty ~~well~~ quickly nowadays. Beecham only competant. Irritatingly ungiving. Poor singers – like singing under an ill-balanced Metronome.[66] But what music! The Love Duet esp.

Wednesday 9 May

Spent most of morning & aft. making copy of pft. part of my two 4.pt songs. Shop immediately after lunch, for Robert, Mum & Self. Bit of cricket with boys before & after tea. Listen to wireless after tea. Bax Symphony 5 (didn't interest me much – too full of notes & clichés – still I can't judge – bad wireless & I didn't really concentrate). Horowitz gave a very brilliant, but rather insensitive show of Tschaikovsky concerto, a work which I admire but cannot like very much – only because I have heard it too often[67]

Friday 11 May

Finish pft copies & send scores of pt. songs off to B.B.C. in aft.[68] Write a school song (Newington) in aft.[69] Also walk abit with Marjorie & John. Write letters after tea & short walk with Robert. Listen to bit of B.B.C. concert under Walter (on very good newly hired wireless). Schubert 7th Symphony[70] was spoilt by exaggeration, & lack of taste. Don Quixote[71] (with Feuerman as a first-rate soloist) was very good indeed, but not inspired – the wind variation wasn't successful, tho' the end was extremely beautiful. What lovely music most of this is – the introduction & end esp.

Tuesday 15 May

I write a short song in morning (New Year Carol)[72] & also walk abit shopping. In aft. write letters & help amuse kids who can't play cricket because of vile weather – wind rain.

After supper we 3 (R.M. & I) go to coffee at Browns. Listen to Mr. B's wireless – very good – bit of Schwanda[73] from Cov. Gar. which seemed amusing, but not particularly original.

Thursday 17 May

Sketch a song – but it comes to nothing – & take Huggil for a pft. lesson in morning. Do organ ~~pft.~~ part of an org. & pft arr. of F.B's Moonlight in aft. & after tea.[74] Before tea go down to field to help with Boys at cricket. Letters & walk also with Robert before supper. After supper at 9.45. Mr. Holgate fetches Robert & me & takes us in his car to Mostyn Iron Works (of which he is works manager). Shows us all over it, & we see a cast taken at 11.0. It is extremely interesting & thrilling, & the colours & shadows of the flames were incredible – Violossal! Back at 11.30.

Sunday 20 May
I move down to dormatory to sleep (there are no boys there of course)[75] – Beth comes in to nursery from Ryle's room (he has been away since Friday but returns to-night) – This means much moving which is done in morning while Robert is at Church with kids. Beth & I go for walk before lunch up hill – very windy & occasional rain. Laze & read in aft. Letters after tea – walk to post with R. Finish arr. of F.B. mov III before supper after which we all play Lexicon.

Tuesday 22 May
Finish pft part of Moonlight & walk shopping with Beth. Pack in aft. & go to field with boys. Weather suddenly brightens after tea, so Beth & I go for a lovely long walk right over hill – this before supper.

After, general laze, talk & bit of Lexicon. I shall be sick to leave this place; & am so fond of the school & the kids that I dread going back to the void at Lowestoft[76]

Wednesday 23 May [London]
Beth & I catch 8.59 for town, arr. 1.15. I am really sorry to leave. I go st. to Bridges – leave all my luggage, & then go to B.B.C. for a run through of my 2 pt. songs with wireless Singers & Leslie Woodgate. Go pretty well, & I meet a man from Hawkes who likes them???[77] Go back to Bridges & before dinner we go to see very amusing French Film – Prenez Garde à la Peinture.[78] After ~~sup~~ dinner, we 3 go to B.B.C. at 9.35 where F.B. conducts an orch. concert. V. sensitive perf. of Mozart E♭ Symph. Franz Osborn plays Franck Symp. Var – very hard – & insensitive. F.B's Charming summer & a riotous perf. of Dvorak Carneval make up rest.[79]

Thursday 24 May
I meet Moeran at Hawkes at 11.0 & play with him the duet version of his Suite Farrago[80] to Ralph Hawkes – publisher. Meet Barbara for lunch at 12.45 at Kilburn. Shop in aft. F.B. drives us down to the country starting at 5.30. Very lovely drive as the country is heavenly. Arr. at Friston at 8.0. app.

Monday 28 May [Friston]
Long talk about matters with F.B. in morning. Play some tennis with T. Brosa after that. Laze in sun in aft, a spot of tennis before tea; after which the Bridges take the Brosas into Eastbourne to catch 5.25 to London. I write abit & a ~~spot~~ bit of tennis practise before supper. After this, listen to Act II of Meistersingers from Cov. Garden What music! Makes me feel small[81]

Wednesday 30 May [London/Lowestoft]
Pack after breakfast & take my luggage to Liverpool St. in a taxi. Since I have heard from Foss that he's not going to print my Oboe quart. I see Ralph Hawkes about it (& Sinfonietta & two part-songs) at 12.30.[82] I now await his decision. Lunch at an Oxford St. Restaurant & then go up to Beth's to help Mum to Liverpool St. with her luggage. Catch 3.15 down. Quick but filthy journey. Walk with Caesar before dinner. It is good to see him again, but it is an effort coming here again with the empty space.

Friday 1 June [Lowestoft]
Don't do much all day except shop abit for Mum, practise pft occasionally, odd jobs abt. house (rearrange ~~furnitly~~ furniture – trying to make everything look as different as poss. from what it was before) & walks with Caesar. Meet Barbara at 8.4 from London – consequently dinner late. Phyllis has already left (beginning of May); to-day May & Ruby go (May's own & Mum's notice for Ruby). A temporary cook (from Miss Astle) & Mabel parlour-maid come to-day.[83]

Saturday 2 June
Practise pft. most of morning with a short walk before lunch with the dog. In aft. I play cricket with South Lodge up at the playing fields. Tea with the Sewells, & after that play 'tip & run' with boys in playground. After dinner listen to wireless – including a bit of 9th Symphony from Hilversum – conductor luckily unnamed – very bad, tempi ridiculous, grosely over-scored (re-scored) & ill-balanced.

Monday 4 June
Long & arduous pft. practise all morning – short walk with Mum before lunch. In aft. I do some rewriting of kid's songs. Fernande Sewell comes to tea. Long walk with Caesar after that. After dinner I go for a bit of Heathcote Statham's organ recital at St. Johns – sheer duty because I loathe org. recitals. He doesn't play badly – but, like most organists with practically no rhythm. He played some ludicrous music – Widor etc.

Thursday 7 June
Pop's estate comes to abt. £15,000 (death duties £900). Mum doesn't want it put in papers for family reasons.[84]

Work all morning & abit in aft. Miss Turner comes to tea. Walk with dog after, & abit of time in playground at South Lodge with boys. After dinner Mum & I go to Astles for coffee. Heavy Thunderstorm abt 8.^{pm} & much rain all day.

Sunday 10 June

Beth & I exercise hound after breakfast. Then we go up & fetch a Morris 10 car from Watson's garage which we hire for day. Take lunch with Mum, of course, into a wood at Sotterly. Laze in gorgeous sun until 3.0 when we go to Chartres for lazy tennis & for tea. Back by 7.0. Car cost 9/6 (3d per mile + extras). Listen to a very fine performance of Don Quixote (Strauss) from Hilversum (Conductor:Van Beinum[85] Cello: R. [Raphael] Lanes excellent). More imaginative than Walter's show – but not such good ensemble.

Monday 11 June

See Beth off back to town by 9.58. Work in morning & aft. with walks before lunch & tea. After tea get some tennis with Laurence & others at north end Club. After dinner listen to a very fine performance of Act. 2 of Rosenkavalier from Dresden via Brussels. What music! I have never heard such sounds.[86] Also, after a short walk, listen to Toni Brosa & Phillipowsky give a rather stiff perf. of Elgar's Violin Sonata.[87] Brosa played, of course, as he always does, but P. was somewhat lacking. How I wish I could like this music Of course it's beautifully done but says nothing that Franck & Brahms haven't said before – not that I even want the latter.

Thursday 14 June

Work all morning at kid's songs – I shall be jolly pleased when they are finished & done with. In aft – cut back-lawn, & more work & abit of piano practice. After tea play tennis with Laurence etc – vilely. Listen to an interesting but mediocre play 'Quartet', at 8.0[88] – also a very lovely show of Parsifal prelude from Paris under Abendroth.[89]

Friday 15 June

Usual morning's work & walk. Tennis at Porteous' in afternoon.

After dinner listen to an excellent studio performance of Hansel & Gretel from Huizen, complete of course. What Heavenly music this is – perfectly done. I simply revel in it. Some of it, I could ~~have~~ wish performed otherwise – I wish they could get simpler voices for the children – but on the whole a good show.[90]

Tuesday 19 June

Practise with Mr. Coleman in church 10–11.30. Letters & short walk. Work abit in aft. & long thinking walk with Caesar before tea. Bathe with Pounder – not too cold – but not warm. There is some heavy rain from 6.30–7.0, but otherwise fine tho' dull.

Listen to Arthur Rubenstein give a remarkable display in Chopin's F min concerto from Hilversum at 9.45.[91] Delightful pft. writing, & some delicious things – but not great Chopin.

Friday 22 June

John Pounder takes me over to Lingwood by 11.0 where I have lunch & much talk with E.J. Moeran & his parents. John calls for me at 2.30–3.0, & we come back to Lowestoft + Mrs & J. Moeran in their car J.M. – J.P. & I bathe, & we all have tea with Mum here. They go after tea, & John & I walk & putt + Peter Walker. After dinner listen to a Holst Memorial concert. I wish I could think he was great![92]

Tuesday 26 June

Practise pft. & do some work & walk in morning. Ditto in aft, + hair-cut Mrs. Priest comes to tea with Mum. After tea I walk, & go up to North End to fetch a forgotten Mac. Have a wire (reply paid) from B.B.C. about rehearsal, & decide to go up to-morrow.[93] Mr Abell comes to dinner, after which Bazil & Boase come in to listen to wireless – a good show of F.B's Lament from Manchester, & F.B. conducting a B.B.C. orchestra at London Ravel's Rhap. Espagnol – Tristan prelude to Act III & Dvorak's lovely 4th Symph.[94] – all in the inimitable F.B. style.

Thursday 28 June [London]

Do some work in morning – here & then go off to see Grace Williams. Have lunch out with her – & then go up to Brompton Arcade to get a Tennis raquet (get a 1st class one cheap at 45/-. Queens) Go at 4.30. to a rehearsal at B.B.C. (St. George's Hall) with Clark of Sinfonietta. Not good – he doesn't know the work. Go to a News' theatre for an hour before meeting Beth, & eating with her. Then we go to see Elizabeth Bergner in Margeret Kennedy's 'Escape me never!' A very int. play – well acted. Bergner is all that is said about her & more – I have never seen anyone like her.[95]

Friday 29 June

I go to B.B.C. at 10.0 for a rehearsal – but the Diaphenia of Van Dieran takes too much time, & mine isn't done. Lunch with Owen Mase, Hely-Hutchinson etc. at Pagani's. In aft. I pack and take my things to Beth's Flat; she goes off home by 4.54. Tea at Bridges – they come back to-day. Rehearsal at B.B.C. at 7.45. Clark does the work better. Show at 9.0 – Contemporary Concert. Van Dieran (v. long) – Lucas Partita (welcome after the V.D. but not much in itself, – tho' Sarabande is quite lovely.) & my Sinfonietta – which the orchestra plays quite well, considering all.[96] Quite well received.

Personally I am bucked with it. Have supper with Mangeot & Anne MacNaghten, & return to Beth's flat by 12.0.

Tuesday 3 July [Lowestoft]
Mrs Nicholson takes Mum to Norwich for lunch. She shops & maid-hunts. I rehearse with Mr Coleman, & bathe in sea & sun before lunch. In aft. I continue with arr. of Finale from Mozart E^b Symph – for Monday.[97] Tea in garden. After which I play tennis with Mr Gillespie (new St. John's Curate) at his Club (Golf club). After dinner Mr. Coleman comes in intending to hear Tschaikov. Concerto from Stuttgart. But for some reason it isn't done – possibly Wührer who was to have played it has been shot by Hitler – in his new Revolution.[98]

Monday 9 July
Rehearse with Mr. Coleman in morning. Sun bathe, & bathe with John Pounder in afternoon. Practise pft in church after tea. Mr. Boase comes to dinner after which I go down to church, & with Mr. Coleman give a Piano & Organ recital. Quite full – very hot – I play most of time in just tennis shirt & trousers. We do Schumann conc. – 1st mov.[99] I play Slow mov. of Beethoven Appassionata & 6 small Schönberg pieces, & then with Org. my arr. of F.B.'s 'moonlight' Then we struggle thro' Tschaikov. 1st mov. – Mr Coleman plays Bach E min. pre & fug. I do L'isle Joyeuse, & both finish off with Mozart E^b Symph. Finale – my arr.[100] The Colemans come back to coffee

Friday 13 July
Write abit more T.D. [*Te Deum*] in morning. & have a bathe before lunch with Stephen Abel. In aft. in spite of pouring rain I go to tennis at Tamplins'. We get a good many sets. Listen to Brosa quartet after dinner; they play what appears to be a very dull & gloomy quartet of Kodaly, but the atmospherics ruin this & the Hindemith no. 3, which they play very finely. I enjoy this (having score) & think most of it really fine & beautiful. I was sick that owing to bad ~~timeng~~ timing the Final Rondo had to be omitted[101]

Sunday 15 July
Mum goes to St. Johns to Church at 11.0. I spend most of morning Sun & sea-bathing at hut with Muriel Cameron & K. Mead, & J. Pounder. In aft. Tony Jones, & Piers Dunkerley (South Lodge Boys) come. ~~to tea~~. Spend aft. on ~~bathe~~ beach & bathe with P.D. Back to tea in garden, + Colemans. After tea I putt with the boys. After supper letters gram. (La Mer of Debussy, lent by Moeran) & Wireless.

Wednesday 18 July

Have a simply great time on the Broads with Roger Porteus in the morning. He is lent a yacht & we both sail up to Somerlayton – bathe & have lunch – & then drift back without wind, into a gale at Oulton. After this I change at his & both go on to Woodgers for tennis party given by Schillings – cannot play at all brilliantly, & it is rather an anti-climax, to the marvellous morning.

Gramophone after dinner. Mum goes out to Cobbolds for tea with Meads.

Saturday 21 July

More ~~copy~~ copying in morning, & very exhilarating bathe with K. Stone & C. Reeve before lunch. In aft, among rain, we have the Annual South Lodge Old boys match – dismal show. They beat us (a vigorous O, & a wicket & a catch being my share) but we were only 7 strong + of course substitutes. Fed up with the game. John Pounder (who isn't playing – the disgrace!) takes me to see very amusing & entertaining Lubitsch-Coward Film – "Design for Living" at Marina after dinner.[102]

Monday 23 July

Helen Boyd takes me over to Norwich at 10.30, where I go to lunch at the Boileau's at Ketteringham Park to meet Roger Coke. He is not exactly of my opinion in musical matters (having to stop at Elgar)! but I enjoy myself & meet alot of actors – all preparing for a Masque to be held there this week. Back by 5.0 ~~for~~ by train. Play some good singles with John Nicholson ~~at~~ on their court – 6.0–7.30. After dinner listen to a great Beethoven concert from Vichy – conducted (Leonora 3, & Sym.5) by Mrs. Weingartner [Carmen Studer] & (Prometheus & Eroica) by Weingartner himself. Mrs. W. is poor, & W. not 1st class – but the indomitible value of the work does the trick.

Tuesday 24 July

I go to lunch at Mrs. Chamberlin's (train to Brudell – Ferry – car). Talk over Orch., & play some quartets with her & Friends (Mozart pft. G min – me playing Vl. part on Vla!).[103]

After this we go to a tennis party at a friend of hers, but it is ruined by rain. John Alston is there, & he brings me right back here in his car – arriving about 7.0. Mum is in most of the day. After dinner listen to Wireless – an interesting concert by Hague Orch. from Hilversum – a Fantasia of Debussy for Pft. & orchestra (brilliantly played by [BB leaves gap here]) L'aprés-midi with some heavenly Oboe playing – & an exotic show of Ravels' brilliant 'La Valse'[104]

Thursday 26 July

Lot more copying in morning & afternoon. Walk before lunch with Mum. In aft. Mrs & Jack Moeran come over for tea. J. & I bathe before tea.

After dinner Mum goes up to Sewells for coffee, to meet Mr & Mrs S. Senior. I have wireless & gramophone, & also go down & play with South Lodge seniors on the playground.

Caesar gets lost coming from hut before tea, but I find him guarding the hut by dinner, but v. dejected.

Bathe before breakfast (v.early – 7.45) with Ethel Boyd. V. cold.

Sunday 29 July

Mend landing clock in morning before going & sitting on beach with Barbara & Helen. Alice (late cook & sister of Nanny) comes to see us before lunch. I am supposed to be going to Kessingland with a party of boys from South Lodge, but rain prevents it. Read & write instead. Barbara & I go down to station to see Helen back ~~by~~ to town by 5.25. Bathe with 6 South Lodge Boys (Dunkerley, Palmour, Hamlyn, ~~Pebbl~~ Peebles, Grant & Ison) before supper; a lovely bathe. Listen to Allanah Delias playing Mozart C maj. concerto from Huizen – (see Anne MacNaghten a few years ago). after supper

Monday 30 July

Hair cut & Copy abit of School songs before Barbara & I catch 12.0 to Reedham where Jack Moeran meets us, & takes us to lunch at Lingwood. Talk music etc & we 4 (+ Mrs M.) play a game of croquet after lunch. J.M. brings us 3 (with Mrs. M.) back here in their car, & we bathe & have tea (with Mum) on beach.[105] They go by 6.30. Boase comes to say good-bye to me before dinner He is leaving S. Lodge & going into business. The Astles come in after dinner. After they go I listen to Act III of Tristan from Vienna (the Salzburg Festival).[106] It doesn't come over at all well.

Tuesday 31 July

Very wet morning, & windy, but I bathe before lunch with Roger Porteus & Mrs Gordon. Write many letters before this. In aft. copy, & listen to broadcast of spasms of challenge round of Davis Cup – Perry beating Shields to retain Cup. Barbara goes over to Farnham to spend day with Alice & Nanny. // Mrs. Morphy comes to tea. // Bathe again with same two at 6.0. // After dinner listen to Vaughan Williams' Benedicete[107] – music which repulses me, as does most of Brahms. (solid, dull).

Wednesday 1 August

Usual morning – bathe before lunch with Roger Porteous. In aft. cut back-lawn, & then go down to ~~beach~~ hut; Mr Gillespie (St. John's Curate) Kathleen Mead, & Audry Enraght come to tea & bathe. We all + Barbara bathe before tea. Mrs Reeve also comes to tea. After dinner, spend most of time trying to fix up tennis for Saturday on 'phone. Letters & listen to Act II of Oedipus Rex of Stravinsky. From what I could hear, this seems (From Rome, conducted by Casella) a remarkably impressive work, & highly original. I should like to hear & see it in full. A lovely show of De Falla's El Amor Brujo to end with.[108]

Saturday 4 August

Bathe at 7.30 at hut with Beth – again at 11.30 with Barbara & Mrs. Gordon, & again at 12.45 with Beth, J. Nic, Roger Porteous. These 2 + Marjorie Phillips come to lunch on the beach with us 4. In aft. Mrs Woodger gives a tennis party for us at her court – J.N., R.P., David Boswell, Teddy Rogers, K. Mead A. Enraght, & pt. time M. Cameron come. Mum stays at home, but Barbara comes to tea. After dinner listen to a radio reconstruction of the events preceeding Aug. 4. 1914.[109] Very well done, it brings back the helplessness & horror of it all most terrifyingly.

Sunday 5 August

Sun & sea bathe in morning – Beth, Barb, Muriel Cameron & I. Mum goes to Church.

Mr & Mrs. Chartres come to tea & stay on to supper.

Bathe with Mr. C. before tea. After supper listen to F.B. conducting a string concert. (B.B.C. Section E) at 9.5. Handel Concerto grosso; his own lovely Suite in E; Arthur Benjamin plays Jacob's efficient but shallow concerto v. brilliantly; 2 lovely little Bizet pieces (1. from L'Arlesienne – Adagietto; 2 Duo from Jeux Denfants; Holst St. Paul's Suite.[110] The orchestra played brilliantly as far as possible for them.

Wednesday 8 August

Begin a simple Jubilate in morning[111] Also a good bathe. Play ½ hr's tennis at Club with Beth after lunch – frightfully hot – before bathing & tea with Piers Dunkerley & Robert Ferris (S.L. Boys) at hut. Mum & Beth too.

Go to a Scavenging party at Pounders at 7.0 – very amusing scouring country & town for a hair from a Cow's tail, 1926 penny, and a slug etc. I do it with Margaret Talbot who is very efficient – back by 11.0

Thursday 9 August

Work in morning & afternoon. Bathe with John & David Boyd in morning & with Beth before tea which we + Mum have on beach. Beth & I scratch from a Kessingland Tournament in aft. on acct. of work. We play abit of rotten tennis at Club with Laurence before dinner.

Listen to a flabbergasting show of Act III of Götterdämmerung from Bayreuth. Leider & Max Lorenz (Siegfried) were worthy of the music, & Elmendorff rose to the occasion magnificently – I have never heard the Funeral March better played – the rhythm so strict & stern. Atmospherics were troublesome, but could not upset my enjoyment of the work.

Saturday 11 August

Beth goes to Ipswich to stay with Hockeys – Aunt Janie etc. I work in morning – copy out more of school songs etc. I stay at home in aft. to work & to keep Mum company. Bathe ~~with~~ after tea & short walk with John Pounder. Listen to 1st Promenade of Season at 8.0. A good many popular items are scuttled through, including a very hectic show of Till Eul.[112] Most of these performances don't stand careful listening. I don't wonder that the orchestra is dead at the end of the season – because Wood is an absolute vandal.

Monday 13 August

Filthy day – windy & very rainy practically all the time. Work in morning – with walk up town for Mum, & after lunch. The Moerans, J. & Mrs, come to tea. I bathe with J., but it is fearfully cold. He lends me a very fine record of Sibelius' very impressive Tapiola. Listen to a typical Wagner Prom., including the most incredibly garish arr. of the Song of the Rhinemaidens – bad taste even for Wood.

Trape down to station in rain at 10.50 to meet Beth.

Tuesday 14 August

Another filthy day – with heavy rain all morning. I work in morning with short walk with Beth, & play some tennis with Teddy Rogers at Club in aft. Have tea with him & more tennis after tea. Robert, Marjorie, & John (who is perfectly adorable now) arr. by 6.50. I attempt to listen to a prom. including La Mer, & 3 Wozzeck extracts but the wireless is impossible.[113] What I did hear of it was very mediocre (Debussy esp.) What does Wood imagine that Lento means? & similarly the Jeux des Vagues became a funeral march[114]

Friday 17 August [Lowestoft/Norfolk Broads]

Final touches to preparations in morning – hair cut & shop, with a bathe before lunch.

In aft. Mr. Porteous takes Lucy, Roger & me over to Repps where we pitch tent etc. Beth comes on later by train at 6.46 (missing con. at Yarm. [Great Yarmouth]) to Potter Haigham, with Gwen & Edward Rice – we meet them eventually & cart luggage along river to House Boat. A good evening & a jovial supper and so to bed – Females sleeping out by Boat & we in tent

Saturday 18 August

We all six go up to Sutton by bus to fetch Yacht I – Puddleduck lent by a Col. Simon friend of Lucy Crowdy, as it is very still, & the only wind there is is slap against us. We don't get back until abt. 7.30. Bobby & Marjorie meanwhile go to Horning to fetch back a hired Int. Dinghy for us. They arr. before us, but have supper before going back to Lowestoft by bus & train

Sunday 19 August

Much more windy with bright intervals. In morning go for a long sail up Bure (.S.) until about 2.15. Ed. & I go in Int. D. & the rest in Puddleduck. Laze in aft, & R.B.G. & I go into Potter Heigham in dinghy (rowing) before supper – wind absolutely dropped.

A Camp fire is a great success after supper.

Monday 20 August

A fearfully windy day – tho' sunny in spots – ~~almost~~ quite a gale. Attempt to take dinghy out in morning nearly ends in disaster, but Roger does manage to get P'duck down to Potter before lunch – but is the only craft on the river.

E.L. & I walk & shop in Potter before 'supper-tea' [bracketed above by BB] (combined) as our meals have been abit behind times today – vis. 10.15, 3.15 8.0.

Thursday 23 August

We set out intending to get to Hickling for lunch – but a broken tiller stops us at Potter. Rain also stops us at lunchtime. Actualy we do sail into Hickling B. in aft; Back after tea (we took both meals) by abt. 6.20 – having had to row – no wind. Lovely but cold evening, eat outside & listen to a glorious concert from Salzburg (Vienna Phil. cond. Toscanini).[115]

Saturday 25 August [Norfolk Broads/Lowestoft]

Bathe before breakfast – which is not very early. Very desponantly, ~~be~~ we pack up & Mr. Porteous & Parr (taxi-man) arrive about 11.0. to fetch us away. It has been a great holiday, & it is sickening to have to go back to civilisation again. ~~It hasn't~~ We haven't put much more than 30/- each into the communal purse for all expenses. Lucy, Edward & Gwen, have lunch here & catch 2.32 back to town after. Beth, Bobby, Marjorie, John & Mrs. Jackson (nurse) go to a very quaint tennis party at the Priest's – in a car sent by them to fetch us. After dinner, Beth & I go to an amazing Film 'Catherine the Great' with Bergner, Flora Robson, & Douglas Fairbanks Jun. B. is everything imaginable in an actress & the whole film is a high artistic achievement.[116]

Monday 27 August
Do some more copying of my Te Deum in morning. Bobby & Marjorie are playing in Bungay T. Tourn. this week – I am personally quite releived not to be. John Alston turns up, & we (Beth & I) shop with him in his car. In aft. Henry Boys (see R.C.M.) arrives to stay fortnight in Lowestoft. Bathe with Beth & him, & he stays to tea on beach (+ Mum, Aunt J. – who leaves at 6.46 for Ips. – John & Mrs Jackson). In evening Mum & I go to pt. of a recital at St J.'s by Peter Upsher & John Hammond. I come out in middle as U. simply has not an idea of singing. Mrs & Mr Chamberlin come in to coffee afterwards.

Wednesday 29 August
A very hectic day. I finish & copy in morning & evening – 'There was a Monkey' – last, thank Heaven, of school songs. Mum, Beth & I catch 11.25 to Moeran's where we have lunch. He comes back with us & bathes & has tea + H. Boys. He also takes me to Bungay by 5.20 where I conduct 1st rehearsal of Str. orch. arr. by Mrs. Chamberlin – not expert but v. good experience. Meet Robert & Marjorie from tournament & return with them by bus. arr. 9.6. Have a meal – letters – copying & pack before bed.

Thursday 30 August [London]
I get up early & catch 8.30 to town. Travel up with Laurence S. & have breakfast on train I go straight away to see Foss about things at O.U.P. Back to lunch with Bridges (Brosas there too) & see Ralph Hawkes abt matters at 2.30. Shop after that & meet Barbara for tea & a walk in park. After dinner go to Prom. with Mrs. Bridge. Hear 3 prize-winning works of D. Telegraph ov. comp. – [Arnold] Cooke (3rd). [Frank] Tapp (2nd) [Cyril] Scott (3rd). Pretty bad but Cooke's was exhilarating & certainly up to date.[117] Toni Brosa plays Prokofiev Vln concerto simply incredibly – never heard such technique. A skew-wiff show of the lovely 2nd Borodine Symphony to end with.[118]

Friday 31 August [London/Hastings/Friston]
I catch 9.10 from Victoria to Hastings where I spend day with Bartons. It is very good to see them again, especially old Francis (see S. Lodge days). Lunch; after which F. & I walk the front – & spend money on side shows –

including a very rough speed-boat trip, in which we both get soaked through. After tea we take F's luggage to station – he goes to-morrow to join up in the Marines, – & then he & Joy & Madeline bring me to Friston whence the Bridges have come by car this morning. Have dinner at Miss Fass'.

Saturday 1 September [Friston]
Work abit & some letters in morning, before going into Eastbourne to shop with Mr & Mrs. F.B. Bits of tennis with F.B in aft. & a bathe at Burling Gap with them (3) before tea. More tennis before an early dinner – after which Mrs Bridge & Miss Fass go into Eastbourne to Theatre & F.B. & I stay in – listening to an interesting Strauss concert (Don Juan, Don Q, Burlesque for Pft & end of Salome – Oda Slobodskaya – v fine)[119] – & much & long talking. Much fine lightning before bed.

Tuesday 4 September [Lowestoft]
See people, odd jobs, long Vla & Pft. playing with Henry Boys & short walk with Mum in morning Great thrills at lunch because an Eastern Counties bus sinks a whole deep into the road outside here – a portion of the road is discovered to be hollow.

Go with H.B. to a tennis party given by Audry Enraght at Woodgers court. Some quite good tennis. H.B. comes to dinner – have much int. talk & gramophone after – esp. Stravinsky Symphonie des Psaumes & Beethoven Mass in D – both incredible masterpieces.[120]

Wednesday 5 September
Bazil returns from 2 months in France & Germany. Long talks with him & a bathe before lunch. Play some amusing & energetic tennis with Henry B. in aft – he's very good. Charles Coleman takes me over to the 2nd rehearsal of the Bungay String orchestra. It goes better than last week – partially because I have got some easier things for them to play. Back for a late dinner at 8.40. // It's Mum's wedding-day – 1st for 33 years without Pop – and she is a marvel.

Monday 10 September
Letters, odd jobs, bit of writing, walk shopping & sit of 'on Beach with Boys & Mum – Sea too untempting to bathe. In aft. I go to tennis at Tamplins. Good fun but I play piffle.

Boys comes in after supper. Listen to a Fragment of a Wagner prom. I shouldn't have thought that anyone could make the Love Duet from Tristan, dull & cheap – but Wood, M. Blythe & P. Jones achieve this feat. Also an absolute Kapelmeister perf. of the Siegfried Idyll.

Wednesday 12 September
Another lovely day – have a bathe with Doris Tamplin ~~before lunch~~ at hut, before lunch. – this after a spot of work, for a change. In aft. H.B. & I go to Bungay to tennis & tea at Gledhills. After that I conduct a rehearsal of the String Orchestra, which is almost improving. We do some very hard work at the Bach Suite. Charles Coleman brings us home. After dinner at 8.45; Mum & I listen to a very good show of Verdi's Theatrical but very effective Requiem from Rome.[121] Some of it is perfectly superb.

Start Gertrude Stein's entertaining Autobiography of Alice B. Toklas.[122]

Friday 14 September
H.B. comes rather early, & we have a final run through of F.B.'s Vln Sonata – it is a great work to play.[123] Bathe after with Doris T. at hut. Go down to station to see H.B. off by 3.33. Walk up town after. After tea in garden with Mum & Miss Hayes, I cut grass, & then go down to beach & bathe with David Boyd; walk & go on boats in Kensington Gardens with him. Listen to a typical Wood – Beethoven Prom after dinner – violently fast & rhythmless.

Hear I've been elected as a member of the Performing Right Society in morning.

Saturday 15 September
I do odd jobs, try unsuccessfully for umpteenth time to settle down to piano pieces for Hawkes. Finally have a lovely rough bathe with Doris before lunch. I go to Tamplins' to tennis in afternoon – but we all play like pigs – owing to very hot & stuffy afternoon partly.

Monday 17 September
I have to write some piano pieces for Boosey & Hawkes.[124] To-day I make a great effort – staying in practically all day (except for a lovely rough bathe before lunch) & putting off tennis at Tamplins. The result isn't satisfactory tho' – & will all have to be scraped. I finish a neat copy of my libelous Te Deum.[125] Letters & wireless after dinner, before which Mum & I go for a walk.

Thursday 20 September [Lowestoft/London]
Mum & I have early breakfast & catch 8.30 to London. Arr. at 11.30 at Liverpool St, & go straight to Harrods where we have a look at second hand pianos. Choose a likely one (a Mason & Risch) at 72 g's.[126] Lunch there, & after Mum shops & goes to see Beth, & I go to see Foss, R. Hawkes, shop (buy a ~~see~~ soiled copy of Stravinsky's Duo Concertante), meet Grace Williams for tea, & go to Liverpool [Street] to meet Mum & catch 7.42. home. Beth sees us off – have a meal on train which is very slow, & arrives

with us pretty dead at 11.20. As there arn't buses, at that hour we must walk home, & feel much better for it.

Monday 24 September [Lowestoft]
Have an early breakfast with Beth, & escort her to station where she catches the 8.31 back to work again. I work in morning & actually start a piano piece. Endeavour, not very successfully to continue this in afternoon after having seen Barbara off by 2.30, to a bit of a holiday in Kent before starting her new job in Hampstead next week. Long walk after tea, in spite of rain. Listen 7–8 to some broadcasts of Grace W's work from Wales. Parry Jones sings 3 v. interesting songs with Orchestra. – v. gloomy all three & then she accompanies him in 8 folk songs she has arr. most beautifully[127]

Tuesday 25 September
Mr & Mrs Coleman take me over to Gorleston in morning to see a prospective viola player for Bungay – a certain Miss Weston the quaintest little person of 40–50, who addresses her mother as 'Mummy' and waits for her word of command & permission. Try in vain to continue these hellish pft pieces & walk frantically up & down the beach trying to think. This in aft. & after tea. Letters after dinner & as last night read abit of German with Mum in preparation for our visit to Vienna etc.

Wednesday 26 September
Letters, anything but work in morning & aft. Also walks as usual. Listen to Broadcast of largest liner (534 – Queen Mary) being launched by King & Queen in aft.[128]

Charles Coleman takes me to Bungay for orch at 5.30 as usual; also taking Miss Weston, & 4 of his choir boys, who sit at the back with & on top of me. Crushed but warm – & it is a cold day. Good rehearsal; & back rather late (at 9.0).

Friday 28 September
The whole house is crammed with workmen this week – electricians (separating practice from private current) & builders (laying in a new 'Cook & Heat' stove).[129] In aft., to the accompaniment of hammers I write a unison song – for Statham & the Year Book Press[130] – merely because I cannot for the life of me do what I want to the piano line & one must do something. Mrs & Jack Moeran come over for tea. J. & I bathe (very warm considering) before tea. Walk after. Miss E. Astle comes in after dinner. Interesting discussions.

Saturday 29 September

Odd Jobs; rewrite bits of things & start to copy out kid's song 'Now is the month of maying'. Also walk – this in morning. In aft. I go to tennis party at Boyds – Chartres & Griffins. Pretty ghastly tennis. Gram. & wireless after dinner. Berlioz' interesting Corsair Ov. & Irelands meandering Pft concerto. The form is so loose & it really is only cheap ballade music (attractive in its way) touched up. Helen Perkin doesn't make it sound as effective or snappy as she might.

Thursday 4 October

Walk – shopping – & then write all morning – with a cold & very rough & dangerous (strong currents) bathe before lunch. Mrs Chamberlin comes to lunch to talk over matters abt. orchestra. K. Mead comes to tea, after which we play a four at tennis on Clyffe Court with Laurence & K. Gillespie. Too windy to play seriously, but fun. Listen to Concergebouw orch. from Hilversum, evening – simply perfect orchestra under Bruno Walter – I am not a worshipper of Walter – many things he does I don't like. But as an interpretation of Walter's ideas it was a consummate show. Mozart's superb G. min (surely the loveliest bit of music ever conceived) & Mahler's 5th Symphony – Enormously long but I was interested & thrilled for the full 1 hr & 10 mins.[131]

Sunday 7 October

Beth & I pick apples in garden in morning while Mum goes to her Christian Science at Gorleston &, Lilian to her R.C. Meet L. & walk with her. In aft Moeran comes over for a bit; after that Alec Hawkridge (South Lodge Boy) comes to tea We all 4 bathe – + John Pounder – but it is too cold to be pleasant. Ethel Boyd, also comes to tea. Ping-pong after. Letters before supper. Listen to the Vienna Boys' Choir. I have seldom heard such superb singing – rhythm – intonation, purest tone, & lovely taste.[132]

Monday 8 October

We all have early breakfast at 7.40, instead of 8.30 as usual, and I go down to station with Lilian & Beth who catch 8.30 to town. Spend morning altering bits of pft-pieces & trying to start a third. Walk with Bazil Reeve before lunch. Have some lovely tennis 3–5 with 2 Gillespies & K. Mead. After a bath at 6.0 I do actually get down to a pft piece which seems almost promising.

King Alexander of Ugo Slavia & M. Bartout are assasinated at Marseiulles – I wonder what this forbodes?[133]

Tuesday 9 October

Quite a satisfactory day. I finish 3rd piece & it's the best so far – this working most of morning & aft. with a walk before lunch. After tea I go for a Marathon walk along beach to Kessingland – lovely, cold evening & the beach is heavenly – no one about – thinking thoughts. Letters & wirless after dinner (the latter a mediocre concert conducted by Malcome Sargent) & a walk with John P. before bed.

Thursday 11 October

A somewhat hectic day. I finish 4th piece in morning so the suite is more or less complete[134] – rather less because there is much clearing up to be done. Moeran comes over for lunch & a walk. Play through the F.B. Fiddle Sonata with him. Mrs. Bridge is staying with Audry Lincoln Sutton-Alston, & they both come over to tea. They go abt. 6.30, when Charles Coleman comes in & we play a Mozart Vln & Vla duet.[135] After dinner listen to the Concertgebow orch. playing the attractive 3rd concerto of Prokofiev with the composer at the piano (v. fine) & Bruno Walter. After that write a severe letter ~~who wrote~~ to Roger Coke who lent me all that Rachmanov stuff.[136]

Monday 15 October [Lowestoft/London]

Finish packing & catch 10.8 to London. Correct proofs all way & arrive at 2.5. – Having lunched on sandwiches in train. See publishers in aft – Foss at O.U.P., & Hawkes – who takes my piano pieces.[137] Meet Grace for tea – and information on Vienna[138] at 5.15. Then Back to Burleigh House where Mum & I are putting up. Mum comes up by 2.28 – arr. 6.0. Beth & I eat at Brasserie Universelle & Mum at Barbara's, & we all meet at the latter's for coffee.

Tuesday 16 October

Much phoning about arrangements etc for shows (I hope!), & I dash all over the place for money (registered Marks) etc. Iris Lemare comes to lunch to talk over arrangements for a show of my 'Boy'.[139] Mum & I leave Victoria at 4.20 by Anglo-Swiss Express. Cross Folkestone Boulogne 6.15–7.40 (approx). not calm, but very interesting – a lovely moon & rough sea. Mum lies down below, but is not ill. Catch through Basle train from Boulogne & have meal on train. Sleep abit.

Wednesday 17 October [Basle]

Arrive at Basle at 5.5 (6.5 Swiss time) when Bethley Kauffman-Mayer, & her stepfather Herr. Reinhart meet us. ~~Go to~~ Have breakfast with Bethley at

Station, & after a walk with her we both have some sleep. We are staying with B's parents at Parkweg 18. After dinner, Mr & Ms Reinhart drive us out & take us to tea. B. comes to supper & takes us to a pianoforte recital by Ernst Levy – who has brilliant technique, but almost no rhythmic sense & absolutely ~~not~~ no musicianship

Thursday 18 October

Sleep rather late & then Mr. R. takes us to an ~~expedition~~ exhibition. Then we go to lunch with the Eisingers (Bethly's sister, & her husband & child). B. also comes. After lunch we go for a long drive all over the place – mountains and all, seeing Roman remains at Augst. They are extremely kind, but speak no English. But it is very good for our French & German. We go to dinner with Bethly, & Lisel Suter-Schlotterbeck (who with Bethley was in England with us) & her husband are there too.

Friday 19 October

Not so late to-day – up by 9.0 I try to work abit in morning, but can only sketch & cross out. We go to Lisel's to lunch – her husband & son – Peter aged 9 – are there too. In aft. see her Cinema, which is very good. After, we go round the town & see the Cathedral, & have tea. She drives us in her mother's lovely Hudson. Back to Reinharts' for dinner, & Mum & I go to Theatre with Md. R. to see Ibsen's strange & wonderful 'Peer Gynt', excellently done (in German) with Wunderbares scenery. Greig's music is, of course, ideal. It was rather hard to follow, but very enjoyable.

Sunday 21 October

Not up too early. Letters, before going to see an exhibition of young Swiss painters' work – with Bethly, Mde Eisinger, Mum. Don't understand very much of it, tho'. Lunch with B, to which Frau R. comes as well. In aft go to see a very Modern Church (R.C. St ~~August~~ Antoneuskirche), which is very beautiful & impresses me more than anything I've seen for a long time. Tea with Frau R., & Mum goes to a Christian Science show. B. & I go with her & while she is there go for a long walk round old Basle, seeing everything. We have supper in the Station Restaurant – M. & Mde R. B. Mum & I – the usual luxurious Swiss meal, with heavenly hors d'oeuvre.

Monday 22 October

Much business after breakfast – letters about pft pieces, & make first real beginning of Magnificat for Boys' voices.[140] Go to lunch at Suters, & make great friends with Peterli – Lisel's son aged 8. In aft, with her mother – Mde Schlotterbeck, Lisel takes us out in the car to Dornach where we go over the

Goethe arnum – the Centre of Anthroposophy. Very very interesting, & very lovely. Drive abit afterwards in the heavenly country. Go to dinner with Yvonne Lichti-Clar (who was in England in 1929 with us) & her husband, cousins (Millwoods) & parents at their Casino.

Tuesday 23 October

In morning we move to the Eisingers (Schaffhauserhimery) where we are staying for the rest of our visit to Basle. We arr. there for lunch – to which Bethley also comes. After that, Mum goes with Lisel to the Clars for a tea party & I go for a shop & a long walk around the place. After dinner at the Eisingers, Bethly takes Mum & me to see Rigoletto at the Stadtheater with Georges Berklanoff as R. Quite a good show, & B. is splendid – with a very charming (to look at, & musically) Gilda (Irma Handler). What lovely music tho' – just right.

Wednesday 24 October

Do alittle more of Magnificat before going to a colossal lunch at Lisel's parents – the Schlotterbecks. Bethley & her parents, Lisel & Dr Suter & Peter are there. I've never seen so much good food. After, much ~~food~~ talk while we recover, & then Lisel takes us for a trip right up the – the highest spot near Basel & it is the most soul stirring sight – Alps in distance, & the trees the most heavenly Autumn colours. After tea at the Schl. we have dinner at Bethley's where we meet Herr Straumann & his wife, who are musical nobs here – he looks at some of my stuff, but is not v. helpful or communicative. But they are nice people, & Bethley of course is an angel.

Thursday 25 October

Work abit in morning. Lunch here, to which Frau Mayer (Bethley's brother's divorced wife – a terribly sad case) comes. In the aft. she takes us for a heavenly drive, & to tea in her lovely house in the hills at Dornach. I go to see Felix Weingartner (whom H. Eisinger knows) at the Conservatoire – but he is not very helpful – tho' charming of course. In the evening we go with Lisel & the Eisingers to a very lovely show of Zauberflöte at the Stadtheater. I haven't enjoyed anything like this for along time. Perf. very good – delightful Pamina & Papagino (E. Franscher & A. Weltner). A delightful staging, & orch. playing quite good. Of course nothing can be said abt. the music. It is just great from beginning to end. Heil, Mozart!

Friday 26 October

In morning go to see some very Fine Holbein pictures [141] – also money business. Go to lunch with Yvonne Clar & her husband Charles Lichti at their lovely flat. Go to tea with Lisel, who first takes me over the Zoological gardens – very interesting – while Mum rests. Back to dinner at the Eisingers, to which Bethley also comes. A nice quiet evening.

Saturday 27 October

Lunch with Lisel, Dr. Suter & Peter. Go to Cooks in aft. for tickets & money etc. Tea & Dinner with Bethly & her Husband (the architect – home for the week-end). In morning I go to the final rehearsal of a Symphony Concert to which Mum goes with me at 8.p.m. Weingartner conducting the very fine Basel orchestra (only a few instrumentalists needing revision). A. Strauss programme – Macbeth, Heldenleben & 7 songs (delightfly sung by Elizabeth Schumann, that great artist – ~~allth~~ although they were badly chosen – not enough variety). W. does not like Strauss, consequently the ensemble was occasionally slack, the music was stilted, & ~~not~~ had, more often than not, no vitality. Luckily alot of it plays itself & Heldenleben had some really thrilling moments The love section was stiff & cold (for Strauss) – but what a work! Inspite of its egotism, I admire it now whole-heartedly. MacB. v. int. but not best S.[142]

Sunday 28 October

Go with Bethly, husband, Fr. Eisinger & Mum to an exhibition of modern paintings (esp. some v. lovely ones by Barraud). Lunch (all of us + Rosemary Eisinger) at Bethley's, & in aft. Mum & I (tickets from Bethley) go to see Aida (– very well conducted by Weingartner). A lovely show – with an especially good Amneris in Res Fischer. This isn't as good as late Verdi, but very lovely stuff.[143] Dinner at the Eisingers – to which Bethley, Flansi (Barbara's nickname for B's husband), Mde & M. Reinhard come. Pack after.

Monday 29 October [Basle/Salzburg]

Get up fearfully early, & Md. & M. Eisinger take us to Station in their car to ~~each~~ catch 6.50 to Salzburg. Lisel, Bethley & Flansi see us off too. Have a most heavenly journey – incredibly beautiful & awe-inspiring Mountains & rivers all the time. Go all thro' the Austrian Tyrol. Arr. at Salzburg at 5.28, & go to Hotel Hapsburg where we are staying. Letters & early bed after dinner.

Tuesday 30 October

Letters in morning & after dinner in evening. Spend rest of morning in Mozart House – where the great man was born. Exceptionally thrilling. See more of it after lunch. Long walk all over the lovely town with Mum after tea.

Wednesday 31 October
~~Mum &~~ I have my hair cut at a Friseur ~~round~~ near the hotel after breakfast, & after that Mum & I go for a long walk up to Hoher Salzburg and see the Castle. Come down in a Seilbahn.[144] In aft read & have an early tea after which we walk up to see the little hut (removed from Vienna) where Mozart wrote Zauberflöte. The scenary is incomparable. The hotel is filled with soldiers in evening, having a grand party or something. Any how they make a beastly noise & the place is very uncomfortable.

Friday 2 November [Vienna]
In morning Mum & I go for a long walk up to Pötzlainsdorf to see a friend of Lisel's – Frau & Herr Laube – very nice people. Back to lunch. Afterwards, I go for a long walk all round the opera house – what a place this is!! After an early tea in our rooms, Mum & I go for long walk – seeing Pensions but finding none decent or so decent enough to justify our moving from here, now that they will reduce their terms so much (to 12s). Letters after a good dinner.

Saturday 3 November
Mum & I walk about town in morning – seeing people (~~some of~~ and missing ~~them~~ others – shopping (I buy Mahler 4th symphony).[145] Read in aft & walk after tea. Early dinner & we go to opera at 7.0 to see Fledermaus (J. Strauss). Superb show – never have I heard an orchestra play like that – incredible rhythm, precision, & eagerness. And the singers too. Everything was worthy of the inimitable, delightful work – inspired from the beginning to the end. A marvellous introduction to the Wiener Oper.

A rather uninteresting Sinfonia of J.C. Bach begins the programme – but it is very beautifully & crisply played.

Sunday 4 November
Mum has a very nasty fall in her room while washing. ~~She gets up~~ She comes down to breakfast, but goes to bed soon after for the rest of the day. So I have to go to the Philharmonic Orch. concert alone – this at 11.30 – conducted by Mengelberg. Little can be said abt. the orchestra – I've never heard the like. M. doesn't impress me so much. He rescores Beethoven's lovely Pastoral Symphony in places almost out of recognition – & even Mahler's 4th Symphony (M. of all people knew to the nth degree what he wanted). But I enjoyed this work enormously – I know it's long – but not too long (except perhaps the 3rd movm.) for me. Elizabeth Schumann sings the lovely solo incomparably. // Read in aft – many letters after tea & short walk after a latish dinner.

Monday 5 November

In morning I go to see Dr. Heinsheimer of the Universal Edition – introduction from Foss. He is very nice indeed: I go to see a man about cheaper opera tickets after, but without success. In aft I sketch a work for Violin & pft.[146] After tea a long walk, all round the Ring & along river – very interesting. Letters after dinner. Mum is better, but in bed until Supper time.

Tuesday 6 November

In morning Mum & I go for an excursion round the town – all over palaces & things & see everything 'worth seeing' & are told everything 'worth knowing'. Personally I get bored with palace after palace – but it was interesting seeing the town. Work in aft – & a Mrs Koller, a Christ. Science friend of Mum's comes to tea. After dinner I go to the opera with this Mrs Koller – in a box with some friends of hers. See 'Cav. & Pag'[147] – very fine operas – but after the other things I have seen lately I couldn't make myself thrilled, though I enjoyed them. I fancy the orchestra felt that way too.

Wednesday 7 November

Mum is still abit wobbly after her fall. Short walk with her in morning, & she then shops while I return to work – don't do much good. Also try in aft, & write letters after tea, which we have as usual in Mum's room. After dinner we go to Falstaff at the opera, & I am more thrilled than I have been for ages – & so was the audience. 1st perf. at opera and the applause lasted for nearly ¼ hr. Clemens Krauss conducts splendidly, & the orch. was simply a miracle of perfection – Falstaff was played by Jaro Prohaska, who was a great singer, & gave a delightful character study. The whole cast sang & acted splendidly, esp. Mrs Quickly (Fr. Anday). The scenery & ballet at the end were enchanting. But the greatest honours go to great old Verdi – for his glorious score – humour, tenderness abounding, & the glorious fugue to end. Hats off, Gentlemen!![148]

Friday 9 November

Mum & I go to Zentralfriedhof in morning – very lovely place, & with graves of Beethoven, Schubert, Wolf, Mozart, ~~etc~~ J Strauss, etc. In aft. I work, finishing March mov.[149] We go to Opera at 7.30 – R. Strauss – Arabella – a sad work for him. Beginning was terribly slow & meandering, & he simply couldn't clinche matters at all – of course it was well done & scored in his own way – but there was little music in even the best bits – the animated 2nd act, with ~~some~~ its warm & luscious love music. Orch. good under Krauss, & singers quite good Arabella (Fr. Ursuleac), being fine.

Saturday 10 November

In morning Mum goes to opening of an exhibition at Kunthistorisches Museum. I go to see Dr. Erwin Stein at Universal edition.[150] He is very nice & interesting. Shop after (picking up Les Noces 2nd hand). In aft read, & sleep – feeling rather wuzzy. After tea, letters & after dinner 'Carmen' at the Volksoper. Of course it wasn't like the 'Oper' [151], but not half a bad show – Carmen being the incredible Maria Olszewska (a guest) who rather overshadows the rest. Orchestra quite good & whole show very lively. Of course the Music is from the beginning to the end just 'it' – & that's all that can be said

Tuesday 13 November

Feel better in morning [after a stomach bug], & tho' pretty wobbly, get up for lunch. Rest in aft, & have a~~n early~~ late tea at 5.0 (eggs & things) & go off to opera to see Meistersinger. Any trace of illness is then obliviated by the Prelude, & we enjoy a wonderful evening. Krauss conducted very well – one or two speeds wern't mine but on the whole, fine – the orchestra superb as usual. Prohaska was a very lovable Sachs, who poured forth volumes of lovely sound, & acted excellently. Ursuleac lookd & sounded very lovely as Eva. As Walther, Kalenberg wasnt so good – looked nice & acted well but too small a voice, Beckmesser (Wiedemann) & David (Zimmermann) both first-rate actors & singers, the first rather pathetic in his comedy, the second lively to the utmost degree. The five hours of the music didn't seem as many minutes; the incredible vitality, modernity, richness & lovely melody, humour, pathos in fact every favorable quality. As a stage show, just 'it'; esp. the glorious Act 2

Thursday 15 November

Mum & I walk in morning to see Museums (all of which are either shut or it is a 'pay'-day), & shop (buying second-hand min scores of Siegfried & Bruckner 4), & see sights. In aft read most of Siegfried. ~~Early dinner~~ late tea at 5.30, & we go to opera at 6.30. A lovely show of Siegfried, the only snag being that S. while being a lovely person to look at & a fine actor – hadn't the first idea of singing – literally painful (Schubert). Mime (Zimmermann) was magnificent, a wonderful singer & actor – quite the best. The others good but not astounding. The scenic effects were wonderful, & the dragon fight, far from being ludicrous, was very exciting; & the last act was touchingly beautiful. The orchestra, under [Krauss] wasn't as impeccable as usual, but the horns (esp. the horn call) were just incredible. And the Music . . . .!!!

Meet Robert Hiller, a friend of Grace and an American friend of his ~~after~~ at the Concert.

Saturday 17 November

Mum & I go to Schubert's Geburtshaus & v. interesting Museum in morning.[152] I after go to see Dr. Kalmus as well as Dr. Stein again at Universal Ed. at 12.0. Frau Koller, a very nice friend of Mums, comes to lunch at 1.0. In aft Mum & I go to Philarmonic Orch. concert at Music Verein – Knappertsbusch conducts. Not first-rate, & terribly affected and extravagant in detail, & uncontrolled. But does some things well. The audience went mad over the Bruckner 4th Symphony – why, I cannot imagine, as I find it a dismal work, with very very few redeeming patches. Certainly the orch. played it and the Tschaikov. Pathetic, which followed, magnificently – I have never heard such string playing or such horn tone, or many other details. But I felt they were being so wasted on this frantically boring Bruckner stuff. Tea with Mum out after, & correct proofs etc. after dinner.[153]

Sunday 18 November

Mum goes to see Spanish Riding School in morning. I work for abit & then go up to Pörtslainsdorf to see Dr. Erwin Stein. Have a lovely walk with him on the hills – & talk long & interestingly. Stay to lunch after which I go by various trams to see Robert Hille & his American friend at a summmer House his parants have at Dornoch. Very lovely. Have tea there & walk abit after. See their flat in town. Back here for dinner. Letters after.

Monday 19 November

In morning Mum & I do all money businesses – drawing more & buying tickets & do general business, at the Inevitable Cooks.[154] In aft. try to write abit. P. Pooley, whom we met in Wien on Sunday, from Holt, comes to tea. After that Mum & I go to Götterdämmerung at the Opera. The orchestra wasn't at its best; the horns not being at all Wiener Philharmonische standard. Brùnhilde (Konetzi) was very fine indeed – Kalundberg as Siegfried not coming up to her at all. The scenery was fine, tho' the end was distinctly lame for the music, but then what wouldn't be? Krauss was fine, but somehow alot of the Act III was disappointing; notably the funeral march.

Thursday 22 November [Munich]

I am not having my 21st birthday until I get back ~~from~~ to England But Mum has a few presents to give me – notably a score of Fledermaus (J. Strauss). In morning we do all our money transactions at the Banks here. I work abit in aft, & have birthday tea. Walk & letters after tea. After dinner, at which we are getting used to the 'school' arrangements, a young American singer one Virginia Pratt comes in to talk etc. – interesting, if a little too full of herself.

Saturday 24 November

In morning Mum & I go to the Alte Pinakothek[155] & see some wonderful pictures – notably some lovely old Dutch masters, & some heavenly Murillos. Shop abit before lunch. Read & write in aft – hair cut & shop after tea. Early dinner & we both go to the opera to see Strauss' incredible Salome. V. finely done, with a superb Salome – Hildegard Ranczak – who sang and acted in a first rate manner. The rest of the cast was good – with a few exceptions – & the orchestra played v. well under Hans Knappertsbusch, who isn't so bad when he can't be seen. Of course the idea & the music, are too thrilling & horrible for words. A great & epoch-making work.

Have a nice supper in our rooms when we get back at 10.30

Sunday 25 November

In morning we go for a long walk all over Munich with this Miss Pratt, who is very good & shows us many things – including very lovely War-memorial & Frauenkirche.[156] In aft. write & read, & have a good tea. Lohengrin at 6.0 It is a lovely work – but not Wagner at his height of course, & there are some dull & bad patches. But alot of it is first rate stuff – most, perhaps. A good show – Orch. not too good & conductor (Fischer) ditto. A very lovely Elsa [BB leaves gap], and a disappointing Lohengrin [BB leaves gap]. The others are all good tho' not super. Staging very fine, and most of the acting good – tho' the duets not convincing.

Tuesday 27 November [Munich/Paris]

Up at 6.0 and breakfast before catching 7.38 to Paris. Supposed to be a Schnellzug, the electric current fails after about an hour, & we are held up for an hour, & are two hours behind at Stuttgart. Terribly slow in spots after, & no restaurant after 2.0, so we are pretty tired & dead when we arrive at Paris Est at 9.10 instead of 7.30. Go to a Cook's Hotel. Grand Hotel Suisse in Montmartre, which seems decidely queer. Interesting though, as there is a large demonstration of apparently War-wounded men, parading the streets, with almost more police than demonstrators.

Wednesday 28 November [Paris]

In morning go to Imperial Airways & fix about tomorrow, & also to banks for money. Walk about Paris abit. Lunch at a Hotel, & then have a lovely (& quite cheap) trip all over Paris in a taxi – seeing things. Work abit back at hotel in aft, & a short walk by myself. Rudolph Holfman comes to see me – he is a young composer I met in Florence. He, Mum & I go & have tea at a nice though expensive Restaurant. Mum & I go to Opera after for Gounod's Romeo & Juliet – not very great stuff, but charming – I'm afraid we were both too tired to enjoy it – esp. as the show was rather dead.

Thursday 29 November [Paris/London]
Up early & leave hotel at 8.15. to catch 8.45 bus to Le Bourget where we catch 9.30 plane to London – very lovely journey although we couldn't see anything of the ground – through the clouds. But it was thrilling in the extreme, & so easy & convenient. Mum liked it too – Fare abt. £5–15s, extra luggage about £4. Arr. Croyden[157] at ~~12~~ 11.40 & to Victoria in bus. We are staying at Burleigh House. In aft. I go to Betty Humby's to see how the pieces go.[158] Stay to tea. See Grace, & thrill over my (& her) beloved Wien before dinner to which Barbara & Beth both come – it is good to see them again – though I can't say I'm pleased to be back.

Friday 30 November [London]
Go to Betty Humby's at 10.30 & she really plays the 'Tales' splendidly. After that with Mum I go to Wigmore Hall abt. tickets, via Bond St to see the decorations for yesterday's Royal Wedding (George & Marina).[159] In aft. I go to Bank to see abt money transactions. Mum goes to tea with Beth, & I work abit here. She & Beth go to dinner with Barbara, & I go with Iris Lemare to the rehearsal of my 'boy' [160] after at 8.0. It don't go well. I dash to the Wigmore Hall at 8.45 to hear Betty H. play my pieces well, but the audience doesn't like them very much.[161] Kit Welford who is living here, drives Beth back to her flat, where we all, + Mum, Barbara, Miss Wheatly from here, & I) have tea etc.

Memoranda [opposite entry for December 1]

Have good 21st birthday presents Share in Pft. from Mum – the rest being the legacy.[162] Music case from Barb. – Viola case from Beth. Shelley from Bobby, John & Marjorie. German books from Bethley. Gold links from Miss Turner. Oscar Wilde's works from Helen Hurst. A Lexicon from Käti. Pansies (D.H. Lawrence) from Mrs. Hurst. Gram. records from Lazy, & Laurence Sewell. £5 from Uncle Sheldon & Aunt Jul., £1 from Aunt Nellie, 10/- from A. Flo. Book Voucher from J. Pounder. Pélleas & Mélisande[163] from Bridges Beethoven songs from Miss Fass.

Sunday 2 December [Friston]
A filthy day – so that we don't go out at all except for dinner at Miss Fass' where we have much music inc. gramophone. Miss Fass comes here to

lunch. Much talk of course. ~~We write~~ They put into words for me a letter ~~fo~~ to the Mendelssohn Committee about the £50 grant that they give me. See 1932. For that large some they propose to call me Mendelssohn Scholar, instead of for the full £300 per annum[164]

Tuesday 4 December [Friston/London]

Yet another filthy rainy day. Our super weather of abroad has broken with a vengeance. Stay in all morning – correct proofs & such like – early lunch & Mr & Mrs. B. drive me back to town with them in aft – arr. 4.0. Much telephoning & arranging before dinner. Dash off to Iris' rehearsal of my 'Boy' at St. Martin's Rectory at 8.0. Hear abit of that, & then go to concert of ~~Inter~~ Contemporary music society. Sylvia Spencer & the Grillers play my oboe quartet very beautifully; not perfectly, but with imagination, and spirit. It goes down well, ~~and~~ after that they play the Prokofiev Quartet brilliantly – it is a wonderful piece of writing, but not a very satisfactory shape.[165] Mum, Beth, & Kit Welford, & Mrs Bridge are there among others

Thursday 6 December

A very hectic day. Go to see Bridges immediately after breakfast to show them the Mendelssohn Schol secretary's rather cringing reply. Back – to pack (most of which is done by Mum), correct proofs, see Iris Lemare, & shop; have lunch with Mum & Beth at Selfridges & shop in pelting rain after. Also go to Boosey & Hawkes to see Ralph. Dash back to 173 Cromwell Road; meet Mum & pick up luggage & travel home by 4.54. having tea on way. Home looks very nice, but the people ~~here~~ in this town don't make me feel very glad, at having put Wien behind me!

Thursday 13 December [London]

Finish copy of Waltz & take it along to Betty Humby in morning. Shop in aft. & see Boosey & Hawkes about matters. After an early dinner I go ~~to~~ with the Bridges to a concert of the Audrey Melville orchestra which F.B. conducts. The orchestra isn't good – the prof. wind being appalling. But even then we had good shows of the Leonora 3 & Borodin's lovely 2nd Symphony. Thelma Reiss plays the Dvorak Vlc concerto, with very lovely tone but not quite musically enough. Back to the Bridges for food & talks.

Saturday 15 December

Filthy wet day. I correct proofs & parts and things in morning, and then go up to Boosey & Hawkes with them. Go to lunch & spend afternoon with Betty Humby. Temianka (Vln) is there rehearsing, & they play my recently concocted Suite. T. is a brilliant fiddler.

Beth comes to dinner, & we both go to a very amusing party at the Hartridges where Käti is 'digging' at the moment. 'Murder' & 'Charades' etc. Back by last train at 12.30.

David Layton (with his sister Margaret who sings in the choir) ~~tak bring~~ take Barbara & me home after.

Monday 17 December

Rehearse abit with Betty Humby in morning at Wigmore Hall – then see people at Performing Right's Soc. and Ed. Clark at B.B.C. In aft. I go to see a Herr Peter Stadlen (A Viennese pianist) who may play some of my things. Beth & I have dinner with Barbara and Helen, & we all go off to Wigmore Hall to hear Betty Humby play my 3 pieces with Temianka – considering that they've only had them such a short time, they go excellently (T. being esp. good).[166] Dash off – with Bridges – to the Mercury Theatre where Iris Lemare conducts a show of my 'Boy'.[167] Mostly very poor I'm afraid – Herod being esp. wobbly. I came out after it, not being able to stand the strain![168]

Funnily enough so many people liked the work. The boys (St. Alban's Holborn) were very, very good and beautiful.

Tuesday 18 December

See F.B. about matters for a long time in morning, & then Grace for a talk. Have lunch at Pagani's with Walter Legge (critic) & hear some int. gram. records after, back at Columbia's with him. Have tea at Strand Palace with Arnold Cooke, Henry Boys, + Baba also being there.

Dinner with Bridges, & go to see that brilliant, & witty in the extreme, film of Réne Clair's – Le Million.[169] A work of art. It was preceeded by a terrible concoction with Conrad Veidt in F.P.I.[170]

Wednesday 19 December [London/Lowestoft]

Go, in vain, to Somerset House & then to King's Coll. to try & find out what the exact details of the Mend. Schol. are. After, go to see Foss, & have a real tussel over performing rights.[171] See Ralph Hawkes after, also, about these things. Phone people, arr. matters, & pack before catching 4.54 home. Beth brings a parcel for me to take back – arr. only 3 mins before time! Tea on train. Mum meets me. After dinner, have on my new Mahler Kindertodten records,[172] which are very lovely.

Friday 21 December [Lowestoft]

My neck's not really much better, so I stay in bed for breakfast. Practise pft, & viola, Gram. for rest of day. Bazil comes for a short walk, tea, & gram. & viola & pft. duetting. In evening listen to an E.M. Delafield play 'the Little

Boy'[173] which began well, but petered out rather badly. Also a Contemporary concert of Hindemith – Concert Musik for Pft, Brass & Harps. (which contains some of the best Hindemith, & Mathias the Painter, a new symphony[174] – hard to judge, thro' wireless, & because of a scratch performance. I get so sick of these shows without any precision or conviction – technically not bad, but that's all. (The work had some nice things but seemed to wander at times).

Sunday 23 December

Long walk with Barb, Beth & Effie along cliffs in morning. Mum & Flo. go to St. Johns. Read (starting Oliver Twist)[175] in aft. & walk with dog, Letters etc. after tea, and listen to a bit of Hänsel & Gretel from Berlin, but wireless is v. bad. Beethoven's Mass in D comes over better from Hilversum at 8.0–9.45. An excellent show (as regards playing & singing), the best Solo singing I've ever heard in this work – & orch & Chorus superb. Mengelberg who conducts, leaves alot to be desired – so[me] of it is very much out of the picture – not even being effective (end of Gloria & Credo), but the Agnus Dei is a great show. Of course one daren't talk about the work. It is just above criticism.

Monday 24 December

Shop abit with Beth & then with her & Barb. spend ~~most~~ rest of morning decorating St. John's. In aft shop. At 6:0 go to St John's with Mr. Coleman, who is a help, trying over the organ part of my Te Deum. At 10.30–11.0 we set out Carol Singing – organised by Marjorie Philips & me. 11 come (inc. Beth, Aunt Effie, & 3 Backs), inspite of windy & cold weather. Great but hoarse fun. Finish singing at abt. ~~12.0~~ 12.45 with a small supper here in kitchen.

Tuesday 25 December

Beth, Aunt Effie & I go to St Johns at 8.0. (Barb. is rather laid up with a sore mouth after an extraction yesterday.) Presents, as usual, at Breakfast. I go to St Johns again at 11.0 with Aunt Flo & Beth. Read & Listen to int. broadcast – round Empire – after lunch.[176] Walk with hound before tea. Entertain maids after.[177] An attempt at a gay Xmas dinner wasn't so bad considering the circs.,[178] but none of us felt particularly merry!

Wednesday 26 December

Many "Thank-you" letters in morning & after tea. Walks with Barb before lunch. Beth before tea. Read much Oliver Twist at various times during the aft. and evening. It has great things in it – not all perhaps ~~the~~ 1st class – but

90% of it is terrifying in the extreme – & extremely well done. Beth & Barb. go to a subs. dance at the Blowers – in a large party with Welfords, Chartres, Reeves, – I got out of it successfully. Listen to a light orchestral concert cond. by F.B. He really is a great cond Di Ballo. Ov. of Sullivan – a lovely show of Casse Noisette (lovely work) & [*Ouverture de fête*] of Saint Saens ending with his own original, brilliant & I truly believe great Sir Roger de Coverley[179] Orch. at its best.

Friday 28 December

Good pft. practice and much letter-writing, also a short walk with dog & later Mum in morning Go to Badminton on S. Pier with Beth 2.30–5.30 – many there but fun. In evening, Beth & Aunt Flo go to a film, but I stay and listen to a B.B.C. orch concert, conducted (atrociously) by R.V. Williams. Grace has 2 Psalms done – not her best works but definitely musical, & far away the best of the programme which inc. dreadful concoctions by E. Maconchy, R.O. Morris, Robin Milford, & R.V.W. (5 dreadfully boring mystical (?) songs). It is concerts like this which make me absolutely despair of English Music and its critics.[180]

Sunday 30 December

Long walk with hound along beach in morning – in pelting rain – it never seems to stop raining now-a-days. Read, wireless (some lovely Meistersinger records) & walk with Beth in aft. Letters after tea – & Mum & I see Beth off by 7.5 to town. After supper – the family's dwindled to 3 now – I play gallons of Debussy's lovely Pelléas – latest present from F.B.

Monday 31 December

See Aunt Flo. off by 10.8 to town with Mum. Shop abit after. Then Mr. Coleman very decently reads through proofs of my Holiday Tales on pft. In aft. Badminton on S. Pier.

As Marjorie Phillipps, Doris Tamp. & Tuttles are there we get some really lovely Badminton.

Listen to whole of Die Fledermaus from Vienna Opera in evening. It doesn't come over too badly. What a lovely show! Kern was again marvellous as Adéle. And the orchestra! F.B. rings up from Friston about O.U.P. matters at 8.0.

1935

Tuesday 1 January [Lowestoft]
Correct proofs letters etc. in morning before Basel Reeve comes for walk & talk. In aft, letters & Mrs. Chamberlin (also Mr. Cates) comes to tea, & to bring her 2nd Viola which she is giving me for a 21st birthdy present. It is a lovely instrument compared to my old one. Play it alot after they go at 5.30. Then some walks with Mum & dog. After dinner more of new viola, together with some with Mum on piano.

Thursday 3 January [Lowestoft/Norwich]
Charles Coleman comes in to inspect and to give his approval to the new Viola, which is flourishing. Much proofs after that – finally finishing Holiday Tales (though how many more mistakes there are in them, Heaven only knows), & sending them off. Walk also. More proofs – Sinfonietta this time; in aft. Early tea & catch 5.20 to Norwich where John Alston ~~takes~~ meets me & takes me to the Sutton's house where I spend the night. They have a small but diverting & entertaining party in evening. John's Friends Bill Wakeford (with whom I sleep) & Peter Woodard, and Christopher A. and of course Mrs Sutton are there. Go to bed at abt. 12.45, but don't settle for sleep until abt. 4.0, because of much serious, & heart-searching conversation with Bill.

Saturday 5 January [Lowestoft]
Spend much time trying to prepare text for a new choral work in morning & after tea.[1] Odd practisings besides. Walk in foul rain & wind before lunch & in aft with John Pounder, who comes back here to tea. After dinner, wireless – including a very interesting 'Conversation in a train',[2] a part of a popular 'Prom' Tschaikovsky Pft. concerto & Berlioz Faust pieces[3] (lovely things) played in a dreadfully slap-dash, off-hand way – & of course received with rapturous applaus.

Sunday 6 January
Mum goes to Christian Science 'do' at Gorleston in morning. I walk along beach with dog, in among the legions of long-shore fishers on the beach. Letters, gramophone, & abit more walk before tea, to which Mr., Mrs, &

Charles Coleman come. After Mr. & Mrs C. go Charles and I play the duets for Vln & Vla. of Mozart – which it is lucky that Mozart couldn't hear! John Pounder comes in to supper. Much talk – discussing opera plots etc.

Tuesday 8 January

See Mr. Coleman in morning about re-taxing his car (it not being in his means) at the expense of the Bungay Orch. Committee for taking over Charles and me on Wednesdays. Also write to Foss – deciding to let him have my 12 School songs – but this is my last work outside the P.R.S. – the O.U.P. not being members. In aft. Bazil Reeve & Christopher Gledhill come over to tea – play much Vla & Pft with Christopher. My 3 Vln pieces[4] (arr. viola), Stravinsky Duo Concertant, Bartok 1st Rhapsody & Franck sonata (all arr. for viola as I go along). The two Misses Astles come in to dinner. Very amusing evening – music & Lexion.

Thursday 10 January

Pft. practice – as well as daily task of de-tangling Caesar – in morning. A very lovely – though very cold morning, & I go for a very long walk with Bazil along Pakefield Beech to Kessingland – 11.30–1.0. Proofs in aft. and abit in evening. Mrs. Chartres comes to tea with Mum. After tea I go in to have some games with David Boyd who's been sick these last few days. After dinner listen to a thrilling, & quite well done, play called 'In the Shadows'[5] – a quasi war play. Also a moderate show of Berlioz' 'Rom. & Jul.' from Paris.

Friday 11 January

Working hard, most of morning & aft. I finish 3 sets of proofs & despatch 2 of them, only to see arrival of 2 new sets (Oboe Quat parts & final proofs of 'Holiday Tales). Long walk, shopping before lunch. Go for a very short tea at S. Lodge – for ½ hr of an old boys' gathering. Then take Teddy Rogers & David Boyd to the Grand at 5.15. See 'The Lost Patrol' – with Victor Maclagen.[6] A very good effort at atmosphere, with some very fine photography, but not satisfactory enough as a whole. Teddy & David come back to dinner at 7.45.

Sunday 13 January

In the morning John fetches Mr. James ('cellist) & Meg. O'Farrell (who plays 2nd Vln on her Viola) from Norwich & we spend morning playing piano quintets (F. Bridge, & arr. of Strauss Fledermaus waltz) & the Fauré C min quart.[7] Great fun. I play Vla, except in Strauss where Audry surrenders her pos. of leader to me & plays Vla. John really proves an excellent chamber music ~~player~~ pianist. In aft. go to Framingham Earl Church, all of us, where John plays the organ. Back to tea, to which A. Batchelor[8] comes. More music after tea, until 6.45, when John brings me back here in time for supper, to which Mr & Mrs. T.J.E. Sewell come. Much talk (abt. S. Lodge etc.) and a little music.

Tuesday 15 January

Spend most of morning, aft, & evening arranging Strauss Du & Du Waltz for the B.B.B.B. (Benj. Britten Bungay Band, alias the 'Hag's Band').[9] Walk with Cyril Reeve before lunch. The Enraght Family were due to tea, but failed to arrive. H. Boyd turns up however.

Listen to Wireless after dinner. General relief at definite result of Saar Plebiscite (90% maj. for return to Germany), but disappointment at loss of power of League, in Status Quo.[10] Also a talk on Judia by Lady Layton.[11]

Wednesday 16 January

More arranging in morning, together with some proof reading in aft. A short walk with Cyril Reeve before lunch. Charles Coleman takes me over to Bungay rehearsal at 5.30. Owing to Fog very few are there – 9 only – and the playing is execrable. It is no use trying to rehearse them – the only advice worth giving them is 'Go away & learn to play your instruments'. Dreadful journey back – running out of water, in the thick fog. However a good dinner, and the Mahler gram. records (Kindertodtenlieder) restores my faith in life.

When F.B. conducts the chief advantage is to be able to listen to the music without bothering about the interpretation. The shows are always 'just right'.

Thursday 17 January

Finish Ob. Quart. proofs in morning & aft. Long walks & talks with Cyril Reeve before lunch & after tea. Listen to wireless after dinner. An amusing concert from Basel – Bekker cond. the v. good Symphony orchestra in J. Strauss & Offenbach (the difficult Polka v. good). Then F.B. conducting Section C (or E) & a Serenade Conct. The orchestra isn't good enough, but even then he gave a very brilliant show of Bizet's Adorable Jeux d'enfants & the Prince Igor Dances; and a very lively Seraglio Ov. The Orch. wasn't up to the Midsummer N.D. Scherzo though. (The Dirge in the 1st work was rather lovely).[12]

Friday 18 January

Don't seem to do anything in morning, except a little pft. practice & proof-reading & a walk with Caesar. Badminton in aft. – some quite good stuff tho' Marjorie P. can't be there. Meet Beth from town by 8.4. Listen to a Contemporary B.B.C.concert. I can't judge the Suite (Black Masquers) by Roger Sessions – ~~tho'~~ it seemed very hysterical & over elaborate, tho' int. Arthur Bliss's Mèlée Fantasque was dull and unoriginal. Gerschwin's 2nd Pft & Orch Rhapsody was in the typical style. By far the best work was a Dance Symph. by Aaron Copland.[13] Most of this was really beautiful & exhilarating.

Saturday 19 January
I'm having great difficulty in finding Latin words for a proposed 'Hymn to St Cecilia.[14] Spend morning hunting. Walk with Beth in pouring rain. Have one of my periodical Liver attacks in aft – so don't go to tea with Fernande & Laurence Sewell as Mum & Beth do. Am much rewarded as I hear some v. int. Gram. records on wireless and also a v. fine show of Berlioz L'Enfance du Christ from Paris. There is some marvellous music in this. After dinner more wireless, including a recital by T. Brosa. Some lovely fiddling, but a disappointing show of the Franck Son. As the pianist (Manheimer) is as dead as mutton – and not even technically efficient.

Sunday 20 January
I'm having a thrilling time reading Pepy's diary.[15] It is a marvel. Last night I dreamt a most sensible dream imagining myself with him at a Ball as young Monmouth with Lady Castlemaine, and discussing most distincly, Bach, but adding 'then of course, he's not alive yet'. // Usual Sunday, long walk with Beth in morning. Wireless, reading, letters, work at other times of day. F.B. conducts a lovely B.B.C. Orch. concert at 9.20. Hadyn 99 Symphony – v. beautifully played – Schönberg's lovely Verklärte Nacht – which the strings played splendidly. A rousing show of his own thrilling Enter Spring, with the heavenly tune in it. And a brisk finale in Coq D'or Wedding March[16] Act. the hall's a bit too resonant, but otherwise it was a fabulous concert.

Wednesday 23 January
Long walk along beach after breakfast to collect my thoughts, while my room is being spring-cleaned or something. Work after, & in afternoon. Charles Coleman comes to tea, & takes me afterwards to Bungay, where I make the orchestra work very hard at the Fledermaus waltz. It does them no end of good too. After a consequently late dinner at 8.30, listen to a Symphony in C minor by Shaporin.[17] This work has the disadvantage of being written for two or 3 orchestras, several choruses & about 15 brass bands (I've never heard such a row), & music has to be esp. good to stand

that. This was terribly dull & reminicant, I hope U.S.S.R. can produce better stuff than this

Friday 25 January
Still my writing won't go right. I have been trying off and on for about 18 months to finish a quartet suite,[18] & I am still as stuck as ever-; I can't begin the extra mov. to the Vln suite; and I have the scheme but no notes yet for my St Cecelea Hymn.

Try all morning, and after tea. Go to Badminton for abt an hour in aft. Listen to wireless, & usual pft. playing after dinner. A wicked night – very windy, & rain & sleet.

Saturday 26 January
Strange to say – what work I do at rewriting the old St. Qu. in morning dosn't seem entirely worthless. Long walk in aft – & more proof correcting. Charles Coleman comes to tea & takes me to the Suttons where we play, with Audry A (Vln 1) & Mr James (Vlc) the 1st Beethoven Quartet. Start at 7.0 – arrive at 11.45 with a run through of F.B.'s Sextet, via a practice at his Pft. Quintet with John A at the Pft. (Meg OFarrell, 2nd Vla).[19] Great fun – though we arn't a great quart. yet! It is a very snowy and haily day – with terrific wind in spots. Drive home (arr. 1.0) very lovely – but necessarily very slow.

Sunday 27 January
A similar kind of day – but a bit more blizzardy. Walk (in the fine spots) with John P. in morning. In aft. Mr. & Mrs. Firth (Vl.I & Vlc) come over at 2.15 and with Charles (Vln II) we play quartets (with a gap for tea & supper) until 9.15. Haydn (op. 3–5 – Emperor & Horseman)[20] & my own Simple Symphony. Great fun, likewise. After they go listen to what seems a fine perf. by B.B.C. orch. under Oskar Fried (tho' without the suavity & rhythm of the Wien Phil) of Mahler's wonderful 9th Symphony. I could listen to this for hours. The End is really very moving

Bobby's birthday, & he 'phones from Prestatyn to say 'how d'you do'.

Monday 28 January
Spend the entire morning over the 2nd Oboe Quart. Proofs. In aft. go to Badminton for 1½ hrs. Not very good stuff – tho' a strenuous single with Kath. Tuttle. Letters & pft practice after tea. I have finally decided, as Foss seems so querilous & doubtful about them, to give the school-songs to Boosey & Hawkes (see Jan 8th). F. has been for ages enthusiastic, then withdrawn by turns; besides there is always so much bother & hold-up about

O.U.P. publications.[21] My Simple Symphony has already been printed over 4 months & is not out yet! Much piano & a little lovely gramophone.

Tuesday 29 January
Spend all morning & alot of aft. in rewriting the 1st mov. of my S.Q.[22] Not much use, though. Walk before lunch – heavenly spring like day – tho' cold – & in aft. to library, where I get a very interesting & moving life of O. Wilde.[23] Mrs. Hutchinson comes to tea with Mum. After dinner listen at 8.0 to a reconstruction (by W. Wilson) of the trial of Lady Alice Lisle – by Judge Jeffreys, who seems to have been an amazing man, tho' very ruthless.[24] F.B. (who phones about 9.0) conducts at light L.S.O. concert at 10.20. A lovely show of Ravel Pavane (d.I.) & Tsh. very entertaining Cap. Italien. The orch. hadn't settled down in the Rim. Korsakov ov. May night. Anyhow it is rather a scratch lot of players. Massenet's Scénes Pittoresque – quite amusing.[25]

Letters also after dinner. Francis Barton – Hawkes etc.
Thursday 31 January
Spend a long time in morning on the beginning of a last movement for Vln Suite for the umpteenth time. Not much use. Long walk along beach before lunch – lovely day. Pft practice etc. in aft. before Christopher Gledhill comes over for tea – & to play Vla & Pft. & Pft duets. He is going to do some proofs for me. Listen to Beecham & L.P.O. doing Mendelssohn Italian & Sibelius 4th Symphonies. Much in common – both saying very little – 1st very charmingly the 2nd very coldly & uncompromisingly. But then Sibelius is probably beyond me.

Saturday 2 February [Lowestoft/London/Friston]
Early breakfast with Mum & catch 8.30 to town – where I go straight to Bridges, where I have lunch with Mr. & Mrs, Miss Fass, Mrs L. Sutton & John. After that we all go to a concert at the Albert Hall – Royal Choral Soc. where among other things F.B. conducts quite a good show (all considered) of his sincere & touchingly beautiful Prayer.[26] Malcolm Sargent conducts a virile (but not much more) perf. of Walton's Belshazzar's Feast – which seems to wear worse & worse – the 2nd half particularly being threadbare. Dyson's In honour of the City wasn't worth doing – being aenemic both in material & craftsmanship.[27] He waved the stick for this. // Back to Bedford Gardens to tea, after which John A. & I leave for Friston in a very bad Ford 8 hired, & the others follow in the Bridges car (Miss F. having left by train.) We arr. at 9.5 25 mins before them. John & I sleep together at Friston Field, & Audry along at Miss Fass.

Sunday 3 February [Friston]
Barbara came [to Lowestoft] on Sat. for Week-end. To-night Mum goes half-way back with her as far as Ipswich, where Mum is going to stay for 3 or 4 days with Aunt Jane

Not up exactly early. Much talk in morning. Miss F. comes along for lunch. John goes back to town by his car in aft. & Audrey, Frank, & I walk for abt. 4 miles over the Downs in very blustery but lovely weather. Tea at Miss Fass' & many lovely records. Back to Friston Field for dinner, & much very serious & interesting argument (civilisation ~~to~~ – war via (of course) religion). After escorting Audry back at 10.15 – talk until past midnight – F.B. about his life, a matter of the Will'o the wisp character of his success both as composer & esp. as conductor[28]

Monday 4 February [Friston/London]
In the morning F.B. gives me a lovely long talk about my school-songs & quartet.[29] He really is a marvel at putting his finger on the bad spots. He & Mrs. Bridge take Audry & me to Polegate & we go to town via Brighton – in the fast electric train arr. in town at 3.25. Have tea in the M.M. Club with her & John, May Mukle & Rebecca Clarke. Grace Williams come to dinner at Burleigh House where I am staying, & after we both go to the Mercury Theatre to the Iris Lemare concert. Orch. Nothing of much interest, except a Suite of Grace, which has some good things in – esp. 1st & 2nd mov, & a ballet on an amusing subject – Great Agrippa by Elizabeth Maconchy – some doleful arrangements of forgotten dirges, & a long clumsy immature, work of Elizabeth Lutyens finishes the programme.[30]

Wednesday 6 February [Friston]
Finish copying two very old part-songs which I take to R. Hawkes at 12.0.[31] He is going to print them – in the hope of making some money. After that have lunch with John A. and Bill W. (see Jan 3.) at their flat – lunch cooked by B. Afterwards they take me to a film (~~Great~~ Mighty Barnum)[32] at Marble Arch – but tisn't very good. Tea there too. On way back – are accosted by a mad woman, who accuses us of being murderers & gangsters. Via Bridges they take me to Barbara, where I have dinner and dash off to B.B.C Q. Hall concert. Very deadly show – a typical, ignorant, listless Boult concert. Elgars' 'Int & Allo.' which I don't like at the best of times. A new & unimportant [?] Scherzo of Holst – Gieseking is disappointing in a dull show of Beethoven's adorable 4th Concerto – tho' technically some of it is perfect. Brahms impossible 2nd Symphony is made even thicker & muddier than it is.[33] A supper back at the Bridges with John A. and the Brosas, cheers us abit.

Thursday 7 February

Go to a rehearsal of the Audry Melville String Orch. with F.B., who conducts, in morning. Very instructive & interesting (Bach, Handel F.B., Arensky). Back to lunch with them. Meet Henry Boys at MM Club at 3.30; long talk & abit of a walk with him, after. Then go up to Hampstead for dinner with Howard Ferguson. Play much pft. duet after – Ravel, Mozart, Debussy.

Sunday 10 February [Lowestoft]

Long walk with John P. in morning whilst Mum is at St. Johns. In aft. read, begin to arrange photos taken abroad, & short walk with dog. Letters after tea & listen to Shakespeare's Troilus & Cressida – which has some very strange & wonderful passages, but is very difficult to follow. John comes to supper & listen to King David (Honnegger) after.[34] A very fine scheme, with some lovely music – though not equally distributed. Caesar is very ill in the evening – seems to have something in his throat – or some poison. But nothing we do seems to help

Tuesday 12 February

2nd Proofs ~~arrive~~ of Te Deum arrive. Much work at correcting them in morning. Also pft. practise, short walk before early lunch at 12.40, after which Helen Boyd takes me to Norwich. I have to see Harrington Kidd about my Viola. Also see Meg O'Farrell at the Gift Shop & have tea with her. Get ~~by~~ back by 6.20. Early dinner & John Pounder takes me to see (with Mr. & Mrs. Pounder) at The Playhouse 'The Man that knew too much'. Prod. by Hitchcock, with Edna Best, Leslie Banks, [Peter Lorre] & Nova Pillbeam (a little darling, and a 1st-rate actress); it is the best English Film I have ever seen.[35] Most delightful comedy mixed with most tense drama, so that even now (12.0 ~~am~~ midnight) I am dithering with excitement. A masterpiece of film-work – superb in every detail, & glorious acting.

Wednesday 13 February

Spend most of day practising piano very hard – but the snag is that I can do no other work at the same time. Have a long walk in aft. along cliff trying to get a little thinking done. Mr. Ernest Banks (org. of St. Margaret's) was found yester in the sea. He had been very depressed of late – abt.~~hel~~ health. // Listen to 'Scrap-book for 1921' in evening – very entertaining – having tried in vain to get Bruckner's 4th from Leipzig. Get most of Dvorak's Adorable 5th later from from Huizen.[36]

Thursday 14 February

Practise in morning & two thinking walks with Caesar. Proofs in aft, & a ditto walk after tea. Go to badminton at St. Peters Hall with Laurence – energetic if nothing else. Back at 6.15 for a run-through of the Franck Sonata with C. Coleman. Early dinner, after which listen to two masterpieces worthily performed. From Vienna, Mahler's adorable 4th Symphony – the lovely Vien. Symph. under Zemlinsky, with Annie Michaldey, as a lovely soloist A truly sensitive show. Then from Regional – F.B's last trio well played by the Grinke – full of great stuff, with impeccable workmanship. Hats off – gentlemen, even if they have to be forcibly removed! Now for war!!

Saturday 16 February

Very windy & warm day. Usual morning – long walk with Beth before lunch. In aft. practise viola & walk with Beth & dog again before tea. Bath before dinner – after which get Acts III, IV, V of Pelleas & Melisande from Huizen – a very fine performance with Concertgebouw Orch. under Pierre Monteux – unfortunately the atmospherics often dreadful, so alot of the delicious music was lost. It is marvellous stuff – but so sensitive & intangible.

Tuesday 19 February

A usual proof-practice-walk day. Mum has Mrs. Owles & Mrs Woodger to tea. After which I spend 1½ hrs knocking at people's front doors up this road – delivering Peace Ballot papers.[37] A foul job – but it may do a little good, and make a few people use their brains. But of course it would be my luck to get allotted ~~such~~ a road just packed with die-hards – Indian Colonels, army widows, typical old spinsters etc!

Have been reading 'Scissors' by C. Roberts[38] – but don't think much of it – either material or workmanship

Wednesday 20 February

Very rough, windy, & later on rainy day. Proofs all morning a abit in aft; consequently can do nothing else. Charles takes me over to Bungay at 5.30, to the Orchestra – but as there are several other events taking place the orch. of course must come last – only 11 there.

Listen to abit of Acis & Galetea [Handel] on the B.B.C. – but A. Boult's reading of it killed whatever beauties it contains – and they arn't a few either.

Thursday 21 February

A completely Oboe-quartet-proof-infested day, the only gaps being a short walk before lunch with Mum, ditto before tea with dog, & ditto before dinner with J. Pounder.

After dinner listen to Wireless which is very bad. Get a bit of Bax's Viola Sonata[39] which I dislike. Debussy's Cl. Rhapsody[40] had some lovely things in it, but I can't see what he's driving at – finally a bad show of Prelude & Liebestod [*Tristan*] from Paris.

A heavenly spring-like morning & aft.

Sunday 24 February

Listen – partly here & partly at John's to a v. fine perf. of Handel's Ode to St. ~~Cel~~ Cecilia's day, from Germany; it is a very lovely work, I think. After, a v. long walk with John, who after lunch takes me with his family for a long & lovely country drive in their car. Mr. & Mrs Chartres come over to tea & supper with a long walk in between. It is nice having them. Listen to Stravinsky's Appolo Musagete – which has some v. lovely things in it & also T. Brosa's wizard playing of the Prokofiev Vln concerto.[41] Long walk in wind & rain with Caesar before bed.

Monday 25 February

Final alterations of 'A Hymn to Virgin'[42] in morning & letters & pft practise & short walk paying bills. Badminton in aft & leave early to go round collecting Peace Ballot papers. Beastly job as many people are so apethetic – perhaps they will be 'interested' if they found a gas-bomb on their door-steps. Letters after dinner, and listen to a fine show of Byrd's 5-pt. Mass. I am not educated enough in this way really to like it all. He makes some lovely sound, but to my mind it is so dreadfully long & monotonous. Probably my ignorance tho'.

Florence (cook-general) is ill, & now at home. So her younger sister is taking her place v. efficiently.

Thursday 28 February

Go to Library in morning to change books etc. Back to work – but not much use. Christopher Gledhill comes over in aft. Long walk & talk with him; then back, to Piano & Vla. & Pft. duets, to which Charles adds his fiddle after tea – do some Bach, Boyce, & my old arr. of a Beethoven Rondo.[43] After dinner listen to wireless – a most terribly mediocre programme of forced & self-conscious 'light' music by the bright young things of English Music – H. Hutchinson, A. Benjamin, G. Jacob, C. Lambert. etc. etc. // Mum 'phones Bobby who is in trouble re illness – Marjorie & some of the boys.

Saturday 2 March

Write a song (A Poison tree of W. Blake) in morning – but it's not much good – more an exercise than anything.[44] This occupies me all the morning – a short walk before lunch. Mr & Mrs Firth (from Beccles) come over with their Violin & 'cello, & Charles C. with his Vln & we play quartets from 2.30–7.30 – with a short interval for tea. Great & marvellous fun – work hard at the incredible Beethoven F minor (95), & at F.B's very lovely Noveletten. At times we almost begin to resemble a quartet. Also do Emperor Var. (Haydn), 2 1st movs of 1st Razumovsky & last mov. of 3rd.[45] A glorious afternoon. Somewhat exhausted in evening, so only read & wireless.

Sunday 3 March

It being a very fine & lovely morning, John P. [Pounder] & his parents take me for a lovely drive in the country – Mum won't come but goes to church. In aft. two splendid & delightful boys – R. Ferrier & Tribe (from S. Lodge) come to tea – & I walk alot with them before. Miss Nora Back and a friend (Mr Wrigly) come also in to tea. Ping-pong with boys after. Letters before supper, to which John P. & John Nicholson come. Rather a difficult evening, since the latter has become, from being a timid & ordinary school-boy, a sophisticated & affected young gentleman of the (so-called) Lowestoft Society – with many opinions & few reasons – so different from the other John – open, intelligent & unconventional. However, gramophone records keep us otherwise occupied – have J.N's [John Nicholson's] 9th Symphony [Beethoven] – cond. by Albert Coates – though I never should have thought any one could be so bad, & ignorant as A.C. is here.

Monday 4 March

Don't seem to do much in morning – nothing seems to move in writing now-a-days. However get some good piano practice. Mr. Voke comes over to see me – & wastes a good ½ hr talking about himself. Badminton in aft. with some lovely games. Go out to collect some more Ballots after that – but little success. Perhaps things will brighten up after the B.B.C. Discussion – Lord Cecil (pro) & Rt. Hon. Amory (con). Tho. Amery spoke very plausibly & had the last word – ~~tho~~ but he had no case if you thought about it. // Also a very amusing & interesting sketch of Sacha Guitry – Dinner for two

Wednesday 6 March

Mendelssohn Committee have capitulated completely[46] – I now need not ~~keep~~ be called Mend. Scholar, can keep my £50 – & am requested to 'let bygones be bygones' and try again for the Schol. in June – I don't know yet. // Great sensation at MacDonald. White paper – £10,000,000 more on armaments this year. Germany has stoped negotiations with John Simon – rightly I feel – It violates every ~~point~~ creed of League of N.[47] // Usual day – usual unsuccess of work. Dreadful Bungay rehearsal – end of day cheered by Mahler's glorious Kindertodtenleider.

John comes to the Suttons too – & brings Mum & me back by 12.0.

Thursday 7 March

Abit of a pft. practice & a shop for Mum before we both go off to Norwich by train. Have lunch + John P. with Meg O'Farrell at her Gifte Shoppe and then go to St. Andrews' Hall for a Phil. Concert – the Roth Quartet. Very capable players (tho' not startling) but they do some bad things – esp. in the Death & the Maiden – lovely work. The Ravel was played well in spots – but the St. A Hall is far too large for chamber music.[48] I came out before the Brahms – I can't stand B. these days. Tea at Meg's & then we go back – separatly – to Audrey's and play chamber music – she, me, Mr James (Vlc) & Nora Back (Pft.). I do the Franck Sonata with Audry (I do pft) as well – & do Pft Quartets by Mozart, Lovely, Schuman good in small spots – Brahms (C minor) bad in large spots.[49]

Wednesday 13 March [Lowestoft/London]

A hectic morning – hair cut, shop, abit of writing, letters & pack with help of Mum. Catch 2.35 to town in aft. arr. 6.0. Repair to Burleigh House (transformed – lift, wash-basins etc.), whence Beth comes to dinner – after which we both go to Queen's Hall to hear the Wiener Sängerknaben.[50] Of course it was a different thing from Monday night. True the intonation and attack was sometimes bad in the first group of motets – but the tone & phrasing was always lovely. The 20 children did a splendid show of Mozart's Bastien & Bastienne – with most finished acting & singing, but so gloriously ingenuouse. The final group of Schuman (Zigeunerlied), Brahms, Schubert (a bad arr. of Wiegenlied) & two delightful Volklieder were just perfectly sung – the two young soloists have voices I have never heard equalled by any one – any age. But the climax of the evening was the encores. Two Strauss waltzs (Wienerwald, & Blau Donau) sung with verve & élan – a touchingly naïve show of Mozart's Sch'afe, mein Prinzlein – an incredible bit of ensemble in a Strauss Polka (?) – & a cheeky A.B.C. Superlatives are useless referring to the finish of these shows – & the incredible vitality. Hats off Gents – Genii!

<u>cont.</u> Ov. & Venusberg Music – Pier Gynt no 2, Dvorak's lovely E min Slav chorus, & Chabrier's España[51] – the beginning of it all. Mrs. Brosa also comes – much talk before a 1'o'clock bed

Friday 15 March [London]

Pack, correct some proofs, & deliver luggage at Bridges – where I am staying tonight. Then on to see Foss at O.U.P. about matters. See the Epstein (and Proctor) exhibition at Leicester Galleries after. His 'Behold the Man' impresses me terribly, both by the sublime simplicity & the seriousness of the thought. A great work.[52] The other bronzes are wonderful, but the other over shadows all.

Go to get Gramophone records (Wycks) & 2nd Hand music (H. Reeves) but not much success. Tea at F Bridges & supper – after which go to Maida Vale Studio where F.B. conducts a lovely & typical concert – the orch. playing as usual much better under him than anyone else. What is so fine about his shows are that he is content to give us the music – without the stunts of a Mengelberg or a Koussevitsky or the ignorance of a Beecham or a Boult. [Programme details continued above date]

Tuesday 19 March [Lowestoft]

I spend most of the day copying out the 1st mov. of the quartet, which has been a nuisance now for about 18 months – I do this to try & give me some self confidence in it, by seeing it look nice on paper, instead of on little scribbled scraps. This in morning & aft. (with walks before lunch with Mum, & before dinner John P. – lovely day) & evening. I am thrilled with my new records Mahler & Strauss (R) songs.

Wednesday 20 March

A marvellously warm day – typical summer weather. A long walk (7.15–8.30) before breakfast with John along cliff. Rest of day finish copy of the 1st mov. of S.Q. and letters. Go to Bungay for a typically miserable rehearsal. After a late dinner listen to first perf of Berg's Lulu Extracts. B.B.C. orch. under Boult.[53] Some of it seemed rather dull – but knowing Boult's performances of works one does know, it isn't fair to judge (this also applies to May Blyth who sang the solo badly) But even then, bits of it – esp. the Ostinato, & the Final Adagio were marvellously impressive, & alot very beautiful & simple.

Thursday 21 March

Another tropical day. John calls for me at 7.30, & we have a lovely walk. Work at parts of S.Q. all morning & aft. Walk to Library before lunch. Mum has her Care of Girls (Moral Welfare) Annual General Meeting, & as usual does all the work & gets none of the credit. I go for a long thinking walk along cliff before dinner – very lovely. Listen to a very good show of the Matthew Passion from Haarlem (via Huizen) cond. by Robert[?]. Some of this music is a bit tedious, but 90% of it is tip-top – the dramatic choruses, some of the recitatives, & the glorious end.

Monday 25 March

Rewrite parts of the Mov. of S Quart in morning[54] – I think it is all right now. Also practise pft. Walk before lunch. Badminton in aft., but not much good – play in a rabbit fashion. Walk with dog after leaving early. ~~After~~ Have dinner in drawing-room so that we can listen to ~~the~~ a concert cond. by F.B. 7.0–8.0 & the Wiener Saenger-knaben from Strasbourg at 8.0–9.30. F.B's show was very lovely – only section E[55] – so the playing wasn't very finished but full of vitality – programme inc. Merry wives of W. ov. – wonderful Rhythm Naile [?] Valse, Steppes of C. Asia, Saint Saens Tarantelle, & 3 lovely Slav. choruses of Dv.[56] The Boys as before sang some of their Motets out of tune – but, oh! the Zigeunerleider, & the Strauss Waltz!!!!!!!!

Wednesday 27 March [London]

All morning at BB.C. with L. Woodgate rehearsing 'I lov'd a lass' & 'Lift-boy' with Wireless Singers – me supplying the piano part. Lunch with Edwin Benbow at present – assistant choral-master there – this, a[t] Brasserie Universelle. Shop in aft. & see Arthur Benjamin at R.C.M. Back to change, & then tea with F.B. at Bedford Gardens. To B.B.C. at 7.15 for a short rehearsal before show at 7.30–8.0.[57] It goes v. well, but I have nerves somewhat. Grace comes here, & to B.B.C. Symph. Concert. cond. by Weingarten [Weingartner] at 8.30. His new finishing of Schubert E min. [major] Not very thrilling S. & mostly W. Lamond plays Beethoven C min. Pft conc. as dully as the orch. A better show of Liszt's Dante Symphony – which I really enjoy – It has some wonderful things in it.[58]

Thursday 28 March

See F.B. almost immediately after breakfast. Talk & go with him up to West End. Then see Boosey, – get Sinfonietta now published & take L.B. the very old song 'The Birds' which he's doing[59] – & then Frank at O.U.P. – get Te Deum now finished. Then lunch with John Alston at M.M. Club (which I am now joining) & then in aft see Charles Laughton in 'Ruggles of the Red gap' – a magnificent new film – acting & production 100% & Laughton being a genius.[60] Then see Barbara's new flat in Chelsea – meet Beth for a Lyon's supper & then go to Gallery to see Barnet's Folly, an unassuming & amusing play – in which Muriel Aked is outstanding – not great but v. charming[61]

Sunday 31 March [Lowestoft]

Music of to-day – on gramophone, the Sanctus – Benedictus of Beethoven D maj. Mass – for me perhaps the most lovely & greatest music of the world; some lovely Mahler & Strauss songs – on wireless, bits of Beethoven's Fidelio (thrilling); Brahms A min. quartet – bad workmanship & mostly dull; a bad show of Act I & II Fledermaus from Brussels; Shoshtakovitch's 1st Symphony – a miracle for a boy of 17, very uneven, but with some splendid imagination – This under Malko from London // Rest of day, walks with Beth – Colemans to tea, & letters after.

Tuesday 2 April

A typical spring day with violent rain & hail storms, interspersed with lovely warm sunshine. Walks before lunch & before breakfast & a lovely long one after tea along cliff – ending by being drenched. Work at Quartet – patching mostly – too many holes at present that it would be indecent to let it appear in public.[62] // John Pounder & I go to see Grace Moore in 'One Night of Love' at Playhouse after dinner. She is a very lovely singer, & off the operatic stage a good actress; but on it, she becomes stilted and too full of manerisms. Some of the lighter parts were splendidly done – n.b. Giovani – but the story had too many impossibilities – such as the 'double' conducting of Butterfly. But it was a treat to be given whole sections of Carmen & Butterfly, not little snippets – & the orchestral playing was fine[63]

Thursday 4 April [Lowestoft/Norwich]

Make an attempt to start mov. III of Quartet in morning – but it comes to nothing. Early lunch and catch (in evening dress) 1.46 to Norwich – where I meet Mrs Nora Back, Gwenneth B, Jack Moeran, & Robert Nicholls (a very nice man) at Andrews Hall, at a rehearsal of the evening concert. Go back to the Back's at 6.0. Play over with J. the 1st mov. of his new Symphony on the piano.[64] Dinner there, & then go on to the Phil. concert at 7.45. They do J's new Nocturne to a poem of R. Nichols, chorus well, & orch. better than expected. It is rather lovely – tho' v. influenced by Delius, yet somehow stronger.[65] Then they (cond. by H. Statham with I. Bailley, & R. Henderson) do V. Williams Sea Symphony – utterly dated – much too long – the truth is that I haven't been so bored for ages. After the concert I go back to a party at the Stathams, but only for ¼ hr The Colemans brought Mum over (she sat with me) & they bring us both back by 12.0 – & come & have some food here.

The printed parts of my Phantasy arrive – with one stupid mistake –
all the pages with rests contrived so that the violas may turn with ease
have been put at the left side instead of the right; which means that

they must be reprinted, or rather re-set. [written across entries for 5 and 6 April]

Friday 5 April [Lowestoft]

In the morning I write a short piece for oboe & piano, for Sylvia Spencer (Grasshopper)[66] but it isn't much use. In the aft. I go to Badminton – but the aft. is marred by my breaking Marjorie Phillips' best racquet against a radiator too close to the back line – costs me 25/-. Bill P. comes too – but the badminton is not excellent. After dinner Mum works at curtains or something, while I gramophone – Beethoven Mass, bits of Tristan, Till E., & some Mahler. Miss Ethel drops in for a short talk.

Saturday 6 April

Hunt for some words without success in morning as I feel in the mood for song writing – however let's hope it will last. Meet Beth from London at 11.39 – she has some fittings to do here. Our wireless conks in the aft. so we can't listen to Cambridge walking over Oxford [Boat Race] for the umpteenth time. Walks with Beth, & up to Cemetary – not that I think anniversaries mean a thing – what is one day worse than any other?[67] To the Astles in the evening; very pleasant – Miss Ethel presents me with all the Beethoven trios – very welcome indeed.

Monday 8 April [London]

Mum Beth & I all catch 8.30 to L'verp'l St. Very crowded journey. After depositing our luggage at Burleigh House (Beth going back to work) Mum & I go to see Elizabeth Bergner (who is just 'divine' – the only word for her) in Escape Me never[68] – a great show – overwhelming, with Bergner at her very best, & that's saying alot. This, at 1.0–3.0 – with Sandwiches in the place. M.M. Club to tea after until 5.0. Then Mum goes to Barbara to dinner – I go to a Lyons for food – then to a News cinema to see some Walt Disney masterpieces – a Silly Symphony (clock-shop) & Two-guns Mickey – Both lovely. Then go to Barbaras to collect Mum – Beth also comes for abit. Then back here in pouring rain, which alternates with lovely sun all day.

Min. score of Ob. Phantasy arrives v. nice

Tuesday 9 April [London/Prestatyn]

Mum & I take taxi to Euston to catch 10.30 to Prestatyn – very good journey – no change; lunch at 12.0 before Crewe. Bobby meets us and takes us back to Clive House.[69] See John in the afternoon – he is a fine lad – remarkably bright & intelligent for 2¾. Marjorie has been overworking but seems well now. Long walk with Robert after tea. Much talk after dinner – even a Peace discussion!!! and a bit of wireless.

Wednesday 10 April

A violent S.W. Gale all day – so fierce than when in aft. Robert & I go for long walk to top of the highest peak round here we actually can't keep our feet. Much pft. practise during day – I can't start my oboe pieces yet. A prospective parent comes to school – with possibility that nos. may be up to 20 next term. Listen to bit of B.BC. concert – an infernally dull & badly played Sonata for brass by Gabrielli – & a ditto Symphony in F min. by V. Williams (1st & I hope last perf.).[70] He has now 'developed' & is writing everything in a contrapuntal mixture of worst Bach-Cherubini-Stanford with rhythms of early Stravinsky – but Lor', the scoring!!! Harmoniums arn't in it!

Friday 12 April

I try again at Oboe pieces for Sylvia – but though I am nearer than I was – it still won't do. Walk with Mum down the village before lunch, & again in afternoon for Robert. Letters also at odd times. With John after tea – also cut lawn. Read, play pft. & listen to Contemporary concert after dinner. I may be a fool but Eisler's Kleine Symphonie & C. Darnton's Harp concerto seemed piffle to me – not even amusing – all this material ought to be in the waste paper basket. After this the Stravinksy Octet & Renard were heaven-sent. Not his best works – but so ~~efficient~~ confident & capable. The last especially is a gem of humour. Perf. hearty but moderate.[71]

Mum sends me (for Easter) a lovely box of candies and a Book 'And now all this' – very funny.[72]

Friday 19 April [Friston]

Have breakfast in bed – and spend most of morning suffering from effects of pill taken last night. In morning & after tea F B. gives me a great lesson on some of quartet – a good help. In aft. go for long walk with F.B. and Bi Oliver a girl – staying with M. Fass. Francis Barton comes over to see me & arr. about things for Tuesday after tea – (from Hastings). Listen to wireless (bit of St J. Passion[73]) & talk after dinner.

Saturday 20 April

Write some letters, and begin copying pft part of Grasshopper before going into Eastbourne to do some Easter shopping with the Bridges. Another lesson in afternoon with F.B. Antonio Butler & Mr & Mrs. Hiawatha Coleridge Taylor – who are all staying at Allfriston nearby – come to tea.

After tea, play about with balls on the fields opposite – & general fooling before they go at 7.45. A very lovely evening – while Mrs. B. goes along to see Miss Fass (still in bed), F.B. & I sit & talk & talk and watch the twilight & the lights on the downs.

Monday 22 April [London]
F.B. has B.B.C. rehearsal in morning. I do some work & have lovely walk in Kensington Gardens – Round Pond. In aft. we all go to see Cicely Courtneidge in 'Things are looking up' – a screaming Film with some superb acting from her.[74] Late tea – walk – late dinner & then F.B. conducts a string concert at Broadcasting House.

The orch. really isn't good enough – some of the fiddles being really bad – but alot of the concert is good. Arensky Tsch. variations – FB's Sally & Cherry, – Dvorak Serenade – too long, but some good things in it.[75] Mary Jarred bellows some good Deutschesreich-somes[?] – a fine voice, but nothing much besides.

Thursday 25 April [Hastings/London]
Up betimes, & Francis & I catch 10.10 to town – I incidently having revenge on my last night's Draughts defeat in the train[76] (on Mrs. Bridge's Easter present – a portable board etc.) arr. 12.2. I take him to lunch at M.M. Club & then deposite him on 1.30 to Plymouth.

Then I see Owen Mase at B.B.C. about Jobs – I shan't be there for a while, I fear. Back to deposite luggage at Burleigh House – a news theatre (lovely Silly Symphony – Peculiar Penguins), meet Beth 6.45 – Lyons – The Old Ladies[77], play by R. Ackland after H. Walpole. Spendedly acted with E. [Edith] Evans – the sole cast being 3 old ladies – it was eerie & frightening beyond belief – so much so that I go back to Beth's to sleep!!

Friday 26 April [London]
Get back from Beth's about 10.15. Odd jobs – shopping – then to Boosey's to see L.[Leslie Boosey] about matters – M.M. to lunch with Dorothy Wadham (very int. & amusing). 3.0. to Brechin Place to rehearse Grasshopper & Wasp with Sylvia Spencer – she is fine & I am very pleased with the little pieces. There to tea, after which I meet Walter Legge at the MM. Club at 5.45. long interesting talk. Then I go to dinner with Barbara alone at her flat. Back here by 10.45; then a little tea with Miss Wheatley.

Saturday 27 April
A most surprising day. Edward Clark's secretary 'phones at breakfast saying would I get into touch with a certain film impressario, M. Cavalcanti,[78]

which I do, with the result that I lunch with him (and another director Mr. Coldstream) at Blackheath – where the G.P.O. Film studio is – and that I am booked to do the music to a film on the new Jubilee Stamp[79] – only half-serious luckily. Talk much about this – go to Lewisham for 2 hrs (see a good Mickey Mouse) then back to the studio to see some 'shooting' – but I can't get definite instructions enough out of them to start work yet. Back by 8.0 – dinner – then spend evening with Barbara – Mrs. & Amrid Johnston also being there.

Monday 29 April

Go up to Soho to G.P.O. films[80] at 9.0 – see about things & then Horton (2nd in command) takes me down to Croydon to see an organist about details of a Cinema organ – in vain as we arr late (being held up for 20 mins in a broken down bus). Lunch there & return to Soho Square & more discussion.

Tea at M.M. Club & then I go to Academy to see 'The Man who knew too much'[81] again (& it wears very well – A. Benjamin's music is very apt) & a lovely little film 'Son autre amour' with some delightful children.[82] Walk most of way (having ham sandwiches) through Park to Bridges at 8.30 & then go with them & Brosas to B.B.C. where F.B conducts a typical concert at 10.0 – in which ~~a~~ lovely shows of Semiramide ov (lovely work) & Polonaise from Coppelia stand out. Buy some sandwiches & eat them outside a coffee stall near Kens. H. St. on way back in car.

Tuesday 30 April

Go to see Cinema Organist at Davis C. Croydon at 11.0. – very fine instrument but there isn't time in this film to get accustomed to it as an inst. Then come back lunch at M.M. Club late (owing to impossibility of any rapid movement in the tremendously crowded streets). I come back here in aft. & then set off for Blackheath at 5.0 to see what is so far ready of the film & to talk & to get scenario. Back here at 9.15 – via a meal at Lyon's Charing X corner house. Long 'phone talk with Beth.

Wednesday 1 May

Literal hell of a day. I spend the whole blessed day slogging at the film music in my room – with a watch in one hand and a pencil in the other – trying to make what little ideas I have (& they are precious few on this ~~Good~~ God-forsaken subject) syncronize with the Seconds. Have a short break for a walk after tea ~~But otherwise~~ (meeting Mrs. Johnson of the Princes Square days – in the park), but otherwise I slog away until abt. 11.0 at night – trying to concoct some rubish about a Jubilee Stamp.

Thursday 2 May

at 10.30 I go to Soho Square to see Cavalcanti about the film & have all my plans changed – I now have until Tuesday to write the music & all yesterday's panic was for nothing. Shop after this – go to Tatler cinema for an hour (2 Mickey Mouses – 2 Silly Symphonies & Life of a Gannet by Julian Huxley – v. fine).[83] Lunch at M.M. Club – meeting all the Alstons – Ethel Hobday – Jan van der Gucht – & Rebecca Clarke. Walk most of way back here. Go to Covent Garden at 6.30 for Tristan & I. Owing to a mistake I spend 1st Act standing in gallery, only to discover that Stall ticket had been left for me by Walter Legge in wrong office. So spend 2nd Acts in acme of luxuary. Leider, Melchior, Jannsen (Kurneval) Kipnis (K.Marke) [BB leaves gap here] (Brangäne) all at their bests. Leider is just a miracle – that heavenly voice – lovely acting – she was just born to be Isolde. Melchior was also fine – tho' not 100% in actual singing. Beecham wasn't bad, but not good enough. Some of it was bad & the orchestral playing not sensitive enough (not accurate either) But what a work! Heil Richard – that Act 2 love duet is heaven – all of it too

Saturday 4 May [Lowestoft]

Practise pft. and try & put thoughts in order for 'J. Stamp', but so far I can make no tangible improvements on Wednesday's work – tho' there are plenty to be made.

Long walks with Beth shopping before lunch & via the Cemetary in afternoon – which I loathe. Play a short amt of tennis (my 1st of season) 6.30–7.30 with her. Amusing but not excellent tennis. We're having fights about decorating our house for Jubilee (as everyone else); at present I don't think its right – too nationalistic.

Monday 6 May

Accession of King George V, 1910

The Jubilee is frightfully lucky in having such a heavenly day. We listen to broadcasts of a bit of the procession & service, but it's not thrilling. I am up pretty early, trying to think – but no luck all day.

Mum hires a car for us, & we all three take out lunch to Sotterly – & lie baking in the Sun. In aft. we go to Chartres – have some tennis with Beth & after tea with Clive C. Only see Clive & Mrs. C. – the others jubilating in the park with the villagers. Back (me driving part of way) by 7.30. Latish supper. Talk & late bed after packing & a 'phone talk with Kerstie.[84]

Wednesday 8 May [London]
Much telephoning & arranging matters at various times of the day. This 2^{d} a call takes an enormous amount of money. The whole day is spent in trying to improve on what I've already written of the film & in writing new stuff. Not very satisfactory in either case. Long walk at tea-time to Round pond. Go to dinner with Barbara. Long talks about troubles of life – rather overwhelming at the moment – she is very good & nice on these matters.[85] Walk home – lovely night.

Thursday 9 May
More sketching after breakfast, in afternoon & after tea. Go to see Bridges back from country at 11.0 on the way to Whiteleys for a hair-cut. Go to tea with Grace – who is just off to Covent Garden. Dinner with Bridges & go with them to one of H. Samuels Bach concerts in his week of Bach.[86] Very lovely playing – deliciously rhythmic – tho' personally I don't like all this amount of Bach at once. Then back to Bedford Gardens with them to listen to abit of Act III ~~from Cov~~ of Siegfried from Cov. Garden. Then much talk, & walk back here by 12.45.

Friday 10 May
Sketch abit more & score title music in morning. 'Phone calls. Lunch at M.M. Club with John Alston. I can do no more at Film stuff until I actually see the film completed. So take off afternoon & see at Academy Cinema 'The Brothers Karamazov' of Dostoievsky[87] – brilliant film by F. Otzep with Anna Sten, Fritz Kortner, Fritz Rasp – mostly good. Unfortunately it was cut, so very difficult to follow – because of censor. Go up to Beth's at 6.0 & play singles at her tennis club with her 7.0–8.15. Eat after at her flat. Back by long & very wandering bus-ride – because of colossal crowds to see flood-lighting.

Saturday 11 May
Have a very long & lovely walk in glorious weather round Serpentine in morning – trying to think. In aft. I do a little work before setting off for Blackheath at 3.15. Have tea there before seeing what is done of film – but I cannot yet get definite times & lengths. Walk on Blackheath after – very lovely. Come back in dense crowds – because of Jubilee. After a late dinner Miss Wheattly, Barbara, Beth & I all go to see Flood-lighting all along Embankment – St. Pauls (lovely) St. James Park etc. – fabulous crowds – so much so that we have much difficulty getting back & Beth misses – in spite of a taxi dash – the last bus – coming back here at 12.30 to sleep with Miss Wheatley, on a mattress on her floor!

Monday 13 May

Sketch abit in morning – but it is useless until I actually get the lenghtes of film.[88] Lunch with John Alston at MM. Club. Go down to Blackheath at 3.0. Hang about until about 7.0 (although I do measure some of the stuff myself) until I can get the actual timings. Get back here about 9.0 after a meal at Lyon's Corner House. Listen to abit of Götterdämmerung with Leider as a wonderfu Brunhilde – a long talk with a Miss Baillie – a pupil of Schnabel – tea with Miss Wheatly, before bed.

Friday 17 May

Finish copying what I did last night by 11.30 this morning – besides many telephone calls. Walk abit; lunch early; Mr. Rowe sends back what he has done of the copying by 1.45 & I go off to Charing X to meet Howard Ferguson who is playing 2nd pft for me (I play 1st & conduct – 3 inst. who work for G.P.O. often – Flute (Picc.) – Clar. & percussion). Work at recording from 4.0–9.30. It goes quite well – & is good fun to do. Cavalcanti is most charming & a marvellous director. Considering the hurry of everything, I think it is quite effective stuff & suits the film. Back via M.M. Club where I get some food by 11.0 – Tea with Miss Wheatly & bed – ah!!

Saturday 18 May [London/Lowestoft]

After doing a good bit of phoning & then pack my things together – I go down to Blackheath by 12.0. to hear the 'rushes' of yesterday's recording. Most of it sounds quite good. Then watch Cavalcanti & Stocks synchronising it before & after lunch with them. It is a marvellously clever work. Then dash back to town & to Liverpool St. & catch 4.54. back here. Mum meets me, & then dinner at 8.15. Beth arrived this morning. The Chartres come in after – Beth is making a dress for Mrs.

Sunday 19 May [Lowestoft]

Lovely day in which I do just nothing. Walk abit (with Beth & Mum before lunch) & with John P. before supper – read abit, & gramophone also slightly. Play hundreds of Strauss Waltzs & Polkas on the piano – relieves ones feeling – a definite fly in the ointment tho' is that I have picked up a flea in the train (they always are fascinated by me) & it is giving me absolute purgatory.

Monday 20 May

Find some words for another song to go into my boys' songbook (there having been a bother about some copyright) – but don't write any music.[89] Walk with Mum before lunch – Beth having gone back by early train. Walk up town in aft. to Morlings – get alovely book of Strauss Waltzs. After dinner John P. comes in to hear Act III of Tristan from Covent Garden – with Furtwängler – Melchior & Leider etc. A lovely show (tho' orchestra not 1st rate) – but rather spoilt by the fine enunciation of the prompter the whole time.

Wednesday 22 May [London]
Letters – telephoning – abit of work – thinking about fresh movement for Vln Suite.[90] Go to Boosey & Hawkes about various things: then I lunch with John Alston at M.M. See Trevor Harvy & go to B.B.C. with him – ther I go through my Simple Symphony with him – which he's doing at Oxford on Saturday – In the afternoon. Go to Howard Ferguson to tea at Hampstead – play 2 pft duets with him (La Mer – Debussy) – then have a meal at a Restaurant with Beth. Spend evening with Barbara & Helen & Mrs. Hurst at their flat in Chelsea

Thursday 23 May
Have a go at Moto Perpetuo for Vln & pft. in morning & aft. but not much good is forthcoming. Lunch at Bridges, up for a bit. At 4.0 go to Boyd Neel's Studios near here to hear his orch. rehearse my Simple Symphony for Sat. It is quite a good little orch. – but rather in need of a first rate conductor & musician to train in. Meet Beth & Lilian Wolff at MM Club for a snack dinner & then with Miss Wheatley go on to see 'Tovaritch' at Globe[91] with Cedric Hardwicke & Eugenie Leontovitch. Some splendid acting, but not a very good play Quite charming in spots but very slow.

To-day takes place the incredible Jubilee Concert at Albert Hall, arr. by dear Walford Davies. Needless to say, no serious musicians go.

Friday 24 May
Go to Soho Square G.P.O. Film offices at 10.30 to see some of the G.P.O. Films with Cavalcanti. A very lovely one on 'Ceylon' with good musical effects – tho' not perfect – some of the music not particularly int.[92] A lovely little comedy by C. 'Mr Pitt & Mr Pott' work of genius – which the charming English Distributors won't buy! – it being too silly![93] Also the famous 'Weather Forecast'.[94] Lunch at M.M. Club with John Alston & Mr & Mrs. Brosa. Practise pft. abit in aft. – the drawing-room being free for a wonder. Then up to Beth's Club for some amusing tennis – 6.45–9.0 Supper with her, & back here by bus at 11.15.

Saturday 25 May

Busy morning – 10.0. Go to see Mr. Arthur Elton at the Gas Light & Coke Co. about film jobs – but nothing materialises yet. After that have long talk again with Cavalcanti at GPO. & see some more films (inc. Spring on the Farm[95] – very charming & lovely). Then at 12.30 go to B.B.C. for a short rehearsal with B. Neel. Snack lunch at M.M. & go up to Beth (via B. House to fetch tennis kit) & have some good tennis at club. Bit of a meal at her flat at 7.0. & then she comes with me to Broadcasting House at 8.0, where the B. Neel orch. do my Simple Symphony really very well in a String concert. After that we refresh ourselves with tea at the MM. & then go to see a Mickey Mouse (v. good Silly Symphony – Bird Store) at a News Theatre – back by 11.45.

Monday 27 May

Spend morning at Queen's Hall at rehearsal of to-nights London Festival concert (B.B.C. orch.) Kousevitzky conducts – very impressive in the Sacre, but not so musicianly in the Pathetic.[96] But he knew his job, & wasn't afraid to say so – must have done this orchestra a world of good. Lunch M.M. Interview at Soho Square with Cavalcanti in aft. ~~after~~ about job. Meet Stephen Crowdie at 5.0. See Sanders of the River[97] at Empire – not very good; much too slow & boring with too much mediocre music quasi spirituels with Robeson. But saw for 2nd & 3rd times Walt Disney's Masterpiece The Band Concert. Eat in Lyons. Back at 11.15.

Tuesday 28 May

Go to Soho Square at 10.30 to meet Cavalcanti, Coldstream, & a Mr. Hudson of G.P.O. & we go to the Central Telegraph Office to see some details about new S.O.S. film.[98] Back to Soho Square where we see some of the Show copy of 'the King's Stamp'. The rest of it we see after lunch which I have with Grierson, (chief here) Cav. & Cold. It seems quite good. Then down to Blackheath to see bits of films to be remade. Back here for dinner. Just talk, with Miss Wheatly & sister & others after.

Wednesday 29 May

Walk abit & write abit (struggling with Moto Perp.)[99] before going to Blackheath via. a meeting at Soho Square before lunch, with Cavalcanti. Etc. Odd jobs at Films before a committee meeting on scrip of film on Mining[100] in aft. Grierson comes down to see about films after tea. Get Back to town at ~~7.45~~ 8.0 & eat at Bertorelli's with Coldstream. Back at 9.45 – cards play some Strauss Waltzs to relieve my feelings – & 'phone Beth.

Thursday 30 May

Work hard at M.P.[101] after breakfast before going down to Blackheath at 11.15. Stay there all aft. – working at script of 'Miners', but seem to waste ages of time as usual there – everyone is so slow, except Cavalcanti of course. Get away soon after 5.0 to meet Mum at Liverpool [Street] & she comes back here with me. Beth comes to dinner & Barbara soon after. Much talk before they go, about 10.15.

Friday 31 May

Mum shops & goes to Beth for lunch & tea. I go to Blackheath about 10.30 & work at script with Legg, Bond & Cavalcanti. This takes all day until 6.30 when Cavalcanti comes with me to the M.M. Club to meet Mum & Beth & we eat there together. At 8.0 we all go along to Soho Square to see the periodic 'Joints', shows of recent G.P.O. & other important films. See Stamp Film, many shorts, a very early 'Garbo' 'Joyless Street'[102] & a very lovely French one about 3 years old – by [Jean Vigo], Les Jeunes Diables à Collége – a perfect masterpiece, a revelation in many ways.[103] Back by 12.30.

Monday 3 June

Go off to Soho Square at 10.30 – & leave Mum to lunch here & catch 3.10 to Ipswich to stay with Aunt Jane. Spend morning & aft. at Soho & then to Blackheath 4.0–6.30 working at libretto of Mining film, with various people, & getting the full attention of none – hopeless job. Then eat at M.M. with Howard F. & to Queen's Hall for B.B.C. orch. under Toscanini – ticket from H.F. Rather unfortunate programme, as two works are anathema to me – Brahm's 4th & Enigma Var. of Elgar – tho' there were splendid shows of them. Cherubinis Anacreo [*Anacréon*] ov. also well played. But the climax of the evening was the Siegfried Funarel march which was overwhelming. T. has a flair for right tempi & the orch. played better than it ever had done under him – tho' even now it is not 1st class – sometimes not even capable.

Wednesday 5 June

Go to Soho Square at 10.30 – meet Coldstream – & then spend another morning at libraries etc. searching for appropriate words. This time however we are more successful & after lunch at M.M. we go down to Blackheath & work all aft. at the script – also with Cavalcanti. Some ping-pong before getting back to town at 7.0 – snack supper then dash to Covent Garden & queue for gallery – meeting Wykes an old Greshamian there & sitting with him; See Weinberger's splendid 'Schwanda' a super-show from beginning to end with most rolicking polkas etc. Lovely show. Elizabeth

Rethberg as Dorote & P. Schoeffler as Schwanda being superb. Heger conducted brilliantly – altogether a great show.

Thursday 6 June

Spend morning sketching music for 'Mining' film & also do abit more of Moto Perp. In aft. go, via Hawkes to see abt some proofs, to Chalk Farm, where Coldstream & I interview a Mr. Glyn Evans, a Welsh miner, ~~about the~~ for material for the film. He is a charming man & most helpful. Back to Soho Square where we work until 7.30 on the stuff. Then I go to Cinema House to see a very entertaining new American film 'Captain Hates the Sea' – with some lovely things in it.[104] Have sandwich at M.M. back 10.30 – tea with Miss Wheatly.

Saturday 8 June [Lowestoft]

Work most of morning & alot of afternoon at Moto Perp which I finish tho' it will have to be altered alot I'm afraid. Walk with Beth & Mum before lunch. Lovely sun tho' fearfully windy. Mum & Beth & I go to South Lodge sports (I very late) much against our wills in afternoon & are thoroughly bored, chilled & annoyed. Leave as early as is decently possible. Walk with Beth up town after. After dinner gramophone & listen to all the B.B.C. can spare us of Bohéme (3rd Act, ½ hr) Grace Moore as Mimi – lovely voice & in this stuff fine; but I should hate to hear her in anything more serious. Couldn't hear enough of others to judge.

Wednesday 12 June [London]

~~After~~ Up early & do some more copying ~~of~~ 8.30–9.30, then go to Blackheath via the city to get a further book on mining, at 11.0. Work down there on the script with Coldstream & Cavalcanti. Lunch at the local pub. Back to Soho at 5.30 with them; work there abit. Back here to dinner at 7.15. After that, finish the copying, & do further alterations; listen to Toscanini doing Le Mer of Debussy – an astounding performance of a really wonderful work. Also play pft duets with a Miss Bailey living here – Walton Facade.

Back by taxi soon after 1.0.

Thursday 13 June

Work all morning & as much of the afternoon as is free from 'phone calls (6 to the Studio!), at Coal-face film music. It's not going well yet. After dinner here I go to Queen's Hall with Cavalcanti & Walter Leigh – Szigeti vln recital (C. being a great friend of S.) Marvellous vln playing – In Bach C maj sonata especially. Ravel also was very good – & incredible virtuosity in smaller pieces after. Go afterwards to Mrs. Woodhouse's to a party with

Cavalcanti etc. to meet Szigeti – and meet hosts of very charming & interesting people.

After concert, go with F.B. & Brosas & friends to M.M. Back here at 1.15.

Friday 14 June

Work all morning & aft. Go at 6.0 to meet Szigeti (& daughter & accompanist) again at Soho Sq. while Cavalcanti shows him a film or two. He takes some of my music away to look at. Then after a hurried meal at M.M. I meet F.B. & go with him to last Toscanini concert. Mrs B. is staying with Miss Fass who's very ill, so I use her ticket. Mozart Haffner Symphony, Debussy La Mer; Mendelsohn Midsummer N.'s D – Nocturne & Scherzo & Beethoven 7th.[105] Of course he is a very great man – La Mer ~~was~~ is really great, & although the B.B.C. orch. isn't good enough for him (strings being really disgraceful, the Mozart was fine. But he did such strange things in the B. & M. The Trio of the Symphony was scarcely slower than the Schezo (thereby loosing much of it's point & all its grace), & the speeds of the Nocturne & Schezo were mad (the N. developing into a Waltz & the S. into a scramble – of course the orchestra couldn't play it). It may have been that he was worried, esp. as on Wed. the speeds were apparently even more erratic. Of course the crowd went mad, & of course they were right, he is agreat man.

Tuesday 18 June

~~Go~~ Do some more work at music 8.30–10.30. Then correct parts which arrive in morning. Steam down to Blackheath for lunch (approx.) & then spend afternoon on making sound effects for a 'Great line fishing' film[106]; to which Grierson's doing commentary. St. back to Poland St. Rehearsing rooms where for 4 hours (about 6–10) I struggle to make 18 members of the Covent Garden chorus fall in with my ideas – with some success in the end. Every one's very pleased with the stuff, & I must say that it comes off. Eat at Bertorelli's after with Coldstream, Bond & Hudson. Back by 11.30.

Wednesday 19 June

New parts arrive in morning. Copy parts of stuff I did yest. morning & correct & get down to Blackheath at 11.45 to continue in the music of 'Great line Fishing'. Finish this before lunch. In aft. prepare matters; then percussion, piano (Howard Ferguson) & two extra perc. from Blackheath Conservatoire[107] (to play chains, rewinders, sandpaper, whistles, carts, water etc.) arr. at 4.0; choir at 5.30 & 6.30; then with commentator – we rehearse time & again & gradually record, finishing with men at 12.0, & with commentator at 12.30. Return (like the rest of the crowd) by taxi at 1.30. with Cavalcanti & Grierson – absolutely dead.

Thursday 20 June

Go up to Soho Square to hear the Rushes from yesterday – mostly very good, but one or two disappointing. This with Coldstream, Cavalcanti & Grierson (who seems pleased). Then spend 1 hr at Tatler & lunch at M.M. Down to Blackheath with Cavalcanti to help him out. Meet David Green at 7.0. – dinner at Vicini's(?) – then with Beth & Barbara go to Haymarket to see the incomparable Ruth Draper. To hold the concentration of an audience for 2½ hours is in itself a feat, but to do it with such wit & real artistry is a miracle. The Jewesses, & Debutant[108] were like the rest 100%

Back here by 11.30 where I find John Pounder has arrived. Talk for ages.

Wednesday 26 June

Spend morning phoning & also do alot of work at Vln Suite. Lunch here, & straight down to Studio after. Here do abit more recording (sentance omitted by commentator) – & see film as it now stands in cutting. Basil Wright brings me (& Cav. & Grierson) back in his car, & we (2) eat in Charlotte St. & he comes to BBC. to here concert of Milhaud's works. Very charming & pleasant, but singularly unedifying – the most striking works being 5 Jewish Songs (splendidly sung by Mark Rapheal).[109] Back to M.M. after where B.W. & I have amazing (1st time for me!) game of Snooker with Mr & Mrs Brosa.

Saturday 29 June [Lowestoft]

In morning practise pft. parts of Stravinsky & Prokofiev Vln Concerti to play with Brosa next week.[110] Also do alot of re-writing of Vln Suite. Bathe & sit on beach with Beth & Doris Tamplin before lunch – Mum & Mrs T. also there. In aft. Kathleen & Peter Brook fetch us & take us to Chartres for tennis. Lovely afternoon – but play like the world's rabbit. Back before dinner at 8.0. After – while Beth 'fits' Helen Boyd have great discussions with Mum on her future – oh, these problems![111] Lights downstairs conveniently fuse before bed.

Monday 1 July [London]

Go to G.P.O. after over-sleeping – spend morning arranging matters & seeing people. See Ralph Hawkes before lunch at M.M Club. In aft. go to rehearsal of Oboe Quart. at Mangeot's, with Alec Whittaker (1st B.B.C. oboe. very good technique; but thin & piercing tone & bad intonation). To G.P.O. Unit at 6.0 to see Cavalcanti. Back here to Dinner – then after go to Bolton's

Cinema with John P. to see Duvivier's lovely Poil de Carotte with the glorious Robert Lynen. Lovely show – tho abit to long in spots.[112]

Tuesday 2 July
Last night was a night-mare – violently oppressive heat with tremendous rain, & occassional thunder. Let's pray that to-night will be better. In morning go to G.P.O – after working here – to see a Mr. Taylor abt. future 'short' on telegram.[113] Eat back here – in aft. André Mangeot takes me to play tennis at Melbury club – 3.15–6.45 – very amusing, but play vilely (partly because of smashed racquet). Then back – bath – & go st. up to dinner with Mr & Mrs. Brosa. Eat out at a restaurant nearby & then after, play with Mr. B. – my Suite & other things inc. Stravinsky Vln. Concerto. He is a superb. Vlinist. Back by 12.30.

Thursday 4 July
After much telephoning, business & rushing I go to Brosas at 11.0 for a run through the Suite, & then he comes with me at 11.45 to Boosey & Hawkes where he plays the work to Ralph Hawkes & Edward Clark. He plays it so beautifully as almost to persuade me it is a bit of music. Lunch at a Lyons with him. Go down to Blackheath for aft. working all time on B.B.C. band of Coal Face. Coldstream & I make an effort to go to a Cocktail party at Bazil Wrights – but arrive too late. Am late to dinner at 8.30. Letters & a few billiards with John before bed

Have a quick hair-cut before Basil Wright calls for me in his car at 10.0 & takes me down to Colwall (near Malvern). Very lovely journey
Friday 5 July [Colwall]
via Maidenhead, Oxford, Tewkesbury. Arr. 1.45 – lunch at Park Hotel where we put up. We come here to talk over matters for films with Wystan Auden (who is a master at the Downs School here – incidentally, Bobby was a master at the Elms, another school in Colwall). Auden is the most amazing man, a very brilliant & attractive personality – he was at Farfield, Greshams, but before my time. Work with him in aft. & then tea in Malvern. After that, watch the boys have a rag – with remarkable freedom – and then eat at the Park. After that have a drinking party with most of the Downs' Masters (about 7) – but very boring.

Saturday 6 July
Walk about the village – to the Elms & elsewhere – with B.W. in the morning. Also up to the Downs for 11'ses with Auden. Have lunch with the school in the dining-room – they are a remarkably nice lot of boys – very free with

the masters, but yet discipline is maintained – very sensibly dressed – most of them just in shirt & trousers. After lunch the Art master (Mr. Feild) shows us many of the boys' ~~draw~~ paintings (all in oils) & they are some of the most vital & thrilling things I have ever seen in modern art – so much so that B.W. & I prevail on some of them to give us specimens, & we leave with 7 or 8 priceless ones each. In the aft. there is a match versus the masters. We stay on & watch, as it is such a heavenly day & the grounds look so lovely with the white-clad little figures prancing about on the green field. One lad (David) makes a very fine century. After tea on the field, B.W. & I leave at 6.30 & go on to Whiteshill where Beth & Lilian Wolff have gone this aft. to see Aunt Flo. who gives us a meal, at 8.0. Go for a lovely walk over the Cotswolds for abit after & eventualy leave at 9.30 (B. & Lil. staying for week-end). Go, via Cirencester, Newbury, Guildford, Brighton, Newhaven, to the Wrights' cottage on the Downs just outside Seaford. Very lovely journey – arr. 2.30. ~~Ha~~ Tea, & welcome bed.

Wednesday 10 July [London]
Go to Soho Square in the morning to see Taylor & Cavalcanti about films – I have to do the sound for Taylor's abstract,[114] & make a short light suite out of some lovely Rossini songs (Soirée Musical, – which I hunt for in ~~the~~ many music shops before lunch at M.M. Blackheath in the aft measuring & finding out about the film on the 'Moviola'.[115] After dinner here – letters, abit of copying & try & get my accounts in order.

Thursday 11 July
Spend morning working at new Abstract film – it is a brute, fourteen small sections of about ~~eight~~ 8–20 sec. each. In afternoon, I go to the Bridges to meet Mr & Mrs. Eugene Goossens. T. Brosa comes too, & we play G's Lyric Poem,[116] & my Suite, & everyone seems very pleased. Stay to tea, & after that they take me to Selfridges where I buy a stop-watch. Very hot evening & I entirely succumb to hilarity with John Pounder – do no work & feel very guilty about it.

They take Bazil back to Hampstead (where he's staying) & then I have some refreshments at their place before they deliver me here.

Monday 15 July
Finish scoring of Telegraph music in morning[117] – it's too hot tho' to-day. Lunch at an Express diary [Dairy]. Work abit in aft. but succumb to heat & play billiards with John P. from 3.30–5.30. Then attempt to work until dinner. Bazil Reeve comes with me to the Bridges, who take us on to Maida

Vale B.B.C. Studio for a concert which F.B. conducts. Very small orch. (only 4 1st Vlns, 2 Vlas etc.). but even then some of it's not bad – esp. Beethoven 2nd Symphony & FB's lovely little 'Willow', Rosamunde ov. & Dvorak Slav dance in C complete programme.[118]

Tuesday 16 July

Work all morning at Rossini arrangements (complete March started yesterday, & do Canzonetta[119]). Go to Blackheath in aft. to see Cavalcanti about matters. Back to town with him by 6.30. Spend ½ hr in Nat. Gallery (see a lovely Cézanne & some thrilling El Grecos). Eat at a Lyons; back here soon after 8.0. Then working 8.45–11.45 do most of Tarantella arr. After that play billiards with John P. until 1.0 & then we tea with Miss Wheatly before bed.

Wednesday 17 July

Arrange more of Suite in morning – Mrs. Rowe comes to collect alot of it for her husband to copy, at 11.30. Work again in aft, & also go with John to Kensington Library to do some reference work. At 8.0 I go down to Blackheath, & thence on to Eltham to his home with Patrick Jackson (one of the staff of the Unit). Play tennis – lovely stuff – hard-hitting – I beat him although actually he is 15 better than I. Play 6.45–9.0 – cold bath with him, dinner, & back by 11.45. Do some more arranging (nearly finish last mov.) before bed at 2.0.

Thursday 18 July

Finish Suite at 11.45, & then chase round Hammersmith, looking for a copyist to finish work – find a Mr. Goldsmith, who seems satisfactory.[120] Back here – & do title Music for Legge's C.T.O. film. In aft. begin search for Clarinettist – eventually wiring to Manchester to Stephen Waters – tho' he can't do it. Blackheath at 6.0 to rehearse with Boys for Sat. – Blackheath Choir (choirmaster, a Mr. Cooper, there part of time. They are splendid little musicians & lap the stuff up esp. the Rossini Tarantella. Eat ices after with them. Back here at 9.30, buy some food, & have a little billiards with John before bed.

Saturday 20 July

Go down to Blackheath by 9.30 for recording. Instruments, Fl: John Francis; Ob: Sylvia Spencer; Cl: Johnston; 2 percussion from Blackheath (quite good) & Davie at pft. (rather disappointing) Starting rather late after 10.0 we rehearse and sychronise 'Telegrams' until 11.30. Then working at full speed with only hasty runthroughs record my Rossini Suite (which pleases me alot) & title music to C.T.O. In the Tel. & Ros. Cooper's 4 Choir-boys sing & speak splendidly. This is all done in such enormous speed because Sylvia had to catch a train to France from Vict. at 2.0. We actually finish at 1.15. Back to town, & then with John in aft. see Claire's very amusing 'Le dernier Milliardaire' at the Embassy[121] – dinner here & after trying various shows unsuccessfully – go to News Theatre & back here to Billiards & bed.

Tuesday 23 July

Go down to Studio on Soho Sq. where I meet & talk alot with Cavalcanti. At Studio work with Mac (Macnaghten)[122] for along time on cutting of Telegram abstract & B.B.C. band of Coal Face. Back to Town at 6.30. Spend ½ hour in Nat. Gallery (where I meet Arthur Benjamin), & then meet Henry Boys for dinner at S.F. Very entertaining evening. Back at 10.15 – 'phone Mum & Beth, then start to pack – oh! what a job!

Wednesday 24 July [London/Lowestoft]

Finish packing in morning & then at 11.0 John helps me take the baggage to Liverpool Street Cloak-room, & I then go down to Blackheath. Work there (arr. for B.B.C. a Suite for Stamp Music[123] among other things) with Mac. & Coldstream, & Spottiswood until 4.0. when I dash to Liverpool St. & catch 4.54. Back to Lowestoft. Mum meets me, & we have dinner about 8.30. Talk much after It is good to be cool.

Sunday 28 July [Lowestoft]

In morning Mum goes off to Gorleston to C.S. I work abit then bathe with Mr & Mrs. N. Vere-Jones – very interesting couple – ardent Communists. In aft. work slightly, then Piers Dunkerley & John Nevill come to tea. Bathe with Piers, & play cricket on beach with them. Tea with Mum in garden & afterwards, putt with them opposite. They are nice lads – & I am sorry that Piers is leaving. Play singles up with John Nicholson only play putridly – owing to bathes & tiredness. He brings me back & stays to supper.

Monday 29 July

Very windy & rather cold day. Work all morning – finish decent copy of Moto Perpetuo[124] & do bits of alteration in other movements – still tons to be done – this in aft. as well. Listen to abit of broadcast of Davis Cup doubles – in which Hughes & Tuckey beat Alison & Van Ryn [6–2, 1–6, 6–8, 6–3, 6–3] – thereby G. Brit. keep Davis Cup. Long walk after tea – part-way with Mum & then with Mr. & Mrs N. Vere-Jones. Wireless & Letters after dinner.

Thursday 1 August

Spend about 1 hour in Library, first thing in the morning looking up names for my Suite. Letters – many of them after that. In aft. Piers D., Honor Sewell (who might be a nice girl if she had been brought up sensibly – not 1 girl among 60 boys), & a very nice little French boy Pierre come to tea & bathe at hut. At 6.0 go up to Nicholsons for evening tennis and supper – to which Mum also comes – but play like a pig – when shall I ever get better?

Friday 2 August

Final version of boys' song in morning.[125] Before a bathe & read (Fascism, by Palme Dutt)[126] in sun on Beach. Go to tennis with Marj. & Bill Phillips at Vere Jones in aft. & play, most irritatingly, like the world's worst rabbit. Letters after dinner, & try to talk communism with Mum, but it is impossible to say anything to anyone brought up in the old order without severe ruptions. The trouble is that fundementally she agrees with me & won't admit it.

Sunday 4 August

Beth drags me out of bed before breakfast for a fiendishly cold bathe from hut. Gramophone, read, & generally slack in morning – except walk with Beth before lunch – & ditto in aft. Laurence Sewell, Fernande, her mother (Mde. Coronelle, who speaks no English), Teddy & Bobby come to tea. Listen at 5.30 to Alec Whittaker, André & his quart. playing my Phantasy – not so badly, except for wrong speeds at beginning and end, & a fearful swim inthe middle. After ~~dinner~~ supper Noggs & Mary Vere-Jones come in and we talk alot & play Lexicon.

Monday 5 August

After a little revising work after breakfast, we all depart about 11.0 in a car hired for day by Mum for Walberswick beach. Spend heavenly day, sun bathing &, sea-bathing Lunch, tea. Back by 8.0. (Beth drives there, & I drive back), in time to listen to Frank. conducting a lovely concert from B.B.C. The orchestra plays better than I've ever heard it, & F.B. is well on form which is saying alot. Parry's ov. was thrilling, & lovely rhythm in Weber-Berlioz Invitation to the Waltz – lovely work. but the climax was Tsch. very lovely & thrilling Romeo & Juliet – superbly balanced. Berlioz Faust pieces to round off with.[127]

Tuesday 13 August

Work at Violin Suite in morning & after lunch. Also pft practise in morning Lovely rough bathe – with David & Hilary Reeve. Long walk with dog in aft.

& singles with Teddy Rogers up at club 5.30–7.30. After dinner, Letters & listen to a fraction of Prom. Henry J. Wood is ~~becoming~~ a public menace – & ought to be shot quickly, before he does much more murdering of classics ancient & modern

Thursday 15 August

Try & work at Oboe Suite[128] in morning but no good. Practise pft. until 11.10 when Mum & I listen to Toscanini cond. Vienna Phil. from Salzburg Festival – what playing! Rossini over. Scuola di sieta [*Scala de seta*] & Mozart G. minor which was just superb.[129] // Bathe after with Reeves (Cyril & Hilary). Mum & I go with Marjorie Phillips to tennis at Tuttles at Oulton – Spashetts there – nice tennis. Listen to bit of Prom – Debussy & Ravel.[130] Maggie Teyte sings enchantingly – & Marcelle Meyer plays Ravel's distinctly attractive pft concerto brilliantly. Rest of programme (Lovely stuff – Mére L'oie, L'Aprés midi, La Mer) best forgotton because of H.J.W.

Friday 16 August

Piano – odd jobs (press shorts) – shopping walk – bathe with Hilary & another (very cold) swimming lesson, in morning. Tennis (very poor) at Boswells in afternoon – Tuttles there. Try to Listen to Tristan from Bucharest in evening but it isn't audible. Listen to a 1st perf. of a violin suite by Jean Francaix',[131] but not very distinguished, tho' pleasant French music, tho' 1st movement was very attractive. // Down to Station about 11.0 to meet Barb. & Beth from London.

Tuesday 20 August [Norfolk Broads]

Holiday rather spoilt for me by wires & telephone messages from D.F. Taylor in town about new music for a film. Spend long time in Potter [Heigham] in morning with Molly seeing about things. In aft. have a very lovely sail in Mayflower with Beth & David, accompanied by Puddleduck with Lucy & Marjorie – up to South Walsham. We all in evening drive over to Yarmouth & spend much money on Pleasure Beach. Have great time – esp on Scenic Railway which has some great moments. Back by 12.0.

Thursday 22 August

Another very windy day. We six (Stephen & Phillip go off working) take the two boats (Lucy Beth & I go in Puddleduck & return in the other) up to Ranworth Broad. Very exciting – Mayflower aground, drastic 'jibes', & we are rammed by a motor yacht while moored. But we have a heavenly sail back in Mayfl. – really thrilling sailing – underwater. Go for a short sail with Stephen before supper at 7.0. After which Lucy, David & Beth drive me back to Lowestoft – whence I must return for business. We go via the Scenic Railway at Yarmouth on which L, D, & I go four times running.

Monday 26 August [London]
The medicine [caster oil] having had its required effect (more or less, as it lasts all day!) I catch 10.0 to town. Go straight to Burleigh H. (where I must stay, till I find a flat) – various 'phone calls – eat out – go to Boosey & Hawkes on business – see Cavalcanti at G.P.O. (Soho Sq.) where it turns out that my holiday is u.p., having to work for them beginning next week. See parts of the new film of Taylor[132] (he is actually away) at 5.30 at Wardour St. Dinner at Bridges – very interrupted by our A.W. gang [?] – so much so that we three (F.B. Mrs. B & I) go to the Embassy to see a poor film with Anna Stern – Lady of Boulevards.[133]

Tuesday 27 August
Taylor can't see me till afternoon when I talk over matters with him & see the film etc. In morning I go to G.P.O. & see people – lunch with Coldstream. Lauricella comes to see me here at 5.0. Patrick Jackson takes me out to a Restaurant for a meal & I take him to the Prom. at 8.0 at which Brosa plays the Stravinsky concerto just splendidly. I think it is a good work – so musical & such style. F.B. conducts his early Dance Poem after the interval – some very very charming things in it – perhaps abit too obvious, but very beautifully scored.[134] Afterwards Mr. & Mrs. Bridge, Mr. & Mrs. Brosa, Edward Clark & friend, Pedro Morales & I all eat at Café Royal. Miss last bus back & have to walk most of way arr. about 1.30.

Thursday 29 August
With tremendous effort I get the film finished[135] – & off to copyists by 4.0. Then up to G.P.O. unit, to see Grierson & Cavalcanti. To Tatler Cinema – to see 5 Walt Disneys (bliss!). Then eat & to packed Prom. to Schubert Concert – stand – horrible! Meet Moeran – whose pleasant Rhapsody no. 2 is done – not really the kind of music I dote on, tho! Elizabeth Schumann sings alot of songs just superbly – with lovely sense of style & rhythm, but with an almost chronic sharpness which spoilt a little of it. But Morgen [Richard Strauss], & Du bist die Rüh [Schubert] were just A.1.

Saturday 31 August [Lowestoft]
Beth & I walk along cliffs with Victor about 10.30–11.0. Then another walk with her up town before lunch. Mum takes Beth & me to Playhouse in aft. to see Katherine Hepburn (who is very lovely) in Little Minister [136] – a very sweet picture, with some lovely shots – but overlong & spineless. Listen

to Fidelio from Salzburg – under Toscanini – with Lehman & Hellitsgruber, Jerger etc. – very lovely cast. A superb show – with wonderful orchestral playing (Vienna Phil) – but what a work. Astounding characterisation.

Monday 2 September [London]
Tremendous commotion to get Robert & fam. off to catch 10.3. to Prestatyn. I catch 10.0 back here. Go straight to G.P.O. at Soho Sq. after lunch to work at Negro film[137] with Auden (new recruit to G.P.O.). Coldstream etc. After tea with Auden I go to Wimbledon to see Elton about some more film music. Back here (Burleigh House) by 8.0. After sandwiches, John Pounder (arrived here to-day) Miss Wheatley & I go to a News Theatre.

Tuesday 3 September
Correct parts of Gas abstract[138] 'music' in morning & go up to G.P.O. to work abit with Coldstream. Lunch with him in Soho. In aft. record the gas. film music – 2.30–4.15 – it was very difficult to synchronise, & I am hopelessly inexperienced in such matters. Have tea after with John Francis & his wife Millicent Silver (Fl. & Pft for me). After dinner here, John P. & I go out to see Becky Sharp [139] (with Miriam Hopkins – very lovely & fine actress) – first full length colour film – some very lovely shots – esp. long distance ones. Flesh isn't good yet. Rather slow moving film – but some fine things in it

Wednesday 4 September
I go, after some 'phone calls, to Unit at 11.0. & work there, & in book-shops, gramophone shops (Levy – Whitechapell) & elsewhere with Auden at the Negroes Film. He is a remarkably fine brain. Meet John P. & Miss Wheatley at 7.30 & then go to see Bernard Shaw's Pygmalion at Cambridge Theatre by Maidon Players. It is, of course, a great & witty play – splendid stage craft. On whole, well done – Esmé Percy being splendid as Higgins

The V.W. was played by Tertis, with forced tone, bad intonation & no style whatsoever.

Thursday 5 September
Spend morning with Elton at Wimbledon about film music. Work with Auden in aft at Soho Square. John & I go to prom in evening (ticket from BB.C.) – vile, the only interesting things being Busoni's Rondo ~~Ach Archles~~ Arleschinesco – which was very exciting & of course R.K's Cap. Espagnol which was pure gold after the exaggerated sentimentalilty & nobilmenti of Elgar's 1st symphony, I swear that only in Imperialist England would such a work ~~by~~ be tolerated – tho' of course it is well done – which is more than

could possibly be said of Vaughan Williams Viola Suite[140] – bad in work & idea.

Friday 6 September [London/Lowestoft]
Spend day at G.P.O. working at Script. See Taylor after lunch – trying to get more money (a mistake in the fee given me, & for copyist) – but without sucess – £10 for a film like that, seems rather ridiculous to me – & others. Meet David Green & John P. who takes us down to Lowestoft ~~by~~ in his new [car] (a very nice B.S.A.[141]) – starting at 4.30. Arr. after very pleasant tho' rather cold (it's an open car) at 9.10. Beth & Mum at home

Saturday 7 September [Lowestoft]
Spend most of morning taking down the best of Cavalcanti's. S. American folk-song records. for Negro Film. Kit Welford comes over for lunch. He, Beth, Mum John P. & I go down for a bathe (I, as a matter of fact, undress, but water is so cold, that I don't bathe). In aft. tennis at Woodgers, & tea at Meads. Beth, John Nicholson, Kit, Kathleen M., two very nice French – Simon & Clement (staying with Walkers.) Beth & Kathleen Mead go off for a film after dinner – K. coming for that here. Mum & I listen to wireless – a very fine and interesting programme on American Negro – by Alistair Cooke.[142]

Monday 9 September [London]
Work with Auden all morning first at Spender's (a friend of his) and then at Bridges (whose piano I use. Lunch with him. Go to BB.C. for rehearsal with Wireless Singers (under Woodgate) of my little 'Hymn to Virgin' in aft. It goes quite well. Tea there – shop after & hair cut at Whiteleys. John & I go to dinner at Bridges and to B.B.C. at 10.15 – where F.B. conducts (brilliantly) a concert with the small orchestra. The tour de force was a glorious piece of Busoni from Indianishes Tagebuch (dance of the Spirits) a fabulous piece of colour & design. Also Mendelssohn's very charming & really beautifully wrought Italian Symphony. Orchestral playing not bad – considering –.

Thursday 12 September
Work all morning at 'Title music – & many arranging telephone calls. See Coldstream at Soho Sq. & have Lunch with him. In aft. I take out young Piers Dunkerley. John P comes too. We go to '1066 & all that'[143] which is riotously funny – tho' perhaps abit consciously superior in its humour – tho' the episode at 'Poonah' is one of the funniest ever (Strand Theatre) We have tea at Strand Palace after & go most of way back to Battersea with

Piers – he is a very nice lad John & I go to first half of prom – actually proming. I haven't been so insulted for ages as to have to listen to Arthur Bliss's new Film music – 1935.[144] Not even amusing – dull – violently badly scored & outraging every principle of taste – & – Lord, what chances he had! Kodaly's brilliant Hary Janos Suite & Berlioz 'Carneval Rom.' were only bright spots in programme. (Soloman played – brilliantly enough – Rachmaninov's efficient tho' intellectually vulgar 2nd concerto)

John Francis (Fl.), Alan Frank (Cl) Walter Price (Vln), Bernard Richards (Vlc) – Millicent Silver (Pft) play for me at session

Monday 16 September [Friston/London]

Mr & Mrs. B. take me in, through pelting rain, to catch 9.36 to town – actually train is late in starting & I get to town 20 mins late at 11.30. Back here – correct parts, & business. Meet Alan Frank for lunch & then go down with him to Wimbledon at 2.30 – for recording of my 3 title musics & Vict. sequence (I dreamt that I dwelt) for Elton at Gas Company. It goes quite well. Back here after tea out. After dinner, letters, & David Green takes me (John P. comes too) to meet Beth from train at Liverpool St. at 9.59. He takes her back to Finchley road where she gives us tea. Back here by 12.0.

Tuesday 17 September

Spend day with Coldstream & Auden in Soho Sq. & British Museum etc. Doing work for Negroes. I always feel very young & stupid when with these brains – I mostly sit silent when they hold forth about subjects in general. What brains! // Go with A. to the Westminster theatre where the Group theatre are doing some of his plays[145] – go at 6.0 but don't stay for any of the rehearsal. Beth comes to dinner & after, she, John Miss Wheatley & I go to see Jack & Claude Hulbert in a bad but funny film Birthday Jack

Thursday 19 September

Work all day with Auden & Coldstream. Things go much better & we make alot of decisions (notably, to have commentary sung as a recitation). John P. & I go to Prom. in eve. (tickets from B.B.C.). Russian pro. makes a brilliant flying start with Russlan & Ludmilla ov. Oda Slabodskaya sings (badly) 3 Mossolov songs – rather uninteresting – some squibs that don't quite come off. Helen Perkin plays competently, but without initiative Prokofiev's very attractive 3rd Conc. then Shoshtakovitch's 1st Symph which has some fine things in it, (notably in 1st mov) but is obviously the work of a very young man – of whom very great things are expected.[146]

Mr & Mrs Sewell (S. Lodge) come in for coffee & stay till 12.0.

Saturday 21 September [Lowestoft]

Go to see Laurence Sewell about some dental trouble at 10.0 Luckily not much to be done – but more later. Play & practise pft. alot in morning & aft. Walk with Barbara & Mum before lunch. Aunt Q. is at work at some portrait painting (Pop for Aunt Flo.). Putt with Barbara in aft. I develop a foul cold. Walk with Aunt Q. along beach – after tea, she is very nervy & suffers from a terrible inferiority complex poor thing.[147]

Wednesday 25 September [London]

A very disturbing day. I do one title music in morning when I am sent for by Cavalcanti (back from Portugal) & who wants to see what we have written of Negroes – not very much. Spend afternoon with him, Auden & Coldstream seeing films, discussing plans (I hope to be able to put off the recording of this film from next Wed (!) to 16th). Also Cavalcanti shows me his lovely silent film 'En Rade' which I am to improvise for (1 hr in length!) next Friday.[148] I feel as depressed as sin consequently. Do some writing (one new title music) & play cards with John, Miss Wheatley & niece, after dinner

Friday 27 September

Finish Legg's stuff & post it to copyist in morning; then to Soho & work & lunch with Cavalcanti on Negroes. Again in aft. Back here at 4.30 & practise pft. Suffering violently from nerves. After dinner early John comes with me up to Joint – where show takes place besides Cavalcanti's lovely 'En Rade' – they show Taylor's 2 Abstracts (my music), Coal Face (ditto) Elton's Housing Problem (v. fine), Rotha's Face of Britain (so-so) & some quaint old French Films of 1904 (3 shorts). My improvisation to En Rade goes better than possibly could be expected – since it lasts over the hour! I honestly enjoyed it – tho' I wish I could have seen it more than once (& then without pft). It caused quite a sensation! I also play little scraps during the French films

Tuesday 1 October

Spend all day at Blackheath – 1st recording in morning, with Legg – telephone apparatus noises & after lunch title musics & 2 sequences for 5 documentary G.P.O. Films (Fl, Ob., Cl., Fg., Perc., Pft – John Francis, Sylvia Spencer, Alan Frank, Cecil James, Mr. Plowman & Millicent Silver). It goes quite well. After that try a bit of commentary for Legg. Then back – in my absent mindedness sailing out to Peckham Rye. After a meal, John & I go to Tatler Theatre for a very enjoyable Walt Disney ~~evening~~ hour inc. 5 very lovely shows. not. Water Babies & [illegible] olden times.

Wednesday 2 October

Business & correct parts in morning – also go up to Levy's to hear more Negro records. In aft. I go down to Wimbledon to record Eltons 1935 sequence (Men behind Meters) – Sylvia Spencer takes me. (Fl. Ob, Vln, Vlc, Pft. Perc – A. Marriot, S.S., Eileen & Olive Richards, Leonard Isaacs & Mr Plowman). It really sounds rather lovely. Practise pft. alot when back – & letters. Go for a short time to cocktail party at Spencers at 6.30. Meet David Green & go to Ballet: de Léon Woizekovsky (who is supberb). Best of All Stravinsky Pulcinella – superb all round. El Amor Brujo – disappointing in setting and altered for the worse in choreography. Divertissement very charming & a really riotously abandoned Prince Igor dance

Thursday 3 October

After having appealed to the League [of Nations] since January – Abbyssinia is to-day attacked by Italy.[149] Great indignation & excitement in London – Evening Newspapers doing a roaring trade. // Go up to Soho Square in morning & work with Auden & Coldstream on Negroes – much of which has to be altered for Grierson, as being too 'flippant' & subjective. Lunch with them & work again in afternoon, this time with Legg on other films. Meet Beth & tea with her & Auden, after which she & I flat hunt without success. I eat with David Green & two friends of his – Taylors – nice people, after which we go to Ballets Jooss. which are very good in spots – Big City & Green table[150] – having lovely things in them – poorer music, but some good dancing & lighting.

Friday 4 October

The War continues, enormous number of casualties – Abyssinian reverses – to general sorrow. So [No] sign of League activity as yet. Still enormous excitement – esp. round Soho. I have lunch with a German Jew refugee – Robert Turner, a very intelligent communist – who has some interesting projects ahead. I work with Coldstream at Joint & abit here in aft. In morning go to rehearsal of Betty Humby & Stratton Quartet – for whom I turn over in the evening at Grotrian Hall. They play an interesting & very young 6^{tet} (Vln, 2 Vlas, Vlc, Cb & Pft) of Mendelssohn – very immature, but surprisingly original. Very capable writing too. Good old Dvorak 5^{tet} too.[151]

Saturday 5 October

Work at Negroes music in morning. Go up to Beth's for lunch & for long & wearying flat-hunt in aft. All over Hampstead – but more [?] success. In

1 The Britten family home in Lowestoft from 1908 to 1936. Benjamin's caption: 'Back to Lowestoft / December 1934 / 21 Kirkley Cliff Road'. Photo: BB.
2 Benjamin's parents, Robert Victor and Edith Rhoda Britten, in the garden at Kirkley Cliff Road.
3 Benjamin and John Pounder in the garden at Kirkley Cliff Road.
4 Benjamin, summer 1928, aged fourteen.

5 J. R. Eccles, Headmaster at Gresham's School, Holt, 1919–35. Portrait by Hugh Riviere.
6 Benjamin's music tutors at Gresham's: Miss (Joyce) Chapman, Walter (Gog) Greatorex, and Hoult D. F. Taylor, photographed outside the music room.
7–9 Gresham's School Chapel, with Benjamin from Farfield House photographs taken in the summer of 1929 and 1930.

10 John Ireland, Benjamin's composition teacher at the Royal College of Music, 1930–33.
11 Studio portrait of Benjamin aged seventeen. See diary for 2 May 1931. Photo: Boughton, Lowestoft.
12 Benjamin's private teacher and mentor, Frank Bridge, with Marjorie Fass and Ethel Bridge, at the Paris Exhibition in 1937. See diary entries for 1–5 October 1937. Photo: BB.
13 Arthur Benjamin, Benjamin's piano teacher at the Royal College of Music, 1930–33, photographed outside the RCM on Prince Consort Road.

14 Studio portrait of Benjamin aged twenty, inscribed to his first music teacher: 'To Miss Ethel / Everlastingly gratefully / Benjamin Britten'. See diary for 27 November 1933. Photo: Swaine, London.

15 Robert Victor Britten with Caesar, the family's Springer Spaniel.

16 Barbara Britten (right) with her life partner, Helen Hurst, Lowestoft, July 1934. Benjamin's caption: 'Barbara & Helen Hurst on beach'. Photo: BB.

17 Bobby and Marjorie Britten, with their first son, John, Lowestoft, August 1934. Photo: BB.

18 Edith Rhoda Britten at Kirkley Cliff Road, 1934, the summer after she was widowed. Benjamin's caption: 'Mum / in garden: / Aug 26th'. Photo: BB.
19 Benjamin and his 'paramour' Francis Barton, Hastings, 1934. See diary for 31 August.
20 Piers Dunkerley and Kit Welford on Frinton beach. Benjamin's caption: 'Kit & Piers D fooling'. See diary for 6 September 1936. Photo: BB.
21 Benjamin escorting Beth into Peasenhall Church for her wedding to Kit Welford, 22 January 1938.

22 W. H. Auden, Hedli Anderson and William Coldstream, Colwall, June 1937. Photo: BB.
23 Benjamin and Sophie Wyss, Crantock, August 1936. Benjamin's caption: 'Self & Sophie looking at Hunting Fathers'. See diary for 26 August 1936.
24 Peggy and Antonio Brosa in Barcelona at the 1936 ISCM Festival. Britten's caption: 'Toni & Peggy Brosa on Tibidabo'. See diary entry for 22 April 1936. Photo: BB.
25 Ralph Hawkes, Chairman of Boosey & Hawkes.

26 Alberto Cavalcanti, producer, director and sound engineer of the GPO Film Unit, 1933–40.
27 John Grierson, Head of the GPO Film Unit, 1933–37.
28 Montagu Slater, poet, playwright, and librettist of *Peter Grimes*. Photo: Enid Slater.
29 Rupert Doone, co-founder and chief director of The Group Theatre, 1932–39.
30 W. H. Auden and Christopher Isherwood, China bound in 1938. See diary for 19 January. Photo John F. Stephenson.

31 Lennox Berkeley, Crantock, July 1936. Benjamin's caption: 'The composers at work'. For the companion photograph of Britten, taken by Berkeley, see *Pictures from a Life*, Plate 86. Photo: BB.

32 Wulff Scherchen at The Old Mill, Snape, 1938. Photo: Enid Slater.

33 Peter Pears in the late 1930s.

34 Benjamin Britten in the late 1930s. Photo: Enid Slater.

evening John & I go to Westminster Theatre to Group Theatre season. See Rubert Doone's ~~season~~ production of T.S. Eliot's Sweeney Agonistes & W.H. Auden's Dance of Death. Both very exhilerating & interesting shows, splendidly put on (Décor & very lovely masks by Robert Medly) & acted. A's play is a very serious contribution to literature. I go back with Doone & Medley to their flat after the show & talk till 1.30 about possible music for Timon of Athens[152] – very nice men

Sunday 6 October

Misty day, which after gets out to & very fine but cold. Go up to club with Beth for tennis (quite good) 11.30–5.0 – with lovely walk along Hampstead Heath before coming back here for a meal.

The Abyssinian war continues a pace. Adowa apparently being captured – tho' the general opinion is that Italy will get the worst of it. The League meanwhile falters & hum's & ha's. Will meet again on Wed to decide who is the agressors!

Monday 7 October

I write at film all morning here – & go up to Soho Square in aft. to see Auden & Coldstream about ~~the~~ various details. Also see a negro Harry [BB leaves a gap here] about a Calypso which he sings very well – and take it down.

In evening, I go to trade show of Eltons new gas films[153] (to which I have done music). They are very lovely, most of them – especially 'Gas Production'. This at Prince Edward Theatre.

Tuesday 8 October

The Italians begin to use poison gas in their 'civilisation' of Abyssinia.

I go up to G.P.O. after working here all morning in afternoon. to work with Auden & Coldstream. Lunch with Bernard Richards to fix about continuing our trio.[154] Also 5.30–7.0 rehearse with Lauricella at Bridges. He is a very silly person & an awfully bad musician. Mum comes up to town from Frinton – where she's been staying – to see the place. She's staying here. In evening Grace Williams comes in to coffee. She is a very nice person.

Wednesday 9 October

I go up to Soho Square after breakfast. Coldstream takes in our completed script of Negroes to be 'corrected' by Grierson.[155] There is an amount of diverging opinions on this question! Lunch with Auden, & Rupert Doone in Soho. Some nice talks. I work back here at film – most of afternoon – feeling very livery tho'. Mum spends day with Beth, who comes back here for dinner & the night. Barbara also comes after dinner.

Friday 11 October [London/Lowestoft]
Sanctions are being discussed at last at Geneva. General opinion seems to be of disgust that so much time has been wasted. They ought to have been discussed in January.

After working all morning, Mum & I go up to Hampstead Heath. Meet Beth at 1.30 to look at a possible flat. I come back to Unit at 2.30 & work abit with Auden – who is off to Switzerland for the week-end. Then meet Beth & Mum at Liverpool Street to catch 4.55. & travel home arr. 8. odd. It's cold here. Feel pretty groggy inside.

Monday 14 October [Lowestoft/London]
Beth & I catch 8.30 back to town. Have lunch (bread & cheese) in my room back here. Work at Negro film abit before going to B.B.C. for rehearsal of 'Hymn'.[156] Then via Hawkes & Unit to Draper's Hall (Throgmorton St.) for a rehearal by Dr. Darke & his St. Michael Singers of my Te Deum – not a bad choir, but non-pro. consequently little balance. This at 6.0. Dash back to B.B.C. in time to hear Leslie Woodgate do my Hymn to the Virgin – with 2nd choir singing thro' echo room – which really sounds lovely. Otherwise it was a good show too. Eat out. 'Phone Mum when back here. very early bed

Tuesday 15 October
Work at Negroes film all morning. Lunch at M.M. with Auden & Mr. Cooper (Choirmaster). In aft. go down to Studio & work with Legg & Pawley (sound electrician) on general Sound problems. Also work with MacNaughten (sound cutter). Back here for many letters, bath & go to Bridges for dinner. After dinner & much talk go with them to Maida Vale BBC. Studio where he conducts a concert. Best orchestra – but terribly lethargic, & slack. Mozart 'Eine Kleine Nachtmusik'. Marcelle Moyse (the most heavenly flautist) plays Ibert's dull but competent Flute concerto brilliantly. But the orchestra (in spite of F.B's sensitive guidance) can't get anywhere near the subtleties & incredible beauties of the 2nd Nacht musik from Mahler's 7th Symph. // A wisdom tooth of mine starts trying to come through – very unpleasant sensations.

Wednesday 16 October
Up betimes and catch 8.15 to Norwich. Breakfast on train & am met at Norwich at 11.11 by Rubert Doone & Robert Medley who came down last night to work on Timon of Athens with Nugent Monck who is producing it for the Group Theatre in Nov. I am doing what little music there is. We work with Monck on it, both before & after lunch at his house. He is a very

pleasant but acid man, with a quick brain. Catch 3.40 back to town with, R.D. & R.M. Dinner in – feeling dead to the world with this infernal tooth. However with much doctoring Miss Wheately manages to expel some of the pain.

Atmosphere – France, Italy & England seems to get thicker every moment.

Friday 18 October

I eventually (having tried one man – too busy) go at 10.30 to see Barbara's London dentist Mrs. Harwood – very efficient – who just says it's a wisdom – tells me what to do, washes & generally eases it. After which I work back here all day – except for an excursion 3–4 to Whiteleys for haircut. Go out to dinner with Alan Frank & wife – a very nice evening, esp as Adolph Hallis comes in for coffee – a very entertaining man.

Saturday 19 October

David Green takes Auden & me down to Blackheath by 9.30 to give us some practical help in the new recording of Telegram Abstract film (Fl, Ob, Cl, Xyl. & Glock, Perc. & Pft) with Cooper's lads – one of which Harold [blank] does all the talking & very efficiently & dramatically too. This takes all the morning. In aft. after a late lunch here, I go up to Beth's & eventually ~~after lunch~~ go up to tennis. But violent winds prevent us playing much & we shop abit – eat out & finally[?] at 8.45 go to Group Season at Westminster to see Besier's very witty & artificial comedy 'Lady Patricia' with Phyllis Nealson Terry in a first-rate character study.

Tuesday 22 October

Go, at 10.0 after having finished a respectable copy of the Dance, to see Doone at Group theatre. He likes the Dance, but after much discussion we decide it's not suitable & must be redone. See Coldstream after this, & then meet at Oddenino's a Mr. Lortorov for whom I am probably going to do some music soon – films again. Then after some food at a Lyon's, I go up to see the owner of the flat we are looking at (West Cottages). & who agrees to most of our requests Thereupon decide to take it. 3.30 go to ~~Group~~ Westminster Theatre to see Medley's lovely sketches for costumes of Timon of Athens. Then to Bridges house, where I practise 5.30–7.15. Letters after dinner & early bed, to make up for last night.

Wednesday 23 October

Spend morning at Unit – talking over many things – finding incidently that Lortorov, with whom I am negotiating, is probably nothing but a crook! In aft. Cavalcanti, Coldstream, Auden, & Wright & I go up to Highpoint, Highgate

(W's rooms) (with Mr Stern a possible tenor solo) to try over & discuss the Negro music. Not very fine results. Back & more discussion with Auden & Coldstream. I take A. out to dinner after which (but not because of which) he is very sick, but better after, & then he comes with me to Queen's Hall for B.B.C. concert under Boult. Berg's Lyric Suite (3 movs.) arr.for Str Orch. being attraction. But the performance was only a Kensington drawing room apology for the wild, sensuous & beautiful music. [Continued above date] Carl Flesch, gave a deadly dull Deutscher professor show, with a suet-like accompaniment from Boult & his boys of the Beethoven Concerto. After this we fled.

Saturday 26 October

Tremendous rush all the morning. Have to see Doone (which I do at Bridges) about Timon. I know my ballet is still unsatisfactory, but it is very difficult to please these people with preconceived ideas. Meet Beth at 12.0. But don't have time to do much furniture shopping. Try to play tennis at Hampstead in afternoon, but too cold & dark to do much. Meet Henry Boys in evening – he is a nice person. Eat with him & see Mae West in Goin' to Town. She is a very great personality.

Tuesday 29 October

Spend morning at Westminster Theatre – seeing Herbert Murrill (Musical Director of Group Theatre season) & Rubert Doone about Timon music. The latter is pleased now. Lunch with him & Robert Medley. Long pft. practise in aft. Then I have a bath, change into tails (ugh) & after dinner here, go with Rubert Doone to opening night of Michel St. Deny's production of Giono's lovely 'Showers of the Hills' at the Westminster. A truly beautiful & thrilling show.[157] I escape before the general party after and when I get back (by 11.0) Miss Wheatley gives me tea in her room – very pleasant too.

Friday 1 November

Work at Timon music until 3.0 in aft. – but don't do anything decent – then go up to play for Ballet for Rubert Doone until 4.30 at Group Theatre. Here some Harpichord records after that (with Herbert Murrill) trying to find out what it really sounds like. Then a long talk on infinite subjects with Ralph Hawkes. I go to Contemporary music concert at B.B.C at 10.20 with Grace Williams – more ~~to trim~~ for duty than for pleasure, as the concert (entirely Krenek) was just the acme of pedantic dullness.

Monday 4 November

Am very prolific for 2 hours after breakfast, when I write 2 funeral marches for Timon. After that, go up to G.P.O. & see Cavalcanti. There is absolutely no money now; I seem to be out of a job there, & Negroes seems definitely off. Very depressing. However I play my Timon music to Rupert, & Nugent Monck who are very pleased. Lunch with them. I spend afternoon hunting for furniture & general shopping After dinner, John & Miss Wheatly both come up to flat & help me (& Beth later) finish staining floors.

Wednesday 6 November

Spend morning working with ~~an~~ spasmodic packing & sorting. Get up to ~~Beth's~~ the flat by 1.30 via Soho Square. Spend afternoon until 4.30 here collecting furniture, laying carpets etc. Then go to Boosey & Hawkes to collect proofs of my Violin Suite. Back to Burleigh House to dinner – after which I meet Grace & take her to B.B.C. Symphony Concert – Harty conducting – efficiently not always in best of taste tho', being somewhat extravagant.

A mod. exagerated show of Don. Juon. And 1st. complete Perf of. Walton Symph.[158] A great tragedy for English music. Last hope of W. gone now – this is a conventional work, reactionery in the extreme & dull to a degree. .

Sunday 10 November

One snag about this flat life is the time taken up by household jobs. Certainly we arn't up early (breakfast at 10.0 – up at 9.15) this morning but even then there is no time for anything except washing-up, bed making etc. before leaving for Barbara's at 12.15. Perhaps when our incomes are larger we'll be able to afford help in this line. Had lunch & tea with Barbara (all 3 of us) I go to S. Ken. Nat. Hist. Mus.[159] with her in aft to see some very lovely Nature photos. Back here by 6 30. I work alot at Timon. Aunt Effie comes for evening meal. After, I listen to wireless (certainly the best way to make me like Elgar is to listen to him after Vaughan Willliams) Also write 50 odd change of address cards.

Monday 11 November

Have a colossal day – finishing score (20 odd pages) of Timon & getting it off to copyists – arrainging about performers, about future films (if any), & numerous things to do with flat. Mum stays here all day – except for shopping excursions – & works at flat. Mrs Trainer comes in 6.0–9.30 to clean & cook our dinner. Do accounts after dinner – so far I have spent just on £40 on flat, Beth £30 odd & Mum £13 – not bad considering that we had practically nothing.[160]

Tuesday 12 November

I go down to Tring with Watt, Pat. Jackson etc., to do with G.P.O. film – T.P.O.[161] – in order to shoot some railway sound. Spend an interesting but very chilly day at the Station. Back to flat & warm bath by 7.30. Mum is here, has shopped & met people all day. After dinner & washing-up I do proofs, proofs, proofs, nothing but proofs – of Violin Suite. Consequently – late bed at 11.45.

Back to flat with Mum, to find Beth dealing with a severe leak of pipe through our cealing – this incurs plumbers & things & general confusion. But we have a pleasant if late evening.

Wednesday 13 November

In morning – after household oddments go to Westminster Theatre for rehearsal – getting cues right etc. Lunch with Rubert Doone, Robert Medly, & Ernest Milton. In aft. I go to Boosey & Hawkes to play over alot of Shosteckovetch's very fine Lady Macbeth[162] – to Ralph Hawkes (He may become agent for it). Also he mentions a possibility of my having a settled income from B & H. Then to St. Michael's Cornhill, with Barb. & Mum – Harold Darke gives a fair show of my Te deum (which makes me blush) at his Festival. Also some dire works by WH Harris & Darke himself & mod. one of Bax.

Friday 15 November

Stay in all morning; odd jobs & correct proofs of Suite – a very long job. Go to Theatre soon after lunch (by 2.30) & have to settle many things with Greenwood (a director) & Murrill the musical director – it is frankly impossible to get good players to play for £5 a week – which is all the Theatre can put up. To G.P.O unit after to see Cavalcanti & Coldstream about things – then back here. Barbara comes to dinner – a hot one as Mrs Trainer is here. Proofs, talk, & 'phone Mum about odd things – inc. pft. – after.

In evening after we shop Beth goes out with Kit Welford, & I go up West with Pat – eat & a news theatre – but above all – much very good talk.

Saturday 16 November

Work very hard at Suite proofs in morning before taking them up to Boosey's at 12.0. Then along to Lewis' Westbourne Grove, where I decide to have the £50 gôr & Kallman piano I looked at the other day – I wanted a 2nd hand Steinway, or Blüthner – but the flat wouldn't take it – actualy the men have a tough job when they bring this piano in aft. But it seems a nice instrument & a bargain. Pat Jackson comes in aft. for tea & a long walk on heath with Beth & Howard Ferguson who turns up.

Sunday 17 November

Not up early, & by the time we have cooked, cleaned, & washed up it is 11.0. Then work at Timon music till lunch. Kit Welford comes to lunch & Beth has the greatest difficulty in getting him gone before supper to which Lucy & Stevan Crowdy come & for which there is of course, just the right amount! In the afternoon I go from 2.30–6.30 to West. Theatre for first band rehearsal – everything goes wrong – bad playing, & of course a small spinet isn't powerful enough & there isn't room for a larger . . . .!!!

Monday 18 November

I start work at G.P.O. Films again to-day. Work – first at Soho Square at 10.15 & then later at Blackheath on a new film T.P.O (Railway Post) with ~~Cavl~~ Cavalcanti & Watt.[163] Meet Herbert Murrill at 4.30 & go instrument (harpsichord or like)–hunting until 6.45 without success, with the result that at 8.0 (after a meal with Mr & Mrs M.) with dress rehearsal ready to start we have no instrument! However a brain~~way~~wave of H.M. save situation – we stick drawing pins into the hammers of the theatre piano & result – a fine harpsichord of considerable power & volume! The rehearsal doesn't go badly – as rehearsals go. Back here by 12.0.

Tuesday 19 November

To Soho & Blackheath during morning & early aft. to work on T.P.O – but very little is done as yet. Back here by 5.0 to rehearse a little Vl. & pft with Lauricella. Beth comes with me at 8.30 to 1st night of Group Theatre production Timon of Athens at Westminster theatre – Nugent Monck production. Ernest Milton – Timon (very fine esp. in 2nd half). Harcourt Williams as Apemantus. Ballet by Rubert Doone, very lovely decor by Robert Medley, music by me – played by Sylvia Spencer, Miss Mellier, (Oboes & Cor Anglais), Mrs Murrill (Piano – harpsichord!), Tony Spergeon (percussion) under Herbert Murrill – it goes very well – Beth & I don't stay long at party after – so as to catch last 'bus home.

Thursday 21 November

Go to G.P.O. in morning for a talk with Cavalcanti about things. Then I go with Coldstream to Bluthner Studios to hear two Viennese pianists (Rawicz & Landauer) who wish to do some film music – brilliant pianists but indifferent musicians. After lunch a time with Booseys. Back here in aft – to think about some title musics for G.P.O. Grace Williams comes in after dinner (which Mrs Trainer cooks for us) to talk & help me with my violin Suite proofs.

Wednesday 27 November

Go to Office all morning & afternoon & work first with Cavalcanti – & then with Miss Spice for whom I am doing a new film probably – until 5.0 when

I come back here & rehearse with Lauricella. He has a meal with us – Beth going out afterwards, & he stays on until 9.30. Listen to Bliss's new Music for Strings[164] – dull, remenescent (stinks of Elgar) conventionial, dated before it was born. This music won't do at all.

Friday 29 November [London/Lowestoft]
Household jobs, shop & then catch 12.25 from Liverpool St. to Lowestoft with Remo Lauricella. Lunch on train – Doris Tamplin meets us, & takes us home to tea. Rehearse abit at Royal Hotel, dinner at home (Beth there at 6.0 too) & Remo & I then give recital for Mum's Lowestoft Ass. for Moral Welfare at R. Hotel. Over 100 there – & it goes really well, tho' personally I suffer badly from nerves esp. in my solos (Ravel, Jeux d'eau, Chopin Nocturne & My fun-fare[165]). R. plays some solos, & with me, Handel A. Son My Suite (3 movs) & Nardini E min Concerto – + encores galore. After – Mum gives small party – to which Kirsty Chamberlin & Meg O'Farrell come too.

Sunday 1 December [London]
Up betimes (with aid of Mum's Xmas [birthday?] present to me – a fine repeater alarm clock) at 7.30 – eat alittle, & leave here at 8.0 – & don't arrive at Blackheath before 9.20, on account of lack of transport. From then till 12.30 help Watt record stuff for his T.P.O Film – which done up to town to help Miss Spice with hers at Whiteleys[166] – hundreds of children in Xmas department & I have to look after many, but interesting very poor ones. This lasts till 9.0. when we eat, & I get back here at 10.30. We should have gone again to Blackheath for Watt, but he lets me off – thank Heaven!

Monday 2 December
Go to Soho Square in the morning & spend most of time talking – music, & film-music in general – with Wright, Watt, Cavalcanti etc. Have lunch with Montagu Slater at Bertorelli's, & talk over sounds for his new Easter play. Then in afternoon to B.B.C. to have a talk with K.A Wright & Clark about my future music. See Slater & his orchestral leader again before going to Marble Arch Pavillion to see [Walmsley's] Call of the Tide with A. Benjamin's not very good music – this film has some fine things in it – Lovely shots & some splendid types in – but is for me mostly impressive in what it suggests (sea that I adore so much) than what it actualy presents.[167] In evening listen to a light concert cond. by F.B. including Vaughan Williams, rambling & interminable Lark Ascending

Tuesday 3 December
In morning I write a short sequence for Slater's Easter 1916 play. Also shop – & practise pft.

In aft. go up to G.P.O. Unit & see Watt & Cavalcanti etc. Then on to Ralph Hawkes for a short interview about my royalty guarantee & also to play over to him some Glière – which he wanted to hear. Mrs Trayner cooks me a meal before I go out to Timon again at West – Mr & Mrs Bridge come too. I should have gone to Basil Wright's to a party after but I leave the Westminster too late.

Wednesday 4 December
Go up to Soho Square after breakfast & see people. I am only working 3 days there this week (£3 per week). Then back here to begin scoring my Rossini Suite (partially changed) for small & large orch. simultaneously (for B & H). Very interesting & helpful lunch with Bridges. Back here to work in aft. David Green comes for food & then he goes with me to Islington Town Hall to see Slater's Easter 1916 in a try out show before the A.E.U.[168] There are some excellent realistic scenes in it.

Back here at 8.0 – Beth has Elizabeth Nicholson to a meal – after she's gone much talk – discussing undiscussable subjects

Friday 6 December
Go up to Soho Square after breakfast to find I'm not wanted until this aft., so see Boosey & Hawkes about matters & come back here for a work on Rossini & lunch. Basil Wright takes Cavalcanti & me to Blackheath to discuss T.P.O film music – & I have as a result, as usual, a pretty violent inferiority complex – these people know so much! – but this is somewhat eased, by my going to a rehearsal of Goodall's choir of St. Alban, Holborn when I take them through my Te Deum – & they are flattering to say the least.

Saturday 7 December
Very foggy to start off with, but it clears later with rain – but, thank God, it's a bit warmer than the last week or so – I have never known such cold, gas fires make no difference – the trouble of having been brought up in the lap of luxury! Work at Rossini all morning – shop (household goods) in aft. at Golders Green with Beth. Barbara comes to dinner, which Beth cooks – joint, greens, potoatoes – fine work: then we 3 go to Last night of Timon – but very depressing audiences – almost but not quite enough to damp the excitement of the superb 2nd half.

Sunday 8 December
Up late, at 10.0 – breakfast 10.45 – much household work, continued by Beth after I go up to Phoenix Theatre at 12.0 for band rehearsal – back by 2.30 – meal (sort of tea) letters etc. meal at 5.45 (sort of dinner) then to Ph. Th. again for another short rehearsal before show at 8.0 – Slater's Easter 1916 – a much tighter show than Wed. tho' still it needs some pulling up & revision – it shows S is a newcomer to the stage in many ways – but it has some great things in it & a good sense of audience. A fine house & reception with a moving speech & appeal for Left Theatre by Ellen Wilkinson after.

Monday 9 December
Work all day at sound of T.P.O at Blackheath with Cavalcanti & Pat. Jackson – with whom at 5.0 I go past Harrow to listen to trains themselves – in pouring rain & very wet grass. He comes back here for a meal at 7.0 which we prepare ourselves. Listen to Pro Arte playing Milhaud's new 8th (or is it 80th) Quartet – which seems heavy & dull. Lennox Berkeley's new one seems just dull too – but witty & bright ending to 1st mov. Sophie Wyss also sings charmingly.

Wednesday 11 December
Spend whole day in (apart from little shopping jaunts) working (a) in office hours on T.P.O sound (b) on Rossini. Meals in, too – have slight tragedy in cooking potatoes, which boil dry. In evening, go with Grace Williams to Queen's Hall to hear A. Boult sterilize Purcell's very lovely King Arthur – what a lovely style of prosody Purcell has! and fine sense of instrumental colour. Performance (apart from BBC Chorus) was scandalous. Super refinement – without style or taste – string playing as dead as nails – Boult at his worst & most typical

Thursday 12 December
Work here all day – copying parts of new T.P.O. sequence & when thats done go on with Rossini – all in living-room here with fire – as it's best way of thawing these days. Bernard & Irene Richards come at 4.10 for short Trio rehearsal. Go to a meal at Bridges before going up to Clerkenwell for an AM.O. concert which FB. conducts – the only place for hearing really good string playing nowadays. ~~A~~ lovely shows of In der Natur (Dvork) Francesca da Rimini (thrilling) & a good one of Brahms Sym. 2 which is anathema to me now.

Colossal indignation of all parties – on the preposterous 'Paris-Peace proposals for Abyssinia. Cabinet endorses them & tries to induce Italy & Abyssinia to accept them. [written above 16/17 December]

Monday 16 December

Tremendous Household matters (fire clearing, breakfast setting, getting & washing up, bed-making, washing sorting, & sending away etc.) from 7.30 to 9.30. Then to Blackheath all day – seeing about sound for T.P.O. Then at 7.0 to dinner with Barbara and Helen at their flat – good & large dinner and very interesting talks after – but I talk too much & too long these days & don't leave till 10.40 so am not back till 11.30.

Tuesday 17 December

Spend morning till 1.30 at Studio. Go to a Walt Disney show at Cameo News Theatre on way back to Joint (Soho Sq.) at 3.15. More business there & back here for a bath & more work at 5.30. After dinner listen to a B.B.C. (pretty poor) show of Mahler's wonderful Fahrenden Gesellen songs – absolute peaches. Toni & Peggy Brosa come in to coffee at 9.45–11.45 – very lovely & amusing people.

Dramatic news at midnight of resignation of political scape-goat – Foreing Secretary – Samuel Hoare.

Wednesday 18 December

Go to Blackheath (via business at Soho Square) all morning to prepare for afternoon's recording of train noises (realistic imitations ~~but~~ by compressed steam, sand-paper, miniature rails, etc.) for T.P.O. It goes well. Also have a tiny scrap of re-dubbing for old 6^{d} Abstract – for which a Blackheath little boy comes along to talk. After, at 6.45 meet Henry Boys & bring him back here for a meal & much very pleasant discussion. Beth & I talk & discuss very late – till 1.0 – generally get annoyed (tiredness), but it helps our brains abit.

Thursday 19 December

Spend morning & aft. at Soho Sq & Blackheath, hearing disappointing 'rushes' of film music of yesterday – fault of technicians, I'm afraid.

Go to rehearsal with Goodall's boys[169] at Holborn 7–8 – they're good. Back here for meal – & listen to very disappointing account of the Socialist's loss of to-night's debate / also long talk with F.B.

Friday 20 December

Blackheath all morning – seeing films, talking etc. After lunch to town – to B & H. & then to Soho Square to talk finance & performing rights.

Satisfactory. Then 6–7. go to St. Albans to take the choir boys thro' my 'Boy'. Eat – Newstheatre – meet Rudolph Holzman (see Florence, & Paris) & his brother & Bazil Wright at B.B.C. & ~~then~~ go to Contemporary Concert – Paradise Lost of Markievitch.[170] Very capable & brilliant young man – but with rather a stereotyped & conventional mind – as strict as Cherubini & people. A very nice party at MM. after – till 1.0 – + Bridges & Brosas. Basil takes R. & me back home in his car

Monday 23 December [Lowestoft]
Write a long letter to Mrs Chamberlin (Kersty) in defence of Communism – not a difficult letter to write! It has shocked alot of people that I am interested in the subject! Shop 12–1.30 – Xmas Presents. I am preparing two Grocery (& Coal & meat etc), parcels for poor families here – Barbara helps me choose them in aft. Shop after with her too. Do up parcels, letters after tea – Mum meets Robert, Marjorie & John & Aunt Effie off 6.0 train (1½ late). somwhat disturbed evening.

Go for a very long & mysterious walk – 10.30–11.30. Think alot about Alban Berg.

Tuesday 24 December
Deliver two parcels to my two poor families one in morning & other in aft. Very depressing – & so unnecessarily so. Help to decorate St. Johns most of the morning with Barbara & the Phillips. Shop in aft & long walk with Basil Reeve. Beth arrives by 8.4 (1 hr late) after dinner. I meet her. Hear that Alban Berg dies. This makes me very miserable as I feel he is ~~the fi~~ one of the most important men writing to-day. And we could do with many successors to Wozzeck, Lulu & Lyric Suite. A very great man.

Sunday 29 December [London]
After much house-work for me, Henry Boys arrives at 11.30 & we then go for very long walk to Hendon where Bridges tell me the Marguerite recording studios are. Eat at Hendon & bus back here & spend afternoon talking (Berg), gramophoning (Mahler Kindertotenlieder) & playing (Berg – Wozzeck). Tea with Bridges – very nice, & a drive after; eat before going to BB.C. at 9.25 for show of my Boy was Born by BB.C. Chorus under L. Woodgate & St. Alban's boys (fine) Apart from a contretemps in Finale it goes well – beginning fine & some very exciting. I can't help but like this work, as I feel it is genuinly musical. Woodgate takes us after to Maida Vale where F.B. conducts a concert. Then back (+ Brosas) to Bridges & good food & talk – then Bridges drive us back by 1.45.

Tuesday 31 December

In all morning – force myself to write a title music for T.P.O. Film Lunch in (Bread & cheese) & after Auden comes & we work here all afternoon on the sound of T.P.O. I go to Prom. concert at Queen's Hall with Remo Lauricella (having eaten first with him) for Tschaikovsky evening, in which Toni Brosa plays the Vln Concerto – qua violin, marvellously – the slow movement being a ~~miral~~ miracle of beauty – but excessive virtuosity & speed robbed the music of something in places. The rest of the programme was popular Tsch. but very great & lovely. This man is of course maligned & scoffed at out of all reason now. So it is really rather fun admiring him so – more than their 'National' Moussoursky – the Vaughan Williams in excelsis (tho' of course of infinitely more value!). I refuse the pressure of the Brosas to go and be merry at the M.M. Club – because I hate these shows. Instead I come back here & listen to alittle of my Boy records in bliss. Outside people seem very merry & bright – but only surely because 1935 is departing – <u>much</u> reason for <u>rejoicing</u>.

Notes: 1934–1935

NOTES: 1934

1. Work continues on *A Simple Symphony*.
2. A recording with the Berlin Philharmonic.
3. *Tommy and Grizel* (1896), semi-autobiographical novel drawn from the author's own marriage, by J. M. Barrie (1860–1937).
4. Though Mrs Britten never withdrew her attendance and support for St John's Church, there is evidence that, encouraged by Ethel Astle and clutching at straws in the face of her husband's advancing illness, she turned to Christian Science as a last hope.
5. *Nijinsky* (1934), biography by his widow, Romola de Pulszky Nijinsky (1892–1978), assisted by Lincoln Kirstein.
6. A production from the Vienna State Opera conducted by Clemens Krauss.
7. The ISCM Festival to be held in Florence in April 1934; see 5 April.
8. Cinema House, Oxford Circus, London W1.
9. This was the world premiere of Bridge's *Phantasm* for piano and orchestra (1931).
10. Ireland *Legend* for piano and orchestra (1933).
11. Moeran *Rhapsody* No. 2 in E for orchestra (1924; rev. 1941).
12. Rossini *William Tell* Overture; Tchaikovsky *Chant sans paroles*, Op. 40 No. 6; Gounod *Funeral March of a Marionette*; Offenbach 'Barcarolle' from *Les contes d'Hoffmann*; Louis Ganne *Marche Lorraine* and *Le Père la Victoire*.
13. Bridge Violin Sonata (1932).
14. Hindemith Trio No. 2 for strings (1933).
15. Beethoven Trio in C, Op. 87, for two oboes and cor anglais; Serenade in D, Op. 8, for string trio.
16. Britten was to abandon this project and the manuscript has not survived. It reminds us that writing concert overtures to order was never Britten's forte. The two 'Occasional' overtures of 1941 and 1946 (the first written in America for Artur Rodzinski, the second for the launch of the BBC Third Programme) both remained unpublished during his lifetime, and *The Building of the House*, Op. 79 (written in 1967 for the opening of the Maltings Concert Hall at Snape) is perhaps one of his least successful and infrequently performed works of the 1960s.
17. A radio adaptation of *Trent's Last Case* (1913), the detective novel by E. C. Bentley (1875–1956), the first in which his gentleman sleuth, Philip Trent, appears.

18. The Suite, Op. 15a, for tenor, baritone and chamber orchestra, from Shostakovich's satirical opera in three acts, *The Nose* (1928), a dramatisation of the classic Gogol novel.
19. *Bloody Mary's* (1934), novel by Geoffrey Dennis (1892–1963), written as an autobiographical account of a young schoolboy in an English public school around the turn of the century. Despite Britten's unhappy experience of life at Gresham's, he nonetheless enjoyed such novels.
20. Woodgate was to conduct the premiere of *A Boy Was Born* on 23 February 1934.
21. *Hell Divers* (1932), early MGM aviation film with Wallace Beery and Clark Gable.
22. From '*Go play, boy, play*'.
23. *The Red House Mystery* (1922), novel by A. A. Milne.
24. The Viennese string quartet led by Fritz Rothschild, formerly a member of the Kolisch Quartet.
25. *Whither Britain* (1934), a series of talks for BBC Radio by George Bernard Shaw, in which he exploited the medium to air his controversial views on social equality and the evils of capitalism.
26. Britten could be particularly harsh about his fellow musicians, even those close to him and whom he admired. It became clear over time that he was a greater admirer of Brosa's technical virtuosity than his musicianship or interpretative gift for the classics.
27. A BBC Radio adaptation in English of Kästner's *Emil und die Detektive*.
28. This initial meeting would eventually result in Britten's collaboration with W. H. Auden on the orchestral song-cycle, *Our Hunting Fathers*, Op. 8; see 25 September 1936.
29. Weber Overture to *Oberon*; Brahms Piano Concerto No. 1 in D minor, Op. 15; Vaughan Williams *Job, A Masque for Dancing*, ballet conceived by Geoffrey Keynes and Gwen Raverat, based on William Blake's *Illustrations of the Book of Job*, (1927–9).
30. Wagner Overture to *Der fliegende Holländer*; Borodin *In the Steppes of Central Asia*; Saint-Säens *La fiancée du timbalier*, Op. 82, a setting of Victor Hugo for mezzo-soprano and orchestra; Tchaikovsky Symphony No. 4 in F minor, Op. 36.
31. *Liebelei; A Tragedy of Love and Honour* (1933), romantic melodrama directed by German film-maker, Max Ophüls (1902–57).
32. *A Boy Was Born*, Op. 3.
33. The premiere of Britten's choral variations, *A Boy Was Born*, Op. 3, given by the BBC Wireless Singers octet, BBC Wireless Chorus (Section A) and the Choristers of St Mark's, North Audley Street, conducted by Leslie Woodgate, at a BBC Concert of Contemporary Music in the Concert Hall of Broadcasting House, London W1.
34. Members of Mangeot's International String Quartet had given both the broadcast and concert premieres of Britten's *Phantasy*, Op. 2 with Leon Goossens (for whom it was written) in 1933, but they were not available for

the ISCM Festival performance on 4 April 1934, which would be given by Goossens with members of the Griller String Quartet (Sidney Griller, violin, Philip Burton, viola and Colin Hampton cello). Britten was clearly put out by this, even though he could be very critical of Mangeot's violin technique, as many of his diary entries show.

35. More tales from the ghost story writer, A. J. Allan, much loved by the young Britten.
36. Unidentified.
37. The cast also included Walter Widdop, Tudor Davies, Parry Jones and Mary Jarred.
38. Britten has by now reverted to the original title, 'Alla marcia', for this revision of the new *All'introduzione* movement of '*Go play, boy, play*'.
39. Britten was writing his programme note and personal biography for the ISCM performance of his *Phantasy*, Op. 2 in Florence.
40. Lalo *Symphonie espagnole*, Op. 21, for violin and orchestra; Debussy *Nuages* and *Fêtes* from *Nocturnes* for orchestra (1897–9).
41. Holst *Lyric Movement* for viola and chamber orchestra (1933).
42. The department store on Oxford Street, London W1.
43. *De Vriendt goes Home*, a fascinating novel by the German/Jewish pacifist writer, Arnold Zweig (1887–1968) that explores the themes of religious tolerance, pacifism and homosexual persecution, all themes close to Britten's own life and work.
44. *Reunion in Vienna* (1931), popular romantic drama by Robert Sherwood (1896–1955), playing at the Lyric Theatre, Shaftesbury Avenue, London WC2.
45. *Lo scoppio del Carno*, medieval Easter festival event at the Duomo in Florence.
46. *1860* (1934), epic film directed by Alessandro Blasetti (1900–87) made during Mussolini's rule to spur patriotism, celebrating the exploits of Garibaldi in the liberation of Sicily from Bourbon mercenaries.
47. *The Way to Love* (1933), romantic comedy directed by Norman Taurog (1899–1981).
48. For the ISCM Festival performance of his *Phantasy* oboe quartet on Thursday.
49. Giuseppe Muré *Two Sicilian Songs* and Alfredo Casella *Introduction, Aria and Toccata* for orchestra (1926).
50. Thirty years later Britten was nonetheless inspired to write his very fine *Nocturnal after John Dowland*, Op. 70, when confronted with the special gifts of the guitarist Julian Bream.
51. Britten *Phantasy*, Op. 2; Henrik Neugeboren *Piano Trio*; Richard Sturzenegger *Cantata* for mezzo-soprano, flute, oboe d'amore, lute, viola d'amore, viola de gamba and cello; Leopold Spinner *Quartettino* for strings; Jaroslav Jezek Sonata for violin and piano; H. E. Apostel *Cinque liriche* for voice and piano; Lars Erik Larsson *Sinfonietta* for strings.
52. *Fra Diavolo, or The Devil's Brother* (1933), a Laurel and Hardy spoof, based on the Auber opera about the famous Italian brigand leader. This chance encounter with 'Young Wulff Scherchen' was to have a greater and profound

significance, when Wulff resurfaced in Britten's life in the summer of 1938. See Postlude.

53. His father's long drawn-out illness, as painstakingly documented in Britten's diaries since 20 May 1932, was finally diagnosed as Hodgkin's disease, a cancer of the lymphatic system. He finally died of a cerebral haemorrhage in the final stages of lymphadinoma.
54. Bach *St Matthew Passion* (BWV244): 'In tears of grief, dear Lord, we leave Thee'; Britten 'Jesu, as Thou art our Saviour', Variation 3 from *A Boy Was Born.*
55. William Hockey battled with a drink problem for much of his life and was eventually hospitalised; it was a problem that also plagued Mrs Britten's mother, as Beth Britten recalled – see *My Brother Benjamin*, p. 17.
56. Bizet Overture *La Patrie*, Op. 19; Grieg *Peer Gynt*, Suite No. 1, Op. 46.
57. Debussy *Jeux*, ballet written in 1913 for Diaghilev's Ballets Russes, one of Debussy's most progressive scores.
58. Stravinsky *Mavra*, one-act opera buffa with a libretto by Boris Kochno after Pushkin (1922); *Les Noces*, dance cantata for soloists, chorus, four pianos and percussion (1923).
59. A final revision of *A Hymn to the Virgin*, the first of *Two Choral Songs* (1930), into the version that we know today, published by Boosey & Hawkes in 1935.
60. Britten is now revising the second of his *Two Choral Songs* (1930), *I Saw Three Ships*, revised again in 1967 as *The Sycamore Tree* and published by Faber Music the following year.
61. Leonora's powerfully dramatic recitative 'Abscheulicher! wo eilst du hin!' (Accursed one! Where hasten'st thou!) and aria 'Komm Hoffnung' (Come, hope!) from the end of Act I of Beethoven's *Fidelio.*
62. 'Mir ist so wunderbar', the Act I quartet for Leonore, Marcellina, Rocco and Jacquino.
63. Conducted by Thomas Beecham.
64. For *Friday Afternoons*, probably 'There Was a Man of Newington' and 'The Useful Plough'.
65. Britten's characteristic analysis of what he perceived to be the shortcomings of Brahms's orchestration.
66. Beecham's cast was led by Lotte Lehmann (Leonora), Franz Völker (Florestan), Erna Berger (Marzelline), Alexander Kipnis (Rocco), Herbert Janssen (Don Pizzaro) and Alfred Jerger (Don Fernando). Britten was always acutely aware of conductors who were incapable of breathing with a singer or providing the flexibility required to support singers as they phrased and placed the voice, something that he himself was highly adept at.
67. Britten's admiration for Tchaikovsky extended to the symphonic poems and the works for the lyric stage, but on the whole not to the concertos and symphonies.
68. Fair copies of the revised versions of *Two Part-Songs* (1932, rev. 1933), eventually taken up by The BBC Wireless Singers and broadcast under Leslie Woodgate on 27 March 1935.

69. 'There was a Man of Newington' for *Friday Afternoons.*
70. Schubert Symphony No. 9, D944 – the 'Great' C major. Britten refers to the old numbering of Schubert's symphonies common at this time.
71. Strauss *Don Quixote*, fantastic variations on a theme of knightly character, for cello, obbligato viola and orchestra, Op. 35.
72. 'A New Year Carol' for *Friday Afternoons.*
73. Jaromir Weinberger *Schwanda the Bagpiper*, folk opera in two acts with a libretto by Milos Kares (1927).
74. Britten was arranging 'Moonlight', the third movement of Bridge's orchestral suite *The Sea*, for the concert that he gave with C. J. R. Coleman at St John's Church, Lowestoft on 9 July; see *Pictures from a Life*, Plate 69.
75. It is interesting that Britten feels it necessary, even within the privacy of his own diary, to make this fact clear, perhaps fearful that someone else might read it, get the wrong impression and consider it inappropriate.
76. It must have been very difficult for Britten to face returning to Kirkley Cliff Road after the death of his father, after the welcome escape of staying with Robert at Clive House School: here, as throughout his life, the company of children and the world they inhabited provided respite from the complexities and conflicts of the adult world.
77. Though Britten fails to name the Boosey & Hawkes representative at this run-through, the company published the *Two Part-Songs* in 1934, their very first Britten publication.
78. *Prenez garde à la peinture* (1933), directed by Henri Chomette (1896–1941), based on the play by René Fauchois – the story of a French bourgeois family.
79. Mozart Symphony No. 39 in E flat, K543; Franck *Symphonic Variations* for piano and orchestra; Bridge *Summer*, symphonic poem (1914–15); Dvorak *Carnival Overture*, Op. 92.
80. Moeran *Farrago Suite* for orchestra (1932), a pastiche of English Renaissance and Baroque styles (inspired by Warlock's *Capriol Suite*) but later withdrawn, despite receiving a successful BBC broadcast and a Promenade Concert performance in 1934.
81. Britten was never lacking in perspective, however confident he was in his own abilities.
82. Ralph Hawkes decided to take all three scores: the *Two Part-Songs* were published by Boosey & Hawkes in 1934, the *Sinfonietta*, Op. 1 and the *Phantasy*, Op. 2 in 1935; and in January 1936 Britten signed an exclusive contract with Boosey & Hawkes that would run until 1963.
83. The family begins the difficult transition after the death of Mr Britten with the children now all living away from home. Mrs Britten starts the painful process of change at Kirkley Cliff Road that would ultimately lead to her final move to Frinton in Essex.
84. Mrs Britten was perhaps concerned that relations on both sides of the family were sometimes inclined to prevail upon her good nature and be a little too dependent on her sense of charity.

85. Eduard van Beinum was to conduct the premiere of Britten's *Spring Symphony* with the Concertgebouw Orchestra at the 1949 Holland Festival; see *Pictures from a Life*, Plates 245–6.
86. Britten greatly admired *Der Rosenkavalier* and is known to have studied the score while working on *Peter Grimes*. Indeed the Act II quartet for Ellen, Auntie and the Nieces ('From the gutter') is more than a little influenced by the famous Trio from Strauss's final scene.
87. Elgar Violin Sonata in E minor (1918).
88. Possibly a dramatisation of *Quartet* (1928), a novel by the modernist writer, Jean Rhys (1890–1979).
89. Hermann Abendroth – see Personalia.
90. It is entirely characteristic that Britten should have preferred simpler, more natural voices for the children in these roles. Even when casting adult sopranos for the children's roles in *Albert Herring* and *The Turn of the Screw*, he was careful to choose singers capable of producing the most youthful and natural of sounds.
91. A Netherlands Radio broadcast of Chopin Piano Concerto No. 2 in F minor, Op. 21.
92. Britten's appreciation of Holst grew over the years, especially after Holst's daughter, Imogen, became his music assistant and co-artistic director of the Aldeburgh Festival in the 1950s.
93. For rehearsals and broadcast of *Sinfonietta*, Op. 1.
94. Bridge *Lament* for strings (1915); Ravel *Rapsodie espagnole* (1907); Wagner Prelude to Act III of *Tristan und Isolde*; and Dvorak Symphony No. 8 in G, Op. 88, known at this time as No. 4, as the first four in the canon were infrequently performed.
95. *Escape me Never* (1933), play by Margaret Kennedy based on her novel *The Fool of the Family* (1930). The great stage and screen actress Elisabeth Bergner was making her UK stage debut in this production.
96. Van Dieren *Diaphonia* (1916), a sequence of unpublished settings for baritone and orchestra of three sonnets by Shakespeare; Leighton Lucas *Partita* (1934) for piano and chamber orchestra; Britten *Sinfonietta*, Op. 1.
97. An arrangement for organ and piano of the finale of Mozart's Symphony No. 39 in E flat, K543, for the St John's Church concert on 9 July.
98. The German violinist Friedrich Wührer was one of the many Jewish musicians persecuted by the Nazi party.
99. Described in the programme as the 'Fantasia in A minor', reflecting the fact that Schumann originally wrote this movement as a free-standing *Phantasie* in 1841, and was persuaded by Clara to expand it into a three-movement concerto in 1845.
100. As well as the piano parts in his own arrangements of Bridge and Mozart, Britten played the solo parts of the Schumann and Tchaikovsky concertos (accompanied by Mr Coleman on the organ) and three further solo items: Beethoven Piano Sonata No. 23 in F minor, 'Appassionata', Op. 57; Schoenberg

Sechs Kleine Klavierstücke, Op. 19 (1911); Debussy *L'isle joyeuse*. See *Pictures from a Life*, Plate 69.

101. Kodály String Quartet No. 2, Op. 10 (1918); Hindemith String Quartet No. 3 in C, Op. 16 (1920).
102. *Design for Living* (1933), romantic comedy directed by Ernst Lubitsch (1892–1947), based on the 1932 stage play by Noel Coward.
103. Mozart Piano Quartet No. 1 in G minor, K478.
104. Debussy *Fantasie* for piano & orchestra (1889–90); *Prélude à L'après-midi d'un faune* (1894); Ravel *La valse* (1919–20).
105. See *Pictures from a Life*, Plate 68.
106. A Salzburg Festival production, conducted by Toscanini.
107. Vaughan Williams *Benedicite* (1929), a setting for soprano, chorus and orchestra of the well-known canticle from the Apocryphal 'Song of the Three Holy Children' and the poem 'Hark, my soul, how everything' by John Austin (1613–69).
108. Stravinsky *Oedipus rex* (1927), opera-oratorio with a libretto by Jean Cocteau; Falla *El amor brujo* (Love the Magician), ballet for orchestra with mezzo-soprano solo (1925).
109. The day on which German troops invaded neutral Belgium and Britain declared war on Germany, at the outset of the First World War.
110. Bridge Suite for strings (1909); Jacob Concerto for piano and strings (1927); Bizet Adagietto from *L'Arlésienne* Suite No. 1, Op. 23 and Duo from *Jeux d'enfants*, Op. 22; Holst *St Paul's Suite*, Op. 29 No. 2 (1912/1922).
111. Britten *Jubilate Deo* in E flat for chorus and organ, which he completes on 10 August.
112. Strauss *Till Eulenspiegels lustige Streiche*, Op. 28, tone poem for orchestra.
113. Debussy *La mer* (1903–5); Berg *Three Wozzeck Fragments* (1924).
114. 'Jeux de vagues', the second of Debussy's 'three symphonic sketches', *La mer*.
115. In 1934 Toscanini famously snubbed Germany's Bayreuth Festival to conduct at the Salzburg Festival, where, together with Bruno Walter, he presided over one of the most glorious periods in the Festival's history, a golden era brought abruptly to a halt with the Nazi annexation of Austria in 1938.
116. *The Rise of Catherine the Great* (1933), directed by Bergner's husband, Paul Czinner.
117. Arnold Cooke's *Concert Overture* No. 1 for orchestra was awarded first prize in this competition, but Britten mistakenly writes '3rd' in his diary entry.
118. Prokofiev Violin Concerto No. 1 in D, Op. 19; Borodin Symphony No. 2 in B minor (1877).
119. Strauss tone poems *Don Juan*, Op. 20 and *Don Quixote*, Op. 35, the *Burlesque* in D minor, Op. 85, for piano and orchestra, and the 'Dance of the Seven Veils' from *Salome*.
120. These Stravinsky and Beethoven scores were highly influential for Britten.
121. Britten's love of Verdi grew as the years went by, and his scores were highly influential on Britten's output after the Second World War, particularly

Falstaff (on *Albert Herring*), *Otello* (on *Billy Budd*) and the *Missa da requiem* (on *War Requiem*).

122. *The Autobiography of Alice B. Toklas* (1933), Gertrude Stein's account of life in Paris in the 1910s and 1920s with her lover, Alice B. Toklas – the narrator of the book, hence its title.
123. Bridge Violin Sonata (1932).
124. *Holiday Tales*, Op. 5 (1934), later retitled *Holiday Diary*.
125. *Te Deum* in C major for solo treble, choir and organ (11 July–17 September 1934). Britten's self-deprecating comment is perhaps a reference to the influence that Stravinsky's music exerted on him around this time, particularly *Symphony of Psalms*.
126. It was routinely the practice in the UK at this time to price quality goods in terms of guineas, a sum of one pound and one shilling in pre-decimal currency.
127. A broadcast given by the Western Studio Orchestra, conducted by Reginald Redman on the BBC's West Region Station. Britten wrote to Grace Williams after the broadcast with a detailed critique, penetratingly analytical about the Parry Jones songs and generous in its praise of the folk-song arrangements. See *Letters from a Life*, Vol. I, Letter 55, pp. 345–7.
128. King George V and Queen Mary.
129. Mr Britten's partner in the dental practice, Laurence Sewell, bought the practice after Mr Britten's death, but Mrs Britten remained at the house for a time before eventually moving to Frinton in Essex, so the services of the residential and business parts of the house had to be separated.
130. The completion of *May: Now Is the Month of Maying*, unison song with piano.
131. Mozart's Symphony No. 40 in G minor, K550; Mahler Symphony No. 5 (1901–2).
132. Britten was later to write his vaudeville for boys and piano, *The Golden Vanity*, Op. 78, for the Vienna Boys' Choir in 1966.
133. King Alexander I of Yugoslavia (1888–1934), the unifying ruler of the kingdoms of the Serbs, Croats and Slovenes, was assassinated during a state visit to Marseilles by a Bulgarian revolutionary, Vlado Chernozemski. The French foreign minister, Louis Barthou, was also killed in the gun attack, though in 1974 it was revealed that this was as a result of a stray bullet from a French police officer.
134. 'Night', the final movement of the piano suite, *Holiday Tales*.
135. Mozart Duos in G, K423, and B flat, K424, for violin and viola.
136. Britten was never an admirer of Rachmaninov, whose music he considered to be sentimental and cheap.
137. Britten dedicated *Holiday Tales* to his piano teacher at the RCM, Arthur Benjamin.
138. Grace Williams had studied with Wellesz in Vienna in 1930 and 1931 on an Octavia Hill Travelling Scholarship; Britten was about to make his very first visit to the city while on a European tour with his mother to Basle (17–28 October), Salzburg (29–31 October), Vienna (1–20 November), Munich (21–6 November), and Paris (27–8 November).

139. A performance that would eventually take place in a Macnaghten–Lemare Concert at the Mercury Theatre, London, on 17 December 1934, conducted by Iris Lemare.
140. See *Letters from a Life*, Vol. I, Letter 56, pp. 348–9.
141. The Kunstmuseum in Basle boasts one of the finest collections of the paintings of Hans Holbein the Younger (1497–1543).
142. Strauss *Macbeth* (1886–8), his first tone poem for orchestra, described by Strauss himself as 'the precise expression of my artistic ideas and feelings'.
143. Though *Aïda* (1871) is considered to be the first of Verdi's last three great operatic masterpieces, Britten was a greater admirer of *Otello* (1887) and *Falstaff* (1893), and the revised versions of *Simon Boccanegra* (1881) and *Don Carlos* (1886).
144. The Salzburg cable car.
145. Britten's score survives in the archive collection of the Britten–Pears Library in Aldeburgh.
146. First sketches for the Suite, Op. 6 for violin and piano.
147. Mascagni *Cavalleria rusticana* and Leoncavallo *Pagliacci*.
148. Britten's love and admiration of *Falstaff* made manifest in his own words.
149. The first movement of the Suite, Op. 6.
150. When Erwin Stein later fled Europe for the UK with his family, he became Britten's key representative at Boosey & Hawkes.
151. The Vienna State Opera.
152. The Schubert birth house, Nussdorferstraβe 54, Vienna.
153. Most probably for the *Sinfonietta*, Op. 1, the first major work by Britten to be published by Boosey & Hawkes, early in 1935.
154. A Thomas Cook travel bureau, an essential agency for foreign travel in the 1930s.
155. The Alte Pinakothek, one of the oldest galleries in the world (housing one of the finest collections of Old Masters), situated in the Kunstareal in Munich.
156. The Dom zu unserer lieben Frau (Cathedral of Our Blessed Lady), the largest church in the Bavarian capital, which suffered severe damage during the First World War, but underwent restoration after the war – a long-term project eventually completed in 1994.
157. The main London air terminal at this time was in Croydon, well before the development of Heathrow or Gatwick.
158. *Holiday Tales*, Op. 5.
159. The marriage of Princess Marina of Greece and Denmark to Prince George, Duke of Kent, fourth son of King George V and Queen Mary.
160. For the Macnaghten–Lemare concert on 17 December.
161. The Wigmore Hall premiere of Britten's *Holiday Tales*.
162. From the proceeds of Mr Britten's estate.
163. Debussy *Pelléas et Mélisande*, opera in five acts with a libretto adapted from the symbolist play by Maurice Maeterlinck – yet another example of Bridge opening up Britten's musical horizons.
164. The drama that ensued is painstakingly documented in *Letters from a Life*, Vol. I, Letters 56, 62 and 67, pp. 348–68.

165. Prokofiev String Quartet No. 1 in B minor, Op. 50 (1930–1).
166. The Suite, Op. 6 is a rare occasion of Britten failing to meet a deadline. The first performance by Henri Temianka (violin) and Betty Humby (piano) at the Wigmore Hall on 17 December 1934 was of movements 1, 3 and 4 ('March', 'Lullaby' and 'Waltz') only. The 'Introduction' and 'Moto perpetuo' followed later and the piece was not completed to Britten's satisfaction until 27 June 1935. Even then, the entire suite would be further revised between July and September 1935. The first complete performance of the Suite was eventually given by Britten and Antonio Brosa, in a BBC broadcast on 13 March 1936.
167. The choir for this performance was unnamed in the programme, but the boys were Reginald Goodall's choristers from St Alban the Martyr, Holborn.
168. Variation 2: 'Herod' (Anon. 15th century) for double chorus.
169. *Le million* (1931), French musical comedy directed by René Clair (1898–1981).
170. *F.P.I.* (1933), science-fiction fantasy directed by Karl Hartl (1899–1978).
171. See *Letters from a Life*, Vol. I, Letters 54, 60, 63, 64, pp. 344–63.
172. A classic recording (and one of the very first on 78s) of Mahler's orchestral song-cycle, *Kindertotenlieder*, sung by the German baritone, Heinrich Rehkemper, with the Berlin State Opera Orchestra conducted by Jascha Horenstein.
173. *The Little Boy*, radio play by E. M. Delafield (1890–1943).
174. Hindemith *Mathis der Maler* Symphony (1933–4).
175. *Oliver Twist* (1838), novel by Charles Dickens.
176. Christmas music and messages from around the British Empire.
177. A Britten family tradition at Christmas, no doubt encouraged by Mrs Britten's charitable nature.
178. The first family Christmas since the death of Mr Britten.
179. Sullivan *Overture di Ballo* (1870); Tchaikovsky Suite from *The Nutcracker*, Op. 71a; Saint Säens *Ouverture de fête*; Bridge *A Christmas Dance: Sir Roger de Coverley* (1922).
180. Britten's taste in contemporary music is by now firmly focused on Continental Europe, embracing Mahler, Schoenberg, Berg, Debussy, Ravel, Strauss, Hindemith and Stravinsky.

NOTES: 1935

1. Britten was looking for a suitable Latin text for a proposed Hymn to St Cecilia; see 19 February.
2. *Conversations in the Train* was a series of scripted debates on philosophical issues, broadcast by the BBC on Sunday evenings during the thirties.
3. Berlioz 'Marche hongroise', 'Ballet des sylphes' and 'Menuet des folles' from *La damnation de Faust, légende dramatique* for soloists, chorus and orchestra (1846).
4. The 'March', 'Lullaby' and 'Waltz' from the Suite, Op. 6.
5. Unidentified.
6. *The Lost Patrol* (1934), war adventure starring Victor McLagen and Boris Karloff, directed by John Ford (1894–1973).

7. Bridge Piano Quintet in D minor (1904–12); Johann Strauss II 'Du und du' waltz from *Die Fledermaus*; Fauré Piano Quartet No. 1 in C minor, Op. 15.
8. The Arthur Batchelor lectures on music and the visual arts at the University of East Anglia in Norwich are named after this individual. Amongst the distinguished guest speakers over the years was Sir Peter Pears, who gave the 1980 annual memorial lecture.
9. Britten was arranging the 'Du und du' waltz in an attempt to provide repertoire to suit the limited abilities of this amateur band.
10. The League of Nations conducted a plebiscite in the Saar in accordance with the Versailles Treaty. Approximately ninety per cent of the voters demanded reunion with Germany and rejected a union with France or continued League administration. The National Socialists mounted a massive political campaign in the Saar, but popular opinion clearly supported a return to Germany.
11. A talk on the ancient Kingdom of Judah (the large southern section of Israel and the South Bank) given by Lady Layton (wife of Sir Walter Thomas [Teddy] Layton, Editor of *The Economist*) whose second son, David, was at Gresham's with Britten.
12. Bizet *Jeux d'enfants* (Children's games), Op. 22, for orchestra; Borodin 'Polovtsian Dances' from *Prince Igor*; Mozart Overture from *The Abduction from the Seraglio*, K384; Mendelssohn 'Scherzo' from the incidental music to Shakespeare's *A Midsummer Night's Dream*, Op. 61.
13. Sessions Suite from *The Black Maskers*; Bliss *Mèlée fantasque*; Gershwin *Second Rhapsody* for piano and orchestra; Copland *Dance Symphony* – performed by the BBC Symphony Orchestra conducted by Edward Clark and Arthur Bliss, with Solomon as soloist in the Gershwin.
14. Seven years later Britten was to make his now famous setting of Auden's *Hymn to St Cecilia*.
15. The private diaries kept between 1660 and 1669 by the English naval administrator Samuel Pepys (1633–1703), a unique primary source for the period of the English Restoration.
16. Haydn Symphony No. 99 in E flat (Hob.I:99); Schoenberg *Verklärte Nacht*, Op. 4, for strings; Bridge *Enter Spring*, Rhapsody for orchestra (1926–7); Rimsky-Korsakov 'Wedding march' from Act III of *Le Coq d'Or*.
17. The Symphony in C minor, Op. 11 by the Soviet composer, Yuri Shaporin (1887–1966), performed by the BBC Symphony Orchestra conducted by Albert Coates.
18. *Alla Quartetto Serioso: 'Go play, boy, play'*.
19. Beethoven String Quartet No. 1 in F, Op. 18 No. 1; Bridge String Sextet (1909–12) and Piano Quintet in D minor (1904–12).
20. Haydn String Quartet in C, 'The Emperor' (Hob.III:77) and String Quartet in G minor, 'The Rider' (Hob.III:74).
21. This remained a problem and frustration for Britten, and one that persisted well after his death.
22. *'Go play, boy, play'*.

23. Probably *Oscar Wilde: His Life and His Confessions* (1916) by his friend Frank Harris, whose biography of George Bernard Shaw Britten had read in 1934.
24. The trial of Dame Alicia Lisle, who had harboured John Hickes (a Non-Conformist minister and a fugitive from Monmouth's army) in the wake of the Battle of Sedgemoor, and was found guilty of treason. She was sentenced to death by burning by the infamous Judge Jeffreys, but after the intervention of James I she was beheaded in Winchester marketplace.
25. Ravel *Pavane pour une infante défunte*; Tchaikovsky *Capriccio Italien*; Rimsky-Korsakov Overture to *May Night*; Massenet *Scènes pittoresques*.
26. Bridge *Romeo and Juliet: A Prayer*, for chorus and orchestra (1916).
27. Dyson *In Honour of the City*, fantasia for chorus and orchestra (1928).
28. This conversation was no doubt at the back of Britten's mind when he wrote his *Variations on a Theme of Frank Bridge*, which he conceived as a character portrait of his beloved teacher.
29. *Friday Afternoons* and *Alla Quartetto Serioso: 'Go play, boy, play'*.
30. Williams Suite for chamber orchestra; Maconchy *Great Agrippa*, ballet for fourteen instruments and percussion (1933). The Lutyens, like all her music from this period, was withdrawn.
31. *Two Part-Songs* (Wither and Graves) for chorus and piano (1932) that were soon to be published by Boosey & Hawkes.
32. *The Mighty Barnum* (1934), biographical comedy about the showman P. T. Barnum, directed by Walter Lang (1896–1972).
33. Elgar *Introduction and Allegro* for strings, Op. 47; Holst *Scherzo* for orchestra (1933–4); Beethoven Piano Concerto No. 4 in G, Op. 58; Brahms Symphony No. 2 in D, Op. 73.
34. Honegger *Le roi David* (King David), symphonic psalm for narrator, soprano, mezzo-soprano, tenor, chorus and orchestra (1923).
35. *The Man Who Knew Too Much* (1934), classic thriller directed by Alfred Hitchcock (1899–1980).
36. Actually Dvorák's Symphony No. 9 in E minor, 'From the New World', Op. 95; Britten uses the numbering of Dvorák's symphony common during the 1930s.
37. A nationwide questionnaire organised by the League of Nations Union to find out the public's attitude to the League of Nations and the policy of collective security.
38. *Scissors* (1922), novel by Cecil Roberts (1892–1976).
39. Bax Viola Sonata (1922).
40. Debussy *Rhapsodie* for clarinet and piano (or orchestra) (1909–10).
41. Stravinsky *Apollon musagète*, ballet for string orchestra (1928); Prokofiev Violin Concerto No. 1 in D, Op. 19.
42. In readiness for its imminent publication by Boosey & Hawkes.
43. Beethoven *Rondo a capriccio* in G, 'Rage over a lost penny', Op. 129. See 1 and 18 April 1931.
44. This early setting of Blake's 'A Poison Tree' (for baritone and piano) was

published posthumously by Faber Music in 1994 as the first song in the collection *The Red Cockatoo & Other Songs*. In 1965 Britten set it again, in his masterly *Songs and Proverbs of William Blake*, Op. 74, for Dietrich Fischer-Dieskau.

45. Bridge *Three Noveletten* (1904) for string quartet; the second movement of Haydn's String Quartet in C, 'Emperor' (Hob.III:77); the Allegro from Beethoven's String Quartet No. 7 in F, 'Rasumovsky', Op. 59 No. 1 and the Allegro molto from the String Quartet No. 9 in C, 'Rasumovsky', Op. 59 No. 3.
46. See *Letters from a Life*, Vol. I, Letters 47, 53, 56, 62 and 67; pp. 334–68.
47. John Simon (First Viscount Simon), Foreign Secretary in Ramsay MacDonald's National Government.
48. Schubert String Quartet in D minor, *Death and the Maiden*, D810; Ravel String Quartet in F (1903).
49. Franck Violin Sonata in A; Mozart Piano Quartets in G minor, K478, and E flat, K493; Schumann Piano Quartet in E flat, Op. 44; Brahms Piano Quartet in C minor, Op. 60.
50. The Vienna Boys Choir.
51. Wagner Overture and Venusberg Music from *Tannhäuser*; Grieg *Peer Gynt* Suite; Dvorak Slavonic Dance No. 2 in E minor, Op. 46 No. 2; Chabrier *España*.
52. Jacob Epstein's famous carving in Subianco stone of a Christ-like figure was on exhibition at the Leicester Galleries, St James's, London SW1.
53. Berg *Lulu* Suite (1934), five symphonic pieces from the opera, for soprano and orchestra.
54. Britten still battling with the 'Alla marcia' of *'Go play, boy, play'*.
55. BBC Symphony Orchestra (Section E), probably without most of the principals.
56. Nicolai Overture to *The Merry Wives of Windsor*; Ravel *La valse*; Borodin *In the Steppes of Central Asia*; Saint Säens *Tarantella*, Op. 6, for flute, clarinet and orchestra; Dvorak *Slavonic Dances*.
57. The first broadcast performance of Britten's *Two Part-Songs*: 'I Lov'd a Lass' (Wither) and 'Lift Boy' (Graves).
58. Weingartner conducted Beethoven's Piano Concerto No. 3 in C minor, Op. 37, Liszt's *A Symphony to Dante's Divine Comedy*, and his own 1934 reconstruction of Schubert's complete sketch for a symphony in E major (D729), the work generally considered to be the seventh chronologically. Britten's slip of the pen, and reference to an E *minor* symphony, was presumably because he had Schubert's other, more famous, 'Unfinished' symphony (in B minor) at the back of his mind.
59. Leslie Boosey agrees to publish Britten's early song 'The Birds' (Hilaire Belloc), in its revised version for voice and piano (June 1929–21 June 1934).
60. *Ruggles of Red Gap* (1935), film comedy directed by Leo McCarey (1898–1969).
61. *Barnet's Folly* (1935) by Albert J. Coles was playing at the Theatre Royal, Haymarket, London SW1.

62. This process of revision to *'Go play, boy, play'* would persist for another year, until the prospect of a Wigmore Hall performance by the Stratton Quartet in February 1936 provides a final focus.
63. *One Night of Love* (1934), romantic melodrama in an operatic setting, starring Grace Moore and Tullio Carminati, directed by Victor Schertzinger (1890–1941). The role of Giovanni was taken by Luis Alberni and the film features the voice of the soprano, Joan Cross, who was to become one of Britten's favourite singers and collaborators after the war.
64. Moeran was working on his Symphony in G minor (1935); Britten and Moeran were presumably playing the draft of the first movement from Moeran's compositional sketch.
65. Moeran's *Nocturne* (Robert Nichols), for chorus and orchestra, was commissioned by the Norwich Philharmonic Society for this concert, at which it was receiving its premiere. It was dedicated to and conceived as a eulogy for Delius, who had died the previous year.
66. The first of five such pieces that Britten sketches for Sylvia Spencer.
67. The first anniversary of the death of Britten's father.
68. *Escape Me Never* (1935), romantic drama directed by Bergner's husband, Paul Czinner.
69. Robert Britten's preparatory school for boys in Prestatyn, North Wales.
70. Vaughan Williams Symphony No. 4 in F minor (1935), considered by many to be one of his most innovative scores. Vaughan Williams himself famously commented, 'I don't know whether I like it, but it's what I meant.' Despite the power and originality of the score, Britten could never get beyond what he believed to be its poor technique and bad orchestration.
71. Eisler *Kleine Sinfonie*, Op. 29; Christian Darnton Harp Concerto (1934) with Maria Korchinska; Stravinsky Octet for winds (1923) and *Renard*, burlesque for four pantomimes and chamber orchestra (1916). This well-documented concert was considered by those involved to be an unmitigated disaster. Experienced orchestral players were in short supply that evening, rehearsals had been stormy, and all concerned had underestimated the difficulty of the programme. Darnton himself designated it 'the worst performed programme in the annals of Broadcasting House!'
72. The sequel to *1066 and All That.*
73. Britten was to conduct performances of Bach's *St John Passion* and make an extremely fine commercial recording for Decca in 1971.
74. *Things Are Looking Up* (1935), riotous comedy directed by Albert de Courville (1887–1960), in which Cicely Courtneidge plays identical twins – one a circus owner, the other a strict schoolmistress. It also includes one of Vivien Leigh's very first appearances, as a schoolgirl.
75. Arensky *Variations on Tchaikovsky's Legend*, Op. 54 No. 5, for strings; Bridge *Sally in Our Alley* and *Cherry Ripe* for strings; Dvorak Serenade in E for strings, Op. 22.
76. Britten, ever the competitor.

77. *The Old Ladies* (1935), psychological drama by Rodney Ackland (1908–1991) after the novel by Hugh Walpole.
78. Though there have been various explanations as to how Britten was recruited to work with the GPO Film Unit (including conflicting accounts from the composer and Film Unit personnel themselves), it seems clear from this diary entry that the recommendation came from Edward Clark at the BBC.
79. *The King's Stamp* (1935), directed by William Coldstream.
80. The offices of the GPO Film Unit, 21 Soho Square, London W1.
81. *The Man Who Knew Too Much* (1934), thriller directed by Alfred Hitchcock. Arthur Benjamin wrote a cantata-like score, entitled *Storm Clouds*, for the famous Albert Hall scene.
82. *Son autre amour* (1933), French romance directed by Alfred Machard (1887–1962) and Constant Rémy (1882–1958) who also starred in the film.
83. *The Private Life of the Gannet* (1934), pioneering natural history film by the British biologist Julian Huxley (1887–1975), brother of the writer Aldous Huxley.
84. Mrs Kersty Chamberlain, one of the founders of the Bungay orchestra that Britten conducted in 1934.
85. Britten seems to have found it easier to talk to Barbara about personal matters than to his other siblings. She was in a same-sex relationship (with Helen Hurst) that was to last for almost sixty years (the two women eventually dying just a year apart), so she would certainly have understood his coming to terms with his homosexuality.
86. A celebration of the music of J. S. Bach in London in 1935, launched with the Winter Promenade Concerts.
87. *Der Mörder Dimitri Karamasoff* (1931), German film directed by Erich Engels (1889–1971) and Fyodor Otsep (1895–1949), after *The Brothers Karamazov*, Dostoevsky's last novel – a masterpiece of world cinema.
88. *The King's Stamp* (GPO, 1935).
89. Britten had to replace his setting of Irene R. McLeod's *Lone Dog* (the first song setting for *Friday Afternoons*) at this late stage of production, as it had proved impossible to clear the copyright of the text. The song is included as an appendix to the 1994 edition of the score.
90. 'Moto perpetuo', the third movement of Britten's Suite, Op. 6, for violin and piano.
91. *Tovaritch* (1933), stage comedy by Jacques Deval, playing at the Globe Theatre (now The Gielgud) on Shaftesbury Avenue, London W1.
92. *The Song of Ceylon* (GPO/New Era, 1933–4), directed by Basil Wright, with music by Walter Leigh.
93. *Mr Pit and Mr Pot* (GPO, 1934), directed by Alberto Cavalcanti.
94. *Weather Forecast* (New Era for GPO/New Era), directed by Evelyn Spice.
95. *Spring on the Farm* (New Era for EMB/New Era, 1933), directed by Evelyn Spice.
96. Stravinsky *Le sacre du printemps*; Tchaikovsky Symphony No. 6 in B minor, 'Pathétique', Op. 29.

97. *Sanders of the River* (1935), adventure drama directed by Zoltan Korda (1895–1961).
98. *C.T.O., The Story of the Central Telegraph Office* (GPO, 1935), produced by Stuart Legg.
99. For Britten's Suite, Op. 6.
100. *Coal Face* (GPO/ABFD, 1935), directed by Cavalcanti.
101. The 'Moto perpetuo' again.
102. *The Joyless Street* (1925), directed by G. W. Pabst, a dark social drama about a family in Vienna struggling after the end of the First World War.
103. *Zéro de conduite: Jeunes diables au college* (1933), a comedy short that would have appealed to Britten, as it tells of a full-scale revolution by boys in a grim boarding school.
104. *The Captain Hates the Sea* (1934), comedy with Victor McLaglen and John Gilbert, directed by Lewis Milestone (1895–1980).
105. Mozart Symphony No. 35 in D, 'Haffner', K385; Debussy *La mer*; Mendelssohn 'Nocturne' and 'Scherzo' from the incidental music to *A Midsummer Night's Dream*; Beethoven Symphony No. 7 in A, Op. 92.
106. *On the Fishing Banks of Skye* (GPO, 1935), produced by John Grierson.
107. Blackheath Conservatoire of Music and the Arts, Lee Road, London SE3.
108. Two of Ruth Draper's famous monologue sketches.
109. Milhaud *Chants populaires hébraïques*, Op. 86 (1925).
110. Stravinsky Violin Concerto in D (1931); Prokofiev Violin Concerto No. 1 in D, Op. 19.
111. Possibly a difficult conversation about Mrs Britten's future, as a result of her husband's death and the expense of running the family home at Kirkley Cliff Road, now that her children had all left home. However, Britten may also have been concerned that Mrs Britten had been encouraged to move to Frinton by newly acquired Christian Science friends, and her developing interest and commitment to the Christian Science movement may have been the topic of this conversation.
112. The central role in this poignant film about an abused and neglected boy was played by the eleven-year-old Robert Lynen.
113. *H.P.O. or 6d Telegram*. Though Britten wrote some music for this Lotte Reiniger short, the film was finally released by the GPO in 1939, with music by Brian Easdale.
114. *The Tocher* (GPO, 1938) a silhouette film described as a film ballet, animated by Lotte Reiniger and produced by Cavalcanti.
115. Invented by Iwan Serrurier in 1924, this was the first professional machine for film editing that allowed the film editor to actually view the film while in the editing process.
116. Eugene Goossens *Lyric Poem* for violin and piano, Op. 35.
117. *C.T.O – The Story of the Central Telegraph Office* (GPO, 1937), produced by Stuart Legg – Britten's contribution was solely the title and end music.
118. Beethoven Symphony No. 2 in D, Op. 36; Bridge *There is a Willow Grows*

Aslant a Brook (1927); Schubert *Rosamunde* Overture, D644; Dvorak Slavonic Dance in C.

119. An arrangement of 'La charité' from Rossini's *Choeurs religieux* for Lotte Reiniger's film ballet, *The Tocher*.
120. Might this have been the composer Berthold Goldschmidt (1903–96), recently arrived in London having had to flee Nazi persecution in Germany?
121. *Le Dernier milliardaire* (1934), comedy directed by René Clair (1898–1981).
122. Film editor Richard Q. McNaughton, who had joined the GPO Film Unit in 1934.
123. *The King's Stamp* (GPO, 1935).
124. Britten was revising the Suite, Op. 6, for violin and piano.
125. 'Begone, Dull Care', a new first song for *Friday Afternoons*.
126. *Fascism and Social Revolution: A Study of the Economics and Politics of the Extreme Stages of Capitalism in Decay* (1934) by Rajani Palme Dutt (1896–1974).
127. Parry *Overture to an Unwritten Tragedy*; Weber-Berlioz *Invitation to the Waltz;* Tchaikovsky *Romeo and Juliet*; Berlioz 'Marche hongroise', 'Ballet de Sylphes', and 'Menuet des Follets' from *La damnation de Faust*.
128. Britten had intended writing a suite of five pieces for oboe and string orchestra for Sylvia Spencer, but completed only 'The Grasshopper' and 'The Wasp' (13–16 April 1935) as pieces for oboe and piano.
129. Rossini Overture to the opera, *The Silken Ladder*; Mozart Symphony No. 40 in G minor, K550.
130. Ravel Piano Concerto in G and *Ma mère l'oye*; Debussy *Prélude à L'après-midi d'un faune* and *La mer*.
131. Françaix Sonatina (1934) for violin and piano.
132. See 3 September.
133. *Nana* (a.k.a. *Lady of the Boulevards; 1934*), directed by Dorothy Arzner (1897–1979), with the Russian actress Anna Stern in the title role.
134. Bridge *Dance Poem* for orchestra (1913).
135. Probably for *Gas Abstract* (see 6 September) though it has been impossible to match the manuscript with this title. The music may have been intended for *Men Behind the Meters* and Britten may well have been using his own shorthand in labelling his manuscript sketch.
136. *The Little Minister* (1934), a film adaptation of J. M. Barrie's stage play starring Katharine Hepburn, directed by Richard Wallace (1894–1951).
137. This film was produced under the working title *Negroes*, but not completed and released until 1938, under the title *God's Chillun*.
138. A film produced by the GPO Film Unit for the British Commercial Gas Association.
139. *Becky Sharp* (1935), the first feature-length three-colour film, based on *Vanity Fair* by Thackeray, directed by Rouben Mamoulian (1897–1987) with Miriam Hopkins in the title role.
140. Vaughan Williams *Flos Campi*, suite for viola, wordless chorus and small orchestra (1925).

141. Probably a 1935 BSA (Birmingham Small Arms Company), Series 1.
142. Alastair Cooke began broadcasting for the BBC in 1934. After his move to the United States in 1937, he began the regular broadcasts to the UK that led to his weekly *Letter from America* – a British institution, broadcasting without a break from 1946 to 2004 and completing almost three thousand editions.
143. A theatrical revue by Reginald Arkell, based on the spoof history book of the same title – 'A memorable history of England, comprising all the parts you can remember, including 103 Good Things, 5 Bad Kings and 2 Genuine Dates' – by W. C. Sellar and R. J. Yeatman.
144. The score for *Things to Come* (1936), the film adaptation by William Cameron Menzies of H. G. Wells' novel, *The Shape of Things to Come.*
145. Two of Auden's plays, *The Dance of Death* and (in collaboration with Christopher Isherwood) *The Dog Beneath the Skin*, were produced by the Group Theatre in 1935.
146. Britten was a lifelong admirer of Shostakovich and his music, and the two composers became good friends after their first meeting at London's Royal Festival Hall in 1960.
147. Britten's aunt continued to be plagued by anxiety attacks and subject to bouts of melancholia.
148. *En Rade* (a.k.a. *Sea Fever*; 1927), a love story directed by Cavalcanti with Catherine Hessling and Georges Charlia; its coastal setting and seafaring subplot presumably stimulated Britten's imagination in a way that would indeed sustain sixty minutes of improvisation.
149. See subsequent diary entries for 4, 6, 8 October and 7 March 1936, for Britten's personal assessment of the Abyssinian crisis and his response to the steadily worsening international political scene.
150. *The Green Table* (1932), a topical ballet satirising the failing international diplomacy that was leading Europe to war, choreographed by Kurt Jooss (1901–79) with music by Friedrich Holländer (1896–1976), who had earlier written the music for *The Blue Angel* (1930) in which Marlene Dietrich had immortalised his song 'Falling in Love Again'.
151. The Sextet in D (1824), written when Mendelssohn was just fifteen; Dvorak Quintet in A, Op. 81.
152. Britten was indeed to write the music for Rupert Doone's production of Shakespeare's *Timon of Athens*, the first Group Theatre enterprise for which he was engaged.
153. *Gas Abstract, Dinner Hour* and *Men Behind the Meters*, made for the British Commercial Gas Association.
154. Britten was clearly finding Lauricella a problematic and unsympathetic chamber-music partner, so for a time Britten and Bernard Richards established a trio with Richards' sister, Irene.
155. Grierson's intervention as Head of the GPO Film Unit, and the divergence of opinion over the script, perhaps reflects the sensitivity of the subject at a time when issues of diversity were not so freely debated.

156. The first broadcast performance of Britten's *A Hymn to the Virgin*, given by the BBC Singers (A and B) under Leslie Woodgate. This recital is likely to have been Peter Pears' very first broadcast of a Britten work, as a member of the BBC Singers.
157. It is characteristic of Britten's very eclectic taste that he should have enjoyed Mae West's latest vamp movie, *Goin' to Town* (1935), in which she plays a saloon singer ('A woman of very few words and lots of action') determined to crash high society, on one evening, and then attend the Group Theatre transfer by Michel St Denis of his original *Companie des Quinze* production of Jean Giono's first play, *Lanceurs de graines* (1932; *Sowers of the Grain*) the next.
158. Walton began his First Symphony in the summer of 1932, but the fourth and final movement was only completed in August 1935, so the symphony was receiving its first complete performance.
159. The Natural History Museum, Cromwell Road, London SW7.
160. A diary entry that amply demonstrates Britten's strong work ethic, and the professionalism and efficiency he applied to everything he undertook.
161. *Travelling Post Office* was the working title of what was to become one of the GPO Film Unit's most famous documentary titles, *Night Mail* (1936), directed by Harry Watt and Basil Wright, with words and music by W. H. Auden and Britten.
162. Britten was one of the most passionate early advocates for this score in the UK.
163. *Night Mail* (GPO, 1936) produced by John Grierson, directed by Basil Wright and Harry Watt, sound supervisor Alberto Cavalcanti.
164. Bliss *Music for Strings*, Op. 54.
165. From Britten's *Holiday Tales*, Op. 5.
166. *Calendar of the Year*.
167. *Turn of the Tide* (1935), based on Leo Walmsley's 1932 novel *Three Fevers*: a tale of feuding rival families, set in the North Yorkshire fishing village of Robin Hood's Bay, directed by Norman Walker (1892–1963). Britten was clearly struck by the film's setting, one not so far removed from Britten's first opera, *Peter Grimes*. Interestingly, in both the film and the opera, the 'gansey' (a fishing jersey with an embroidered pattern unique to the family, designed to help identify corpses washed up on the coast) plays a crucial role in the drama's denouement.
168. The Amalgamated Engineering Union.
169. Reginald Goodall's choir at St Alban's, Holborn; a rehearsal for the broadcast of *A Boy Was Born*.
170. Igor Markevitch *Le paradis perdu*, cantata for soprano and male-voice chorus, a setting of a French translation from Milton's *Paradise Lost* (1933–5).

Awakening and international successes

Every artist except the supreme masters has a bias one way or the other. The best pair of opposites I can think of in music are Wagner and Strauss. (Technical skill always comes from the bourgeois side of one's nature.)

For middle-class Englishmen like you and me, the danger is of course the second. Your attraction to thin-as-a-board juveniles, i.e. to the sexless and innocent, is a symptom of this. And I am certain too that it is your denial and evasion of the demands of disorder that is responsible for your attacks of ill-health, i.e. sickness is your substitute for the Bohemian.
W. H. Auden, writing to Benjamin Britten (New York, 31 January 1942)

If Britten can be said to have hit the ground running in 1935, as his portfolio of work with the GPO Film Unit and The Group Theatre intensified, then 1936 saw him really getting into his stride. Though some of his earlier works had been published by Oxford University Press (the *Three Two-Part Songs* of 1932 and *A Boy Was Born* in 1934) and Boosey & Hawkes (the *Two Part-Songs* in 1934, the *Sinfonietta*, Op. 1 and the *Phantasy*, Op. 2 in 1935), in January 1936 Britten had the good fortune to sign an exclusive publishing contract with Boosey & Hawkes, with a guarantee of royalties. He set to work on a final revision of movements from his *Alla Quartetto Serioso: 'Go play, boy, play'* (1933), now refashioned as his *Three Divertimenti* for string quartet, with the promise of a Wigmore Hall premiere by the Stratton Quartet on 25 February. And there were a number of smaller projects throughout the year, including his *War and Death, an Impression for Brass and Orchestra* (published posthumously as *Russian Funeral* in 1981), a pair of *Lullabies* for two pianos (published posthumously in 1990), *Two Ballads* (settings of Slater and Auden) for two female voices and piano, and the *Temporal Suite* for oboe and piano, published posthumously as *Temporal Variations* in 1980.

Amongst these lighter and/or shorter works from 1936 were two scores of much greater substance. The first of these was *Soirées Musicales*, Op. 9 – a suite of five movements from Rossini, three of which were re-orchestrations from his 1935 *Rossini Suite*, written for Lotte Reiniger's short animated silhouette film *The Tocher*. Together with the later Rossini suite, *Matinées*

Musicales (1941), this score was used for Balanchine's ballet *Divertimento* for the American Ballet Company, first staged in the Teatro Municipal in Rio de Janeiro on 27 June 1941, during a South American tour. Both Rossini suites have retained their popularity down the years and are rare examples of Britten letting his hair down, realising the possibilities offered by light music of quality, and bringing it off supremely.

More characteristic of Britten's creative temperament, however, was the other major work from 1936 – indeed, his most important project of the year and his first serious collaboration with W. H. Auden: the orchestral song cycle, *Our Hunting Fathers*. However one chooses to approach this piece, its significance is profound – not for nothing did Britten refer to it as his 'op. 1'. The work (which is dedicated to his publisher, Ralph Hawkes) is an essay on man's inhumanity to man, a subject ever close to Britten's heart, which uses cruelty to animals as a metaphor. Auden helped Britten select the texts (two are anonymous, the third is by Thomas Ravenscroft), and provided his own lyrics for the Prologue and Epilogue. It is unquestionably the most radical score Britten had penned to this date, not only in terms of its uncompromising message. The experimental nature of much of the vocal writing (extremely demanding in tessitura and vocal flexibility, particularly in 'Rats away!' and the 'Dance of Death') and the extraordinary virtuosity and technical demands of its orchestration are evidence, if any were needed by now, of Britten's searing technique and theatrical imagination.

But this was just the tip of the iceberg for Britten in 1936. In April he attended the ISCM Festival in Barcelona, where he and Brosa gave the first complete performance of his Suite, Op. 6. During the Festival he also attended the premiere of Berg's Violin Concerto, a work that made a lasting impression and remained a favourite for him amongst Berg's music, along with *Wozzeck*. In autumn 1936 Britten conducted the premiere of *Our Hunting Fathers*, with Sophie Wyss and the London Philharmonic Orchestra, at the Norfolk and Norwich Triennial Festival (on 25 September), and in October he moved into Beth's flat at 559 Finchley Road, his first London base since his college accommodation at Burleigh House on the Cromwell Road.

And then, of course, there were his ongoing commitments to the film and theatre industry, 1936 being particularly prolific in this respect. In this year alone Britten wrote incidental music for *Night Mail*, *Calendar of the Year*, *Men of the Alps*, *The Savings of Bill Blewitt*, *Line to the Tschierva Hut*, *Message from Geneva*, and *Four Barriers* (GPO Film Unit); *Peace of Britain* and *The Way to the Sea* (Strand Films); *Stay Down Miner* (Left Theatre); *Around the Village Green* (Travel and Industrial Development Association); *Love from a*

Stranger (Capitol Films); and Louis MacNeice's *The Agamemnon of Aeschulus* (The Group Theatre).

In some respects, this period of Britten's life proved difficult in terms of his family relationships. He had not had a teenage rebellion, but as he entered his twenties he began to assert himself more, and become more independent, artistically and politically. This sometimes led to tension with his siblings, notably Robert. He was much more liberal in his views than his family, more avant-garde in his artistic tastes, more left-wing and outspoken in his politics, and through the diaries we begin to witness at first hand his response to the rise of Fascism in Europe, his dismay over the fortunes of the Spanish Civil War and his bewilderment and horror over the progress of the Nazi party in Germany – he is forever lamenting the Baldwin government's mishandling of international affairs.

Britten was also troubled by the discovery that, during his father's long illness, his mother had been influenced by Ethel Astle to embrace the Christian Science movement in a desperate attempt to save her husband. According to Britten's diary, Ethel Astle actually visited his ailing father in 1933, to give 'healing counsel', and as Mr Britten's health declined, so Mrs Britten's commitment to the faith became stronger. Indeed, her eventual move to Frinton in Essex was influenced by her Christian Science friends' discovery of a small community of followers in the town. The move did not in itself cause particular concern for Britten, beyond the sentimental tug of having finally to sever ties to the family home at Kirkley Cliff Road, as he recognised the need for his mother to move on and re-establish a life for herself. But the change in the nature of her faith did trouble him, and it is around this time that Britten himself stops attending church (notably on Easter Sunday, 12 April 1936), despite having been a regular attender throughout his childhood and college years. Certain topics of conversation – all the usual ones, one suspects: politics, sex and religion – are now out of bounds. Certainly Britten's growing awareness of his own homosexuality, and his struggle to come to terms with this, might equally have caused tension, on his side at least.

Nonetheless, 1937 seemed to be full of promise, and Britten was riding high as the year began. Tragedy struck, however, within the first month. Britten's sister Beth developed a particularly pernicious form of flu, which then developed into pneumonia. At Britten's request, his mother travelled up from Frinton to stay and help nurse Beth, but she herself developed pneumonia within days of her arrival. With Beth still in her sick bed and too ill and weak to be told what had happened, Britten's mother died in the next room at Finchley Road, on 31 January.

This was a devastating blow to Britten, who remained haunted by the incident and the loss for some time to come, as many references in his diaries attest. And he may well have felt guilty for having asked his mother to look after Beth under these circumstances. Slowly he returned to work, as much for escape as anything, and it is interesting to note that the first score he worked on after his mother's death – for the Group Theatre premiere of the Auden–Isherwood play, *The Ascent of F6* – includes a particularly touching song for the 'Mother' in the cast, which is addressed to her son, the play's hero, Michael Ransom. *The Ascent of F6* was premiered by The Group Theatre on 26 February, at London's Mercury Theatre, and with this project now behind him, Britten began immersing himself in a number of further projects and domestic matters. The three most significant original compositions of this year were the *Variations on a Theme of Frank Bridge*, written for the Boyd Neel Orchestra for the 1937 Salzburg Festival; the first volume of his Auden settings for high voice and piano, *On This Island*; and *Mont Juic*, the orchestral suite of Catalan dances he wrote with Lennox Berkeley, inspired by their visit to Barcelona for the ISCM Festival the previous year.

Needless to say, there was still a steady flow of commissions for incidental music, notably for the Left Theatre production of Montagu Slater's *Pageant of Empire* (in February), and for the Group Theatre production of Louis MacNeice's *Out of the Picture* (in December). By now Britten's music was receiving regular attention from the BBC, and works such as the *Sinfonietta, Soirées Musicales*, the *Frank Bridge Variations* and *On This Island* were frequently broadcast. But in 1937, the BBC also got wise to Britten's skill as a fluent and imaginative writer of incidental music for dramas and features. One wonders why it took them so long, as it was the Corporation that had recommended him to the GPO Film Unit in the first place – but once the BBC did recognise Britten's flair for such work, they showered him with commissions. In 1937 alone he wrote music for D. G. Bridson's historical pageant play, *King Arthur* (March–April); the radio feature *Up the Garden Path* (June); R. Ellis Roberts' Michaelmas programme, *The Company of Heaven* (August–September), and the historical feature, *Hadrian's Wall* (November). And this flow of work from the BBC continued well into 1938, with a series of four programmes devoted to national and international communications, *Lines on the Map*, in January; *The Chartists' March* for a features production by John Pudney in May; and *The World of the Spirit* for another substantial R. Ellis Roberts production, this time a Whitsun programme, broadcast on 5 June. Also in 1938, Britten received his first Promenade commission, for a Piano Concerto that he was to premiere with the BBC Symphony Orchestra under Sir Henry Wood at the Queen's Hall on 18 August 1938.

But of more lasting significance than perhaps anything from this period was the friendship that Britten began with a young tenor in the BBC Singers, whom he first met on 6 March 1937 over lunch with Trevor Harvey and Basil Douglas. Peter Pears, then a jobbing singer, had been at Lancing with Peter Burra, whom Britten had met during the 1936 ISCM Festival in Barcelona – a valued mutual friendship. Pears was a very good friend of Burra's and was, in fact, sharing a cottage with him: Foxhold, in Bucklebury Common near Reading. Britten's friendship with him was newer, but there was certainly an attraction there. Just seven days after the lunch with Pears, Britten stayed with Burra at Foxhold for the weekend, during which time (as he confides in his diary) he felt he had found a soulmate. Tragically, Burra died in a flying accident just six weeks later, and Britten and Pears were thrown together by this, both volunteering to go down to Foxhold to sort out his private papers and belongings.

This sad occasion brought the two men closer as friends, and they began to see more and more of one another, eventually choosing to share a flat in London. They were no more than friends at this time, as is clear from the diaries. In fact, for much of this time Britten was living in Peasenhall with the Welfords, the family of Beth's fiancée Kit, whose architect father was supervising the conversion of the Old Mill at Snape that Britten had acquired with the proceeds of his family bequest. Pears, meanwhile, had left the BBC Singers in October 1937 to tour the United States with the New English Singers, and on his return to the UK he joined the Glyndebourne Festival Opera chorus for the 1938 season. But the friendship of these two men continued to grow and prosper, and Britten began to recognise Pears' potential as a singer and an artist. Indeed, he wrote his first song expressly for him – an orchestral setting of Brontë for the BBC broadcast of *The Company of Heaven*.

It has generally been accepted that they gave their first recital together around this time, and in later life (though uncertain about the date) Pears thought it might have been a concert in aid of Spanish war relief at the Cambridge Arts Theatre in 1937. However Britten's diaries show no trace of this and the two recital dates in Pears' appointment diary for 1937 – both in Oxford, on 16 May and 24 October – find Britten in Gloucester and Suffolk. In fact, the first concert date on which the two men's appointment diaries actually agree is 17 February 1939, at Balliol College, Oxford, so this may indeed have been the very first Pears–Britten recital.

So as we enter this final phase of Britten's life during the 1930s, as witnessed by his private journal, the journeying boy who set out from Lowestoft in September 1928 reaches a crossroads, and is confronted with one major life experience after another: the loss of both his parents within three years; an intense and liberating exposure to the cultural elite in London; growing dismay at the state of European politics and culture; and the need, finally, to come to terms with his sexuality. These factors come into play to bring focus to his journey of the soul, and lead to a decision to journey geographically even further afield – to the United States in 1939. To understand why he eventually felt this to be necessary and inevitable, read on.

Diaries: 1936–1938

Awakening and international successes

Autograph composition draft (pencil) for the climax of *Messalina*, the second movement of the symphonic cycle, *Our Hunting Fathers*, Op. 8. © The Britten Estate Limited. See diary entries for 4–5, 8 June 1936 and 30 April 1937.

1936

1936 finds me infinitely better off in all ways than did the beginning of 1935; it finds me earning my living – with occasionaly something to spare – at the G.P.O film Unit under John Grierson & Cavalcanti, writing music & supervising sounds for films (this one T.P.O. Night Mail) at the rate of £5 per week, but owing to the fact I can claim no performing rights (it being Crown property) with the possibility of it being increased to £10 per week or £2 per day; writing very little, but with the possibility & ideas for writing alot of original music, as I am going under an agreement with Boosey & Hawkes for a £3 a week guarantee of royalties;[1] having alot of success but not a staggering amount of performances, tho' reputation (even for bad) growing steadily; having a bad inferiority complex in company of brains like Basil Wright, Wystan Auden & William Coldstream; being fortunate in friends like Mr & Mrs Frank Bridge, Henry Boys, Basil Reeve (& young Piers Dunkeley – tell it not in Gath) and afar off Francis Barton;[2] being comfortably settled in a pleasant, tho' cold, flat in West Hampstead with Beth, with whom I get on very well; doing much housework but with prospect of having a woman in more than twice a week in evenings & once in mornings. So for 1936.

Thursday 2 January [London]
Go to Soho Square in morning to work with Auden & Wright on T.P.O. – the first 'correction' of our Tuesday's work. Meet Robert (on his way back to Prestatyn with Marjorie & John) & Beth for lunch at Lyon's new Marble Arch Corner House (esp. for R's benefit). To Blackheath in aft with Wright & Auden for 2nd 'correction' (now completely altered) of T.P.O work – by Watt (director of film). Auden comes back here for a meal at 7.30. We talk amongst many things of a new Song Cycle (probably on Animals) that I may write.[3] Very nice and interesting & pleasant evening. Preparing for early bed when Frank B. 'phones and talks from 11.0–12.0 unceasingly. Very nice tho' – he is one of the world's marvels & dears.

Friday 3 January

Go up to Soho Square in morning for more discussions as to T.P.O. Sound. Now to complicate matters the Producer (Wright) can't make suspicious Watt (director) see the point of Auden's lovely verse. So we make in the afternoon at Blackheath a rough 'take' of the verse alone (spoken by [Stuart] Legg) to cut the film roughly to, first. I go to see Ralph Hawkes to put a cap on the discussons on my agreement with him & also to Whiteleys for a hair-cut. Back here to dinner in evening with Beth – she does the food part – heats up some Steak & kidney pie. After, listen to wireless (Wood racing thro' Beethoven's fantastic & very great 8th, and most of a play on Anderson's lovely Snow Queen)[4] – untill Mr & Mrs F. Bridge come at 9.30 to hear my records of 'A Boy was Born' (towards which F.B. gave me £1) & seem very pleased. Certainly I adore them. They go by 11.0.

Monday 6 January

Early up – because there's so much to do – Laundry to prepare besides usual stuff. To Soho Square by 10.0 where I meet Wright & Cavalcanti – after much delay down to studio at Blackheath in Wright's car. There we cut in the test-bands for T.P.O. Spend whole day until 6.45 there. Back here late for dinner, after which write alot of over-due letters – & a little gramophone before bath & bed ——.

~~The Abs~~ Mussolini's Abassynian Adventure doesn't seem to go well at all. It seems to be raining there now again. General indignation seems to be growing – especially since the dual bombing of Ambulance & Red X Hospital – when some Swedes were killed. But unfortunately the execrable Paris Peace Plan (of which Hoare was the scape-goat) seems forgotten – although Baldwin's prestige is very much lowered.[5]

Tuesday 7 January

Another Blackheath day – after helping Beth shop in Kilburn & some business at Soho Square. Basil Wright takes Cavalcanti & me down by car – & we spend all day on T.P.O. there. Very interesting – but annoying that the music will have to be rushed owing to this delay. Also help Auden about one or two things with his film (Calendar of the Year).[6] Back here to dinner which Mrs Traynor cooks, and to which Barbara & Helen Hurst come. A nice evening – have some of my gramophone records on. Phone 'Mum – she's not coming to morrow as planned – but on Thursday.

I have had a lot of praise – letters & innumerable people met – about my Boy's broadcast. But I doubt if the work can ever become popular in spite of what musical value it may have. Until all choirs are professional and/or are become musicians, it will scarcely be done more than once or twice a year, if that. One result – a letter from Joseph Williams & Co asking for works to print! Of course impossible since Hawkes agreement.

Wednesday 8 January

Mrs. Traynor can't come everyday as Beth & I now want so we are seeing other people. One, Lena Magnus comes at 8.30 this morning – she certainly is not prepossessing & has a loud & somewhat raucous voice – but she is so eager to come & so willing to do everything wanted, that Beth & I practically decide to try her. It is so hard to say no to obviously poor & pitiful cases.

I go to Blackheath with Wright & Cavalcanti all morning – at last get instruction for T.P.O. Sound. Meet Adolph Hallis for lunch – & talk over our proposed light 2 piano-duets for B.B.C.[7] ~~Also~~ Go to Boosey & Hawkes about many matters – my agreement with them is all but settled. Also 'phone R.C.M. & B.B.C. about future matters – things certainly are beginning to move! Back here by 4.30 & work alittle on T.P.O. After dinner 'phone Mum about bringing some music for me (Quartet 'Go play, boy, play' to be rewritten ~~by~~ for Feb. 25th)[8] – innumerable other 'phone calls – & also work on Rossini for a bit till about 12.0.

Friday 10 January

Work vigourously & solidly all day at Film music – not daring to look back on the previous page – for fear I should want to alter anything! Not bad considering. Mum shops but is in to lunch. I leave at 5.30 – & go up to Piccadilly to meet Piers & Daphne – collect twelve chairs & take them all up to Coldstream where Auden & he shoot a sequence ~~from~~ for Miss Spice's film 'Calender of the Year' – this being a New Year's party of a typical respectable upper-middle-class family. Beth, Lilian Wolff, & brother, the 2 Romilly's are among the sixteen or so. It is amusing to watch – & to talk to Olive Mangeot – also there, watching – although I feel Auden made some mistakes in choice – some being definitely Bohemian! Over by 11.30 – tho' I dispatch Piers & Daphne (who make a success) by 10.45. Piers makes friends with Giles Romilly – not too great, I hope, tho' Giles seems nice, & may broaden Piers mind alot – which he needs – but he is a nice lad for all that. Back by train – to find Mum waiting up patiently & with a meal for us – which we don't want, having 'snacked' steadily all the evening

Saturday 11 January

See in the Telegraph that the International Jury (including Webern & Ansermet) have chosen my Violin Suite for performance in the Barcelona (Contemporary Music) Festival this April. Very pleasing.

Work hard until 11.15 – then shop with Mum & Beth. Lunch out & after, while Beth & Barbara go to an 'old girls' reunion', go to Leicester Square to see Réne Clair's very amusing & brilliant 'Ghost Goes West' with Robert Donat – very charming – & Eugène Palette brilliant. A very witty satire, tho' not particularly Claire – but wonderfully well made. Also a lovely Disney – Music Land – & a glorious slap-stick Custard Pie – Keystone Hotel.[9] Back here for a meal at 7.30 – Barbara comes too. Our new char comes – is a queer degraded person – seems efficient, but oh! so loud & rough. Still she is a poor thing & it is a kindness to have her.

Sunday 12 January

Breakfast at 10.0 – & Mum goes off to her Christian Science meeting at 11.30. Beth does chores about the house, & I finish off the film music. Late lunch. In aft. have nice laze – read alot of Carroll's wonderful fantasy 'Sylvie & Bruno'[10] which for sheer magical charm beats anything I know. After tea I play Mum my 'Boy' records – which I confess I love more each time. Go to Barbara for a meal – all 3 of us – after which I take Beth to the 1st performance of Auden's (& Isherwood's) Dog Beneath the Skin – a Group Theatre show at Westminster. There are some first rate things in this – Auden's chorus's are some of the loveliest things I know & the best part of the show was the speaking of them by Robert Speight. As a whole the show was marred by Rupert Doone double-~~dotting~~ crossing the 'ts' & underlining every point – leaving nothing to the imagination – Some of the sets were lovely[11] – notably the Red Light scene. Of course it was very much cut – but even might be more so – alot of it moves to slowly I feel. Murrill had done the music very competently, but adding nothing to the show, I'm afraid. It was just clever & rather dull jazz – not as amusing perhaps as the original – a common fault with satirists. Pick up Mum at Barbara's after.

A very cold day – again.

Wednesday 15 January

Up early & get to Soho Square at 9.45. Some bother over parts for orchestra, but I eventually get down to Blackheath at 11.0 for big T.P.O recording. A large orchestra for me – Fl. Ob. Bsn. Trpt. Harp (Marie Kotchinska[12] – very good), Vln, Vla. Vlc. CB, Percussion & wind machine – a splendid team. The music I wrote really comes off well – &, for what is wanted, creates quite alot of sensation! The whole trouble, & what takes so much time is that over the music has to be spoken a verse – kind of patter – written by Auden – in strict rhythm with the music. To represent the train noises. There is too much to be spoken in a single breath by the one voice (it is essential to keep to the same voice & to have no breaks) so we have to record separately – me, having to conduct both from an improvised visual metronome – flashes on the screen – a very difficult job! Legg speaks the stuff splendidly tho'. Recordings last from 11.0–2.30 – lunch – 3.15–5.30. So pretty dead. Beth & I prepare meal here – nice one – & after – much 'phoning (to F.B. notably) & then work at Te Deum for a bit – too late tho' & not to bed till 12.0 – & it's so difficult to get up in the mornings!

Thursday 16 January

Very foggy & cold day disolves into heavy snow after mid-day. Go to Soho Square by 10.30 – have long talks with Auden about proposed song cycle & also hear 'rushes' from yesterday – not at all bad. Lunch with Auden, Coldstream, Cavalcanti & Wright at a little French Soho restaurant – very good. Take afternoon off to see Piers Dunkerley – take him to a cinema (only see a very poor Tom Walls-Ralph Lynn show – saved by two good Disneys 'Music Land' & 'Pluto's Judgment day')[13] & out to tea. I have a lot to talk to him about – he being to all intents & purposes fatherless & obviously having a difficult time – poor lad. Giles Romily isn't too good for him I fear. However he unburdens his soul in a long walk across Hyde Park after tea at the Criterion – & I do feel I've helped him abit. But what a boy to help! So splendid in brain & form – and delightful company. Back here to a meal at 7.30 with Beth. Afterwards talk, wireless, 'phone, letters, & on with the Te Deum score until mid-night —

Friday 17 January

Still more snow all day – lying heavily Beth goes home in afternoon. I go off early to Blackheath to help cut in the sound & also join voice & orchestra into rhythm – incidently discovering that by mistake I was given wrong bands to conduct from, in some cases the voice not fitting the orchestra at all – so Pat Jackson & I start a lovely job of patching which lasts so long that I cannot keep a dinner date with Trevor Harvey at 7.30. Get back here soon after 8.0. & do abit of boring scoring of Te Deum until I meet Basil Wright, Basil Reeve & Henry Boys at BBC. at 10.20 for Contempory concert at which F.B's 1930 Oration for 'Cello[14] (Florence Hooton – splendid, young as yet & perhaps abit immature, but with lovely technique & control) & orchestra is played.

Monday 20 January

To Blackheath all day until 6.0. when I eat out & come back here to work for the evening. Beth is back from Lowestoft, where she found Mum not too well – very highly strung – obviously from over-work. She (B.) is out for evening tho'. Very dramatic announcement from B.B.C. at 9.38 – 'King dying'. All stations close down except for an impromptu service Ps.[Psalm] 23, a colossal prayer.[15] Further ~~Bulletins~~ announcement at 9.45 – when Bulletin is repeated – Stuart Hibbert getting more awed & quavery than ever – ditto at 10.0.–10.15–10.30–10.45 (feelings are now working off a bit) – 11.0–11.15 – (definitely cool now, tho' Hibbert still emotional) – 11.30, – 11.45, – 12.0 (really this King won't die') so I switch off & continue my work till 1.45 (finishing score, thank God!)[16]

Wednesday 22 January

Fetch parts of Te Deum from copyists after breakfast & take them (thro' immense traffic blocks & diversions on account of Proclamation of New King at St. Jame's Palace) to R.C.M. for first rehearsal with Goodall.[17] Considering we have only one string to each part they sound very well. Back to lunch with Auden in Soho – & down to Blackheath with Wright in afternoon (in his car, with Auden & Coldstream). [Incidently at lunch & after A. & I discuss at great length the psychology of teaching art in combination – & possibility of an Academy of Combined art.] Spend aft. there re-cutting the musical end to T.P.O. Back here by 7.30 & get a meal with Beth. Lovely laze in evening – listening to what little Broadcasting there is (owing to King's death) – only a very dull concert of BB.C. orch. under Boult – a vilely bad show of Egmont. Ov. – a Meditation of Hindemith (concocted since the death of King) on a Bach Chorale – very dull.[18] Phone Mum – seems well – & others. Bed at 11.0.

Friday 24 January

To Soho Square before Blackheath with Wright in his car at 12.0. Odd jobs there, before lunch in the Pub, after which we spend afternoon re-recording (i.e. putting Commentary band & music band together on one band, by recording combined sound at varying degrees of strength) the last sequence of T.P.O Back to town with Wright – before I go to a rehearsal of Te Deum with Reginald Goodall & his choir at 7.0 (having eaten abit). They sing it very well, except for the Solo boy who is bad. He is quite new on the job – apparently the old good one has been taken off by some man to live with him – for obvious reasons – & Goodall is rightly indignant.[19] Back here by 8.30 when I rehearse with Bernard &

Irene R. until 10.30. Beth is out for the evening & is at the moment not back – 12.15.

Monday 27 January

Practise pft. for a change in morning & also do alot of business – much overdue – bills & letters. Go to lunch with Kenneth Wright (programme director B.B.C.) & Adolph Hallis at Pagani's for the sole purpose of talking about our two-piano duets. The land lies very favourably, although I personally dislike K.W. pretty thoroughly. But – business is business! Go down to Blackheath in aft. with Basil W. & see projections of last section – laze about, while he does alittle cutting – & see it again. Back to town by 5.30. Back here – bath. Auden comes for a meal – & after Beth, he & I trail up to Mercury Theatre for Iris Lemare's concert – a dismal concoction of odds & ends, played in an amateur way. This is the last year of my connection with these shows! I play viola in Reginald Goodall's quite competent show of Te Deum – which goes to show attitude of these concerts! Auden flees at interval, & Beth & I soon after – having heard some quite promising Essays for Pft. by W.E. Glasspool. // I should have had broadcasts of my 'Lift-Boy' & 'Lov'd a lass' but – 'decency forbids'!!!

Tuesday 28 January

To-day is the funeral of King George. The public hysteria reaches its climax; after days of trooping past the 'lying in state' at Westminster (800,000 have done it in 4 days – some waiting all night till 6.0), myriads of people turn out to see little or nothing of the funeral procession – composed of six kings all dressed in military garb. – infinite foreign potentates (Lebrun from France – Litvinov from Russia) & representatives of all the regiments & naval & air batallions in the world. Great protectors & war preventers! Two minutes silence at 1.30 – but procession was ½ hr late. All shops closed & all in deepest mourning – the nation has lost a father – what . ., what. // Beth & I take advantage of general holiday, & stay in bed till 9.0 or later. I work in morning – walk with Beth on heath. Lunch & spend afternoon with Edric Cundell – who is to do my Sinfonietta with his orch in March.[20] Back for another walk – pretty considerable tea. Ber. & Irene come 7.0–10.0 to rehearse. Miss Wheatley to coffee & goes at 11.0.

Wednesday 29 January

Piano tuner comes after breakfast – my new piano was much in need of ~~it~~ him. // Go to Toni Brosas at 11.0 to rehease & to decide what to play at our broadcast in March. Rehease the Beethoven op. 30 in G.[21] Very lovely, but, I find it very hard to play with such lovely playing. This till 2.15. I go then to see Wright etc. at G.P.O. I am not working there for 2 or three weeks – there being no more work for me to do. Very late lunch at 3.30. Shop after & come back here – change, 'phone (Lortonov about the prospective film job – which seems as far off as ever – rather luckily considering what I've to do) & piano practise before going to dinner with Bridges at 7.15 – very pleasant. Then we go to B.B.C. concert at Queen's Hall (I meet Basil & he has my other ticket – from B.B.C.). All the musical world is there to hear Lambert's new work 'Summer's last Will' – fine ~~Nassh~~ Nashe words[22] – personally, I went for the Mendelssohn Walpurgisnacht[23] – which has some great things in it. But the Lambert was a disappointment even for him. I detest this kind of music – sensational – full of clichés & thoroughly bad workmanship. Text spoilt. Performances wern't good – the M. being quite badly conducted – even for dear Adrian B. Chorus (Philharmonic) – weak & uncertain – tho' the Lambert was ungrateful enough.

Thursday 30 January [London/Lowestoft]
Pack in morning – shop & hair-cut. Meet Bernard & Irene at Liverpool St. & catch with them 12.25 to Lowestoft. Lunch on train – write for amusement to words of Menu a canon (to be read upside down – table music) which we sing with gusto.

Mr. Coleman meets us in his car. They are staying with us. After tea with Mum we walk on beach & along fish-market. Then to Royal Hotel for rehearsal – waste much time in getting platform arranged – organisers forgetting that fiddlers & 'cellists have to bow (boh). Eventually home by 7.10 – hurried change – I have a quick run thro' of Fun Fair on pft. as I have been suddenly asked fora solo – gulp some food & we are down at Royal on stroke of 8. Play Schubert B^{b} (we are terribly nervous & it doesn't go too well – nothing serious, but unsteady) – Beethoven op. 11 & Bridge Phant. go as well as we have ever played them & we really enjoy them.[24] Megan Thomas sings some ballads. After – various people (inc.Kersty, C. Gledhill & Lee – (Norwich critic)) come back to supper.

Friday 31 January [Lowestoft]
Ber. & Irene have to catch 8.30 so we all have breakfast at 7.40 & I go to station with them: Spend morning doing nothing in particular & enjoying it alot. Play my 'Boy' records & enjoy them on the good gramophone. Shopping walk with Caesar (meeting dreadful people – 'Oh, last night was just lovely!') before lunch. In aft. Mum has 1st of Farewell parties [prior to her move to Frinton]. Fernande Sewell comes to help.

Rather a dull lot (16 altogether) – tho brightened by Marjorie Phillips & Reeves.

They go (except Fernande) by 5.30 luckily. A lovely example of necessity of scandal in provences was Mrs Palmer's presence – she has a great weakness for spreading people's secrets. Meet Beth by 8.4 from town.

I am reading (Auden's friend) Christopher Isherwood's Mr Norris Changes Trains. It is splendidly done – & very exciting; I feel he over accentuates the importance of the sex episodes – necessary as they are for atmosphere.[25]

Monday 3 February [Lowestoft/London]

Mum has had & is having a terrible time – tremendous business, both in this house in at Frinton, to be arranged. Considering ~~it~~ all, she is very well, if highly strung at times. But I hate leaving her there alone. I stay until the 2.36; spending morning doing odd jobs – including a walk along the cliffs (some useful thinking, too). & one with Mum shopping. Play my 'Boy' on the gramophone (& (pppp) revel in it!!).

Arrive in town after a long & tedious journey at 5.55. Have some tea on the journey & some buns, but rather because of the very nice little restaurant-boy who brings it along & talks abit. Quel horreur!! But I swear there's no harm in it! Dinner here (Lena, the beautiful & silent, cooks it for us) & spend after in writing letters (to Piers, (my protegé) & Francis Barton – this is getting bad!)[26] & telephoning.

Saturday 8 February [London]

Spend morning in – writing – but my teeth give me hell – but luckily again clear up in the evening. I finish the march of the quartet which seems better than I had expected. In afternoon Grace Williams comes – & I have a lovely walk right across the Heath to Kenwood with her – ~~though~~ it is fearsomely cold, though hard & sunny. Back here for tea – with Beth (who had to work this afternoon – a real 'Spring' rush) – after which Grace & I talk for ages. She is scoring two of her songs – & I am helping her – (or leading her astray!) – about the technique of the instruments & balance.

Beth & I go out to Baker Street for a meal – intending to go on to a film; but it gets too late & we come back. Read poetry – revel in some Shakespeare sonnets, & ~~Ket~~ Keat's lovely dreams.[27]

Monday 10 February

Go off early to Sloane Street to see Mrs. Harwood (back now) about teeth. Not very much result – except general cleanings. Walk back across park – back here at 11.0. Begin Waltz (from Quartet) – don't do much – find it difficult to get on. Go to Brosa in aft for rehearsal & tea. Enjoy myself alot. It is another fiendishly cold day – howling gale of the most freezing kind. Thank God we have enough money for fuel – what people must suffer who are cold & can't get warm at home or in bed. After dinner (Lena – at her most voluble) write letters – many of them – & listen to wireless – Frank's 2nd Trio played capably, but hard-ly, by Pougnet Morrison Pini Trio.[28] It is a fine work – genuinely musical & really inspired I feel. Perhaps a weakness is the restriction of harmonic & melodic language, which becomes a fraction tedious. It is as if a poet set out to write; & decided to avoid using the verb 'to be'. (This is of course 90% of the trouble of contemporary music). Even so, I feel this leaves every other bit of recent British (& most foreign chamber-music standing.

Wednesday 12 February

Polish up Waltz & take it up to Boosey & Hawkes with the March – which they are to have copied for me. Also borrow a score of Oedipus Rex from them. Alot of business for Hallis at Chesters. Eat lunch here & spend afternoon on Burlesque (mov. 3 of Quartet). Cavalcanti comes for a meal here – Lena cooks it for us 3 (Beth is in & goes out at 7.45 for cinema show). Then Cavalcant comes to Queen's Hall for B.BC. concert with me; & Toni Brosa whom we meet. Ansermet conducts BBC orch. in a slightly dull & somewhat inaccurate show of Mozart's Jupiter – Dohnanyi plays Beethoven's 3rd Conctrio (which was anyhow misplaced in a too long programme) disgracefully – no other word. Then follows a moderate show – Ansermet working like a ~~trogg~~ trojan – of Stravinsky's tremendous Oedipus Rex.[29] A most moving & exciting work of a real inspired genius. Hats off gentlemen. //

Falling to the temptation of playing some ping-pong with T. Brosa, I miss the last bus back & am treated to a taxi by two women in a similar position (turning out to be a well-known contralto & a famous dress-~~deg~~designer – according to them!). Back here to find Beth on door-step having been out to the films & forgotten her key. It's very cold – & she had 40 minutes of it.

Saturday 15 February [London/Lowestoft]

I have to post-pone trio rehearsal at 9.0. as Quartet has to be off to copyists this morning. Finish it at 11.15 – but I dare not think of the quality of the work – sometimes I doubt whether it is better than all the preceding versions – & sometimes whether it is worth all this trouble. Anyhow, we'll see. Then thro' thick fog – take it to Boosey & Hawkes, who are arranging about copying. then on to Liverpool Street to ~~see about~~ meet Beth & catch 12.25 to Lowestoft. Lunch on train – a rotten one too. Arr. 3.30 odd. Mum is up to her eyes in moving & sorting. We start helping almost at once. She seems to [be] managing very well; tho' is pretty tired.

Start the very interesting job (& extremely amusing too!) of turning out infantile letters & photos of family – kept by Mum & Pop. I can't help feeling a jot of pride and pleasure at belonging to such a family – & not bad looking too!!!

Sunday 16 February [Lowestoft]

This – & up to Wed. has to be written on Thursday – I left this book in town so everything has to be written from memory & at a stretch – tiring too!

I spend morning writing an article on Oedipus Rex & [Shostakovich] Lady Macbeth for the first number of World Film news.[30] A curse, & I find it extremely difficult to express myself in passable language. . Result is pretty lousy, but there's little time to think & it has to be off this afternoon. Walk before lunch with Beth. In afternoon read abit, & then walk along beach with dog. Meet some small friends & amuse them by throwing stones an infinite distance for them – at no small strain to my arm. Mrs. Speak & Mr & Mrs Coleman to tea. A farewell one, naturally. Go to see John Pounder after & walk with him to Post. After supper continue with Photos & letters.

Tuesday 18 February [Lowestoft/Frinton]

Up early, with breakfast at 7.30. See Beth off to town by 8.30 & return to find Men (from Wiggs – very efficeint movers) busily taking everything into large vans outside. Have a final run round (in Mr Coleman's car) delivering jumble & oddments to places. Lunch at Victoria with Mr. Graham Goodes (the very objectionable, self-important, ignorant, bumptious & altogether despicable secretary of the Norwich Festival). I find it not difficult to make him come round to letting me do a vocal suite (Sophie Wyss) for the Sept. festival. In fact I'm convinced it was only to give himself airs that he ever queried it. Then at 1.30 Fred, the Woodger's chaffeur takes Mum & me, & a little luggage, & Caesar to Frinton.[31] A lovely ride – there by 3.30. For the moment we are staying with Mrs Hill Forster who lives close to the new house & we have all meals with her. Spend alot of time with Mum superintending the moving of furniture.

Wednesday 19 February [Frinton]

I don't think that Mum regrets leaving Lowestoft. She certainly seems more cheerful than for a long time, & ~~I think~~ it has given her alot to live for in the new house. I personally don't mind a scrap – except for the fact than one suddenly realises that now, one's youth is so to speak gone. An era is passed. 'In Lowestoft when I was young' etc. Purely sentimental – but life is coloured by sentiment.

[BB leaves a line space with and draws a line separating these two paragraphs, as though he was, indeed, finally drawing a line under his childhood.]

Spend all day in the house with the second batch of furniture arriving. Walk in to Walton for things in the morning. Meals with Mrs Forster – her sister Mrs Snelling there too. Judging by talk Frinton people seem to be snobbish, cleaky (cliquey?), & shallow & dull in the extreme. But I hope I'm wrong. Mrs. Forster goes out in the evening & Mum & I have nice meal alone & very early bed.

Caesar seems to be settling down well. Likes Ivy, Mum's new maid.

Friday 21 February [London]
Cold is just as foul as possible – for others besides myself too. Rehearse trio all morning – & thank goodness it doesn't go too badly. Lunch at a nearby Express – & then walk to Alan Rawsthorne's (Belsize Park) to borow a copy of L'isle Joyeuse which I hope to play on Sunday & & think it's about time I re-practised it! Here to work until 4.30 when I go up west to meet a Mr. Whiteley who performs on the 'Theremin' & makes most heart-rending sounds. He hopes to make sounds for films – maybe, but it has to advance a good deal first. Besides who wants new instruments anyhow? Dinner with Alan Bush – to fix about me writing a brass band work for 8th.[32] After to Toni Brosas to rehearse. I should have gone to a Contempory concert at B.B.C. but can't face it with the cold, so I come back & have hot bath & Beth feeds me with hot drinks.

Sunday 23 February [Cambridge]
Up early – shave (it is one of my shaving days (every other day actually)) – breakfast, pack & go straight to Liverpool Str. & just (by 3 mins) catch 10.40 to Cambridge – arr. 11.55 & walk up to Trinity Col. & wait in David Layton's rooms till he comes at 1.0. Lunch in Hall with him & others, & in aft. go for a long & lovely walk with him & another to Grantchester. Back at Station by 4.33 to meet Bernard & Irene from town. Have a run thro' of Bridge in Hall (where we play to-night) & then tea with Michael Everitt (sec. of Trinity Col. Music Club, who are getting us down). After that long talks with David & many other old Greshamians up here – & surprisingly intelligent they seem too – mostly Communists – out to dinner with him (having changed

into tails) & then we perform in Hall at 9.0. Loillet B min, Bridge (1929) Trio – & Beethoven op. 11.[33] we each play solos (I play Debussy L'Isle joyeuse & my Funfair which goes down excellently). Not too bad, & Bridge went well. I enjoyed it – except for the solos. A party after at Gordon someones – a nice person – friend of David's.

I am sleeping in Trinity over David. He is a very good sort – clean, healthy, thinking & balanced. Exceptionally intelligent & modest considering he is captain of 'Varsity Hockey & what that is considered up ~~there~~ here.

Tuesday 25 February [London]

Up not too early. Odd jobs etc. before going at 11.0 to a rehearsal of the Stratton Quartet of my 3 divertimenti.[34] Considering all they don't go too badly, & I am very pleased with them. Beth comes back in morning & I have lunch with her & Barbara at the business flat. In aft. a long & arduous piano practise. The show of quartet is at Wigmore Hall at 5.30 in a so-called Patron's Fund Festival. The Stratton play my pieces, a quintet of Bax & a Brahms – which I do not stay to hear, feeling as I do about Brahms at the moment. The pieces don't go nearly as well as in the morning, and are a dismal failure. Received with sniggers & pretty cold silence. Why, I don't know. Perhaps they are worse than I had hoped. They are not great music – but I did feel that they are interesting & quite brilliant. Perhaps even now they need a little more boiling – but ~~perhaps~~ it may be best if they hop right into the fire! very depressing, & even a cheering evening with Lilian Wolff & Stephen Crowdy to a meal doesn't do much to change my state of mind.

Wednesday 26 February

As I expected the Telegraph (J.A Westrup) gives me a stinking notice on quartet & on my works in general. Tho' Edwin Evans is nice in the Daily Mail – I feel so depressed – in spite of myself – that working on the Russian Funeral March for Alan Bush is almost impossible. I feel like a spanked school-boy – exactly as I used to feel after a jaw – I remember perfectly. It's all silly, as I don't usually care a jot for critics least of all J.A.W.[35] However I manage to do a little march – in all day at ~~at~~ it – tho' I am quite sure it is 'superficial' – ("J.AW"!!)

Out to dinner with Barbara – a nice time & I play piano solidly afterwards – old & new favourites. Find Barbara difficult & unreasonable about Mum at Frinton & being alone at week-ends.

Thursday 27 February

Spend morning rehearsing 2 piano duets with Adolph Hallis at his flat & also making out specimen programmes for the BB.C. I expect we shall get quite a few engagements on this, & our playing isn't at all bad now. Lunch with him & Chantal at an A.BC. & a short walk after in Regent's Park. Back here then & before dinner I finish complete sketch of Russian March. It doesn't seem satisfactory – but it is as good as I can manage in the time I'm afraid.

Letters & wireless after Lena gets us a meal. Beecham & the Philharmonic orchestra. There are some lovely wind players in this band but the strings are pathetically ragged & no sense of style – but alot of this may be due to B's extravagances. His tempo of the last movement of Beethoven's 4th was ludicrously fast. All rhythm was lost. Primrose plays Walton's Viola Concerto disappointingly for a play[er] like him – not at all clean – but it must have been hard with Beecham's wild tempi. There are some fine things in this work – but alot of it wears so thin – especially the scherzo, which is very weak in parts. Most of it is too uncontrolled – & little sense of style – tho' much is quite beautiful. Also Schubert's immature 6th – but some heavenly wind solos in it & some Sibelius – not for me.[36]

Friday 28 February

Up betimes & pack. Then to GP.O at Soho Square, where I discuss sound of Calender of the Year with Miss Spice (director) & Basil Wright (producer). I am to start work here again on Tuesday. This lasts all morning. Before a hurried lunch at a Lyons I go to Chesters to get some more 2 piano music on hire for Adolph & myself to try over. Then to meet Harold Darke at B.B.C. (Maida Vale Studio) at 2.30 – tell him odd things about Te Deum. Back to flat to work on March until the 5.30 train which I catch at Liverpool St. with Beth – to Frinton. Tea on train – quick – arr. 7.10 & Mum meets us. It is strange indeed to come back to 'home' here. But pleasant on the whole, & the house is really very charming & cosy. Definitely good. Mum's maid – Ivy is proving a treasure & is happy with Mum. Much talk in evening & then at 11.0 odd listen to Harold Darke & his Michael Singers doing my Te Deum with B.B.C. orchestra. They don't sing it badly – tho' May Bartlett is a very clumsy soloist. The scoring seemed abit too subtile – but that was only the placing of the microphone. But it made some delicious sounds! Which I am not ashamed of -!!

Saturday 29 February [Frinton]

It is enormously more pleasant that we have not now to be out of dining-room by 9.0 – for 'practice' waiting-room reasons – so we take advantage of this & breakfast at 9.0. I spend morning – re-doing a little of the Funeral & also a bit of arduous piano practice before a walk to meet Mum & Beth from shopping. In afternoon I start scoring the march. After tea a long walk along beach & shopping with Beth. After dinner read alot more 'Farewell to Arms'.[37] I think it is very exicting, tho' very terrible. Also listen to wireless, & hear that the Abbyssians are being routed by the Italians. How we can sit still, quibbling about sanctions – drivelling over increased armaments – being afraid to loose 2^{d} on oil payments, yet being willing to spend £300,000,000 on men-slaughtering machines – beats me. Yet the country detests this war, & says so – vide Hoare-Laval peace plan – but still <u>trusts</u> Baldwin and his dear Government.

Sunday 1 March

Mum goes to her Christian Science meeting in the morning – there is quite a little colony of them here – led by Mrs Hill Forster.

Beth & I go for a long walk along beach to Little Holland – also alot of work on March. In aft – gramophone & wireless. ~~the~~ The King (Edward now) makes a speech to the 'Empire'. I had hoped that he would at least say something interesting – feeling that he is more of a personality than his father – something about the foreign situation or the League of Nations – but I was very disappointed. Work solidly at March until supper & after for an hour or so. Listen to a show of Walton's Symphony[38] – which confirmed my first impression that this is a capable, & undistinguished piece of work. A definite retrogression on the Viola concerto & even Façade. It ~~isn't~~ doesn't so much matter using some one else's medium & methods (Sibelius of course) throughout, but it does matter having no new idea from beginning to end. And dull is not the word for the last movement.

Tuesday 3 March [London]

Off to G.P.O. in morning at 10.0. I am on their staff now for a bit, but only for four days out of the week (£6 salery – not bad) – because I can't manage more. Spend day down at Blackheath working out sound of 'Calendar of the Year' with Miss Spice – who is very nice to work with. Cut away early to go to Wigmore Hall at 5.30. to Patron's Fund concert – given by Brosa Quartet. They play Franks 2nd G minor – a splendidly written work – not perhaps violently important – but streets ahead of the other contemporary chamber music – because it is content to be music & not over ~~conc~~ run with theories of 'great' or 'national' music. The Brosas might have played this & the Beethoven no 6. (delicious work) better.[39] 2nd Vln & 'Cello are definitely weak. I wish Toni were a bit more sensitive to the music too – tho' he is a heavenly fiddler. Lena cooks a meal in the evening for Montagu Slater & myself (Beth out till 9.30). He is a charming person & one of the most brilliant I know. We discuss many schemes – & also the film 'Calendar' which he may work on.

Lunch with Alan Bush at Bertorelli's discussing Sunday's show

Wednesday 4 March

To G.P.O early – & spend whole day hanging about – spending short time discussing sound of Calendar of Year with Cavalcanti & seeing some amateur films – but mostly no one knows what I'm to do yet. However in aft. a pretext of working I go off to Continental Telephone exchange with Bill Coldstream & see about things there – have tea & talk alot. Go to F.B.'s at 6.0 and he goes thro' the Beethoven sonata I am doing with Toni – & helps me alot.

Then after I have dinner with them, we go off to the Queen's Hall to hear Harty conduct colossal B.B.C. forces in Berlioz Requiem & Triumphant Symphony (op. 35). I have never seen so many performers – 22 Clarinets for instance. Certainly – in spite of Harty's unimaginative & insensitive tempi – the Requiem is a thrill – some little weaknesses & conventialities perhaps – but what power & imagination! Lacrymosa especially. The Symphony one cannot judge as it [is] obviously for military band performance in the open air – the ~~did~~ din was colossal. But the Funeral march contains some splendid stuff – even tho' Harty played it like a wedding march. The trombone solo was bad. I go to MM. Club after with Henry Boys – FB goes home. I get back here about 12.0 to find Beth has been to dentist & had ~~feiniting~~ fainting fits & generally seedy

Saturday 7 March

Beth goes off to stay with an old school-friend to stay week-end near Oxford.

I go to Morley College at 10.0 for a rehearsal with Alan Bush of my 'War & Death' for brass[40] – of course the players arn't expert – but it certainly seems to come off. Vladamir Vögel is also there – they are playing his Sturm Marsch.[41] Leave in time to ~~'phone~~ meet Mum at Livrpool Street at 11.40. Back for lunch here – In aft. Ber & Irene Richards come to rehearse the Bridge Trio. Barbara comes to tea – they stay too, & go about 6.0. After Lena cooks us 3 a meal we go off to Carlton, where Mum is extravagant & ~~pla~~ pays

6/- each for us to see Harold Lloyd in Milky Way[42] – a very amusing & well made comedy – not subtle of course but inspite of some slack & slow moments, very effective. Also our 'Night Mail' is put on – & it goes down excellently with the Audience.

The International situation now is ludicrously complicated – Germany now discards Locarno & Versailles & occupies Rhine territory – Italian successes on Abysssian front continue in spite of financial difficulties – Japan owing to the shooting of her statesmen in ~~the~~ last week's revolt is more milataristic than ever – & Russia is pressed on the other side as well by Germany & Poland. Central Europe is a hot-bed of intrigue – and our re-armament plans mount up & up – etc. etc. !!!!

Sunday 8 March

Breakfast about 10.0 – Mum cooks it, & goes off to a Christian S. service ~~by~~ at 11.30. I go to Edric Cundall's Orchestra to hear them rehearse my Sinfonietta – which sounds fine with the larger number of strings.

Back for lunch. I am reading Slater's new play – 'Stay down miner' for deciding about music for it.[43] Read alot after lunch. Then at 3.30 to Brosas – both of us – I to rehearse with Toni. Stay to tea. Back for hurried meal with Basil Reeve too & then he comes with us to West. Theatre for London Labour Choral Soc. show of Expedient[44] (Brecht & Eisler) which is done with fine spirit under Alan Bush. There are some fine things in this work & it is splendidly dramatic – tho' use of chorus is not too satisfactory. The first ½ of programme was my 'War & Death' – during the show of which I suffer more exquisite agony than ever before owing to uncertainty of playing. I certainly have been a bit tactless is giving so thin a texture for nervous players! Alan Bush's serious Songs of the Doomed & Vögels energetic (if weak in fugal episodes) Sturm March. Toni & Peggy come with us, also Grace Williams, Basil Wright, Slater, Cavalcanti too – Murrill & wife & John Ireland in all his gloom.

Listen at 11.45 to Broadcast from Haunted House with Harry Price as investigator in chief. Nothing startling happened except some very queer changes of temperature in the cellar

Tuesday 10 March

A lovely warm & sunny day – how welcome Spring will be after this cold & vicious winter. Work all morning & alittle in afternoon at a Lullaby for 2 pianos[45] – not very good or typical I'm afraid. Lunch in with Mum & Barbara. Much bother in afternoon over our Yale Lock – all the springs being found missing & any thing (even a pen-knife) will open the lock! New one put in at once. Mum goes by 5.30 from Liverpool St. I go with her a part of the way & stop at Brosas, where I have tea & rehearse till 7.0. Play pretty vilely. Then meet Henry Boys for a meal at M.M. & then go to Edric Cundeall's orchestral concert at Aeolian Hall at 8.30. F.B., Grace Williams & Basil Reeve also come. They are rather a scratch team & some of the wind (horns esp.) are execrable. However they play with Spirit – welcome in these B.B.C. days. They do my Sinfonietta not badly – some of the last movement being good – I can't help liking some of this work. It is absolutely genuine at anyrate. One of the worst shows of Siegfried Idyll ever / ~~was then~~ & a quite good one of 'Matin' (Haydn) Symph.[46]

Wednesday 11 March

Finish lullaby in morning, copy 1st piano part – & bit of pft. practise before going to lunch with Slater to talk about his new play – at Bertorelli 1.0. Then in aft. for rehearsal with Hallis until 5.0. Back here for practice, bath etc. before meal with Bridges. After which I take them & Basil Reeve to see Auden's 'Dog' at Westminster Theatre.[47] It is an excellent show – with glimpses of real beauty in the choruses and a lovely sense of wit & satire allthrough. Of course the moral (how W.H.A. loves his moral!) is more urgent than ever to-day – when the world is sick with fear of war, & yet its' bloody leaders are dragging it steadily into it.

Beth goes to Frinton to try & get rid of her seemingly chronic colds & general depression.

Thursday 12 March

Early to Mrs Harwood at 9.30 then on to G.P.O. where I meet Marion Grierson & talk about a new film which I am to do music for. A rather lovely thing about English Villages. Then on to Strand films to talk to Paul Rotha about a short film on peace which has been huriedly commitioned by T.U.C. & League of Nations Union. These two films have risen suddenly & I can't refuse them.[48] Lunch at M.M. with Sophie Wyss & meet Moeran. In aft. for a time to Adolph's to a committee meeting of a new series of concerts of his. Back here for desparate piano practice. Then out to MM. where I meet Rudolph Holzmann back from Germany – he has had difficulty in getting permission to land. With him & John Alston to a News Theatre where the German situation & our own satisfied incompetance is made sickeningly real. Wild ping-pong – & then John P brings me back here in his car by 11.30.

The 'eminent English Renaissance' composers sniggering in the stalls was typical. There is more music in a page of MacBeth than in the whole of their 'elegant' output!

Wednesday 18 March

Finish film music in morning – also have to go down to S. Hampstead for a shave as I have brightly left my razor at Frinton. Lunch in – & go to Booseys to see Ruch about some music and to borrow a score of Lady MacBeth. Rehearse with Hallis in aft. It is going much better – in fact quite well. Back here for a very rushed meal at 7.10 & then go straight to Queen's Hall where I sit with Rudolph Holzman for Shostakovitch's Lady MacBeth opera in concert form. Coates conducts – capably (in so far as the ensemble was good) but unintelligently as regards speeds. Slobodskaya sings beautifully as Katerina, Parry Jones fine as husband & Macklin good as Sergei – passable rest of cast. Of course it is idle to pretend that this is great music throughout – it is stage music and as such must be considered. There is ~~such~~ some terrific music in the entre' acts. But I will defend it through thick & thin against these charges of 'lack of style'. People will not diferentiate between style & manner. It is the composer's heritage to take what he wants from where he wants – & to write music. There is a consistency of style & method throughout. The satire is biting & brilliant. It is never boring for a second – even in this form. Some of the vocal writing is extravagant. But he may have special singers in view After – can't resist temptation of ping-pong with Toni Brosa. John Alston brings me back in his car.

Friday 20 March

Spend morning in – writing many ~~bills~~ cheques for long over-due bills, & letters, & also a good deal of piano practice. Up to Wardour Street to see Rotha & his new peace film at 1.0. M.M. for lunch – short ping-pong after with J.A. before going to Booseys to see Ruch about alot of new music – & to play lots for him to hear – mostly appalling stuff. Leave there at 4.30 a little tea – collect parts of Film music from copyist (Munro) – then to Herbert Hughes – Bond St. photographer for a few 'camera-studies' requested by 'Society Papers'.[49] Probably means a free photo – so that's why I go. Back here for bath & meal. & I go at 8.30 to Aeolian Hall for Toni's recital with Reizenstein. Programme starts with very dull (& not too well played) Hadyn F maj, Schubert Variations, Hindemith's new 1935 Sonata – 'back to the land' 'tone Aryan' Nazis style – & two lovely Sonatas of Dvorak (F) & Debussy – better played – superbly by Toni.[50] Of course the last is a marvel. To MM. for short time with J.A & Rudolph Holzman.

Monday 23 March [Friston]
As it is fearfully wet all the morning – spend it in talking to F.B. Very interesting & deep conversation – I show him Auden's stuff for me and he is impressed. Also find he is very ~~simp~~ sympathetic towards my socialistic inclinations, in fact we are in complete agreement over all – except Mahler! – though he admits he is a great thinker. In aft. we all go in to Eastbourne to see some films – nothing especial~~ly~~ – an amusing American comedy – Lemon Drop Kid, in which Baby Leroy is a perfect winner. An exciting ride back – one near escape – therefore somewhat emotive, tho' justifiably. John A. [Alston] returns up for a late dinner. Listen to Wireless & play light card games. The former includes an incredibly bad show of the Debussy Quartet by André Mangeot and his little colleagues.[51]

Tuesday 24 March [Friston/London]
In morning John & I decide that at it is such a superb day it would be sacriledge to ~~stay~~ leave earlier than mid-day, so I wire Hallis & Dorothy Wadham to cancel engagements (committee meeting & lunch resp.) in morning. Walk with Mrs. B. along downs & with J. to Seaford. After an early lunch at 12.0. J & I leave at 12.30 and after an amazingly quick journey I am at Soho Square by 2.30. Meet Marion Grierson & talk & see alot about her film. Then at 5.0. on to see Rotha about His peace film – which has come off excellently except for the final chorus – & it needs some subtling wangling to get over that. Eat tea at MM. with May Mukle, & back here for dinner at 7.30 to which Rudolph Holzman comes. Talk music & politics chiefly – he is a bright & intelligent person & thoroughly musical. His account of present-day Germany is as depressing as possible. Now of course everyone is hanging on Hitler's lips for his answer to the League proposals. I suppose he will accept & that will postpone war for a year or so.

Germany says – no – to proposals. How can we hedge now?
Wednesday 25 March [London]
Spend morning indoors – although it is a glorious day – & definitely warm. Practice, letters, & continue with arrangement of Rossini suite[52] for B & H. After lunch I go up to B.B.C. to see Rollo Myers & Miss Fairfax-Jones (Clarke's sec.) about an article I have to do for World Film News. Then at 5.0 I see Anstey about a film I may do for him – actually I decide I haven't time (he wants to record it soon next week) & that I will offer it to Grace. After a meal at M.M. and a news theatre. I meet Grace for B.BC. concert – last of series. Bartoks Cantata Profana[53] (I borrow score from B & H) seems a fine & serious work. Performance mediocre. Too much fugato for

my mind however. Then 2nd half a disgraceful show of the 9th Symphony. Dead, wrong speeds, no phrasing, ignorent, – (chorus better far than orchestra) – in fact Boult at his most typical. I should never have thought that it could have bored me. But it did. To MM. after – talk & ping-pong – to recover!

Thursday 26 March

A terrible morning – spend the whole time until 11.45 answering telephone & 'phoning people. It is just impossible to get anything fixed. Calls about films, about World Film News, Barcelona, odd things personal and other wise.

Go at 1.0 for hair cut to Whiteleys. Meet Grace Williams in aft. at 3.0 & take her to see Anstey about the film job. Shop. Then tea with Miss Dorothy Wadham – very entertaining. Rehearse 5.0–7.30 with Toni Brosa – but alot of talk – Hallis coming in to see about his proposals – (to include Toni if pos.). Back for dinner – wireless & more 'phone calls. By-the-way – phone calls to-day inc. Frank Bridge 2ce (Barcelona etc.). Anstey (Film). Marion Grierson (do.). E. Spice (World F. News). Cavalcanti (do.). Hallis 2ce (his scheme) Toni Brosa (rehearsal). D. Wadham (Barcelona). Wayfarers' Travel. Ag. (do.) Grace. (film). Miss Wheatley (nothing in particular). Telegram (answer to Moeran's wire). And mostly ¼ hr at least in length.

Friday 27 March [London/Bournemouth]

Up betimes, pack. & to G.P.O. to see Marion Grierson about film & also Evelyn Spice. Catch 12.30 from Waterloo (lunch on train) to Bournemouth. Go past Southampton Docks at 2.0 just as the Queen Mary (new Cunard Liner largest in world 83,000 tons) enters having come from Clyde. She looks a marvellous thing. Jack Moeran meets me at B. – his parents are living there now. Go for a long walk in afternoon with him ~~most of the~~ to Poole (bus part of way there & back) Harbour. It is a wonderful spot – very thrilling. Walk is not improved by distinct premonitions of 'flu about me. Back by 6.30 for supper & then he & I go off to Festival concert – of Municiple Orchestra which Stravinsky conducts & his son (Soulima) plays his Capriccione for pft. & orch. He plays it excellently – with just his father's style – it is an engaging work. The orchestra does really creditably in this & the delightful Pulcinella suite & the ever fresh (re-orch. & brilliantly done) L'oiseau de Feu suite. A great man is Stravinsky – sans doute. We have to leave in the middle of a show of Tsch.'s 4th under Richard Austin the permanent conductor – whom I meet in Interval & also Dan Godfrey the retired one.

Wednesday 1 April [Frinton]

~~Still~~ Stay in bed [with a bad cold] all day until ~~7.0~~ 4.0 when I ~~half~~ dress & come down for tea. Read all day – looking at odd things – inc. Moliéres Comedies, and hunt through alot of Folksongs & things for the new film.

Listen in evening to Boult & B.B.C. from Glasgow. Literally <u>the</u> worst show of Tsch. 5th ever. No rhythm or shape about 1st movement. Nothing happened as it wanted in the 2nd, & boiled shirts were much in evidence in the little waltz.

They make a brave effort at the Sacre after & play alot of the notes splendidly. But the tempi were pretty wooden & there wasn't much atmosphere about the two introductions. But the work stood up to it – it <u>is</u> a marvel, admittedly some sections arn't equally good, but the pure invention of it. And thank Heaven, Stravinsky has gone on & ~~out~~ on!

Tuesday 7 April [London]

Many long telephone calls in morning – inc. one long one with Primrose secretary of the Travel Association. I have to be very business like & 'grabbing' – but I think I shall get £40 of my money. Practise pft & letters. I'm leaving the film music for a while. Lunch at MM. before meeting Piers Dunkerley – home from school – & taking him to Cinema (Tivoli) to see Chaplin's new Modern Times.[54] Much maligned, but I enjoyed it no end. Perhaps the silence is aggravating, but the material is endless, & makes one think too – although it is very 'defeatest' throughout. But what an actor! Paulette Godard is very charming too. We go to MM. for tea & play alittle ping-pong. Long walk in park after – he needs some help poor lad. Bloxham seems a queer school, & it makes one sick that they can't leave a nice lad like Piers alone – but it is understandable – good heavens![55] Back to a meal here – John A. comes. Beth out with Kit. Talk alot & I go back to his rooms to hear his ~~gramophone~~ wireless. Bed by 11.0.

Wednesday 8 April

Early to G.P.O. & spend morning talking over Calendar of the Year film with Evelyn Spice. // The fuss caused by the Censor not passing that little Rotha Peace film[56] is colossal. ½ centre pages of Herald & News Chronicle, & Manchester Guardian – BBC. News twice. Never has a film had such good publicity! // Eat at a Lyons & then after some business go to see with John A Vielle D'armes at Studio no. 1. a french flag-waving film – but very well done. Annabelle is not one of my favourites tho'. Meet Slater for tea at M.M. at 5.0. & after discuss at length the music for his new play, a little ping-pong after, & with John Alston Dinner back here –

Beth late. Letters & innumerable telephone calls & also a short piano practice – afterwards.

Friday 10 April [Frinton]

A lovely day of rest [Good Friday]. Up ~~early~~ not particularly early – 9.30. & do just no work at all during the day. Spend time going for walks (lovely tho' cold day) playing piano – Mendelssohn's Songs without words – which I discover contain some marvellous things – not at all nothing but drawing-room pieces – gramophone & wireless. Listen to Stravinsky's Symphonie de psaumes (of which I have recently got the small score) on the former & in the evening we hear chunks of Parsifal under Wood from Queen's Hall (BBC.). It is interesting to compare the attitudes of the two composers in writing religious works. Wagner being attracted by the sensuous side of the subject – the incense, ritual, beauty of sound & emotion, Stravinsky by the moral, the psychological side, yet tremendously influenced by the ritual side as well. Parsifal is musically tremendously unequal, but has some first-rate ideas. Stravinsky has written an epoch-making work.[57]

Saturday 11 April

Practise pft. for practically all morning. I am looking at the Stravinsky Duo Concertant now – it is a fine work, but the devil to play! Also a walk. At all moments now I am getting ideas formulated for the Animal work – On walks especially. In the aft. Mum takes us all to Clacton – where we shop, have tea & walk on front. Appalling weather – violently heavy hail-storms & bitter North wind. As the 'Star' poster says – Easter shivers! Back by 6.0. – walk back along beach – v. low tide with Barbara. After dinner in evening we listen to wireless & general laze – oh! it's good to have nothing to do! Before bed we have the periodical row about going to Communion (for to-morrow). It is difficult for Mum to realise that one's opinions change at all – tho it would be a bad outlook if they didn't!

Sunday 12 April [Easter Sunday]

No one goes to Church early this morning. Subject is dropped like lead. Mum goes at 11.30 to her C.S. meeting tho! Barbara goes off for one long walk, & Beth & I go for another colossal one, round by Great Holland (where I stayed with Francis Barton when a kid, years ago) – in fact the whole day seems to be spent in going for long walks – & very pleasant too. Also read abit (I'm revelling in Francis' Merrie Tales of Tournebroche) & listen to wireless (including the adorable Vienna Boys[58] from Vienna) & an infinite amount of piano playing, & accompaning the family in their renaissance of singing – must be Spring, I should think. Mahler's Ich ging mit Lust[59] is the great favourite – & not a bad choice either!

Tuesday 14 April

Beth goes off back to town at 9.53. Barbara & I see her off & walk back along beach. It is a divine day – Sunny & hot tho' a good breeze. I spend morning down on beach, sitting in front of our hut – reading writing letters & sketching the songs at leisure.

My reveries are disturbed somewhat (tho' pleasantly I admit!) by the Forster Grandchild[ren] (minus David away ~~on hol~~ at camp) who play round about. Again there after lunch & the children too. A long walk with Barbara to Walton before tea & after tea I go for along & lovely walk on beach. A heavenly evening. After dinner listen to Boyd Neel & his strings doing my Simple Symphony. They play alot of it well, tho' too much Con Abandone! Sarabande was miles too slow. After that they play the new Schönberg Suite. It is a delightful work to listen too & I should imagine a good deal more. It might be a Hommage to Mahler both in matter & manner – but that doesn't detract from its value – rather adds to it. This seems an unexpected development for Schönberg – but quite natural.[60]

Wednesday 15 April [Frinton/London]

Dulcie Calkin comes to fetch Barbara & me in her car to station to catch 9.53. Great send off with the three children too. Arr. 11.40. Go with Barbara for coffee. Numerous telephone calls – discover that no one can see me this afternoon so 'phone Piers. Back here to dump luggage & do money business (letter of Credit) with Bank. Then meet Piers at 3.0 at Piccadilly & go to Tatler for Disney Season. Some lovely, witty, Silly Symphonies. Adored by all ages & classes. A large tea after (since I missed lunch) & walk & ping-pong with the lad after. He is a nice thing and I am very fond of him – thank heaven not sexually, but I am getting to such a condition that I am lost without some children (of either sex) near me.[61] // Back here for a meal. Poor Beth has many worries – whether to continue at Finchley Road at the end of the lease (June) – if so for how long, whom with, & can she let her upstairs portion. This responsibility!

Thursday 16 April [London]

Up early – alot to do – & to G.P.O. at 10.45. Talk over films with Spice (hers to be postponed till September) & Coldstream (his, end of May) all the morning.[62] Then C. comes with me to M.M. Club to lunch with Montagu Slater (his play to be musicfied by May 10th). After lunch to Fox's Photos to be taken – press purposes – all good advertisement, tho' unpleasant! Meet Mum at Liverpool St. at 3.42 & then after tea she comes with me to Austin Reeds where we proceed to spend all my hard-earned money in buying – new suit shoes, over coat & Goodness-knows what else. All this business with trying on in front of endless mirrors gives me an inferiority complex. Back here for a meal – trouble with Lena because she didn't wait in for the beef, so we have to have bacon and eggs. Very lazy after; Mum & Beth do my packing. Thank heaven for families – sometimes!

Friday 17 April [London/Barcelona]
Up at 6.30. Mum gets me some food & I taxi to Horseferry House to catch bus at 7.55 to Croydon. Meet Dorothy Wadham at Vict. & we both with Hubert Foss whom we meet at Croydon catch Air France plane to Barcelona. Very exciting journey – very bumpy in spots, the weather starts beautifully from London & gets windier & windier to the South. Croydon. 8.45. Paris 10.15. Change planes for Marseilles via Lyons where we stop for food. Fly very high (10,000 ft) to L. & ears hurt considerably on descending. Marseilles at 1.55 (we were early). Then change to Flying boat (Ala litoria) to Barcelona over sea. Arrive ½ late at 4.45 because of high winds & delay in starting at B. & are met by Brosas who've been here for 14 days or so. Go with them & the others to Falcon Hotel where we're staying. Meet E. Clark too & Lennox Berkeley. To a café with them & afterwards walk the town with Edward C. On going back to Hotel at 8.30 run in to Bazil Wright & John Tayler (who've been filming in the Balearic Isles). Spend ev. with them Dorothy, L.B., & Foss. Walk about & in cafés till 12.30. Should meet Brosas at a café at 12.45 but return to bed with the others. Toni eventually phones me at 1.45 about to-morrows arrangements.

Saturday 18 April [Barcelona]
Up & breakfast about. 9.30. Shop abit down the Ramblas after & then Toni Brosa's brother comes to fetch me to rehearse with him up in his flat in Gracias. Just as we start, Basil Wright appears – he should have flown this morning at 5.0. but weather is too bad, & as he must be back on Monday has to go by train. He wants to borrow some money for his & Taylor's fares – so I go with him to Cooks & give him what he needs. To Brosa to rehearse after & stay with him & his family for a typical & very lovely meal. In afternoon to various places with him & Peggy & to the big reception in the Town Hall (Generalidad?) [Generalitat] – with infinite speeches. But afterwards the Saltaders danced to the enchanting music (~~o~~ more powerful oboes (tiglis?) in the Square.[63]

Eat a meal at ~~9.0~~ 8.30 with Dorothy W. Edward Clark & Lennox Berkeley & afterwards go to a concert at 10.0 at Palau by Orfeo choir. Mangnicent singing (boys, men, women) – deadly accurate & exceptionally musical. Mostly old stuff (some lovely Vittoria) & some more modern (19th & early 20th cent), stuff. D.W. & I leave at 1.0 – rather exhausted. The concert doesn't end till 1.30!![64]

Sunday 19 April

Wake late at 10.30. Go to Palau des Belles Artes for concert of Municiple Wind Band with Foss & Brosas. It is an amazing Band of about 65 – all sorts & shapes of inst. & making the most heavenly sounds. Unfortunately a very dull programme – an academic Devise of Vogel (not up to his other works) a most deadly choral & band work 'Joan de l'os' by De Grignon jun. frightfully long & bad Wagner & Massenet, & Schmidt's Dyonisiaques. The conductor De Grignon sen. is a fine musician.

Meet Arnold Cooke from England at lunch. Eat at Hotel with him & D.W. In aft. go (with A.C.) to Brosas to rehearse Suite[65] & back to Palau de Musica at 5.30 for first orchestral concert. The first half of programme (Borck, Gerhardt, Krenek) is completely swamped by a show of Berg's last work Violin Concerto (just shattering – very simple, & touching) & the Wozzeck pieces – which always leave me like a wet rag.[66] After this Arnold C. & I have a good meal, & go for a long walk round the town till 12.30. There is a Mayoral Banquet which we cut. You can't be polite after Berg!

Tuesday 21 April

Rehearse in the morning (after much waiting about) in the Casal des Metges with Toni, where we are playing this afternoon. It goes very well – tho we have sufficient slips to avoid over-confidence. ~~There is a do~~ Back here to lunch and after that go with A.C. up to Brosas to discuss for the xth time what to wear (6. p.m. is an awkward time). Eventually decide that evening dress is impossible (which I've brought) & so I borrow a dinner jacket from A.C. Back via café for shoes to be cleaned (marvellously too) & then a rapid change & to the Casal des Metges at 6.0 where concert is.

Wednesday 22 April

Up pretty late & then Arnold Cooke & I go up to the Brosas & pick them up at 12.0. Then we all four go up to mount Tibidabo where we spend the morning. It is a glorious day & we see much better than on Monday. Stay with AC. up there for a colossal lunch (~~6~~ 7 courses at least) which takes 2 hours (like most Catalan meals) – the Brosas have to go back to Gracias for a meal. Meet them after & then go for a long walk round the harbour &

in the slums. Eat at hotel in the evening before going to Orchestral concert no. 3.[67]

After the concert go with L.B., Peter Burra, & AC. to a night club in Chinatown – my 1st & not particularly pleasant experience – as a young harlot is very keen on picking my pockets tho' I loose nothing. The dancing (mostly male – & dressed as females) is very lovely. But my god the sordidity – & the sexual temptations of every kind at each corner.

Thursday 23 April

To André Mangeot at 11.0 in the morning & we go to the Radio station & rehearse sonatas for tomorrow evening – play some nice things but this isn't the ideal way or performers to play them! After a fine meal at a local restaurant – very cheap 5pt.50 (about 2/10) with him and in the afternoon walk with Arnold C, Lennox B, Peter Burra & a friend (Dan?) round the harbour, on top of Mount Juic – a heavenly view of the town & the sea-side across the aerial railway to the restaurant over the harbour.

Friday 24 April

Up with breakfast at 8.15 & then to Palau da Musica at 9.0 to go on the Montserrat excursion. The first buses with Toni etc. are full, & we have to wait ½ hr for an extra one – i.e. with A.C., D.W. etc. A very long & lovely drive arriving at the Monastery about 12.0. It is a heavenly spot – unlike anything around, with its incredible fingers of stone. It is difficult not to believe in the supernatural when in a place like this, especially as we go to a concert of old church music in the chapel, beautifully sung (a lovely Vittoria canon) in semi-darkness.[68]

Lunch there, & after go up in the funicular to the top – where the wonders increase. Start back so as to arrive about 7.0. Eat at Hotel with AC., & Egon Wellesz – who's staying here. Then go with André Mangeot to Radio Station where we are to play at 10.20. Finally, having rehearsed, & 'balance & controlled', we are told it is off, because of a political speech (Presidential elections) which won't end. After that I go with André Mangeot & A.C. to a *Pelotte match which is one of the most exciting things (& dangerous) I have ever seen. Café & back at 1.30. *It is played by four men slinging a hard ball at wall – in a court of 3 sides about 10 × 60 yds.

Saturday 25 April

As usual breakfast about 10.0 – I cannot wake after these nights – and then after a few cards & letters I go for a lovely walk quite alone (& pleasant!)

thro the town. Spend a ~~lovely~~ long time in the Cathedral – revelling in the sensuous beauty of darkness & incense. Then to the Palau where I meet Lennox & Peter B. ~~Coffe~~ Go to a café with them. Back here to lunch (with a man called Penny) & then go to a café & have my shoes cleaned & heeled (3/6!). Then at 4.0. we all go to Mont Juic[69] for the festival of Folk dances. Meet Toni & Peggy there.

Sunday 26 April

Up pretty late – some cards written – then I go with André M. to Radio Station and we have our postponed broadcast of 3 Sonatas (Purcell, Eccles, Festing) at 12.30. Pretty bad, & very under rehearsed. Then to lunch with the Brosa family[70] – which is very pleasant, as they are dears. In the aft. Toni, Peggy, Peter B., & I go to see the Motor Cycle racing on Montjuice. This is very exciting & interesting to watch – until we are close spectators (& very nearly involved) in a fearful crash – in which a spectactor ~~obj~~ obstructs a competitor, is instantly killed, the rider badly injured & many of the audience by the flying machine. This is terrifying, especially as the crowd gets somewhat out of hand, police get panicky, and the chances of other people getting killed while crossing the track is considerable – the noise of people screaming, hystericly, police whistles & roar of machines. Back to the hotel for a meal & go after to a concert by the Madrid

Monday 27 April

The Brosas go back to London early this morning. Up by 9.30 I go shopping with Dorothy (she helps me by a hat for Beth) & also arrange about money. Then Jack Gordon takes the rest of us (D.W., Peter Burra, Lennox & myself) in a taxi to Sitges the fashionable summer resort of Barcelona. It is a heavenly place – the quaintest odd narrow streets. The weather is lovely, except for rain at lunch-time. The drive along the coast is very beautiful up and down mountains – with a precipice into the sea always on one side – abit thrilling! Back by 6.0. Then Lennox & I go out to a music shop to trace some Sardanas[71] we have heard, but without success. Then pack before a meal in the hotel – settle up the bill (226 pts. about £6) – & then go to a cinema with him. He is a very delightful person, & with sound ideas on music. Back by 12.15 & straight to bed.

Wednesday 29 April [London]

Many 'phone calls all the morning, including an interview with the News Chronicle. I seem to have had an enormous amount of publicity when away – 'photos & all – & everyone has seen something. I can't help feeling gratified, after all the blows before this – and after too I expect. Lunch with Montagu Slater & Wilfred Walters, after a hair cut with my nice hairdresser at Whiteleys, to talk about 'Stay down miner' music this till 3.30. Then I go to Toni Brosa's & play the Benjamin Concerto[72] for him – he's to broadcast it tomorrow. Stay to tea with him & Peggy. Then back to the Group theatre rooms at 7.0 for a committee meeting (I have been put on the executive committee). Don't do much. Rupert Doone & Robert Medley take me back to their flat, where I meet Wystan Auden before he goes off abroad again.[73] Then back here for a late supper at 8.45. Then proceed to write this up as far as I can – as I am quite behind.

Friday 1 May

After some telephoning I go up to see Montagu Slater, & Charles Kahn about this music – make alot of decisions & finally go to see a Harmonium which we may hire – at Chappels. Meet Bazil Wright for lunch & discuss one or two projects. Then in afternoon I meet Toni Brosa & we go & play some knock-about tennis at my club – 4–6. Then to a meal with Barbara & Helen Hurst. Beth joins me at 10.0 & together (& with Brosas & Bridges) go to B.B.C. contemporary concert – Alban Berg in memoriam. Von Weben conducts – not good at all – & orchestra definitely B.B.C.-ish. Two pieces from Lyric Suite – very moving, but less intimate than the quartet version. Then Crasner plays the Violin Concerto – the show not a patch on the Barcelona one – which is again a very moving experience. It certainly is a very great work, & at the end I feel pretty wet with ~~sor~~ anger about losing a genius like this.[74] Then of course the British spirit ~~wa~~ becomes uppermost & they play with great gusto 'God save the King' (as if it mattered compared with the other loss). It took an English institution to do that.

Sunday 3 May [Frinton]

We are cursed with dull weather down here. Yesterday it was lovely until the moment we arrived at the door. To-day it is dull in the morning with a beastly N.E. wind – & the afternoon is sunny until we decide at 4.0 to take tea out to the Naze when it clouds over for the rest of the day. However we have a pleasant time sitting underneath a bank out of the wind. // In the morning I sketch a song for M.S's play & then walk to Great Holland with Beth & Lilian. I copy out a decent copy of the part-song in the afternoon. Back from the Naze at 7.0 – Mrs Forster comes to see us – Bath – supper – talk over endless matters & bed at 10.45.

The Italian-Abbysinian war is nearing its close. Addis-Ababa is in a state of confusion; the Emperor (fine man) has fled & most of his generals & what with the Italians & the native looters it is in a bad way. Mussolini's war of civilization is at an end. What country will be in need of treatment now?

Monday 4 May [Frinton/London]

Up at 6.30 & we make an early start at 7.30. Unfortunately Lilian's car develops some engine trouble before Chelmsford. This & the fact that we lose time in looking for a short cut coming into town. prevents us arriving until 10.30. Back here – do lots of business & do more theatre music before going out to lunch on Heath with Beth & Lilian – lovely sun. In aft. back & finish the stuff – take it up to the Left theatre office – tea & then meet Grace Williams & go to Covent Garden with her (she's given me 'Gallery Slips' tickets) – Parsifal at 5.45. Dinner at Slaters in first interval. It is not Wagner at his best & there are dull passages – but alot of the last two acts are splendid. On the whole a good show – Reiner conducts steadily – Leider as Kundry was great in intention but unfortunately the great voice is going & she is becoming fat – also a trouble with [Tortsen Ralf] (Parsifal) who sang well too. Best of the rest was easily Janssen as Amfortas who sang splendidly & acted as well. Habich as Klingsor also fine. Production pretty lousy. Some of the settings impressive, but the flower maidens in Victorian Bathing dresses with paper caps, & none too slim either, were a slight for the Gods!

Sunday 10 May [London]

My throat is just giving me hell – last night I was pretty nearly unable to speak. But I'm hoping for recovery with the help of Formalin.[75] Apart from that I'm fine. Play tennis after a late breakfast at club (quite good, but play putridly) until a late lunch at 2.15 here. Then in aft. after letters etc. go to Westminster Theatre at 4.30. A short run thro' with the band of bits of the stuff then a show of 'Stay down Miner' at 5.15 & one at 8.15. Beth & various friends come to the 2nd. Considering the state of the dress rehearsal the shows are marvellous. Margeret Yarde is superb. & the whole cast is fine. The music doesn't go badly – little as there is of it. I think the play is really good – very dry & terse, with a strong sense of comedy. The last scene needs to be tightened. A meal in between with Montagu S. & another man.

Monday 11 May

After shopping with Beth I have a good tidy up in my room – business letters etc. writing up accounts as well – & a piano practice (in excelsis – for me). I go to lunch with Rupert Doone (of Group theatre) at his flat – to talk over new projects. A very good lunch, tho he is inclined to be too affectionate.[76] A long walk in the park with him after. Then I do some things up West, go to a news theatre before ~~go to~~ going to Toni B's to rehearse the Stravinsky again. I think it is a very lovely work though a blighter to play. Back here for a late dinner which Lena cooks & to which Miss Wheatly of Burleigh House comes. 'Phone Mum, & she 'phones me.

Tuesday 12 May

Go for a tremendous walk over Hampstead Heath practically all the morning – after an energetic practise – trying to finish 'Rats' in my mind.[77] But it won't work – it is a pig. I get back for lunch & settle down to think in the afternoon – but infinite telephone calls distract me entirely & I eventually go off to tennis at 5.30. André Mangeot I get to come to club – but the tennis is pretty lousy. Stay on with Kathleen Mead for a single after the others go & eventually have a meal at a local restaurant with her. Poor food tho', makes one long for the Spanish one where the food was taken seriously – Back by 10.15 – Mum phones She went to Lowestoft by car to-day.

Wednesday 13 May

Work all morning at 'Rats' & it seems to be going well. Lunch in – bread & cheese, bread & honey & jam or cake, & fruit – as usual – practise after & then go to Toni's for rehearsal at Stravinsky[78] – it is going well now.

After tea there & abit more playing I meet Paul Wright – whom I knew well three years or so ago & whom I've not seen recently – & eat with him at Durands. He is a nice person – very charming & clever & gifted too. After that we go to part of John Francis's (flute) Philharmonic Ensemble concert at Aeolian Hall (although I inadvertantly go to wrong Hall first – 2nd time recently!) – with Kokchinskia as a good harpist. They play a charming Mozart Flute 4^{tet} – Arnold Cooke's quintet (some good ideas, but a student work) & Roussel Serenade.[79] – charmingly scored but rhythmically weak & musically very dull & full of French clichés. Back by 10.15 Eleanor Bond is staying the night here.

Monday 18 May

Rehearse – (1) light stuff with Hallis in morning – two pianos (2). Stravinksy & my suite with Toni B. 3.30–6.30. (1). bad (2) better. Then back here to listen to Act. I of Tristan from Covent Garden with Kirsten Flagstad as Isolde – her first appearance in England after her sensational American shows.[80] She certainly is a wonder – marvellously accurate – scarcely a semiquaver wrong ever & a great voice with a tremendous variety of tone.

Melchior was singing splendidly too. Reiner was an accurate if uninspiring conductor – but infinitely better than Beecham's erractness. This finishes at 8.0 when Rudolph Holzman comes to dinner. Talk after – there is much to talk about – Barcelona, his Soirées de Brusselles (where a work of his was played), state of music & politics in the world ~~its~~ & in England in particular etc.

Wednesday 20 May

Rehearsal with Toni all morning. Lunch at MM. with Paul Wright. Then in the aft. to the Academy where I meet Murrill & try piano for to-morrow. Late in leaving & have to taxi to Fullers. Victoria to meet Mrs. Hurst for tea. She is very outspoken in her opinions on modern art – quite refreshingly so, & we get on like a house on fire! Take one hour by bus to come from Victoria back here – spend over ¼ hr waiting ~~for~~ at Marble Arch in a traffic block. This is a very urgent problem as every year is best – & you don't cure it by keeping motorists off the road by making the driving test unreasonably difficult. David Green & his friend Herbert Tayler come for a meal. Beth goes out afterwards & we stay in & talk till 11.0. Then listen to a bit of the Mendelssohn Octet – last mov. very thrilling too – & a lovely broadcast song of the Nightingale[81]

Thursday 21 May

Spend morning in, & most of the time practising. In aft. go to Toni for a rehearsal & then at 5.30. we go to Royal Academy New Music Soc. where we contribute ½ the programme (the other ½ being piano solos of Berg – Norman Demuth). Toni & I play the Stravinsky Duo Concertant & my Suite both of which go well & are well received mine especially – tho' I hear after that my critic friend J.A.W (Westrup), who is there is despondent about the future of British music! That is as may be! A meal after at MM. with Toni, Peggy, John Alston & Rudolph Holzman.

Then I go to Rheingold at Covent Garden with Grace Williams – in the Gallery Slips as usual (hearing good, but seeing not so good – & seats hard & 2½ hrs without a break would try most posteriors!) A good show (tho' Orchestra pretty bad under Beecham). Bockelman is on wonderful form as Wotan & Kremer's Loge, & Weber's Fasolt were fine. The English contingent (inc. Farmedge & Wrey) were pretty wretched – lack of tradition & practice partly. // It is a great priviledge going to this Ring. The plan of it is so fine that one should really do nothing else all the week.

Sunday 24 May [London/Surbiton/Epsom]
Very late breakfast as I am not particularly energetic & Beth is tired after a very late night. Then odd jobs about the place – make beds (Lena only comes to cook a meal on Sundays) & then I go off to Surbiton to lunch with the Gyde family (Sophie Wyss, husband & son – Arnold). Very pleasant afternoon talking in the garden & then after tea we all go in the car to Epsom Downs where the place is seething with excitement about Derby day next Wednesday.[82] The gypsies are very prominent & the atmosphere of 1850 is prevalent.

Before & after dinner Sophie sings alot & very beautifully too. We also discuss points about the new song cycle. The small son aged 9 is a delightful lad – as full of animal spirits ~~of~~ as 4 ft of person could be. Very intelligent too – & enthusiastic. His parents are charming & interesting of course. Back here by 11.0. Beth played tennis this afternoon & in this evening.

Monday 25 May [London]
Spend practically all the morning trying to get my business accounts in order – I didn't keep them last year & I fear me the income tax man is round the corner. In the afternoon I walk for 2 hours on Hampstead Heath – thinking but not too satisfactorily – It is impossible with all this music round me to do much – however next week I start in earnest. Go to Covent Garden for Walküre at 5.45 with Grace. Unfortunately the show is marred by Bochelmann's cold (– his Wotan was non-existant, for he couldn't sing a note. Apparently no other was to be found), and the execrable orchestral playing. Flagstad's Brünhilde was thrilling except for some of the quieter lower passages when there wasn't much legato – but she ~~loke~~ looked a god; Very different from poor Rethberg as Sieglinde (Grace said that when she came in in Act II she was scared that Siegfried might be born any moment), tho' her singing wasn't too bad. Melchior is a fine Siegmund, and Zantho a great Fricka – as before the less said about the conductor & orch. the better.

Tuesday 26 May
In morning stay in (I should have gone to Hallis for rehearsal but it is 'off') & practise pft. much business – telephone (incessantly) & letters. Then go early to Soho Square & have lunch with Basil Wright & talk about a Ballet which we may do together (possibly 'Golden Asse').[83] Then in afternoon I spend whole time discussing music for 'Calendar of the Year' with Miss Spice (mostly at the M.M. Club where we have tea). Back here at 6.30. Pat J. should have come to tennis but he can't at last moment, & I go up on chance to club – & am rewarded with some pretty hopeless stuff. Back here at 9.0 for a

bath, & then a meal with Beth. Letters after – among my large correspondance (inc. letters from Piers & Francis) was one from a Miss Nettleship (relative of Augustus John) about a possible cottage for us in July & Aug in Cornwall. Sounds good.

Wednesday 27 May

Beth and I go down early to Hatch End with John Alston in his car to look at a Lagonda car going for £6 at a garage there. Eventually we decide to buy it as it seems in such ~~cond~~ good condition. Probably fool-hardy, but the offer is tempting. This takes most of the morning. I do a little work but its impossible with 'Ring' behind & in front of one to work much. Listen to Derby broadcast. Pretty exciting. Then to Whiteleys for a hair cut & then Mrs Bridge comes to Act. I of Siegfried in place of Grace who can only manage Acts II & III. A meal with Charles Brill in first interval. A much better show than Walkure. The new Wotan (Roth) not too good, but better than a bad Bochelman. Siegfried (Melchior) ~~was~~ is really splendid – in spite of many faults. A young & joyous actor – amazingly so. Mime (Fleischer) ~~was~~ is also splendid. Flagstad looked radiant in Act III as Br. – & sings like a God. Perhaps not intimate enough in the quieter parts, but the end (from both) was a blaze of glory. Erde (Szätho) again great. But the hero of the evening was the composer. This must be the greatest of the ring. The variety, power, humour and incredible invention.

Friday 29 May

Much business – letters etc. early in the morning before going to Westminster with John A. to get car licence. Lunch with Charles Brill in Soho. He is extremely pleasant & charming to me, which I find impossible to resist tho' I feel he is a doubtful character & really self-seeking. But then I know my weakness for charm and/or flattery. Meet Grace in the aft. and she helps me buy a wedding present for Sylvia Spencer. – book-ends – quite plain & pleasant. Then to Covent Garden to Götterdämmerung – last lap of the great adventure – musically great & overwhelming. A fine show. Flagstad sings in an extraordinary way ~~, Melchior,~~ 'tho the Brünhilde is a trifle meek at the end, ~~tho~~ but the curse in Act II (perhaps the finest music of all) is terrible. Melchior has never sung better, & the others (inc Weber as Hagen, Habich as Alberich) were all good. Orchestra & Beecham both erratic. I feel exhausted entirely at the end. The Wagner fever is as strong as ever on me, but less hypnotic than before I hope. Now I more appreciate the colossal dramatic & musical skill, sheer invention in every direction. Grace & I have a meal with Lennox Berkeley just back from Spain & Paris in first interval. It goes well considering the intense opposites of their two characters.[84]

Tuesday 2 June [Frinton]
Beth goes off back to town alone in the car. She leaves at 9.45 & when we 'phone in the evening we learn that she didn't arrive until 2.30, owing to very bad (skiddy) roads, very bad brakes, filthy weather & on top of all that the ignition pin comes out & she spends 1 hour ~~having~~ finding a garage & having it put right. So much for 2nd hand cars!

I work abit in morning, walk abit too, down to town before lunch, but it is only in the afternoon & after tea that I really get going, rewriting what little I've already done, & continuing with my 'rats'. Not too bad so far. In the evening, play piano alot – Beethoven sonatas – & listen to a really wonderful show of Tristan act III with Melchior & Flagstad right at the top of their lovely forms. True I missed Leider, but what a voice this Isolde had, & what serenity in the Liebestod. Jannsen is superb of course. But what music! It gives me such an inferiority complex & yet makes life worth living with such art – words as well as the incredible music.

Thursday 4 June
Spend most of morning doing a short article for World Film News – on BB.C. programme for July. Also do alot of revision of yesterdays work on Rats. In aft. at 2.30. Millicent Silver plays my Holiday Tales from London – really excellent playing; one or two little details perhaps, but she has caught the spirit absolutely, & she has excellent fingers. After that re-start Messalina – & go for a long walk after tea (Mum has some visitors) to think about it. Decide it's not very good, & Rats also, so have a bath & dinner & listen to wireless trying to forget it. Go for a long walk in the woods nearby, & get back to find that Beth's 'phoned to say she's had a smash in the Lagonda, & mucked up one wheel. A bus ran into her thro' no fault of hers apparently; but it seems doubtful whether we shall get the insurance since we're only on third party.[85]

It takes a lot of Beethoven sonatas (mostly early ones, op. 14, 22 – 96 [?])[86] to cheer me after <u>that</u>!

Friday 5 June
Spend morning & most of afternoon writing practically finishing Messalina – but spend rest of day thoroughly depressed not being able to decide whether the stuff is the best or worst stuff I've ever written. Most probably it's neither – that's the trouble! Write long letter to Bazil W. about the ballet

in afternoon – long thinking walk after tea, but not to much purpose. Life is a pretty hefty struggle these days – sexually as well. Decisions are so hard to make, & its difficult to look unprejudised on apparently abnormal things.

In the evening Mum & I go to see Shirley Temple in the little Colonel in Walton with Mrs Forster. Very entertaining little star-vehicle. Certainly she's an attractive little girl – but then, children . . . . ![87]

Sunday 7 June

Very dull & rainy day until late in the afternoon when it decides it will be civil to the workers from London & show some sun. Walks in morning – car in dock to have wheel changed – abit battered – sit & play on beach in afternoon & drive after tea (in the garden.). Have lots of bother with Mum – saying things (Rosemary [Pollard] is delightfully free in her conversation!) that arn't polite, conventional, or innocent. It is very difficult always to curb one's tongue!

Monday 8 June

Up at the very crack of dawn to drive Rosemary to station to catch 6.58. Beth & Lilian leave soon after at 7.30 after breakfast. It is a heavenly morning & I quite envy them their drive to town. Mum & I breakfast at 8.20. In the morning & aft. I swat at the end of Messalina & the Rat's middle section (3rd edition).[88] Former I think O.K. latter definitely N.B.G. [no bloody good] yet – I am just stuck with it. I am thinking hard about Hawking[89] but no very concrete ideas come yet. (This, in a long walk after tea with hound). Listen to Clifford Bax' Socrates[90] – which makes quite a good play really – after dinner. It is the tremendous value of the actual material of course that makes it possible nevertheless his end was very naturally & simply managed.

Beethoven's op. 110 to cool my troubled thoughts before bed[91] – rather spoiled by Caesar being violently sick in hall.

Thursday 11 June

Work at Hawking morning & afternoon & on a walk after tea. Lovely day, tho cold evening. Work goes much better, indeed I feel quite cheerful – almost excited – about it later in the day. After dinner I play it over alot & describe it in detail to Mum. She disapproves very thoroughly of 'Rats' – but that is almost an incentive[92] – ~~not~~ no actual insult to her tho'.

Walks are spendid along the beach in the evening. Sea & light are gorgious & one is kept alive by dodging cricket balls from the youth of Walton & Frinton! I am reading Butlers Erewhon, & enjoying it immensely. Other recreation is solely playing Beethoven piano sonatas & reading Mahler scores. Symp. I, V, & Lied von der Erde.

Thursday 18 June

The weather broke with thunder last night – & to-day is very close & rainy – but it lightens & brightens towards evening.

I work at end of Hawking all day solidly. I <u>think</u> it's good. It is pretty exhausting tho! Listen to Mozart's Figaro from Glydenbourn[93] acts I & II as a respite 7.0–8.40. I should have gone to dinner with Mrs Forster, as Mum does, but I decide to listen to this instead (& my god it was good) & then go for a long thinking walk. I go there at 9.45 for a short talk.

Lennox Berkeley sends me a copy of his Jonah[94] – like a dear.

Friday 19 June

Mum goes to Clacton to shop in morning. I write letters & then try & get on with Epilogue – without any success. Write abit of it in aft. & after tea, but not much use. Walks after tea & before lunch. Read – Gulliver[95] – after dinner & then inspite of a colossal thunderstorm nearby, try & listen to Lennox' Jonah from B.B.C. From what one could tell (& having score of course) there are some very good things in it. To its advantage it is under Stravinsky's influence of course, but the harmony is extremely personal. A weakness is a comparative dullness in the vocal line. Some of the choral writing is extremely beautiful – especially at the end.

The storm gets pretty bad towards early morning. Very unpleasant.

Monday 22 June

Up with the lark (but not feeling like one) ~~at~~ to take Beth & Grace to station to catch 6.58. I am having the Lagonda here this week. It is another lovely day – very hot, but good breeze. I work alot at Rats (getting the middle right I think) and abit at End which isn't good yet. Various short walks – clean car & oil etc. after tea. After dinner Salome (Strauss) from Paris. It is exciting inspite of its extravagances – & ~~but~~ perhaps the best Strauss.[96] Performance all over the place. I attempt to listen to abit of V. Williams piano concerto[97] – but it is too bad even for him – & I go to bed with a nice (if erotic) taste in my mouth from the Adagietto of M.[98]

Poor Caesar is very bad to day – sick & what-not. Won't ~~mot~~ move from the garden & is generally dejected & miserable.

Friday 26 June

I take Mum down the town for a long shop soon after breakfast & we arn't back till 11.30. But it is good fun driving round in the Lagonda. Back here &

until lunch and in aft. I work on piano score of 'Rats' which I post to Sophie after tea. Long thinking walk after tea – I'm getting further with the Prologue. After dinner play piano a lot – strange mixture, Chopin Waltzs & Czerny Fingerfertigkeit.[99] Musically of course the latter has it, but they are both supreme piano stuff.

I like Fridays because apart from the daily paper there is the Radio Times (occasionally World Radio too) & New Statesman. All good to read, tho' no news is good to read now. The Goverment has definitely decided to stop sanctions – on the principle that Abyssinia is lost & nothing will bring her back again. Forgetting entirely the punitive value of them. Alas for collective security. If Mussolini can get away with it, what for Hitler? O God, this National Government!

Tuesday 30 June [London]

I go up to Boosey & Hawkes at 11.0 to introduce Lennox Berkeley to Ralph Hawkes & Leslie Boosey – hoping to get them to publish some of his stuff, which I think they will.

Then to M.M. where I meet John Alston & lunch with him. In the aft. I go to G.P.O. & work on the ballet script with Basil Wright. We do some good work & it seems to be shaping very well. Then I go to the P.R.S. where F.B is at a meeting, & wait for him & then we go to Victoria & have a snack meal before he catches a train back to Eastbourne at 6.45. I go to a news theatre & then back here for a meal with Kathleen & later Beth. Listen to Part II of Zaüberflöte from Glyndebourne at 9.30. It is one of the heavenliest works ever. Performance fine, with a glorious Pamima – Aulikki Rautawaara.

Wednesday 1 July

After shopping, & seemingly endless telephone calls spend morning copying out Epilogue for Sophie. Then lunch with Rudolph Holzman – who is being driven out of the country because of his nationality. He is going to Italy now because that is the only place which will accept German currency now, & he is forbidden to make money here. It is a bloody shame as he is a fine musician, to say nothing of being such a delightful person. Go to a news theatre before meeting Mum from Frinton at 4.57. She goes with me to Barbara's where she is putting up & then after that meet Beth for a meal, & then with Kathleen Mead we all go to Haymarket to see the inimitable & lovely Ruth Draper in some fine sketches.[100] The very finest mime possible, & so much of it is moving to tears almost, especially the miner's wife. The 3 women & Mr. Clifford is as good as ever & in a Florence church is a great experiance.

Thursday 2 July
Copy the Prologue for Sophie & then go up to B. & H. to discuss the Ballet of Cupid & Psyche with Ralph Hawkes – i.e. Basil Wright & me. He likes the idea. I also play him & others the Hunting ~~Farthes~~ Fathers, but it is impossible to do anything on the piano with it – & the only comments ~~were~~ are, or could be, 'interesting' & 'striking'. However, at the moment I love it all. Lunch with Montagu Slater – who is a dear & exceptionally intelligent of course. We are thinking of a ballet on Gulliver – Lapente [?].[101] Then to Sophie at Surbiton for tea & an early dinner. Work at the songs abit which she will do splendidly, I know. Arnold – small son – is there & as attractive and entertaining as usual. S. is to have a baby in Aug. so is consequently not working hard at the moment. Back to meet Brosas for a cinema at 9.0 – but they fail to turn up & I return here. // Mum goes to Worcester to stay with Uncle Sheldon & Aunt Julianne.

Friday 3 July
Odd jobs – seeing about car – infinite telephoning & I go to see Adolph Hallis & Chantal at 12.0. Then on to Lennox Berkeley's to lunch with his friend Greenage (?)[102] in Bloomsbury. Very charming flat. Talk alot & play him my 'Fathers' – & he seems thrilled. Then back here to tea to which Harry Morris – the little boy Barbara found – comes (& Barbara for about ½ hr). He is getting on with his fiddle, & sings very nicely, & seems very intelligent. He is terribly keen on everything – especially gym at the moment – he shows me some of his especial tricks. Then to Grace at 6.30. Play her 'Fathers' & then eat with her & to Covent Garden for the De Basil Ballets. All old stuff of course – classic in its way tho'. The lovely Lac des Cygnes – perhaps loveliest Ballet music ever – Thamar in the Bakst glitter – L'Ápres midi (which I hate – but love the dancing & the music – the combination is wrong) & a wild & vigorous Prince Igor to finish with Danilova in Cygnes, Lichine in Thamar & L'après M. & Shabelevsky in Prince Igor were outstanding – some of the cor[ps] de ballet rather poor, but on the whole good shows. Orchestra not at all bad.

Saturday 4 July [London/Friston]
Rupert Doone & Robert Medley come in morning to discuss doing 'Hunting Fathers' as a ballet. Then I go rummaging in Charing X Road for books to read in Cornwall (Rabelais, Marx, Swift). Back to lunch with Brosas, & then in the afternoon I play a little (bad) tennis at the club with Beth & Kit Welford Etc. Then at 8.0 Beth & I set out in the Lagonda for Friston. Lights on the car are appalingly bad – the off head not working at

all. Consequently the journey is very bad – plus. the fact that we miss the way at Polegate (new roads made) and go to Eastbourne & vile sea mist & fog over the downs. One filthy skid. We share the driving. Mr. & Mrs Bridge come out to meet us a little way to Eastbourne after a 'phone call. Arrive about 12.15 – very thankful.

Tuesday 7 July [London/Crantock]
Up pretty early – finish odd things & Beth drives me to Paddington in the Lagonda (& very well too, she does it) to catch Cornish Riviera at 10.30. Very lovely & exciting journey – first stop Plymouth – & I arrive at 4.30 at NewQuay, where I am met by Miss Ethel Nettleship who takes me out to Crantock where I am to live in a hut in her grounds. It is perfectly glorious country – a glorious little village – and, o, the sea view! – so I can foresee a pretty pleasant month – working at Hunting Fathers – reading alot & walking the neighbourhood.

A Mrs. Hughs is getting my food – I order what I want & she does it. Have very good meals to-day. A long read (Marx) and a long walk on beach before bed at 10.30 – well content.

Wednesday 8 July [Crantock]
Mrs. Hughes comes at 9.15 to give me my breakfast – but I am up well before that. While she does my room I go to village to pay for the food she ordered for me this morning – it is going to be no cheap job this living alone – & to buy a paper. I then come back &, working all morning & afternoon, complete the scoring of the Prologue.[103] It is a horrible rainy day, but after tea I put on shorts & old clothes & brave the elements, & go for a long walk along the cliffs & beach. It is heavenly this bay. After dinner I read alot – Beer's Marx, & begin Rabelais' Gargantua.[104] Both of which I enjoy, but in very different ways. I am also pouring over Mahler symphonies etc. and Beethoven later quartets & there is a tremendous amount in common in these I feel. Also letters at odd times.

Sunday 12 July
A simply wild day – the weather has been just putrid all this week – Curse it – but I brave the elements & go for a 3 hours walk in morning over the common to Holywell Bay – a heavenly walk (marred only by the fact that one has to trespass so much – enormous stretches of uncultivatable land marked 'Private' for Sale – ~~oh th~~ with no sign of any life on them – oh this Capitalist System!). Back by 2.0. In aft. read & spend a long time at accounts (Business ones – somewhat behind hand) & then after tea go to a service at

the local church – lovely little place – but a miserable little service, with a stupid slack parson. Long walk after that – & back to a meal at 8.0 – when I have some Cornish pasties (v. good) made by my Mrs. Hugh – this with Cornish cream, cherry tart is getting me down inside at the moment! After that more accounts – read, meanwhile the wind rages & rain pelts outside – I hope I'm not going to be blown away!

Friday 17 July

An incredibly violent day – wind, & rain – exhilarating in a way – it would be miraculous if one could discard all ones clothes & walk miles in it. I do walk miles before dinner – but it gets so uncomfortable – water in shoes, trousers clinging to one & rain dripping off hair down neck.

A bad day for work – I go to Newquay in morning – to get odd things – Miss N. takes me in her car – which takes most of the time. Lots of letters in aft. – village to post – early tea (conditions are abit strained here to-day as people are moving in and out in immense quantities) work for 2 hours after & abit after dinner. Then give it up & read.

// Tremendous sensation in papers – the King was shot at by some Irish ½ wit at yesterdays Presentation of Colours. A bad business, as the direct result is that of increased affection thro' abhorrence of the crime. Although looking at it calmly, why an 'attempt on a life' should cause so much fuss in a display to commemorate & encourage 'attempts on millions of lives' – beats me entirely.

Two delightful little cockney boys on beach at Holywell – show me the Holy Well with great glee. It is a fascinating spot – but unfortunately I hadn't got a bent pin on me – which creats the 'luckiness' in the wish!

Sunday 19 July

After a dull & wet early morning the weather at last clears & the evening is heavenly. I am terribly worried (& injured – so hermit-minded have I become!) by new arrivals in neighbouring huts. Too many signs of life – and a gramophone. Too much like civilisation. I eventually go out for a terrific walk along cliffs well past Holywell – starting at 11.0 don't arrive back till 3.30. I have never enjoyed a walk so much – and the climax is when I find a colossal chasm in the rocks – miles away from civilisation – climb an enormous distance down to rocky shore & undress & bathe stark naked. The sheer sensual exstasy of it! – ~~cop~~ coupled with the real danger (currents & submerged rocks) & doubts whether I shall be able to climb the tortuous path to the top. Utter bliss. Eat – read (finish Erewhon – the end (Machines) is superb – & is almost convincing!!)[105] – accounts – ~~for~~ and another short walk – for rest of the day. But it is hard to think that this morning is real.

Monday 20 July

I work hard at scoring – nearing the end of Hawking[106] – & very excited – do 13 pages to-day. – working, morning, aft., & after dinner. The weather is execrable to start with, but afternoon & evening are superb. Have a good bathe after tea with Miss N – surfing with a board for the first time – & good it is, too.

Incidentally, Lennox Berkeley writing this morning (saying he's coming here on Sat) tells me to listen to J. Françaix's Piano Concertino[107] this evening (not specifying time). Which of course, as I have no wireless – nor know anyone here who has, is impossible. However – ~~after~~ coming back thro village after a heavenly beach-walk at 10.45 – I hear a wireless, stop & listen, hear announcer say – 'You will now hear a Concertino by J.F. . . .' & so hear whole thing. It is very charming & what with wind in trees & cool of Summer evening it makes a delicious effect. Perhaps too much like the other works I know of his (Trio, Vln Concert.)[108] – but nevertheless – musical.

// Spanish revolution – those bloody fascists trying to get back into power. However it seems as tho' the government & people have the situation in hand.[109]

Thursday 23 July

Rather a beastly day – spoilt by Spanish news. There has been alot more fighting & the government doesn't seem entirely on top – there seems to be a lot of dirty work going on – rich people outside helping those bloody fascists. There has been alot of fighting round Barcelona – and hundreds are dead.

I actually finish the score of H.F. working till 11.30 at night – owing to these disturbances I don't work well & I'm very doubtful about the end.

Frightful morning – howling gale & pelting rain. The wind stays but the rain stops & there is alot of sun in the aft. I go down to Porth Joke for a nice surf bathe with the Bangays before tea.

Friday 24 July

News from Spain still bad, tho' government seems to be gaining ground abit – it varies with what paper one reads. One thing is certain is that Fascists are executing hundreds (literally) of Popular Front or Communist members – including many boys of 14–16. Marvellous to have opinions of that strength at that age. I can't help feeling that not until that 'political ~~conscience~~ consiousness' is more general that the world will get out of this mess. Apart from that I am exhilerated at having finished Hunting Fathers. Spend day – numbering pages, doing titles, index, cueing, general expression & tempo marks etc. – which is good fun, especially as I am at the moment thrilled with the work.

A glorious bathe after tea with the Bangays – a lot of wind so surfing is exciting.

A long walk after dinner, after which I sketch a bit of a funeral march to those youthful Spanish martyrs.[110]

Sunday 26 July

After rain in the morning it turns out a heavenly day tho' with enough wind to be good for surfing – I am becoming the complete surfist now! We bathe at 11.30 with the Bangays before they part at 1.0 for London – it has been nice having them here – in a way – for they are cheery folk – but it is somewhat of a worry having to be continualy facetious in small talk. However – final impressions are ~~differ~~ definitely good – even if affectionate!

I have lunch in with Lennox & after a short read – he, my H.F., & I his Jonah & also Wozzeck (marvellous work) we go for a glorious walk via Holywell (tea) on to Hoblin's Cove – my famous spot of last Sunday – and even further. He is a dear and we agree on most points & it is nice to discuss things we don't agree on! Get back for meal at 8.30 – talk read & an early bed – exhausted!

Tuesday 28 July

A mostly filthy morning. It pelts & there is a vile wind so we stay~~at~~ in – Len. writes letters & I get on with the vocal score – or rather the duets portions so as to be able to try them with him. It clears in afternoon & we have a glorious bathe & then lie together on the beach partly naked – sun bathing. Heavenly. After tea a long walk down the Gannel to look for tennis courts – in vain. Work hard after ~~tea~~ dinner & late bed & even later to sleep. Lennox has brought with ~~the~~ him scores of the new Walton (B^b) & Williams (F min) symphonies[111] & we spend most hysterical evenings pulling them to pieces – the amateurishness & clumsiness of the Williams – the 'gitters' of the fate-ridden Walton – & the over pretentiousness of both – & abominable scoring. The directions in the score too are most mirth condusive! It isn't that one is cruel about these works which are naturally better than a tremendous amount of English music – but it is only that so much is pretended of them, & they are compared to the great Beethoven, Mozart, Mahler symphonies.

Wednesday 29 July

After normal down the village jaunt in morning I work & Lennox goes with Miss Nettleship to see about a piano for us, which we go to in the aft: but it is a very poor instrument & the effect of Our Hunting Fathers & Lennox' new organ & piano pieces on it is beyond description! Have a bathe (with Miss N. as well) after tea – surfing poor – as it is a heavenly day – first day here without any rain!

After dinner – much walk & talk with Lennox & then we drive into Newquay with Miss N. & pick up ~~the~~ some friends of hers (mother, aunt, child) from a concert-hall – & we afterwards till 12.0 odd have tea with them. Long talks before sleep – it is extraordinary how intimate one ~~bef~~ becomes when the lights are out!

Same Spanish news – there seems a steady Government push – but one feels that something terrific will happen within the next few days – 'il faut reculer pour mieux sauter' – kind of thing.

Thursday 30 July

Miss N. takes Lennox in to catch 11.45 up to town. I go with them & we partake of a very sorrowing farewell. He is an awful dear – very intelligent & kind – & I am very attached to him, even after this short time. In spite of his avowed sexual weakness for young men of my age & form – he is considerate & open, & we have come to an agreement on that subject. // We have decided to work alot together – especially on the Spanish tunes. Back here for lunch & work after as well as lots of letters & a bathe – with poor surf tho'. Work again before & after dinner – with a sherry & coffee from the Banfords (now staying in the bungalow.). Early to bed – but admittedly quite lonely!

Saturday 1 August

Seem to spend whole morning arranging matters & shopping – certainly the mornings are short when breakfast's not before 10.0!

Work at piano score more in afternoon, & after a good Cornish cream tea, Mum & I bathe with Miss Nettleship – quite a good surfing one too. Work again after dinner, which Mrs. Hugh gets for us – she is doing for us & the others in the quarry as well.

The Spanish Revolution drifts on & on – hopeful Government successes published by the left papers (Herald, Chronicle, New Statesman etc.) & the Tory press (Times, Telegraph, Beverbrook & Rothermere filth etc.)[112] magnifies everything to Red Terror – Times actually saying that the whole is manufactured by Moscow – i.e. Soviet encouraging a reactionary military force! Very likely!!!

Thursday 6 August

Another filthy day. Wind & rain continuosly except for a brief period in the afternoon when John [Alston] takes me over to Porth; but this is short lived & after tea when we decide to bathe it becomes as black & dismal as ever. In morning play ping-pong at Forsters & then John takes Mum & me to Newquay for a shop. Have a lovely walk in Porth along shore & over rocks in aft. Ping-pong & no bathe after tea as intended. After dinner – work abit (also before afraction) & then with John, Mum, & Miss Nettleship we play odd games.

Spanish news still as doubtful as ever. Government seems to be gaining in the north & the Rebels are marching on Madrid. International situation seems to be calmer with neutrality being sworn by all interested countries – but who believes for a moment that Italy & German will keep their promises – what about past history?

Saturday 8 August

Spend all morning – starting at 8.30 – finishing & revising piano score. Then in aft. Miss Nettleship takes Mum & me to Newquay & I post it off to Boosey & Hawkes. Bathe & sunbathe(!) after tea with Mum – it is a heavenly day, only a slight breeze – almost summer! Beth & Robert are supposed to be coming from town to-day – at the moment (10.0) they haven't arrived & may be staying on the road somewhere.

Still no Spanish news – only the Government seems to be gaining slightly. All the Right wing (including the Gutter press – Bever. & Rother.) are well on the side of the 'Insurgents' & 'Rebels'. now. It is a comfort to read the New Statesman, & News Chronicle.

Sunday 9 August

Another heavenly day. We take down lunch to Crantock Bay & lie & run about & bathe in glorious sun getting browner & browner (& of course sorer & sorer!). Back for tea after which I walk into Newquay with Robert. – rather a difficult walk as we think differently on practically every subject (politics especially) & are both very keen on them that arguments are liable to be extremely fierce! After supper – a glorious evening; talk & gramophone (some lovely Duke Ellington & J. Strauss).

Thursday 13 August

I must say that it is pleasant to have finished all ~~plea~~ pressing jobs – although at the back of my conscience there is the Rossini suite[113] to be done for B & H. But it is just a breather before proofs come to be corrected.

Long political arguments with Robert after breakfast – but, for a wonder, quite peaceable – partly because there is one subject of which we both have abhorrence – war.

Ping-pong at Forsters after – Miss Foster is infuriating in her steadiness – it takes me hours to recover my temper! In aft. read (Passage to India – E.M. Forster[114] – great, so far), & walk with Robert. Ditto with Beth after tea. In eve. R. goes to village dance – which we personaly refuse, but we have a very pleasant evening with Miss Nettleship – after having driven him there.

Sunday 16 August

A general laze day – very pleasant, but weather unutterably dull. Letters, walk in morning – Bobby & Mum go off to church in Cubert. Read in aft – finish Passage to India (haven't been so impressed for a long time) – bathe after tea (poor surfing) – & after dinner tea with Miss Nettleship in her lovely caravan in the old quarry.

Spanish news magnified into a Patriot ('fascist'!!) success by all the tory & capitalist press – although I doubt whether it is as near as that yet – but to think of all these totally unnecessary deaths – all caused by the greed of a few elderly 'gentlemen' – egged on by Musso & Hitler.

Monday 24 August

First news of morning was that Uncle Sheldon died last Thursday while playing croquet at Hunstanton while on holiday with Aunt Julianne. We are terribly sorry for her, because she is such a cripple & so dependent on him[115] – nothing is yet known as to what she'll do. He was a nice man in a lot of ways, & as far as we knew him we respected him. Spend most of morning sending wires etc & letters, tho' I manage to get a bit of work done & Beth & I bathe with Mr Gyde before lunch – another lovely day, very hot.

In aft. I go to tennis in Newquay with Miss B Foster – have some quite good games, but mostly against stone wallers – good for ones technique, but bad for one's temper! Work again before Supper – actually finishing the Suite – apart for many alterations to be done. I'm terribly pleased with it – it is such heavenly music – (better than I ever hoped to write!) – tho' I'm afraid it may be more complex than Ralph Hawkes bargained for.

After supper the Madges (Mr, Mrs, & Uncle) come in to tea to arrange about tomorrow's rounders match.

Tuesday 25 August

A very eventful day. First of all, by post arrived proofs of Our Hunting Fathers – very smart – & also letter from Rotha asking about music to a film

– a relief since I have no G.P.O. job in sight yet. Wire about this, write 3 letters, umpteen postcards, & alittle revision of Rossini (Soirées Musicales) before Beth & I go down to beach, bathe & lunch – it is a glorious day – no wind, lots of sun & lovely surfing. In aft. it is the return match of the rounders, & our side (Cpl. Mr Madge) wins by 12–0. – (I feel pleased as I make 7!). After a bathe we all have tea, & then a good rag with all the kids, 4 Madges, Rodney Jenkyn & Willy Ride, & then another bathe. Leave at 7.30 to find I've lost all my money from my pocket (6/-) – return with Beth to seek – in vain – back here to find telegram from Boyd Neel about another Film – this time Elstree! Dash to P.O. & wire about that – another urgent one – looks as if my holiday is up – curse it. After dinner, inspite of exhaustion!, spend 2 hours revising & altering Soirées Musicales. And so to bed – & thankful!!

Wednesday 26 August

Have a long rehearsal in Village Hall with Sophie at Our H.F. – she is beginning to sing it very well indeed. Then after waiting for a wire from Boyd Neel, I phone him at Elstree. He wants me to do the music for a film,[116] but gives no details. He wanted me to meet the Director on Friday but I think I've got it put off until Monday. Then we set out for a picnic (12.30) with Fosters – following them to Truro. Actually we run out of petrol between here & Truro & have to wait ½ hr while some is brought from nearest garage – on to Truro at 2.15, wait for them & hunt for ½ hr. then on in stages to the Lizard where we discover them at 4.30! Fine day of picnicing! However Beth & I have a good bathe in Housel Bay – lovely spot – tea & have to leave for home at 7.0. Good first part of journey – but when it gets dark it is lousy, as our lights are practically non-existant. Back by 9.15 – tired, bad tempered, & hungry – the last is counteracted by a good Beef-stake & Kidney pudding, the first by bed, but the middle seems to persist still!

Tuesday 1 September [London]

Up to G.P.O. at 10.0 when Rowland Lee & Boyd Neel see some of my films, & are suitably impressed – but even to-night nothing is finally settled, curse it. After that work abit with Miss Spice on the Travel Association film I was doing; coffee with Bill Coldstream – nice person –; & then lunch with Basil Wright. Spend long time on business in Boosey's in afternoon & then back here to tea & bit of work. Meet Boyd ~~Nell~~ Neel for a meal & then we go to Prom together to hear Rubensten play Ireland's piano concerto. Of course he plays it brilliantly, although last movement didn't go well – lack of rehearsal. But the work wears terribly thin – bad scoring & construction; & all the lush beauty of the 1890 Ballades dressed in modern clichés. Also in programme Dvorak's great 5th & L'apprenti Sorcier[117] – but performances were incredibly rough.

Wednesday 2 September [London/Frinton]
I spend morning doing business in flat – bank, sorting & get on alot with proofs before going to lunch with Rupert Doone & Robert Medley at Albany Terrace at 1.30. Discuss new Hunting Father's Ballet, & Agamemnon[118] (for which I may do music for Group Theatre). I also finish my proofs there, take them to B & H – have tea with Coldstream from GP.O. then to Van Wyck's to hear new recording of Berg Lyric Suite (by Galimir Quartet (Vienna)) – which I fall & buy – partly on strength of new Capitol Job, although as I haven't had a wire from Boyd Neel to night, I'm afraid it's off. Dash then & catch 6.39 to Frinton – even if I will do this film there is nothing to be done this week. Beth meets me in the car at 8.30 – it is good to be out of the heat of London.

Thursday 3 September [Frinton]
Of course now I have every reason for being delirously happy. My film job with Capitol is fixed – I haven't to return to town till Monday (after 2 telephone calls to town) – spend a good day here; bathe in morning; blackberry in Gt. Holland in aft; picnic-supper near Horsey Is. with the Alexanders – pleasant anticipation of Piers coming to-morrow – besides the facts that I shall have a pretty large amount of public shows next season in town – I have written a work of which I admit I'm proud – have ideas for many others, & opportunies to write & have them performed – financial aspect is rosy, with films & Boosey & Hawke's royalty continuing – BUT it is entirely clouded ~~when~~ by the continued disastrous news from Spain. To think of these massacres (2000 estimated dead each day in battle) of ordinary men & women like this family & people next door – & all because of the bloody greed of a comparatively few old men.

Sunday 6 September
Weather still impossible – we go for a very long walk in the morning (Beth, Kit Piers & I) to Great Holland. Play ping-pong on an improvised table upstairs in aft. & then a fiendishly cold bathe (really a challenge!) before tea. Play some cricket on the beach with Kit & Piers before dinner. As we prepare to see Kit off to town in his Riley about 9.30 we suddenly decide, that, ~~better~~ rather than face an early start – & most probably a late arrival – in the

Lagonda in rain & wind to-morrow – we had better all pack in & go with him. Which we do at 10.30, & after a very rapid journey arrive at 12.45. Kit & Piers both sleep here – Kit in the sitting room, & Piers shares my room – in my bed, & me on a camp-bed.

Monday 7 September [Frinton/London]
Slept only periodically last night so very weary all day. Beth, Kit & I, having sorted out the house, have breakfast (got by Mrs Nun) at 8.45 but we let Piers sleep till past 10.0. I don't have to meet Boyd Neel till 12.0 – so I spend time until then with Piers. He's a charming person & it has been nice having him – very exhilarating with his constant prattle – and more than that too; often he makes very sensible remarks. Of course he's suffering from the usual Public School Education but he will soon get over that. // To Denham with B. Neel & lunch with him in the charming village Pub. See (after 1½ hrs weary wait) Rowland Lee who tells me there's nothing to be done yet – so I return to Boosey & Hawkes by 5.0. Then back to see Beth in great anguish since she has been summoned for hitting a taxi on July 7th – & what's worse she didn't receive either of the summonses – so she ~~was~~ is 'escorted' to the police station this afternoon. However we have fixed with solicitor to explain matters to-morrow & it simplifies things. Back here to a meal cooked by Mrs Nun & letters after – 'phone Mum.

Tuesday 8 September [London]
Storm breaks when we go to Mr. Elvin – solicitor at 9.45 – he is good & helps Beth alot; but luck is all against her – the worst magistrate for motoring cases is sitting, & costs for the previous hearings (when she failed to arrive) have ~~added~~ accumulated. However when I return from fetching my cheque book at 12.0 – it is all over & she was fined £1 – and £4–10–6 – costs – better than we feared. But Solicitors' £5–5 makes it up to a tidy little sum – an expensive lift she gave me to Paddington that day! // I go off to see Ralph Hawkes after that. Talk over many things with him. Lunch at M.M.. To GP.O. in aft. & Strand Films. See Coldstream for tea. Tatler cinema for 1½ hr after. Back here for bath & dinner. Listen to bit of Prom concert – Elizabeth Schuman singing some Mozart with glorious style.[119] Rupert Doone, Robert Medley & Richard Wood come in just before ten when I discuss with them the proposed music for Agamemnon which I may do for them. They leave before 11.30

Wednesday 9 September

I go up to Soho Square by 10.0 and work until 12.30 (with gap for coffee) with Evelyn Spice on the rest of the music I am to do for Village Film[120] (Travel Association). Then I go to Boosey & Hawkes to see Ralph Hawkes about my new Capitol Film arrangements. He's acting as my agent. Back here for lunch late. Odd business's in afternoon & also begin a new sequence for the Village Film – Pub scene. Up to M.M. Club at 6.30 to meet Paul Wright, with whom I play some ping-pong & then back to his flat. We eat out on the embankment & return to his flat to talk & play. He is a nice thing – very intelligent & I feel [h]is poetry is going to be very good. At 10.30 we walk round to see Barbara just in town for one night on the way to Frinton. She's been in Worcester helping Aunt Julianne – who's bearing up well, but who is terribly crippled poor dear.

Beth's out with Kit – theatre & dinner, and apparently supper after, as she's not back yet – 12.15.

Thursday 10 September

My brain is getting completely fogged with so many different activities. Forinstance (1) I write some more of the music for Travel Association Film after breakfast (2). I go to Ralph Hawkes at 12.0 to arrange about Capitol film (3) I rehearse with Sophie (back from Bognor) 'Our Hunting Fathers' for Norwich before lunch – & she sings it well . . . . lunch with her & Arnold (son) – & alittle ping-pong with them after . . . . . (4). I spend aft. discussing music for Group Theatre prod. of Agammemnon with Rupert Doone & he reads the whole play (3.30–6.30) (5). I get 'phone calls & letters about articles for World Film News (6) I try also to get together some ideas for the Ob. & piano work for Hallis concerts (7) & Our H.F. proofs are to be done. It's just abit too much – but my fault for never saying 'no' to anyone. However a very pleasant evening with the Bridges cheers me. After a meal with them I go to a concert which he conducts on the B.B.C. – rotten programme including Vaughn Williams impossible (even for him!) effusion – old King Cole'.[121]

Friday 11 September

I seem to becoming a journalist as well – nowadays. After writing alittle Pub scene & business arr. at B&H. I go to G.P.O & do article on B.B.C. programme for Oct. for World Film News. Then after lunch with Coldstream (& short pleasant & cool visit to Nat. Gallery with him) I go to As You Like It film[122] – Czinner production with Bergner (a glorious actress, but perhaps too sophisticated for Rosalinde), Olivier (a good Orlando) etc. – at Carlton, to critisize Walton's music – there being very little to critisize. Back at 5.30 to G.P.O to do this. Then back to flat where David Layton comes at 7.30 for a meal & we 3 go to see Marx Bros. in 'One Night at the Opera' – very very funny. Harpo M. is a real genius – & the opera scene is hair-rasingly funny!

Thursday 17 September

Corrections in morning – finish string parts & deliver them to Covent Garden at 11.30. Back to GP.O. to continue a little with Wind & Percussion parts – lunch & a little Ping-pong with Coldstream – & back here to get on with them. Tea with F.B. who is up here for a few days & discuss with him the abominable rehearsals I've been given for this festival. Then on to G.P.O unit where Basil Wright picks me up & takes me to his Highgate Flat for dinner, which he cooks – splendidly. There is also a German-Spanish refugee staying with him

After the meal we discuss the Ballet project & really get very excited over it. He brings me back here in his car by 11.45 & I settle down to the Devil's own job till 2.30.

Friday 18 September

Hectic scramble to complete corrections & up to Gt. Russel St. to plead with Heathcote Statham about the rehearsals. On to Cov. Gard. to pick up more to be corrected & back to rehearse with Sophie at 12.0. Lunch after at M.M. & to see Boosey & Hawkes. More corrections before I take Piers with Sophie & small Arnold Gyde to see Disney Season at Tatler – very lovely of course. Tea after & more corrections (at GP.O – most convenient spot) before Piers & I walk to Covent Garden to deliver the last batch to the secretary – thank God. Meal at MM. & Piers comes with me to Prom. Concert. It is a Beethoven programme (Coriolan, 3rd Symph.) – Wood is really a marvel considering the amount he has to do – & F.B. conducts his two really charming Poems.[123] Piers seems to enjoy it alot – it's a very new experience for him; but he's not a scrap bored. I take him round to see F.B. after & he's very thrilled. I don't go back with them after as I must come back & sleep

Saturday 19 September

After endless business arrangements I go up to Boosey & Hawkes to sign my contract with Capitol. After that shop at Mappin & Webb[124] (discount thro' B & H) to by christening present for my god-child! Beth meets me at Waterloo at 1.30 & we go down to Surbiton (sandwiches in train). A very pleasant afternoon with the Gydes – Humphry is christened & I officiate. At 6.0 we (Beth, Sophie & Arnold I) come back to Covent Garden & there begins the most ~~catasth~~ catostrophic evening of my life. Waiting till 8.30 to begin the rehearsal of Our Hunting Fathers – the orchestra (~~third~~ fourth day of 9 hours rehearsal) is at the end of it's tether – no discipline at all – no one there to enforce it. I get throughly het up & desparate – can't hear a thing in the wretched Foyer. I get alot of the speeds wrong & very muddled – but I'm glad to say that in spite of the fooling in the orchestra & titters at the work – the 'Rats' especially brought shreaks of laughter[125] – the rehearsal got better & better. But it was impossible & it takes all Arnold's optimism and kindness when he & S. take Beth & me to a nice meal at Strand Pal. to cheer me at all – but I'm feeling pretty suicidal.

Sunday 20 September

Sleep late – & Beth brings me breakfast in bed. Up about 10.30 & after many telephone calls I get down to a bit of the Agga. music – but (owing to exceedingly depressed mental state) result is lousy. Go up to Beth's working flat to inspect the overhead quarters which we may decide to move into as she can't re-let them. Back here for lunch & after that I go & see Frank B. about last night's debâcle. I try & persuade him to come & do it for me, but he won't consent & gradually talks me round till I reluctantly say I'll go on with it, but only if I get the extra rehearsal that Statham half promised me. This I 'phone him about in the evening & get it settled. After, the B's take me to Golders Green & I go to the tennis club, where Beth has proceeded me, & start playing when we are stopped by rain. Evening spent in arranging things & letters etc. Early bed – we hope (this as written 9.45).

Monday 21 September [London/Norwich]

Up betimes – & to Liverpool St. – meet Sophie W. and we catch 9.48 together to Norwich. Most of the orchestra are on the train & after Saturday's catastrophe I don't feel too inclined to meet them. Audrey Sutton (Alston) meets us & we both go out to Framingham Earl (where we are staying with A) for lunch & she takes us back to Norwich for a rehearsal (½ hr) in the aft – when I am relieved to say things improve alot. Back to Framingham for a high tea (Jack Moeran & Patrick Hadley also there) & then back to St. Andrews Hall for a grand 'rehearsal' (with packed audience). I fear I don't take much notice of the audience & rehearse as hard as the one hour permits. It dosn't go perhaps so well as the aft. but the orchestra were a bit more tired I suppose. Some people are very excited over the work.

Tuesday 22 September [Norwich/London]
Catch 10.23 with Sophie back to London – & lunch with her at M.M. Club. I see Boosey & Hawkes in aft – there is some bother about my Capitol film job as the cheque hasn't arrived & there are rumours of the company going smash – serious as I am very over-drawn at the bank.

Back here & work abit at the ballet for Agamemnon. Heny Boys arrive at 6.0 & we talk abit – meet Grace at Earl's Court for a meal – and at 9.0 John Alston takes me & Guy Johnstone (pianist) to Wembly to see third Evening of the 6-day Cycling race at Wembly – very, very thrilling to watch & speed is amazing. Piet van Kempen being especially miraculous. Back by ¼ to one.

Wednesday 23 September
Busy all morning with arrangements & finish a rough draft of Agamemnon Ballet – but it is very bum – I know. Meet Montagu Slater for lunch in Soho – he is a lovely person & I always enjoy lunches with him. Afterwards see B & H – still no Capitol cheque – see Grace Williams at her flat & talk over Aga. as she is to help me. She comes with me to see Rupert Doone at Group Theatre rooms at 5.0 & we talk – then she comes back here to dinner. Talk – play H.F's – discus Aga. – letters – bath – bed.

Friday 25 September [Norwich]
Breakfast at 9.0 after which Sophie & I have abt. ½ hrs work on the H.F. & then alot of us go in to the first half of the morning programme in St. Andrews Hall (me already rigged out in full morning dress – most uncomfortable!). I sit with F.B. & E.E.B – Mum & Beth (1st staying with Mrs. Chamberlain in Surlingham, & 2nd in Lowestoft with Sewells) – sitting together elsewhere. Jelli D'aranyi plays the Brahms (handicapped by Stathams laboured conducting) & V. Williams conducts a very successfull show of his 5 Tudor Portraits (1st perf.) – not my music, but obviously the music for the audience. After a hurried lunch at Fram. we go back to the hall – & I conduct 1st perf. of my Hunting Fathers with Sophie Wyss – who is excellent indeed. The orchestra plays – better than I had dared to hope – tho' one or two slips. I am <u>very</u> pleased with it & it goes down quite well – most of the audience being very interested if bewildered. A very complimentary & excited gathering in the artists' room afterwards – including F. Bridge & Mrs. B., – Vaughan Williams, J. Moeran, Patrick Hadley, Ralph Hawkes, Basil Wright, J. Cheetal Rupert Doone, Robert Medley, Alstons galore Mum & Beth, Ronald Duncan etc. etc.

Back to Fram. after that – a spirited game of tennis with Christopher A. before early meal at 6.30. after which we go back to ev. concert of Delius Mass of Life. Sit with Mum & F.B. – & am very bored. Too much of same style & mannerisms. Back & a large party – enjoy myself, but pretty tired.

Saturday 26 September [Norwich/Frinton]
Notices of my work vary from flattering & slightly bewildered (D. Tel.) – to reprehensive & disapproving (Times) – but I am pleased, because what would be the use of a work of this kind if the narrow-minded, prejudiced, snobbish Colles (forinstance) approved? See Sophie off in Norwich at 10.23 – & back at Framingham F.B & EEB[126] go off at abt. 11.30. Then Christopher & I have a short game of tennis & after lunch Audrey takes me in to Norwich in her car – goes on to the Festival (last concert) while I go to see Bill Wakeford in ~~thei~~ his 'Gift Shop'. Catch 3.40 to Frinton – meeting Mum & Beth at Colchester – arr. here at 6.39 (!) & go up to house in the old town-bus – really a decrepit old horse carriage!

Monday 28 September [Frinton/London]
Up early – 7.20 breakfast & Beth & I catch 7.58 to town. Horrible getting up, but not so bad when one is in the train. I come back here & spend morning 'phoning & then do final sequence of Travel Association music for Miss Spice. After a snack lunch here, I go up to B & H. see Ralph Hawkes & learn that inspite of repeated promises the Capitol Film cheque is not here. So I go to G.P.O. & talk over things to do in the meantime with the 'Calendar of the Year' (with Spice) & a new Swiss Film (with Cabalcanti).[127]

Spend after dinner (cooked by Mrs Nun) doing Accounts – Income Tax in – & letters & phoning. Feel depressed economically in spite of the fact that B & H. have given me their £13 a few days early. There is so much to come in & nothing seems to come.

Beth is in a dreadful way too – Solicitors letters from creditors! But she will no doubt recover from this effect of the hols.

Wednesday 30 September [London]
Work at Aga. in the morning before going up to Boosey & H – still no cheque. Lunch at M.M. with Peter Burra, & Paul Wright & after that I go with Miss Spice & Stocks (ass. director) up to Bishopsgate to get material for Blackpool sequence sound – Carnival novelties etc. By mistake we go into ~~the~~ a factory warehouse & find most appalling conditions of work – young boys (not more than 11) working in airless & dark places – probably under the connivance of the police too. And this is 20th century – but probably not

~~the~~ in advance of the 2nd, because look at the Spanish Tragedy – still dragging on, 1000's slaughtered day after day. Government is gradually loosing ground because of lack of any arms – & the other democratic countries stand & look on, while the Fascist countries openly land arms – e.g. the Italians in Majorca. This is all confirmed & enlarged upon by Toni Brosa with whom I have a meal at 7.30 & long walk after. // I have tea at MM. with Jack Moeran & then go back to GP.O to discus sound further.

Thursday 1 October

I work all morning at odd bits of Agamemnon music – amid a ceaseless flow of 'phone calls. Lunch at Café Royal with Auden & meet with him Christopher Isherwood & Louis MacNeice & a young boy John [gap] who wants to start in the music trade – silly mutt! After this to B & H & on to Grace where we work abit on the Agamemnon stuff & back to Group Theatre rooms where we meet Rupert Doone & a Mr. Nieman who is helping us on the stuff. Then to M.M. Club where Grace & I have a meal with Jack Moeran (slightly the worse for drink, but very amusing!) & go back to G.T. rooms after for a rehearsal of the Ballet music. Leave there at 10.30.

Saturday 3 October [London/Essex]

I spend morning on the Rossini Suite here. Kit Welford arrives & shops abit before lunch – buying food for ~~lunch~~ week-end. After lunch here Beth, he & I set off in his car for Colchester arr. there about 4.0 & park the car. Catch bus for W. Mersea & then we board his yacht – the Curlew. I go & fetch water & parrafin etc. nearly getting stuck in the filthy mud. We are supposed to be making for Harwich to night, but there is so little wind that we get only as far as the river Blackwater & anchor there for the night. The plans are to get Woodbridge & put the boat away there – train to Colchester tomorrow evening & pick up car there. But with this lack of wind & tides being abit wonky – it looks doubtful.

Tuesday 6 October [London]

I work at title music[128] after ~~bed~~ breakfast for abit before doing my income tax ~~form~~ returns – with extra help from Bank. To lunch at MM with Nieman to talk about Group Theatre work – G.P.O after to see about Films – & then B & H to see ~~after~~ about 1001 things. Back here for some more work on title music – a big job this.

Mrs Dunkerley (Piers' mother) comes to dinner & Lilian Wolff too. I had never met Mrs D before & she is a very charming person – very like Piers. She is head buyer at Peter Jones & helps Beth & Lilian alot afterwards in talking business. They go by 10.0 & I write letters after & in bed by 12.15.

Wednesday 7 October

Straight down to studio in morning with Grace Williams & Kit Welford who come to help me in the recording of the Blackpool sequence from Calendar of the Year – for Spice. We have good fun with all the Carnival noises & Kit plays his accordion. Lunch with them, Spice, Coldstream & Bond. Stay for other business (including a recording with Prince Monolulu, a famous Derby tipster, which fails to materialise as he walks out because of money) until 4.0 when I go to meet Mum at Liverpool [St.] at 4.57. Back here by bus – slow because of strike on.

Peter Burra & his sister[129] come to a meal (Beth out, Mum in) – & are very charming & pleasant – & after go to the Van Dieren memorial concert – which I ought to go, but feel I must get on with the Rossini arrangement. Listen to a show of the Bliss Viola Sonata,[130] which for flamboyant rubbish must certainly be unexcelled.

Wystan Auden sends me a copy of his & Isherwoods latest – Ascent of F6 – on first glance it looks exciting & good.

Thursday 8 October

The cheque – mirabile dictu – arrives in the morning [from Capitol Films] – & now I have to see whether it'll be returned or not. Still it's good, so far! Work at title music, & then at Rossini in morning. Mum shops & comes back for ~~me in the~~ lunch with me. More work in aft. before going with Mum to inspect new flat over Beth & then tea with her – then to R.A.M. New Music Society Stravinsky concert of chamber music. Rather too much of same period – Pergolesi Suite ('Cello & Piano – Florence Hooton (excellent)) Piano Sonata (a dull work for me) – 4 Russian Songs from 1918 (– wonderful songs) – & then 1st perf of the Concerto for 2 pianos – which is of course wonderfully done & very interesting – but it isn't best Stravinsky.[131] Invention seems to flag at moments. Then on to Café Royal where Mum Beth & I have a celebration dinner – very good. Then on to Group Theatre for a Ballet rehearsal – very boring – meet Alan Bush & Alfred Nieman after & eat at a Lyons with them & other communist friends till 11.30 & back here – pretty tired.

Saturday 10 October

I work at Title music for Calendar of Year in morning & then at 12.30 see Spice at GP.O about Travel Association Film[132] – & see the Film. Then lunch at M.M. with Pat Jackson. We play a little ping-pong after & then tennis at Club with Beth & others. But it gets dark early & there are some bad players there. Change & down to MM with Pat for a snack supper & we play a little ping-pong before going down to Piccadilly where I meet Teddy Rogers (now in town in a bank) & also George Hockey (cousin) & Beth (sister!). We then go to Forum to see Unfinished Symphony[133] a ~~charing~~ charming & sentimental film on Schubert – by Willi Forst & most beautifully made. Then 'Bed & Sofa'[134] the epic of Russian silent days by Alexander [Abram] Room – & my God it is a film. A most moving experience. Some coffee at Lyons to recover from it.

Sunday 11 October

Spend whole of light day up at Club with Henry Boys too, & we really have some lovely tennis. Henry comes back to supper here & we talk & talk music etc (mostly pro-Mahler & anti-Brahms), & play Wozzeck. I should work but this is good.

After he goes at 10.45 I work till midnight on getting my correspondance for last 3 or four years straightened out & destroyed.

Monday 12 October

I stay in all morning & aft. working a little on Rossini (out of G.P.O hours!) & then on Winter Sequence of Calendar. I feel lousy tho' as I have a foul cold arriving, which breaks with violence in the evening. I go to G.P.O to see Spice about films at 5.30 & then we & Shaw (Film drictor too) go with Cavalcanti to his house in Stanwood for a very pleasant evening. Very good food, good gramophone records (mostly French low songs), good conversation & agreeable company. Back at 12.30 feeling like hell.

Tuesday 13 October

Stay in all day – trying to write Spring sequence in cold day with a running cold, & interrupted by dozens of long & complicated 'phone calls. However what I do isn't so bad.

After dinner Jack Moeran comes with his new Symphony[135] – it has some excellent things in it, but terribly under the Sibelius influence – mood, ideas & technique. ~~It~~ This is going to be almost as bad as the Brahms influence on English music I fear.

Wednesday 14 October

After numerous telephone (business) calls, I have to go up to a Group Theatre rehearsal at Leicst Sq. It is bad, but I cannot arouse any interest at all in this production – everything is onerous to a degree. Probably because

I have so much else to do – more interesting – & it is abominably irritating to be treated like this when one is giving one's services. Because of this I don't exactly hurry to the rehearsals! However after that I have a very pleasant lunch with Montagu Slater of whom I'm very very fond, & full of admiration – one of the nicest people I've met in town.

Down to Blackheath in afternoon to see Spice & Cavalcanti – about yet another bit of ~~recording~~ stuff to be written before Thursday's recording – one cannot really put any thought into all this gallons of stuff to be poured out. I work all after dinner until 12.0 at Calendar music.

Friday 16 October

I spend morning hurriedly concocting some stuff for Cavalcanti's new film[136] which I rush off to copyist's after a quick lunch here. Hair cut in aft. after that at Whiteleys. Back here to work again before I change & go out to dinner & to Ballet at Sadler's Wells with Ralph Hawkes. The shows are Rake's Progress – Gavin Gordon [music and scenario] – a very effective Hogarth setting with only effective & rather affected music; – Beethoven Prometheus Music – lovely music is not matched by the choreography, which is not stylised enough; & Tsch. Casse Noisette act. 3, dream of music, but very slackly played & consequently not too vivaciously danced.[137] But the Corps de Ballet is on the whole excellent & [blank] is fine.

The evening itself is my first taste of excessive wealth, & I don't find it over good, tho' certainly wizzing thro' London in a 37 h.p. Hispano Suiza[138] has it's points! R.H. is supremely natural & charming, but it is a bit ironicle to park this kind of car outside the sort of houses that surround Sadlers Wells.[139]

Saturday 17 October

I have a very bad nose-bleed (a real pourer) in the middle of last night – & it doesn't stop oozing all the morning, which I spend idoors doing nothing (by command of Barbara). So I 'phone a Dr. Moberley who examines me & prescribes for me in the afternoon. Overwork & excessive nose-blowing with the cold. So I'm to do nought this week-end. Very enjoyable!

Elsie Hockey (cousin) comes to spend night here, and in the evening Beth & she go with George (her bro.) to a dance. She is very trying; very provincial & attempting to make a good (& fast) impression – & incredibly snobbish. Still she has suffered a lot in her youth (with her father).

In the evening Grace Williams comes for a meal with me, & we spend a pleasant time talking (arguing over Sibelius) & listening to Schönberg Verklärte Nacht – a lovely (tho' unequal bit of music).

Sunday 18 October

Apart from walks on the heath in afternoon (solo) & with Beth after tea – spend day in doing nothing but read – Compton Makenzie (Carnival[140] – very entertaining), & endless Mahler Berg & Schönberg – & also listen to wireless, deadly programmes except for the Kindertotenlieder in the evening – a very bad show of that, Kipnis being far too clumsy & too close to mike, & Boult as slow, dull & ignorant as is his wont. Even then they stand as supreme – music that I think I love more than any other. Early bed, & bath.

Tuesday 20 October

After much business I go down to Blackheath by 11.30 & correct parts & discuss matters before lunch. In aft. I record incidental music for 3 films (mostly Calendear of Year (Spice), & some for Fishing Village (Watt) & Swiss Telephone (Cavalcanti)).[141] Everything goes swimmingly because of splendid~~ly~~ little band of 10 (got toether by John Francis, inc. Kotchinska (harp) & Brosa 4^{tet} – without Toni who's ill) & we finish all this music in 3 hours including a good deal of synchronis-ation. Basil Wright brings me back with him in car & I get back here by 7.15. Spend evening doing odd things & writing letters – Piers included

Wednesday 21 October

Up to Soho Square at 10.0 to work with Spice at Travel As. music before going with her & Maclan [Maclaren, assistant to Spice] to Star offices to record Newsboy stuff. This 11.0–11.45, quite successful. Then back to G.P.O where we hear sound from yest. recording & it is lousy & completely bum – bad recording & all that good playing wasted. This is the last straw – what with all this stuff to think about & above all the Group theatre to try & organize I go then in the aft (after Boosey & Hawkes for abit) & see Rupert & really tell him I cannot do everything. So we hunt round & find no one.

However I get much cheered up at 6.30 by the recording for the Travel Association (music I wrote mostly back in April)[142] – all arrangements of Folk & traditional tunes (some from Moeran) – lovely stuff, & I must admit my scoring comes off like hell. Of course we have 16 slap-up players – whole Brosa quartet inc. Everyone's very bucked. After, at 9.30 we all (inc. Beth & Peggy B. who comes to recording) go to M.M. Club – i.e. Brosa quartet & us – for riotous supper & ping-pong, till 12.0. Come back feeling that life is worth living inspite of Group Theatre – if one doen't think of Spain, of course.

Friday 23 October

After a quick scribble of some stuff for Group Theatre, I go at 10.45 to Boyd Neel & he takes me down to Denham (Capitol) Studios where I see people & see the sets for 'Love from a Stranger'[143] & Ann Harding at work. Very interesting, but apparently there won't be anything for me to do for ages. Back to lunch to M.M. with Brian Easedale – discover at 1.45 that I haven't brought stuff I've done for G.T. & have to dash back here to fetch it – accursed memory! Go then for a short rehearsal before going on to G.P.O. where I see & have tea with Spice. At 6.0 I go to see film at Acadamy – Der Singender Jugend[144] – a film about the Wiener Sängerknaben. Tho' well made & beautifully shot it is grossly sentimental & sloppy – embarrassingly so in fact – but I'm afraid the combination of the gorgeous singing, the Vienna element, & the lovely little boys wins me over completely! // Back here by 9.15 & supper with Beth; & infinite telephone calls – including one from Mrs Vince (the B's housekeeper) – saying that F.B. is very ill down at Friston. 2 Nurses & Doctor from town. If anything happened to my musical father I don't know what I should do.[145]

Monday 26 October

I stay in all morning – apart from some shopping – & do a new sequence for G.T. & then get on with the long overdue Piano conductor[146] of my Rossini suite. Lunch at MM with Brian Easdale, & in afternoon down to Blackheath where I help with endless bits of recording etc. – Recording lots of small boys shouting for swimming bath sequence; ~~& bit superf~~ supervising a recording of commentary etc. etc. Back to town by 7.15 & spend evening at 559 – staining floors with Beth. Working till 11.0 we give the floors done yesterday a second coat. Back here by 11.30 pretty tired I must say. Good news of Frank continued.

Europe in a ferment because Russia seeing the farce of the non-intervention in Spain has decided to do something at last (probably too late) & is sending arms there. Great appeals from Germany for 'friendship' against common enemy of Communism.

Wednesday 28 October

A very hectic morning – I endeavour to get the Rossini done by lunch to deliver it to B & H, but I get so many 'phone calls & other distraction that I can't manage it. I go up to 559 for lunch with Beth, & Lilian takes her & me after to Lewis' where we choose curtains for the enormous windows of the new place. Meet Grace at 3.0 & go to some lovely picture shows – one by Richard Eurich, very promising young man, with a really pleasant gift. Some great Christopher Woods as well. Then on to the French exhibition, which is a revelation – some great Manets (Garçon au chien), Van Goch's (L'arléssienne), Renoirs & Degas – but greatest of all are the Cézannes – Mardi Gras, Baigneurs, Garcon au Filet Rouge, St. Victoire & miracle of miracles the Chateau Noir – a very exhausting exhibition. After a meal at Schmidts we go to Vienna Symphony Concert at Q.H under Kabasta. This is a really great orchestra, & it is a miracle to hear real orchestral playing. Perfect ensemble & intonation in the Leonore 2 & Haffner Mozart Symp. A most thrilling virtuoso show of Til Eulenspiegel – a wonderful show. Bruckner's 7th does not convert me. The organist in his loft dreamily improvising – very lovely sounds the occasionally lovely ideas (the beginning is lovely) – but the construction, the aimless wandering, the appalling lack of invention. An encore show of the Meistersing overture puts me in a right mood for the departure!

Thursday 29 October

Still lots & lots of business about the flat. I get the Rossini thing finished. Lunch here & I go up West at 2.0. Have a look at the Felicia Brown exhibition (she was killed fighting for Government in Spain abt a month ago) & buy 3 lovely drawings of hers. To B & H, where I see Ralph H Then tea with Brian Easdale about Group Theatre. Rehearsal with Boyd Neel of my Simple Symphony. at Earls Court. Back here by 7.45 for a meal & more arrangements. Dash up to Q.H. for 2nd half of Phil. concert where Julius Harrison (with Sinby (tenor) & Jarred (alto) 1. good. 2. excellent) does Lied vn der Erde. Boyd Neel takes me & we eat after to recover from the show, which, all things considered (lack of rehearsal, lack of ability of orchestra, lack of real understanding by conductor) isnt bad. But what a work – it moves me more than any other music – certainly of this century. He seems to be gaining a large public here – which is almost annoying – one doesn't want to share ones beauty spots! Back here by 12.0, but there's lots to be done before bed.

Friday 30 October

The men from Green & Schrands arrive at 8.30 to begin our move. I stay in till 11.30 to superintend their packing (also get a section of music for Group Theatre written at the same time, written on any odd bit of furniture that escapes their clutches) when I go up to 559 to superintend the moving in. This takes all the aft. (I'm supposed to go down to Denham, but there isn't time) until 4.15 when I dash to Liverpool St. to meet Mum (who's staying with Barbara) & dash back by 6.0. The place is beginning to look very smart – carpets down, but no curtains yet. It is much larger, but I think it's going to be fine. I go out immediately after dinner to Wigmore Hall – concert by the Boyd Neel Str. Orchestra. I sit with Toni Brosa & Henry Boys. They play a mixed programme inc. my Simple Symphony (which goes swimmingly, & gets a rousing reception!) & the wonderful new Suite of Schönberg[147] – a miracle in every way – very striking & full of deep passion & content. It goes down very badly, but H.B. & I have coffee out after still raving over it!

Monday 2 November

Mum does gallons of work in the flat all day – staining all the stairs & Kathleen's room – tho' K. gives it a 2nd coat after dinner which she has here with us. I do business, shop, & do a new sequence for Cavalcanti before lunch. To Boosey & Hawkes, & G.P.O. in aft. Also buy a copy of Auden's new book of verse 'Look Stranger!' which has I think some splendid things in it. He has written two for me included in it.[148] After dinner letters, & also some work (parts altering & rewriting) for tomorrow's recording.

Tuesday 3 November

I spend a long time in morning 'phoning, business etc. ~~until~~ and arranging & sorting music. Then at 11.45 Spice 'phones & asks for a lot of music (just under 2 mins.) for to-days recording. I say I'll look for something, but of course can find nothing of right length or scoring. So I sit down at 12.15 & with only a rough pencil sketch (for piano) score out this bit (for 11 inst – Fl, Cl, Tpt, Trb, Harp, percussion, 2 Vl.s, Vla, Vlc, Db.). Work in taxi (I make no score but write straight out into parts) on way to pick up Toni Brosa & his 4tet – all way down in Mannuci's car – getting stuck for ½ hr in Park Lane in traffic jam (opening of parliament – & about time too!) – finishing it at 2.15! without lunch. The recording goes quite well, but there is too much to do & colossal strain. The new bit sounds fine. Get back here by 7.0 just about done in. However a bath & good meal prepared by Mum revives me & spend a pleasant evening reading. Boyd Neel 'phones from Dundee (touring with his orchestra) about Capitol Films, at 11.0.

Thursday 5 November

I meet Phil Green (a jazz-merchant who is writing the jazz for Love from a Stranger) at Baker St at 10.0 & together we depart for Denham. Arrive after a tortuous journey – four changes, everlasting waits, Snail-like travelling in antique trains when we do eventually move – ~~then~~ at 12.15!! These English suburban railway- systems. Spend whole day on the set, waiting to see Lee about the music for the Paris sequence – which we don't actually do till 4.0.

I stay on till 6.0 seeing Daviicheosky – the publicity agent. Back here by 7.30 & spend evening writing letters.

Madrid bombed by air for umpteenth time. No. of children killed not specified. 70 were killed in one go the other day. What price Fascism?

Friday 6 November

I attempt to work in morning & afternoon back at flat – but telephone calls & other business interruptions are so numerous that I get only the theme of the oboe & piano Variations roughly sketched out. After a bath, change, & shave I go out to Ralph Hawkes' flat where I meet him & a Mrs [gap]; have some good food & other essence of luxury (Rolls & chauffeur) go with them to Covent Garden in a box to hear Richard Strauss conduct his Ariadne auf Naxos with the Bourgeois Gentilhomme prologue. The Dresden State Opera season. Excellent cast & orchestra & setting & production (inspite of the Jew, Communist, & Intellectual purge, there is still a good deal of talent left in Naziland) – Ariadne (Marta Fuchs) & Zerbinetta (with her high A trill!)[149] are fine. As a ~~show~~ work it is impeccably written – delicate & refined to a degree & it is a treat to hear such workmanship. But it is 90% of it very thin music, a pale reflection of what [h]as gone before. But what vocal writing! // After this we all go to the Café de Paris, eat in the luxurious surroundings see a first rate caberet (4 Yacht Club boys) & Mayfair generally fiddling while the world is burning. It seems pretty ironical to have a menu given one, priced 21/- minimum, when 21/- will feed a poor family in comfort for a week. Back here (by cab) at 2.0.

Saturday 7 November

Up early & catch 10.10 from Marylebone to Denham. Here I meet the pianist, Jack Phillips, whom Phil Green has sent down to try over some new numbers for the Paris Caberet sequence.[150] We spend whole day till 4.0 hanging around – waiting for verdicts. A wicked waste of time. Eat various meals with him & Dariszeoski with whom I come back to town. Find Kathleen Mead & Kit Welford here for tea & ~~supp~~ dinner (Mrs Nun cooks it well for us); After it listen to a B.B.C. concert of chamber music – Sophie singing some Fauré most beautifully, & Isolde Menges 6tet playing (not so well) Schönberg Verklärte Nacht (which makes my spine wobble) & Franks 6tet [for strings, 1906–12] which is a <u>very</u> very beautiful work. Beautifully written & some lovely material in it. The slow movement is a gem.

Sunday 8 November

Up nice & late (10.15) & do nothing in morning but talk with Mum & Beth, make my bed, & play piano. Barbara comes to lunch. In aft. laze & read – what bliss! – until 4.0 when Beth & I go for a walk with Kit who comes to tea. Lennox Berkeley (back from Parris) is added to the party for supper which is amusing. After, Beth, Len. K. & I go off to Group Theatre show of Agamemnon – (MacNeice's Trans. my music) & it is far & away better than I had dreamed of. Certainly the music is badly played, but considering all Easdale has done a very good job of organisation. It is a good show & perhaps the best & simplest thing that Rupert or the Group theatre have ever done. Toni & Peggy Brosa come too & afterwards we all have some tea & back here by 11.30.

Monday 9 November

Mum goes back to Frinton, but via Lowestoft for this night. It has been lovely having her & things have gone very smoothly. She has done lots to help us get straight. I have to go off very early to Denham – breakfast (got by Mum) at 8.0, leave at 8.25, 8.55 from Marylebone & at the Studio at 9.30.

I spend whole day on the set, on & off, supervising music being played during a Paris night club. But in the afternoon I get away frequently enough to be able to write a duet to some words of Montagu's (Mother Comfort). Much has to be altered, but I feel there is a foundation of a nice little number there. Back here by 8.15 – have a meal – 'phone odd people – talk & bath & bed soon after 11.0.

Tuesday 10 November

I shop, 'phone & other business matters in morning before going up West to see Ralph Hawkes at 12.0. There is a bother with Mr. Rouche – who runs the orchestral light department – about my Rossini Suite because he thinks it is not nearly direct enough or simple (in scoring) for the market. I of course defend it stoutly & R.H. keeps the peace, but we ~~hav~~ don't reach an agreement (it is difficult for the ages of 60 odd, & 20 odd to agree over scoring). Lunch at M.M. with Mosco Carner, & Gerald Abrahams – v. pleasant, & after odd business matters – to G.P.O – back here by 4.0 & do some work on yesterday's duet before leaving for Ralph Hawkes' flat at 6.15. Meet there his brother Geoffrey (charming) & two female friends a Mrs Osborne (a society creature) & a Signora . . . . (whose Spanish fascist husband's just been shot by the Gov. in Spain – so one has tactfully to avoid the subject – difficult these days when Franco is bombing the innocents in Madrid.) We go on to Covent Garden by 7.0 for Rosenkavalier. A box. This glorious opera (sickly agreed, but beautifully done, & adorable once in a while) is very well played by the Dresden Co. whose team work is excellent. Cebotari as Sophie, both looked & sang divinely. Ochs ([gap]) was great, & sang & not bawled his part. After that we all, plus a group of nice Americans over here completing a good business deal (electric Organ) with B. & H., go to the Mayfair for a suppper & dance – I also dance to Ambrose's band! Lap of Luxury of course & I admit I enjoy it – splendid caberet by 2 little black boys – Nicholas Bros. Back by 2.30.

Wednesday 11 November

In the morning I go with Montagu Slater up to ~~the~~ a meeting of the International Peace Soc.[151] (Film, Theatre & Music section). at Vaudeville Theatre. There arn't many people there – everyone is enjoying remorse ~~at~~ & glorifying the noble milatry profession at the Cenotaph. However it gives one some satisfaction that something is being done (in 33 countries) to propagate pacific settlement of disputes (if disputes there be) – as outlined by Alan Bush – general sec. of Section. Back here for lunch & work all aft. at duet. After dinner I go (having changed) up to Covent Garden & meet Ralph Hawkes & two friends. Figaro to-night & it is without exception the loveliest thing I have ever seen on any stage. This simple beauty (expressing every emotion) is withering to any ambitions one might have – & yet it is good to have lived in a world that could produce such perfection. It is a glorious production – not a weak spot – Cherubino (Marte Rohs) looked like the mischievous rascal he is – Susanna (Cebotari) is enchantly beautiful & lively. Countess (Teschemacher) looked lovely & sang better – as did the previous ones. Figaro (Schöffler) & Count (Ahlersmeyer) both fine. Orchestra was lovely (very small 8 Vlns, 2 Vlc, & 2 Cb.) & Böhm was a superb conductor – right feeling & delicacy, so that the soloists never had to strain. Shohbach excellent producer – but, best of all was Mozart.!

Straight back home to-night – no night club, luckily, but I'm extravagant & take a taxi – you can't scramble on a 13 bus after Figaro!

Thursday 12 November

I stay in all day & work at my oboe suite[152] but it doesn't go well at all – however I manage to do one complete movement which may be usable after alteration. At 7.15 I go up to Bloomsbury & after a meal with Lennox Berkeley, we meet Grace & go to a recital of the Organ Music Society – at St. John's, given by André Marshal, the blind French organist. First part of programme all ord. organ stuff, well played I suppose, but not to my taste. The 2nd half was a Symphony Improvised on themes by 4 English

Composers (Fugue, Alan Bush – Scherzo, me – Adagio, Walton – Toccata, Lambert). It is amazingly clever & inconceivable since he is blind. My scherzo was a quaint odd little thing, very French & exotic.

Friday 13 November

I work here all morning – rewriting odd things, but not successful in progressing further with my Suite. ~~In aft~~ After lunch at 12.30 – I go up to Harold Reeves & buy a Min. score of Figaro complete – which is haunting me beyond words. Wed. night was a land-mark in my history.

At 2.15 I go down to Denham with Boyd Neel, who is back from his tour round Scotland & N. England with his orchestra – He's played my Simple Symph all over the place with great success – But there is nothing doing there in the music way yet, so we have tea & come back. Beth out at millinary in evening, Kathleen Mead, who is installed here now in our extra room, goes out after dinner, but I stay in all evening & enjoy it – doing 'phone calls & lots of letters. I should have gone to a B.BC. contempory concert but cannot face it (show of a new V. Williams work). // Spanish news more hopeful than for 6 months – Madrid still holding out & a tremendous attack is being launched on Franco's butchers.

Saturday 14 November [London/Frinton]

After breakfast I put my odd things together & then go to meet Ronald Duncan up at Oxford Circus to talk over the Marching Song[153] for Shepherd's Albert Hall meetings that we've got to do. After that I go to Van Wyck's to get some Figaro records – which I play often later in the day, & adore more than I can say. ~~Afte~~ Meet Beth & catch 12.35 from Livpool St down to Frinton – meal on way, usual rotten one for 2/6. Mum has Aunts Queenie & Effie with her – ~~the two~~ two of the down & outs of the family (tho' the latter works very hard – for little or no pay – but has no job at the moment). It is rather a trial – relations usually are. However Mrs Foster & the Alexanders come in to tea & it is all very bright & cheerful – except for a slight political argument which I foolishly start! Walk with Beth before dinner – & talk & 'Figaro' after.

Sunday 15 November [Frinton]

Queenie is really a most dreadful trial – she is terribly self righteous, prying, & a general busy-body. She means well, but rubs every one the wrong way – being a religious maniac, everything controversial (even the subject of U.S.S.R!!) has to be avoided. One is sorry for her, as she must have a lonely life – but by jove she is irritating!

Effie is a dear & a brick – work's like a nigger;[154] has it is true got funny ways & talks without ceasing (a Hockey failing) – but is a comfort after Q.

Beth, Effie & I go for ride in Lagonda & exercise Caesar on Marshes. Windy & boisterous day, but very exhilarating. Rest of time – read, gramophone (Figaro; Rosenkavalier; Berg, Lyric Suite etc.), & after dinner sort out photos & manuscripts (for Capitol, they want an early M.S. to photo, & a contemporary photo!).

Tuesday 17 November [London]

Hear from Boyd Neel in morning that we've got to start work on the Capitol Film stuff to-morrow, which means that it is all up for the other stuff (for Hallis) for a bit. However in desparation I write a duet (Auden's words) in the morning & early afternoon[155] – very light & Victorian in mood! Barbara to lunch. Auden I meet for tea at the M.M. & discuss odd things. Grace comes after dinner for coffee & to hear my duets, which she approves off, which is a relief!

Wednesday 18 November

In morning I do some work at the yesterday's Duet – & alot of business as well. Bank & Hair cut at Whiteleys. M.M. Lunch. In aft Boyd N. & I go down to Sound City (Shepperton) to see Reels 1 & 2 of Love from a Stranger & to decide over music – which is going to be dammed difficult. I get down to it after dinner here, but do some bloody awful stuff. Go to bed early in desparation in the hope that to-morrow's labour will bear some better fruit.

Thursday 19 November

Up pretty early and at the work – with occasional walks to help the muse. Out to lunch in Soho with Ranje Danisharski, the Capitol Publicity agent. Go on to Zwemmer's gallery for a bit with ~~them~~ him afterwards.

Back about 3.30 & work till 7.0. I find it's not going too well, so I 'phone Lennox Berkeley, with whom I'm supposed to be eating at the Café Royal (with E.J. Dent) & cancel it, & also to Mrs Robert Mayer, ~~who~~ saying I can't attend her party for Nadia Boulanger to-night. A pity, but it can't be helped. After a walk & food, I get down to the stuff with better results. Bed at 12.45.

Friday 20 November

Meet Boyd at 9.45 & go with him to Shepperton where we spend the day with Rowland Lee seeing the picture (or first 4 reels of it) & measuring it. There of course is a colossal rush on the film, & recording must be done by Wednesday! – very likely! ~~since then~~ with all these gallons of stuff to be done, scored & copied.

After tea with Boyd I come back here & start at it – scarcely stopping for meal (Mrs. Nun in, Beth out at Theatre with Meads) until 3.0 a.m. in the morning. I get the title music finished & scored.

Tonight I should have played the piano part of a work of Lennox's at the French Embassy under Nadia Boulanger – but it is cancelled owing to general mourning in France (owing to suicide of Savengro, minister, because of Calumny of Right wing Press).[156] It is put off till Tuesday, which I can't manage, so that I spend ages finding a pianist to deputise for me. Eventually get Millicent Silver.

Sunday 22 November

My birthday, but not spent in a very festive manner. Up late & don't breakfast till 11.0! Then work till lunch at 1.30 & after. Beth goes out with Kit again & Grace comes in afternoon to help me as yesterday. We have a nice walk on the heath after tea as a respite from the drudge. Work on till 2.30 – but Grace leaves at 10.0 – having helped me enormously.

// International situation worse & worse – Franco going to blockade ships entering Barcelona – England as in 1914 hums & has before commiting the people of Spain to even further agony. Madrid inspite of frightful bombing is still hang[ing] out by the skin of its teeth.

Wednesday 25 November

Up betimes – meet Boyd (& Grace who comes down for interest) at 9.0 & go down to Pinewoods Studio (Iver) where the 1st recordings of 'Love from a stranger' music takes place. A large orchestra – composed mostly of Boyd Neel Strings (with William Primrose, & Cedric Sharpe) & odd wind (Bassoons bad) – of about 20. Considering the pace at which the music was written it comes off marvellously – some of it is pretty difficult, & Boyd synchronises it without any difficulty. The long Channel sequence for which I've written a long Viennese Waltz is the most successful, & comes off like hell. Some rather good tunes, I think! Back by 6.30 with Boyd. I have to pack up the duets to Sophie & sister[157] & take them to Golders Green to post, – this before dinner. After, write yet another sequence, & other odd jobs.

Friday 27 November

Up early & with Boyd to Iver where we spend morning recording Phil Green & his very competant band ~~reco~~ playing too numbers for the Paris Café scene. After lunch we have the second orchestral session – & it is amusing if surprising to see difference in attitude between the 'hot' & the 'straight' bands – the former all keen & there ¼ early – the latter dull & slow & few there before 2.15.

However it goes well when we get started – take another playing of the Channel crossing Waltz & all the other odd stuff. Back with Boyd – pretty tired, but mostly reaction, by 7.30. Bath, dinner, 'phoning & bed.

I become very extravagant & buy the full score of Berg's miraculous Violin concerto My god what a sublime work.

Monday 30 November

I go to B & H in morning & then Ralph Hawkes takes Boyd Neel & me down to Iver in his superb Cadillac (we do 85 on the Western Avenue!) to hear some of my stuff for Love from a Stranger. I feel very disatisfied with it – as I feel it is just ordinary film stuff, but appantly Max Schach (head producer & manager of Capitol) is not of that opinion & thinks they've discovered a new Stravinsky!! Back by lunch (MM.) & after a news theatre (bad) I come back here for tea with Ronald Duncan & together we work on a Marching song for Dick Sheppard & his league.[158] Between us – he words, me tune – we do practically the whole of one between 4–6.30! Bernard Richards comes – Beth he & I walk on Hamptd Heath before a meal to which Irene also comes. After that we rehearse the trio – Beethoven D maj (lovely) & Brahms A minor (foul – I can scarcely bear to play it).[159]

Apparently the Crystal Palace is burning to the ground tho' we can't see it from here. I have never seen the place close to, so am not very moved – but BBC calls it London's most disatrous fire ever.!!

Tuesday 1 December

After breakfast I go up to B & H to pick up my cheque from Capitol – £200 (2nd & 3rd payments) – less £30 to B & H for agents fees. Back here & work the rest of the day on the oboe suite – it goes quite well, but one cannot dash off this kind of thing like Film music.

Wystan Auden arrives at tea-time to stay for a time while we work on the Strand Film.[160] It will be nice having him, if I can conquer this appalling inferiority complex that I always have when with vital brains like his. After dinner he tells me he's decided to go to Spain after Xmas & fight – I try to disuade him, because what the Spanish Gov. might gain by his joining is nothing compared with the world's gain by his continuing to write; but no one can ~~alte~~ make W.H.A. alter his mind.

Wednesday 2 December
Wystan & I go up to Strand Films to see Rotha (producer) & Holmes (director) about the 'Way to the Sea' film which we're doing. See the various sections and then discuss projects with them after.

Lunch with Grace – she is going to help me alot with the oboe suite – copying & editing Back here with WHA in aft & work together on lengths of commentary & music to be done.

He goes out to dinner with Basil Wright, who comes to fetch him – I should have gone too, but stay & work at oboe work instead.

Thursday 3 December
Colossal sensation to-day in papers, as it has all come out about the King wanting to marry Mrs. Simpson (American & twice in divorce courts) as we had all known for ages. The Cabinet says 'no' & a 1st class crisis is the result. Papers filled with photos & life stories of Mrs. S.

We go up to Strand Films for more discussion in the morning – back to Golders Green for lunch & work on in afternoon.

A strange, strange evening – John Carter, the lad & friend of Wystan's who I've been helping to look for a musical job, has an uncle who invites Wystan & me out to a meal at Café Royal & to a pub first. Strangest people there too, a young man with a 'professional' fiancée, a very intellectual young woman, & this rather lewd, & jolly old man. Strange mixture.[161] Back after coffee to recover at 11.0.

Saturday 5 December
Try & work until 11.0 when the Richards come to rehearse – but the 'phone is ~~so~~ incessant & I get nothing done. Go in aft. with Wystan to see Green Pastures at the New Pav.[162] – it is a very moving show – & very well done (except for one or two sects). Back here after tea & then Sophie & Arnold Gyde come to dinner (Grace comes after.) & we have a very amusing evening.

Sophie sings Hunting Fathers to Wystan & then goes on to sing (beautifully) lots of Fauré, Mahler, & Mozart. until about 11.30.

Monday 7 December [Frinton/London]
Wystan, Beth & I come back by early 7.58 train – sorry to leave Mum & to return to the awful rush of this week. – go to copyist on arrival & then back here via B & H. to work all day. W. is out to meals. Then at 5.0 we meet at Strand Films to try out a commentator (recommended by T.S. Elliot) named Tandy – (from Science Museum & looking the image of a stage

bug-hunter) – who will do. Then to Golders Green where I give W., & Lennox Berkeley & Peter Burra dinner & then come back here for sherry, gramophone, & a few mild & amusing games of cards, winding up with a little music. After they are gone Wystan & I talk late into night & he is a great comfort. He is the most charming, most vital, genuine & important person I know & if the Spanish Rebels kill him it will be a bloody atrocity.

Wednesday 9 December

~~Have~~ Spend morning having rows with people on telephone. Talk to Ralph Hawkes about my doing this film to schedule, & he says it's impossible & then 'phone's Rotha who says it's impossible to change the date of recording & that I should manage it (if these people only realised how many notes one has to write for a minutes music!) However I phone him & get things straightened & the 2nd recording fixed for Wed. week.

Write all the rest of the day before going out to dinner with Henry Boys in Soho & then on to Queens Hall with him to hear Krasner do the Berg. Violin Concerto (B.B.C. orch. under Wood, both lousy & hap-hazard). It is a grand work – & has an extremely moving effect on me like no other stuff. It is so vital & so intellectually emotional. A complete contrast to the frightful 2nd Symphony of Brahms which proceeded it – applied music – dull, ugly, gauch.

It was difficult after the Berg to have to come back & write a movement (Waltz) of my Oboe Variations, but it had to be done.

Bed at 2.0.

Thursday 10 December

Bernard & Irene Richards come to rehearse for to-nights concert in the morning. I don't know the stuff (the Brahms I don't want to know) & not being 'in' with the piano is very diffiult. However the show at 9.0, at the Mignon Club Bayswater – run by rich spinsters & retired Colonels, goes quite well – surprisingly so.

The great event of the day of course is the Kings Abidcation – announced in the afternoon. Not being allowed to marry the woman he loved, obviously being incapable (naturally in such a strained position) of continuing without her, the only course is abdication. But parliament still have put no charges against her. It would have been good politically to unite England & U.S.A. – she would have been an excellent Queen democratically & (being divorced typical of the age). But obviously they wanted to get rid of a King with too much personallity & any little excuse surficed.

Have to work as usual till about 1.0.

Friday 11 December

Go to Adolph Hallis at 9.15 for a short rehearsal of the sections of oboe work already done & hear Sophie & Betty Bannerman try over the 2nd duet – which I think will be fine. Then straight on to Strand Films at 10.0 where I run thro' stuff I've already written on a small piano in the cutting room, watching the picture on the Moviola. It fits well & I come back here to do some more. Work at it all afternoon & then do some more to the Polka of the suite in the evening – which I think will do now.

The event of the evening is the farewell speech of the ex-king Edward (variously termed, Prince Edward, Mr. Windsor & the Duke of Windsor) at 10.0 which is really a most moving affair. Very well spoken, very simple & direct – containing some good home truths only slightly disguised & ending with a terrifying 'God save the King' that made one shiver in ones shoes. If he had only been allowed to broadcast a week ago (as he wished to, but as it now transpires, the Ministers didn't think it 'advisable') there would have been no abdication.

Saturday 12 December

Another solid day of work – luckily ~~not~~ this rushed period won't last for ever.

To Strand Films early – work there all morning on new section. Late lunch in Soho with Holmes (director) – to Grace in afternoon where I do more work – back here for dinner (to which George Hockey comes & is interesting about dancing at which he's expert) & after that do the final 'Resolution' of the oboe suite which I hope will pass muster tho' I can never judge till the next day. It is a relief to get it finished – but I'm not sure of the ~~value~~ standard of work in it.

Sunday 13 December

Not early up – as I can't wake, but I get alot of work done in morning – copy Oboe parts of oboe work & do some sections of Film stuff which I continue after lunch. Rehearse commentary for to-morrow with Tandy & Holmes at Strand Films at 4.0 & then on to Adolph Hallis for a rehearsal of the Oboe work with him & Natalie Caine – it seems to be going quite well tho' she is abit clumsy. I think it comes off – doubtful movements – Polka & Exercises. Meet the Gydes & Colette Wyss here to sing Die Serenaden of Hindemith[163] – excellently too.

Back here for supper & work till 10.45 – then an early bed – earliest for weeks!

Monday 14 December

Interrupted incessantly by telephone, I manage to do a section more of Film before meeting Holmes for lunch at 12.30 & then with him to the recording of Section III of the Film. Music accompaning commentary (spoken by Tandy) very closely – which is the devil to synchronise consequently it takes 2 sessions (6 hours) to get it done. However tho' exhausted ~~one is~~ I am pleased with the result – although God forgive me for some of the music I've written (including the slow Waltz & Military march) – tho' ~~why~~ I don't see why, because it will give unprejudiced people pleasure – & it is quite well done – & clean at that.

I decide that I can't go out to dinner with Wright to meet Jaubert (French Composer) to-night as I'm abit buggered up – & I have this other stuff to get done. So I come back, meal with Beth, & then work on afterwards – at 'The death of Nelson'.[164] But I'm getting a genuine affection for the best Victorian music.

Tuesday 15 December

After writing some more stuff I go up west to Copyist & then on to Wigmore for rehearsal of to-ngith's concert. Lunch after with Hallis & Christian Darnton & then back here to write final piece of Film stuff – thank God. Then meet at 7.15 Wystan Auden & Louis MacNeice for a meal – very rowdy & pleasant. W. being slightly drunk & arguing hard with the Waitress about 2nd helpings (having always a collossal appetite). The[n] we go on to Hallis concert at Wigmore Hall. This is run by him on a Subscription basis (all partakers buying up a certain number of seats). Sophie Wyss & Colette Wyss (her first appearance here) Shadwyck Str. Quartet Natalie Caine & Adolphe take part – as well as Betty Bannerman who takes Colette W's place in my duets as she is scared of the English.

Main works were Hindemith Serenade – some good things, but too many formulas & dull devices to make it great. Fauré's Bon Chanson (Sophie singing exquisitely) – a delight. My Oboe Suite which they play well if not brilliantly & which goes down very well – surprisingly – as also do the duets – Montagu Slater's & Wystan's words.[165] After the concert Wystan, Louis M., Peter Burra & Lennox Berkeley, Beth & I all go to Café Royal & have nice supper – back by 12.45.

Wednesday 16 December

I leave pretty early & go to Strand Films where I try over my music with the film to see how it fits for this afternoon – then hear Monday's stuff & discover that the sound Engineer has got all the balance between music &

commentator wrong for some of the stuff & it is alot of it unusable Therefore we decide to do some of it again which means a tiny bit of rescoring & lots of 'phoning for the extra players. The recording is an awful strain as I'm pretty dead & there's lots to be done. However I get thro' somewhere & finish by 7.0. Then go to a nearby pub & over some sherry discuss world in general, art & politics in particular till 8.30 with Geoffrey Tandy the scientist who's done the commentary. Back here by 9.0. & Beth leaves her dressmaking downstairs to talk to me while I eat. At about 10.0 she goes to do some more work down stairs – discovers much smoke pouring from work-room & we find iron (which she'd left on) lying on floor with board & linoleum in flames – we extinguish it luckily, having discovered it soon enough, but it does alot of damage & gives us a hell of a fright.

Thursday 17 December

It is glorious to have no work to do – & I spend all morning telephoning to people, & getting my business in order & letters written – which has got hopelessly out of hand these last weeks. Up west & eat at Le Diner Franciais with Arnold Cooke in town at the moment. Shop in aft. Tea with the Bridges – F.B. has recovered sufficiently to conduct at the B.B.C. to-night. He's looking well, tho' week, but a good deal over [older?]. He don't remember anything of his fortnight's wandering of brain[166] – but apparitly he was perfectly 'decent' & incredibly lucid in it. – mostly 'being in Spain – worrying abot the revolution & Toni B. –' runing thro' music, talking French to Marge, & slanging audiences at Norwich for not taking my 'Hunting Fathers' more seriously!! // Spend evening with Pat Jackson dinner at Liberal Club, & Ping pong at MM. & then back in time to hear F.B. do his String Suite.[167]

Saturday 19 December

A very expensive day, but it is great fun spending money when you've got some to spare.

In morning I do odd business here & then lunch with John Alston (back from his first term at Denstone) at M.M. In the afternoon Barbara & I escort Aunt Julianne (she is crippled with Rhum. Arthritis – made no better by the death of Uncle Sheldon in Aug.) from ~~Worc~~ Paddington to Livepool Street to catch 4.57 down to Mum. It is very slow business, but the porters are charming & help with bath chairs etc. Back with Barbara to a news Theatre (5 Disneys) before I meet Grace Williams & Piers Dunkerley (back from Bloxham) – eat with them & then take them to Sadlers Wells where we see quite a good show of Hansel & Gretel[168] – glorious work – I adore every bar. Edith Coates[169] was outstanding as the Mother & none of the others were really bad except the Sandmäunchen. Corbett conducts, competantly – but, oh, how dully & slowly! // Piers comes back with me to spend the night, as Beth's away to a dance with Kit & Kathleen's gone home.

Sunday 20 December

Up at 9.15 & get breakfast for Piers & do odd household jobs. He & I go for a short walk on the heath – he goes back home (Battersea) by lunch time & I come back here feeling as dead as mutton. Foul throat & completely tired – reaction from the last ~~night~~ weeks I suppose. I don't lunch with Lennox or dine with Pat as intended but stay in for rest of day & early bed. Beth & Kit come back in aft & seem very quiet & moody & it afterwards transpires that they got engaged last night. What momentous days we live in! But I hope she'll be happy as I think she will, as he's very nice.

Monday 21 December

Stay in – feeling pretty low – all morning, doing business, letters, & 'phoning people putting off this week's engagements as I've definitely decided to go home to-morrow. Go out shopping in the afternoon – to book-shops & music-shops for presents. Meet George Atkinson of South Lodge – who has improved out of all knowledge & become very intelligent & interesting it seems. Feel very dead about 4.20 so I take a taxi to MM & recover with the aid of some tea. Back here more dead than alive by 6.0. Lennox comes to dinner & we have a cheerful evening discussing Spanish work & playing Vla. & piano duets. He's a dear & we both feel better for the evening.

Beth, poor thing, is feeling absolutely bewildered – 'as if she's been run over by a bus'. But, not surprising, as one dosn't become engaged every day.

Tuesday 22 December [London/Frinton]

I stay in all morning – pack & post Xmas parcels galore. Then I'm juston leaving to catch 1.30 to Frinton, when Barb. arrives for lunch & kindly points out that I shall have to wait a long time – as it only runs on Saturdays. So I wait till 3.42. Feel very flu'y & very glad to be down here & finished with work. I have a bath & go straight to bed – & Mum brings me a nice supper & I spend the evening with a Dorothy Sayers.[170]

Mum has Aunt Julianne here – it is appalling what disease makes people bare. And think of the amount the country spends on means to destroy people when there are medical research-men in need of funds.

Thursday 24 December

Up for breakfast – better, but cold & head still pretty lousy. In morning I endeavour to make the old Lagonda move, but she's as obstinate as a mule & it takes an other car from the garage down the road, pulling her, to start her in the Afternoon. After that I run her round the place to warm her up.

Walk down town for final shopping in morning. My gramophone records of the 'Battle Symphony'[171] come – & I am very pleased with them. There are some very exciting & picturesque things in it – & the end is gloriously naive.

Barbara arrives by 2.20 (30 mins late) – & I meet her. Beth is brought by Kit in the aft. – but the engagement is still to be kept secret.

Thursday 31 December
In the morning I set some very nice verses of Lamb (Philip's Breeches) for mixed voices[172] – actually to sketches made in Cornwall. But I don't think it matters much – but quite nice. Take Mum out shopping in Lagonda (running well, but a bugger to start). Sophie Wyss sings some rather dull Balikirev very well 6.40.

Thank God there is no more 1936 to be gone thro'. Of all the frightful years. Tragedy after tragedy – vile hippocracy of State & Church – with only the miraculous Madrid stand,[173] & at home F.B's recovery to brighten it. Anyhow Lucy Houston's dead, so that's <u>one</u> stumbling block removed.[174]

1937

Friday 1 January [Frinton]
A happy new Year! – faint hope of that with the International situation as black as approaching thunder clouds. Being selfish (a universal failing) I feel it cruel, as I have had a good year & think that next year ~~will~~ would be even better – with a very hopeful future, given normal conditions. Ralph Hawkes is a splendid publisher & general patron & I am getting not so bad a number of performances & have lots of ideas for the future. No prospect & little inclination for marriage, tho' unsettled by Beth's proposed change of state. But with plenty of friends old & (mostly) young.

However with this religious war upon one – one only prays for courage enough to give one's life to the most useful & necessary cause, & for guidance in that direction. So help me God![1]

Letters, & rewrite bits of Temporal Suite & 'Philip's Breeches' in morning[2] & aft. David & Jean Calkin come to tea (aged 15 & 10) & we have a grand time fooling about & playing games. They stay till past 7.0. After supper the

Alexanders come in to play Monopoly – which we all do somewhat hilariously till 11.45.

Saturday 2 January

A little work before I go down to Snellings to play ping-pong with David & Jean. We go in the car, & drop Mum on route – they are much ticked by the £6 Lagonda!

In aft. I meet Beth off 3.20 from town. Long walk with her after tea. She seems satisfailed [satisfied], but not over-confident about the engagement. Monopoly again after dinner. Aunt Ju. seems to be enjoying herself heaps here – a good thing as she doen't get much fun in life with that dreadful ~~infir~~ illness.

The bloody Germans dish everyone's hopes of avoiding 'direct' intervention in Spain ('indirect' means only 15,000 troops!) by seizing a Spanish Government cargo boat. Otherwise the loyal cause prospers.

Wednesday 6 January [London]

Spend morning correcting parts of Soirées Musicales – & pretty bum they are too. Lunch in Soho with Danischewski – the Capitol Publicity man – who is nice, but he has this awful flu, that is such a plague at the moment. Apparently one out of every four persons has either had it, has got it, or about to have it. In the aft. Beth & I chase from garage to garage looking for a suitable 2nd hand car to replace the Lagonda. Find possibililties but no certainties.

Back here for a meal after which I go across to Montagu Slater's & spend the evening with him & his wife, so spend a very charming & amusing evening – playing with plastacine, discussing projects & just talking. Back by mid-night.

Kathleen's back to-night.

Ralph Fox is the latest victim to Fascism in Spain – shot in action. He was a very good writer & a great loss.

Thursday 7 January

Spend morning correcting Rossini Suite Parts & then go up for lunch at Baker St. with Bill Coldstream – he is a grand person & we have lots to discuss – sit for ages & get steadily more depressed (~~as~~ which one cannot avoid these days) & naturally talk alot about Wystan.

At 3.0 I go to Ralph Hawkes & play him (& Leslie Boosey) the duets – which pleases alot. Also discuss lots of other projects. Back here for more work & then bath & change. After an early dinner, Beth & I go by Taxi up West & at London Pavillion meet Barbara & Boyd Neel for first Gala performance of 'Love from a Stranger' – also a grand Disney – Count[r]y Cousin, one of the best ever. The show goes down well – & people are thrilled – but I felt that it somehow misses being a complete knock-out – the middle & beginning is too slow – anyhow I feel that more music ought to have been used (tho' I say it who shouldn't) as it is a true melodrama. Ann Harding & Rathbone are splendid in it – tho'. After this Boyd & I go to a celebration party (given by some people inc. the Neels & Max Schach) at the Savoy. Quite fun, & back here by 2.0.

Friday 8 January

Hurriedly do some more parts (Sinfonietta, this time for further reproduction) before meeting Wystan Auden at Tottenham Ct. Road. He goes off to Spain (to drive an ambulance) to-morrow. It is terribly sad & I feel ghastly about it, tho' I feel it is perhaps the logical thing for him to do – being such a direct person. Anyhow it's phenomenally brave. Spend a glorious morning with him (at Lyons Corner House, coffee-drinking). Talk over everything, & he gives me two grand poems – a lullaby, & a big simple folky Farewell – that is overwhelmingly tragic & moving. I've Lots to do with them.

Meet – feeling very sore – Peter Floud, late of Gresham's, a great friend of mine there – at Café Royal, & he is very nice, but naturally it's hard to appreciate anyone feeling like this. At 3.42 meet Mum & Aunt Julianne from Frinton (Ju. goes to Louise at Bromley) – bring Mum ~~her~~ back here after tea – & then back to meet Francis Barton (my paramour at South Lodge) at Charing X at 7.0. Then eat in Soho with him. He is still a grand person – utterly different from anyone I ever meet & quite refreshing in many ways. Meet Beth, Mum & Kathleen & see "Love from a Stranger" again at Pavillion.

Sunday 10 January

Up pretty late, but make up for lost time on parts, but working solidly all morning, aft. & after tea on them – eventually finishing them. Also I write out in full the Pacifist March.[3]

Spend evening, i.e. Mum, Beth & I, with Barbara.

Wystan hasn't yet gone – expects to go to-morrow – because the Medical Unit he was going with was stopped by the Government. Fine non- intervention that, which even stops medical aid as well as arms, to the legal Government.

Monday 11 January

After business here & at bank (much extracting of money!) I go up to discuss music for F6 with Rupert Doone – he is very difficult, wanting me of course to write the music for nothing, & even to play the piano in the show for a fortnight, also gratis! Nothing doing! Then lunch at Café Royal with Ronald Duncan, Nigel Spotteswood & Scott Goddard. About the Pacifist March. Don't decide much, & the Lunch is a pretty hectic affair, S.G. being incredibly lively to cover his obvious depression & decadence. Not a favourite of mine! In aft. Henry Boys & R.D. & I collect tickets for to-morrow, & Henry & I meet Mum for tea at M.M. Shop after.

In evening – after business & letters before dinner – Mum, Beth & I go to Green Pastures[4] at Marble Arch. It confirms the impression it made on me at first – but perhaps mostly ~~by~~ because of the marvellous music. Pack – Bed. – feeling desparate.

Tuesday 12 January [London/Paris]

Up pretty early & after breakfast I meet Henry & Ronald at Victoria & we catch 10.5 via Newhaven & Dieppe (quite calm, but very cold) and arrive in Paris (St. Lazard) at 6.0 about. Then take a taxi to Hotel Indo-Hollandais (recommended by Ronald) in Rue d'HauteVille.

We eat in the little restaurant next the hotel (very good & very cheap, 8F.). – Afterwards decide to go to Opera, but on arrival there discover that there is nothing on to-night – so go on to Folies Bergérs – but as we arrive ½ hr. early, we are taken by one of the commissioners to 'another little show' – fools I admit to go, but a mixture of ignorance & curiosity made us follow. Anyhow we are taken to a large house a few yards away, & there are presented in the most sordid manner possible ~~without~~ with about 20 nude females, fat, hairy, unprepossessing; smelling of vile cheap scent, & walking round the room in couples to a gramophone. It is revolting – appalling that such a noble thing as sex should be so degraded. We are given cheap champagne, but decide that we've had enough, & to the disgust of the fat proprietress, take a hasty departure – it cost us 100F too. After this disgusting little exhibition, we are in no mood for the Folies, & as it turns out it is incredibly bad – just chocolate box pornography back-stage, alternating with feeble comedy front stage. Besides Josephine Baker is as old as the hills, & can neither dance, sing nor act. So we leave here at ½ time & after wandering the streets for abit make our way to Notre Dame, which is indeed a sight for sore eyes. It gives one hope that humans can erect a building such as this. Terrifying with its disdainful gargoyles but superb in its perfection. Stay here till past 12.0 & then back to hotel.

Wednesday 13 January [Paris]

Up really very late & then go up to Montmatre – inspect this very good Church (Sacré Coeur) & then have a late lunch ~~in the~~ in a very lovely little square – a miracle of perfection, and a miracle of a lunch as well. Then down again to Notre Dame which is as grand as we thought last night. Back to hotel & then off again to Theatre Champs Elysés for Fidelio (the Opéra is being cleaned at the moment). This is a very deep religious & exhilarating experience. Well as I know the incredible music, I did not realise what a tremendous dramatic thrill it was. Not a weak spot from beginning ~~to end; whe~~ with the delicious Marcellina (best of all the cast, Lotte Schöne) comedy passing thro' the ~~collect~~ gathering thunder clouds to the glorious sunshine of the end. The F major 'O Gott welch' ein Augenblick'[5] is the most ecstatic moment of all. // All this too with a not too exact performance; but the vitality on the stage made up for some slackness in the orchestral pit. Feeling slightly dazed we wander & then have some coffee before returning.

Thursday 14 January
Up again pretty late & go (with the others of course) to the Louvre where we stay quite a long time. It is a grand place with the most amazing amount of real achievement on every wall (the Fra Angelicos & Goyas, & Rembrants impress most), but too much to be seen in a year. Then in the aft. we go up to Cimetiére Paris looking for Wildes grave, which is apparently elsewhere – then to Tour Eiffel, which is shut – an aft. of disappointments. Back here via numerous cafés & of course in a taxi (we are living a life of excessive luxury, never walking or bussing!) & then change, wash & shave & go out for a late meal. Walk, shop & coffee & back here by 11.15. // While wandering the shops, Ronny & I see a Gargantua & Paraguel illustrated ed. by Dubout[6] – limited edition – knowing his name & seeing the quality of the drawings we purchase both vols. not examining them closely till we arrive back. When we do look at them – we are as appalled by the coarseness of it (being still pretty 'green'!), as we are impressed by the skill of it. Certainly we are having some experiences – what is one to make of an animal that can produce the hideous pornography of Tuesday evening, Notre Dame, Fidelio, & give rise to these filthy & brilliant satires?

Friday 15 January [Paris/Dieppe]
Up early – after an uncomfortable night – sleeping with another person is a mixed blessing (Henry & I share beds, while Ronald has the sofa) – at 6.0 & then we all three go to see Notre Dame at dawn – & it is well worth the effort. This is on the way to the Gare de Lyons, where we see R. off at 8.5 to Marseilles on the way to India, where he is to see & talk with Gandhi & Tagore. He is indeed a brave little man & both Henry & I have become most fond of him. Spend rest of day walking about Paris, Boulevards & Tuilleries

& Quais, & in Notre Dame again of course. Go to a cinema & see a pleasant little film ~~before eating~~ (L'amour En Cage)[7] before eating at 7.30. at the little restaurant adjoining the Hotel. Then at 8.57 we take our sad departure via Dieppe & Newhaven. We are both very tired & feel the journey very trying–

Saturday 16 January [Dieppe/Newhaven/London]
We try & sit up during the sea-journey but succomb & descend to the 3rd Class Salon, which has the appearance & atmosphere of a Morgue. There is besides an attendant who is suspiciously attentive, but I wake apparently unharmed (!) but very bad tempered at the strictness of the Douanes. However there is no trouble about Gargantua & Paraguel. Arrive at Vict. at 6.15 & breakfast there. London is dank & dark, & we feel furious at being back with realities again. This feeling is accentuated, when I get back here at 8.0 & find Kathleen with the bad Flu plague, & Beth sickening for it.

Odd things in morning & sleep solidly from 11–2. Then to BBC. Maida Vale Studios where Joseph Lewis rehearses my Rossini Suite – it goes well tho' the ~~performance~~ conductor is not exactly sensitive. Back here by 4.30. Kit is here. Beth goes to bed with temp of 101 at 7.0. My broadcast of Soirée Musicales goes well & I love the work. Phone Mum who's coming tomorrow to help nurse. Kit stays – till 10.0. I try & listen to Milhaud's Christophe Columb,[8] but tho' I'm very interested there are too many distractions – telephone, arrangements galore–

Bed by 11.0

Monday 18 January [London]
As I've got a filthy cold & I must prevent it developing into this plague I 'phone Dr. Malcom Sargent that I cannot go to his rehearsal of my Sinfonietta at the R.C.M. this morning. So stay in & make hundreds of 'phone calls & start scoring the 'pacifist march'. In the evening I have a slight temperature so have a bath & an early bed. Kathleen's up to-day & dressed. But Beth's temperature is still high. // The Soirées Musicales seems to be well liked.

Long talks to Frank & E. Bridge. They are going to the Memorial for Harold Samuel – who died last Friday – this afternoon. I am sorry not to be able to go to pay tribute to a great little man who was always so grand to me.

Tuesday 19 January
Tho' my temp's down Mum makes me stay in bed all day – & certainly I'm not loth to do so as I'm feeling desparately stuffed up with it. So read most of the day – finishing Firbank's brilliantly amusing 'Cardinal Pirelli'.[9] The

stuffy sensual atmosphere of these Sanctuaries moves me alot – I feel that it wouldn't take much to turn me R.C. They are so incredibly peaceful, so absolutely devorced from realities. But ~~they~~ then in days like these, with threats of war, conscription on every side, one is terribly inclined to become defeatist & escapist.

I get up (not dressed) & come down for dinner. Mum's not feeling too well (terribly tired) & Beth's no better tho' quite cheerful.

To bed about 10.30 & we all spend a very wretched & restless night.

Wednesday 20 January

Beth is much worse – we send for the doctor who actually doesn't come till 5.0. Meanwhile Mum is down with the Plague, & so she moves into my room. I get up & dress after breakfast & stay in all day looking after them. Mrs Nunn is as usual an angel. Barbara comes to lunch & confirms our fears about Beth. Dr Moberly, when he comes at 5.0, says it's pneumonia. We must have a nurse. So Kathleen (now back at work) moves from her room, & Barbara (back from work) takes me down to a friend of hers (Mrs Hibberd) where I'm to spend the nights, & also to borrow necessary linen. Nurse arrives after dinner & the Doctor back again. He doesn't seem overworried, but of course we've got to be terribly careful. Meanwhile he's proscribing the most drastic treatment – wide open windows – little or no heating. Seems very sensible to the laymind. K & I spend a hectic evening satisfying these people's wants from the chemist & elsewhere.

Then at 10.30 I ~~go~~ come to my new quarters – she seems a very decent woman.

Friday 22 January

Back again to flat soon after nine feeling pretty grim. Dr. again says Beth's holding her own, but Mum's no better & a roaring temperature (104+). Barbara doesn't come in the morning but 'phones, but Kit's here all day. I'm afraid that I've got this Plague – temp. 102 mid-day: however I don't go to bed – as there's no where to go! – until after dinner when I go in the sitting room. [Kathleen has gone home for the week-end; she's been sleeping in the sitting room.] Barbara stays till late evening when Muriel Bond fetches her.

Saturday 23 January

In bed all day but much better, thank God. – & nearly normal temperature.

The others are about the same. Dr. seems satisfied that Beth's holding her own – of course she's desparately ill – but the illness is taking its normal course. Mum, we're very worried about. She seems to be developing

Bronchitis – a risky thing when one's her age (60 odd) – her temperature is still way up in the heights. It is so difficult too when there are two seriously ill patients in one house. We change the Night nurse to-day as Beth didn't like her overmuch – but the Day nurse is fine & will be permanent we hope.

Barbara stays all day, & Kit does too – he sleeps in the little room (in Elspeth Biede's quarter) downstairs.[10] B. goes home about 10.0.

Monday 25 January

I get up after breakfast. Barbara comes for a few hours in morning & then back again at 5.0. for evening. Mum definitely has bronchial pneumonia & is completely ~~wonder~~ wandering all the time. Beth no better, but no worse apparently tho' breathing is terribly fast & shallow. Poor dear, its frightful to see her – indeed both of them. Kit here all day – after shopping & buying the ring for Beth in the morning.

Write a good many letters & cards to people & relations – it's amazing how many friends one has & how decent they are, in times of trouble & stress.

Tuesday 26 January

A miserable wretched day. Neither patients so well in fact we all are terribly worried ~~aft~~ about them.

Mum is incoherent all day, but Beth is terribly & pathetically alert. However the Doctor after his 2nd visit in aft. decides to call in Sir Maurice Cassidy again & he makes suggestions. Then (in evening) they give Beth oxygen & this makes a definite improvement & he (Cass) also makes reassuring comments. So we feel more cheerful in evening.

But definitely a kind of day to be avoided!

Aunt Effie comes in afternoon – she is free for a few months & is helping us with the catering which will be an enormous saving & pleasure as she is a 1st-rate cook & cheering as well.

Thursday 28 January

The doctor's evening verdict is that Beth is now out of the wood – very ill still, but definitely progressing now. Mum is not so well – but he says there's a fine chance for her. I spend alot of the day with her, but she mustn't talk much, much as she wants to.

I write hundreds of cards in answer to letters that are pouring in by every post. People are very good.

Read lots of poetry (Shelly, Elliot, Auden, & Spender) & also music (principally Mahler). I'm still sleeping down the road with Mrs Hibberd – Kit in the downstairs room, Aunt Effie in sitting room & Mum in Kathleen's room. Barbara still comes for all the mornings & then from 5.0 for the evenings till Muriel Bond fetches her about 9.0.

Saturday 30 January

Robert is supposed to be coming up to-day but as he has 'flu – it is postponed till to-morrow. Barbara is staying in Hampstead this week-end – with Miss MacDonald, her secretary, who has a lovely house in E. Hampstead. I go there for the night too – she is a charming woman. News about the same. Beth still slightly better, temp. coming down. Mum slightly better too – tho' completely delirious – still she says 'good-night' to me & apparently recognises me.

Sunday 31 January

We get a 'phone call at 7.30 in the morning – Mum not so well – Barbara & I half run the distance – taking ¼ hr, there being no taxi. Then we find when we arrive that Mum had a heart attack at abt 7.0 & died in about ten minutes without being at all conscious or suffering – thank God. So I lose the grandest mother a person could possibly have – & I only hope she realised that I felt like it. Nothing one can do eases the terrible ache that one feels – O God Almighty–

Poor old Beth musn't be told, so we have to act, which makes things 1,000,000 times worse. ~~Still~~ We have to make hundreds of 'phone calls – luckily Barbara is here to help with & to organise everything – a grand comfort. Get in touch with Nicholson (Lowestoft Solicitor – Mum wants to be buried there with Pop of course), & the authorities here, & of course all relatives. Robert, better but not well yet, is coming up to-morrow. I go back with Barbara with Miss Macdonald, to-night – she is a grand woman very practical.

God – what a day!

Monday 1 February

The ghastly farcical acting is kept up still – because Beth mustn't know, but she becomes more & more suspicious all day – the deathly silence after Mum's continuous chatter. But by evening the Doctor realises that sooner or later ~~she~~ it must dawn on her, & we decide to tell her. The Doctor does it very beautifully & Barbara & nurse stand by. She takes it terribly pluckily – perhaps too pluckily, – tho' it must be a terrible shock. She doesn't shed a tear, until actually I go up myself & considering that we were together so much with Mum (more than the others) she does break down a little.

The undertakers come to take the Coffin away to-night – the darling body but that really has no relation to Mum herself. It is the most heartrending thought that I shall never set eyes on her again. Robert arrives at mid-day & comes back to Miss Macdonald with me at night.

Tuesday 2 February
Another terrible day of hanging about & doing nothing definite. Every day one feels completely exhausted. Beth is not so well – temperature varying abit & Empyena[11] is feared. Cassidy comes again in evening & gives a pretty favourable report. Hopeful anyhow. Many wreaths arrive – lovely ones – only it is so annoying that Mum shouldn't see them, as she adored flowers so – of course people say that she can see them, ~~becaus~~ which I only trust & hope ~~believe~~ she can't; for if she is conscious of earthly happenings, then she realises that the Madrid agony is dragging on & on – besides hundreds of other agonies.

Wednesday 3 February [London/Lowestoft]
Robert & I come back here before going to Lowestoft with Aunt Effie (& from Ipswich Elsie Hockey) for the Funeral. Barbara we meet at Liverpool Street too. The Nicholsons ~~fetch~~ meet us & feed us before the show. It is a terrible strain – Barbara nearly faints, but we succeed in holding out. It was a fitting service for darling Mum – Mr. Reeve, Mr Gillespie & Mr Phillips officiate, & Mr Coleman plays suitable music (including my little 'Birds' which was written for her).[12] Many people come up to Kirkley Cemetary after. We go back to the Sewells (Laurence) for tea & it is a rest after the strain. Barbara & Robert stay with Nicholsons for the night to do business, while I come back to London with Effie. Have the appalling news when I get back that Beth appears to be forming an Empyena – & operation is considered necessary. Really there is no end to the bloodiness of this hellish world. However Miss MacDonald is comforting when I get back there – but no earthly comfort is can possibly fill this ghastly blank.

Thursday 4 February [London]
Cassidy says that Beth musn't be moved so Moberly is going to make a suction from the lung to-morrow with a local anaesthetic. She seems better in herself to-day, thank God. Barbara & Robert come ~~over~~ back in aft. Aunt Flo came yesterday to sit with Beth – she is in town with Louise at the moment.

Friday 5 February
Moberly makes his asperation on Beth & Kit goes off to St Thomas'[13] to examine the stuff, & as far as he can see it is quite sterile – a tremendous

relief. All this time Effie is doing all the catering & cooking most wonderfully for us. Barbara comes every day & all day – Robert is of course here, & I'm sleeping with him at Miss Macdonald – who is grand.

I go to Mercury Theatre to see Rupeet Doone & Ashley Dukes about F6.[14] Settle quite alot.

We sort the myriads of letters that people have sent us in the evening – & as Mum laboured so long with the letters on Pop's death that we feel we must do these all by hand.

Saturday 6 February

Barbara & Robert go down to Frinton to-day to begin to settle matters – see Bank-manager & Agent & gardener etc. & to sort things in house. Robert returns in the evening while Barbara stays on with the Fosters.

I ~~go~~ come back here to Beth, & Kit & Effie & I am here all day. I try to do a little work on F6. ~~by~~ but it isn't much good. ~~The ro~~ My room upstairs (with darling old Mum had) was fumigated yesterday & I am using it as much as possible, so as to be able to sleep there to-morrow (for sentimental not hygenic reasons, of course).

We go back to Miss Macdonald's abot 10.0 to see David Layton who is a great friend of her niece, Elizabeth Grey. Talk alot to him, & walk abit on the heath – he is a grand lad & I'm very fond of him.

Sunday 7 February

Pack up after breakfast as Robert goes back to Prestatyn at midday, – after moving the whole of my room's furniture round (with the help of Kit & Mrs Nunn) to disguise the place a little, I am to sleep in it to-night. A filthy day – vile rain & dank weather. I go to tea with Rubert & Robert to see about F6. Stay till 6.odd. Do alot of work. Barbara gets back from Frinton after a heart-rending & depressing day of arrangements & packing up.

Monday 8 February

Aunt Florence comes in morning to see Beth before she goes off to country again. The Doctor comes in morning & gives Beth a thorough overhaul: – tho' she is cheerful, & better in herself, the heart is giving alot of trouble (a flabby heart) & the lung isn't clear of fluid. So an Xray is to be taken on Wed. & the Doctor predict's at least a month's more bed for her – poor child.

I tidy this room & work abit at F6 in afternoon. Sit with Beth alot & Barbara comes to dinner. Beth spends her time doing jig-saw, a little reading, wireless & gramophone.

Begin answering the myriad of letters (well over 60) in evening. A depressing job.

Tuesday 9 February

The X ray people arrive at 5.30 – & take the photo. The result doen't confirm the Doctor's fears, but on the other hand is not particularly cheerful. There are unresolved patches on both lungs & some fluid in one. No cause for alarm but the progress must be necessaraly terribly slow.

Kit goes off to Peasenhall before dinner – to stay for abit – he's looking very tired & it should buck him up abit.

I work abit at F6 & succeed abit.

Brian Easdale who's doing the musical directing comes to lunch & to arrange matters.

Wednesday 10 February

I work alot at F6 but don't do very much – merely finish off the Dance of Death started yesterday.

The Night Nurse leaves us – & that in itself is a hopeful sign. Beth doesn't seem too happy about the night, but there is a bell to the day nurse's room. Montagu Slater comes in after dinner to see me & talk about matters – it helps one to forget the awful gap to do work again, not that one is ever or can be ever unconscious of it.

Thursday 11 February

In the morning & aft, I do alot more F.6. – including a little Mother's song.[15] Brian Easedale comes at tea time to collect this.

I go for a long walk on the Heath with Effie after tea – very lovely, & almost makes one forgets one's horrible troubles (including the terrible Spanish one – now raging at it's most ghastly).

Beth is not so cheerful in the evening – when Barbara is here – but I believe these little periodic collapses are a natural occurrance – tho' distressing. At the present moment I feel as if I can't stick any more worrying.

Friday 12 February

O God, I wish something would ease this awful ache – whatever I do (and I do alot to-day – write alot for F6 until late in the evening) and tho' I have good news of a B.B.C. commission for music for a pageant[16] & Beth is going on well, tho' slowly, nothing takes this consciousness of a terrible gap – that that heavenly presence is with us no longer. Why, oh why, if God is a beneficient God, does he do it. Its more than the likes of me can understand. So young, so useful, & so healthy too – and so incredibly wanted.

Sunday 14 February

Very disappointing but Beth's improvement dosn't continue as it should. Her temp. is up – first time for 9 days and pulse & respirations similarly. & she has much pain. The doctor doen't come more than once for fear of frightening her, but we will know the worst to-morrow. There is just no end to this bloody business. I work at F6 alot all day – finish another number – but I can't think what I'm writing. Walk with Aunt Effie after tea.

A fortnight ago to-day . . . .![17]

Monday 15 February

Doctor comes & examines Beth in morning – suspects fluid in Left lung – but when he does a aspiration (needle) into it in the evening there is nothing there so he diagnoses an attack of pleurisy. Not serious but uncomfortable.

I go to BBC. in afternoon to see Val Gielgud & Laurence Gillian about the Arthur Pageant. It looks a good size job anyhow if not exactly to my taste. To Mercury after – to see how things are going – & it appears to be good.

Barbara comes in for tea – she's had a good week-end, but one needs 2 months not 2 days to recuperate from this sort of thing.

Wednesday 17 February

There seems to be no improvement, worth speaking about, with Beth – temp down in morning (97) but 100 at night. Doctor Moberly comes but cannot suggest much.

I spend morning at Mercury at rehearsal & the music is going quite well – what there is written of it!

Then in afternoon I go to see Michel Saint-Denys about a possible connection with his Theatre Studio up in Islington.[18] Very interesting, but I'm doubtful whether there is going to be time for me to fit it in too.

Work at odd moments at more F6 music.

Thursday 18 February

Beth 99 all day – Dr comes in evening & 'needles' her – giving her considerable pain – but still finds nothing. I expect he'll be calling in Cassidy again soon – & it would be a relief to know the cause of this extra trouble.

Work all day at F6. Don't achieve much – it is abominably difficult when one feels defeatist & fatalistic about everything – art, politics, personal matters, sex – and with this appalling ache & loneliness too.

Peter Burra comes to tea – it is nice to see him, but it gives one contact with the world outside (mostly political) with its abominable intrigues – & that isn't so pleasant, as realities seldom are.

Saturday 20 February

In morning I work at music for the Left Review – Montagu Slaters very amusing & ~~provocko~~ provoking Pageant of Empire. I finish sketching three or four little Music Hall songs. Barbara to lunch. Rehearsal at Mercury all aft – very annoying, Rupert is really beyond all endurance sometimes – his appalling vagueness, & quasi-surrealist direction – completely impractical for all his talents.

Beth seems better to-day – & Doctor more pleased.

Sunday 21 February

Doctor really pleased with Beth to-day – the lung is at long last resolving & temp. is well down & pulse too. Now for some progress.

Work at Left Theatre stuff in morning & Montagu comes to tea in aft to hear it & discuss it. Then I spend a hectic evening copying & sketching more stuff for ~~the left the~~ F.6.

Barbara is here for Tea & dinner & I have a good long blow on the Heath in the aft. with Stephen Crowdie, the first for ages.

Three weeks[19] – but thank God I've got somuch to think about!

Monday 22 February

Beth is still wonderfully better – doctor is very pleased – tho' he unfortunately shows his pleasure by interminable visits – talking 15 to the dozen – & generally wasting our & his time by somewhat bragging & self satisfied conversation – tho' ~~what~~ I suppose he has reason to congratulate himself – over Beth at anyrate – But . . . .

I spend day at Mercury – rehearsing & then come back here after tea & at 6.0 I start work on the F6 overture – to last five minutes about – I work till 2.30 & then exhausted chuck it, tho' it is nearly done.

Tuesday 23 February

Finish the overture & copy parts in morning & then at 2.0 I go off to M. Theatre for a short rehearsal. Back here for tea to which Grace Williams comes to see Beth. Then back to Theatre at 6.30 to play percussion (Vera Dart being engaged elsewhere) for dress rehearsal. Everything goes abominably – Rupert drives me crazy (I'm dog-tired after Sunday & last nights) by saying in dozens of places "We must have more music here & here & here" – regardless of the fact that it takes time to write & rehearse music.[20]

Back here by 12.30 – & find telephone messages of frantic nature ~~clamouring~~ from Left Theatre Clamouring for more music. – Oh God.

Wednesday 24 February

A very very black day. Wake with a vile head (feeling the reaction after Beth's steady recovery) to a telephone call about Left rehearsals – & one from Vera Dart with 'flu – & a letter from Malcolm Sargent saying he cannot play my Sinfonietta after all in the Cortauld-Sargent concerts (time limit – he says, but I suspect dirty work) – which is a hearty blow as it would have meant two first rate shows. Then spend morning playing for a ghastly Left Theatre rehearsal – dash (without lunch) to Mercury where I rehearse abit & learn (to my anguish) that they intend to cut the big final scene – including a lot of the best music – including the Blues[21] – my protests are unavailing. Back here to work – work – work – at scoring piddling bits of music-hall stuff for Sunday[22] – & to-bed feeling as desparate as a Communist in Germany, & as lonely – well – – as a person who has lost a beloved mother & who is going to loose a very dear sister into marriage in the near future.

Thursday 25 February

I go up to the B.B.C., after dashing to bank & other business, to discuss the music ~~with~~ for the King Arthur pageant with C. Raybould (conductor), Gilliam (producer) & Bridson (author). Decide a little. Then on to Collins Music hall for a little bit of the dress rehearsal for Left Theatre revue on Sunday – lunch with Slater afterwards. Then on to Mercury where I see Brian about odd points & have tea with Christopher Isherwood & Rupert Doone. Back to flat & then after an early dinner Aunt Effie (& Grace & Lennox B.) come with me to dress rehearsal of F.6. at Mercury. It goes better – but at the end of it (11.0) we decide that lots of things have to be rehearsed & bits of music altered & added – so rather than have to come back to-morrow the whole cast stays on & works there & then. I get back to the flat at a quarter to four – & pretty tired too.

Friday 26 February

Finish score of Left Theatre stuff in morning & take it up to copyist after lunch – I have held them up so long with this orchestral stuff, but it has been a difficult time. Rehearse a little with Toni Brosa (for a concert on 4th) at his studio in aft. Back here & change for to-nights first performance of F6. to which Peter Burra comes with me. It goes down very well, & I think is pretty sure for a long run. I feel it is a grand play – spoilt by the ommission of the end scene (but if it is transferred to the West End that may be remedied.) After the show we all have a good party at the Theatre & then feeling very cheerful we all sing (all cast & about 20 audience) my blues two or three times as well as going thro most of the music of the play! Then I play & play & play, while the whole cast dances & sings & fools, & gets generally wild. In fact have a good & merry time (& me not far from being the centre of attraction strange as it may seem!).[23]

Back, after coffee out, about 2.30

Saturday 27 February [London/Friston]
Early up in the morning & to the Bridges by 9.30 when we leave in their car for the country. Sorry at leaving Beth (who is, however, going on marvellously – having sat out of bed for an hour both yesterday & Thursday), but so glad to get away from London & that ill-fated flat. The weather is pretty bad & gets worse towards the afternoon when F.B. & I go out for a long walk along the top of the Downs & get literally soaked to the skin. However a warm bath & a good tea restores ones circulation. Anthony Collins does a good show of my Sinfonietta after dinner with his Mozart Orchestra (Regional prog.)[24] – tho the speeds were a bit odd in spots.

Sunday 28 February [Friston]
Don't get up till 12.30 – it is grand to have such a rest & as the day is a perfect hurricane don't go out until after tea when we attempt to fetch the Nurse (who looked after F.B. when in bed recently) from Eastbourne for the evening. However the car is running badly & has to be overhauled before returning her at 9.30. Sit & talk politics (mildly for me) most of the day.

It is great to have nothing to do – but it somehow makes the ache a little more obvious & hurtful, – being able to think about it more – I suppose.

Monday 1 March
Up about 10.30 & then have a long & lovely walk along Downs with F.B. before lunch. Grand Conversations – he is a fine thinker, but not so domineering as to prevent any observations from myself. I feel that he has a rather precious & escapist view of art – but that is typical of his generation – & eminently excusable. But his enthusiasm for music & his understanding of the classics is a tremendous virtue.

We go into Eastbourne after tea for a show of Hitchcock's Conrad film – Sabotage.[25] A very well-made thriller with some sophisticated humour & fine acting by Oscar Homolka & Desmond Tester (miscast as a boy of 10 or 11). But the whole thing is rather meaningless & only valuable as pure entertainment.

In the interval are some incredibly bad child discoveries on the stage – a 'boy' organist (dressed in an Eton Suit with well developed buttocks that suggested ~~well~~ advanced adolescence – spot lit in a most suggestive way!), &

singing page & crooner Usherette. – all equally talentless & devoid of any attractions.

Tuesday 2 March

Don't wake until 11.30 – practically 12 hours sleep – reaction probably after the past few weeks.

Lovely day – & in aft. I go for a long drive round Newhaven & Seaford with F.B.

Many long talks – mostly about the appalling blackness of the outlook for the world – disarmament finally burried – Fascism triumphing as the democratic & leftwing opposition breaks – & war threatened with more than usually severity in mid-Europe (Czhecho-Slovakia).

Wednesday 3 March [Friston/London]

Up early & we leave in their car at 8.0 for town – glorious morning, mild after the previous rain (how I sympathise with romantics who would compare it to the 'pathetic sweetness after a child's tears'!). Argue hotly about politics on the journey – & I fear their talent doesn't lie in that direction – still I know I am horribly intolerant in a youthful hot-headed way & I curse myself for having done or said anything hurtful to ~~the~~ people who have helped & are helping me in every way possible.

Back at the flat by 11.0 – Beth seems to be progressing well & is cheerful. Gallons of correspondance & telephone calls have accumulated. Lunch up West with Charles Brill – interview with Ralph Hawkes in aft. & back here for odd things & a little piano practice. Letters & sit with Beth after dinner. Feel desparate tonight – there are bothers about Biltmore[26] which Mr Nicholson advises us to sell at once – I can see Beth & me (especially me too) as the 'homeless orphans' very soon.

Thursday 4 March [London]

Very busy day – after much business & 'phoning here I go to rehearse with Toni Brosa at his ~~flat~~ studio all morning. Lunch with him – he's not at all well – like many people upset by this vile & perpetually wet weather. BBC. to see Gilliam in afternoon. Then at 3.30 I go to the Wine Dive in Gt. Russeill St. to try & buy some sherry, but it being a free country I have to leave empty, as I can't buy any till 5.30.[27] Tea with Montagu Slater – a meeting with Barbara Nixon on Left Theatre matters – & then back here – travelling in a tube that ~~it~~ is so vilely overcrowded so as to merit the Daily Mail adjective of 'typically Russian (or Bolshevic).[28] Christopher Alston & Peter Burra to dinner & Barbara too – & after that we all (+ Barb. & Effie) go to Golders

Green Musical Society concert at which I assist Toni – mixed programme including my Suite which goes like blazes. A nice concert – & grand fun. Coffee after with them all – except for Toni who has to leave at once for B.B.C. where he's broadcasting to Empire at 12.0.

Friday 5 March

Day starts very cheeringly by a 'phone call from Wystan now in London – back from Spain – apparently unharmed. Reason not given yet – shall know to-morrow, but any how its a grand relief. Other cheering news is gain of Labour party in L.C.C. elections – in spite of the vile propaganda in the Right wing papers (Morning Post – & Daily Mail).

I lunch with David Green – who is very decent – & emphasises the point (very truly) that now is the time for me to decide something about my sexual life. O, for a little courage. Boosey & Hawkes on business in afternoon. Back to tea. Mrs Bridge comes to see Beth & to tea in afternoon – she is the world's darling. Mrs Bramwell (also very nice) comes too. I don't go to BBC. for Frank's nice concert (L'Apprenti Sorcier – & his Jeffrey's poems)[29] – but stay here with Beth. Listen to the Busch playing – not perfectly – too Brahm[s]ian & roughly for my taste – the impeccable B^b maj (op 130) quartet.[30] It is works like this that make one decide to go on living after all.

Saturday 6 March

Rather miserable kind of day – as Beth gets better, & ~~the~~ her discomfort & my worry decrease, we both feel more & more sad. This coupled with, for me, an almost innumerable number of activities, none without anxiety, makes life fearfully difficult. I rehearse with Trevor Harvie & the BBC. singers Lovd a lass, & Lift boy in morning. Lunch with T.H., Peter Piers, & Douglas – at their flat[31] – with interesting tho' snobbish & superficial arguments. Back to Beth for tea – & then meet, Auden, Isherwood & Bill Coldstream at BBC. – we have the very competent performance of my partsongs at 7.0 – miss Johan Hock's show of the Simple Symphony on the Midland Regional as there is nowhere to listen – but eat with them at Piccadilly. They are nice people – but I am not up to their mark to-night, feeling dazed, stupid & incredibly miserable – & so leave them at 9.0 with an overwhelming inferiority-complex & longing for bed – if it wern't so single.

Sunday 7 March

However, sleep till 10.15. Sit with Beth in morning & don't go out in the blustering snow. Robert comes up from Prestatyn by 1.35 & comes here with

Barbara (train late (2.30)), before going down to Lowestoft later in the afternoon. We are very much divided on the question of selling the house – Barbara & Robert (with few prospects of using Biltmore) wish to sell at once – Beth & I (hoping to be there in April & May) wish to hold on to it until Sept. Various other pros. & cons. However as they are executors they will obviously win. They are going to see Mr Nicholson about it.

David Layton comes to tea & then we both go to see ~~part~~ rehearsal of 'Blimp's parade' section of Left Revue.[32] It goes quite well. George Hockey comes to supper – Beth & I very annoyed & sad, so we have Mrs Bramwells bottle of champagne which ocomes our emotions & we behave as badly as school-children & it does us no end of good.

Monday 8 March

I go up early to London Theatre Studio & see a Mde. Magito who runs the music there at present. They want me to write the music for their performance of a play on Judith at the end of this month – I have to decline tactfully owing to lack of time – but I suggest Henry Boys who seems grateful. Back here for lunch & in the afternoon I work on the Arthur Pageant. Meet Robert & Barbara from Lowestoft & have tea with him (only) at Euston before he goes back to Prestatyn at 6.10. They have decided to sell Biltmore at once – well, on their heads be it. The finances are pretty good – there is for us four £13,000 odd – including all the property – a colossal amount,[33] but nothing compared to the appalling gap which we are suffering from – & which seems to get larger rather than the reverse.

I don't go out to Hedli Anderson as planned in the evening as Wystan can't go (he wires from Southampton) & there is too much to do & think about here.

Tuesday 9 March

After hair cut & bank – I write a little bit of the Vln virtuoso piece I'm to do for Toni B.'s recital.[34] Then meet Grace Williams up West for Lunch – she is a grand woman. Then Poppy Vulliamy for the afternoon – she tells me her most thrilling & hair-raising experiances behind Franco's lines in Cadiz & Seville. Being a Communist (unknown to them) she was keen to find out things – but was continualy shadowed & eventually had to fly the country when desparately suspected. She is amazingly brave – & admirable, as well as being charming & grand company – While at the MM with her, I see Jack Moeran & Audry Alston (Lincoln Sutton).

Meet Henry Boys for ~~supper~~ dinner & talk over plans. Back here & talk to Beth for evening.

Wednesday 10 March

Work all morning at Revieille – when I'm not sitting & talking to Beth – a temptation when she's feeling rather blue in this long convalescence. Lunch with David Green at MM

Back here latish in the afternoon – after business at Boosey & Hawkes – Miss Wheatly is here to tea.

Miss Macdonald comes to dinner – & I go with her to see F6 after – which is going splendidly – tho' the end is definitely unsatisfactory. Rupert is there – & is a confounded nuisance with his grumbles about vague & abstract matters – like a spoilt child that feels neglected & wants to make a fuss about something.

Miss M. is a charming & intelligent person.

Thursday 11 March

Work here in morning – before going to lunch at MM with Ronald Duncan, back from India where he has had some amazingly interesting experiences – staying with ~~Gahn~~ Gandhi & Tagore. The conditions are frightful – & it is just a military camp. In fact the whole outlook now everywhere is so bad (Coronation week is zero-hour) that one feels desparate, & in this condition one doesn't want to stop at anything.

The London Theatre Studio in the aft. & Henry Boys & I see St. Denys & others about the music he's doing for them – I go in an advisory capacity. Lennox Berkeley comes to dinner – he is a dear, but I feel pretty blue & stupid.

Friday 12 March

Work on piece in morning & after tea – it goes better but not well. Lunch with Basil Wright – & pleasant talk. Back in aft to flat – & tea with Beth, who's still getting on well, tho' slowly. Then after dinner I meet Lennox & we go to the B.B.C. Contemporary concert – at which Alan Bush's 'Cello piece (very dull & terribly academical), & the New Schönberg 4^{tet} is played.[35] This is the work of a true master & some of it is marvellously ~~play~~ beautiful. The Kolisch play it with the greatest of finish & beauty of style. In between Marya Freund, a very lovely singer of great experience, sings some Poulenc – very musical & quite delightful – Szymanowskis, interesting – & Berg (early) which are great & exstatically lovely.

A large audience of intellectuals that clapped everything moderately. F.B. is there – & I have coffee after with Lennox at MM

Saturday 13 March [London/Bucklebury Common]

I catch 10.45 to Reading where Peter Burra meets me – he takes me to his lovely little cottage in Bucklebury Common. It is a heavnly day & it is grand to be in the country after all this time in London. We go & look at a charming little cottage nearby – which I'm thinking of taking as it is a such a heavnly part of the country. After lunch we go into Thatchington [Thatcham] & Peter initiates me into the wonders of Squash which I find completely captivating & I curse myself for not having played it before. Back here for bath & tea & a long lovely walk over the common after.

After dinner play piano duets & talk till a late hour – I have a kindred spirit in thousands of ways (one way in particalar) here.[36]

Sunday 14 March [Bucklebury Common]
The glorious weather stops & the awful weather resumes its reign – we have blizzards & then slush. So instead of walking Peter & I go into Newbury & play squash again – this time I progress (I actually beat him about 6–3!) & really enjoy myself alot – so much so that in my over eagerness I sprain my ankle pretty severly & hobble about the rest of the day with a stick – very pathetic, but secretly (I'm ashamed to say) pleased as it draws attention to my prowess at Squash, which Peter is proud of – & which I feel adds to my glamour!!

We have lunch with rich friends of Peters, the Behrends nearby – charming & cultured people who have done a tremendous amount to help artists (besides Peter – Lytton Strachey, & Stanley Spencer among others) in general. We spend afternoon too there – & see Spencers impressive little chapel they erected for him after the war. Back at 'Foxhold' – we play piano & violin (Schumann, Mozart, Franck – swapping parts & making the most extraordinary noise) & then talk till mid-night – Peter is one of the world's dears.

Monday 15 March [Bucklebury Common/London]
Can't move much to-day – so I finish my Reveille for Toni in morning while Peter plays with his new toy, the motor Bike which symbolises his craving for the normal or 'Tough' at the moment.[37] Then early lunch – Julie Behrend calls for us both at 12.15 – lunch & then set off for London. Arrive here in time to hear the Scottish Orch. under Guy Warrack do my Rossini Suite[38] – not too well – speeds wrong. They both stay to tea, to which Poppy Vulliamy (a marvellous person, one of the most admirable I know) & Ronald Duncan come. Talk fifteen to the dozen.

Christopher Isherwood comes to dinner – a grand person; unaffected, extremely amusing & devastatingly intelligent. He stays nice & late.

Beth is going on well – but gets very tired.

Tuesday 16 March [London]

I don't go out as the ankle must needs be rested. So in morning I do business & help to entertain the Nicholsons for Beth (Elizabeth N. is having her wedding trousseau made here & B. has to see to it alittle). Also rewrite & copy the violin part of Reveille. – this in aft. too. Tony & Peggy Brosa both come to tea (Molly Fermer – & friend of Beth's too).

And after tea he & I work at the Reveille which needs only slight adjustment (bowing & fingering) in one or two places – which is pleasing considering it is such a 'specialist' virtuoso piece – but anyhow I adore inventing tricks for instruments. It sounds very lovely, I think, & shows him off to perfection. They stay till 8.0.

After that dinner – & letters.

Beth is too tired to-night – the business this morning was too much for her – but if she hadn't officiated at all, she would have worried & fretted up here.

I still just cannot realise Jan. 31st – & that there isn't that glorious, warm, mature & adorable person down at Frinton, there for us when ~~for~~ we go & always at our call.

Wednesday 17 March

Aunt Flo comes to see Beth. I do lots of business & also some work on King Arthur. Then after a very pleasant lunch at MM with Ronald Duncan & Peter Burra I spend afternoon with Val Gielgud & D.G. Bridson working at King Arthur from 2.30–5.30 – discussing all sounds. Back then to flat where Elaine (cousin) is seeing Beth. Barbara in to dinner on this last night of nurse Cullinan. It is sad to say good-bye to her because she has been a grand woman, – excellent in duty & company. We couldn't have had a better nurse – & I hope we shan't lose touch with her.

I listen to Part 2 of Busoni's Dr Faustus (concert Version from BBC. concert)[39] – as it is all I can manage to hear. But I am enormously impressed by it – the marvellous invention & really dramatic feeling. I feel it is so intensely musical – much more so than would be expected from so high an intellect.

Thursday 18 March [London/Friston]

A most hectic morning – go thro' all my correspondance (long overdue) – go to bank & to garage, to arrange about disposal of the Lagonda (to a dump heap – we shan't keep it on as it needs too much doing to it to keep it possible to use), then up West to Boosey & Hawkes & on to lunch at Café Royal with Dorothy Wadham & Lennox Berkeley – very entertaining & interesting consequently. Then after a bit of shopping at Austin Reeds I scuttle back to Hampstead to find the Bridges already packing Beth into their car previously to bringing us both down to Friston. Aunt has packed for me over lunch-time – an efficient person!

Beth stands the journey down remarkably well, tho' is very tired on arrival & goes straight to bed. It is good to be away from London & that fated flat – & the B's are paragons of virtue & affection.

Sunday 21 March

The B's come back from town in the morning. Write more Arthur stuff during the day – very boring, but I suppose it's got to be gone through with – & it's not going too badly.

Their Nurse (who looked after F.B when so ill) comes over to tea; she is a dear but her rather obvious form of humour wears rather badly. We all take her in to Eastbourne ~~in the~~ after tea & drive along to Beachy Head which is grand in the light of the setting sun.

After dinner, Beth is phoned by Kit back from India – & there are consequent rumpus'es as she tells him he can't come down tomorrow to see her. I like the way he stays away for a month on holiday (while she is so bad & needing him) & then expects everyone to put themselves out for him on his return! He is a very nice person, but very thoughtless – the result of having had everything he wants all his life – product of the Capitalist System![40]

Tuesday 23 March

A grand day – but fearfully cold wind. Beth goes out with me but it is too cold for her. Work abit on Arthur sketch a Psalm & Galahad music[41] (can't do much with <u>that</u>, tho', – subject doesn't interest me!) Kit arrives in evening & we pass a pleasant evening with light prattle.

Thursday 25 March [London/Frinton]

Up not to early & 'phone people – then up to Hampstead to see that things are OK at the flat – see Lilian & do lots of other things. Then back to Bloomsby for lunch with Lennox & John Greenich (whom he lives with). Then we both go to BBC for a long talk over things with Trevor Harvey & Robin Whitworth to talk over music for shows in general & about Whitsun[42] in particular – for the not immeadiate future. Then we go to Trevors flat & here recorded examples of past efforts – not edifying but interesting in what not to do. Then back to Lennox' Flat – collect luggage & to Liverpool St. to catch 6.39 to Frinton. Lousy journey, crowded, ¾ hr late, no restaurant car as advertised only a crowded (to a stifling state) Buffet car – & then the dreadful arrival to ~~Frinton~~ Biltmore with it's heartrending gap. It seems worse than ever to-night – Barbara, Beth, Effie & Kit are all here – but it dosn't eleviate much of the agony.

Monday 29 March [Frinton]
I do alot more music for Arthur & also copy out most of the Reveille for Toni Brosa. Barbara & Robert get down to the sorting of furniture & inventories etc.

Relations are still fine – in fact riotously so – but this is rather because we are all so keen to keep the peace at any price (especially with tomorrow looming ahead) that we go to the other extreme perhaps.

Tuesday 30 March
We settle down in morning – the four of us – & in afternoon too, to dividing all the furniture & things in the house.

Picking one thing in turn starting from Barbara. It all goes very amicably, & there is no disturbance or even discussion – people being extremely unselfish – which is a blessing. We all get good things – me of course with an eye to the future – cottage & flat of course – Beth to marriage & Robert for school – Barbara sticks principally to smaller things. It is a relief to get it done; – but oh what an accursed thing to have to break up this charming little home after only a year. And Mum had got it going so well & was so ~~lovely~~ loving it. It is damnable.

Wednesday 31 March
We spend the morning doing the Books – dividing them between us four; ~~I think~~ this arouses some bitterness, for I think ~~do~~ none of us can bear to be parted from any of the books that have surrounded us all our lives. I get some of my special wants tho'.

Barbara goes in the afternoon – Robert, Beth & I take her in his car to Colchester.

Do a little more Arthur stuff – nearly finished the sketches – but I'm hopelessly behind with any other business.

Another month gone after that fatal Sunday[43] – & the unpleasant thing is that the ache, the literally physical pain doesn't seem any the less.

Thursday 1 April
After abit of work we all, except Beth who spends the day here with Kit, go out with Robert in the car – first to Ipswich where we see Hockeys (Mum's brother's wife & daughter) – Elsie & dear old Janie, for lunch & in the afternoon we go onto Farnham (nr Saxmundham) via Capel – where we spend so many deliriously happy Summers when we were very, very young. Robert & I

are completely bowled over by the country, & by sentimental memories – in fact my choice of a cottage is becoming damnably complex. At Farnham we have tea with Nanny [Scarce] & Alice [Pratt] (very late of 21 K.C. Rd) & they are both absolutely the same – very real bits of our youth – and, o, how valuable at this moment. Call in at Cauldwell Hall, Ipswich, on the way back & see Poppy Vulliamy.

Friday 2 April
I am now getting down to the scoring of King Arthur stuff – having finished the sketches – it is frightfully hard work – tho' Robert is helping me alot with the ruling of lines – I do need my apprentice so terribly. Poppy comes over to tea in the afternoon – she is a splendid person & it is grand to have such a brain as hers backing one in arguments (political) which we have so fircly. Work after dinner till 1.45 – feeling like hell as it takes so long to do.

Sunday 4 April
Work alot in morning & do endless business matters for the rest of the day.

After dinner Robert & I go thro' my records of My 'Boy' – & he is marvellously appreciative. In fact this time I have felt much more warmth towards him, in spite of his obstinate conservatism in so many ways. Actually on our evening walks we have had very intimate discussions & he hasn't been shocked by, but even helped with sympathy & advice, my 'queerness'.

Monday 5 April [Frinton/London/Painswick]
John wakes me (he's sleeping in the adjacent room) pretty early with his vigourous chanting & singing & so I get up betimes. Robert takes me to the station & I catch 10 to 10 to London. Straight to flat where I see to things & 'phone innumerable people. Then in aft. I go via Paddington to drop luggage to see Ralph Hawkes about things in general & the BBC job in particular. And then catch the lovly express train at 5.0 to Stroud arr. 6.40 – wonderful train – Lennox Berkely meets me & we drive together to Painswick where his friend Miss Bryans is putting me up with him. Spend a pleasant evening playing violin (!) & piano.

Tuesday 6 April [Painswick]
Lennox & I get down to work on the Spanish Suite[44] in the morning. He has sketched two movements which we discuss fully & alter accordingly, & then while I sketch a third (having settled form etc) he makes out a rough score of the first. Everything goes very amicably & tho' of course we don't agree on everything at once I feel the final arrangements are satisfactory. Certainly the music seems nice.

In the afternoon we go for a long drive with Miss Bryans thro' Gloucester – & tea in Gloucester coming back. The country here is grand – tho' it is misty & we can't see far. See the really lovely cathedral.

Walk with Lennox across hills after – & arrange many things. After dinner (they, having borrowed a viola for me) we play trios & such-like – a noise but inestimable fun.

Thursday 8 April

I get on with the Arthur music in morning – there is still lots to be done, but Lennox is being sweet & helpling me copy etc.

In the afternoon we go for tennis to Mitchelhampton to the Paynes – nieces etc. of Miss Bryans. But it is too windy to be possible tennis & I still don't know whether my 'rabbits' ' disease is chronic or not.

Pamela Payne comes back with us to a dinner party which Miss Bryans gives for us & Mr & Mrs Ore – local people & he a musician of some slight note (composer & musicologist) & she's a charming person – an amateuer actress. We have a very nice evening – P.P. sings some Fauré quite charmingly – & I scribble down a little round for us all to play – Miss B (Vln) Mr. Ore (Voice), P.P. (Soprano), Lennox (Pft) & me (Viola).

Sunday 11 April

It is a curse having to go on & on with this awful bore of Uncle Arthur – especialy when we are here especially to work together on the Spanish Suite. However one must live – but we get alot of the Spanish Question settled before lunch.

As it is a heavenly day – first real perfect one so far here – we all go over to Mitchehampton to some cousins of Miss Bryans to tennis. For a wonder I play quite well & we have a very pleasant four – then the drive home is perfect across the hills. Certainly there isn't much to touch the luxury of this scenary. Then the Hills (Mr & Mrs) come over for the evening, which is a pure Mozart one – as I play gallons of Figaro & we play the Vla trio (E^b)[45] & generally rave about him – Mr. H. is an enormous enthusiast.

Then before bed – long & deep conversation with Lennox – he is a dear & I am very, very fond of him; nevertheless, it is a comfort that we can arrange sexual matters to at least my satisfaction.[46]

Monday 12 April [Painswick/London/Frinton]

Spend morning sorting music, returning the borrowed viola (to Miss Clissold along the road) & packing. Then Lennox & I catch 12.20 to London from Stroud. Lunch on train. Straight to BBC. for a meeting & partial play thro' of Arthur music with Val Gielgud – producer, & Clarence Raybould, conductor. This lasts till 4.45 when I catch 5.30 from Liverpool Street down to Frinton, where the actual move of furniture is to take place. Beth has gone to Peasenhall to spend a long week-end with her future parents-in-law & Barbara has come here to prepare for the move. Robert etc are still here; & Effie too, of course.

Things are well in hand it seems; & going smoothly. Long walk with Robert in the evening – he is a very difficult person, with an entirely dupal nature. Marjory is having a very difficult time with him.[47]

The Toscanini concerts with the BBC orchestra are announced this morning – & by this evening it is rumoured that all seats for the six are sold! It gives one hope that a man of such stolid worth is appreciated in this days of fashion.

Tuesday 13 April [Frinton]

The railway men come to fetch the Prestatyn furniture in the morning & get everything done very quickly & efficiently. The family depart in the afternoon – by car & ~~talking~~ taking Caesar with them; we couldn't really have him in London, it isn't fair on a dog.

For the rest of the day we pack, & I do a certain amount of work at Arthur. We feel very depressed as this is the last day of Biltmore; but Barbara buys some wine which bucks us up abit.

Wednesday 14 April [Frinton/London]

Complete chaos – we are ready for the removers at 9.0 – they don't arrive till nearly 11.0 which makes them correspondingly late the other-end. They are hopelessly under-staffed – only 3 men & one small van for all this stuff; consequently they muddle all our methodical labelling & grouping. If it weren't for the Alexanders who let us use their house as a refuge at all hours & the Forsters who give us lunch I think we would have collapsed. We leave by the latest possible train – 5.49 – leaving them to finish under the superintendency of the very efficient gardener – Warren

Travel more dead than alive to town – eating when we get here – Effie & I; Barbara goes to Chelsea.

Listen by accident just before bed to the Tannhaüser overture which gives me an enormous kick – haven't heard it for ages & hadn't dreamed that it was so good. Beth is back here from Peasenhall where she got on well with her future in-laws.

Thursday 15 April [London]
Another chaotic day. ~~Firstly~~ I have to work at all possible hours & to a very late hour to finish King Arthur for the BBC; & I have to do this in the middle of the landing of all our sections (Beth's & mine) of the Frinton furniture – into this already completely furnished flat! We are sending a certain amount into store ready for the cottage, but all the china & pictures & all the stuff that nobody could decide about is dumped here.

Effie is an absolute brick & works with Mrs Nunn like a trojan. Eventually a little order is established – but as I write (in bed) the room is strewn with boxes, carpets, tables, books, music & all kinds of junk – & the other rooms are worse too.

Saturday 17 April [Lowestoft/London]
In morning Mrs Mead & Kathleen take us about in their car – see the Nicholsons & the Sewells & then in pouring rain & vile wind Beth & I visit our two beloveds' grave at Kirkley – but the blustering weather dosn't allow us to do much or stay long (perhaps luckily) – but it is looking neat & suitable to their dearest of all memories. Lunch at the Woodgers – & the wedding of Elizabeth Nicholson to George Barradel-Smith at St. Margerats afterwards. Very dull – really – music slow & ~~extremely~~ mediocre tho' the dresses were good if not superlative. We don't go to the reception after – on the plea of Beth's illness & strain. So I meet John Pounder for a long walk & much 'queer' talk – he's a sympathetic dear – & then Beth & I tea at the Sewells. Laurence & Fernande come to the station with us – & we catch 6.44 back to town again – there being no Restaurant car (o, this civilised L.N.E.R.!) – Fernande gives us some sandwiches. Extravagently but justifiably take a taxi back here – to the chaos which Effie has been working hard to alleviate.

Monday 19 April
My business matters are hopelessly behind hand – ~~in fact~~ I've done very little since the middle of Jan – so much so that a tradesman calls for his money in the middle of the morning. This gives me incentive to start clearing everything up – so I spend morning & some of the afternoon in writing letters & cheques & sorting papers. Also do a final bit of King Arthur music after tea. Lennox Berkeley comes to dinner & after we listen to Otello from Covent Garden (on the new wireless – on 'appro'. – the other one in the old Radio Gram. is D.C. instead of AC.

This performance – mediocre as it is (except for Otello – Martinelli – & Iago & one or two others – Beecham being the real culprit) – goes to justify any claims that one hears made for the work – in that it shows Verdi's great art – at its most warm & fluent, besides being the apotheosis so far of all that is glorious in the Italian – & vocal in general – tradition.

Wednesday 21 April
Odd things in morning before lunch with Lennox in Soho, & then he comes with me for first orchestral & choral rehearsal of the King Arthur music. It all comes off like hell, so there's nothing to worry about – likewise nothing to be jubilant about. However people are very nice, & tho' one doesn't like to admit it, that is a very pleasing thing. Very tired in evening – so listen with Beth & Effie to wireless (including a fascinating Act (2) from Donizetti's Don Pasquale). & early to bed – & to Firbank's 'Flower beneath the Foot'.[48]

Friday 23 April
Early to the BBC. at 10.15 for full rehearsal – it goes quite well, apart from a few misunderstandings – tho' the actual play irritates me more than I can say – its stilted dialogue, a pale pastiche of Malory – its dull Tennysonian poetry, & not nearly as good as that either – & its complete divorce from realities or humanties. In the afternoon a further consultation with Raybould (who conducts really very well) & then I go to see Christopher Isherwood who has been in bed for a time, & then a rushed visit to Piers, who is now out of hospital [after a knee operation] & looking very fit. But he has become suddenly extremely mature – having turned 16 – & more adult than adults themselves! Then back to BBC for the King Arthur show – at 7.30. It goes very well – but I still feel the same about it. The music certainly comes off like 'hell' & the orchestra & Lennox Berkeley (who comes with me, & with whom I eat at Café Royal after) are enthusiastic about it.

Sunday 25 April [Surbiton/London]
It is a heavenly spring-like day, & Beth & I go off to Surbiton to the Gydes in the morning – for lunch, tea & dinner. Sit in the garden for most of the time (tea, there too) & before dinner we go to Hampton Court which is just heavenly inthe dimming light. To lunch there is Geoffrey Dennis, who with Heinemann's (who publish his book Coronation Commentary)[49] is being sued by the Duke of Windsor. He has quoted libelous opinions itseems, tho' hasn't expressed any definite subjective opinions. But the law of libel is a scandal. The book itseems is a brilliant piece of topical journalism.

I rehearse Hunting Fathers with Sophie – & it goes well. Altogether a first rate day – we are both ~~fon~~ exceptionally fond of Mr & Mrs – Arnold junior is of course a special pet of mine – & Humphrey, my god-child, tho' not really at an interesting age – is growing fast.

Beth & I come back by 8.30 & we go to the Left Revue – to which I did the music of Montagu Slater's little Pageant of Empire. I feel that this is the best form of propaganda – guying the other side – especially when as most of tonight it is hilariously funny. A little descrition might be added here & there (such as regards length & overstatement), but the talent was very obvious throughout.

Tuesday 27 April

Go to bed feeling desparate as I've just heard that dear old Peter Burra has been killed in an Air smash near Reading – flying with one of his 'tough' freinds. He was a darling of the 1st rank, & in this the short year & a bit that I've known, him he has been very close & dear to me. A first rate brain, that was at the moment in great difficulties – tho' this is far too terrible a solution for them. Nothing has leaked out yet how it happened. This is a bloody world, & nothing one can do can stop this fatal rot. Here is Franco in Spain blowing thousands of innocent Basque & Castilliains to bits. I'm glad that Peter is out of all that – he felt it so terribly.

For the rest of the day – business, with Hawkes & Brian Easedale up West in morning – lunch afternoon & evening with Piers – see a rotten, provocking film Elephant Boy[50] in aft. (lovely photographs coupled to a beastly story, with lousy music & worse sentiment) – Sherry party at Dr Moberly's – John Alston in after dinner, & Barbara to the party & dinner.

Wednesday 28 April

Tho' feeling desparate I hurridly finish off the last Spanish tune before going to Lennox Berkeley to work at them all. This we do fairly satisfactorily. Lunch with him. To the BBC. in aft with Sophie Wyss for a run thro' with piano, for Adrian Boult's benefit. See Ralph Hawkes about the Spanish tunes after & he is very pleased indeed.

Dinner with Barbara & Helen Hurst They do me excellently & we have an interesting time, but interruppted many times by 'phone calls for me dealing with Peter's death, which casts a complete shadow over the day's doings.

Thursday 29 April [Bucklebury/London]

Lennox & I go off to Bucklebury, by train from Paddington, bus from Reading & private car from Wolhampton. Arrive for Peter's funeral which is at 12.0. Quite alot of people there – I have never known anyone who had somany friends as he had. Apart from his great talent for writing, his genius lay in making first rate friends – to which he was Father Confessor, of course, being so sweet & sympathetic.

The Behrends – his great friends – bring Lennox & me back to London, giving us a sandwich lunch on the way. They are charming & first-rate people. To cheer ourselves up we go to a new & exhilarating Picasso exhibition (1930–34) – & an adorable little Constable one, that makes me long more than ever for Suffolk. Tea with L. & Vere Pilkington & back here for dinner to which Brian & Freda Easedale come. Then with them to the Little Theatre for a dress rehearsal of F.6. which is opening there to-morrow. I leave at 12.0 – exhausted, but the play was only ½ finished. But it was going quite well.

Friday 30 April [London]

I have a rehearsal with Boult of H.F at BBC at 11.30 – it goes quite well, tho' he doesn't really grasp the work – tho' he is marvellously painstaking. Sophie of course sings well. Lunch after with her & Arnold jun., & John & Millicent Francis. Then I meet Poppy Vulliamy & have long talks with her. She goes off to Spain very soon to look after the evacuated children from Madrid & Malaga. I have agreed to adopt one & pay for him for a year. Back here in aft. & then out to dinner with Peter Piers[51] & Basil Douglas – very nice, but sad as we have to discuss what is best about Peter Burra's things. BBC. Contempory concert after cond. by Boult – BBC orch They do my Hunting Fathers very creditably – I am awfully pleased with it too, I'm afraid. Some things don't satisfy me at the moment – but it's my op. 1 alright – The Leighton Lucas work I miss – but I hear Rubbra's Symphony 1[52] I don't like this kind of music – infact I disapprove of it – but it is very well done of it's sort – & much more admirable than Walton or Williams. A huge audience – I meet Toni & Peggy & eat afterwards with them at Café Royal.

Saturday 1 May

General bus strike starts – reasons, general conditions, & demands 7½ hour day, & alterations of the admittedly cruel schedules. Public opinion seems 50% with them, & 50% annoyed at the excessive inconvenience – especially before the Coronation! Incidently an excellent time to strike I feel. Anyhow it is good for one to walk – as I have to to the bank in morning & with Lennox & Aunt in the aft. to tennis. Stay there a very long time & have some quite good games. Beth goes with Kit to Mersea (where Yacht [*Curlew*] is) for week-end.

Sunday 2 May

Not up too early as may be imagined & spend morning (what there is of it left!) & aft. in sorting things & old letters to be answered. Grace Williams comes to tea & we have a long walk on the heath in the lovely sun. I go to an evening meal with Howard Ferguson – whom I haven't seen for ages. He is very nice but I don't think that any two people have ever disagreed on quite so many subjects! Have to walk there & back (other side of Hampstead).

Tuesday 4 **May**

More letters in morning – a vain effort to catch up all the lost time. Lunch with Charles Brill up west & then spend very interesting afternoon with Henry Boys – talk & talk – he seems in a strange position at the moment – his philosophy seems to have divorced him utterly from realities & he is completely occupied with meanings & 'consciousness' – We go together to a very large & comprehensive Artists' Congress exhibition for Peace & Democracy in Grosvenor Square. Some very interesting Surrealist pictures there too.

Then walk the whole way back – & a darned long way it is too!

Letters in evening.

Wednesday 5 **May**

A successful day with the 'muse'. In the morning I set a serious poem of Wystan's (from Dog – Skin) – Nocturne, & inthe afternoon a light one for Hedli Anderson – Johnny.[53] After this mental effort I go for an hour's knock-up at the club with Molly Fenner. Stephen Crowdie with Beth fetches me in his car (relief from this endless walking) & eats here. After dinner letters & proofs (duet – Ballads).[54]

Thursday 6 May [London/Bucklebury]

Sketch another song for Hedli in the morning. Lunch & excessive political arguments with Peter Floud at Baker Street – I am in a damned muddle trying to compromise between Pacifism & Communism. Back here in aft. & then meet & walk with Harry Morris – a charming kid – protegé of Barbara's who is very keen on music & very good draughtsboy.

Then after tea Kit takes us round looking for car's – find a possible Lee Francis[55] in Highgate. Kit stays to dinner – having delivered the child to his home in Hampstead. After dinner general slack & then Kit drops me at Paddington at 10.45 & I meet Peter Pears & travel with him in a packed dirty train to Reading where we arrive about mid-night – & set out for the Behrend's house (Burclere) on his motor-bike, in the pouring, pouring rain. After wandering helplessly in the maze of roads over the common – very cold & damp, to our skins – & me pretty sore behind, being unused to pillion riding – we knock up people in the only house with a light in we meet at all, & get some rather vague instructions from them. Wander further & quite by accident alight on the house – at about 1.45 or 50. Have hot baths & straight to bed. The Behrends themselves are in town.

Friday 7 May [Bucklebury/London]
After a 9 o'clock breakfast Peter & I go over to Peter Burra's house (Foxhold) to spend day sorting out letters, photos & other personalities preparatory to the big clean up to take place soon. Peter Pears is a dear & a very sympathetic person. – tho' I'll admit I am not too keen on travelling on his motor bike! Catch 5.35 up to town, & I have to walk from Kilburn Park Station – but it's all for the good of the cause & so far there's no likelihood of an immediate settlement. Spend evening writing letters & sketch another song for Hedli

Saturday 8 May [London]
A sad & also considerably inconvenient bit of newsis that our Mrs Nunn is seriously ill – small Geofrey N. comes to tell us about 10.0. Hedli Anderson comes to see the new songs I've sketched for her (do another before she comes) & seems very pleased. And the two Bridges come & fetch me for lunch & deliver me back in the afternoon – it is good to see them again as they are such 1st-rate people. A little cold & very bad (consequently) depressing tennis in the afternoon. Then at 7.30 Beth & I go to BBC. (Maida Vale) studios for a light concert conducted by FB. – a lovely one including Tschaikovsky's deliriously good Caprirccio Italien – magnificently played too. Then Beth & I go on to Toni Brosa & Peggy for dinner & have a good time indeed – playing darts too.

Sunday 9 May
Barbara is staying with us for the weekend because of the strike which will persist – inspite of the half-hearted efforts of the Government to reach a compromise.

Wet & filthy day. In aft. I go with Peter Pears to the Left Book [Club] meeting – Musicians circle i.e. Some very good & some equally boring speeches. The secret is, I suppose, that while the issue is most terribly serious & urgent, the means are most terribly dull & unsympathetic. Anyway it makes us as depressed as purgatory & it takes all the wonders of Lyons' cream 'Gateaux' to cheer us up! Kit is here to a meal.

Feel terribly lonely for Mum to-night – it is so hard to realise that this all has happened. I have some gramophone records on – but can't bare many, because it is through music that our contact was perhaps greatest.

Monday 10 May

Barbara stays the night & returns to work this morning. Hedli comes with her accompanist in the morning & we go thro' the songs – now completed by me – they are going to be hits I feel! Walk to Bank after lunch – this exercise is fine for one's figures. Then the man (agent) comes to see us about the Lea Francis & we take the plunge – probably mad.

Then in evening I walk over to the Coldstreams for a meal. They (Nancy & Bill) start the evening by quarrelling like hell – it's not only slightly uncomfortable but not very exhilarating company for me. However towards the end things brigthten, & I end by enjoying them alot. Bill – a grand man – walks all the way back with me.

Wednesday 12 May

Coronation day – & by jove don't they let us know it! Continuous broadcast of the ceremony from 1.0–5, & everything one sees & hears is but a repetition of the same bla, bla, bla – of empire, loyaltes one big family (that is 'fine feeling' if expressed by the upper classes – 'damned cheek' if by the lower!). We, with Kit who stays here the night, escape into the country for a picnic lunch; but oddly enough (& valuably too) the weather is rotton, & it rains solidly from the afternoon onwards, after having been depressingly dull all the morning. Listen to a coronation revue in the evening, after the coronation address by the King (the poor man masters his stutter well), & coronation news – In fact spend a coronation evening, writting coronation letters & retiring to a coronation if lonely bed.[56]

Thursday 13 May

Not up early. Kit goes off in morning – actually without saying 'good-bye' to either Effie or myself (actually the providers of his entertainment) – he is admittedly a very nice person, but he is very much lacking in ~~a tremendous amount of~~ polish, & manners which make life so much easier, I feel.

Business practically all day – trying to square accounts & bring them up to date. Mrs Hibberd, with whom I stayed so much during the crisis, comes to tea. Listen at 6.0 to a very finished performance of my Rossini Suite by B.B.C. orch under Joseph Lewis. Laulie, Miss Austen, my godmother – comes to dinner – up from Liverpool. She is a dear, & does a tremendous amount of really good & interesting social work up there, nevertheless it is difficult to make much contact with old family friends.

The Lee Francis comes in the evening, & Beth & I drive it about a good deal (mostly she) – it is difficult to manage, but will be satisfactory we hope.

Saturday 15 May [Whitehill/Cotswolds/Bath]
O – the bliss of doing nothing.

Walk abit in morning. In aft. we all three go over in the Lee Francis to see Aunt Julianne staying in a hotel in Bath. It is good to see her, but she is a terrible cripple, & had a beastly accident with scalding tea (when alone & unable to get up) the other day.

Also walk round Bath which is a wonderful place – the glorious crescents & squares. Back under the hour.

Look at photos alot after supper – heart rending one's of Mum & Pop included, – Mum being shown as an absolute beauty, such a girl as even I could lose my heart too.

Sunday 16 May
A beautifully fine sunny day – first for ages; we sit out in the garden all aft. & have tea – very pleasant. I adore the sun to do nothing in.

Walk with Beth over glorious hills in morning, & with Aunt [Flo] as well after tea. I love this country – but actually not with the same affection as Suffolk. I always feel that Suffolk is the genuine article, while this is aspiring to something that is outside its compass.

Tremendous discussions – Aunt is very provocative & I am intolerant so we go at it on all subjects (art-religion-politics). But she is a dear & so like Pop to command everlasting respect.

Friday 21 May [London]
Still feeling very rocky. Don't go out in morning – finishing up accounts.

But in afternoon Lilian Wolff takes me up to the West End in her car – with Beth to see Ralph Hawkes who is as nice & helpful as ever. This, in afternoon. Listen to Act II of Götterdämmerung after dinner (to which Lucy Crowdie comes). It is grand music this. Perhaps the best of the Ring. Letters. after.

Saturday 22 May
The day is completely blighted by the Police notification that they are going to prosecute me for Dangerous driving – blast their eyes.[57] It's infuriating, because I know I was in the right. However with solicitors I may get off – but there is the infernal bother & worry of it all to be faced.

I spend morning in – & then before lunch Hedli Anderson & Henry Boys (who is going to play for her) come – lunch & then we run thro' the songs.[58] Walk in afternoon with Henry (Hedli goes to the theatre) & tea in Golders Hill Park. Beth & Aunt Effie go to F6.

Record after record after dinner – trying in vain to dispel~~l~~ depression.

Monday 24 May

Barbara goes off to work pretty early & I walk with her to S. Kensington station. Then later I walk all the way to Oxford Circus – a very hot & summery day – where Henry Boys & Hedli Anderson rehearse the caberet songs – & Ruth Taylor comes along to ~~coach~~ give Hedli some advice on mime etc.

Lunch after with Henry – & a film (Ammer Konig – a charming, naive little Austrian film, beautifully done, & with a childlike innocence – this is the film which the Censor won't give a certificate to – & yet Loyalties[59] (the supporting film) is allowed to go on its degrading, disgusting, & depraved way unmolested). I play for an audition (Paramount) for Hedli & then back here for dinner. Poor old Aunt Queenie is here – she is a pathetic case – now in a most depressing home & miserable – yet with plenty of alternatives & no strength of mind to go to them.

Wednesday 26 May

Work at a new song[60] in the morning & alittle in the afternoon – by W.H.A. – middle is bad tho' beginning & end good. Ronald Duncan & I have lunch at Dutch Oven – it is good to see him; & we exchange miseries, & revel in Schadenfreude.

After dinner Peter Pears gives me a ticket for & I go with him to the first of the London Musical Festival BBC. orch. concerts with Toscanini. He certainly is a first-rate man – not always perhaps absolutely as one feels the works – but so marvellously efficient & sensitive with the orchestra – like no one else. The Busoni Rondo Arlechinesco was electrifying (a grand work – perhaps Busoni's musical invention didn't always ~~his~~ equal his ideas) – the Daphnis & Chloe was a revelation; it can never have sounded like that before – all the colours melted into each other, & never was the colour all important. Coriolan – great – & Brahm's 1st was as good as it could be – but it is a very bad work – desparately ugly & pretentious & not redeemed by its several good patches. But the Beethoven stood out from all by its colossal welding inspiration, technique, & philosophy.[61] One of the number one works of the world.

Peter is a dear

Thursday 27 May

I work on the Auden song in morning – but it doen't go write. Disturbed ½ way by piano tuner – so I talk (½ hr as usual) to F.B. on 'phone. In the afternoon I set another Auden song – complete this time & more satisfactory (Now the leaves are falling fast). Tennis in the evening with Mr Archdale – but play like a pig – too much to think about these days – curse it.

Weather still hot – but not the tropical stuffiness of Sun-Wed.

Letters – wireless (Eugène O'Neill – Emperor Jones[62] – v. moving) – etc. in evening.

Friday 28 May

Lunch with Juley Behrend who has written me appealing & sentimental letters about setting a charming little poem of Peter Burra's. She lets me pay for an expensive lunch at S.F. tho'. Rehearsal & tea with Hedli & Henry after – My songs go splendidly. Engagement no. 3. is a 2nd tea with Lennox over from Paris for a few days – he seems as pleased to see me as I do to see him – quite considerably that is. Then a ~~wast~~ cocktail party at Anne Woods – a friend of Peter Pears with whom I also go after to the BBC. Orch. concert cond. again by Toscanini. Not such a good programme – & tho' T. himself is 100% the orch. isn't really up to scratch for all he wants. Elgar, Intro. & Allegro – not for me. Cherubini D maj. Symph. – nice but spotty. A trivial but amusing set of variations on Carnival of Venice by Tommasini. ~~Highl~~ The High Lights of concert are a fantastic show of Berlioz Queen Mab & the Meistersinger overture.[63]

Eat with Peter after at Café Royal.

Tuesday 1 June [Friston/London]

They [Frank and Ethel Bridge] take me to Eastbourne to catch 8.36 to town. When in town I go straight to see Mr. Tunncliffe[64] about complications about the smash. No summons actually as yet, but fears. Back here for lunch, with Barbara too. Then a little work in aft. & then tennis at 4.0 at intervals until dark. Beth, Kit & Effie come up with food & we play some pleasant games.

Back here & listen, enraptured I admit, to Act III of Götterdämmerung – with Flagstad & Melchior & Furtwängler – really superb singing & conducting. There is really something super human about this music. Tho' not with the serenity of Mozart, Beethoven or Mahler, it is on ~~another~~ different plane from life.

Wednesday 2 June [London]

I spend all day with the investigator (a Mr Don) from the firm of solicitors who are dealing with the case for me & for the insurance. He comes here at 11.0 & we talk of it for ages; & then he drives me down ~~for~~ to the scene of the crime & we re-enact the whole thing & see the poor wrecked car. Then back here where he takes long statements from me & Beth – departing at 5.30. He seems pretty sure of us getting off alright.

Then in evening – Beth goes to Ballet – listen to a Toscanini concert – Rossini – Italian in Algiri (orch. only moderate, as it was during the whole evening – but T. is gloriously rhythmn) & a really good show of the Pastoral Symphony. What a heavenly work this is. No. 1 of the Symphonys for me at the moment. After the interval the music wasn't worth the antispretation – Brahms-Haydn, & Tod & Verklärung.[65]

I finish a song before a late bed.

Thursday 3 June

I copy some of the Auden songs for Sophie Wyss[66] & then see Ralph Hawkes about matters before lunching with John Cheatle at 1.0. in various pubs. Spend afternoon alternativly listening to his pornographic history & doing pleasing research for the B^{c} programme – ~~Down~~ Up the Garden Path.[67] Tea with Sophie & then meet Arnold Gyde & we then eat at Paganis. They are 1st rate dears.

Back here to telephone, bit of Act III Figaro, letters & bed.

Friday 4 June

Letters & business in morning – & also look up things for Cheatle's programme. After lunch I start rewriting no. 3. of Auden's Fanfare song[68] – but tho' it is nearer, it isn't there yet. I go along to Highpoint – Highgate – to see Cheatle about the programme at 4.30. Back here at 6.0 – change – try to hear (without much success) a broadcast of Simple Symphony from the North Regional – then to Langham Hotel for dinner with the Behrends, & then they take me to Toscanini BBC. concert. Two Symphonies – Shostakovitch no. 1. & the Eroica.[69] The S. is an important work – more perhaps in what it stands for than what it is. It is charming – vital – enterprising & deliriously free – makes all our Sibelius's & the saletites [satellites] look like the old Tories they are. It infuriates many people – as the Eroica did. But what a work <u>that</u> is! Toscanini gave it a fine, simple & direct performance. All that is in the work was there – except perhaps a little more finish in the orchestral playing. Straight back after.

Saturday 5 June [London/Colwall]

Work and odd jobs – including sketching abit of F.B. variations[70] (for Salzburg?) – before meeting John Cheatle at Paddington & catch 12.45 with him to Malvern. Arrive there about 3.30 & find no connection to Colwall – so wait for bus, which is full, so have to taxi. Meet Wystan Auden (who is teaching in a prep school – Downs) & see about the place & talk with him. He has another friend staying with him – a Brian Howard, a very clever, intellectual but surprisingly foppish & affected. But definitely amusing. Eat at hotel in the evening & then go to the music rooms where we play & sing (bellow) the bad music I've found for the 'Up the Garden path' that we are here to work on.

We (C[heatle]. & I) are staying at the Park Hotel.

Sunday 6 June [Colwall]
Up early & walk down to see Elms school (where Robert taught) before breakfast. Work hard at the programme in morning with WHA & J.C. – Doing some good stuff.

Then at 12.30 I give a small concert to some of the boys – delighting their simple hearts with fireworks of the most superficial & Victorian manner (var. on Home Sweet Home – Polkas & Galops etc). But they are splendid kids. We all have lunch with the school. Work again in afternoon. Eat with school in evening & then in hotel – fool about quite irresponsibly – Brian H. is the promoter of this. As can be imagined the conversation (owing to the vicinity of the school) lies in rather specialised lines – but it is treated with such enthusiasm, with delicate synonyms & epithets, & with such genuine taste, that it doen't aggravate.

Wednesday 9 June [London]
Tennis in morning with Peter Pears – both on form – grand fun in boiling sun. Lunch with him & Charles Brill up West & then in afternoon I go to Dennis Arundell's flat for a run thro' of the music of 'Up the garden path' – with Cheatle, Charlotte Leigh & Clinton Baddeley. Then to BBC. for further run thro'. It goes quite well – but rather hindered by uncontrollable laughter. Letters & work at odd moments.

Thursday 10 June
Spend a long time in morning running round second-hand music shops looking for an item for the Sunday programme. Then for a time to BBC. Lunch with Boyd Neel in Soho – he is a charming person & very kind – but I only wish he were a little more proficient a musician.

Shop & then back to flat & then work before an early dinner. Up to tennis for about ½ hour before we are ~~disturb~~ plunged into the middle of a colossal thunder-storm – the result of the heat-wave. Take refuge for about 1½ hours with Bramwells.

Friday 11 June
Rehearsal of music for 'Up the Garden Path' at 10.0 at BBC. Some difficulty as some of the singers <u>won't</u> see that some of the music (Victorian solemn

& pompous 'Night Hymns at Sea') arn't bad – so facile in expression & so cliché'd. But the light stuff (in its way so good – goes so well. Lunch with John Cheatle & walk with him in afternoon.

Eat in evening at Waldorf with Ralph Hawkes & then he takes me to the Stalls at Covent Garden for Fliegende Hollander – a grand work, splendidly done – with the wonder – Flagstad as Senta, Janssen as a superb Dutchman Weber as the father etc. & Reiner an efficient conductor. Eat afterwards in Soho & see a depressing brawl in the street – two women fighting a man – 'jealousy' – everyone said.

Sunday 13 June [Friston/London]
The weather changes most suddenly & the morning is pouring wet – inspite of which Christopher [Alston] & I go for a long walk to Beachey Head along the cliffs. Very exhilerating & he is a splendid person. In afternoon it clears enough for ~~me~~ us to get a little tennis, & to make it doubly hard to return to London – which I have to do by 6.36. Straight to BBC. Eat with John Cheatle & then back there for broadcast of 'Up the Garden Path' – which goes spendidly & is really very very funny. Auden's & my collaboration with a very ~~exle~~ excellent production by Cheatle is quite successful. Back here & early to bed – in fear & trepidation about to-morrow.

Monday 14 June [Burnham/London]
Mr. Donne, the investigator for Crockers, my acting-solicitors, calls for Beth & me at 8.15 & takes us down to Burnham Police-court. There ~~with~~ we meet Mr. Edgedale the council & talk over matters. After a few small cases before the bench – my case comes up: – two of us – the villain in the grey car (Mr Bartlett) are prosecuted for dangerous driving. I am taken first & all the witnesses give evidence that is 'for' me – & my council makes great use of that & my case is dismissed without Beth or myself even going into the witness box. The other man is convicted by ~~the~~ daming evidence. We both feel very relieved – & Mrs Welford, who came up specially takes us to Slough for lunch, to revive us, & drives us back here. Shop & see BBC. people in afternoon. & Cheatle. Then after a meal here I go to Toscanini concert with Peggy Brosa – & very exciting – only quite a lovely show of the Mozart G. minor – a dreadful arrangement of Respighis of C min Passacaglia. – Iberia was given a splendid performance – a worthy show of a great adorable piece of music. Sibelius En Saga, was as bad as that was good (in every way) & Hungarian March from Faust to end[71] – more exciting than authoritative. After the early end of the concert. I go with Peggy to Coliseum where Toni is leading the orchestra – & see act III of Coppelia. Eat after & back here at 1.0.

Wednesday 16 June [Colwall]

Spend day making alterations in the caberet songs & also in giving concerts to the boys of the Downs school – one in lieu of a French lesson – Wystan is a very unconventional master! The boys & staff (mostly) are charming – & things go with an immense swing.

Play a little tennis with Bill [Coldstream] – terribly steady stuff. Tea with Miss Woodhams – music mistress – a charming person.

After dinner at Hotel we all go along to Mr Feilds – the art-master – who is very intelligent & pleasant. Here we play & sing indefinitely. We lunch with the boys. Everything is going swimmingly – we couldn't be a better suited or happier party – Wystan's brilliance, Hedli's intelligence & art, Bill's integrity & dry wit – & my dullness (or youth – my only virtue) as a complete foil.[72]

Thursday 17 June

A tremendous amount of work – rewriting things doing a new version of F6. blues[73], which we try on the boys – & a great success it is too.

The place is grand, & weather lovely & company as good as ever. Wystan is terribly pleased with my straight songs for Sophie.

My rooms are nice (5/6 bed & breakfast) tho not many conveniences – but nice people & comfortable beds, not to speak of the colossal breakfasts.

Monday 21 June [Peasenhall/London]

Mr Welford takes us into Saxmundham to catch 9.25 to town. Straight back here – & do alittle work before early lunch.

Afternoon with F.B. at BBC. (Maida Vale) – he's conducting a show including my Sinfonietta after a good many runs-through it goes quite well. Back for a meal with him (& Mrs. B & Margery Fass) & then we all go to concert – Meeting Henry Boys there too – at 8.20. It goes well (but some of the playing isn't all it should have been) – he gets right into the work – which I can't help liking for all its immaturity. Then we all go onto a ~~rest~~ bit of Felix Salmond's recital at Wigmore Hall – he is a grand 'cellist but it's a doleful programme (mostly ghastly Brahms). Afterwards – leaving with Henry – I get an awful nose-bleed in Wigmore St. – a real pourer. So I taxi back here – but it doen't stop till nearly 1.0.

Wednesday 23 June

Early to the Bridges, & we all (including Marjory Fass) go to Covent Garden for the dress rehearsal of Goossen's new opera 'Don Juan de Manera.[74]

(Drive up in their car which is a terrifying experiance). The opera is completely wrecked by Bennett's inane, & ~~complete~~ absolutely unsingable libretto. Their are some good ideas in the music, but little or no continuity. It falls heavily between two stools – neither super-realism or real artificially (which, to my mind, opera should be).

Back for tea – a little work – some tennis after dinner – & then my nose bleeds fast & furious. This gives me a completely ~~restly~~ restless night – & I only get a couple of hours sleep.

The War scare is being worked ~~over~~ furriouly at the moment. The government has dared to say 'No' to Hitler, & everyone is scared of his next movements.

Friday 25 June

In all day working at Variations ~~& then Boyd Nee~~ until afternoon when I walk over to Keat's Grove for tea with Louis MacNeice – he gives me his new play 'Out of the Picture' ~~for~~ to look at – I'm doing music for it. Then he brings me back here (via Nancy Coldstream to see about title pages) & Boyd Neel comes to hear what I've done of the Variations – is terribly pleased and decides about them for Salzburg.

I meet Christopher Isherwood for a meal & have a grand evening, sitting, walking & talking with him. He gives me sound advice about many things, & he being a grand person I shall possibly take it. Back soon after 12.30.

Beth goes down to stay with some Aunts of Kit's for week-end.

Crisis with Germany & Fascists in general still damnably serious – doen't look as tho' I shall get ~~the~~ summer holiday.

Saturday 26 June

Work and business in morning – then up West for lunch with Trevor Harvey. Discuss a certain BBC. proposal. Back to Golders Green & spend a very enjoyable afternoon with Harry Morris on Hampstead Heath – tea here and talk after – he is a splendid little boy & I hope I'll beable to do something for him.

Then after an early eat – I go to Otello at Covent Garden with Trevor – Stalls from BBC. It is a grand show (Tibbett as Iago being really superb 100% – Martinelli as Ot. not so good in voice but a splendid artist) of a supreme work – & most moving. Eat long & entertainingly with T.H. & C. Brill – & walk back along way home arriving abot 2.30.

Monday 28 June
Lunch with Montagu Slater at Bertorelli's – after a short meeting with Max Plowman at Shepherd's P.P.U.[75] – to arrange a possible Music show for them and ~~al~~ the Basque children.

In the afternoon Nancy Coldstream & I go to Wimbledon to see the tennis. Get in to a good place at Court. no. 1. & see good people like, K. Stammers, Budge, MaGrath (who gives B. a good game, but no one can beat him this year I feel) Hengel (unpleasant) & Parker (America's no. 2. – a perfect Adonis with great technique).

Back to dinner to which Barbara comes to settle family matters.

Tuesday 29 June [Peasenhall]
I go down to Peasenhall to stay with the Welfords for four days. Object – to go through the myriads of names sent to me by Agents in my cottage quest. Everyday Mrs. W. & often Mr. W. too take me in one of their cars to visit places – but nothing is any good, until we find on Friday a Mill at Snape[76], which seems to have possibilities – but alot of alterations to be made.

The county is grand – none in England like it – & I feel I'm infinitely wise in choosing this place.

The Welfords treat me very well – & are kindness itself. I do a certain amount of work but not ~~alot~~ as much as I should. I want to sleep all the time.

Saturday 3 July [Peasenhall/London]
Mr. Welford takes me to Saxmundham, I catch 9.15 to town. I lunch with Lennox & tell him all about Snape & he seems pleased. Tennis in afternoon with Kit & Beth at club – but wretched stuff.

After dinner I go out with Christopher Isherwood, sit for ages in Regent's Park & talk very pleasantly & then on to Oddenino's & Café Royal – get slightly drunk, & then at mid-night go to Jermyn St. & have a turkish Bath. Very pleasant sensations – completely sensuous, but very healthy. It is extraordinary to find one's resistance to anything gradually weakening. The trouble was that we spent the night there – couldn't sleep a wink on the hard beds, in the perpetual restlessness of the surroundings.[77]

Monday 5 July [London]
F.B. has to come up to town for a few hours for P.R.S. meeting. Henry & I play tennis hard in morning & after tea. Have some grand, but not very serious games. I start to write out the score of the not yet completed Variations in afternoon.[78]

It is grand to see two people click (mentally) like Henry & F.B. They talk for hours, but I go to bed & leave them.

Thursday 8 July [London/Peasenhall]
Back to the flat in morning & work hard at score – deliver most of it to B & H to be copied, before meeting Lennox at Liverpool [Street] at 1.0. to catch train to Saxmundham. Mrs. Welford meets ~~our~~ us & takes us in car to see the Mill. Not so impressive to-day – it seems noisy & messy. Feel depressed.

Back to Peasenhall – tennis (not too bright) & then talk & discuss possibilities with Mr. Welford, of houses & alterations which I hope he'll do for me.

Friday 9 July [Peasenhall/London]
After some tennis in the morning with Lennox, in which he vainly tries to be serious, he & I catch 11.0 from ~~Peasenhall~~ Saxmundham (Mrs. W. takes us in). Lunch in city. I go to see Mr. Tunnicliffe about various matters – car insurance, & possible house buying. Then back to Hampstead, where Christopher Isherwood has tea with me & Harry Morris – who is a charming boy, & C. wanted to meet him.

Beth & Kit to dinner – they are off to Peasenhall to-night. I meet Christopher again & we see the dull Nazi propaganda film Der Herrscher[79] – with Jannings hopelessly overacting all the time. Back to flat & work on score till very late.

Sunday 11 July [London/Snape]
Barbara & I go early to Liverpool St. & catch 10.15 to Saxmunham. Eat a 2nd breakfast on the train – quite a good meal for L.N.E.R. [London & North Eastern Railway] which is deficient in everything a railway should be – one of the snags of proposing to live in Suffolk – but there are plenty of virtues to make up for it.

Kit, Beth, Barbara & I all go over to the Mill after tea – with Mr. Welfords proposed plans. The place seems definitely good to-day, & I almost decide to make them an offer. The others seem impressed too.

Kit's car conks. & they have to go back to town by train; poor wretches having to leave this lovely spot.

Monday 12 July [London]
I spend the whole of the day writing the score (from a very rough sketch from Saturday) of the fugal end of the Variations. I feel rather proud of my 11 part fugue with Canto written straight into score in ink![80] After a tremendous effort scarcely stopping for meals I get it off to copyist by 6.40 post.

Laze & recover in evening, while Mr. W. reads us alot of the very amusing Kai-lung stories of Brahmah's.[81]

Wednesday 14 July [Peasenhall/Lowestoft]
More letters in morning. Then after an early lunch Mrs. Welford Takes me over to Lowestoft – having first given me carte blanche to take any flowers & plants from the Peasenhall garden. These we plant up at the Kirkley cemetary – & spend a time there. It brings everything back with a horrible rush, & I become hopelessly morbid ~~at~~ & sentimental about Lowestoft & its associations. Walk on the front & see the glorious sea; sunny & blue but rough & choppy in the inimitable Lowestoft manner. See the Sewells but no one else. We come back by car about 5.0 –, have a little tennis. They both go out for dinner, & I walk the grand garden & read – Orlando (V. Wolff)[82] which is first-rate & very entertaining.

Thursday 15 July [Peasenhall/London]
I catch 11.0 from Saxmundham; park luggage, eat at Nottinghill Gate, & then on to rehearsal of the Boyd Neel Orchestra at 2.30. I take them thro' the Variations, which will be successful I think. Much time is spent in correcting parts & things, but the work is grateful to play, & the orch. themselves (a charming crowd) are very enthusiastic.

Back to flat after – pretty exhausted. It has been a devilishly hot day, & when one doesn't conduct often, it is a strain.

Kit's here to dinner.

Saturday 17 July [London/Newbury]
I go over to Hampstead E. to see Harry Morris' parents about his coming to Cornwall with me. They are charming & terribly keen for him to come with me. Then Beth & I catch 12.30 down to Newbury, where Mr. Behrend meets us & takes us back to the Grey House. A nice week-end party; Peter Piers, a Mr. Bernays (of the treasury, and a Mr. Alan George (advertising) as well as occasional visitors. We play lots of good tennis – & talk 19 to the dozen, & then after dinner (& what a dinner! – Mrs. B. is a superb housekeeper, & Mr. B knows all about wines) play & sing to a late hour.

Sunday 18 July [Newbury/London]
Still more tennis & bathing (2^{ce}) in their private bathing pool – good meals (naturally) & interesting talk – which at dinner becomes a regular marathon for me, for I have to stand up to the whole company to defend my (& all our set) ~~opi~~ 'left' opinions – the chief protaganist of theirs was a cabinet minister, Robert Bernays, who was charming but a supreme Parliamentarian &

evaser of points! Anyhow, I am not at all vanquished, but maintain my points – & even obtain from him a promise to find anyone I know a job who has left school & cannot find one at all – under the age of 35 too. We'll see!

Alan George brings us back in his car & we arrive soon after 11.30.

Monday 19 July [London]

I have a suit fitting in the morning – then on to Charlotte St. to discuss with Trevor Harvey a programme I'm doing for the B.B.C. Lunch there too, & meat a strange woman (a musical patroness) called Deneke. Back in the afternoon & work abit – then Brill comes to go over the Rossini Suite which he's doing on the BBC. on Aug. 3. Then I go out to dinner with Alan George at his flat in Kensington, & after that on to Uday Shan-kar – the Hindu dancers. This is a most tremendous experience. Judged by Western standards, the music is highly ~~sublte~~ subtle, developed & consequently marvellously beautiful. The dancing is the same – & technique of everyone beyond conception. I can't speak of the philosopy of it, because I know nothing of it – but I have the intuition that I was taking part in a very significant festival. Beth & Kit, go also to the show, but we sit apart for slightly similar reasons! Alan brings us back here in his car.

Tuesday 20 July

Work in morning & then lunch with Cavalcanti in Soho. Talk about films & future jobs at G.P.O. Then see some of their latest stuff – mostly pretty dull.

Then back here at 5.30 & play tennis up at Club – first of all singles (very energetic) with Teddy Rogers (see Sewells of Lowestoft) – & then doubles with Peter Piers, & Pat Jackson. Quite good tennis, tho' fearfully erratic. It is interrupted rather irritatingly by the appearance (alone) of the club rabbit who insists on thrusting herself in the middle of our set – she is a horrible person as well as deficient utterly at the game – still that's one of the snags of clubs.

Wednesday 21 July

Go early to rehearsal of Boyd Neel Orchestra. They spend 1½ hr on my work – Boyd taking them thro' it. It is going much better, but still alot to be done.

I lunch at Baker St. with Adolph Hallis – & have a satisfying grouse by the state of music in general, & the BBC. executive in particular. Fitting of suit after – I don't like the ceremony actually, too much prodding & poking – tho' they take a tremendous amount of trouble.

Then I meet Mrs. Bridge & her young niece ('Bon' Lüderes) over from Germany – see a news film & have tea.

Ralph Hawkes for a short bit of business. Back here for dinner.

Then go to a show of 'Mde. Boveray' at R.A.D.A.[83] with Rupert Doone & Robert Medley. Not very well done – even for students – pretty dull talent. The play has some good moments – but, at any rate in this production, Acts II & III are disappointing after Act I. I must read the orginal Flaubert tho'.

Otherwise the evening's a success

Friday 23 July [London/Prestatyn]
Business here before going to see Mr. Tunnicliffe (Solicitor) about the Snape house – there are lots of formal things to settle – buying a place is not so simple as I thought! Then lunch with Henry Boys & Peter Pears in Soho (Barcelona restaurant), after which I collect my posh new suit from Haymarket & Henry comes back here with me where I pack & write letters – & we have a little gramophone (the inevitable Stravinsky & Mahler). Then Beth & I (the usual taxi-dash, & she gets held up over work) catch 6.10 from Euston to Prestatyn. Eat on the journey with a boy called John Pooley (late of Clive House School) – a nice lad – but otherwise the journey is slow & very boring. Robert meets us at 11.24 & removes us in car to Clive House. Marjory – in spite of her 'expectations' – is well & it's good to see them.[84]

Sunday 25 July [Prestatyn]
They certainly have a charming set of boys here – & the three boarders – Brown, Preston, & Musgrave – are delightful kids. I walk to church with them & Robert, & then I return for a walk with Beth & young John, who is a grand kid; most grown-up & in the school now, his name was read in the school lists yesterday! Have sherry with the Prices (more friends of R's), in the afternoon going via St. Asaph – to see an Organist – Dr. Stokes – we four & John go for a long car ride along the coast to Llandudno – which is very impressive – & right round the Great Orme & back. Grand scenary. When back I take Caesar (who is living here with R. for the moment) & Brown & Musgrave for a long walk up the big Hill. Lovely walk with splendid company – actually I keep them out too long, & we all get into a row on return. Spend evening discussing the future of the school – a difficult decision. It seems a pity to drop it now as they've got it going so well – but Robert's quite considerable talents seem wasted on this poor, (literally) school with little or no scope for experiment. He's fine with the kids.

Monday 26 July [Prestatyn/London]
Great end of term ceremonies. The weather is foul as usual. Odd walks & packing in the morning. After lunch I play with the boys alot – young

Brown is a splendid boy & we make great friends. He comes to see us off at Station. Robert & I have a long walk over the hills talking 19 to the dozen – (we get on much better now, even tho' he is very much out of things, & considers me very 'free'!!) – & then after tea, Beth & I catch 5.8 to town. Good journey & have dinner – back at flat before 10.0. Find Effie here & desparate with Queenie who has a bad attack – no where to go, no money, & won't take advice. Insoluble problem.

Tuesday 27 July

Get down to business etc. in morning – & also in getting F6 music ready for future hirings.[85] Barbara comes to lunch & discuss all the depressing family affairs as usual – what a family we have inherited (the Hockeys being the worst specimens). In the afternoon Ronald Duncan up from Cornwall, rings up in despair from Chappells – in the middle of buying a piano & doesn't know which. So I go up West to help him & his girl friend.

Back for tennis at club with Peter Pears, Teddy Rogers & Archdale. Quite good fun – play for once quite well on form.

They both (P.P. & T.R.) come back for a meal.

Result no. x. of the appalling British Foreign policy is now starting: – just as she before raped Manchuria, as Italy raped Abyssinia, as Fascism in general is raping Spain, ~~China is now~~ Japan is now getting her filthy military clutches onto Pekin.[86]

Wednesday 28 July

Work in morning – or as ~~for~~ much as is possible in among the myriads of 'phone calls. Hair cut – & then lunch with William Walton at Sloane Square. He is charming, but I feel always the school relationship with him – he is so obviously the head-prefect of English music, whereas I'm the promising young new boy. Soon of course he'll leave & return as a member of the staff – Williams being of course the Headmaster. Elgar was never that – but a member of the Govening Board. Anyhow apart from a few slight repremands (as to musical opinions) I am patronized in a very friendly manner. Perhaps the prefect is already regretting the lost freedom, & newly found authority!

Back here in afternoon – & Peter Pears comes – play songs for him, & also run thro' the Variations[87] for his benefit.

Dinner with Lennox at his Reform Club – much talk. He is a dear & I'm glad I'm going to live with him.[88]

Thursday 29 July
More F6. work in morning. Lunch with Ronald Duncan & Henry Boys in Soho – to discuss with them the musical policy of R's new Magazine – Townsman. Then at 3.30 I go to B.B.C. where we have a prelimnary meeting to discuss Michaelmas programme[89] with Trevor Harvey (conductor) & Ellis Roberts (Author) It's going to be pretty boring, I'm afraid.

Then see Edward Clark about some Left film music – then on to eat with Christopher Isherwood in Soho. He is an awful dear, & I am terribly tempted always to make him into a father confessor.

Friday 30 July
Work in & lunch in; then I take Piers Dunkerley – back from [Bloxham] School – to see the new Marx Bros. film – a roaring farce called 'A day at the races'.[90] With some genuine inspiration in the humour direction, is some really beautiful & fantastic stuff – e.g. Harpo seducing the negro colony on his 1^{d} whistle; & again smashing the piano & removing the strings to play 'quasi arpa'.

Tea after with Piers at Criterion – & walk after. He's a charming kid – essentially normal & healthy – most refreshing.

I meet Alan George & he takes me out to a good dinner at Spanish Restaurant, & then drives me all over London – down to E. India Docks (which are very beautiful & romantic) & then I go back to his flat until rather late. He brings me back here by 1.0 – & I decide to end this little friendship.[91]

Saturday 31 July [London/Fawley Bottom]
Business & more work in morning. After an early lunch I meet Christopher Isherwood & catch with him the 3.18 to Henley (& Brian Easedale, whom we meet on the train) – where we are met by various delegates of the Group Theatre congress which is taking place at Fawley Bottom Farm House (residence of Mr. & Mrs. John Piper – artist). Pretty grim out-look – house filled with people – I have to sleep on floor – no accommodatory luxuries – however Wystan & Stephen Spender arrive, so it may not be so bad.

Have first discussion in evening, which is pretty tense as Rupert Doone puts point-blank questions to the Authors (W, Christopher, & Stephen) which have to be answered by an uncompromising 'no'.

Sunday 1 August [Fawley Bottom]
A terrible day of meetings & ultimata. Rupert asks for a guarantee of play-rights from the authors, which of course they are not willing to give – lack

of confidence in the present G.T. organisation. Rows – & more rows, – Rupert always taking things personally – but eventually an agreement is arrived at – & a directing committee is formed (by the authors) which, to all intents & purposes, will have control of the Theatre. And a good thing too.

We go over to a lovely house nearby for some tennis (lousy) – but this doesn't really relieve the misery.

Monday 2 August [Fawley Bottom/London]
One more meeting in morning – & that, thank God, finishes the business.

I smoke two cigarettes (first since adolescent efforts at school) with disastrous consequences in morning. Never again.

Stephen & brother authors go off at mid-day, but Brian Easdale's wife, & Coldstreams & Louis MacNeice come over which improves matters. We play tennis & bathe in afternoon.

There is a beastly party in evening, but don't see much of it. Eventually in despair I pack up & leave with the Coldstreams & L. MacNeice in their car about 10.0 Back at Flat at 12.0. Robert [John?] Moody is in the car too, & he's a very nice man.

Wednesday 4 August [London]
Work – accounts & letters – much behind in them – in morning. In afternoon I take Harry M. to a news theatre – it is grand to treat a poor kid to these things – his first trip to Piccadilly! His face is a picture

In the evening I eat with Louis MacNeice at Café Royal – & also Bill & Nancy Coldstream. Do a certain amount (after, at the Coldstreams) to the music of his new 'Out of the Picture'.[92]

Saturday 7 August [Peasenhall/London/Peasenhall]
Mrs. Welford takes me early to Saxmundham & I catch 9.19 to Liverpool St. – a slight mishap which makes train ¾ hr late, the excessive heat, & apalling crowding of the train makes it a lousy journey. Arrive & go straight to Queen's Hall, where I just play thro' my Soirées Musicales on the piano to Sir Henry Wood – for his benefit for Tuesday next. Lunch at the flat with Beth – Aunt Effie's gone to Cornwall, whence Robert & family are also gone to-day.

Beth's finished with work & the girls are all packed up & gone – & she's not feeling to happy about it.

Shop with her & meet Barbara for tea at Golders Green – & then catch 4.54 to Sax. – same kind of journey as before & train ¾ hr late – poor Mrs Welford who meets me!

Sunday 8 August

I sketch out a bit of the Michaelmas programme which I'm doing for Ellis Roberts & the B.B.C. A little non-energetic tennis in the afternoon heat, & after tea Mrs. Welford & I have a lovely drive to Minsmere & a grand walk over it – talking all kinds of intrimacies – I win Mrs. W.'s heart – but partly for a purpose, as I want to discover their reaction to Beth – which I ~~discover~~ find's not as bad as I expected, tho' not altogether favourable.

Monday 9 August [Snape/London]

Mr Welford & I spend morning & afternoon taking all the measurments possible at the Mill – a grand job, & very exciting planning everything. Gradually all the pig-stys are being removed & opening up fascinating new ~~vistas~~ views of the river & country.

Unfortunately I have to catch 7.33 back to a hot & dirty London – & a miserable solitary flat – of really ~~terryi~~ terrifying & heart-breaking associations too.

Tuesday 10 August [London]

10.0 Rehearsal at Queen's Hall with Sir Henry J.W. & the BBC. of my Rossini Suite. It goes as well as can be expected in a Prom rehearsal. See various BBC. personages. after – notably the Woodgates & Trevor Harvy, Lunch with John Moody (of Group Theatre) – very pleasat.

Back here & rest from heat & exhaustion. Eat in the evening with Christopher Isherwood – & then go on to Queen's Hall for Second half of Prom concert – when Henry W. does my Soirées Musicales. It don't go so badly – but not a rousing success with Audience unfortunately. However – there we are. Feel ill & sick after – so drift about with C.-Isherwood – Stephan Spender, whom we meet – go home for a bit with C.I. & then taxi back here – & straight to bed & to forgetful sleep!

Wednesday 11 August

Not up early – then business – then see Barbara's Kilburn centre[93] for a bit – she is very impressive as a Matron & I'm filled with admiration. It is strange how difficult it is to imagine members of one's family in positions of authority. – The snag of having grown up with them I suppose. It's the same with Robert's school.

Lunch with Ellis Roberts at his club (Oriental – 'for Reform') & talk (he is interesting) much, & also discuss programme for BBC. Dash back here & John Noel (pft. teacher) & Charles Brill come to tea. Similar dash to Chelsea for dinner with Barbara & Helen Hurst – I stay there the night.

O – for Cornwall & rest!

Thursday 12 August
Back here early. Then to Barnes to get tickets for to-morrow (bliss!). On to Marx Bros. with B. Easedale – enjoy it even more than ever. Lunch at Café Royal – see Wystan, Christopher, & Stephen S. and also Rupert Doone – with whom I spend the afternoon (at the Nat. Gallery) & walking about London. Back here at 6.30 & write letters – then desparately begin to pack. Harry Morris comes at 8.30, in preparation for to-morrow. But he goes to bed early & I don't follow for a long time.[94]

Friday 13 August [London/Cornwall]
Harry has a wretched night – very homesick, & I have to stay with him a long time until he goes to sleep. However in the morning he's much more cheerful, & excited at the prospect of train journey & Cornwall. Catch Cornish Riviera from Paddington at 10.30. A wonderfully quick journey & it is exhilerating to see his face when he sees things for the first time. Perhaps the meal in the dining car is the most tremendous experience! We arrive at Newquay at 4.40 – Robert & Marjorie meet me. (They have been here a week – at Miss Nettleship's bungalow at Crantock. Effie's been with them, & Beth & Kit arrived on Monday). They don't seem too pleased to see us – Harry is going to be a bit of a nuisance they think.[95] But I suppose they never think of doing anyone a good turn. Get a grand bathe & a surf at Crantock bay before supper. It is grand to be away from London & in the cool & quiet.

Saturday 14 August [Crantock]
Effie goes to-day. The holiday for the first week goes well – no quarrels, to any extent; certain antagonism as Robert will insist on asking his newly made & very intimate friends in, & no one likes them. Weather patchy, but some good surfing. We go about a certain amount but mostly stay in Crantock or Porth Joke. Harry sleeps in the double room, Robert & family in the little N. one – Beth, Kit & I on verandar. We have a girl in to do cooking & washing for breakfast & dinner (ev.) – a Swiss girl, Margurite, staying with Miss Nettleship; efficient & charming – but we all help alot.

Tragedy to-day is that Kit's wireless fades soon after the beginning of a supreme show of Verdi Requiem from Salzburg with Toscanini. That also means that I can't use it to hear Toni Brosa play my Reveil to-morrow.[96]

Tuesday 17 August
My plans for Snape arrive – they look fine – & it is very exciting planing things.

I am doing a certain amount of sketching for the Michaelmas BBC. programme.[97]

Wednesday 18 August

Beth, Kit, Harry & I, go over after lunch to Perranporth – where we meet one of Beth's working-girls (Lena [gap]) & her sister – Have a fine bathe & surf, tea, walk, & then we stay on to supper & 4 of us go to see ~~Pett~~ Peter Bulls' players do quite a pleasant 'sophisticated' comedy, called 'Lovers-leap'[98] – done with much fluency & style, without which it would have been unbearable. Harry is terribly struck by this his first visit to a theatre! He is getting on very well with us. Very quiet – it is difficult for him having us all around all the time, – but useful.

Monday 23 August [London]

Arrive in London early morning. Go to Hairdressers etc. for shaves – & then I go with Robert to see some school agents. My rehearsal (final) with the Boyd Neel Orch. is in the afternoon & it goes excellently. Frank & Ethel Bridge come from the country to hear it – also Miss Fass – & they are very excited – in fact we have celebration – dinner etc. & when I go along after to Barbara's flat to pick up Robert preparatory to our return to Crantock – it is a bit of a come-down to find them all wild with 'in loco parentis' wrath at my so-called conceit & bumptiousness – etc. etc. So we have (R. & I) a first-rate bust up, & part for rest of evening – I to a restaurant for a meal – & he to wander London.[99] Catch 2.0. train.

Tuesday 24 August [Crantock]

Rest of Holiday – split is very marked we never join for anything – always, Kit, Beth, Harry & me – & John, Marjorie & Robert. Personally I'm not distressed.

Wednesday 25 August

Tryarnon bay to-day (our section K.B.H. me) & day is spoilt by our being mixed up with 2 bathing tragedies. The surfing is fine, but there is a devil of a cross current.

Listen to Boyd Neel broadcasting the Variations from Hilversum[100] – they go very well.

Wednesday 8 September [London]

Work here in morning (BBC. programme) & then lunch with Peter Pears in Kensington. He's a dear – & I'm glad I'm going to live with him.[101] Piers Dunk. then takes [me to] film (Souls of the Sea)[102] & to tea – then back here, where Peter & Boyd Neel come to dinner.

Have a good time – talk – & general gramophone. My work seems to have gone frightfully well at Salzburg.[103]

Peter stays the night – talk till a late hour.

Friday 10 September
Before Peter leaves in the morning he runs thro' my Emily Brontë song[104] (for Michaelmas programme) that he's going to sing – & he makes it sound charming. He is a good singer & a first-rate musician.

Beth comes back from Peasenhall with Mrs Welford (on her way abroad) & they both have tea here. My tooth ache returns – curse it. Kit is here to dinner – & I leave Beth & him tactfully alone as much as possible. But they're very good to me.

Saturday 11 September [London/Friston]
I meet Piers Dunkerley at Victoria & we catch 10.45 to Eastbourne. F.B. & Mrs. B. meet us & after shopping abit take us back to Friston. Tennis in afternoon when the Eardley Holland girls come over. In the evening they take us both into Seaford – with Marge to see a film – Winterset,[105] that appeals to me politically, but not aestheticly so much.

Piers is getting on with the Bridges like wild-fire. They adore the rough, awkward school-boy that he is at the moment. Certainly he is a grand lad.

Sunday 12 September [Friston]
Bathe (or rather the others doit – my back & the cold prevent me from venturing) at Seaford in morning. I take hundred's of photos of them at various angles. In afternoon – tennis – the Spiers (Ferdy & Dorothea) come over – as well as back permits.

Tremendous discussion about my dedication of the Variations to Frank. Both Mr. & Mrs. B. say I can't put it – but fail to produce any good reasons – save that of privacy of such things – but Marge & I stick out for it.[106]

Tuesday 14 September [London/Surbiton]
After working I go at 12.0 to dentist (Mr. Harwood – Mrs. H. not there) & he discovers fresh trouble. Meet Beth & Peter Pears for lunch – tooth getting worse – see News Film (an appalling one of the Chinese war – massacre of civilians in Shanghai – only the effect of this on public is to make them want to keep out of this at all costs) – & then Beth & I go down to Surbiton to spend afternoon with the Gydes. My god-child Humphrey's a grand little boy. Kit comes in to dinner there.

But it's frightful how completely a bad toothache focuses one's attention. It's impossible to think of anything else.

Wednesday 15 September [London]
Up from 4.0 onwards with this blasted ache. I go at earliest moment to see Mr. Harwood – though, remembering Pop at home, & considering the

dentists feelings, I restrain myself from 'phoning till 9.0 – & he removes the offending tooth by gas. Has a terrible time as it crumbles to bits. Gas sensation not bad – but do everything to music (the Michaelmas programme too – can't get away from it even with gas!). Suffer horribly with the soreness & stiffness for rest of day. Beth's very good & attentive. Kit comes to dinner.

Thursday 16 September

Work at scoring of BBC. stuff in morning & all afternoon & evening. Lunch with Sophie Wyss, & show her the stuff she's got to sing – the BBC. have let me call her in to the programme at the last moment.

Beth goes to Gwen Rice's for the afternoon.

Friday 17 September

Wystan & Christopher wire that they're coming up from Dover where they've been writing their new play 'On the Frontier'[107] – dedicated to me with a grand little dedication. I meet them & spend morning with them. Back here in afternoon & work solidly at score all the time.

Sunday 19 September

Work – score & some household – (Mrs Nunn doesn't come on Sundays) – in morning. Mrs Welford, back from Germany – (with some entrancing presents – a real Deutscher pair of knickerbockers for me!) comes to lunch, & in the afternoon we then go down to Pinner for tea with the Crowdys. We stay on to supper & Peter Welford (also there) brings us back to town. Stephen C. has just got a first rate lecturing job in Trinidad & is off there next Saturday. It is sickening how so many decent people go abroad.[108] Lucy's going soon – & we four (S.,L, Beth & I) always have the grandest giggling parties together.

Monday 20 September

Continue scoring in morning, & then at 12.30 I rehearse Sophie Wyss abit in her part. Lunch with Lennox at the Barcelona – I always feel better towards L.B. when I am with him. In afternoon I take Sophie & young Arnold to cinema – they are a grand couple, & he is a most charming kid. Tea afterwards, with them, & he insists on me helping him to choose him a suit at Harrods.

Group Theatre executive meeting at 6.30, & dinner with Rupert Doone & Robert Medley after. Tremendous self-justifications from R.D, but Robert is the one I'm fond of. He brings me home as I'm feeling so dicky.

Tuesday 21 September

Spend just the whole day working without stopping. Beth has Elinor Bond here staying, but they are out nearly all the time.

I'm getting so bored with 'The Company of Heaven' that I find in the evening that I can listen to the Strauss 'prom'. (with E. Schumann) & continue the scoring without slackening speed.[109]

Wednesday 22 September

I finish the work in the morning & deliver it to the BBC. in the afternoon – thank God. Now if only I could wash my hands of it & not go thro' with the show . . . . .

Tennis (playing on form for me – except for back being bad ~~stif~~ still) with Peter Pears ~~6–7~~ 5.30–6.30. Then spend a very pleasant evening with Christopher Isherwood. I have read their new play the last few days & ~~It~~ it is just terrific. The best so far. We eat & see a New's Theatre.

Thursday 23 September

Letters & other business in morning – it's a treat to get some time to do it. See Leslie Boosey too about things. Work in afternoon – still letters. I go to dinner with Peter Pears & together we go onto the Debussy-Stravinsky prom. H. Wood does La Mer – & not too well; but I suppose considering it's Prom season it was creditable. But really the man is a vandal too often. Soulima Stravinsky play's his father's really lovely ~~capp~~ Capriccio[110] brilliantly. I meet him after with Lennox, & have supper after at the Café Royal. I spend most of the concert with Sir Arnold Bax & Harriet Cohen (the inseparables of course). He seems nice, but she talks more uneadulterated drivle than anyone I've ever met.

The Chinese massacre (3000 people reported dead in the Japanese raid on Canton) is sending people silly with disgust here & elsewhere. I hope that even our National Govt. won't take <u>this</u> lying down.

Friday 24 September

Spend morning at BBC. with Robin Whitworth (producer of 'Company of Heaven') going thro' my music. He seems pleased – so I suppose it's the kind of stuff he wants. Lunch with ~~hymn~~ him & Peter P. – & see a grand Viennese Film – Episode[111] (with that lovely Paula Wessely, & a first rate bevy of males). Back here & take out Beth & Effie (jobless – & back here to our discomfort – tho' one must be kind I know) to see the charming Sacha Guitry film – Roman d'un tricheur.[112] It is grandly witty.

Saturday 25 September

Up by mistake rather late, so I don't do all the work I want to. However – I have time to do about 6 versions of the beginning of 'Florid Music' one of W.H.A's songs[113] – & all of them N.B.G. [no bloody good] – I have never had such a devil as this song. Lennox comes in aft. intentionally to play tennis – but it rains – so we talk, play (viola duets) – including my String Variations, which he's very keen on, – & gramophone. Grace Williams & Kit come to dinner & we talk & gramophone – [Mahler] Das Lied – agreeing that it is one of the worlds No.1. works.

Sunday 26 September

Robert Medley, & Rupert Doone take me by car down to Croutch in Kent where Brian & Frida Easdale have a cottage. It is a heavenly day & the country's refreshingly beautiful after yesterday's rain & ~~the~~ permanent London gloom. Lunch there & ~~tea~~ a grand walk in the afternoon. Jack Moeran comes over in the afternoon – & we all go to the old Golding Hop pub. & I get rather drunk on the most potent cyder – & I'm afraid behave somewhat freely! Back in town by 11.45.

Monday 27 September

Beastly day of strains – work & business in morning (see Ralph Hawkes on matters – just back from his surprise marriage) – lunch with Brian Easdale & discuss matters (also about his room which Beth & I may rent this year – which I see afterwards).

Afternoon with Rupert Doone discussing music for Louis Macneice's New play[114] – then 6–8. chorus rehearsal for 'Company of Heaven' – my stuff all comes off like hell, but the chorus (BBC. professional) of course cannot sing really warmly enough – all too polite & 'English-church'.[115] Then dinner with Chantal & Adolphe Hallis. They are having a terrible time with their brilliant young daughter, Claire, who is on the verge of becoming either a/. mad or b/. a genius – & at the moment quite violent. I found her tractable but terribly excitable. The other two are dears – Chantal esp. is charming.

Tuesday 28 September

Spend all day at BBC. Full rehearsals – recordings & post mortems for tomorrow's show of Company of Heaven. My music comes off like fun, but tho' the production & drama side approve mightily of it the religious (Iremonger etc) is ~~is~~ definitely sceptical. – too modern & complicated – ~~the~~

over-dramatic etc. etc. 'give us the genuine hymn tunes' etc. I am quite frantic, but don't have to give way over many points.

Spend evening recovering – with Trevor Harvey.

Wednesday 29 September

BBC. rehearsal all morning – make one or two alterations, but keep well away from the drama section! Back here for lunch. Wystan comes in afternoon to talk about things – & also to play duets etc! I & he go to dinner with Mr. & Mrs. Ellis Roberts (he is the compiler of to-nights programme) – her mother & Miss Nettleship are also there. We have a grand dinner & nice amusing time. Then we three (E.R. is ill with Heart & cannot come) go to B.B.C. at 10.0 for the Michaelmas broadcast, for which I've done the music.

My side of it goes marvellously – & I do like some of it. People are enthusiastic (the orchestra even affirming that it's the best incidental music they've ever played!) – but the poetry side of it is pretty lousy. I don't understand the programme really – I cannot see the significance of it. What interests me is that I have nice words to set. Peter Pears, & Sophie Wyss both ~~set~~ sing their songs beautifully. The War in Heavn is thrilling.

Lots of us go to the Café Royal after – & have pleasant time.

Thursday 30 September

In all morning – many telephone calls about last night. People seem pleased. I spend time writing letters – a testimonial for Miss Ethel Astle who's setting up in Frinton (how that name makes my heart ache!). In afternoon I go up West to see a Baroness Hughwinkle – a slightly potty person who's dying for me to set her nice whimsey Ballet to music. Then tea with Christopher Isherwood, Wystan Auden & William Walton – a distinguished gathering in Dobrins – Baker St. Then see Wystan off by 6.55 to Birmingham. Meet Henry Boys & spend riotous evening with him. Pack before late bed. Beth out.

Aunt Effie goes to-day – to Wimbledon to intensify job-hunt – but really, it is too expensive a luxury, keeping aunts.[116]

Friday 1 October [London/Paris]

Early to Victoria & catch 10.5 to Newhaven – here I meet the Bridges & Miss Fass & we cross channel (like a mill-pool) arr. at Dieppe about 3.0 & go on to Paris. They are taking me and – the dears – paying for everything. We stay at a nice hotel (De Nice) in the Rue des beaux Arts across the river. We wander along to see the Exhibition after dinner – it is a wonderful spread, & we see some exciting fireworks – grand therminated fountains. Not too late back to bed.

Saturday 2 October [Paris]
The best thing about the exhibition is the pictures actually. We spend most of to-day in the Petit Palais seeing the independant modern artist's exhibition – an enormous collection.

The Utrillos, Picassos, Suzanne Valedon (never known by me before) Braques impressed

Tuesday 5 October [Paris/London]
Catch 10.0 from St. Lazare & have pretty fierce crossing – leave Bridges at Newhaven & get back to flat about 6.30. Beth comes with me to Wigmore Hall, when Boyd Neel does my Variations – not too good to-night – speeds were pretty cock-eyed. They go down well – much spontaniou's applause in the middle. Leave at interval with Behrends for Leeds in their car.

Stay night on Great North road in a pub – very nice.

Wednesday 6 October [Leeds]
Arrive in time (leaving at 6.0) for morning concert of festival.[117]

Rossini (little Solemn) Mass[118] pleased enormously – a grand work. But the new Walton (City of London ode)[119] was desparate – typical W. admittedly – but full of mannerisms & frightful lack of invention.

Here [hear] L'Enfance du Christ (Berlioz) in evening – & it is a magnificent work – fearfully good – every moment.

Must buy & study.

Thursday 7 October
No concert in morning – instead, the Behrends take me to Haworth where we look over the Bronte Parsonage.

Appallingly dark & bleak country – all stones are black – no wonder that Wuthering Heights ensued! On to Scarborugh for tea. & back in time to hear Lennox's Jonah[120] – which he conducts very well, & has a good show. It has some good things in it & is even more promising for the future. A party of sorts after.

Saturday 9 October [London]
My cold develops to-day & so, feeling pretty grim I stay in all day & amuse myself by writing songs – one little one of Peter Burra's, & a longer one (As it is plenty) of Wystan's.[121]

Beth & Kit to an evening meal – they go to a dance which Barbara & I should have gone to, but both being indisposed, we can't.

Sunday 10 October
Peter Pears comes to lunch & to stay for the week here. We both walk over to see Barbara in the afternoon, & back after an evening meal at ~~Stran~~ Regent Palace – amusing because so many interesting types of people there – but lousy over-cooked food.

Tuesday 12 October
I rewrite one Auden song in its entirety (Let the florid music) & write another new one (Seascape).[122] Also go to see at 6.0 some new Gas Light & Coke. Co. documentary films (mostly dull, but a nice bright one on Children at school by Basil Wright)[123] with William Walton.

Wednesday 13 October
Moving business in morning; ~~and~~ a poor wretched musicologist (if one is to believe him) – who is willing to do anything, from orchestrating a symphony to translating a song from the Japanese, – & who is completely penniless & foodless – comes to see if I have work for him. I, soft heartedly, give him £1 in advance & my Hunting Fathers to translate to French; heaven knows it's hard to refuse them.

I go to lunch with the Group Theatre Committee (R. Doone, R. Medly, Stephen Spender, & self) with D. Beddington, the new business manager at his office in Shell New house. We discuss the position of the committee & Rupert in particular.

Tea with Bryan Easdale, & see Lennox Berkeley after – about my new songs which he likes.

Back to dinner. Peter's in after – much talk until very late.

Thursday 14 October
Peter & I go to the Beecham show (with the very fine Leeds Festival Chorus) of the Mass in D[124] – & it is a tremendous disappointment. – not that one really expected anything really good from that irresponsible man. Every speed was just wrong – the work is obviously alien to the vandal – the Crucifixus was scandalous.

Even then the work stood out as one of the supreme masterpieces of all time.

Peter & I come back after & sing my songs till very late.

Friday 15 October
Bung [Begin] packing & things – after dinner Lennox B & Christopher Isherwood come to coffee to hear Peter sing my new songs & are considerably pleased – as I admit I am. Peter sings them well – if he studies he will

be a very good singer. He's certainly one of the nicest people I know, but frightfully reticent.

I spend the afternoon – after lunch with Trevor Harvey in city – with Ellis Roberts, discussing how we can turn the Company of Heaven into a concert work. He's been very ill, poor man, with heart-trouble; a wearing thing, with the unpleasant feeling that one may drop dead at a any moment, which is still unpleasant even in these days, of car accidents & almost universal war.

Saturday 16 October

Up to Ralph Hawkes the morning – he is about to launch on many of my things – printing of Variations, Rossini Suite, Spanish Suite (when finished – as also the songs). He's charming, & it's good to have a publisher like this.

Barbara & Kit come for week-end – Peter goes.

I'm buying clothes (& a football yesterday) for my little Spanish boy[125] – to-day pyjamas & pullover. I'm enjoying the responsibility tremendously.

Sunday 17 October

Tremendous turnings out etc.

In all day – Pat Jackson coming to tea being the only diversion.

This row of mine with Robert is subject of a discussion after supper – notably with Barbara. I still feel adamant about it – I may have been partly to blame, but the fact that it was such a bitter one & such things were said by a comparative stranger, shows that there is a complete lack of understanding between us.[126] I don't say that we must always be melodramatic enemies – but never more than aqaintances.

Monday 18 October

The removers come early to take Piano, some furniture to the Easdale, where I'm taking a room to use occasionaly in London, & where we can plonk some of our more frequently used belongings.

Back here after & busy turning out until ca 6.30 group theatre meeting up west – & a stormy one too – on the new constitution, & new chairman etc. etc. A meal after with Brian & Freda Easdale, jolly one. Back immediately after in the thick fog – first of winter, & jolly unpleasant it is too.

Mrs Welford comes up to town by car to stay with us over the move – & to help us generally.

Tuesday 19 October

I go with Lennox to Queen's Hall Courtauld Sargent concert to hear 2nd English performance of Jeux de Cartes of Stravinsky (whom I meet in ~~the evening~~ afterwards).[127] It is a charming & delightful work – worthy of the master. His conducting is excellent too. Back immediately after in preparation for to-morrow, & address some 100 change of address cards.

Wednesday 20 October [London/Peasenhall]

The moving men (Green & Edwards) are here at 8.30 & chaos (apparently) reigns till 5.30 when they depart, having stripped the place of everything movable. They are damanably efficient. We leave soon after, Mrs Welford driving Beth & me down to Peasenhall. Unfortunately we meet a most disgusting fog, & we have a most worrying journey – I have to walk in front of the car quite a way, & we get hopelessly lost. Strange that in this world of marvels they still ~~have~~ know nothing to penetrate fog.

I am heartily glad to be rid of 559 Finchley Road – it might have been a nice house, but all these memories are too bitter – The loss of Mum & Pop, instead of lessening, seems to be more & more apparent every day. Scarcely bearable. No where to look for help or comfort – & I am weak enough to want them very often.

Thursday 21 October [Peasenhall]

We go over to Snape early, by 9.30, & find the men waiting to put the stuff in to the Engine house to be stored till the house is ready for us. It goes in well. Beth & I ride back with the Men on the lorry & arr back here ~~till~~ soon after lunch.

Then we sit down & thank God that it's all over. Certainly it is difficult not to have any home, but the Welford's are sweet, & we can use Peasenhall in loco domus (except that I've forgotten all my latin).

Friday 22 October

I spend all my time in the next few days working over at Rhino (the house over the garage) in inimitable quiet (a). copying the Auden songs for Sophie Wyss. (b.) writing new ones (either before ~~brea~~ breakfast, or just before bed) (c) and starting the scoring of Lennox' & my Catalan suite[128] which seems to be working very well.

Apart from this we go about a little with the family in the car; to Snape, where the Mill's looking fine, or round the Country.

Tuesday 26 October

Sophie Wyss sings (beautifully) two of my Friday Afternoon songs in a programme for children this afternoon (1.0).

Frank conducts a concert at BBC. in the evening, including his Sea Suite (which pleases me enormously – although it's not as interesting as the later stuff) & Blow out you bugles[129] – which of course has good things in it, but even tho' I'm so fond of him, I dislike it – partly because of the pompous sentiment of the words (Brooke), & because as music it's not my 'cup of tea'.

Wednesday 27 October
In the afternoon we go (Beth & I are taken by Mrs. W. in her car) over to Lowestoft, & have a lovely time watching the fishing, smelling the sea & the kippers, & watching the Scotch girls gutting the herrings – all of which makes me homesick in the extreme.

Saturday 30 October [Peasenhall/London]
I am taken to Saxmundham where I catch 11.0. to London. I go straight to the Isherwoods (where I'm staying for a few days) in Earl's Court, to leave my luggage.

Then I go with Christopher, first to the private view of the London Group Pictures[130] – where Bill Coldstream's pictures stand head & shoulders above the rest – tho' Robert Medley's are striking; then to a Zersky [?] exhibition of Camera studies – wonderful, but tiring – so many examples of (to me) the same kind of thing.

Dinner at the Isherwoods, & then I go to the Queen's Hall with Basil Douglas to the Toscanini Brahms concert. Tragic Overture, & Requiem.[131] Some how the efficientcy & ~~skill~~ inspiration of T. seems to make Brahms even thinner than ever. T. obviously sees what was at the back of B's mind, & what he hadn't the skill to put on paper.

Sunday 31 October [London]
C. & I go to rehearsal of my Variations with Boyd Neel at the B.B.C.; after a certain amount of work on them they go much better. I spend afternoon with Barbara, & have tea with her at her flat.

After supper at the Isherwoods I go with the Bridges to the Maida Vale studio to Boyd's concert. The Brosas, Spiers, Ursula Nettleship. Lennox Berkeley brings Nadia Boulenger (who is sweet), come too. My piece goes very well, & I do feel pleased about it. The audience like it too – can it be that I am going to have a success with it? Small party at Bridges after.

Monday 1 November
Group theatre meeting & then supper with William Walton in his Chelsaea flat – he is very nice & we have a grand evening.

Tuesday 2 November
lunch with Brosas & Lennox.

Play them the Catalen Suite in afternoon. Hair cut. meeting at G.P.O. Films – on to Group Theatre party (Masefield speaking) – & then spend evening ~~at~~ with Alan George at his flat – difficult, must stop this friendship.[132] Back to Isherwoods – where it is very pleasant indeed to stay. Christopher's one of the nicest people I know.

Wednesday 3 November
Toscanini and the 9th & 1st in evening.[133] Disappointing. Of course he knows his stuff – & gives a magnificent example of disciplined playing – the 1st was grand. The 9th was so dramatic (1st movement raced along & all majesty was lost) – but the Scherzo was terrific, & of course the end was glorious.

Back to Lennox to-night.

Thursday 4 November
Meet Montagu Slater in morning & lunch with him & Lennox.

Tea with Dorothy Wadham.

Go with Lennox to Nadia Boulenger's concert of Monteverdi & Fauré (mostly). The latter's Requiem was serenely beautiful.

Friday 12 November [Painswick]
Spend our time playing trios & duets (Vl., Vla, Pft.) & also I do some sketching for Wystan's Hadrian's Wall programme & scoring of the Catalan Suite.[134]

Monday 15 November [Painswick/London]
Back to London by a mid-day train.

Rehearse with Sophie Wyss at 3.0 at Weekes studio – my Auden songs, & then catch 6.10 train to Birmingham where Wystan meets me & I stay at the Audens.

Wednesday 17 November [Birmingham]
Play lots of Mozart (Viola & piano – & piano duet) – at odd hours – Wystan's passion. I like his parents enormously, in fact things are very pleasant.

Friday 19 November [London]
Lunch with Ernst Schoer of the Opera Group.[135] Rehease at BBC. in aft.

At the Contemporary concert at 9.0 odd I play the piano part of my 'On this Island' songs (Vol. 1.) – with Sophie Wyss who sings them excellently – tho' her English is obscure at times. They have a public success, but not a succés d'estime – they are far too obvious & amenable for Contempory music.

Wystan comes & we – with the Gydes, W. Walton, & Lennox Berkeley, have a party after. Wystan comes back to the Gydes after – but as the car misbehaves, we don't get back till past 3.0.

[The diaries' entries become little more than appointment reminders from this date and BB made no further entries after 26 November for this year]

1938

Friday 7 January [London]
Lunch L. Berkeley – rehearse F.B's Phantasm with Kendall Taylor (to play it on 22nd).[1]

Dinner at Hedli Anderson (Wystan A. also there) – leave at 9.0 for Contemporary Concert at BBC. (Bartok – music for strings & perc. – very interesting)[2] with Christopher Isherwood – & supper after. Then back to Hedli's for 1 hour or so.

Saturday 8 January
Record Negroes[3] at Blackheath for G.P.O. in morning. Joe Lewis gives 1st perf. at BBC. (Maida Vale) of Lennox' & my 'Mont Juic' suite. Comes off O.K.

Saturday 15 January [London/Lowestoft]
To Lowestoft in afternoon

After much thinking begin Wystan's song 'Fish in the ~~Unf~~ Unruffled Lakes[4]

Tuesday 18 and Wednesday 19 January [Peasenhall/London]
Early train to London with Mr. Welford.

Record (1–4) Lines across Map stuff.[5]

Then I go to Isherwoods where I'm staying. Change Dinner with Stephen Spender etc. (John Lehman & Humphrey S. there) – colossal row – on phone Christopher & me v. Rupert Doone – eventually go on to Party given in honour ~~by~~ for Wystan & Christopher at Trevelyan's in Hammersmith. Beastly crowd & unpleasant people. Christopher leaves in temper & I spend night with J. Pudney in Hammersmith. Early to Isherwoods – & I go ~~with~~ to Victoria to see him & Wystan off to China.[6] Lunch with Peter Pears (back from America)[7] – & shop with him & Beth. Hedli sings Wystan's & my Cabaret Songs to Ralph Hawkes with great success.[8] Catch 7.42 back to Peasenhall.

Friday 21 January [Yoxford/Lowestoft]
Robert, Flo, Lilian Wolff come & we all (family) move to Yoxford for night. Sophie Wyss & Arnold Gyde (jun.) spend night at Peasenhall. Barb. Beth & I go over to Lowestoft in aft. to visit the graves at Kirkley.[9]

Saturday 22 January [Peasenhall]
Wedding at Peasenhall Church. 2.15. Recept. at Hall after – about 115 people come. V. good success. I give Beth away – Barb. & Robert act as Hostesses – 2 small girls (Griffin & Ann White) Bridesmaids – (dressed ex. like Beth) – 2 Pages – Arnold Gyde & Bobby Sewell (like Kit) very pretty. Party lasts till 6.30 – with Dancing. Stay in in evening – staying night at Peasenhall. Sophie sings my 'Birds' in service.[10]

Thursday 27 January [Peasenhall/London]
To London (after packing & sorting clothes in morning) in afternoon – via Ipswich (where I choose fittings for Mill).[11] Stay in Harley Mews[12] with Peter Pears, with whom I go to Phil. Concert – Mengelberg (v. good – if too temperamental) – with L.P.O. – grand show of Tschaikov. 5th – & also bits of ~~Pscheyé~~ Psyché (Franck) which was surprisingly good.[13]

Friday 28 January [London]
Spend day flat-hunting (without success) with Peter.
Dinner with Barbara – Helen & Muriel Bond there too.

Saturday 29 and Sunday 30 January [London/Surbiton]
Go down to Surbiton in aft. (after a film – 100 men & a girl[14] – with Peter & Barbara) – to the Gydes. I am rehearsing for Tuesday with Sophie. Have a grand domestic time with the family – two kids (Arnold – aged 10 – Humph. – 1½– both first rate specimens).

Tuesday 1 and Wednesday 2 February [London/Liverpool]
Sophie & I leave early for Liverpool (Euston 10.40) – & when there (met by Secretary & A.K. Holland – critic & sponser of concert) we rehearse a little in hall. Tea where we are being put up (me with Websters, S. with Whitmores) – & concert starts at 8.0. A long solo recital by Sophie – old English & French Group – Mahler – modern French – & my five.[15] Grand reception – my 'Plenty' being encored. Beth & Kit came to concert last night, & to party after at Whitmores. To-day Sophie & I (& Robert, & John from Wales) see them off by Casanare[16] to Jamaica (for pt. 2 of honeymoon). Back to London (me to Peter's flat) late in evening

Monday 7 February [Peasenhall]
Start piano concerto in morning[17] – it dashes along full-speed.
Walk at Minsmere with D.W.[18] in afternoon – very lovely.

Tuesday 8 February
Continue the concerto in morning – still haring along.
To Snape in afternoon. They go out in evening – I'm left alone to hammer on the piano, & listen to the wireless and 'Scrap's'[19] lugubrious howlings (for D.W.).

Wednesday 9 February [Peasenhall/London]
Up to town by early train. Lunch Trevor Harvey. Hear play-back of Lines on Map. no. 1 to which I wrote music. 5.0 Boosey & Hawkes Chamber concert with Henry Boys & Anne Wood. Dinner (feeling groggy) with Behrends at Pagani's & on to Q. Hall for Mahler's 8th.[20] Execrable performance (under H. Wood) – but then even the work made a tremendous impression. I was physically exhausted at the end – & furious with the lack of understanding all around. Sleeping with Peter P.

Thursday 10 February [London]
Mrs. Welford comes up & helps us (Peter & Me) look for flats. It's lucky she does as I couldn't have managed it on foot – the Mahler & my stomach are too much for my health. Look unsuccessfully for flats for us – successfully for Beth & Kit. Barbara makes trio into quartet for dinner – & pleasant evening.

Monday 14 February [Peasenhall]
~~Concerto in morning – it's going quite well~~ – To Snape in morning – it's going marvellously & will be fine for us to live in.[21]
To Aldeburgh after tea – see roads washed away – it's impossible to get from Slaughdon onwards.[22]

Tuesday 15 February
Over to Aldeburgh again all morning – as the tide is up – the road to Slaughdon is impassable. Chunks of cliff down at Dunwich.[23]
Work at Concerto in aft. – it's swimming along.[24]

Thursday 17 February
Concerto hard all morning – quite pleased.
To Lowestoft again in aft. with D.W. See by day-light the damage to Pakefield. ~~It's~~ The Cliff's gone appreciably since we left – & ~~is very~~ the Church is very near the edge now.

Wednesday 23 February [Friston/London]
Long walk in afternoon – & then in afternoon go in see Miss Fass (who is seedy again). I am having the Hunting Fathers translated into French by a French Poet (Pourchet) & Miss Fass is helping me. To London in time for dinner with Lennox at the Reform Club. Then he & I & Henry have some music – finally he (H.) comes back to Peter's Flat, because he can't get in anywhere else, & sleeps on sofa.

Thursday 24 February [London]
Peter comes back in evening from Dublin.

Business in morning & in the afternoon I go & see the Morris family about Harry's future – architect or butcher – butcher wins. Take Harry to Film. Proofs in evening.

Friday 25 February
In morning Peter & I sign up a flat – Neve[r]n Square – Dick Wood's late place.[25] 2 very nice rooms. Probably a rash decision, but we must get settled. Lunch with Ursula Nettleship in Sloane Square. See 5.0 the first full length Disney 'Snow White'[26] – grand entertainment & some terrific incidents.

Son born to Robert & Marjorie.[27]

Saturday 26 February [London/Peasenhall]
Spend most of morning in Boosey & Hawkes. Lunch & spend afternoon with John Pounder

Catch 4.54 to Peasenhall. Welfords meet me, & after a hurried dinner we go over to Aldeburgh to see Captains Courageous[28] – a grand film with splendid acting. Most moving

Wednesday 2 March [Peasenhall/London]
Up to London mid-day. See Basil Graves oculist in afternoon. Suddenly lose voice before dinner, so at the dinner I have with Basil Douglas, talking has to be done by writing. See after, 'Dead End'[29] with him, one of the most moving films I've ever seen. Documentary film (almost) of appalling conditions in New York.

Monday 7 March [Peasenhall/Lowestoft]
John [Pounder] goes back to town by 8.30. I see him off. Go up to Kirkley in morning to put flowers on graves. Lunch at Royal Hotel with Marjorie Phillips & walk in aft – she is having a rotten time since her mother died.

Back to Peasenhall in evening.

Tuesday 8 March [Peasenhall]
~~Work hard at getting business done & translation of Hunting Fathers copied in etc.~~ Pleasant walk with D.W. at Minsmere in the evening.

In morning I write a small Duet for Anne Wood & M.[Mary] MacDougal – Cradle song[30] – not too hot.

Saturday 12 March
Hitler marches into Austria, rumour has it that Czecho.S. & Russia have mobilized – so what! War within a month at least, I suppose & end to all this pleasure – end of Snape, end of Concerto, friends, work, love – oh, blast, blast, damn . . .

Sunday 13 March
Beth & Kit go off to London in aft. Glorious day, & bloody news from Vienna – to think of Wien, under Nazi control – no more Mahler, no lightness, no culture, nothing but their filthy, lewd, heartiness, their despicable conceit, & unutterable stupidity.

Monday 14 March [Peasenhall/London]
Up to London in afternoon – Peter's back from Prague – safely, but with grim news of Germany under Nazi rule.

Tuesday 15 March [London]
Peter's furniture is moved into flat. I have lunch with Ellis Roberts about Whitsun BBC programme.[31] Beth helps us arrange matters & furniture at new flat.

Sleep in Harly Mews one more night.

Friday 18 March [London/Peasenhall]
~~Pett~~ Peter, Beth & I go to Christopher Wood's complete exhibition.[32] A rare & vital talent – very memorable – especially the boats. Kit, Beth, Peter & I go down to Peasenhall in Kit's car. Arrive about 1.30. Good, tho' cold run.

Monday 21 March
Work at Concerto when I've got a second.

It's not going too well. Stuck in 2nd movement – which is poor stuff.

Tuesday 22 March [London]
Meet Ernst Schoer about proposed opera schem (I was/am to write one for June) for Interational festival (eventually this falls through thr' lack of

money). Peter & I go to Stephan Spender's play 'Trial of a Judge' at Unity Theatre (Group Theatre production) in evening.[33] Michael [Patton-Bethune] (Peter's friend) comes too.

Wednesday 23 March

Lunch, Lennox, Montegu Slater, & 2 Binyon sisters re new puppet plays etc.[34] Tennis with J. Nicholson in afternoon. Peter & I go to dinner with ~~Sop~~ Gydes – Patrick Hadly there Much singing & playing. Grand food & drink.

Thursday 24 March

Work alot & write abit. Not too good. Grace Williams comes in evening & I go thro' her new Welsh variations.[35] These composers are very rocky in their scoring, whatever their gifts.

Friday 25 March

Spend afternoon & evening at BBC; Pudney's broadcast 'Lines on Map' (no 3) with my music. Goes well. My Sinfonietta's done at Grotrian Hall – but don't go – not too keen on my childish works.[36]

Saturday 26 March

Lennox comes in afternoon to show me his Ballet.[37] It's very good – but I make lots of orchestral suggestions – which should improve it. BBC. rehearsal of my Film music (Telegram stuff for GPO) in morning.[38] Show is in evening. It goes well. Then see 'Trial of Judge' with Lennox again. It is 100% better 2nd time. Really grand poetry in it.

Tuesday 29 March

Meet Rupert Doone for tea – supposed to be 'having it out' – re. quarrel ~~wit~~ which continues. Not satisfactory – as I have little respect for his abilities, & it's on these that our acquaintance must depend. Lunch with Peter & Sophie W. Barbara comes to dinner – or rather we eat out at our usual 'Continental' & spend evening in.

Wednesday 30 March

Work in all day. In afternoon Lennox & I go to Costa's [Howard Coster] the celebrated 'Photographer of Men' to be taken – most amusing.[39]

Friday 1 April

Lunch with Slaters (Montegu & Enid) at Café Royal – ~~but~~ very pleasant – but gilt off gingerbread because I find I'm landed with the bill (21s.) unexpectedly which breaks me for abit![40]

Saturday 2 April
Boat race party at Mrs Pudney's parents (A.P. Herberts). I go with John Pudney. Most distinguished people inc. Sir John Simon, Cochran Kennedy[41] (U.S.A. Ambassador) & children, John Squire etc. Go on river with J.P. & one of A.P.H's sons (John). Spend evening with Piers Dunkerley now back from school – & John Pounder.

Wednesday 6 April
I play for Sophie in a recital of songs on BBC at 6.40. Schubert, Mahler & one of mine etc.[42] Then dinner with W. Walton & F. Ashton (of Sadlers Wells). There's some talk of me doing a ballet for them.[43] Very good evening but a little too much drink!

Thursday 7 April
Foul cold – but nevertheless play tennis with André Mangeot at Melbury in morning (good for beginning of season). Lunch Beth. Group Theatre Audition (some singers to hear). Dinner Ronald Duncan back from France – various plans.

Friday 8 April [London/Peasenhall]
See Ralph Hawkes in morning – back from U.S.A. Very pleased with life – & me too. Lunch Boyd Neel. Rehearse with Sophie 5.15 – & she (& Young Arnold) eats with Kit, Beth & me – before we (3) leave for Peasenhall in Kit's car. Arrive 12.30.

Saturday 9 April [Snape]
The great move into Snape begins. Have lots of people all working. Most of Welford family – 2 maids, 2 gardeners. & Bye family. Things are chaotic.

Wednesday 13 April
I pack & come over to Snape. The workmen leave – but the place isn't really complete yet. It's going to be good, but a bit of a shambles as yet. Lennox's furniture arrives. Mostly stored

Thursday 14 April
I have bought a 2nd hand Morris 8 – for tootling about the place. So far it's going well. I shop in Sax. in morning & then Barbara arrives at 2.31. She needs a rest. The place is improving – the rest of my furniture arrives from store. Shop in Saxmundham again in evening.

Friday 15 April
Do a certain amount of work on house – sorting the ton of crockery & silver. Walks. The country is heavenly & the view from the Mill superb. Beth comes

over from Peasenhall (she & Kit are spending Easter here) for tea & dinner. Barbara & I run her over ~~afte~~ about 9.0. [Added by BB in a small rectangle beside the date for this entry, as an afterthought, but clearly belongs to the evening] – Mr. Blowers, 20 years inn-keeper at Sotterley, which we knew so well when at Lowestoft, ~~is~~ keeps the Pub here. He is a grand man & comes for a drink before dinner.

Monday 18 April

Weather has been cold all Easter & now it's raining too. But it's ~~fe~~ been fine all over the move, so mustn't grumble. In afternoon Kit & Beth come over to tea. I run over to Farnham to fetch Nanny [Scarce] & Alice [Pratt] (née Walkers) who have tea with us. They are dears & it's nice to have them so near.[44]

Thursday 21 April [London]

Lots of business at BBC. and elsewhere. Rehearse with Sophie (for Boosey & Hawkes).

A party in evening at Trevor Harveys – films etc. Not exciting. But I see Piers Dunkerley in afternoon & with Peter, Hedli Anderson & him we shop & tea. Also choose new wireless which R. Hawkes is giving me.

Friday 22 April [London/Snape]

Lunch with Trevor Harvey after session with J. Pudney at BBC. In afternoon I meet Andoni Barrutia who is going to live with me at Snape.[45] With Beth we go down in evening. Pick up car at Sax

Monday 25 April [Snape/London]

I have to come up to town in morning – abit doubtfully as I don't know how Andoni will fare. I play for Sophie at Boosey & Hawkes party – 5.0. My 5[46] & others. Piers comes & eats after with Sophie & Arnold. Peter has now gone to Glyndebourne[47] & John Pounder is living at Neven Square.

Tuesday 26 April [London]

I have to stay up to-day as well. With John Pudney at BBC. & a long session at Harvey's flat with Trevor & Robin Whitworth about Whitsun programme.[48] Lots to be done. Eat at Dunkerleys in evening – see Barbara & back at flat about 10.30. Lunch with Cavalcanti and see some GP.O films in morning.

Wednesday 27 April [London/Snape]

Back to ~~Peasenhal~~ Snape after lunch. I go back to an acute crisis. I have been gradually placed under an obligation to the Bye family – they care-took for me etc. etc. – & now they are working here Mr. Bye (10/- week in garden) Mrs. Bye (10/- week helping Mrs Hean)

Thursday 28 April [Snape]
Master Bye (~~2/6~~ 5/- week – furnaces). Mrs. Welford sees to that they are doing nothing for this – sees that I shall be ruined, & offers to come & help organise if I sack the lot. I talk things over in great detail with her to-day on Minsmere, & in the afternoon I sack them all. What an effort.

Friday 29 April
Repercussions are great – Andoni (who's position gets more awkward everyday – Mrs. Hean doen't like serving ~~him~~ his meals with mine since he does coals & scrubbing for her) is fond of Mr. Bye & objects. Mrs Hean says she can't manage. Mrs. Welford spends days over here re-organising everything.

Saturday 30 April
Mrs. W. & Mr. W. come over in afternoon (David Green drops in and helps) & we get things straight & settled. Everyone's in an acute state of flap. I get no work done although Whitsun & Concerto call;[49]

Monday 2 May
Mrs. Welford's over to-day. Mrs. Hearn gives me notice – re. over-work & Andoni principally. Another worry is that Andoni is lonely & wants me to be with him – just crisis after crisis.

Tuesday 3 May
Decide after 'phone call with Poppy Vulliamy (who got me to take Andoni from her Basque camp) that A.B. must go back to the camp. He's upset. Lonely here, but has good time. Depressing atmosphere – & I'm sorry for the kid. I take him over to Wickham Market at 5.0–7.0 to see some of his compatriots at a camp there.

Wednesday 4 May
I pack Andoni off to London where Beth meets him & packs him off to Farringdon. I breathe a sigh of relief. Lunch at Peasenhall & dinner too. The Welfords are an oasis in this desert of misery. Mrs Hean becomes easier & will stay if we get help – which we promise to & search in Sax. for it in afternoon. [Leslie] Heward broadcasts my Var: at 6.0 from Birmingham.[50] They sound quite good

Thursday 5 May
The Search for help goes on – I go & get a name from Nanny & Alice in Farnham. Lunch at Peasenhall. Take Mrs. Hearn for a jaunt to Leiston – & return to work like hell. I've done lots the last few days as my mind's clearer.

I get the new wireless – a present from Ralph Hawkes – fixed up. It is as good as any I've ever heard.

Friday 6 May
Spend lovely day – in alone all the time – working hard; a little gardening and wireless. A real Snape day – the first of many I hope.

Saturday 7 May
Beth & Kit come over from Peasenhall to help me sort Junk in the Engine room. Spend ½ day here. Listen to broadcast of two Dictator's mutual admiration society in Rome to-night.[51]

Monday 9 May [Snape/London]
Up to London after lunch. In morning I go over to Lowestoft to see Mr. Nicholson (solictor) about income tax. Straight to Group Theatre meeting at 6.0. Then back to flat to dinner with John Pounder. To Beth's to hear 'Electra' from Covent Garden after – it is good Strauss & clear & consise – but weak. Daily Mirror emotion.[52]

Tuesday 10 May [London]
Work abit in morning – to Boosey & Hawks for business. Lunch Trevor Harvey. Rehearsal for Chartist March.[53] 2.30–5.30. BBC. I conduct my march for chorus. Back for rapid change & dinner then to Sadler's Wells for Gala performance of Ballet – inc. Lennox' new one. (Judgment of Paris) – very good. After to party with Freddy Ashton – the dancers – & C. Lambert, at Mr's. von Hofmanstall – very good too.

Thursday 12 May
Group Theatre meeting 11.0 to meet Stanley Bate. Lunch with the dear Brits (F.B. & E.E.B.). See 'Boys will be boys'[54] – Will Hay early Film – in aft. with John Pounder & Beth. Then 6.0–9.0 – BBC. rehearsal – & dinner after with John Pudney who produces, & J.E. Miller who wrote it. & is a brilliant sort of fellow. The rehearsals are complicated by the fact that each section comes from a different region, London Scotland, Birmingham, Manchester, Wales

Friday 13 May
Rehearse songs for Thursday with Sophie 12.0–1.0 & a grand lunch with her at Café Royal after. See with her & John P. – Le Roi S'amuse[55] – very amusing too – & BBC. 6.0 rehearsal & 9.0 show. It goes well & is exciting to do & listen to.[56]

Monday 16 May [Snape]
Over to Lowestoft in morning to Nicholson's again – lunch with them, & back here soon after 5.0. Then work solidly till late bed. As I go to bed – the noise of the birds is deafening – Cuckoo, Nightingale, Sand Piper, & Shell drake[57] – truly this is a grand spot – & domestic things are easier too.

Wednesday 18 May
Work – scoring the Whitsun programme – very boring stuff all morning – aft & evening Shop in Sax. before lunch – pouring wet. There is a fearful Underground smash at Charing X – 6 killed & dozens injured – a shock because one never dreamed of accidents there.

Thursday 19 May [Snape/London]
Catch early train to town & after seeing Ellis Roberts about Whit programme, I rehearse with Sophie for a recital I give with her at 5.0 at Acadamy of Music – of modern French songs. After that I go back with her & Arnold to dinner to meet Mr. Yeomans of Decca. Nice dinner.

José – Lennox. .
Saturday 21 May [Snape]
Great International Crisis – war more than ever likely – if only this Government would have a policy. José [Rafaelli] (Lennox's Paris Friend) & L. come down by mid-day train. To get his things sorted.

Monday 23 May [London]
Crisis seems averted for the moment – because our Govt. almost said she mightn't be entirely neutral if Germany seizes Czecho-Slovakia. Marvellous! F.C.B. [Francis Barton] is fencing at Olympia in the morning. Lunch with him & Montagu Slater at Café in Aft. see films (Snow White – Disney, V. fine) & René Clair's pretty poor [*Break the News*] with Chevalier & Buchanan.[58]

Tuesday 24 May
Finish off Whit programme in morning & deliver it to B.B.C. Lunch with Francis & new's flick. He is a great contrast to most of my friends – being in the Marines, a Tory, & conventional, but he is so charming & ingenuous, that he is decidedly bearable! To Barbara's after dinner – John P. too.

Thursday 26 May [Snape]
Do odd jobs about the house & garden. In afternoon F. & I go over to Lowestoft & have some grand tennis on Cliffe Courts. F. is pretty good, & we are fearfully energetic.

Go out in evening to hear the nightingales do their stuff at Winterton. [-on-Sea, Norfolk]

F.CB away

Friday 27 May

Francis goes after an early lunch & I am desparately miserable after he goes.[59] However the Alcocks who live at Orford ring up & I go over to tea with them & we have a good time playing chamber-music, piano & viola – trios by Beethoven.

Monday 30 May [Snape/London]

After a morning at accounts & things I go up to town in afternoon to Toscanini's show of the Verdi Requiem. Heaven itself. A grand show – with soloists fine, chorus good, & orchestra not too bad. There was nothing wrong with Toscanini – & a good deal right with Verdi! What a work. Sincere & deeply felt from beginning to end.[60]

Thursday 2 June [London]

Spend most of day rehearsing at Maida Vale Studios & B. House. It goes fairly well considering lack of time – but ~~the~~ a record is made of the last run through which is not good – & consequently the dramatic side complain about the quality of the music.[61] Dinner with Trevor Hardy.

Friday 3 June

I go to Toscanini rehearsal in morning – Mozart Jupiter & Schubert C maj.[62] – suffice it to say that Toscanini is worthy of such music – the highest praise. The rest of day is spent in hysterical crises at BBC. the production people <u>won't</u> see that the music sounds bad only because of no rehearsal – finally I threaten to withdraw it – which causes a little sobriety. Very, very disturbing.

Sunday 5 June [Snape/London]

up early & catch 8.16 to London. Rehearsal for Whit programme goes well – & they are reconciled – all of them. Then evening show goes better – & I'm invited to do the next of the Series – shows what a little Temperament can do. Lunch with T. Harvey, R. Whitworth & E. Roberts & Ursula Nettleship – tea with latter, & the Roberts give a dinner party at the Reform

Wednesday 8 June [Snape]

Up early & leave 7.15 for Harwich by car (take man from Garage to bring back car) & join Ralph Hawkes on his Firebird (16 metre cutter) for 2 days racing. It is bewildering since I've had nothing ever to do with boats this size – 4 paid hands & 4 more to run her – but it is good fun – Race to Southend. 2nd. in.

Thursday 9 June

Race today is round Mouse & Naze. Don't do well – but enjoy ourselves. Up to town before dinner with R.H. – he's as grand a publisher as one could have.[63]

See Barbara after dinner.

Friday 10 June [London]

Rehearse Violin Suite[64] with Grinke in morning. Lunch J. Pudney & Beth – see 4 Marx Bros in 'Horse Feathers'[65] – old but grand film – go to Toscanini show at Q. Hall – grand in lousy progamme – Brahms & Sibelius in D maj.[66] Go with J. Pudney.

Monday 13 June [Snape]

Finish off Puppet music & then get down in earnest to Concerto. Finish off 3rd movement.[67]

The Alcocks (Mr & Mrs) come over to play Chamber music (Pft Quartets & string trios) in evening – irresistable fun.

Tuesday 14 June

Lot more work. Lennox's sister comes over – she is a nice person – but embarrasingly flattering (& susceptable!).

Wednesday 15 June

Work in morning. In aft. D.W. comes over & we plan alittle garden work to be done. Poppy Vulliamy (& usual trial of Basque boys) drops in. Spend evening at Alcocks (Sudbourne) scraping at Chamber music. Energetic if nothing else.

Notes: 1936–1938

NOTES: 1936

1. For a young composer at this time, this was a remarkably good weekly income, Britten's salary from the GPO Film Unit and his Boosey & Hawkes retainer amounting to more than twice the average national earnings for 1936. Britten's career as a full-time composer took off from this point: unlike most of his contemporaries, he would never have to depend on income from teaching or working as a copyist or editor.
2. It is clear that both Piers Dunkerley and Francis Barton held a very special place in Britten's heart at this time and both were to remain lasting friends, though Dunkerley died tragically young. The closeness Britten felt for these two boys, in particular, was probably the earliest manifestation of his homosexuality. There were twenty-two references to Dunkerley in his diaries in 1935 alone – Britten played the role of older brother and counsellor to the fatherless Piers – and Barton was referred to on one occasion as his 'paramour'. See *Letters from a Life*, Vol. I, pp. 401–8 for Donald Mitchell's very considered analysis of this important dimension of Britten's sexuality, and also John Bridcut's ground-breaking Faber publication, *Britten's Children*.
3. *Our Hunting Fathers*, symphonic cycle for high voice and orchestra, Op. 8.
4. Beethoven Symphony No. 8 in F, Op. 93; *The Snow Queen* (1845), fairy tale in seven stories by Hans Christian Andersen (1805–75).
5. Rejecting the League of Nations' plan to protect Abyssinia from Italy's military forces, Mussolini ignored the League and ordered his army and Blackshirt legions to invade in September 1935. Sanctions threatened by the British House of Commons never materialised and Sir Samuel Hoare, the architect of a further peace plan that simply enabled Mussolini to retain those parts of Abyssinia already conquered, was swept from office by the force of public opinion.
6. *Calendar of the Year* (GPO, 1936), produced by Alberto Cavalcanti.
7. *Two Lullabies* (10–16 March 1936) for two pianos, composed for Britten's BBC audition as a piano duo with Adolph Hallis on 19 March 1936. Unpublished during Britten's lifetime, they first saw the light of day on 22 June 1988 when Peter Frankl and Tamás Vásáry performed them at Snape Maltings during the Aldeburgh Festival. They were subsequently published by Faber Music in 1990.
8. Britten was to revise his *Alla Quartetto Serioso: 'Go play, boy, play'* as *Three Divertimenti* for the Stratton Quartet's Wigmore Hall concert.
9. *The Ghost Goes West* (1935), British romantic comedy starring Robert Donat and Jean Parker, directed by René Clair (1898–1981), Clair's first English-language film; *Music Land* (1935), an amusing Disney short about the

marriage of jazz and symphony; and *Keystone Hotel* (1935), a slapstick silent classic starring Ben Turpin, directed by Ralph Staub (1899–1969). Towards the end of Britten's life he programmed a short season of three René Clair films at the 1971 Aldeburgh Festival, including *Le million* (1931).

10. Lewis Carroll's magnum opus, *Sylvie and Bruno*, a Victorian social novel and fairy-tale sequel, published in 1889 and 1893. Britten was presumably reading the second volume, in view of his reference to its being a 'wonderful fantasy'.
11. Rupert Doone's lover, Robert Medley, was resident designer of The Group Theatre and a very accomplished artist in his own right.
12. Maria Korchinska was later to premiere the revised version of Britten's *A Ceremony of Carols* with the Morriston Boys' Choir at the Wigmore Hall on 4 December 1943, conducted by the composer.
13. Tom Walls and Ralph Lynn made three Ben Travers comedies together in 1935: *Foreign Affairs, Fighting Stock* and *Stormy Weather*, each directed by Walls (1883–1949).
14. Frank Bridge *Oration, concerto elegiaco* for cello and orchestra (1930).
15. The BBC has always made elaborate and well-rehearsed plans for the death of members of the Royal Family, and King George's demise was widely anticipated after long periods of ill health.
16. Britten completes his orchestration (begun on 14 January) of the *Te Deum in C* (11 July–17 September 1934).
17. Reginald Goodall conducted the first performance of this orchestral version of the *Te Deum* with the Choir of St Alban the Martyr, Holborn and an unnamed orchestra in a Macnaghten–Lemare concert at the Mercury Theatre, London on 27 January 1936.
18. Hindemith was in London to play the solo part in his viola concerto based on German folk songs, *Der Schwanendreher*, with the BBC Symphony Orchestra. King George V died the day after his arrival, making the performance of this somewhat extrovert piece inappropriate, so the BBC invited him to compose something appropriate for the situation. His *Trauermusik* (mourning music) for viola and strings (premiered in this broadcast) concludes with a harmonisation of the Bach chorale *Vor deinen Thron tret ich hiermit, O Gott* (Before Thy throne, O God, I stand).
19. A reminder of how common such occurrences were in those days and how disapproving Britten himself was, despite his attraction to what Auden later described as the 'sexless and innocent'.
20. In February 1936 Britten was to make an orchestral version of his *Sinfonietta*, Op. 1 (with the addition of a second horn and adapted for multiple, rather than solo strings), and Edric Cundell was to conduct the premiere of this version with his orchestra on 10 March 1936 at London's Aeolian Hall. This was the only performance of this orchestral version during Britten's lifetime.
21. Beethoven Sonata in G, Op. 30, for violin and piano.
22. Constant Lambert *Summer's Last Will and Testament* for baritone, chorus and orchestra, after the play by Thomas Nashe (1936).

23. Mendelssohn *Die erste Walpurgisnacht*, Op. 60, cantata for mezzo-soprano, tenor and bass soloists, choir and orchestra, a setting of Goethe.
24. The concert included Britten's 'Fun Fair' from *Holiday Tales*; Schubert Piano Trio in B flat, D898; Beethoven Piano Trio No. 4 in B flat, Op. 11 ('Gassenhauer'), the alternative version with violin of the trio for piano, clarinet and cello; and Frank Bridge's *Phantasie* Trio in C minor (1907).
25. Britten's prudish side coming through and an indication of his reluctance fully to embrace the physical side of his homosexual nature.
26. Britten's susceptibility to the charms of younger boys surfacing nonetheless, despite his awareness of the dangers – a theme to which he was to return in his last operatic masterpiece, *Death in Venice*, based on the Thomas Mann novella.
27. Britten was to return to these sources for the final settings of his two nocturnal song-cycles: Keats's great Sonnet ('O soft embalmer of the still midnight') drawing the *Serenade* for tenor, horn and strings (1943) to a serene close, and Shakespeare's Sonnet 43 ('When most I wink then do mine eyes best see') providing the exultant climax to the *Nocturne* for tenor, seven obbligato instruments and string orchestra (1959).
28. Bridge Piano Trio No. 2 (1929), played by the Pougnet, Morrison, Pini Trio; see Personalia.
29. Stravinsky *Oedipus Rex*, opera-oratorio with a text by Jean Cocteau, the title-role of which was to be a signature role for Peter Pears, who first sang it under Stravinsky's baton for concerts and a commercial recording in Belgium in 1952. Pears later performed and recorded the role again, under Sir Georg Solti.
30. Britten's admiration for these works and indeed for both composers remained undiminished throughout his life.
31. Mrs Britten was finally making the move to settle in the Essex village of Frinton-on-Sea.
32. *War and Death, an Impression for Brass Orchestra*, written for a London Labour Choral Union Concert and first performed by the South London Brass Orchestra at the Westminster Theatre on 8 March 1936, conducted by Alan Bush. The work was posthumously published by Faber Music in 1981 as *Russian Funeral*, the title a reflection of the fact that the main theme is a Russian revolutionary song 'You Fell in Battle', while the middle section is based on the *Komsomol Fleet March* of the Soviet youth naval fleet.
33. Jean-Baptiste Loeillet (of London), Piano Trio in B minor – Alexandre Béon's arrangement of Loeillet's C minor Trio sonata for recorder, oboe and basso continuo.
34. The Wigmore Hall premiere of *Three Divertimenti* for string quartet, the revised version of three movements from '*Go play, boy, play*'.
35. Jack Westrup, then chief music critic of the *Daily Telegraph*.
36. Britten's ambivalence towards Sibelius was nothing if not constant.
37. *A Farewell to Arms* (1929), semi-autobiographical war novel by Ernest Hemingway (1889–1961).
38. Walton Symphony No. 1 in B flat minor (1935).

39. Bridge String Quartet No. 2 in G minor (1915); Beethoven String Quartet in B flat, Op. 18 No. 6.
40. *Russian Funeral* for brass and percussion.
41. Vogel was a Swiss composer of Russian descent, a disciple of Skryabin and pupil of Busoni.
42. *The Milky Way* (1936), comedy vehicle for Harold Lloyd, directed by Leo McCarey (1898–1969)
43. Britten writes the music for the production of Slater's play, which premieres at London's Westminster Theatre on 10 May 1936.
44. *Die Massnahme* ('The Decision' or 'The Measures Taken'), a polemical play written in 1930 by Bertolt Brecht, with music by Hanns Eisler.
45. The first of the two *Lullabies* Britten wrote for his BBC duo audition with Adolph Hallis.
46. Haydn Symphony in D, 'Le matin' (Hob I:6).
47. The Auden–Isherwood play, *The Dog Beneath the Skin*, then in production by The Group Theatre.
48. *Around the Village Green* (GPO, 1937), produced by Marion Grierson and Evelyn Spice, and *Peace of Britain* (Freenat Films/Dofil, 1936), produced by Paul Rotha.
49. See *Pictures from a Life*, Plate 61, where this Hughes Studio portrait photo is wrongly assumed to be from Britten's student days at the RCM.
50. Haydn Violin Sonata No. 7 in F (Hob.III:81); Schubert Introduction and Variations on 'Ihr Bluemlein alle' (originally for flute), D802; Hindemith Violin Sonata in E (1935); Dvorak Violin Sonata in F, Op. 57; Debussy Violin Sonata. Britten's comments on the Hindemith reflect the fact that Hindemith was considered by many at the time to be a Nazi supporter, as he had sworn an oath to Hitler, conducted for an official Nazi concert and accepted a position on the Reich Music Chamber. However his relationship with the Nazi party was ambivalent at best and in 1938 he emigrated to Switzerland, largely because his wife was Jewish, and the full horror of what was unfolding in Germany became clear to him.
51. Britten's views about the Mangeot Quartet were clearly hardening, though it is clear from earlier diary entries that he had long held serious misgivings about the quality of these players, and his judgement could often be harsh.
52. Britten was adapting his earlier Rossini arrangements (for Lotte Reiniger's animation film *The Tocher*) as an orchestral suite, which Boosey & Hawkes were later to publish as *Soirées Musicales*, Op. 9.
53. Bartok *Cantata profana*, for tenor, baritone, chorus and orchestra, which had received its UK premiere by the same BBC forces two years earlier, on 25 May 1934, conducted by Aylmer Buesst. Britten clearly felt that Boult had not got the measure of the piece.
54. *Modern Times* (1936), the classic romantic comedy of the day, starring Charles Chaplin and Paulette Goddard, written and directed by Chaplin (1889–1977).
55. More evidence of Britten's great affection for Piers Dunkerley.

56. The censorship issue rested on the film censor's assertion that it included War Office footage, which it did not, but the publicity stimulated by the issue drew disproportionate attention to the film and helped no end in its promotion.
57. Britten's admiration for Stravinsky, particularly the works of this period, knew no bounds.
58. Britten's admiration for the Vienna Boys' Choir was no less enthusiastic, and in the summer of 1966 he was to write *The Golden Vanity*, Op. 68 (a vaudeville for boys and piano after the old English ballad) for this exceptional choir.
59. 'Ich ging mit Lust durch einen grünen Wald' (I went happily through a green wood) from *Des Knaben Wunderhorn*
60. Schoenberg Suite in G (1934) for string orchestra – indeed a somewhat surprising departure for the composer of *Pierrot lunaire*!
61. As Britten notes, 'thank heaven not sexually', but this need for children around him was to remain with him till the end of his life. One suspects that if he had been born into a different generation of gay men, he would have found the need to adopt a child, as so many gay couples do today.
62. *Calendar of the Year* and *The Fairy of the Phone*.
63. Britten is referring here to a type of shawm, the *tible* (Catalan for treble), commonly used in Catalonia along with the *tenora* (Catalan for tenor) and other instruments, to accompany the traditional Catalan circle dance, the Sardana.
64. Barcelona's famous and exquisite Palau de la Música was designed by Ramon Muntaner, and is the most important Modernist example in Ciutat Vella. It was the headquarters of the *Orfeó Català*, the oldest Catalan choir. The programme included *profana i religiosa dela segles XIV, XV & XVI*.
65. Britten's Suite, Op. 6, whose first complete performance Britten was to give with Brosa the following day at the Casal del Metge, during this ISCM Festival season in Barcelona.
66. Britten's profound admiration for the Violin Concerto and *Wozzeck* was to have a lasting impact on his music, not least on his own Violin Concerto (written for Brosa in 1939); *Wozzeck* cast its own long shadow over much of *Peter Grimes*.
67. Britten leaves seven lines blank here, as if planning to insert the details of Orchestral Concert No.3, in which Pedro Sanjuán, Ernest Ansermet and Bartolomé Pérez-Casas conducted music by Ruggles, Roussel, Martin, Halffter, Mihalovici and Palester.
68. Monserrat is the site of a Benedictine abbey, Santa Maria de Monserrat, associated by some with the location of the Holy Grail of Arthurian myth. It is also the home of the world famous Monserrat Boys' Choir, one of the oldest and finest cathedral choirs in Europe.
69. This visit to Mont Juic was the genesis for the suite of Catalan dances on which Britten and Lennox Berkeley collaborated in 1937, published by Boosey & Hawkes in 1938 as Britten's Op. 12 and Berkeley's Op. 9. *Mont Juic* was dedicated to the memory of Peter Burra, who accompanied them on this ISCM trip to

Barcelona and was to die tragically in a flying accident in 1937, while Britten and Berkeley were working on their joint score. See *Pictures from a Life*, Plate 83.

70. See *Pictures from a Life*, Plate 84.
71. Research work beginning on *Mont Juic*, no doubt.
72. Arthur Benjamin Violin Concerto (1932), which Brosa had premiered with the BBC Symphony Orchestra under the composer's baton.
73. Auden was to spend three months in Iceland, gathering material for a travel book, *Letters from Iceland* (1937) written in collaboration with his friend, travel companion, fellow poet and playwright, Louis MacNeice.
74. Britten was no doubt reflecting that this represented a personal loss for him, as he had wanted to study with Berg in Vienna while at the RCM, but the College authorities had persuaded his parents that Berg would have been a bad influence on the young boy. One shouldn't rule out the possibility that if he had met Berg at the Barcelona ISCM Festival, he might have asked to study with him. It should be remembered, after all, that Britten was taking his scores to Bridge right up till the time he left the UK for America in 1939.
75. A saturated solution of formaldehyde, water, and typically another agent (most commonly methanol) used as an antiseptic and disinfectant. Britten was to suffer many of these throat infections, the most severe resulting in his having his tonsils removed while he was in America in the early 1940s.
76. Britten showing his British reserve and his lack of real comfort in openly 'gay' surroundings and circumstances. Many years later his partner, Peter Pears, confided to the editor of these diaries that Britten was never drawn to what he described as the 'queer society' in London, and had an abhorrence of camp.
77. Britten had begun work on *Our Hunting Fathers*, with the first setting of the anonymous text 'Rats away!' As was his usual practice, much of the early work was done in his head, during lengthy walks.
78. Stravinsky *Duo Concertante* (1932).
79. Mozart Flute Quartet in D, K285; Cooke Quintet for harp, flute, clarinet, violin and cello (1932); Roussel *Serenade*, for flute, string trio and harp, Op. 30.
80. Having made her Metropolitan Opera début as Sieglinde in February 1935, Flagstad went on to take New York by storm, singing Isolde, Brünnhilde, Kundry, Elsa and Elisabeth, and establishing herself as the pre-eminent Wagnerian soprano of the era. In 1936 she performed all three Brünnhildes in the San Francisco Opera's *Ring* cycle, so her arrival at Covent Garden was a much anticipated triumph.
81. Stravinsky *Le chant du rossignol* (1917), the symphonic poem Stravinsky based on his opera, *Le rossignol* (1914).
82. See *Pictures from a Life*, Plate 89.
83. Presumably a treatment of *The Golden Asse* by Lucius Apuleius 'Africanus', available in translation by William Adlington. This project did not materialise.
84. Berkeley was from aristocratic English stock and Grace Williams from good Celtic stock, a strong, outspoken and independent Welsh woman. It would indeed have been an interesting evening!

85. A somewhat confusing statement, as the 'third party' insurance should only have come into play if Beth Britten were responsible for the accident. If the bus driver was at fault, the company's insurance should have been liable.
86. Beethoven Piano Sonatas No. 9 in E, Op. 14, and No 11 in B flat, Op. 22.
87. *The Little Colonel* (1935), dramatic comedy starring Shirley Temple and Lionel Barrymore, directed by David Butler (1894–1979).
88. Britten is now completing the second movement of *Our Hunting Fathers* ('Messalina' – a lament for a dead monkey) and still toiling with 'Rats away!'
89. 'Hawking', later entitled *Dance of Death* (possibly Auden's suggestion) is a setting of Thomas Ravenscroft.
90. A BBC radio adaptation of *Socrates* (1930), a play by the British playwright, poet and journalist, Clifford Bax (1886–1962), brother of the composer Arnold Bax.
91. Beethoven Piano Sonata No. 31 in A flat, Op. 110.
92. Signs of Britten finally breaking away from his mother's apron strings, much as his comic hero, Albert, was to do (some ten years later) in Britten's second chamber opera, *Albert Herring*.
93. A BBC broadcast from the third season of Glyndebourne Festival Opera, of the production of Mozart's *Le nozze di Figaro* that opened the Festival Theatre on 28 May 1934.
94. Berkeley *Jonah*, oratorio for soprano, mezzo, tenor, bass, chorus and orchestra, Op. 3 (1935); Berkeley's first major score, later withdrawn.
95. *Gulliver's Travels* (1735), novel by Jonathan Swift (1667–1745).
96. It is interesting to note that Britten thought *Salome* to be the best of Strauss: an opinion held by many, and in keeping with his own antipathy to the bourgeois excesses of *Der Rosenkavalier*, despite his admiration for Strauss's orchestration.
97. Vaughan Williams' Piano Concerto must indeed have come as something of a culture shock for Britten after immersing himself in the musical language of *Salome*.
98. Britten is presumably referring to the Adagietto of Mahler's Fifth Symphony, and it is interesting that he responded to the erotic, not the sentimental, in this music. Interesting, too, that Visconti should have chosen this movement for the sound-track of his famous film adaptation of Thomas Mann's *Death in Venice* – the novel that Britten himself adapted for his last operatic masterpiece.
99. Carl Czerny *Die Kunst der Fingerfertigkeit* (The Art of Finger Dexterity), Op. 740.
100. Later in the century, Draper's mantle as a monologist and comedienne was assumed by the inimitable Joyce Grenfell, who became a big supporter of Britten and Pears and their annual music festival in Aldeburgh.
101. Based on Swift's *Gulliver's Travels*, a project that never materialised.
102. Unidentified.
103. Britten was collaborating with W. H. Auden on this orchestral song cycle; Auden had helped select the texts (two anonymous medieval lyrics and a text

by Thomas Ravenscroft) and provided his own texts for the framing Prologue and Epilogue.

104. *Selections from the Literary Remains of Karl Marx* (1923) by Max Beer (1864–1943); and *La vie très horrifique du grand Gargantua, père de Pantagruel* (The Very Horrific Life of Great Gargantua, Father of Pantagruel), commonly known as *Gargantua*, the second of five related novels by the French Renaissance writer and humanist, François Rabelais (*c.*1494–1553).

105. *Erewhon, or Over the Range* (1871), novel by Samuel Butler (1835–1902), a satire of Victorian society that has been compared to *Gulliver's Travels*. Britten refers here to Chapters 23 to 25, 'The Book of Machines', which rather prophetically deal with the concept of machines developing their own intelligence.

106. Britten refers here to the third movement of *Our Hunting Fathers*, the 'Dance of Death': given the extraordinary virtuosity of this orchestration, it is sobering to think that he was able to complete no fewer than thirteen pages of full score in one day!

107. Jean Françaix *Concertino* for piano and orchestra (1932)

108. Françaix String Trio (1933); *Concertino* for violin and chamber orchestra (1936).

109. A planned military *coup d'état* on 17 July began with an army uprising in Spanish Morocco, spreading to other regions of the country; but it met with serious resistance, leading ultimately to a full-blown civil war with the legitimately elected government in Madrid. Britten's optimism about the political upheaval was to be short-lived.

110. Unidentified, though in March 1939 Britten was to write his *Ballad of Heroes*, Op. 14 (originally entitled *Anthems for Englishmen*) to honour the men who had died in the Spanish Civil War.

111. Walton Symphony No. 1 in B flat minor (1935); Vaughan Williams Symphony No. 4 in F minor (1935) – both works very much of their time, influenced by the onset of war.

112. Britten refers to the fact that Lords Rothermere and Beaverbrook controlled much of the tabloid media through their ownership of the *Evening Standard, Daily Sketch* and the *Sunday Herald*.

113. Britten had clearly fallen behind schedule in his adaptation of his Rossini arrangements for *Soirées musicales*.

114. *A Passage to India* (1924), novel by E. M. Forster, with whom Britten was later to collaborate (together with Eric Crozier) on the Festival of Britain commission for *Billy Budd* (1951) for Covent Garden.

115. Britten's Aunt Julianne (one of his godmothers) suffered from a very debilitating arthritic condition.

116. This was to be Britten's only foray into the feature-film industry. Boyd Neel had been engaged as the musical director for a Trafalgar Films production, *Love from a Stranger* (1937), based on the stage play by Frank

Vosper, which was itself an adaptation of Agatha Christie's *Philomel Cottage*. The film, produced by Max Schach, was directed by Rowland V. Lee and starred Ann Harding and Basil Rathbone. See diary entry for 23 October.

117. Britten again refers to Dvorak's Symphony 'From the New World' (No. 9) using the numbering common at this time.
118. Britten would collaborate with Rupert Doone and the Group Theatre again, on a new production of Louis MacNeice's translation of Aeschylus.
119. Elizabeth Schumann sang Mozart's 'L'amerò, sarò costante' from *Il ré pastore*, K208, and the 'Alleluia' from *Exsultate, Jubilate*, K165, with the BBC Symphony Orchestra under Sir Henry Wood, in this Promenade Concert from London's Queen's Hall.
120. *Around the Village Green* (TIDA/MGM, 1937).
121. Vaughan Williams *Old King Cole* (1923), ballet for chorus and orchestra, written for the Cambridge branch of the English Folk Dance Society.
122. This was Laurence Olivier's first performance of Shakespeare on film.
123. Bridge *Two Poems* for orchestra (1916).
124. Retailers of silverware, fine jewellery, watches and glassware, 132 Regent Street, London W1.
125. By all accounts the players of the London Philharmonic Orchestra behaved so badly during the rehearsal that Vaughan Williams (whose *Five Tudor Portraits* were also premiered in this concert) chose to intervene between rehearsals and persuade the orchestra to be more professional in their approach to this new and challenging score.
126. Frank and Ethel Bridge.
127. *Line to the Tschierva Hut* (GPO and Pro Telephon, Zurich, 1937), produced by John Grierson and directed by Alberto Cavalcanti.
128. For *Calendar of the Year.*
129. Helen (Nell) Burra; see Personalia.
130. Bliss Viola Sonata (1933).
131. Despite Britten's great admiration for Stravinsky, he always judged him by his own (that's to say, Stravinsky's) extraordinarily high standards and achievements.
132. *Around the Village Green.*
133. *Leise flehen meine Lieder* (literally 'gently plead my songs', but known in English as *Unfinished Symphony*), the 1934 musical film biography starring Márta Eggert and Hans Jaray, directed by Anthony Asquith (1902–68) and Willi Forst (1903–80).
134. *Bed and Sofa* (1927), Soviet silent film, a satire on the Moscow housing shortage of the day, directed by Abram Room (1894–1976).
135. Moeran Symphony in G minor (1924–37).
136. *Line to the Tschierva Hut.*
137. Britten's love of ballet during the 1930s, and his interest in pursuing the possibility of writing for this medium of the lyric stage or lending his

repertoire to such use (*Our Hunting Fathers* for instance), makes it all the more surprising that it would be some twenty years until he wrote his only full-scale ballet score, *The Prince of the Pagodas*, Op. 57.

138. The Hispano-Suiza, Spanish-French car that rivalled the Rolls Royce in 1930s England.
139. During the 1930s, this part of North London, and especially the area around the Sadler's Wells Theatre, was not the sought-after residential area that it is today.
140. *Carnival* (1912), melodramatic novel by the English-born Scottish author and nationalist, Compton Mackenzie (1883–1972).
141. A session which laid down the soundtracks for *Calendar of the Year, The Savings of Bill Blewitt* and *Lines to the Tschierva Hut.*
142. *Around the Village Green.*
143. With Britten's great interest in film, this must have been a fascinating glimpse of another dimension of the industry, whose possibilities he would pursue further during his American trip in March 1939.
144. *An Orphan Boy of Vienna* (1936), a touching story (featuring the Vienna Boys' Choir) about an orphan who finds sanctuary as a member of the world-famous choir. The film starred the child-actor Hans Olden and was directed by Max Neufeld (1887–1967).
145. After the death of his own father the relationship between Britten and Bridge was increasingly vital to the young composer.
146. Britten was working on his incidental music for the Group Theatre production of *Agamemnon* while simultaneously preparing a piano-conducting score of his Rossini suite.
147. Schoenberg Suite in G for strings (1934).
148. Britten was to set eight of these poems in 1937 for high voice and piano: five were published as 'volume one' of *On This Island*, Op. 11 (Boosey & Hawkes, 1938).
149. A notorious sustained *tour de force* for any coloratura soprano.
150. For the film *Love from a Stranger.*
151. A characteristic way for Britten, a committed pacifist, to spend Armistice Day. Just nineteen days later he was to start writing his *Pacifist March* (for chorus and orchestra) for the Peace Pledge Union, completing the score on 27 January 1937.
152. Britten resumed work on his *Temporal Variations* for oboe and piano, begun on 15 August 1936; see 15 December.
153. Duncan was providing the text for Britten's *Pacifist March.*
154. A deeply offensive term today, but a common phrase of the day to describe industrious individuals, implying that they worked like slaves.
155. 'Underneath the Abject Willow', written for Sophie Wyss and her sister, Colette, and published the following year by Boosey & Hawkes, together with a setting of Montagu Slater's 'Mother Comfort'.

156. Roger Henri Charles Salengro (1890–1936) had been the target of a poison-pen campaign from an extreme right-wing journalist, accusing him of desertion in 1916; this had led to Salengro's suicide on 17 November.
157. In readiness for the scheduled premiere at the Wigmore Hall with Adolph Hallis on 15 December.
158. Britten and Duncan were writing their *Pacifist March* for Canon Dick Sheppard and the Peace Pledge Union.
159. Even Britten's earlier love of Brahms' chamber music is beginning to wane by this stage.
160. *The Way to the Sea* (Strand for Southern Railway/ABFD, 1936), produced by Paul Rotha and directed by J. B. Holmes, for which Auden was to provide an end commentary.
161. Britten's people-watching was to stand him in good stead as a music-dramatist: think of the vividness with which he sketched the many characters who inhabit the scene at The Boar in *Peter Grimes* or the village of Loxford in *Albert Herring*.
162. *The Green Pastures* (1936), a revolutionary film in its day: an Old Testament drama with an all African-American cast, directed by Marc Connelly (1890–1980).
163. Hindemith *Die Serenaden*, Op. 35, little cantata on romantic texts, for voice, oboe, viola and piano.
164. Britten was working on the incidental music for *The Way to the Sea*.
165. These were published by Boosey & Hawkes as *Two Ballads* for two voices and piano in 1937.
166. Bridge's recent illness had clearly been very serious and life-threatening, and he had been forced into complete physical and mental rest for some six months. Severe vomiting had placed a strain on his heart, bronchitis led to further complications, and he was left with high blood pressure and a weakened heart for the five remaining years of his life.
167. Bridge Suite for string orchestra (1909).
168. One of Britten's favourite operas, for which he retained a great affection.
169. Edith Coates was to create the role of Auntie in the Sadler's Wells premiere of Britten's first operatic masterpiece, *Peter Grimes*, in 1945.
170. The authoress best known for her mystery novels featuring the aristocratic sleuth, Lord Peter Wimsey.
171. Beethoven *Wellington's Victory at Vittoria* (*Battle Symphony*), Op. 91.
172. Unpublished.
173. A glimmer of hope in the all-too grim scene developing in Spain.
174. Lucy, Lady Houston (1857–1936), a typical English eccentric of the day, a noted patriot, philanthropist and adventuress. She was so devastated by the abdication crisis that she stopped eating and died of a heart attack on 29 December, aged seventy-nine. Britten was clearly not a fan!

NOTES: 1937

1. A clear indication of Britten's pacifism being tested by the turmoil of international affairs.
2. Britten was revising his oboe suite and working on a new setting of Lamb.
3. The history of this brief piece is strange in that, despite the characteristic efficiency and flair that accompanied its writing (Britten had completed its orchestration by 27 January), it wasn't considered by Sheppard and the League until a meeting of the Sponsors on 15 September, when it was rejected on the basis that it was not much liked – so to this day it has not been performed professionally.
4. Britten had first seen the film with W. H. Auden on 5 December 1936, when it had made a great impression.
5. 'O Gott! Welch ein Augenblick!' (Oh God, what a moment!), the chorus that accompanies the freeing of the prisoners in Act II of *Fidelio*.
6. Albert Dubois (1905–76), French cartoonist, illustrator, painter and sculptor.
7. *L'amour en cage* (1934), comedy directed by Jean de Limur (1887–1976).
8. Milhaud *Christophe Columb*, grand opera (1928), libretto by Paul Claudel (1868–1955).
9. *Concerning the Eccentricities of Cardinal Pirelli* (1926) by Ronald Firbank (1886–1926), a curious piece of writing that starts with the Cardinal christening a dog in his cathedral and ends with His Eminence dying of a heart attack, naked, while chasing a choirboy around the aisles.
10. The dress-shop premises on the ground floor.
11. A common complication of pneumonia, caused by bacteria, when pus collects in the pleural space between the outer surface of the lung and the chest wall.
12. Britten's early setting of Hilaire Belloc.
13. Kit Welford was studying at the medical school of London's St Thomas's Hospital.
14. Britten had been commissioned to write the incidental music for the Group Theatre premiere of the Auden–Isherwood play, *The Ascent of F6*.
15. The very touching quality of this song (a mother addressing a son) was clearly influenced by the sad circumstances surrounding its writing.
16. This BBC commission was for the historical radio drama, *King Arthur*, by D. G. Bridson, first broadcast on 23 April 1937.
17. A reference to the death of his mother, an agony that haunted Britten for some time to come.
18. The London Theatre Studio in Islington was the first British drama school to incorporate theatre design and the training of directors, stage managers and lighting designers in its curriculum.
19. Britten, still haunted by his mother's death.
20. Christopher Isherwood writes a wonderful little vignette of the young Britten, scribbling music to order in rehearsals for *The Ascent of F6*, in his autobiographical novel, *Christopher and His Kind*, p. 200.

21. Britten's famous setting (in this original version, for chorus, two pianos and percussion) of W. H. Auden's wonderful lyric, 'Stop all the clocks, turn off the telephone'.
22. For Montagu Slater's Left Theatre production of *Pageant of Empire*.
23. The normally reticent Britten enjoying the limelight for the first time, as he was to do so often throughout his post-war career.
24. Anthony Collins had been the second viola in the broadcast premiere of Britten's *Phantasy* string quintet (1932), with the International String Quartet, in an earlier BBC Regional broadcast on 17 February 1933.
25. *Sabotage* (1936), drama thriller about a bombing plot in London, thought by many to be one of Hitchcock's greatest films.
26. Mrs Britten's home at Frinton-on-Sea.
27. Licensing laws dictated at what hours of the day alcohol might be sold.
28. Presumably reflecting the belief that the Communist state transported its citizens like cattle.
29. Bridge *Two Poems* for orchestra (1916).
30. Beethoven String Quartet No. 13 in B flat, Op. 130.
31. This is the first time Britten and Peter Pears meet, at the maisonette Pears then shared with Trevor Harvey and Basil Douglas, at 105 Charlotte Street, London W1.
32. Slater's *Pageant of Empire*.
33. This is indeed a substantial bequest, and points to the success that Mr Britten made of his career, given that neither he nor his wife had family money.
34. *Reveille*, concert study for violin and piano, which Britten completed on 16 March for Brosa's Wigmore Hall recital with Franz Reizenstein on 12 April.
35. Schoenberg String Quartet No. 4, Op. 37.
36. Britten was obviously drawn to Burra.
37. This is probably where he and Burra were not so attuned, as Britten's tastes were for the refined spirit (which he was to find in abundance in his relationship that was soon to start with Peter Pears) while Burra was perhaps more attracted to the more masculine 'toughness' of a very different sort of gay man.
38. It is interesting how quickly his scores were being taken up by the BBC at this time, with two broadcasts of *Soirées Musicales* by BBC orchestras within three months.
39. Busoni *Doktor Faust* (1916–24), his last opera, left incomplete at his death.
40. Kit Welford came from a 'good' family and enjoyed a more privileged life at Peasenhall Hall, a manor house in Suffolk.
41. Britten was working on 'Death Music' and 'Galahad', which are featured in the 'Scherzo' and 'Variations' of Paul Hindmarsh's orchestral suite drawn from *King Arthur*, compiled in 1995 and published the following year by OUP.
42. *The Company of Heaven*, incidental music for speaker, soprano, tenor, chorus, organ, timpani and strings, with texts selected by R. Ellis Roberts.
43. Britten still brooding on the death of his mother.

44. *Mont Juic*, suite of four Catalan dances for orchestra, Berkeley writing the first two movements, Britten providing the remainder.
45. Mozart Trio in E flat for violin, viola and cello, K563.
46. It would seem that Berkeley was keen to take their sexual relationship onto another level, but Britten was resisting any serious physical involvement.
47. The tensions in their marriage were ultimately to lead to divorce.
48. *The Flower Beneath the Foot* (1923), novel by Ronald Firbank (1886–1926).
49. In his book, *Coronation Commentary* (1937), the author Geoffrey Dennis had insulted Mrs Wallis Simpson, and the Duke of Windsor threatened to sue the author for libel. Most of the book had been written in November 1936, but after the abdication and the Coronation of George VI, two additional chapters were added, in the course of which the author had commented that 'For Queen of England [Edward had chosen] an itinerant, shop-soiled twice divorcee with two ex-husbands living . . . She came too far below; she clashed too crudely, with the nation's idea and ideal, dream and myth of feminine royalty. . . . She would not do. The comedown from Queen Mary to Queen Wally was too steep.'
50. *Elephant Boy* (1937), a British film based on Rudyard Kipling's *The Jungle Book*, starring Sabu Dastagir, directed by the documentary filmmaker, Robert Flaherty, and produced by Alexander Korda (1893–1956).
51. Britten persisting in his misspelling of Peter Pears' name, no doubt because the only significant 'Pears' in his life till now had been Piers Dunkerley, to whom he was very close.
52. Rubbra Symphony No. 1, Op. 44 (1936).
53. 'Now through night's caressing grip', an Auden lyric from the Auden–Isherwood play, *The Dog Beneath the Skin* (1936), published as 'Nocturne', the fourth song of *On This Island*, Op. 11. *Johnny*, a setting of a much lighter lyric by Auden, was the first of a number of Auden settings that Britten made for the cabaret singer, Hedli Anderson, who was appearing in the Group Theatre production of *The Ascent of F6*. These settings also included a solo version of Britten's 'Funeral Blues' from *The Ascent of F6* (arranged on 17 June 1937), 'Tell me the Truth about Love' (January 1938) and 'Calypso' (summer 1939). These four settings were eventually published posthumously as *Cabaret Songs* by Faber Music in 1980. Britten is known to have set two further Auden texts as cabaret songs, 'Give up Love' and 'I'm a Jam Tart', and indeed recorded them with Hedli Anderson for Columbia in July 1938 and January 1939, but neither the music nor the recording masters have survived.
54. *Two Ballads* (1936), Britten's settings of Slater and Auden.
55. Classic saloon car of the day.
56. In 1953 Britten was commissioned by the Royal Opera House, Covent Garden, to write a new opera, *Gloriana*, for the Coronation celebrations of King George's VI's daughter, Queen Elizabeth II. By this time the issue of his 'lonely bed' had also been resolved, as he was fourteen years into a partnership with Peter Pears that survived till the end of his life.

57. Britten had a car accident on Tuesday 18 May, while driving in the Cotswolds, but doesn't note the circumstances in his diary – the page for this day is totally blank. When they return to London, he and Beth are examined by Dr Moberly, both being rather stiff and bruised by the accident, but with no serious injuries.
58. As Britten refers here to 'songs' for Hedli Anderson, and at this stage only 'Johnny' (of the surviving songs) was completed, this play-through must have included the two missing cabaret songs, 'Give up Love' and 'I'm a Jam Tart'.
59. *Loyalties* (1933), crime drama based on the play by John Galsworthy, starring Basil Rathbone, directed by Basil Dean (1888–1978) .
60. 'Let the Florid Music Praise!', the first song of *On This Island*, Op. 11.
61. Busoni *Rondò arlecchinesco*, Op. 46; Ravel *Daphnis et Chloé*, Suite No. 2 (1913); Beethoven *Coriolan* Overture, Op. 62; Brahms Symphony No. 1 in C minor, Op. 68. The concert opened with the Corelli–Geminiani Concerto Grosso, Op. 12.
62. *The Emperor Jones* (1920) by Eugene O'Neill (1888–1953), the first American play to feature an inter-racial cast on Broadway, with a black actor in the title role.
63. Elgar *Introduction and Allegro*, Op. 47, for strings; Cherubini Symphony in D (1785); Vincenzo Tommasini *Carnival of Venice*; Berlioz 'Queen Mab' Scherzo from *Roméo et Juliette*; Wagner Overture to *Die Meistersinger von Nürnberg*. Though Britten was dismissive of the Elgar, later in life he was persuaded by his Decca record producer, John Culshaw, to perform and record the *Introduction and Allegro* with the English Chamber Orchestra.
64. The solicitor who was advising Britten on the repercussions from his car accident.
65. Rossini Overture to *L'Italiana in Algeri*; Beethoven Symphony No. 6 in F, 'Pastoral', Op. 68; Brahms *Variations on a Theme by Joseph Haydn*, Op. 56a; Strauss *Tod und Verkärung*.
66. Though the first volume of *On This Island* was dedicated to Christopher Isherwood (Auden's friend and collaborator, who was fast becoming a good friend to Britten also), these Auden settings were written expressly for Sophie Wyss, Britten's preferred singer at this time. She had already premiered the orchestral song cycle, *Our Hunting Fathers* (1936), and Britten was later to write *Les Illuminations* (1939) and his collection of French folk-song arrangements (1942) for her.
67. *Up The Garden Path*, a radio recital of words and music, the verses chosen by W. H. Auden and music by Britten, presented by John Cheatle; a BBC Regional broadcast transmitted on Sunday 13 June 1937.
68. 'Let the Florid Music Praise!'.
69. Shostakovich Symphony No. 1 in F minor, Op. 10; Beethoven Symphony No. 3 in E flat, 'Eroica', Op. 55. Strangely enough, much of the documentation for this concert suggests that Beethoven's Fifth Symphony was originally on the billing, so one must assume that the programme was changed.

70. Britten had been commissioned by the Boyd Neel orchestra to write a work for their debut at the Salzburg Festival: *Variations on a Theme of Frank Bridge*, Op. 10 was dedicated to (and conceived as a character study of) his teacher, using a theme from the second of Bridge's *Three Idylls* for string quartet.
71. Mozart Symphony No. 40 in G minor, K550; Bach–Respighi Passacaglia in C minor; Debussy *Ibéria*; Sibelius *En Saga*; Berlioz 'Rakoczy March' from *La damnation de Faust*.
72. Britten's inferiority complex in such dazzling company was often a problem for him.
73. Britten made his solo arrangement of the 'Funeral Blues' from *The Ascent of F6* for Hedli Anderson on this day.
74. Eugene Goossens *Don Juan de Mañara* (1934); the Covent Garden premiere with Lawrence Tibbett in the title role.
75. The Peace Pledge Union.
76. The Old Mill, Snape, on the hill overlooking Snape Maltings in Suffolk.
77. The long conversation in the park with Isherwood was doubtless about Britten's slow acceptance of his homosexuality, and the 'Dutch courage' consumed in Regent's Street's Odenino's Imperial Restaurant and Café Royal was intended to break the ice for this midnight visit to the Jermyn Street Baths. However, one can't help thinking that Britten was missing the point: those who frequented the Jermyn Street baths in those days were not there to sleep.
78. Britten was nonetheless making extraordinary progress on his complex string orchestra score for the *Variations on a Theme of Frank Bridge*, begun only a month earlier.
79. *Der Herrscher* (1937) was based on Gerhart Hauptmann's play *Before Sunset*, but the screenwriters changed the ending to fit Hitler's agenda for Nazi Germany. In the play, the central role of the wealthy industrialist Clausen (played in the film by Emil Jannings) ended tragically; in the film, he disowns his family and then bequeaths his munitions factory to the German people, dedicating himself to rebuilding Germany's shattered economy.
80. Such was Britten's extraordinary technique and compositional fluency that he had the confidence to embark on such a complex contrapuntal texture in ink.
81. Ernest Bramah's fantasy novels of ancient China, as told by his fictional itinerant storyteller, Kai Lung.
82. *Orlando* (1928), semi-biographical novel by Virginia Woolf (1882–1941), based in part on the life of her intimate friend, Vita Sackville-West.
83. A dramatisation of the novel by Gustave Flaubert (1821–80), given by the students of London's Royal Academy of Dramatic Art at their theatre on Malet Street, London WC1.
84. Marjorie Britten was expecting her second son, Alan.
85. Boosey & Hawkes had agreed to facilitate the hiring of Britten's incidental music to *The Ascent of F6*, though they didn't publish the score as such. These materials are now in the Britten–Pears Library at Aldeburgh.

86. The war between the Republic of China and the Japanese Empire began in earnest on 7 July 1937 with a clash at the Marco Polo Bridge; on 29 July, Peking (Beijing) was surrendered to the Japanese Imperial forces.
87. Britten had completed the *Variations on a Theme of Frank Bridge* on 12 July. The Boyd Neel Orchestra was to give the broadcast premiere on Radio Hilversum in The Netherlands on 25 August and the concert premiere at the Salzburg Festival on 27 August. Though Britten could not attend the Salzburg premiere, Pears was travelling in Europe that summer and would be in Salzburg for the concert.
88. Berkeley was to share Britten's newly acquired Suffolk home in Snape, The Old Mill.
89. *The Company of Heaven.*
90. *A Day at the Races* (1937), classic Marx Brothers comedy starring Maureen O'Sullivan, directed by Sam Wood (1883–1949).
91. It seems from the references in this diary entry to the romantic setting and lateness of the hour that Alan George had designs on Britten.
92. *Out of the Picture* (1937), play by Louis MacNeice, premiered by the Group Theatre in December 1937.
93. Barbara Britten was the matron and health visitor in a medical centre in Kilburn.
94. Britten being careful as ever in his actions and, indeed, his words.
95. It had apparently not crossed Britten's mind that Robert, and particularly Marjorie, might have been concerned that Britten was in the company of a young boy.
96. Brosa was to give the broadcast premiere of Britten's *Reveille* in a BBC National programme the following day.
97. Work progressing on *The Company of Heaven*, for the BBC broadcast on 29 September.
98. Unidentified.
99. There seems to be more to this than meets the eye from Britten's account here. See 17 October.
100. The broadcast premiere of the *Bridge Variations*, the Boyd Neel Orchestra en route to Salzburg.
101. It is important to point out that at this stage in their relationship, Britten and Pears were friends, not lovers, and this domestic partnership in London and their easy friendship anticipated the beginning of their sexual relationship by two full years.
102. *Souls at Sea* (1937), seafaring film starring Gary Cooper and George Raft, directed by Henry Hathaway (1898–1985).
103. Pears had recently returned from Austria and had attended the Salzburg Festival premiere on 27 August.
104. As a member of the BBC Singers, Pears was to be a soloist (alongside the soprano Sophie Wyss) in the broadcast of *The Company of Heaven* on 29 September. The score included a setting for tenor and orchestra of Emily Brontë's lyric, 'A Thousand, Thousand Gleaming Fires', the very first vocal

setting made expressly for Pears and one that already reflects Britten's instinctive affinity with his particular vocal qualities.

105. *Winterset* (1936), political drama directed by Alfred Santell (1895–1981), in which an immigrant political extremist is wrongly accused and executed for a murder, and then railroaded into a conviction because of the public's fear of his beliefs – a contemporary tale if there ever was one.
106. Britten did indeed stand his ground and the dedication reads: 'To F.B. A tribute with affection and admiration.' However he did draw the line at publishing the detailed programme he wrote into the manuscript, showing how each variation helps build up a detailed character study of his beloved teacher.
107. *On the Frontier* (1938), play by W. H. Auden and Christopher Isherwood (dedicated to Britten), premiered by The Group Theatre at the Cambridge Arts Theatre on 14 November 1938. Britten again provided the incidental music for this production.
108. Little did Britten imagine at the time that within eighteen months he too would be fleeing Europe (in the company of Peter Pears) and would spend three years living in North America.
109. It is astonishing to think that Britten could actually score a work for soloists, chorus, organ, timpani and strings while listening to a Strauss Prom!
110. Stravinsky *Capriccio* for piano and orchestra (1929).
111. *Episode* (1935), romantic comedy set in old Vienna, starring Paula Wessely, directed by Walter Reisch (1903–83).
112. *Le roman d'un tricheur* (1936), comedy directed by and starring Sacha Guitry (1885–1957).
113. Frank Bridge eventually found the clue to Britten's predicament. Britten had originally started the song with a descending glissando on the piano as the opening flourish. Bridge told him he was trying to replicate a side-drum and he would do better to write more idiomatically for the piano and replace the glissando with a descending arpeggio. Once Britten had adopted this suggestion, the rest of Britten's setting of Auden's 'Let the florid music praise!' fell into place, based as it is on fanfare-like arpeggios.
114. *Out of the Picture*, for which Britten was to write the incidental music.
115. The BBC Chorus of the day would have been recruited from church musicians and spent much of their time providing the music for the Daily Service, but it must be said in their defence that *The Company of Heaven* frequently sets religiously inspired or biblical texts, so it was not unreasonable of them to think that an ecclesiastical style might be expected of them.
116. It was always to be Britten's lot in life to provide for his wider family.
117. Britten was attending the Leeds Festival.
118. Rossini *Petite Messe Solennelle* for soloists, chorus, two pianos and harmonium, the last of what he referred to as his 'sins of old age'.

119. Walton's *In Honour of the City of London* for mixed chorus and orchestra (1937), a setting of an eponymous poem written for King James IV of Scotland's marriage in 1501 to Mary Tudor. This was the work's premiere, given by Leeds Festival Chorus (to whom it is dedicated) with the London Philharmonic Orchestra, conducted by Sir Malcolm Sargent.
120. Berkeley *Jonah*, oratorio for soloists, chorus and orchestra (1935), whose premiere Berkeley conducted at the Leeds Festival.
121. 'Not Even Summer Yet' (text by Peter Burra), posthumously published by Faber Music in 1994 in a volume of Britten's hitherto unpublished songs, *The Red Cockatoo & Other Songs*; 'As It Is, Plenty', published as the last of five songs in his Auden collection, *On This Island*, Op. 11.
122. The first and third songs of *On This Island*.
123. *Children at School* (Realist for British Commercial Gas Association, 1937), produced by John Grierson and directed by Basil Wright.
124. Beethoven *Missa solemnis*.
125. Encouraged by Poppy Vulliamy, Britten was taking on the responsibility for a Basque orphan.
126. This seems to be a reference to Robert's 'newly made & very intimate friends', to whom Britten refers in his diary entry on 14 August, and implies that the 'bust up' with Robert involved a third party. Worse still, the criticism of Britten might have originated with Marjorie.
127. Strange and a little frustrating that Britten makes no comment about any impression Stravinsky made on him personally, though this was perhaps a very passing encounter.
128. *On This Island* now completed, and *Mont Juic* entering its final stage – Britten completing the scoring of his two movements for the suite on 12 December.
129. Bridge *The Sea*, suite for orchestra (1912), and *Blow Out, You Bugles* (1918), for tenor and orchestra.
130. The London Group is an artists' exhibiting society launched in 1913 (and still in existence today), created to challenge the dominance of the Royal Academy, which was considered unadventurous and conservative.
131. Brahms *Tragic Overture*, Op. 81; *Ein deutsches Requiem*, Op. 45.
132. Clearly Britten had not successfully put an end to this friendship, however much he felt the need to do so.
133. Toscanini's final concert of the season with the BBC Symphony Orchestra and Choral Society at London's Queen's Hall: Beethoven's first and last symphonies. The soloists in the 'Choral' Symphony were Isobel Baillie, Mary Jarred, Barry Johns and Harold Williams.
134. Britten was collaborating again with Auden, this time on a BBC radio feature, *Hadrian's Wall*, while he was completing the orchestration of *Mont Juic*.
135. An enterprise launched by two émigré musicians, the musicologist George Knepler and composer Ernst Schoen, its development halted by the onset of war.

NOTES: 1938

1. Bridge *Phantasm* for piano and orchestra (1931).
2. Bartók *Music for Strings, Percussion and Celesta* (1936), commissioned by Paul Sacher, for whom Britten was later to write his *Cantata Academica*, Op. 62 (1959).
3. *God's Chillun* (GPO, 1938), not one of the more distinguished GPO documentaries, this film is a compilation of an extraordinary array of images, compiled to fit a soundtrack comprising a poem by Auden, and music by Britten with a Caribbean slant. Its lack of success has been put down to the fact that this short half-reeler had three editors and a sound-recordist, but neither a producer nor a director.
4. Possibly intended for a second volume of *On This Island* Auden settings; occasionally sung in place of 'Seascape' in performances of *On This Island* given by Britten and Pears during the 1940s.
5. *Lines on the Map*, a series of four BBC radio programmes dealing with different aspects of national and international communications, written (like *Hadrian's Wall*) for the BBC staff producer, John Pudney.
6. Auden and Isherwood were travelling to China to gather material for their book on the Sino-Japanese conflict, *Journey to a War* (1939). See Plate 30.
7. Pears had been on tour in America with the New English Singers.
8. Despite the success of this sing-through for Ralph Hawkes, Boosey & Hawkes did not publish these cabaret songs and indeed they remained unpublished and largely unperformed (by anyone other than Hedli Anderson) throughout Britten's lifetime, only returning to the public domain after they were published by Faber Music in 1980.
9. Britten making one of his last visits to his parents' graves before the war. Within a year he decided to give America a go, travelling with Peter Pears, and they were not to return till the height of the war, in March 1942.
10. At the marriage of Britten's sister Beth to Kit Welford, Sophie Wyss sang Britten's early setting of Hilaire Belloc's *The Birds*, the song he wrote for his mother. The song dates back to 1929 and was originally written for soprano and strings, being retouched many times before it reached its final published version, for soprano and piano, in 1934. Sophie Wyss gave its premiere in this version, with Britten at the piano, in a BBC National broadcast on 13 March 1936. See Plate 21.
11. The Old Mill, at Snape in Suffolk, which Britten had acquired in July 1937. It was being reconstructed for him under the supervision of Kit Welford's architect father, Arthur.
12. Peter Pears' temporary London flat, at 17 Harley Mews, W1, on loan from a friend, Iris Holland Rogers; Britten did not have a London address at this time and he and Pears were looking for an apartment that they might share.
13. Tchaikovsky Symphony No. 5 in E minor, Op. 64; Franck *Psyché*, symphonic poem for orchestra.

14. *One Hundred Men and a Girl* (1937), musical comedy starring Deanna Durbin, directed by Henry Koster (1905–88).
15. *On This Island.*
16. *Casanare*, a cargo ship built in 1924, in use by Elders & Fyffes Ltd for the banana trade.
17. Britten had been commissioned by the BBC to write a Piano Concerto (his Op. 13, composed between 7 February and 26 July and dedicated to Lennox Berkeley) for the 1938 Promenade Concerts. Britten himself was to be the soloist in the premiere with the BBC Symphony Orchestra under Sir Henry Wood at London's Queen's Hall on 18 August 1938.
18. Dodo Welford, Kit Welford's mother, whom Britten always referred to as 'D.W.'.
19. The Welfords' dog.
20. Mahler Symphony No. 8 in E flat major, 'Symphony of a Thousand' (1907).
21. The plan was for Britten to share the accommodation at The Old Mill with Lennox Berkeley.
22. A common occurrence during heavy rain or high tides, as referenced in Montagu Slater's libretto for Britten's Suffolk-based opera, *Peter Grimes.*
23. Dunwich had been the capital of East Anglia, and was a prosperous sea port and wool trading centre during the early Middle Ages, with a natural harbour formed by the mouths of the River Blyth and the River Dunwich, most of which has since been lost to erosion. Its decline began in 1286 when a sea surge hit the East Anglian coast, and it was eventually reduced through coastal erosion to the village it is today.
24. Britten completed the entire Piano Concerto in little more than five months.
25. 43 Nevern Square, London SW5, the former home of Richard Wood, brother of the mezzo-soprano Anne Wood, who was a member of the BBC Singers with Pears.
26. *Snow White and the Seven Dwarfs* (1937), Walt Disney's first full-length animation.
27. Alan Britten.
28. *Captains Courageous* (1937), adventure based on the novel by Rudyard Kipling, starring Spencer Tracy, Lionel Barrymore, Melvyn Douglas and Mickey Rooney, directed by Victor Fleming (1889–1949).
29. *Dead End* (1937), crime drama set in New York, starring Humphrey Bogart, directed by William Wyler (1902–81).
30. *A Cradle Song: Sleep, Beauty Bright*, for soprano, contralto and piano, a setting of William Blake – a poem that Britten was to reset as the first song of *A Charm of Lullabies*, Op. 47, written in 1947 for the mezzo-soprano Nancy Evans.
31. *The World of the Spirit*, again written for R. Ellis Roberts and of a similar format to the Michaelmas programme *The Company of Heaven*, being scored for speakers, soloists, chorus and orchestra, though this time for the full forces of the BBC Orchestra. Britten began the score in April, finishing the

orchestration on 24 May 1938. The broadcast was on the BBC National programme on 5 June 1938, with Felix Aylmer, Leo Genn and Robert Speaight as speakers, Sophie Wyss, Anne Wood, Emlyn Bebb and Victor Harding as vocal soloists, with the BBC Singers (Section B) and the BBC Orchestra (Section C), conducted by Trevor Harvey.

32. Christopher [Kit] Wood (1901–30), a highly gifted English artist who was addicted to opium and died tragically young, falling under a train, either by accident or design.
33. *Trial of a Judge* (1938), tragedy in five acts by Stephen Spender (1909–95), receiving its first production by the Group Theatre.
34. Britten and Berkeley collaborated in writing incidental music for the Montagu Slater play, *Spain*, to be produced by the Binyon Puppet Theatre.
35. Grace Williams *Fantasia on Welsh Nursery Tunes* (1940), one of her most successful and frequently performed works.
36. False modesty on Britten's part – the score stands the test of time as one of his most impressive early compositions.
37. Berkeley *The Judgement of Paris* (1938).
38. *H.P.O. [Heavenly Post Office]* or *6d Telegram* (GPO, 1938), animation by Lotte Reiniger, the final release of which had music by Brian Easdale, not Britten.
39. See *Letters from a Life* Plate 29b.
40. A characteristic example of Britten's thrift, doubtless inherited from his father, but somewhat at odds with his sense of courtesy and good manners.
41. Father of President John Fitzgerald Kennedy (1917–63).
42. Possibly Britten's recently completed setting of Auden's 'Fish in the Unruffled Lakes'.
43. This never materialised, possibly because of Britten's departure for the US early the following year.
44. Farnham, where Nannie Scarce and her sister had retired, was a very short distance from Britten's new home at Snape.
45. A Basque orphan refugee whom Britten fostered, though the arrangement lasted a very short period of time (just two weeks) because it created such tension with his housekeeper, Mrs Hearn.
46. *On This Island.*
47. Having left the BBC Singers in October 1937 to tour America with the New English Singers, on his return Pears joined the Glyndebourne Festival Chorus for the 1938 season.
48. *The World of the Spirit.*
49. Britten had certainly made life difficult for himself in the midst of fulfilling two BBC commissions, for *The World of the Spirit* and the Piano Concerto.
50. This broadcast of the *Variations on a Theme of Frank Bridge* is yet another indication of how quickly Britten's new scores were being taken up by the BBC Orchestras.
51. Britten refers to Franco and Mussolini and the Vatican's recognition of Franco's Catholic, Fascist Spain.

52. Britten finding this period of Strauss to be rather too rich for his tastes.
53. *The Chartists' March*, another commission from the BBC, for producer John Pudney.
54. *Boys will be Boys* (1935), comedy starring Will Hay, directed by William Beaudine (1892–1970).
55. *Le roi s'amuse* (1909), classic silent short after the Victor Hugo play, directed by Albert Capellani (1874–1931) and Michel Carré (1865–1945).
56. *The Chartists' March*, radio feature on Chartism, BBC National programme, 9.35 p.m.
57. Britten loved birdwatching and listening for bird-calls: see *Pictures from a Life*, Plate 380.
58. *Break The News* (1938), musical comedy starring Maurice Chevalier and Jack Buchanan, directed by René Clair.
59. Francis Barton had been staying with Britten in his London flat and at Snape, and Britten's devotion to him is evident. Their friendship was to endure throughout their lives.
60. A work that was to have a lasting impression on Britten, influencing much of the *War Requiem*.
61. *The World of the Spirit*.
62. Mozart Symphony No. 41 in C, 'Jupiter', K551; Schubert Symphony No. 9, 'Great' C major, D944.
63. Britten was extraordinarily fortunate with his key publishers and representatives, notably Ralph Hawkes and Erwin Stein at Boosey & Hawkes, and later, Donald Mitchell at Boosey & Hawkes and Faber Music – all three became close and valued friends as well as much-respected colleagues.
64. Britten's Suite, Op. 6, for violin and piano.
65. *Horse Feathers* (1932), Marx Brothers film, directed by Norman Z. McLeod (1898–1964).
66. Brahms Symphony No. 2 in D, Op. 73; Sibelius Symphony No. 2 in D, Op. 43.
67. Britten was eventually to replace this 'Recitative and Aria' movement with an 'Impromptu' (which drew on material from his incidental music for *King Arthur*), when revising the Piano Concerto in 1945.

Postlude

The ceremony of innocence is drowned
W. B. Yeats, 'The Second Coming', quoted by Myfanwy Piper in her libretto for Britten's chamber opera, *The Turn of the Screw* (1954)

On 16 June 1938, the daily journal begun by E. B. Britten on 1 January 1928 came to an abrupt and final end. There had already been occasional hiatuses in the progress of the diary in the past – notably on the day of his car accident (a page left blank) – and the 1937 journal peters out entirely, just three days short of Britten's twenty-fourth birthday. Though he continued to use Letts Schoolboy's Pocket Diaries to note engagements throughout his adult life, Britten never again kept anything approaching a daily record of his innermost thoughts. But why stop now? Why, halfway through June 1938? One is tempted to conclude that after a decade of writing about his life, his work, and his deepest emotions, he was now ready to live life to the full, and stop trying to analyse it through a personal commentary. So much had happened in the intervening years. The boy who reluctantly left home to pursue his destiny in London had lost first his father, in April 1934, and then his beloved mother, in January 1937 – at twenty-three, and a very *young* twenty-three at that, he was now, in his own words, an orphan.

For three years, Britten's older, more worldly-wise homosexual friends, W. H. Auden and Christopher Isherwood, had done their best to help him feel more comfortable about his homosexuality, with varying and limited success. Britten's close and often intense relationship with his mother was undoubtedly an inhibiting factor – though it might be argued that the strong moral fibre, work ethic and self-control that his mother instilled in her son, was to stand Britten in very good stead as he faced some of the challenges of his life and confronted some of his own demons.

There had been signs of willingness, on his part, to experiment and find himself, and his friends were certainly sympathetic and eager to help. After a disagreeable encounter with Barcelona's night life on 22 April 1936, the following January Ronald Duncan had tried to awaken any heterosexual inclination that Britten might have harboured during a (not surprisingly) unsuccessful visit to a Paris brothel. Six months later, on 3 July, Christopher Isherwood had got Britten a little drunk during a night out on the town, and treated him to a nocturnal visit to the Jermyn Street Turkish Baths, then a favourite haunt for London homosexuals. As Britten's diary entry for that day attests, it was not an altogether unpleasant experience: 'It is extraordinary to find one's resistance to anything gradually weakening,' he wrote, clearly surprising himself with his new-found valour and his willingness to explore something that had remained in check for so long. On a more private and personal level, it is clear that Lennox Berkeley had been very drawn to Britten, as the diary entries from Crantock in July and August 1936 demonstrate. 'It is extraordinary how intimate one becomes when the lights are out!' Britten writes on 29 July; and it would seem that the intimacy had been significant, as Britten goes on to write the following day, 'In spite of his avowed sexual weakness for young men of my age & form – he is considerate & open, & we have come to an agreement on that subject.' But Berkeley persists in his advances, and we find Britten writing again the following spring, on 11 April 1937: 'before bed – long & deep conversation with Lennox – he is a dear & I am very, very fond of him; nevertheless, it is a comfort that we can arrange sexual matters to at least my satisfaction.' Though this was never to develop into a love affair of any significance, Britten and Berkeley were to remain devoted friends and colleagues throughout their lives, and when Berkeley later married, Britten was to become godfather to his first son Michael – also, as it turned out, a very gifted composer.

A more shadowy character from this period of experimentation, though one to whom Britten was clearly attracted, for a while at least, was the advertising executive, Alan George. He had courted Britten after their chance meeting at the Behrends' house party in July 1937, and the two men met on more than one occasion thereafter. Britten soon sensed that the relationship was not what he was looking for, but perhaps felt the need of the attention and affection, now that he had been somewhat cast adrift – feeling the loss of his parents and, with Beth now engaged to Kit Welford, seeing all three of his siblings in happy relationships.

What is abundantly clear from the course of these diaries is Britten's need to be in the company of children, and the joy he derived from their innocent and uncomplicated friendship. More problematically, one also senses his need to befriend younger boys, in their early adolescence, and here lies a possible clue as to why these daily journals came to so abrupt an end in the middle of 1938. Britten had found the opportunity to talk both to his brother Robert and his close school friend, John Pounder, about his 'queerness', but only in the privacy of his diaries did he confront his need to spend time with much *younger* male friends, with all the dangers this entailed. One must remember that for a homosexual of any persuasion in the 1930s, there was the very real danger of imprisonment and public humiliation, and it is clear that Britten is acutely aware of this when writing his diaries. On more than one occasion he qualifies the information he shares with his journal, particularly in terms of the impetus for certain friendships, or the nature of the relationship, or the detail of sleeping arrangements, or, more explicitly, the absence of any 'sexual' attraction that might tarnish an otherwise pure impulse for a particular friendship. Think back to entries referring to his 'paramour' Francis Barton, or Piers Dunkerley ('Tell it not in Gath'), or Harry Morris, whose presence on a family holiday seems to have precipitated a major rift between Britten and his brother Robert.

W. H. Auden later confronted the matter in a letter to Britten, in which he expressed concern about Britten's 'attraction to thin-as-a-board juveniles . . . the sexless & innocent'. And this was indeed Britten's 'weakness', one that he battled with: later in life, with the loving help of his partner, Peter Pears, he learned to keep it in check, but this was not always the case during this pre-war period. Britten's naivety and sexual inexperience did not always equip him with the antennae to sense the dangers that these relationships brought with them. This is particularly true in the case of Harry Morris, whose abrupt departure from the family holiday in Crantock is not mentioned in Britten's diaries, because he stopped writing altogether for five days. The scenario was later pieced together by John Bridcut, for his award-winning BBC television documentary in 2004, and later publication, *Britten's Children* (pp. 46–53), in which he tells of Morris's belief that Britten had made a sexual advance to him during the holiday. Beth Britten makes a very matter-of-fact reference to the incident in her own book, recalling Britten's surprise and horror at discovering that Harry was going to wear the new pyjamas Britten had provided for the holiday *over* his underwear. Whether this was misconstrued by the boy as inappropriate intimacy, or whether Britten did in fact overstep the mark, we will never know; but the fact that Harry and Britten met again in London, after the holidays, presumably with the blessing of Harry's mother, would suggest that the incident did no immediate damage. Later in life, Harry seems to have become more haunted by the incident, perhaps because Britten's homosexuality was by then more widely known and understood. Whatever the truth of the matter, Britten had, in Bridcut's words, 'bumped into a boundary fence, which reminded him of the moral framework of his upbringing. If there ever was a moment of madness . . . it was never to recur.' One wonders, in retrospect, whether Britten's 'bust up' with Robert during this holiday period was in some way related to his friendship with Harry. It seems that Robert and his wife didn't welcome the boy's arrival in Crantock, if Britten's diary entry for 14 August is to be believed. And a later diary entry, on 17 October, also implies that some level of criticism had been communicated by Robert, originating from 'a comparative stranger' (perhaps the 'newly made & very intimate friends' Robert and Marjorie had made in Crantock), quite possibly about the idea of a twenty-three-year-old man befriending a thirteen-year-old boy.

In this context, the five blank pages in the diaries in the summer of 1937 speak volumes, and in their own way are as significant as any of the entries that touch on these complex and troubling issues in more explicit terms. But Britten's habit of avoiding difficult issues by setting his journal aside might also explain why the 1938 diary comes to so abrupt an end, and indeed why he never resumed his journal thereafter.

The International Society of Contemporary Music Festival for 1938 was held in London, opening on 17 June – coincidentally just a day after Britten stopped writing his journal. During the Festival Britten renewed his acquaintance with Hermann Scherchen, who was conducting the British premiere of Webern's *Das Augenlicht* and Gerhard's *Albade, Interludi, I Dansa*. He discussed the *Bridge Variations* with Scherchen, who was sufficiently impressed by the new score to take it up immediately for his forthcoming concerts in Europe. During the course of their meeting Scherchen mentioned that his ex-wife and son, Wulff, were now living in England, not far from Britten's East Anglian home in Snape. The family had fled Europe because of the growing threat of Nazi persecution; Hermann settling in Switzerland and his wife and son in Cambridge, where Wulff, still a schoolboy, was studying English. Britten immediately recalled a magical day he had spent with Wulff in Siena – in April 1934, during the ISCM Festival in Florence – when they had shared Britten's raincoat to protect them from a shower. As Wulff Scherchen recalled in 1989:

> A light shower caught us as we walked on towards Siena. Ben happened to be carrying a mac, which he insisted we share. He had his right arm in one sleeve, I had my left in the other. We found the experience uproarious, as did the rest of the party. Though nothing of any consequence was said or done at the time, it was an occasion of light-hearted and shared contentment, which I still recall with fondness and pleasure.

The memory was clearly a fond and special one for Britten too. On 25 June, just nine days after closing his journal and his private thoughts from any possibility of public scrutiny, Britten wrote a letter that was to have a profound impact on the next eleven months of his life, and might even have precipitated a move that would affect his fortunes for the next four years. The letter invited Wulff to come from Cambridge to visit him, either at his London flat or at Snape. The friendship that ensued between the seventeen-year-old schoolboy and the twenty-four-year-old composer was significant for both parties, and shattering in its impact on Britten himself. For the first time in his life he had yielded to a love affair with another male and the effects were profound. Enid Slater, the wife of the writer Montagu Slater (with whom Britten was then collaborating on the Binyon puppet-play, *Spain*) observed the relationship develop at first hand and, as a keen photographer, she documented the affair in some of the most telling informal photographs from this period. The relationship that flourished between Wulff and Britten, from June 1938 to May 1939, is painstakingly documented and interpreted with great sensitivity, balance and human insight by John Bridcut in the television film, *Britten's Children*. Two years after making the documentary, Bridcut turned his research and materials into a book of the same title published by Faber and Faber, and I commend this to any reader who wishes to understand this vulnerable aspect of Britten's psyche in a broader perspective. Enid Slater's photographs (Plates 7–10 in *Britten's Children*) speak volumes about the closeness of the relationship: the age difference seems hardly discernible, Britten looking much younger than his years and Wulff looking almost like his contemporary. But as Bridcut points out in his very persuasive narrative, unless Britten was communicating through music with his contemporaries, he invariably found it easier, and certainly more congenial, to be in the presence of young people – and amongst those, boys held a pride of place.

When I was working as Research Scholar at the Britten–Pears Library and Archive in the early 1980s, Donald Mitchell and I paid a visit to Enid Slater at her Highgate home, to interview her for the Archive. She recalled this period in Britten's life as vividly as she'd caught it in her photographs. As Britten's letters to her confirm, she had been perhaps more closely involved in the circumstances surrounding this affair than any other of Britten's circle, though it is clear that he had discussed his feelings for Wulff in some detail with Pears, Berkeley, Auden and Isherwood. Enid Slater was very clear about the implications of such a relationship for Britten and, indeed, the risks involved. Her take on the situation, and Pears' role in its resolution, was precise and unsentimental.

> I had known of – and in one case been involved in – some of Ben's other relationships. One relationship had got difficult before he went to America

> and I used to go and try and sort things out a bit. And when Peter came on the scene, I must say I was very relieved. I liked Peter at once. And I thought this relationship is right, you know, this is absolutely perfect. And I think everybody, all his friends who wished him well, were thankful, because a lot of them didn't know about the other problematical relationships, but could sense that he was searching around a bit, that he wanted some sort of stable relationship in his life.

In fact, very soon Pears did take Britten away from the 'difficult' relationship that was developing (on Britten's side at least) with the young Scherchen – and probably further away and for longer than either man had anticipated. On 29 April 1939 Britten and Pears boarded the *SS Ausonia* in Southampton, bound for North America, where, first by accident and then design, they were to remain until March 1942. They travelled as close friends, not lovers, and there is no doubting from Britten's sometimes desperate letters to Wulff and Enid Slater that he was still as besotted as ever with his young 'Apollo' (as he called him). Indeed, he poured out his ecstatic feelings into a fanfare for piano and strings entitled *Young Apollo* – unquestionably a salutation to Wulff – that he wrote in Canada, at the start of the trip. But life was changing for Britten, and his time in the United States was having a turbulent and maturing impact on this Peter Pan of music. As he travelled with Pears in those early months, the nature of their relationship began to change. While still in Toronto in early June 1939, at the very start of their travels south to New York, they realised that they were falling in love with one another, as Pears later told their friend and artistic collaborator, the opera director Basil Coleman. Travelling on to stay with friends of Pears in Grand Rapids, Michigan (from 12 June) their relationship was at last consummated, as Pears later reminded Britten in two love letters, more than thirty years apart. The first was written just seven months after their trip to Grand Rapids, when they found themselves temporarily apart and Britten revisited the town alone on business – Pears wrote to him from New York, 'I shall never forget a certain night in Grand Rapids. Ich liebe dich [. . .] I'm terribly in love with you.' Then in 1974, towards the end of Britten's life, when Pears was singing in the American premiere of *Death in Venice* at the Metropolitan Opera, his separation from Britten again led him to thoughts of their thirty-five year journey together through life, as lovers and creative partners: 'it is <u>you</u> who have given <u>me</u> everything, right from the beginning, from yourself in Grand Rapids.'

The gradual shifting of Britten's affections, back in 1939, can be clearly traced in the dedications of the individual movements of *Les Illuminations*, the Rimbaud song-cycle he had begun before his departure and completed in the United States. The transition from obsession with Wulff to a deeper and more lasting commitment to Pears – a commitment the singer later referred to as a 'pledge' – is reflected in *Les Illuminations*, whose most famous interpreter Pears, poignantly, would become. Early in the cycle is a setting of Rimbaud's *Gracieux fils de Pan* (*Antique*), which is dedicated to 'K.H.W.S.', Wulff's initials; but later we encounter *Being Beauteous*, 'to P.N.L.P' – Peter Neville Luard Pears. Britten had still to get Wulff out of his system, but it was clear by now that he fully intended to. He even withdrew *Young Apollo*, despite having assigned it an opus number, and suppressed it from publication throughout his life. After a serious illness in February/March 1940, Britten told Beata Mayer – the daughter of their Amityville hosts, and a cherished friend who was nursing him back to health – that 'Peter is a rock.' When writing to friends and family back home, meanwhile, to assure them of his full recovery and fast-improving health, he confided, 'Peter has been sweet & nothing too much trouble for him', '[he] looks after me like a lover.'

And the rest, as they say, is history.

Personalia

ABENDROTH, Hermann (1883–1956)
German conductor, Kapellmeister of the Leipzig Gewandhaus Orchestra (1934–45).

ADDLESHAW, D. H.
German master at Gresham's School, Holt.

AHLERS, Annie (1906–33)
German singing actress.

AHLERSMEYER, Mathieu (1896–1979)
German baritone in the ensembles at Hamburg and Dresden; created the role of Danton in the Salzburg Festival premiere of von Einem's *Dantons Tod*.

ALEXANDER, Misses Agnes and Hannah
Mrs Britten's next-door neighbours in Frinton.

ALFORD, Violet
Fellow lodger at Princes Square; authority on the dance customs of Western Europe and expert on the traditional dancing of the Basque region.

ALLCHIN, Basil Charles (1878–1957)
Professor at the Royal College of Music (1920–47) and College Registrar (1935–9).

ALLEN, Sir Hugh Percy (1869–1946)
English organist, conductor and musical administrator, knighted in 1920; Director of the Royal College of Music (1918–37).

ALLIN, Norman (1884–1973)
English bass.

ALSTON, Audrey [Mrs Lincolne Sutton] (1883–1966)
English violinist, violist and teacher; founder of the Norwich String Quartet; Britten's viola teacher from 1923.

ALSTON, Christopher (b. 1917)
Younger son of Audrey Alston.

ALSTON, John (1914–96)
Son of Audrey Alston and a contemporary and close friend of Britten; a gifted musician who studied at Lancing College, Sussex (at the same time as Peter Pears, who was four years his senior), returning to the school as Director of Music (1948–74).

AMAR QUARTET [Also known as the Amar–Hindemith Quartet]
Licco Amar, Walter Caspar (violins), Paul Hindemith (viola), Rudolf Hindemith (cello).

AMORY, Mr and Mrs

Lowestoft friends; they and their daughter Helen were tennis and bridge partners of the Brittens.

ANDAY, Rosette (1903–77)

Hungarian mezzo-soprano; sang regularly at the Vienna State Opera (1921–61).

ANDERSON, (Millicent) Hedli (1907–90)

English singer and actress; married Louis MacNeice (1907–63) in 1942; performed in the first productions of the Auden/Isherwood play, *The Ascent of F6*, and MacNeice's radio-drama, *The Dark Tower* (1946), both with incidental music by Britten.

ANDREWS, (H)erbert (K)ennedy (1904–65)

Northern Irish music scholar, teacher, organist, composer and editor.

ANDREWS, J. G.

A Farfield House boy at Gresham's, one year Britten's senior.

ANSERMET, Ernest (1883–1969)

Swiss conductor of the Suisse Romande Orchestra; noted interpreter of the French repertory and the music of Stravinsky; later became a champion of Britten's music, conducting the premiere of *The Rape of Lucretia* at Glyndebourne (1946) and the *Cantata Misericordium* in Geneva (1963).

ARNAUD, Yvonne (1892–1958)

French actress.

ARNOLD FAMILY

Lowestoft neighbours and friends; drapers at 95/97a/100 London Road North, Lowestoft.

ASTLE, Ethel M. K. (1876–1952)

Britten's first piano teacher; with her older sister, ran Southolme, the pre-preparatory school at 52 Kirkley Cliff Road, Lowestoft.

ATKINSON, Misses

Fellow lodgers at Princes Square; older sister, Ruby, was a secretary at Hill's, the famous violin dealers in London.

ATKINSON, George

South Lodge contemporary of Britten.

AUDEN, Wystan Hugh (1907–73)

English poet, dramatist and librettist; Britten's many collaborations with Auden include incidental music for *Coal Face* (1935) and *Night Mail* (1936) for the GPO Film Unit; *The Ascent of F6* (1937) and *On The Frontier* (1938) for The Group Theatre; and *Our Hunting Fathers*, Op. 8 (1936), *On This Island*, Op. 11 (1937), *Ballad of Heroes*, Op. 14 (1939), *Four Cabaret Songs* (1937–9), and the operetta *Paul Bunyan*, Op. 17 (1941).

AUNTS: Britten and Hockey

Aunt Effie: see under Euphemia Maud Hockey

Aunt Flo: see under Florence Hay Britten

Aunt Janie: see under Jane Hockey
Aunt Julianne: see under Julie Annie Painter
Aunt Louise: see under (Mary) Louise Fernnie
Aunt Nellie: see under Ellen Elizabeth Harmer
Aunt Queenie: see under Sarah Fanny Hockey

AUSTIN, Henry Wilfred [Bunny] (1906–2000)
British tennis player.

AUSTIN, Mabel [Laulie]
One of Britten's godparents; family friend and amateur musician who lived in Liverpool.

AUSTRAL, Florence (1892–1968)
Australian soprano; great Wagnerian and notable Isolde and Brünnhilde.

AVELING, Elizabeth
Senior pupil and scholar at the RCM; daughter of Claude Aveling, the College Registrar.

BACK, Mr and Mrs
Proprietors of Backs Ltd, Wine & Spirit Merchants, Bevan Street, Lowestoft.

BACKHAUS, Wilhelm (1884–1969)
German pianist and noted Beethoven interpreter.

BAINTON, Edgar (1880–1956)
English composer, pianist and teacher; Director of the Music School in Newcastle-upon-Tyne (1912–33) and an external examiner at the RCM.

BAKLANOFF, Georgy Andreyevich (1881–1938)
Russian baritone at the Vienna State Opera.

BALFOUR, Margaret (?–1961)
English contralto; sang The Angel in Elgar's recording of *The Dream of Gerontius* (1927); one of the original sixteen singers for whom Vaughan Williams wrote the *Serenade to Music* (1938).

BALLS, J. L.
Farfield House boy at Gresham's, contemporary of Britten's.

BANKS, Ernest
Schoolmaster, living at 20 Corton Street, Lowestoft, whose daughter attended musical evenings at the Colemans.

BANTOCK, Sir Granville (1868–1946)
English composer, knighted in 1930.

BARBIROLLI, [Sir] John (1899–1970)
English conductor and cellist, knighted in 1949; while Chief Conductor of the New York Philharmonic Orchestra (1936–42) he conducted the premiere of Britten's Violin Concerto, Op. 15, with Antonio Brosa at Carnegie Hall on 28 March 1940. He returned to the UK in 1943 as Chief Conductor of the Hallé Orchestra, where he remained until his death.

BARLOW, Henry [Harry] (1870–1932)
English tuba-player; principal tuba of the BBC Symphony Orchestra (1930–2).

BARRAUD, Francis (1856–1924)
English painter famous for his painting *Dog Looking at and Listening to a Phonograph*, later renamed *His Master's Voice* and adopted as the image of the HMV Record Company.

BARTLETT, Ethel (1896–1978) and ROBERTSON, Rae (1893–1956)
British piano duo; travelled extensively in Europe and the Americas, married and worked exclusively in duo partnership; Britten wrote his *Introduction and Rondo alla Burlesca*, Op. 23 No. 1 (1940), *Mazurka Elegiaca*, Op. 23 No. 2 (1941), and *Scottish Ballad*, Op. 26 (1941) for them.

BARTÓK, Béla (1881–1945)
Hungarian composer, pianist, conductor and ethnomusicologist; published by Boosey & Hawkes, like Britten; the two men met at the ISCM Festival in New York in 1941.

BARTON, Francis C. (1916–2001)
Contemporary at South Lodge who enjoyed a warm and lasting friendship with Britten, well beyond his school days. The 'Burlesque' from Britten's *Three Divertimenti* for string quartet (1936) is dedicated to Barton. His sisters Joy and Madeline were also part of the Britten family circle. Barton had a successful career in the Royal Marines (1934–66), rising to the rank of Major-General.

BARRIE, J. M. (1860–1937)
Scottish dramatist; author of *Peter Pan.*

BAUER, Harold (1873–1951)
Anglo-German-American pianist.

BAX, Arnold (1883–1953)
English composer, knighted in 1937; appointed Master of the King's Music in 1942.

BBC SYMPHONY ORCHESTRA
Founded in 1930 by Adrian Boult; London's first permanent orchestra and now the flagship orchestra of the British Broadcasting Corporation.

BBC WIRELESS SINGERS
Founded in 1924 by Stanford Robinson as The Wireless Chorus; established as a full-time professional octet in 1927 and renamed The Wireless Singers; expanded in 1934 with an additional octet of singers; the combined forces renamed the BBC Singers 'A' and 'B' in 1935. Peter Pears was contracted to this ensemble from July 1934 to November 1936.

BECK, Conrad (1901–89)
Swiss composer.

BEECHAM, Sir Thomas (1879–1961)
English conductor, knighted in 1916; formed the Beecham Opera Company (subsequently the British National Opera Company) in 1915, the London Philharmonic Orchestra in 1932 and the Royal Philharmonic Orchestra in 1946; conducted Britten's Violin Concerto with Bronislaw Gimpel and the Royal Philharmonic Orchestra at the Royal Festival Hall on 12 December 1951, during the Festival of Britain.

BEHREND, John Louis (1882–1972) and Mary (1883–1997)
Noted patrons of the arts, particularly of English artists and writers, including Stanley Spencer (1891–1959) and Lytton Strachey (1880–1932). Though originally great friends of Peter Pears and Peter Burra, they also became great supporters of Britten and his many enterprises after the war, generously supporting the English Opera Group and the Aldeburgh Festival. They sponsored the first recital Pears and Britten gave on their return to England from America in 1942. Britten's Second String Quartet, Op. 36 (1945) is dedicated to Mary Behrend.

BELLERBY, D
A Farfield House boy at Gresham's, two years Britten's junior.

BENBOW, Charles Edwin (1904–67)
English composer and pianist; assistant chorus master of the BBC Singers (1933–5); professor at the RCM (1927–67).

BENJAMIN, Arthur (1893–1960)
Australian-English pianist and composer, famous for his *Jamaican Rumba* (1938); professor at the RCM (1926–39) where he was Britten's tutor; Britten's *Holiday Diary*, Op. 5 is dedicated to him.

BERNERS, Lord [Gerald Hugh Tyrwhitt-Wilson] (1883–1950)
English composer, painter, author and diplomat.

BERG, Alban (Maria Johannes) (1885–1935)
Austrian composer of the Second Viennese School, pupil of Schoenberg.

BERGER, Erna (1900–90)
German soprano.

BERGNER, Elizabeth (1897–1986)
Austrian-British stage and screen actress.

BERKELEY, [Sir] Lennox Randall Francis (1903–89)
English composer educated at Gresham's (a decade before Britten) and Oxford (where he was a contemporary of W. H. Auden), and with Nadia Boulanger in Paris (1927–32); knighted in 1974.

BERTHOUD, O(liver) C. (1911–72)
A Howson prefect at Gresham's, two years Britten's senior; a fine musician who became a close friend and remained in touch with Britten in later life as headmaster of Trinity School, Croydon.

BILLISON, Mr
Mr Britten's junior dentist at the Kirkley Cliff practice (1928–30).

BISHOP OF LONDON (1931)
See under Winnington-Ingram.

BITTERAUF, Richard (1900–61)
German bass.

BLACK, Mrs and Mrs James Alexander
Neighbours at 28 Kirkley Cliff Road, their daughter Daphne becoming part of the Britten social circle and the subject of the second of his *Three Pieces* for piano (1930).

BLISS, [Sir] Arthur Drummond (1891–1975)
English composer and conductor of American descent, knighted in 1950; Director of Music at the BBC (1942–4), Master of the Queen's Music (1953–75).

BLUNT, Beryl Scawen (b. 1911)
English viola player, student at the RCM, and a member of the Macnaghten String Quartet.

BLYTH, May (1899–1985)
English soprano.

BOCKELMANN, Rudolf August Louis Wilhelm (1892–1958)
German bass-baritone; appeared throughout the 1934 to 1938 seasons at the Royal Opera House, Covent Garden.

BOND, Elinor
Schoolfriend of Beth Britten at the Woodard School of St Mary and Anne, Abbots Bromley, Staffordshire.

BOND, Muriel
Friend and flatmate of Barbara Britten and Helen Hurst at Holbein House.

BOOSEY, Leslie Arthur (1887–1979)
English music publisher, succeeding his father in charge of the publishing department of the Boosey company in 1919, becoming Chairman in 1930 when Boosey's merged with Hawkes' publishers, and President of Boosey & Hawkes on his retirement in 1963.

BOUGHTON, Ernest
Photographer, 54 London Road, Lowestoft.

BOUGHTON, Rutland (1878–1960)
English composer.

BOULT, Sir Adrian Cedric (1889–1983)
English conductor, knighted in 1937; Musical Director of the BBC and Chief Conductor of the BBC Symphony Orchestra (1930–50); conducted the first broadcast performance of Britten's *Our Hunting Fathers*, Op. 8 in 1937, with Sophie Wyss and the BBC Orchestra.

BOWES-LYON, Miss
A member of the Bowes-Lyon family, related to the then Duchess of York, later Queen Elizabeth, consort to King George VI.

BOYD, Mrs Doveton and Miss Elizabeth
Widowed friend of Mrs Britten, whose daughter, Elizabeth, was a friend of Britten's.

BOYD, Misses Helen and Ethel
Next-door neighbours, living at 22 Kirkley Cliff Road; their young nephews, David and John, were friends of Britten's, the latter being the subject of the first of Britten's *Three Pieces* for piano (1930).

BOYS, (Claude E.) Henry (1910–92)
English critic, composer and teacher; fellow student of Britten's at the RCM (1929–33).

BRADLEY, Annie
Matron of St Luke's Hospital, Kirkley Cliff Road, Lowestoft.

BRAIN, Aubrey (1893–1955)
English horn-player and father of Dennis Brain, for whom Britten wrote the *Serenade*, Op. 31, for tenor, horn and strings (1943), and *Canticle III: Still falls the rain*, Op. 55, for tenor, horn and piano (1954).

BRIDGE (*née* Sinclair) Ethel (1881–1960)
Australian violinist; studied at the RCM where she met Frank Bridge, whom she married in 1908.

BRIDGE, Frank (1879–1941)
English composer and conductor; Britten's composition teacher and mentor.

BRIDSON, D. Geoffrey (1910–80)
English playwright, poet and BBC radio producer.

BRITTEN, Alan (b. 1938)
Second son of Robert and Marjorie Britten.

BRITTEN, (Edith) Barbara (1902–82)
Eldest child of the Britten family.

BRITTEN (*née* Hockey), Edith Rhoda (1872–1937)
Benjamin's mother; gifted pianist and amateur singer, member of the National Chorus and Bach Choir in London; Secretary and occasionally soloist with the Lowestoft Musical Society.

BRITTEN, Edward Benjamin (1913–76)
The Benjamin of the Britten family and the author of these diaries, which tell the story of his early years in his own words.

BRITTEN, (Charlotte) Elizabeth [Beth] (1909–89)
Third child of the Britten family; married Kit Welford in 1938.

BRITTEN, Florence [Aunt Flo] Hay (1875–1956)
R. V. Britten's older sister; graduate of the University of London; teacher who established her own school in Malvern with her sisters Louise and Julie Annie; later became Headmistress of the Girls' High School in Bridgetown, Barbados; retired to Creswell Cottage, Whiteshill near Stroud in Gloucestershire in 1923.

BRITTEN, John Robert Marsh (b. 1932)
First son of Robert and Marjorie Britten.

BRITTEN (*née* Goldson), (Helen) Marjorie (b. 1908)
Robert Britten's girlfriend, soon to be fiancée and wife; they had two boys, John and Alan.

BRITTEN, Robert [Bobby] Harry Marsh (1907–87)
Second child of the Britten family.

BRITTEN, Robert Victor (1877–1934)
Benjamin's father; born in Birkenhead, trained as a dental surgeon at Charing Cross Hospital in London; established his own practice in Lowestoft in 1905, first at 46 Marine Parade and then, from 1908, at 21 Kirkley Cliff Road, where he continued to practise until his death on 6 April 1934 of Hodgkin's disease.

BROSA, Antonio (1894–1979)
Spanish virtuoso violinist for whom Britten wrote *Reveille* and the Violin Concerto

(both of which he premiered); he gave the first complete broadcast and concert performance of the Suite Op. 6 (1934) with Britten in March and April 1936.

BROSA, Peggy
Wife of Antonio Brosa.

BROSA STRING QUARTET
Antonio Brosa, David Wise (violins), Leonard Rubens (viola), Livio Mannucci (cello).

BRUNSKILL, Muriel (1899–1980)
English contralto.

BRYANT, H. F.
A Farfield House boy at Gresham's, nineteen months Britten's senior.

BUCHANAN, Jack (1891–1957)
Musical-comedy actor in the 1930s, whose partner was Elsie Randolph (1904–82).

BUCK, Percy (1871–1947)
Organist and professor at the RCM.

BUCKLAND, Sylvia
Fellow lodger at Burleigh House.

BUESST, Aylmer (1883–1970)
Australian conductor.

BURRA, Helen [Nell] Pomfret (1909–99)
Twin sister of Peter Burra; singer and actress who appeared in a number of Group Theatre productions, as did her husband, John Moody (1906–95), one of the founder members of the company.

BURRA, Peter (1909–37)
English writer on art, music and literature, educated at Lancing and Oxford with Peter Pears; died tragically in an aeroplane accident on 17 April 1937, near Buckley Common in Berkshire.

BURROWS, Benjamin (1891–1960)
English composer.

BUSCH, Adolf (1891–1952)
German violinist and composer; brother of the conductor Fritz Busch (1890–1951).

BUSH, Alan (1900–95)
English composer, pianist and teacher; educated at the Royal Academy of Music where he became a professor in 1925; political activist who joined the Communist Party in 1935.

CAINE, Natalie (1909–2008)
English oboist; premiered Britten's *Temporal Variations* with Adolph Hallis (piano) at the Wigmore Hall in London on 15 December 1936.

CALKIN, David and Jean
Grandchildren of one of Mrs Britten's Christian Scientist friends.

CAMDEN, Archie (1888–1979)
English bassoonist for whom Eric Fogg composed his Concerto in D (1931).

CAMERON, (George) Basil (1884–1975)
English conductor.

CAMPBELL, Peggy
Lowestoft neighbour; friend and regular duet partner of Britten's.

CANNEL, Mary
Member of the Lowestoft Musical Society.

CARTER, Kathleen
Schoolfriend of Beth Britten at the Woodard School of St Mary and Anne, Abbots Bromley, Staffordshire.

CASALS, Pablo [Pau] (1876–1973)
Catalonian virtuoso cellist.

CASELLA, Alfredo (1883–1947)
Italian composer, pianist, conductor and administrator; leading Italian musician of the inter-war years.

CASSADÒ, Gaspar (1897–1966)
Catalonian cellist and composer; leading pupil of Casals.

CATCHPOLE, Mr
Member of the Lowestoft Musical Society.

CATTERALL, Arthur (1883–1943)
English violinist; led both the Hallé and BBC Symphony Orchestra during his career; leader of the Catterall String Quartet.

CAVALCANTI, Alberto (1897–1982)
Brazilian-born sound supervisor, producer and director at the GPO Film Unit.

CEBOTARI, Maria (1910–49)
Romanian-Austrian soprano who died of cancer just a year after the death of her second husband, the Austrian actor, Gustav Diessel. The British pianist, Sir Clifford Curzon, adopted their two sons.

CHAPMAN, Audrey
See under Mrs Audrey Melville.

CHAPMAN, Joyce
Member of the music staff at Gresham's (1925–54); Britten's viola teacher at school.

CHAMBERLAIN, Mrs Kertsy
One of the founders of the Bungay orchestra that Britten conducted in 1934.

CHAMBERS, Mr and Mrs
Friends with whom the Brittens used to holiday in Capel St Andrew when the children were young.

CHARTRES, Frederick W. C.
Agent for the estates of Michael E. St John Barnes and Thomas Meakin Marmiloe. The family lived at Willingham St Mary, Beccles, and played a prominent role in Lowestoft's social scene. Their children, Jean and Clive, were friends of Benjamin.

CHEVALIER, Maurice (1888–1972)
French actor.

CLAR, Yvonne Lichti
Swiss *au pair* at the Britten household for four months in 1929.

CLARK, (Thomas) Edward (1888–1962)
English music administrator and conductor; pupil of Schoenberg; husband of composer Elisabeth Lutyens (1906–83); on the staff of the BBC (1923–36); elected President of the International Society for Contemporary Music in 1947.

CLARKS
Family friends from Bromley in Kent; Mr Clark worked at St Stephen's Walbrook (near the Mansion House in London) and they had two sons, Victor and Gordon.

COATES, Edith (1912–83)
British mezzo-soprano, who was later to create the role of Auntie in Britten's opera *Peter Grimes.*

COATES, John (1865–1941)
English tenor.

COBBETT, W[alter] W[ilson] (1847–1937)
Lexicographer, amateur violinist and patron of chamber music; established the Cobbett Music Prize in 1905 for the composition of single-movement chamber works based on the model of the seventeenth-century Fancy (Phantasy). Britten was awarded the Cobbett Prize at the RCM in 1932 for his *Phantasy* in F minor for string quintet.

COHEN, Harriet (1895–1967)
English pianist; premiered the Elgar Piano Quintet in A minor, Op. 84 and many works of Bax and Bridge.

COLDSTREAM, William (1908–87)
Distinguished English painter; educated at the Slade School of Art, London, where he later became Director (1949–75); worked as John Grierson's assistant at the GPO Film Unit, where he worked on three films with Britten in 1935: *The King's Stamp, Coal Face* and *Negroes.*

COLEMAN, Charles Joseph Romaine (1879–1959)
Organist, singing teacher and conductor; Organist and Choir-Master of St John's Church, Lowestoft (1902–40) and conductor of the Lowestoft Musical Society. He later became Organist and Choir Master at Holy Trinity, Bristol (1940–2) and finally St Peter Mancroft, Norwich (1942–59), where he commissioned Britten to write his *Hymn to St Peter*, Op. 56a (1955) to mark the quincentenary of the church.

COLEMAN, Charles (b. 1910)
Son of C. J. R. Coleman; boyhood friend and regular musical partner of Britten, talented violinist.

COLLES, H[enry] (Harry) C[ope] (1879–1943)
Music critic and writer; editor of the third (1927) and fourth (1940) editions of *Grove's Dictionary of Music and Musicians.*

COLLINGWOOD, Lawrence Arthur (1887–1982)
English conductor and composer.

COOKE, Arnold Atkinson (1906–2005)
English composer; pupil of E. J. Dent and Hindemith; professor at the Royal Manchester College of Music.

CORTOT, Alfred Denis (1877–1962)
French pianist and conductor.

COURTAULD, S. M.
A Woodlands House boy at Gresham's, seventeen months Britten's senior.

COURTNEIDGE, Cicely (1893–1980)
English actress; married to Jack Hulbert.

COX, David Vassal (1916–97)
English composer and writer on music; later External Services Music Organizer at the BBC (1956–76).

CRANMER, Arthur (1885–1954)
English baritone.

CRAWFORD, R. S.
Farfield House boy at Gresham's, contemporary of Britten's.

CROWDIE FAMILY
Lowestoft family friends: Molly, Lucy and Steven were contemporaries and tennis partners of the Britten children.

CUNDELL, Edric (1893–1961)
Horn-player and composer; Principal of the Guildhall School of Music and Drama (1938–59).

DACAM, C. Brinney
A master at South Lodge and a good friend of Britten's older brother Robert; in 1927 he wrote a poem, *Liebesfreude*, which Britten set, inscribing it in Dacam's autograph book.

DALMAINE, Cyril (1904–86)
English composer, conductor and broadcaster; chorus master of the BBC Chorus (1932–3).

DANILOVA, Alexandra (1903–97)
Russian-American prima ballerina.

D'ARÁNYI, Jelly (1895–1966)
Hungarian violinist.

DARNELL, A. Beatrix (1873–1970)
Lady Superintendent at the RCM (1919–39), responsible for the general welfare of the College students.

DARNTON, Christian (1905–81)
English composer, writer and educator, with left-wing sympathies; editor of *Music Lover* (1930–4).

DAVIES, Tudor (1892–1958)
Welsh tenor.

DENT, Edward J., (1876–1957)
Composer, musicologist and teacher; Professor of Music at Cambridge University; elected President of the International Society for Contemporary Music in 1922.

DESMOND, Astra (1893–1973)
English contralto.

DIEREN, Bernard van (1887–1936)
Dutch-English composer and writer.

DIGBEY [major], K. H.
A Kenwyn House prefect at Gresham's, eighteen months Britten's senior.

DOCKER, M. L.
A Farfield House prefect at Gresham's, two years Britten's senior.

DOHNÁNYI, Ernö (1877–1960)
Hungarian pianist, composer, conductor, teacher and administrator.

DOLIN, Sir Anton (1904–83)
British dancer and choreographer, knighted in 1981; studied with Nijinsky and danced with the Diaghilev Company; co-founder of the Camargo Society in 1930, appeared with the Vic-Wells Ballet from 1931 to 1935, after which he created the Markova–Dolin Ballet with Alicia Markova; danced with the American Ballet Theatre in New York from 1940 to 1946.

DONAT, Robert (1905–58)
British screen actor.

DOONE, Rupert [Ernest Reginald Woodfield] (1903–66)
English dancer, choreographer, producer and director; started his career as a dancer, appearing in 1929 with Diaghilev's Ballets Russes; founder member of the Group Theatre in 1932 and its principal artistic figure and director (1934–9), directing Vanbrugh's *The Provok'd Wife* (1932), the two Auden–Isherwood plays, *The Ascent of F6* (1937) and *On the Frontier* (1938), MacNeice's translation of *The Agamemnon of Aeschylus* (1936) and MacNeice's *Out of the Picture* (1937); after the demise of the Group Theatre, Doone ran the theatre school at Morley College from 1940.

DORFMANN, Ania (1899-1982)
Russian pianist.

DRAPER, Charles (1869–1952)
English clarinettist.

DUNCAN, Ronald (1914–82)
Rhodesian-born poet, playwright and publisher; like Britten, a pacifist and member of the Peace Pledge Union. Their first collaboration was on the *Pacifist March* (1937) for the PPU, and their professional relationship was sustained beyond the war with five further collaborations. Britten wrote incidental music for three of Duncan's theatre projects, *This Way to the Tomb* (1945), his translation of Cocteau's *The Eagle has Two Heads* (1946), and *Stratton* (1949). They also worked together on the Wedding Anthem, *Amo Ergo Sum*, Op. 46 (1949), for the marriage of Lord Harewood and Marion Stein (daughter of Britten's publisher Erwin Stein), but the most substantial and enduring collaboration was on Britten's first chamber opera, *The Rape of Lucretia*, Op. 37 (1946) for which Duncan wrote the libretto.

DUNKERLEY, Piers Montague (1921–59)
Pupil at South Lodge (1930–4) and Bloxham School, Banbury, Oxford. He served as a captain in the Royal Marines during the war, and was wounded and taken

prisoner in June 1944. A failed marriage engagement led to his suicide on 8 June 1959; Britten considered him to be a casualty of the war, so difficult had he found it to adapt to civilian life and make a career for himself. It is for this reason that Dunkerley is included amongst the dedicatees of *War Requiem*, Op. 66 (1962).

DUPRÉ, Marcel (1886–1971)
French organist, composer and teacher; after the war Britten was to provide Dupré with two themes on which to improvise a prelude and fugue for a public event promoted by the BBC on 24 July 1945.

DUSHKIN, Samuel (1891–1976)
Polish-American violinist for whom Stravinsky composed his Violin Concerto (1931) and *Duo concertante* (1932).

DUTT, (Rajini) Palme (1896–1974)
English communist, political analyst and propagandist; founder-editor in 1921 of *Labour Monthly*.

EATON, Sybil (1897–1989)
English violinist; premiered the Finzi Violin Concerto and Violin Sonata.

ECCLES, James Ronald (1874–1956)
Headmaster at Gresham's (1919–35), having taught at the school since 1900.

EISDELL, Hubert (1882–1948)
English tenor.

ELLIOT, Rev. Wallace Harold
Incumbent of St Michael's Church, Chester Square, London SW1.

ELMAN, Mischa (1891–1967)
Russian-American violinist.

ELMENDORFF, Karl Eduard Maria (1891–1962)
German conductor.

ENGLAND, Leslie (1902–71)
English pianist.

ENGLISH SINGERS/NEW ENGLISH SINGERS
Vocal sextet founded by Steuart Wilson in 1920 and reformed as the New English Singers in 1932: Dorothy Silk, Nellie Carson (sopranos), Mary Morris (contralto), Eric Greene, Norman Stone (tenors), Cuthbert Kelly (bass). Peter Pears was to become a member of this ensemble in 1937.

ENRAGHT, Audrey and Evelyn
Wife and daughter of Rev. Canon Hawtrey J. Enraght (1871–1938), Rector of Lowestoft (1931–8).

EPSTEIN, Jacob (1880–1959)
American-born sculptor.

ERHART, Dorothy (1894–1971)
British harpsichordist and composer.

EVANS, [Dame] Edith [Mary Booth] (1888–1976)
British actress, awarded the DBE in 1946.

EVANS, Edwin (1871–1945)
English music critic who joined the *Daily Mail* in 1933.

EVANS, Dr Harold Muir
The Brittens' family doctor; lived in Turret House, Kirkley Cliff Road.

FACHIRI, Adila (1889–1962)
Hungarian violinist, who made her home in England; sister of the violinist Jelly D'Arányi.

FAIRBANKS Jnr., Douglas (1909–2000)
American screen actor.

FAIRLEY, Mrs
Fellow lodger at Burleigh House.

FALKNER, Keith (1900–94)
English bass-baritone; later worked for the British Council in Italy (1946–50) and as Director of the Royal College of Music (1960–74). He was knighted in 1967.

FARQUHAR, Miss
Fellow lodger at Burleigh House.

FASS, Marjorie (1886–1968)
Close friend and neighbour of the Bridges at Friston in Sussex; a gifted amateur artist and musician.

FERGUSON, Howard (1908–99)
Irish composer, pianist and musicologist; pupil of Harold Samuel.

FERNIE (*née* Britten), (Mary) Louise [Aunt Louise] (1872–1957)
Mr Britten's older sister, married to William George Fernie of Bromley, Kent, with one daughter, Elaine.

FEUERMANN, Emanuel (1902–42)
Austrian-American cellist.

FINZI, Gerald (1901–56)
English composer; professor at the Royal Academy of Music (1930–9).

FIRBANK, Ronald (1886–1926)
English novelist and aesthete.

FISCHER, (Maria) Res (1896–1974)
German contralto; a fine singing actress.

FISCHER, Sarah (1898–1975)
French-Canadian soprano in Beecham's British National and Covent Garden companies.

FLAGSTAD, Kirsten (1895–1962)
Great Norwegian soprano, much admired by Britten.

FLESCH, Carl (1873–1944)
Hungarian violinist and distinguished teacher; a prize in his name has been awarded since 1945.

FLETCHER, Basil A.
Teacher at Gresham's (1922–32); Britten's first housemaster at Farfield (until November 1928) and form-master of the Lower Fourth in 1929.

FLOUD, Mollie (b. 1911)
Daughter of Sir Francis and Lady Floud and twin sister of Peter; studied piano at the Royal Academy of Music and later with Clifford Curzon.

FLOUD, P(eter) C(astle) (1911–60)
Pupil at Gresham's (1924–30) before going up to Oxford; an authority on William Morris; later Keeper of Circulation at the Victoria and Albert Museum in London, 1947–60.

FONTAINE [FONTANNE], Lynn (1887–1983)
Anglo-American stage and screen actress; married to American actor, Alfred Lunt.

FORBES-ROBINSON, Jean (1905–62)
English actress; her second husband, André van Gyseghem (1906–79), directed the Left Theatre production of Montagu Slater's *Easter 1916*, for which Britten composed the incidental music in 1935.

FORSTER, Mrs Hill
Friston neighbour of Mrs Britten.

FOSS, Hubert James (1889–1953)
Founder of the music publishing division of Oxford University Press in 1925.

FOSTER, Arnold (1896–1963)
English conductor, composer and educationalist; founder of the English Madrigal Choir.

FOSTER, Megan (1898–1987)
Welsh soprano.

FOX, Douglas (1893–1978)
English organist, Organ Scholar at Keble College, Oxford and prizewinner at the RCM, where he first met Frank Bridge. Fox lost his right arm in 1917, during the First World War, after which he became an influential teacher to many leading musicians, including Sir David Willcocks.

FRANÇAIX, Jean René Désiré (1912–97)
French composer.

FRANK, Alan (1910–94)
English publisher, editor, writer and clarinettist, married to the composer Phyllis Tate (1911–85); joined OUP in 1927, becoming music editor in 1948 and Head of Music from 1954 to 1975.

FRASER, Patuffy Kennedy
See under Helen Patuffy Kennedy-Fraser.

FRIED, Oskar (1871–1941)
German conductor and Mahler disciple.

FURTWÄNGLER, Wilhelm (1886–1954)
Renowned German conductor of the Berlin Philharmonic Orchestra.

GALIMER STRING QUARTET
Marguerite Galimer, Renée Galimer (violins), Adrienne Galimer (viola), Felix Galimer (cello).

GARBO, Greta (1905–90)
Swedish-born film actress.

GASKELL, Helen (1906–2002)
English oboist, member of the BBC Symphony Orchestra (1932–66).

GATES, Mr
Fellow lodger at Princes Square.

GAUNT, Mrs
School Matron at Gresham's during Britten's first term.

GERHARDT, Elena (1883–1961)
German-British soprano who later became a mezzo-soprano.

GIBBS, Armstrong (1889–1960)
English composer; pupil of Charles Wood and Vaughan Williams at the RCM and later professor there (1921–39).

GIELGUD, Val (1900–81)
BBC Radio drama producer; brother of the actor John Gielgud.

GIESEKING, Walter (1895–1956)
German pianist and a particularly fine interpreter of Debussy.

GILLESPIE, Dr Helen
Fellow lodger at Burleigh House.

GILLESPIE, Rev. Laurence
Curate at St John's Church, Lowestoft from 1934.

GILLETT, Miss
School Matron at Gresham's from 1929, in succession to Mrs Gaunt.

GILLIAM, Laurence (1904–64)
BBC Radio drama producer.

GINSTER, Ria (1898–1985)
German soprano.

GLEDHILL, Christopher (b. 1912)
Son of the Vicar of Bungay and a gifted pianist; involved in the Bungay Orchestra that Britten conducted in 1934.

GODFREY, Sir Dan (1868–1939)
English conductor; graduate of the RCM and conductor of the Bournemouth Municipal Orchestra.

GOLDSMITH, Edmund Onslow
Medical colleague of Britten's father, who was a partner of Hutchinson, Mead and Goldsmith, physicians and surgeons, and a former neighbour of the Britten family when they lived at 46 Marine Parade (the Goldsmiths lived at No. 44); the Goldsmiths were regular visitors to Kirkley Cliff Road, particularly for musical gatherings, and their children, Philip, Terence and Flossie, were friends of Beth and Benjamin.

GOLDSON, (Helen) Marjorie
See under Marjorie Britten.

GOLDSON, Mr, Mrs and Charlie
Parents and brother of Marjorie (Robert Britten's fiancée and later wife) who had become members of the extended Britten family by 1930.

GOODSON, Katherine (1872–1958)
English pianist.

GOOLDEN, D. C. A.

A Farfield House boy at Gresham's, one year Britten's junior.

GOOSSENS, [Sir] Eugene (1893–1962)

English conductor and member of the famous Goossens musical dynasty, knighted in 1955; as conductor of the Cincinnati Symphony Orchestra, he conducted the premiere of Britten's *Scottish Ballad*, Op. 26, with Ethel Bartlett and Rae Robertson, on 28 November 1941.

GOOSSENS, Léon (1897–1988)

Member of the Goossens family and the leading oboist of his generation; Britten wrote his *Phantasy* oboe quartet, Op. 2, for Goossens in 1932.

GORDON, Jack

English producer at Sadler's Wells Opera, responsible for repertory and casting in the mid–1930s.

GOW, Dorothy (1893–1982)

English composer.

GRAHAM-BROWN, Dorothy

Family friend in Lowestoft whose sons, Charles and Herbert, were at South Lodge with Britten.

GRAINGER, (George) Percy Aldridge (1882–1961)

Australian-American composer, pianist, editor, folk-song collector, writer and teacher; much championed by Britten in later life.

GRAVES, Mr

Friend of Marjorie Fass and the Bridges at Friston, a local oculist.

GRAVES, Robert (1895–1985)

English poet and novelist.

GRAY, Cecil (1895–1951)

Scottish composer and critic.

GREATOREX, Walter [Gog] (1877–1949)

Director of Music at Gresham's (1911–36).

GREEN, David

Fellow lodger at Burleigh House during Britten's College days; an architectural student from Lowestoft, where his father was also an architect; partner in the firm of Taylor & Green of London and Lowestoft.

GRIERSON, John (1898–1972)

Pioneering Scottish documentary-film maker; educated at Glasgow University and studied communications media on a Rockefeller scholarship in Chicago in the 1920s; appointed film officer of the Empire Marketing Board in 1927; Head of the GPO Film Unit from 1933 to 1937.

GUI, Vittorio (1885–1975)

Italian conductor and composer.

GWYNNE, Miss

Fellow lodger at Princes Square.

GYDE, Arnold (1894–1959)
Employed by the London publishers, William Heinemann Ltd, first on the editorial staff (1918–39) and subsequently in the publicity department (1939–59); he married Sophie Wyss in 1925.

HABICH, Eduard (1880–1960)
German baritone who sang principally at the Berlin Opera; made guest appearances at Covent Garden and the Metropolitan Opera in the 1920s and 1930s.

HALFFTER, Ernesto (1905–1989)
Spanish composer, protégé of Manuel de Falla.

HALLIDAY, Michael
Orphaned boy, adopted by Miss Peto of Oulton Broad near Lowestoft, and a contemporary and schoolfriend of Britten at South Lodge (1923–7); Halliday was killed in action during the Second World War and is one of the dedicatees of Britten's *War Requiem*, Op. 66 (1962).

HALL JONES, Miss
Fellow lodger at Burleigh House.

HAMBOURG, Mark (1879–1960)
Russian-British pianist; also an eminent teacher in London, who included Gerald Moore amongst his protégés.

HANDLER, Irma (1907–95)
German–American soprano, who created the role of Xanthe in Strauss' *Die Liebe der Danae.*

HANWORTH, Dr Honoria Josephine
Friend at 41 Hurlingham Court, Fulham, London SW6.

HARDIE, Rev. and Mrs
Lowestoft family friends, former vicar in Lowestoft and later Bishop of Jamaica; their sons, Archie and John, were at South Lodge with Britten.

HARDWICKE, Sir Cedric Webster (1893–1964)
English stage and screen actor, knighted in 1934.

HARMER (*née* Britten), Ellen [Nellie] Elizabeth (1871–1945)
Mr Britten's older sister, married to Frederick Harmer; they had two children, Freda and Aldwyth.

HARRIS, Lillian
English composer, Foley exhibitioner and fellow student of Britten at the RCM; awarded the Cobbett Prize in 1932.

HARRISON, Pamela (1915–90)
English composer; student of Gordon Jacob at the RCM (1932–36).

HARTY, Sir [Herbert] Hamilton (1879–1941)
English composer, conductor and accompanist, knighted in 1925; conductor of the Hallé Orchestra in Manchester (1920–33).

HAWKES, Ralph (1898–1950)
Director of Boosey & Hawkes Ltd, and a valued friend and adviser; Britten dedicated *Our Hunting Fathers*, Op. 8 (1936) to him.

HAYES, Edith Ellen [Lazy]
Mr Britten's secretary for eighteen years, known affectionately (and undeservedly according to Britten's sister Beth) as 'Lazy' Hayes.

HEGER, Robert (1886–1978)
German conductor and composer; guest conductor at Covent Garden (1925–35).

HEINSHEIMER, Dr Hans W. (1900–93)
German-American publisher and writer on music; head of opera department at Universal Edition in Vienna; after emigrating to America in 1938 to flee the Nazis, he worked for Boosey & Hawkes, Belwin, Inc., New York and later G. Schirmer, Inc.

HELY-HUTCHINSON, Victor (1901–47)
South African-born composer, conductor, pianist and administrator; as Director of Music at the BBC (1944–7) he was responsible for commissioning Britten's *Occasional Overture* for the launch of the Third Programme in September 1946.

HENDERSON, Nora and Tumpty
Spinster sisters who lived at the same Bayswater lodgings as Britten in Princes Square.

HENDERSON, Roy (Galbraith) (1899–2000)
Scottish baritone.

HENDRIE, Dr A. S.
School doctor at Gresham's, a local general practitioner and keen amateur singer.

HERBAGE, Julian (1904–76)
English conductor, scholar, broadcaster and musical administrator; on the music staff of the BBC, with special responsibility for planning the Promenade Concerts (1927–46).

HESS, Dame Myra (1890–1965)
English pianist; founded the National Gallery lunchtime recitals during the Second World War, which included a number of notable concerts from Pears and Britten.

HEUWINKEL, Baroness (1912–96)
Barbara von Shilling, married to the novelist Roman Denecke.

HEWARD, Leslie (1897–1943)
English conductor and composer; Principal Conductor of the City of Birmingham Orchestra (1930–43).

HIBBERD, Stuart
The BBC's Chief Announcer in the 1930s.

HILL, Sir Leonard Erskine (1886–1952) and Lady (Janet)
English physiologist and his wife, who lived at Chalfont St Peter's and had a holiday cottage at Corton, near Lowestoft, where they were patients of Mr Britten. Their youngest daughter was Nanette (Nan).

HINDE [major], E. J. F.
A Farfield House boy at Gresham's, one year Britten's senior.

HINDE [minor], S. R.
A Farfield House boy at Gresham's, six months Britten's junior.

HINDEMITH, Paul (1895–1963)
German composer, theorist, teacher, conductor and (like Britten and his teacher Frank Bridge) a fine viola player.

HINNENBERG-LEFEBRE, Margot (1901–81)
German soprano.

HOCKEY, Elsie Mary (1902–84)
Britten's cousin, a dance teacher in Ipswich; daughter of Mrs Britten's eldest brother, Henry William [Willie] Hockey and his wife Jane.

HOCKEY, Euphemia [Aunt Effie] Maud (1876–1944)
Mrs Britten's younger sister, one of Britten's maiden aunts.

HOCKEY, Henry William [Willie] (1870–1948)
Mrs Britten's eldest brother; organist of the Tower Church (St Mary-le-Tower) Ipswich, a singing teacher and conductor of the Ipswich Choral Society.

HOCKEY (*née* Holbrook), Jane [Aunt Janie] (1869–1942)
Wife of Mrs Britten's eldest brother, Henry William Hockey; they had two children, George and Elsie.

HOCKEY, Sarah Fanny [Aunt Queenie] (1875–1939)
Mrs Britten's youngest sister and the younger of Britten's maiden aunts; an accomplished artist and miniaturist, exhibiting at the Royal Academy, London. She painted portraits of all the Britten children: her portrait miniature of Benjamin (aged about nine) is now in the National Portrait Gallery.

HOLST, Gustav(us Theodore von) (1874–1934)
English composer of German extraction; his daughter Imogen worked as Britten's Music Assistant (1952–64) and was an Artistic Director of the Aldeburgh Festival (1956–77).

HOLZMANN, Rudolf [Rodolfo] (1910–92)
Peruvian composer and ethnomusicologist of German origin; pupil of Hermann Scherchen.

HONEGGER, Arthur (1892–1955)
Swiss composer and member of *Les Six*.

HORNE, Mr and Mrs Ernest
Dental surgeon at 10 Station Road, Beccles; shared lodgings with Mr and Mrs Britten in Ipswich when Mr Britten worked for the Penraven dental surgery.

HOROWITZ, Vladimir (1903–89)
Ukrainian-American virtuoso pianist.

HOWARD, Brian Christian de Clairborne (1905–58)
American-British poet and literary critic.

HOWARD-JONES, Evlyn (1877–1951)
English pianist, teacher and scholar; friend of Delius, whose *Three Preludes* for piano (1923) and Second Violin Sonata (1923) he premiered.

HOWELLS, Herbert Norman (1892–1983)
English composer; pupil of Parry and Stanford at the RCM, where he himself taught from 1920 until his death.

HOWES, Frank (1891–1974)
English music critic; assistant music critic of *The Times* and contributor to the *Musical Times*.

HULBERT, Claude (1900–64)
English actor.

HUMBY, Betty (1908–58)
English pianist, later to become the second wife of Sir Thomas Beecham, whom she met in the USA during the Second World War.

HUNGARIAN STRING QUARTET
Emmerich Waldhuer, Jean de Temesváry (violins), Tivadar Országh (viola), Eugene de Kerpley (cello).

HURLSTONE, William Yeates (1876–1906)
English composer and pianist; educated at the RCM and recipient of the first Cobbett Prize for chamber music for his *Fantasy* string quartet in 1906.

HURST, Helen (1887–1981)
Social worker and Barbara Britten's long-term partner, fifteen years her senior; they first met when Barbara moved to London to work in Peckham as a health visitor and ended their lives together in retirement in Bexhill-on-Sea, East Sussex.

HUTCHINSON, Donald Henry
Local doctor, magistrate, and partner of Hutchinson, Mead and Goldsmith, physicians and surgeons; an active member of St John's Church.

IDZIKOWSKI, Stanislas (1894–1977)
Polish dancer and a star pupil of Enrico Cecchetti; he danced with Pavlova before joining Diaghilev's company in 1915, with which he remained until 1928. Idzikowski was primarily a character dancer with exquisite technique. Tiny in stature, with an animated face, he had a special gift for grotesque and artificial comedy.

ILES, Edna Amy (1905–2003)
English pianist.

IRELAND, John (1879–1962)
English composer; Britten's composition teacher at the Royal College of Music in London, where he taught from 1923 to 1939.

ISHERWOOD, Christopher (1904–86)
English-American novelist and playwright; collaborated with W. H. Auden as members of the Group Theatre on a number of dramatic works that brought him into contact with Britten.

JACKSON, Gerald
English flautist; principal flute of the BBC Symphony Orchestra (1938–46).

JACOB, Gordon Percival Septimus (1895–1984)
English composer, teacher and writer; studied with Stanford and Howells at the RCM, later professor at the College (1926–66).

JAMES, Ivor (1882–1963)
English cellist; a former student of the RCM and professor of cello and chamber music there (1919–53); member of the Menges Quartet and the English String Quartet, whose viola player was Frank Bridge.

JANSSEN, Herbert (1895–1965)
German baritone and famous Wagnerian.

JOHNSON [major], G. A.
A Farfield House boy at Gresham's, six months Britten's junior.

JOHNSON, Mrs
Fellow lodger at Princes Square.

JOHNSTONE, Armrid
Artist and friend of the Brittens in Lowestoft, who shared a flat with Barbara Britten and Helen Hurst in London; designed the cover for the first edition of *A Boy Was Born*, Op. 3 (1933).

JONAS, Mrs
Fellow lodger at Burleigh House.

JONES, Parry (1891–1963)
Welsh tenor.

JONES, Trefor (1901–65)
Welsh tenor.

JOSEPH, Jane M. (1894–1929)
Composition student of Gustav Holst.

KABASTA, Oswald (1896–1946)
Austrian conductor of the Vienna Symphony Orchestra (1933–8); Principal Conductor of the Munich Philharmonic (1938–45). He was an enthusiastic supporter of the Nazi regime, and after the war he was stripped of his Munich post by the denazification authorities, which led to his suicide the following year.

KALENBERG, Joseph (1886–1962)
German tenor.

KALMUS, Dr Alfred August Uhlrich (1889–1972)
Austrian-British music publisher at Universal Edition in Vienna; fled to England in 1936, where he set up the London office of Universal Edition.

KAUFFMAN-NAYER, Bethley
Swiss student who had stayed with the Brittens as an *au pair* in the summer of 1920.

KENNEDY Sr., Joseph Patrick [Joe] (1888–1969)
United States Ambassador to the United Kingdom (1938–40), father of the Kennedy dynasty.

KENNEDY, Lauri (1898–1985)
Australian cellist; principal cellist of the BBC Symphony Orchestra, and later the London Philharmonic and Covent Garden orchestras; grandfather of violinist Nigel Kennedy.

KENNEDY-FRASER, Helen Patuffy [Mrs Hood] (1889–1967)
Scottish folk-singer and pianist; daughter of Marjorie Kennedy-Fraser (1857–1930), the Scottish singer, collector of folk-songs, and widely travelled international recitalist of Hebridean songs.

KENWORTHY, D. M. de B.
A Howson House boy at Gresham's, one year Britten's junior.

KERN, Adele (1901–80)
German soprano.

KERSEY, Eda (1904–44)
English violinist; a decade later she was to give the UK premiere of Bartók's *Contrasts* (with Frederick Thurston, clarinet and Ilona Kabos, piano) at the Wigmore Hall on 23 September 1942, in the same concert in which Pears and Britten gave the first public performance of the *Seven Sonnets of Michelangelo*, Op. 22.

KIPNIS, Alexander (1891–1978)
Russian bass.

KITTEL, Bruno (1870–1948)
German violinist and conductor.

KNAPPERTSBUSCH, Hans (1888–1965)
German conductor.

KNIPPER, Lev Konstantinovich (1898–1974)
Russian composer.

KODALY, Zoltan (1882–1967)
Hungarian composer, ethnomusicologist and educationalist.

KOHLER, Irene (1912–96)
English pianist educated at the RCM; pupil of Steuermann.

KOLISCH, Rudolf (1896–1978)
Austrian-American violinist.

KOLISCH STRING QUARTET
Rudolf Kolisch, Felix Khuner (violins), Eugene Lehner (viola), Benar Heifetz (cello).

KONETZNI[-Wiedmann)], Amy (1902–68)
Austrian soprano at the Vienna State Opera.

KOUSSEVITZKY, Serge (1874–1951)
Russian-American conductor and virtuoso double-bass player; Music Director of the Boston Symphony Orchestra (1924–49); a champion of Britten's music, who commissioned *Peter Grimes* (1945), via the Koussevitzky Music Foundation, set up in memory of his wife, Natalie, and *Spring Symphony* (1949), for the Boston Symphony Orchestra.

KRASNER, Louis (1903–95)
Russian-American violinist.

KRAUSS, Clemens (1893–1954)
Austrian conductor, friend and outstanding interpreter of the operas of Richard Strauss; Director of the Vienna State Opera (1929–34) and the Berlin State Opera (1935–6).

KREISLER, Fritz (1875–1962)
Austrian-American virtuoso violinist and composer.

KRENEK, Ernst (1900–91)
Austrian-American composer.

KREUZ, Emil (1867–1932)
Eminent viola player and teacher, whose volumes of exercises are bibles for teachers and pupils alike.

KUTCHER STRING QUARTET
Samuel Kutcher, Max Saalpeter (violins), Raymond Jeremy (viola), Douglas Cameron (cello).

LAMBERT, Constant (1905–51)
English composer, conductor and writer; pupil of Ralph Vaughan Williams at the RCM; conductor of the Camargo Society and Music Director of the Vic-Wells Ballet (1931–47).

LAMOND, Frederic (1868–1948)
Scottish pianist and composer.

LANG, Matheson (1879–1948)
English stage actor.

LAUGHTON, Charles (1899–1962)
English-American stage and screen actor.

LAULIE
See under Miss Mabel Austin.

LAURICELLA, Remo (1912–2003)
English violinist and composer of Italian parentage; studied at the RCM and at the conservatoires of Siena and Santiago de Compostela; Britten's unpublished *Fantasy Scherzo* piano trio (later retitled *Introduction and Allegro*) is dedicated to Lauricella and Bernard Richards; after the war Lauricella spent most of his career as a member of the London Philharmonic Orchestra.

LAYTON, D(avid) (b. 1914)
Woodlands House boy at Gresham's, eight months Britten's junior, son of Sir Walter Thomas Layton (1884–1966), economist, editor and newspaper proprietor. Dedicatee of Britten's *Alla Marcia, 'P.T.'* [Physical Training] – the first movement of the incomplete suite for string quartet, *Alla Quartetto Serioso: 'Go play, boy, play'* (1933).

'LAZY'
See under Edith Ellen Hayes.

LEDERER, Louis
Friend of the Hendersons and a fellow lodger at Princes Square.

LEGGE, Walter (1906–79)
English critic, record producer, administrator and musical impresario; worked with Beecham at the Royal Opera House in the 1930s; in charge of ENSA concerts for the troops during the war; founded the Philharmonia Orchestra in 1946; perhaps best known as a legendary record producer for HMV (1927–64).

LEHMANN, Lotte (1888–1976)
German-American soprano.

LEIDER, Frida (1888–1975)
German soprano and leading Wagnerian of her day.

LEIGH, Walter (1905–42)
English composer of light music; killed in action.

LEMARE, Iris (1902–97)
English conductor, teacher, administrator, and co-founder (with Anne Macnaghten and Elizabeth Maconchy) of the Macnaghten–Lemare Concerts for the promotion of new British music; she conducted the concert premiere of Britten's *A Boy was Born* in a Macnaghten–Lemare Concert at the Mercury Theatre in London on 17 December 1934.

LÉNER STRING QUARTET
Jenö Léner, Joszef Smilovits (violins), Sándor Roth (viola), Imre Hartmann (cello).

LEVY, Ernst (1895–1981)
Swiss composer, pianist, and writer on music.

LEWIS, Joseph (1878–1954)
Senior staff conductor at the BBC (1930–8).

LICETTE, MIRIAM (1892–1969)
English soprano.

LICHINE, David (1910–72)
Russian-American dancer and choreographer.

LONG, Kathleen (1896–1968)
English pianist.

LONG, Marguerite (1874–1966)
French pianist; dedicatee of Ravel's Concerto in G (1929–31) which she premiered with the composer in 1932.

LOPOKOVA, Lydia [Lady Keynes] (1892–1981)
Russian dancer, married to economist and writer, John Maynard Keynes (1883–1946).

LORENZ, Max (1901–75)
German tenor.

LOUGH, Ernest (1911–2000)
Immortalised as a boy soprano for a whole generation of music lovers when he made a now famous recording of 'O, for the Wings of a Dove' from Mendelssohn's anthem, *Hear My Prayer*.

LÜBBECKE-JOB, Emma
German pianist, much favoured by Hindemith.

LUCAS, Leighton (1903–82)
English composer and conductor.

LUNT, Alfred (1892–1977)
American stage and screen actor, married to actress Lynn Fontanne.

LUTYENS, [Agnes] Elisabeth (1906–83)
English composer and co-founder in December 1931 (with Anne Macnaghten and Iris Lemare) of the Macnaghten–Lemare Concerts; daughter of the architect, Sir Edwin Lutyens (1869–1944) and wife of the conductor Edward Clark (1888–1962).

LYNN, Ralph (1882–1962)
English actor, noted for his appearances in popular Aldwych farces.

LYTTON, Sir Henry (1867–1936)
English actor and singer, knighted in 1930; a leading artist of the D'Oyly Carte Opera Company.

MacDONALD, (James) Ramsay (1866–1937)
Prime Minister, leading Britain's first Labour Governments (1924 and 1929–31) and then a National Government (1931–5).

MACNAGHTEN, Anne Catherine (1908–2000)
English violinist; pupil of Antonio Brosa and André Mangeot; founder in December 1931 (with Iris Lemare and Elizabeth Maconchy) of the Macnaghten–Lemare Concerts, and the Macnaghten String Quartet in 1932.

MACNAGHTEN (*née* Booth), Lady Antonia Mary (1872–1952)
Anne Macnaghten's mother and wife of the High Court Judge, the Rt Hon. Sir Malcolm Macnaghten (1869–1955).

MACNAGHTEN STRING QUARTET
Anne Macnaghten, Elise Desprez (violins), Beryl Scawen Blunt (viola), Mary Goodchild (cello).

MACONCHY, [Dame] Elizabeth (1907–94)
English composer, awarded the DBE in 1987; studied at the RCM (1923–9) with Charles Wood and Vaughan Williams, and later in Prague.

MAGITO, Suria (1903–87)
Russian-American dancer and director; second wife of Michel Saint-Denis (1897–1971), founder in 1935 of the London Theatre Studio.

MALIPIERO, Gian Francesco (1882–1973)
Italian composer and musicologist.

MANGEOT, André Louis (1883–1970)
British violinist and impresario of French birth; founder of the International String Quartet, the Mangeot Ensemble and the Mangeot String Quartet.

MANGEOT STRING QUARTET
André Mangeot, Boris Pecker (violins), Eric Bray (viola), Jack Shinebourne (cello).

MANSFIELD, Veronica (1904–80)
Australian mezzo-soprano who later taught at the RCM.

MARCHANT, [Sir] Stanley Robert (1883–1949)
English church musician, teacher and composer, knighted in 1943.

MARE, Walter de la (1873–1956)
English poet, short-story writer and novelist much admired by Britten.

MARKEVITCH, Igor (1912–83)
Russian-born composer and conductor.

MARKOVA, [Dame] Alicia [Lilian Alicia Marks] (1910–2004)
British Dancer with the Rambert Ballet Club (1931–3) and founder of the Markova–Dolin Ballet in 1935; awarded the DBE in 1963.

MARSHALL [minor], G(eoffrey) C.
A Farfield House boy at Gresham's, eleven months Britten's senior; Britten was to fag for Marshall's older brother, Alan, in 1929.

MARTELLI, Henri (1895–1980)
Corsican-born French composer.

MASE, Owen
Adrian Boult's assistant at the BBC in the 1930s.

MASEFIELD, John Edward (1878–1967)
English poet, playwright and novelist; Poet Laureate (1930–67).

MASTERSON, Frederick
Tailor to Mr Britten and his sons, 164 London Road South, Lowestoft.

MATTHEWS, S.
A Farfield House boy at Gresham's and Captain of Hockey, two years Britten's senior.

MAWSON, Dr
Doctor at St Luke's Hospital on Kirkley Cliff Road.

MAY, Mr and Mrs (Diana)
Fellow lodgers at Burleigh House.

MAY, Frederick (1911–85)
Irish composer and a contemporary of Britten at the RCM.

MAYER, [Sir] Robert (1879–1985)
German-born patron and benefactor of music, knighted in 1939; founder of the Robert Mayer Children's Concerts and Youth and Music.

MEAD, Kathleen
Daughter of Dr John C. Mead, partner in the local medical practice with Dr Hutchinson and Dr Goldsmith.

MEDLEY, Robert (1905–94)
English painter and stage designer; studied at Gresham's, the Slade School of Fine Art and in Paris; chief designer of The Group Theatre and long-term partner of Rupert Doone.

MENGELBERG, Willem (1871–1951)
Renowned conductor of the Concertgebouw Orchestra, Amsterdam.

MEIKLEJOHN, M(atthew) F. M.
A Farfield House boy and Open Scholar at Gresham's (1927–31), a contemporary of Britten's with whom he shared a study; became Professor of Italian at Glasgow University.

MELCHIOR, Lauritz (1890–1973)
Danish-American Heldentenor.

MELVILLE (*née* Chapman), Audrey
Musical benefactor and founder of the semi-professional Audrey Chapman (later Melville) Orchestra.

MENGES, Herbert (1902–72)
English conductor.

MENGES, Isolde (1893–1976)
English violinist and leader of the Menges String Quartet; professor at the RCM.

MEYER, Marcelle (1897–1958)
French pianist.

MILES, D. H.
A Farfield House boy at Gresham's, one year Britten's junior.

MILFORD, Robin Humphrey (1903–59)
English composer; studied with Holst, Vaughan Williams and R. O. Morris at the RCM.

MILLAR, Mrs
Fellow lodger at Burleigh House.

MILTON, Ernest (1890–1974)
English actor; created the role of Guidanto in the Auden–Isherwood play, *On the Frontier*.

MOERAN, E(rnest) J(ohn) (1894–1950)
English composer of Irish descent; student at RCM (1913–14) and later a pupil of John Ireland.

MONCK Nugent (1878–1958)
English theatre director and producer noted for his Shakespeare productions.

MONTAGU-NATHAN, Montagu (1877–1958)
English violinist and writer on music; Russian specialist who wrote biographies of Glinka, Mussorgsky and Rimsky-Korsakov. He also acted as secretary for numerous musical and arts organisations, most notably the Camargo Ballet Society.

MONTEUX, Pierre (1875–1964)
French-American conductor.

MOOR, Dr
Doctor at St Luke's hospital, Kirkley Cliff Road.

MORLING, Ernest Jabez
Music retailer at 149 London North Road, Lowestoft.

MORPHY, Mr and Mrs
Friends of Mr and Mrs Britten at Gorleston.

MORRIS, (R)eginald (O)wen (1886–1948)
English musical scholar, teacher and composer; studied at Harrow, New College Oxford and the RCM, where he later became a professor (1928–48).

MORRISON, (Stuart) Angus (1902–89)
English pianist and composer; pupil of Harold Samuel and Vaughan Williams at the RCM and professor at the College from 1926; pianist of the Pougnet, Morrison, Pini Trio.

MOULE-EVANS, David (1905–88)
English composer.

MOULTON, Dorothy (1886–1974)
English soprano who specialised in contemporary music; married to (Sir) Robert Mayer.

MOYSE, Marcel (1889–1984)
French flautist and teacher, for whom Jacques Ibert wrote his Concerto (1934).

MURCHIE, Robert (1884–1949)
Scottish flautist; principal flute, BBC Symphony Orchestra (1930–8).

MURRILL, Herbert (1909–1952)
English composer and Music Director of the Group Theatre (1933–6), composing the music for Auden's *The Dance of Death* (1934) and the Auden–Isherwood play *The Dog Beneath the Skin* (1936); joined the BBC in 1936, becoming Head of Music in 1950.

NASH, Heddle (1896–1961)
English tenor.

NEEL, [Louis] Boyd (1905–81)
English conductor; director of the Boyd Neel Orchestra, for whom Britten wrote his *Variations on a Theme of Frank Bridge*, Op. 10 in 1937.

NEILSON-TERRY, Phyllis (1892–1977)
English actress.

NETTLESHIP, Ursula (1886–1968)
Trained as a singer in Leipzig and devoted her life to teaching singing and, above all, to the training of choirs and amateurs. Britten met her in 1936 through her sister, Ethel, who had loaned her house in Crantock to Britten and Berkeley. When Britten and Pears returned from America in 1942 she provided them with a London home by lending them her studio on Cheyne Walk. *A Ceremony of Carols*, Op. 28 (1942) is dedicated to her.

NICHOLSON, John (1914–75)
Fellow pupil of Britten's at South Lodge; he and his future wife, Patricia, were lifelong friends of the composer. John and his older sister Elizabeth (1909–87) were the children of (Joseph) Arthur Nicholson, the Britten family solicitor, and next-door neighbours at 22 Kirkley Cliff Road.

NOBLE, Denis (1899–1966)
English baritone.

NORWICH STRING QUARTET
Harrington Kidd, Jocelyn Bates (violins), Audrey Alston (viola), Charles Finch (cello).

OLCZEWSKA, Maria (1892–1969)
German mezzo/contralto; leading Wagnerian of her day.

ONLEY, Roland Charles (b. 1912)
Violinist; exhibitioner at the RCM (1928–34).

OSBORN, Franz (1905–55)
German-British pianist.

OSTERC, Slavko (1895–1941)
Yugoslavian composer.

OUSELEY, J(ohn) A.

A Farfield House boy and County Scholar at Gresham's (1925–31); contemporary of Britten's.

OWLES, Mr and Mrs Sydney

Neighbours from 41 Corton Road, Lowestoft; Mr Owles was Manager of Barclays Bank, 1–2 Commercial Road, Lowestoft.

PAINTER (*née* Britten), Julie Annie [Aunt Julianne] (1868–1946)

Mr Britten's eldest surviving sister and one of Britten's godmothers, married to the Rev. Sheldon Painter CMS, vicar of St Helen's Church, Worcester.

PARRY, Mr and Mrs

Lowestoft neighbours whose daughters, Lilian and Jean, and sons, Ellis and Jack, often played tennis with Britten.

PATTON-BETHUNE, Michael

A close friend of Peter Pears, and a former pupil from his days as a master at The Grange, Crowborough.

PAYNE, Jack (1899–1969)

British dance-band leader; Director of Dance Music at the BBC (1928–32) and frequent broadcaster with the BBC Dance Orchestra.

PEACOCK, J. R.

A Farfield House boy at Gresham's, one year Britten's senior.

PEARCE, J. Allan

Former Gresham's boy, a solicitor in later life; while Britten was attending the 1934 International Society for Contemporary Music Festival in Florence with John Pounder, Pearce was also there, staying at the Pension Balestri, while travelling with his sister Phyllis.

PEARS, [Sir] Peter Neville Luard (1910–86)

Great English tenor, Britten's life-partner and principal interpreter, knighted in 1978. Pears was educated at The Grange preparatory school in Crowborough, Lancing College, Keble College, Oxford, and the RCM; he began his singing career as a member of the BBC Singers, the New English Singers and Glyndebourne Festival Chorus, before joining Sadler's Wells Opera during the war. His intelligence and artistic sensibility set him apart from most singers and he became one of the greatest Evangelists in the Schütz and Bach Passions, and (in partnership with Britten) one of the finest Lieder singers of his day. He was also Britten's muse, and over a period of thirty years Britten wrote no fewer than seven song cycles, five canticles, two orchestral cycles, four solos in major concert works, and thirteen operatic roles, from the title role in *Peter Grimes* to Gustav von Aschenbach in *Death in Venice*, expressly for him.

PEARSON, H. C. R.

A Farfield House boy at Gresham's, a contemporary of Britten's.

PERNEL, Orrea (1906–93)

British violinist and teacher, a noted soloist and chamber musician.

PERKIN, Helen Craddock (1909–96)
English pianist and composer, student of John Ireland at the RCM (1926–33); she is the dedicatee of Ireland's Piano Concerto, which she premiered in 1930.

PETO, Mrs
A friend of the Britten family, from Oulton, near Lowestoft, who adopted Michael Halliday, one of Britten's South Lodge friends.

PHILLIPOWSKY, Ivan
Russian pianist.

PHILLIPS, Rev. Richmond W.
Licensed Preacher within the Norwich Diocese, who had preceded T. J. E. Sewell as headmaster of South Lodge preparatory school. He and his wife lived in Victoria Mansions on Kirkley Cliff Road; their daughters, Marjorie and Connie, were also family friends.

PIGGOTT, Audrey (1906–89)
English cellist, student at the RCM, and later a professor at the RAM.

PIPER, John [Egerton Christmas], CH (1903–92)
English painter, stained-glass and ceramic artist, and theatre designer; co-founder and director of Britten's English Opera Group in 1947 and one of Britten's principal artistic collaborators, designing all the stage premieres of his works for the lyric theatre from *The Rape of Lucretia* to *Death in Venice*.

PIPER, Myfanwy (1911–97)
English writer, editor and librettist, second wife of the artist, John Piper; librettist of three of Britten's operas – *The Turn of the Screw, Owen Wingrave* and *Death in Venice*.

PIRANI TRIO
Max (Gabriel) Pirani (piano), Leila Doubleday (violin), Charles Hambourg (cello).

POLLARD, Rosemary
Norwich schoolfriend of Beth Britten.

POLKINHORNE, Edwin J. N. (1897–1955)
Bursar at the RCM (1923–46).

POOLEY, H. P. K.
A Howson Prefect and Open Scholar at Gresham's, two years Britten's senior.

PORTEUS, Roger
Friend of Chartres family, who also became a good friend of Britten for a period in the mid-1930s.

POUNDER, John Ward (1915–2002)
Son of the manager of the Lowestoft branch of the Midland Bank; a close South Lodge friend, educated at Charterhouse and law school in London, who later became a solicitor and remained in touch with Britten until the end of the composer's life. It was Pounder who nicknamed Britten 'Little O'Cedar Mop' – a reference to the mop designed for use with the famous brand of floor polish of the day. Britten was sensitive about his wiry curly hair, which took some taming, hence his frequent visits to the barbers.

POUGNET, MORRISON, PINI TRIO
Jean Pougnet (violin), Angus Morrison (piano), Anthony Pini (cello).

PRATT, Mrs Alice
See under Alice Walker.

PRIEST, Mr and Mrs
Patients of Mr Britten and friends of Britten's Aunt Julianne, who lived in Harleston, near Lowestoft, but also had a house in London, near Frank and Ethel Bridge; according to Beth Britten they gave wonderful tennis parties.

PRIMROSE, William (1903–82)
Scottish viola player and founder member of the London String Quartet; Britten wrote his *Lachrymae*, Op. 48, for Primrose, who premiered the work with the composer at an Aldeburgh Festival concert in Aldeburgh Parish Church on 20 June 1950.

PRIOR, May
Sister of Miss Thurlow Prior, a fellow lodger at Princes Square who worked at Central Hall, Westminster; she had sung in the National Choral Society with Mrs Britten and they were old friends; this was probably the reason that Britten began his College years at Princes Square.

PRIOR, Thurlow
Proprietor of the boarding house at 51 Princes Square in Bayswater, where Britten lodged for his first year at the RCM.

PROHASKA, Jaro (1891–1965)
Austrian baritone.

PROKOFIEV, Sergey (1891–1953)
Russian composer and pianist.

PUDNEY, John (1909–77)
English poet, novelist and dramatist; a contemporary of Auden's at Gresham's (1923–5) and a staff producer and writer at the BBC (1934–8).

PURDY, Thomas
A contemporary of Britten's at South Lodge (1926–8) and Gresham's (1928–31); a Farfield House boy six months Britten's junior.

QUEENIE, Aunt
See under Sarah Fanny Hockey.

RALF, Torsten (1901–54)
Swedish tenor, associated particularly with Wagner and Strauss; he created the role of Apollo in Strauss's *Daphne* (1938).

RANDALL, Maud
English pianist, pupil of Dame Myra Hess.

RASP, Fritz (1891–1976)
German character actor with a sixty-year career in the industry, most famous for his portrayal of 'Der Schmale' (The Thin Man) in Fritz Lang's 1927 film *Metropolis*.

RAUTAWAARA, Aulikki (1906–90)
Finnish soprano, a renowned Mozart interpreter and performer of the Sibelius song repertoire.

RAYBOULD, Clarence (1886–1972)
English conductor, composer and accompanist; joined the BBC in 1936, becoming Chief Assistant Conductor of the BBC Symphony Orchestra (1938–45).

REEVE, Basil Leslie (1912–84)
Son of the vicar of St John's Church, a close musical friend of Britten's during his school days in Lowestoft; later educated at Guy's Hospital.

REEVE, (Edward) Cyril Reynold (b. 1913)
Basil Reeve's younger brother, at South Lodge (1925–7) with Britten.

REEVE, Rev. William Ernest
Vicar of St John's Church, Lowestoft (1925–36), who had four children: Basil, Cyril, David and Hilary.

REEVES, George (1895–1960)
British pianist and accompanist.

REEVES, H. Wynn
English violinist and conductor; though not credited on the film, he conducted Arthur Benjamin's score for the original Hitchcock version of *The Man Who Knew Too Much* (1934).

REINIGER, Lotte (1899–1981)
Pioneering German-British film animator.

REISS, Thelma (1906–91)
British cellist who had a distinguished career, but was forced to retire early in 1955 due to ill health.

RETHBERG, Elisabeth (1894–1976)
German soprano.

REUTTER, Hermann (1900–85)
German composer.

RICE, Gwen
Norwich schoolfriend of Beth Britten.

RICHARDS, Bernard Roland (1913–96)
English cellist, a contemporary of Britten's at the RCM (1930–6); he was to remain in touch with Britten throughout his life, frequently performing the Britten repertoire as a member of the RAF, Boyd Neel and Jacques Strings Orchestras, and often under Britten's baton as a member of the English Chamber Orchestra, the resident ensemble for many years at the Aldeburgh Festival.

RIDDLE, Frederick Craig (1912–95)
English viola player.

RIPLEY, Gladys (1908–55)
English contralto.

RITCHIE, Margaret [Mabel] (1903–69)
English soprano who was later to become a member of Britten's English Opera Group, creating the roles of Lucia in *The Rape of Lucretia* (1946) and Miss Wordsworth in *Albert Herring* (1947); Britten's realization of Purcell's *The Blessed Woman's Expostulation* was written for her.

RIX, Anne Winifred [Winnie]
Lowestoft friend and regular tennis partner during Britten's South Lodge days; Winnie (according to Beth Britten) 'loved him dearly' – they even exchanged wedding rings as young children.

ROBERTS, B.
A Farfield House boy and Open Scholar at Gresham's, fourteen months Britten's junior.

ROBERT, Richard Ellis (1879–1953)
English writer and one-time Literary Editor of the *New Statesman*.

ROBERTSON, (Herbert) Stuart (1901–58)
English bass-baritone.

ROBESON, Paul (1898–1976)
Legendary African-American singer and actor.

ROBINSON, Stanford (1904–84)
English conductor; member of the BBC Music Staff (1924–66).

ROBSON, [Dame] Flora [McKenzie] (1902–84)
English actress, awarded the DBE in 1960.

ROGERS, Mrs Fernande
Fiancée and later wife of Laurence Sewell, Mr Britten's assistant; Mrs Rogers had a son Edward (Teddy) by her first marriage.

ROHS, Marta (1909–63)
German mezzo-soprano.

RONALD, Sir Landon [Landon Ronald Russell] (1873–1938)
English conductor, composer and pianist, knighted in 1922.

ROOTHAM, Cyril Bradley (1875–1938)
English organist, teacher, conductor and composer, and former student of RCM; Organist and Director of Music at St John's College, Cambridge.

ROSS, Hugh (1898–1990)
British-American choral trainer and conductor of The Schola Cantorum of New York since 1929; he conducted the premiere of the Britten-Auden operetta, *Paul Bunyan*, Op. 17, in New York in 1941.

ROTH STRING QUARTET
Feri Roth, Jenö Antal (violins), Nicholas Harsanyi (viola), János Starker (cello).

ROTHA, Paul (1907–84)
English documentary film-maker, historian and a much-respected colleague of John Grierson; he joined Stand Films as Director of Productions in 1936, commissioning Britten to write the music for the pacifist film *Peace of Britain* that March.

ROTHENSTEIN, [Sir] John Knewstub Maurice (1901–92)
English art historian, later Director of the Tate Gallery (1938–64); knighted in 1952.

ROTHWELL, Evelyn [Lady Barbirolli] (1911–2008)
English oboist and contemporary of Britten's at the RCM, where she studied with Léon Goossens; she married John Barbirolli in 1939.

RUBBRA, (Charles) Edmund (Duncan) (1901–86)
English composer, teacher and writer.

RUBINSTEIN, Artur (1887–1982)
Renowned Polish-American pianist, one of the great virtuosi of his generation.

RUBINSTEIN, Ida (1885–1960)
Russian prima ballerina.

RUSSELL, Sheridan (b. 1903)
English cellist.

RYLE, Mr
Junior master at Clive House School, Prestatyn.

SALMOND, Felix Adrian Norman (1888–1952)
English cellist.

SAMMONS, Albert (1886–1957)
English violinist.

SAMUEL, Harold (1879–1937)
English pianist, noted Bach interpreter and professor at the Royal College of Music; taught Britten privately in London from November 1928 to March 1930.

SARGENT, [Sir Harold] Malcolm [Watts] (1895–1967)
English conductor, knighted in 1947; premiered Britten's *The Young's Person's Guide to the Orchestra*, Op. 37 with the London Symphony Orchestra as both conductor and narrator of the film *Instruments of the Orchestra* (1946), an educational project made by the Crown Film Unit for the Ministry of Education, directed by Muir Mathieson with a script by Montagu Slater.

SAVORY [major], P(hilip) H.
Farfield House boy at Gresham's (1927–30); contemporary of Britten's who shared a study with him in 1928 and was in the Lower Fourth with him the following year.

SCARCE, Mrs Annie
See under Annie Walker.

SCHARRER, Irene (1888–1971)
English pianist.

SCHERCHEN, Hermann (1891–1966)
German conductor and contemporary music specialist.

SCHERCHEN, Wulff (b. 1920)
Son of Hermann and Gustel Scherchen; Britten became infatuated with Wulff when he and his mother moved to England in 1938.

SCHILLING, Mollie, Jefferson and Richard
Local children of George Shelling, physician and surgeon of Kessingland, Lowestoft; Molly was an occasional piano duet partner of Britten's.

SCHNABEL, Artur (1882–1951)
Austrian-American pianist and composer.

SCHÖFFLER, Paul (1897–1977)
German baritone, a favourite at the Vienna State Opera and the Salzburg Festival.

SCHOENBERG, Arnold Franz Walter (1874–1951)
Austro-Hungarian/American composer and theorist; founder of the Second Viennese School and teacher of (amongst others) Alban Berg, Anton Webern and Erwin Stein.

SCHONE, Lotte (1891–1977)
Austrian-French soprano (originally known as Charlotte Bodestein) who sang in Paris (1933–48).

SCHORR, Friedrich (1888–1953)
Hungarian-American bass-baritone; a great Wagnerian and a leading Wotan and Sachs of his day.

SCHUBERT, Richard (1885–1959)
German tenor.

SCHUMANN, Elisabeth (1885–1952)
Great German soprano and a favourite artist of Britten's.

SCHUSTER, Joseph (1905–69)
Russian-German-American cellist; soloist in Strauss's *Don Quixote* for Leonard Bernstein's famous debut with the New York Philharmonic at Carnegie Hall in 1943.

SCOTT, Charles Kennedy (1876–1965)
English choir trainer and conductor; founder of the Oriana Madrigal Society in 1904.

SCOTT, Cyril (1879–1970)
English composer and pianist.

SEAGO, Edward (1910–74)
British painter.

SEGOVIA, Andrés (1893–1987)
Spanish virtuoso guitarist.

SERKIN, Rudolf (1903–91)
Austrian-American pianist.

SEWELL, Laurence Alleine
Mr Britten's assistant at his dental practice from November 1930 and his partner from 1933. After Mr Britten's death in 1934, Sewell bought the practice, but retained the name 'Britten and Sewell', presumably as a mark of respect and in recognition of Mr Britten's considerable reputation and standing in the community.

SEWELL, Thomas Jackson Elliott (1888–1972)
Headmaster of South Lodge Preparatory School, Kirkley Cliff Road, Lowestoft. He and his wife were neighbours and friends of Britten's parents.

SHABELEVSKY, Yurek (b. 1911)
Polish-American dancer and director.

SHANKAR, Uday (1900–77)
Bengali artist, classical dancer and choreographer; older brother of the sitar virtuoso, Pundit Ravi Shankar.

SHARP, Joan (1898–1968)
English folk musician; daughter of Cecil Sharp, who founded the English Folk Dance Society in 1911.

SHAW, George Bernard (1856–1950)
Irish dramatist, novelist, music critic and polymath.

SHELTON, Mr
Fellow lodger at Princes Square.

SHORE, Bernard (1896–1985)
English viola player.

SILK, Dorothy (1883–1942)
English soprano.

SIMON, Sir John Allsebrook (1873–1954)
Chancellor of the Exchequer in Neville Chamberlain's National Government (1937–40).

SINCLAIR, Arthur (1882–1951)
Irish screen actor.

SKELTON, Mr
Fellow lodger at Princes Square.

SLATER, Enid (1903–88)
Wife of Montagu Slater, part of the artistic circle in which Britten moved in the mid-1930s; a talented photographer who took some of the very best photographs of Britten at this time.

SLATER, Montagu (1902–56)
English poet, playwright, editor, literary critic and prominent left-wing activist. Britten and Slater were to collaborate many times: first at the GPO Film Unit on *Coal Face* (1935), then on two of Slater's plays, *Easter 1916* (1935) and *Stay Down Miner* (1936), and for the Binyon Puppet Theatre production, *Spain* (1938) – but most famously on Britten's first full-scale opera, *Peter Grimes*, Op. 33 (1945), for which Slater wrote the libretto.

SLOBODSKAYA, Oda (1888–1970)
Russian soprano.

SMITH, Cyril (1909–74)
English pianist.

SMYTH, Dame Ethel Mary (1858–1944)
English composer, conductor and leader of the women's suffrage movement, awarded the DBE in 1922.

SNOWDON, Viscount [Philip] (1864–1937)
British statesman, created Viscount Snowdon of Ickornshaw in 1931; Chancellor of the Exchequer in the Labour Government (1929–31) and in the ensuing National Government led by Ramsay MacDonald.

SOLOMON [Solomon Cutner] (1902–88)
English pianist, whose significant career was cut short by a stroke in 1956.

SOMERVILLE, Arthur (1863–1937)
English composer of songs.

SOUTHALL, Joseph Edward (1861–1944)
English artist and designer; member of the 'Birmingham Group' of artists active in the early years of the twentieth century.

SPASHET, George (1884–1943)
Vice Consul of Sweden, Latvia and Germany who lived at Langdale, Cotmer Road, Oulton Broad, Lowestoft; his daughter, Barbara, was a tennis partner of Britten's.

SPENCER DYKE STRING QUARTET
Spencer Dyke, Tate Gilder (violins), Bernard Shore (viola), Cedric Sharpe (cello).

SPENCER, Sylvia (1909–78)
English oboist; student at the RCM (1923–30).

SQUIRE, Sir John Collings (1884–1958)
British poet, writer and historian.

STADLEN, Peter (1910–96)
Austrian-British pianist, writer and music critic.

STATHAM, Heathcote (1889–1973)
Organist of Norwich Cathedral, conductor of the Norwich Philharmonic Society and joint conductor with Beecham of the Norfolk and Norwich Triennial Festival; an old boy of Gresham's.

STEIN, Dr Erwin (1885–1958)
Austrian-British conductor, editor, publisher and writer, and a pupil of Schoenberg; editor at Universal Edition in Vienna before emigrating with his family to Britain in 1938 to escape the Nazis; he joined Boosey & Hawkes in London and effectively became Britten's publisher (and devoted friend and mentor) for the remainder of his life. Britten and Pears lived with the Steins for a while in London and Stein's wife, Sophie, became one of the many surrogate mother-figures to whom Britten turned over the years. Their daughter, Marion, became like a sister to Britten and Pears and a very prominent figure in Aldeburgh Festival circles.

STEUERMANN, Eduard (1892–1964)
Polish-American pianist, pupil of Busoni; played in the 1912 premiere of Schoenberg's *Pierrot Lunaire* and almost every Schoenberg premiere involving a piano thereafter.

STEVENS, Alfred (1818–1875)
English artist and sculptor.

STEWART, Margaret and Joan
Family friends from Bungay.

STILES-ALLEN, Lilian (1896–1982)
English soprano.

STOKOWSKI, Leopold Anthony (1882–1977)
British-American conductor and orchestrator, of Polish/Irish parentage.

STONE, Kenneth
Nephew of Mrs Donald Hutchinson.

STONE, Norman (1890–1967)
English tenor and editor of the music of Schütz and Schein.

STRATTON, George Robert (1897–1954)
English violinist; founder of the Stratton String Quartet and leader of the London Symphony Orchestra (1933–52).

STRATTON STRING QUARTET
George Stratton, William Manuel (violins), Lawrence Leonard (viola), John Moore (cello).

STRAUSS, Richard (1864–1949)
German composer and conductor.

STRAVINSKY, Igor (1882–1971)
Russian composer whose music was much admired by Britten.

STRAVINSKY, Soulima (1910–94)
Son of Igor; Stravinsky wrote the Concerto for two solo pianos (1931–5) for himself to perform with Soulima.

SUGGIA, Guilhermina Suggi (1885–1950)
Portuguese cellist, one-time lover of Pablo Casals, immortalised in a magnificent oil portrait by Augustus John (1878–1961), now in the collection of the Tate Gallery, London.

SUMMERS, Mr
Fellow lodger at Princes Square.

SUTER-SCHOTTERBECK, Lisel
Swiss student who had stayed with the Brittens as an *au pair* in the summer of 1920.

SZIGETI, Joseph (1892–1973)
Hungarian-American violinist.

TALBOTS
Unidentified Lowestoft neighbours; Laurence, the son, would seem to have been a particular friend of Beth.

TAMPLIN, Doris
Daughter of Mrs H. R. Tamplin of Normanshurst, Normanston Drive, Lowestoft, a friend of Mrs Britten and fellow supporter of the 'Care of Girls' charity in Lowestoft.

TAUCHER, Kurt (1885–1954)
German tenor and noted Wagnerian.

TAYLOR, Donald (b. 1911)
English documentary film-maker at the Empire Marketing Board, GPO Film Unit and Strand Films, which he established with Ralph Keene in 1935.

TAYLOR ARCO, Hoult Dutton F. (1903–83)
Gresham's music master (1928–44).

TAYLOR, Kendall (1905–99)
English pianist and teacher; professor of piano at the RCM (1929–93).

TAYLOR, Mrs Sydney
Local violinist of Hillingdon, Gunton Cliff, Lowestoft, who played quartets with Britten, and led the first (domestic) performance of Britten's *Miniature Suite* (1929) for string quartet. She was the wife of a local solicitor.

TEMIANKA, Henri (1906–92)
Polish-American violinist, leader and founder of the Paganini String Quartet in 1946.

TERTIS, Lionel (1876–1975)
English viola player.

TESCHEMACHER, Marguerite (1903–59)
German soprano who created the title role in Strauss's *Daphne* (1938).

TEYTE, [Dame] Maggie (1888–1976)
English soprano, awarded the DBE in 1958; a noted French interpreter and famous Mélisande who also recorded Britten's *Les Illuminations*, Op. 18, in a version with piano (accompanied by John Ranck), in January 1948.

THALBEN-BALL, [Sir] George (1896–1987)
Australian-British organist; Organist and Director of the Choir at the Temple Church, London (1923–81); knighted in 1982.

THIBAUT, Jacques (1880–1953)
French violinist.

THOMPSON, G. R.
Taught maths at Gresham's (1912–36), led the second violins in the school orchestra and was Britten's housemaster at Farfield from November 1928 for the remainder of his time at the school.

THORNDIKE, Dame Sibyl (1882–1976)
English actress; awarded the DBE in 1931.

THURSFIELD, Anne (1885–1945)
English mezzo-soprano.

THURSTON, Frederick (1901–53)
English clarinettist, principal of the BBC Symphony Orchestra (1930–46).

TITTERTON, Frank (1891–1956)
English tenor.

TOSCANINI, Arturo (1867–1957)
Renowned Italian conductor, particularly of opera; ran La Scala before moving to the USA; a great Verdian and Wagnerian, who premiered both Leoncavallo's *Pagliacci* and Puccini's *La Bohème*.

TOSELLI, Enrico (1883–1926)
Italian pianist and composer.

TOYE, (Edward) Geoffrey (1889–1942)
English conductor and composer; brother of the critic and writer, Francis Toye.

TOYE, Wendy (b. 1917)
English dancer, choreographer, actress, theatrical producer and director.

TURNER (*née* Hempson), Ruth
Family friend from Lowestoft, married and living in London.

TUTTLE, Kathleen and Donald
Children of Ernest Tuttle, a local organist who played for the Lowestoft Musical Society.

TYLER, Michael
Lowestoft friend and the subject of the third of Britten's *Three Pieces* for piano (December 1930) which quotes from 'Ragamuffin', the second of John Ireland's *Three London Pieces* – presumably a hidden reference to what attracted Britten to the young Tyler.

URSULEAC, Viorica (1894–1985)
Romanian soprano.

VACHELL, Horace Annesley (1861–1955)
English novelist.

VAN BEINUM, Eduard (1901–59)
Dutch conductor, assistant to Mengelberg at the Concertgebouw Orchestra in Amsterdam, succeeding him as the orchestra's Principal Conductor in 1945; later became a champion of Britten's music in Holland, conducting the premiere of the *Spring Symphony*, Op. 44 with his orchestra at the Concertgebouw on 14 July 1949.

VAUGHAN WILLIAMS, Ralph (1872–1958)
English composer who joined the staff of the RCM after the First World War, a post he held until 1939. Britten's relationship with VW and his music was ambivalent to say the least, though he later performed and recorded *On Wenlock Edge* with Pears. VW was immensely sympathetic and supportive of Britten, made efforts to get Britten's music performed while he was a student at the RCM and later, when Britten returned from the USA at the height of the war, wrote in support of Britten's registration as a conscientious objector and argued for his exemption from military service.

VÖGEL, [Wladimir Rudolfovich] Vladimir, (1896–1984)
Swiss composer of German/Russian parentage.

VOKE, Leon Charles (b. 1900)
American bass, student at the RCM (1927–31).

VRONSKY, (Vitya) Victoria (1909–92)
Russian pianist; wife and duo partner of the pianist Victor Babin (1908–72).

VULLIAMY, Poppy
A friend of Peter Burra, communist and activist who saved countless children from the ravages of the Spanish Civil War, helping Basque refugees relocate to the UK.

WADDINGTON, Sydney Peine (1869–1953)
English composer and teacher of harmony at the RCM from 1905.

WADHAM, Dorothy
Administrator at the International Society for Contemporary Music (ISCM).

WALDEN, Lord Howard de (1880–1946)
Benefactor and first President of the British Music Society (1918–33); a generous patron of the arts.

WALKER, Mrs
Lowestoft friend whose son, Peter, was at South Lodge with Britten.

WALKER, Alice

Sister of the Britten family nanny; Alice joined the household as cook in May 1914 and remained with the family for almost twenty years, leaving in January 1933 to marry and return to Farnham.

WALKER, Annie

She joined the Britten household as nanny in 1907, six months after Robert was born, and remained with the family until 1932, when she too left to marry and settle in Farnham.

WALKER, Mrs

Fellow lodger at Princes Square.

WALLS, Tom (1883–1949)

English actor in the Aldwych farces.

WALSWORTH, Ivor (1909–78)

English composer; student at the Royal Academy of Music where he was awarded the Mendelssohn Scholarship in 1932 and 1933; long career at the BBC, finally as Music Organiser for the BBC Transcription Service.

WALTER, Bruno (1876–1962)

German conductor.

WALTON, [Sir] William (1902–83)

English composer, knighted in 1951; Walton and Britten became friends, though the relationship was not without its frictions, largely due to Walton's jealousy of Britten's international reputation. However, mutual respect sustained the relationship: Britten commissioned Walton's one-act opera, *The Bear* (1967) for the English Opera Group and Walton composed *Improvisations on an Impromptu of Benjamin Britten* (1970), one of his finest orchestral works, as a tribute to the younger composer.

WARLOCK, Peter [Philip Heseltine] (1894–1930)

English composer, editor and writer.

WARNERS

Family friends at Bramerton; the son, Christopher Warner, was a South Lodge boy.

WARRACK, Guy (1900–86)

Scottish conductor and composer; appointed to the BBC Scottish Orchestra in 1935.

WATT, Harry (1906–87)

English documentary maker; director (with Basil Wright) of *Night Mail* (1936).

WEBERN, Anton Friedrich Wilhelm von (1883–1945)

Austrian composer and conductor; pupil of Schoenberg.

WEINGARTNER, Felix (1863–1942)

Austrian conductor, composer and author.

WELFORD, Mr and Mrs Arthur

Arthur and Dodo Welford lived at Peasenhall Hall in Suffolk; their sons Peter and Christopher (Kit) were friends of the Britten children.

WELFORD, Christopher [Kit] (1911–73)
Suffolk friend and medical student at St Thomas's Hospital in London, who was to marry Britten's sister Beth in 1938.

WELLESZ, Egon (1885–1974)
Austrian composer, musicologist and teacher.

WELTNER, Armin
German baritone.

WESTRUP, [Sir] Jack Allan (1904–75)
English musicologist, teacher, critic and conductor, knighted in 1961.

WHEATLEY, Miss
Fellow lodger at Burleigh House.

WHITE, T. A. B(lanco)
A Farfield House boy and Open Scholar at Gresham's, one year Britten's junior, with whom he shared a study.

WHITEHEAD, Percy Algernon (1875–1953)
Piano professor at the RCM (1920–38).

WHITEHOUSE, William E. (1859–1935)
English cellist.

WIDDOP, Walter (1892–1949)
English Heldentenor; soloist in the premiere of Britten's *Ballad of Heroes*, Op.14, at the Queen's Hall, London, on 5 April 1939.

WIEDEMANN, Hermann (1879–1944)
German baritone.

WILLCOCK [major], H(enry) D. (1913–76)
A Farfield House boy at Gresham's, ten months Britten's senior.

WILLIAMS, Grace (1906–77)
Welsh composer; studied with Vaughan Williams at the RCM and with Egon Wellesz in Vienna; she became a good friend to Britten through their association with the Macnaghten–Lemare Concerts.

WILLIAMS, Harcourt (1880–1957)
English actor and producer.

WILLIAMS, Harold (1893–1976)
Australian bass.

WILLIAMSON, A(lexander) R(obert) H(andley)
A Farfield House boy at Gresham's, nine months Britten's junior.

WILLSON, Dorothy Wynne (1909–32)
English author, whose father taught Britten at Gresham's.

WINNINGTON-INGRAM, Arthur Foley (1858–1946)
Bishop of London (1901–39).

WILSON, [Sir] Steuart (1889–1966)
English tenor, knighted in 1948, founder of the English Singers and later Music Director of the Arts Council of Great Britain (1945–8) and Head of Music at the BBC (1948–9).

WITTGENSTEIN, Paul (1887–1961)
Austrian pianist (and brother of the philosopher, Ludwig), who lost his right arm in the First World War and sustained his post-war career by commissioning piano works for left hand only. These included pieces by Ravel, Strauss, Prokofiev, Schmidt and Britten, whose *Diversions*, Op. 21 for piano (left hand) and orchestra (1940) Wittgenstein was to premiere with the Philadelphia Orchestra under Eugene Ormandy on 16 January 1942.

WOIZIKORSKY (WOJCIKOWSKI), Leon (1899–1975)
Polish dancer, ballet-master and teacher; joined Ballets Russes in 1916.

WOLFF, Lilian
Friend of Beth Britten and fellow student at the Paris Academy of Dressmaking, Old Bond Street, London; Beth and Lilian were partners in Elspeth Beide, a dress-making establishment at 559 Finchley Road in Hampstead during the 1930s.

WONTNER, Arthur (1875–1960)
English actor-manager.

WOOD, Charles (1866–1926)
Irish composer and professor at the RCM.

WOOD, Haydn (1882–1959)
English composer.

WOOD, Sir [Joseph] Henry (1869–1944)
English conductor, knighted in 1911; founder (in 1895) of the Promenade Concerts (later the BBC Proms), which he led until the end of his life. Britten was the soloist under Wood in his own Piano Concerto, Op. 13 (1938), in a Promenade Concert in the Queen's Hall, London, on 18 August 1938.

WOODGATE, Leslie (1902–61)
English conductor and Chorus Master of the BBC Choral Society (1934–61); his association with Britten's music continued after the war, when he conducted the premieres of *Hymn to St Cecilia*, Op. 27 (1942) and *Saint Nicolas*, Op. 42 (1948).

WOODGER, Mr and Mrs
Lowestoft friends of the Brittens who lived at North Lodge, 10 Yarmouth Road.

WOODHOUSE, Charles (1879–1939)
English violinist, orchestral leader and conductor.

WRIGHT, Basil (1907–87)
English documentary film-maker and producer, educated at Cambridge; joined Grierson at the Empire Marketing Board Film Unit in December 1929 and moved with him to the GPO Film Unit, where he brought Auden and Britten together for the first time for *Night Mail*. His collaborations with Britten continued beyond the GPO Film Unit: he commissioned him to write the music for *Advance Democracy* when he founded the Realist Film Unit in 1937, and the score for the educational film, *Instruments of the Orchestra* in 1946, when he was producer-in-charge of the Crown Film Unit.

WRIGHT, Kenneth Anthony (1899–1975)
English musical administrator and composer of light music; Assistant Director of Music at the BBC (1936–7), Acting Director of Music (1946–8), later Head of Music Programmes (Television), retiring in 1959.

WRIGHT, Paul Herve Giraud (1915–2005)
A good friend of Britten's during the 1930s; he was employed by the John Lewis Partnership to organise musical events for the staff, for which he sometimes wrote the music and lyrics. In later life he became an eminent British diplomat.

WRIST, Miss
Fellow lodger at Burleigh House, occupying a top-floor room next to Britten.

WÜHRER, Friedrich (1900–75)
Austrian pianist and teacher.

WYNN-REEVES, Joan
Tennis partner in London; schoolfriend of Beth Britten at the Woodard School of St Mary and Anne, Abbots Bromley.

WYSS, Sophie (1897–1983)
Swiss soprano who settled in England in 1925; Britten wrote *Our Hunting Fathers*, Op. 8 (1936), *On This Island*, Op. 11 (1937) and *Les Illuminations*, Op. 18 (1939) for her, and a set of French folk-song arrangements (1942). She married Arnold Gyde in 1925, with whom she had two sons, Arnold junior and Humphrey (b. 1936) who was one of Britten's godsons.

YEOMANS, Walter (1890–1940)
Director of serious music at The Decca Record Company.

ZIMMERMANN, Erich (1892–1968)
German tenor.

Bibliography

Alston, John. Interview with Donald Mitchell, Aldeburgh, 20 June 1988, The Britten–Pears Library.

Anderson, Hedli. Interview with John Evans, Paris, October 1980, The Britten–Pears Library.

Apel, Willi. *Harvard Dictionary of Music*, second edition, London: Heinemann Educational Books, 1979.

Auden, W.H. *Collected Shorter Poems*, London: Faber and Faber, 1966.

– *Collected Poems*, London: Faber and Faber, 1976.

– *The English Auden: Poems, Essays and Dramatic Writings 1927–1939*, edited by Edward Mendelson, London: Faber and Faber, 1977.

– *The Complete Works of W.H. Auden: Plays (with Christopher Isherwood) and other Dramatic Writings, 1928–1838*, edited by Edward Mendelson, London: Faber and Faber, 1989.

Auden, W.H., and Christopher Isherwood. *The Ascent of F6*, London: Faber and Faber, second edition, 1937.

– *The Dog beneath the Skin*, London: Faber and Faber, 1935.

– *On the Frontier*, London: Faber and Faber, 1938.

Blyth, Alan. *Remembering Britten*, London: Hutchinson, 1981.

Boyd, Malcolm. 'Benjamin Britten: Grace Williams: Chronicle of a Friendship', *Welsh Music*, 6/6, Winter 1980–1, pp. 7–28.

Bridcut, John. *Britten's Children*, London: Faber and Faber, 2006.

Britten, Benjamin. *A Catalogue of the Published Works*, compiled and edited by Paul Banks, The Britten–Pears Library for The Britten Estate Ltd, 1999.

Britten, Beth. *My Brother Benjamin*, Bourne End: The Kensal Press, 1986.

Brosa, Peggy. Interview with Donald Mitchell, London, 9 September 1977, The Britten–Pears Library.

Carpenter, Humphrey. *W. H. Auden: A Biography*, London: Allen & Unwin, 1981.

– *Benjamin Britten: A Biography*, London: Faber and Faber, 1992.

Coldstream, William. Conversation with Donald Mitchell, London, 18 November 1978, The Britten–Pears Library.

Evans, John, Philip Reed and Paul Wilson. *A Britten Source Book*, Aldeburgh: The Britten Estate, 1987.

Gishford, Anthony (ed.). *Tribute to Benjamin Britten on his Fiftieth Birthday*, London: Faber and Faber, 1963.

– *The Gresham*, school magazines, Gresham's School, Holt, 1928–30.

– *Gresham's School Register*, Gresham's School, Holt.

Haskell, Arnold L. *Ballet: A Complete Guide to Appreciation, History, Aesthetics, Ballets, Dancers*, Harmondsworth: Penguin, 1938.

Hindmarsh, Paul. *Frank Bridge: A Thematic Catalogue*, London: Faber Music, 1983.

Isherwood, Christopher. *Christopher and His Kind*, New York: Farrar, Strauss and Giroux Inc., 1976; London: Eyre Methuen, 1977.

Jones, Barry and M.V. Dickson. *The Macmillan Dictionary of Biography*, London, Macmillan, 1981.

Kenyon, Nicholas. *The BBC Symphony Orchestra: The First Fifty years 1930–1980*, London: British Broadcasting Corporation, 1981.

Lauricella, Remo. Interview with Donald Mitchell, London, May 1986, Britten–Pears Library.

Low, Rachel. *Documentary and Educational Films of the 1930s*, London: George Allen & Unwin, 1979.

MacNeice, Louis (translator). *The Agamemnon of Aeschylus*, London: Faber and Faber, 1936.

– *The Dark Tower and other Radio Scripts*, London: Faber and Faber, 1947.

– *Out of the Picture*, London: Faber and Faber, 1937.

Medley, Robert. Interview with Donald Mitchell, London, 2 October 1977, The Britten–Pears Library.

Mitchell, Donald. *Benjamin Britten: The Early Years*, BBC Radio 3, 1980.

– *Britten and Auden in the Thirties: The Year 1936*, London: Faber and Faber, 1981.

– 'Britten on "Oedipus Rex" and "Lady Macbeth" ', *Tempo* 120, March 1977, pp. 10–12.

Mitchell, Donald and John Evans. *Pictures from a Life: Benjamin Britten 1913–1976*, London: Faber and Faber, 1978.

Mitchell, Donald and Hans Keller (eds.). *Benjamin Britten: A Commentary on His Works from a Group of Specialists*, London: Rockliff, 1952.

Mitchell, Donald and Philip Reed. *Letters from a Life: The Selected Letters and Diaries of Benjamin Britten, Volumes One and Two*, London: Faber and Faber, 1991.

Nicholson, Patricia. Interview with Rosamund Strode, Lowestoft, 1985, The Britten–Pears Library.

Palmer, Christopher (ed.). *The Britten Companion*, London: Faber and Faber, 1984.

Pears, Peter. Interview with Donald Mitchell for *A Time There Was . . .: A Profile of Benjamin Britten*, two-part film portrait for *The South Bank Show*, produced and directed by Tony Palmer, London: London Weekend Television, 1980.

Pounder, John. Interview with Donald Mitchell, Aldeburgh, 1999, Britten–Pears Library.

Priestley, J. B. *Johnson Over Jordan (the Play) and All about It (Essay)*, London: Heinemann, 1939.

Pudney, John. 'Britten – A Formative Recollection', programme book for *A Tribute to Benjamin Britten*, New Philharmonia Orchestra, 22 February 1977.

Reed, Philip. 'A Cantata for Broadcasting: Introducing Britten's *The Company of Heaven*', *Musical Times*, June 1989, pp. 324–31.

– *The Incidental Music of Benjamin Britten: A Study and Catalogue of His Music for Film, Theatre and Radio*, Ph.D. dissertation, University of East Anglia, 1987.

Reeve, Basil. Interview with Donald Mitchell, London, 3 October 1986, The Britten–Pears Library.

Sadie, Stanley (ed.). *The New Grove Dictionary of Music and Musicians*, 20 volumes, London: Macmillan, 1980.

Slater, Enid. Interview with Donald Mitchell and John Evans, London, 1981, The Britten–Pears Library.

Slater, Montagu. *Easter 1916*, London: Lawrence and Wishart, 1936.

– *New Way Wins: The Play from Stay Down Miner*, London: Lawrence and Wishart, 1937.

Thorpe, Marion (ed.). *Peter Pears: A Tribute on His 75th Birthday*, London: Faber Music/The Britten Estate, 1985.

Welford, Beth. Interview with Charles Ford, Aldeburgh, *c.*1976/7, The Britten–Pears Library.

– Interview with Tony Friese-Greene, 1977, The Britten–Pears Library.

– *My Brother Benjamin*: see under Beth Britten

White, Eric Walter. *Benjamin Britten: His Life and Operas*, revised second edition (ed. John Evans), London: Faber and Faber, 1983.

Index to Britten's works

General index